Main Currents in The History of Education

Main Currents in The History of Education

Second Edition

Edward J. Power
Professor of Education
Boston College

McGraw-Hill Book Company
New York, St. Louis, San Francisco, Düsseldorf,
London, Mexico, Panama, Sydney, Toronto

This book was set in Caledonia by Brown Bros, Linotypers, Inc., and printed on permanent paper and bound by The Maple Press Company. The designer was J. E. O'Connor. The editors were Nat LaMar, and Timothy Yohn. Sally R. Ellyson supervised the production.

Main Currents in the History of Education

Library of Congress Catalog Card Number 73-95821
50581

1 2 3 4 5 6 7 8 9 0   M A M M   7 9 8 7 6 5 4 3 2 1 0

To Thomas, Richard,
Suzanne, and Maryann

Preface

The history of education is a theoretical study. It has the same relationship to contemporary education that general history has to contemporary life. History does not solve our problems for us, although it may illuminate our efforts to find solutions. The history of education offers no guarantee that it will answer the pressing present-day questions concerning goals, curricula, methods, costs, and administration. Offering such answers is not its function. It can, however, provide us with some insights into the way these or similar problems have been handled in the past. We may learn from the past, but we do not look to the past to produce the solutions for today's questions. No teacher or prospective teacher can hope to become a better classroom performer merely because he has studied the history of education. On the other hand, if he has some insight into the educational trends of the past, he will be a more adequate educator and a more thoroughly prepared member of his profession. No one can doubt that the history of education, like any other kind of history, is a relevant study, although it would be inaccurate to make extravagant claims for its direct practical outcomes.

A survey of the history of education takes us all the way back to the beginning, when man first inhabited the earth, and then brings us down to the years that immediately precede our own day. This is an immense expanse of time. To cover all of the developments that have taken place in education during those thousands of years would be impossible in a single volume. This book makes no claim for completeness, and of necessity many details have been omitted. Despite this curtailment, however, every effort has been made to keep in perspective the educational movements—plans, theories, and schools—and the schoolmen that have had the greatest influence on later educational developments and thus on our own time. The principal purpose of this book, then, is to trace the main currents of educational thought and practice down through the ages. It is intended chiefly as a textbook for undergraduate classes in the history of education.

In two principal ways this book is different from other history of education textbooks. First, in treating of ancient education, it attempts to put schools and educational theories, teachers and learners, in direct relation with life. The schools in past days were real—not fictional—institutions, and the students who went to them learned the values that their society had tested and accepted in formal and informal education. In other words, we have tried to make it easy for the twentieth-century student who uses this book to understand that ancient schools and the students who attended them really existed. We have also tried to make the relationship between those schools and the theories of education current in both ancient and modern times clearer and more significant. We are interested to know that Plato and Isocrates had educational theories, but we are even more interested to know the relevance such theories had to the actual practice of ancient education and even to our own education. Second, this book endeavors to give a fuller appraisal of the Christian-medieval period and its relationship to the evolution of the classical heritage. This is a part of educational history susceptible of neglect, and we have tried to pay it due heed.

In the second edition we have added new interpretations in several chapters, written an entirely new chapter on Roman educational theory (Chapter VI), and brought the bibliographical notes up-to-date.

It would be impossible to write any history of education without depending heavily on the special and general studies that have appeared in the field over the past several years. To the authors and publishers whose books were used in preparing this history, and to my colleague, Prof. J. Richard Bath, for helping me read proof, sincere thanks are extended.

Edward J. Power

Contents

Part II   Christian and Medieval Education

cAncient Education

R emote and irrelevant though the subject may at first seem to some, the ways in which early societies educated their young—and thus, to some extent, how they educated future generations—form a truly significant chapter in cultural history which should inevitably prove fascinating to all. If we assume that cultural and educational antecedents make a difference—that the values of the present are somewhat rooted in the past—we should want to know the principal avenues of ancient action. In educational history, this means we should want to know and understand the ideals guiding education in the ancient world, along with the men who framed them, and the policies and practices invented to achieve them.

Primitive education needs only brief notice, for it serves largely as a background against which to measure later ancient educational events. If it is good to begin at the beginning, education among the primitives meets that criterion.

We are looking for a history which has become a more or less permanent feature in the Western world. Thus, once taking notice of the Egyptians, Chinese, and Jews as representatives of pre-Grecian civilizations, and paying due heed to the possibilities of their continuing, if indirect, influence on Western education, we can move forward in time to the Greeks, who, in the last analysis, took a heritage more ancient than their own and abstracted from it values and tools they believed useful to them. There may be elements of historical optimism in the assertion that the history of Western education begins with the Greeks, but there is enough truth in it to allow us to defend our preoccupation with them. So, to begin a more or less detailed study of ancient education (which at best may always be charged with incompleteness if it is done in a one-volume study), we turn to the Greeks.

In Greece we find two principal city states: Athens and Sparta. We look more closely at Athens because therein was born and nurtured the classical heritage to which, in one way or another, Western education has regularly paid allegiance. From Greece the model for the educated citizen was transplanted throughout the Hellenistic world, wherein the classical ways of living and thinking had become remote from day-to-day life. The old inheritance was perpetuated the only way it could have been: by the written word. Thus we meet, for the first time, educational institutions which, through various literary means, kept relatively intact the honored heritage of the past.

Sharing in Hellenistic attitudes, but honoring tested traditions of their own, too, the Romans tried to build an educational program to achieve two diverse objectives: culture and utility. We begin with an educational program among early people that was unequivocally practical; add to it, from among the Egyptians and Jews, a syllabus of culture and spirit; refine this cultural commitment in Greece (although not without some false starts); and end with a Roman determination to produce decently educated men—citizens with cultural refinement on the one hand, and a hard-headed facility for practical achievement on the other.

Through several centuries (if we think only of beginning with the Greeks and ending with the Romans, the span will be from the seventh century B.C. to the early fifth century A.D.) educational theories and practices were tested, accepted, modified, discarded. If there is anything the history of ancient education teaches, it is that men have always been uneasy about the means and ends, as well as the scope and depth, of education. Ideas about what education means, never in short supply, became a regular currency of intellectual exchange in the ancient world. Good men with good minds probed the mysteries and uncertainties of education. We can learn from them.

I

Education in Early Societies

Education among the Primitives

A completely comprehensive history of education must begin with man's inhabitation of earth, when the unfeeling world of flora, fauna, and natural phenomena were all that he had to work with and learn from. Since his mind was occupied largely with the business of survival, mental training, except as it enabled him to cope with everyday issues, was foreign to the context of his existence. In its most general meaning, then, primitive education was for the most part accommodated to the hard facts of living.[1]

[1] See Thomas Woody, *Life and Education in Early Societies*, The Macmillan Company, New York, 1949, pp. 15–19; and Charles Hose, *Natural Man: A Record from Borneo*, The Macmillan Company, New York, 1926.

In historical retrospect one sees varieties of institutions, practices, and theories, so to aim our thought backward through the ages to man's early educational endeavor and to describe and evaluate his achievements, distinguishing the important from the unimportant, the ephemeral from the permanent, is a hazardous undertaking. Educational records from intervening centuries are not especially helpful in this reverse projection, and historical evidence, either obliterated by time or fragmented and overlaid by subsequent events, constructs inadequate landmarks and undependable guides.[2]

Primitive education, centering on the useful arts, was totally practical: The world's first people were untouched by either a need or a desire to preserve and perpetuate a literary inheritance. A literary education was of course unknown, and therefore meaningless; even the most basic elements of reading, writing, and computing were undeveloped because they were unnecessary. Formal education in school did not even belong to the realm of prophetic anticipation.

The term "practical education" should be taken literally: It meant preparation for life wherein primitive men fed, clothed, and protected themselves, and those dear to them, in a world that was hard and hostile. Children should know both their friends and their enemies, but they should know, too, the fundamental arts of survival. Any educational or training program failing to meet the pragmatic test of adequacy—of fitting youth for its responsibilities—was inevitably doomed. On the other hand, an adequate "curriculum" had such obvious recommendations that theoretical justifications were superfluous.[3]

Uncomplicated as it was, this "practical curriculum's" simplicity left room for something besides mastering a huntsman's skills, a herdsman's prudence, a warrior's strength, and a mechanic's craft for inventing crude creature comforts. Even simple men do more than just eat and sleep. Tribes were societies, and their members were welded by bonds of common purpose (which came eventually to be tribal traditions, always worth communicating if social bonds were to stand the strain and tension of community life). And beyond the social horizon

---

[2] The major sources of our knowledge of prehistoric man and his educational endeavors are the relics of prehistoric people, from which anthropologists are able to draw important conclusions, and the study of so-called contemporary primitives. The worth of the latter source is described in some detail by W. J. Sollas, *Ancient Hunters and Their Modern Representatives,* St. Martin's Press, Inc., New York, 1915.

[3] See W. D. Hambly and Charles Hose, *Origins of Education among Primitive Peoples,* St. Martin's Press, Inc., New York, 1926, p. xi; and S. E. Frost, *Historical and Philosophical Foundations of Western Education,* C. E. Merrill Books, Columbus, Ohio, 1966, pp. 5–12.

were spiritual forces which seemed to demand tribute and allegiance. In mysterious and occult ways these forces affected life—made the rain fall, the sun shine, the game plentiful, and the crops grow—and so primitive man, never thinking to gainsay their reality, tried with might and main to placate them.

Tribal lore, embellished by rites and ceremonies, spoke the language of social education and contained the principal values of primitive life. Magical formulas, laden with superstition and fear, usually were the private knowledge of the privileged few who appeased the forces that refused to leave men alone. These gods or spirits if paid proper heed might smile on primitive man; but on him, too, they could vent their anger. So he invented ways of staying on good terms with them, and called his invention "religion." [4]

Without formal agencies for learning, and deprived of professional teachers, society itself was a school, and every tribesman a professor. Good or bad, teaching and learning were informal, incidental, and never-ending. Youth was the time for mastering the most obvious of essential skills, and primitive men were at pains to see their young start on the right track. Only after the essentials were learned was it time to turn to the ornamental and the artistic. Thus, a plain-looking but useful weapon had priority over an ornamental one: An ugly but sharp spear was always better than a beautiful but dull one; a drab but watertight vessel was preferred to one whose art reflected tribal values but which leaked. Only where gods were concerned did primitive men fashion useless works of art, yet consider them useful. Education, then, at this point in pre-history, was shaped by utility and conservatism; the fundamental arts of living—not as it *might* be lived, but as it *was* lived—formed the content of instruction.

Looking more closely at this fundamentalism, we can translate it into four special educational emphases:

1. Food, clothing, shelter, and protection were always and everywhere first on the list, because without means for securing them nothing else had much meaning.

2. In many respects an individualist, primitive man was nevertheless part of a social unit which, with its customs and taboos, made regular demands on him; and because of this, the young were schooled for citizenship in the tribe.

3. Once their basic necessities and social obligations had been

[4] See R. Karsten, *The Civilization of the South America Indians*, Alfred A. Knopf, Inc., New York, 1926, pp. 17–21; and E. B. Taylor, *Primitive Culture*, John Murray, London, 1913, vol. I, chap. 11.

taken care of, primitive men could think of more personal interests, among which was their relationship to the world and to its spiritual forces. Thinking of this sort led them to contemplate unsophisticated and uncomplicated philosophies and theologies of life.

4. Amid his simplicity and superstition, primitive man was awed by his environment—by the majesty and beauty of the world, and by the powerful forces within and upon it. In common with all mankind since, he sought to express, to communicate, his finer thoughts and more profound feelings, and came to use language, music, dancing, ornamentation, and ceremony to fulfill this aesthetic urge.[5]

With these life expectations, the role of education and training— even without schools to help—was clear. Essentials came first, for even an informal syllabus recognized the relevance of learning to live; so with clear objectives, primitive men could turn their attention to method.

And here we meet a technique, met time after time in later educational history, and regularly praised for its efficacy: imitation. Boys and girls watched and learned; what adults did was often translated into fun and games. Through play, children not only amused themselves but mastered skills, strengthened muscles, sharpened minds, and developed keenness of observation, imagination, and invention. No one stopped to theorize about work or play, or to justify the educational value of mimetic games; it was taken for granted that tools and toys could be used interchangeably: Boats, shields, bows, arrows, and spears had a quality of unquestioned utility whether in the hands of a man or a child.[6] It was all so simple, but also so useful.

Growing older, boys and girls continued a training that, if not more carefully organized, at least appeared to be more consciously directed. What we would call schooling was, for primitive man, simply a day's work: Young people helped their parents—the boys by hunting and fishing, the girls in child care and household duties—and, following a most basic and natural method, learned by doing. No one who wanted to belong to a primitive community excused himself from this apprenticeship. But even then life was not all work, and social education, though approached with the utmost seriousness, could have a lighter side. Rituals, ceremonies, purposeful dances, and incantations, even with their burden of social and religious significance, also had elements of distraction from the harshness of primitive life.

Initiation was an awesome but mandatory experience which occu-

[5] Arthur J. Todd, *The Primitive Family as an Educational Agency*, G. P. Putnam's Sons, New York, 1913, pp. 64–70.

[6] Woody, *op. cit.*, pp. 20–23; and Hambly and Hose, *op. cit.*, pp. 332–336.

pied an important role in tribal life and indeed no doubt formed a significant part of primitive man's education. Initiatory format varied from tribe to tribe and, depending on its purpose, within tribes; yet there were common elements, all geared to testing a person's fitness to belong to the group toward which he was aspiring. There were rules (which cannot now be of much interest) guiding the process both for occupational-group membership—the tribe's hunters, for example, may have been segregated into a special class—and for full tribal standing. What is important was the assumption that success in initiation indicated the possession of certain skills and abilities, and in this light initiations were a serious business. Once through an initiatory ordeal, novices had an upgraded status: They enjoyed new privileges, were privy to trade secrets, and were commissioned to keep and guard the rules, taboos, customs, and values of the community.

Accounts of primitive customs reveal various initiatory methods and the fervor of their application. Always painful, the process could be both dangerous and torturous. Initiates were expected to demonstrate their qualifications of social fitness by undergoing the rigorous discipline of such ceremonies. Initiations for girls were usually supervised by older women and those for boys by the wisest men of the tribe. It is possible, without going into detail, to indicate a few fairly distinct initiatory steps, which sometimes extended over a period of several years.[7]

Up to age ten or so, a child was subject only to the relatively mild discipline and tutelage of his immediate family. After his tenth year, however, the tribe became involved, or at least some of its members did, and a long process of initiation prior to tribal induction commenced. To begin with, as a foretaste of worse things to come, he was painted with totemic symbols, flung in the air, and severely beaten. Later he submitted to mutilation: the scarification of the back or breast, the knocking out of the front teeth, the piercing of the nasal septum or lips, the loosening of the scalp—marks that would last throughout life as badges of distinction or tags of identity. Then novices were exposed to smoke and fire to test their courage and physical endurance of pain. During special periods reserved for these proceedings, candidates had to supply their own food. If they wanted to eat they had to hunt, and if they hunted they were expected to bring back bounty useful or necessary to certain ceremonials.

As part of the total process the novice was trained in self-reliance, or better yet was made to demonstrate, under unusual and often

[7] See W. B. Spencer and F. J. Gillen, *The Arunta: A Study of Stone Age People*, St. Martin's Press, Inc., New York, 1927.

extreme social pressure, skills he already possessed. Initiations some-times took months or years before all conditions were fulfilled, and during this long probationary period novices were responsible to guardians appointed by the tribe. Whether guardians were teachers or policemen, or some combination of both, is unclear, but they were more or less constant witnesses to the novice's strength, courage, stamina, maturity, and character. In such a system boys and girls were expected to prove their mettle; once proved they could take their places as full-fledged members of the tribe.[8]

Whether tribal rituals were initiatory or merely social (and the latter were quite possible), they were thought to inculcate moral value and were, therefore, part of a broad, indefinite, and unwritten educational syllabus. Boys were taught to endure pain, hardship, and hunger; they learned obedience and reverence. Social duties and private obligations were impressed on them in a solemn manner. Even initiations, we know, had a social-political side: Totemic symbols decorating novices depicted history and tradition; dances and other ceremonials served a similar purpose or pertained to the mystery religion practiced in the tribe.

Among primitive people, children stayed close to their elders, were aware of adult issues and affairs, and, in general, shared in the activities of the entire group. They were encouraged to grow up fast. This intimate involvement gave them opportunities to learn by contact and observation. Unsheltered from life and enjoying considerable freedom of action, their schools were work, travel, play, and danger.[9]

Unrefined as it was, primitive education had a pedagogy built on the dual foundations of imitation and trial-and-error. Imitation, the more conservative method, held one to the status quo; but trial-and-error was likewise restricted by what offended the community's moral sense or, what was more important, irritated the gods. Imitation and a circumscribed experimentalism were therefore the main techniques for educating each succeeding generation.

In many ways woman was man's equal. Of course her role and status varied from tribe to tribe, but the environment possibly more than anything else suggested or demanded equality or near-equality of the sexes. In general, the status of women was higher among agriculturally oriented primitives than among herdsmen tribes. Usually it was to women that the easier but also the more monotonous tasks were assigned: the care of children and the gathering and preparing of

[8] See A. Moret, *From Tribe to Empire: Social Organization among Primitives and in the Ancient East,* Alfred A. Knopf, Inc., New York, 1926, pp. 90–103.

[9] See Todd, *op. cit.,* pp. 64–70.

materials for food and clothing. While the work of women tended to be confining, man was free to roam about for much of his work and to expand the horizons of his experience. Men were hunters and warriors. Thus the same circumstances that made for equality of the sexes often operated to elevate men to a position of dominance. No primitive tribe could afford the divisiveness of sharp, rigid class distinctions, but, on the other hand, the regularly accepted practices of life with respect to division of labor militated against equality. So, though primitive woman was valued mainly as an economic asset, this attitude did not set her very far below man, who was valued in the same way. Differences in the training of men and women, of boys and girls were natural and inevitable.[10]

Education in Early Egypt

How long man remained in a simple, uncomplicated, primitive state is difficult to say exactly. For our purposes it is not necessary to trace his evolution meticulously. Man made progress. The societies of which he was a part became more complex, and the activities in which he engaged in order to make a living passed from those of hunter and herdsman to artisan and husbandman and beyond. Along with economic and social advancement came new and more carefully organized political units, and with this progress, too, came the creation of social classes. The aristocracies of nature were supplemented by those of privilege, position, and wealth. Men were placed in categories, or their birth placed them there, and the opportunities of life were assigned according to rank in society.

Education was intimately associated with life's goals. The orientation of utility, so obvious among the primitives, was honored and protected by social convention and legal sanction.[11] The kind of education a boy might expect to receive depended now not so much on the skill and training necessary for sustaining life but on the place he or his family occupied in society. The principle of division of labor was recognized to the extent that certain classes in the population of a political unit were acknowledged to have rights and duties consistent with their

[10] See W. T. Corlett, *The Medicine Man of the American Indian and His Cultural Background,* Charles C Thomas, Publisher, Springfield, Ill., 1935, pp. 202–244; H. R. Schoolcraft, *Archives of Aboriginal Knowledge,* J. B. Lippincott Company, Philadelphia, 1868, vol. II, p. 63 and vol. IV, pp. 67–70; and P. A. Means, *Ancient Civilization of the Andes,* Charles Scribner's Sons, New York, 1931, pp. 311 ff.

[11] See Harold I. Bell, *Cults and Creeds in Graeco-Roman Egypt,* Philosophical Library, New York, 1953, pp. 20–30.

station in life. It may seem that the rights too often belonged to the upper classes, the duties to those less fortunately placed in the social hierarchy.[12]

These developments in social, political, and economic life represented man's progress from a less complex existence. They characterized, in most respects, the type of society common in Egypt as early as about 3000 B.C.[13] It was the major function of education in Egypt, as well as in many Oriental countries, to prepare men for life in this kind of society.[14]

ELEMENTARY EDUCATION IN EGYPT

Throughout the history of education, the first level of instruction has, almost without exception, found its objectives in the most fundamental needs of the society responsible for organized elementary education. It is not surprising that this should be so, and there are few good reasons for believing that any other way of determining objectives is possible. But in a society like the one in early Egypt, from about 2000 to 1000 B.C., the organization of elementary levels of instruction was not a simple matter. The various classes in society, each with its own special mission, could not be expected to lend any support to popular and uniform elementary education. Noble people did not live as the military classes lived, nor did they face the same problems; neither of these upper classes needed the kind of elementary training or education that seemed most useful to artisans, merchants, and farmers. Below these classes were the slaves—men, women, and children, captives of war or simply an unranked and underprivileged mass of mankind—for whom any kind of formal instruction seemed entirely unnecessary. In addition to the distinction which could be made in the kind of education appropriate for each class, there was in Egypt a thriving economy and a growing political system which, although completely supporting the class system, needed nevertheless the services of clerks, copyists, computers, and inspectors to keep it going.[15]

[12] G. C. C. Maspero, *The Dawn of Civilization: Egypt and Chaldaea*, SPCK, London, 1901, pp. 326–336.

[13] See J. H. Breasted, *A History of Egypt*, Charles Scribner's Sons, New York, 1912, pp. 32–45.

[14] See G. Rawlinson, *The Story of Ancient Egypt*, G. P. Putnam's Sons, New York, 1888, pp. 40–60; A. Erman, *Life in Ancient Egypt*, Macmillan & Co., Ltd., London, 1894, pp. 105 ff.; and John A. Wilson, *The Culture of Ancient Egypt*, University of Chicago Press, Chicago, 1956, pp. 66–80.

[15] See Breasted, *op. cit.*, pp. 88–98; Walter B. Emery, *Archaic Egypt*, Penguin Books, Baltimore, 1967, pp. 140–180; and Rawlinson, *op. cit.*, pp. 43–51.

The richness of the Nile Valley made agriculture the very core of Egyptian economy. A landlord might have his laborers till the soil, sow the crops, and bring in the harvest without concerning himself very much about their skill in computation or their facility in writing. But someone had to do the computing and writing, for landlords often had vast holdings, and sharecropping was an established institution in the agricultural feudalism of the times; someone had to know the best time of the year to irrigate, and this involved computing the seasons when the river would overflow its banks to make irrigation possible. Whether such computation was simple or difficult, and what degree of skill was needed are not the subjects of our inquiry at the moment. Besides these matters, many other practical considerations could not be ignored. Irrigation was a much more complicated procedure than simply letting the waters of the Nile spill over the fields; dikes, ditches, docks, and bridges had to be constructed and maintained. Mechanics and the sciences basic to mechanics were developed to serve man in his attempts to control or modify his environment.

Before or perhaps while they were learning to utilize mathematical and mechanical means in controlling nature, Egyptians developed, through borrowing and their own ingenuity, the art of written communication. As time passed, they perfected this art to such an extent that it was used to record far more than the needs of commerce, agriculture, and government. Learned men in the society used the art of writing to preserve their profound and elusive thoughts; the achievements of the people's ancestors were transferred from an oral tradition to a literary inheritance; and above all, perhaps, the balance sheet of a man's life was prepared by scribes employed for this purpose, and the scrolls with the record of this life were entombed with the body of a deceased for the gods to read.[16]

Discoveries in science, computation, writing, etc., were not made in elementary schools. But once these sciences and these arts were known, it became the chief function of many elementary schools to adapt them for their use and communicate them to the young. Boys fortunate enough to have an opportunity for formal education—and the majority of boys were not so fortunate—did not gamble away their chances for what would be a fuller, finer, and easier life. Schools were not fun but work, and a boy worked hard to absorb the practical curriculum that was organized for him.[17]

[16] James H. Breasted, *Development of Religion and Thought in Ancient Egypt*, Harper & Row, Publishers, New York, 1959, pp. 155–161.

[17] See Cyril Aldred, *The Egyptians*, Frederick A. Praeger, Inc., New York, 1961, pp. 99–108.

Boys who did not attend elementary schools received whatever education and training was deemed necessary for them from their fathers or masters. Education under these auspices, except the training of apprentice scribes, did not give much attention to the tools of education: reading, writing, counting, computing. Girls in ancient Egypt, as well as in most other countries in these very early years, were not sent to school, nor were they, for that matter, given opportunities for learning anything more than the simple domestic arts. The universal view can be stated succinctly: A woman without ability is normal. No argument was formidable enough to open the doors of schools to girls.[18]

It appears, although authorities on the subject do not always agree, that formal education in Egypt was established very early, sometime between 3000 and 2000 B.C. This formal education usually took the form of schools that were elementary in character. But, as we noted above, such schools were organized to serve a particular class in the population. In spite of the positive assertions of some Egyptologists to the contrary, there is no very convincing evidence that these schools were everywhere committed to teaching reading, writing, and arithmetic. That some schools had such objectives is not open to debate; and strangely enough, such objectives were not out of keeping with a school for poorer boys. The time had not yet arrived when literate men could claim social precedence, or when literary achievements and attainments were the mark of social excellence. The arts of communication in rudimentary form were tools for men who worked and were regarded in the same light as the carpenter's hammer or the mason's chisel. Poor boys could aspire to the occupation of the clerk or the vocation of the scribe without disturbing in any way the rigid social barriers that marked off one class from another. Education, whether for manual or literary skills, was vocational training.[19]

Writing, it is said, was first of all a priestly art. The fact that such a skill came in time to be essential to all or most classes, though not to all people, in no way alters the clearly practical motives associated with priestly writing. This skill, along with all other literary skills, was employed as an instrument for maintaining the position the priestly class enjoyed in the social hierarchy. With such an obviously instrumental character, the tools of learning were communicated to the youth of this

[18] See Maspero, *op. cit.*, p. 320.

[19] See Erman, *op. cit.*, p. 329; Rawlinson, *op. cit.*, p. 45; Maspero, *op. cit.*, pp. 283–298; and C. H. Oldfather, *Diodorus of Sicily with an English Translation*, Loeb Classical Library, Harvard University Press, Cambridge, Mass., 1933, vol. I, p. 81.

class in temple schools.[20] Noble and military classes also came to see the need for reading and writing, and they, too, introduced these skills to the curriculum of their court and military schools. Their method may be thought of as a generalized apprentice system—one which would prepare a royal or noble child to rule and direct, or the son of a military leader to follow his father's career. And in addition to the temple, court, and military schools, the needs of government and economics dictated the establishment of department schools. In these schools the young were prepared for specialized careers in civil government or for business.[21]

In the absence of precise documentation, it is somewhat hazardous to venture beyond what has been said about the kinds of elementary schools that flourished in Egypt. For the most part, however, these schools did not undertake to prepare the scribe. His skill, for which the Egyptians in their business pursuits and in their religious life had a great need, involved preparation in a special kind of writing, but little else. People who built the great pyramids and constructed incomparable obelisks with the afterlife in mind may not have hesitated at organizing schools wherein boys could obtain the skill for writing the history of the dead. One may be fairly certain that master scribes trained apprentices to carry on this work, but it is possible also that schools were founded for this same purpose.

Before leaving the subject of elementary education, we should say a word about the intramural experiences of boys in Egyptian schools. First of all, elementary education, formal or informal, began at an early age; if a boy was going to school, he entered when he was about four. And if the slender accounts that treat of education in Egypt can be trusted, the school day was relatively short; the boys were dismissed at the middle of the day. While they were in school they were taught to write, first by tracing letters and then words; and since Egyptian writing was far more difficult than ours with its hundreds of different hieroglyphics, this was a task somewhat more difficult than one might imagine. The curriculum of elementary education was centered on writing, and the kind of writing that was done in the various schools usually identified the social rank of the students in attendance. Each class in society and often each profession or vocation had symbols and signs which had to be mastered, and the school dealt with the type of writing the students were expected to learn. As we have mentioned

---

[20] See Emery, *op. cit.*, pp. 168–174.

[21] See Breasted, *Development of Religion and Thought in Ancient Egypt,* p. 363; Maspero, *op. cit.*, pp. 301–310; and A. Erman, *The Literature of the Ancient Egyptians,* Methuen & Co., Ltd., London, 1927, pp. 185–186.

above, writing was not a general but a very particular skill; and an elementary school organized its work in writing to comply with the kind of vocational training it was commissioned to give.[22]

It would be difficult to arrive at many general conclusions about the curricula of schools in ancient lands. Although we know more about Egypt than we do about China, Assyria, Babylonia, Sumer, or other countries of the ancient world, we do not stand on very solid ground when we attempt a detailed description of Egyptian schools. Progressively more difficult studies in writing and possibly in elementary science and some mechanics led boys through fiom six to ten years of elementary education. By the time boys were fourteen they were supposed to be ready for life's work. Some had been taught to write; along with writing they had learned something of arithmetic, geometry, and astronomy. Music, too, because it was thought to have some values for moral formation, was taught, and the boys were given an opportunity to learn and sing songs prescribed by the state. Besides this, they were taught to dance, for dancing, in addition to any recreational value it might have had, was often accepted as a form of religious devotion or exercise.[23]

Where teachers came from for these schools, who they were, and what their preparation was for teaching the elements of Egyptian education, we can only guess. It seems clear that the methods they employed were set or fixed and the discipline they imposed strict and harsh. The purposes of elementary training were obvious, and apparently teachers found little or no difficulty in following approved and tested means to achieve these objectives.

SECONDARY EDUCATION IN EGYPT

Modern education—an educational period that began with the humanistic revival in the fourteenth century and terminated about the end of the nineteenth century—has regularly devoted more attention to secondary than to elementary schools. The educational historian two centuries from now will probably be able to write a much fuller and more accurate account of secondary education from 1350 to 1950 than of elementary education for the same period. What may be true of modern education, however, was certainly not true of ancient education in Egypt. Although from certain sources of information we find evidences of secondary education in this ancient land, it is impossible to give

[22] See Stephen R. K. Glanville, *The Legacy of Egypt*, The Clarendon Press, Oxford, 1957, pp. 300–312.

[23] See Wilson, *op. cit.*, pp. 204–212.

either a very full or a very accurate account of it. The art of writing—the heart of elementary education—was, it appears, a staple in all formal secondary education.[24] On this level of education the student could give more attention to the style of his writing and composition; he could follow either the copybooks prepared for this purpose or he could acquaint himself with some of the writings, speeches, or religious pronouncements that had risen to places of respect in Egyptian life and letters. Chief among these were the important writings that made up the wisdom literature of Egypt. It was not the function of secondary education to open any new intellectual worlds or to broaden or illuminate fundamental literary or social issues; this was not the time for inculcating or even defending recognized moral or civil values. Secondary schools were probably little more than continuation schools. Apparently without complaint they assumed the functions of perfecting the work of elementary education and tried to make better craftsmen out of the small proportion of boys who continued their formal education in secondary schools.[25]

A somewhat different picture of secondary education may be drawn from the postelementary activities of the young of the upper classes. But with no notable exceptions, these activities were informal, and their guiding motives were found in the determination of the upper classes to perpetuate their code of manners and morals. Our understanding of secondary education in Egypt would be advanced very little by going into the maze of details on which the culture of the upper classes was built.

In the light of what has been said of secondary education here, and taking into account rather significant but unavoidable omissions, the reader should not be surprised to learn that nothing at all can be said about the teachers of these schools, either their actual work in the schools or their preparation for teaching, or about the organization, administration, support, or popularity of secondary education.[26]

HIGHER AND PROFESSIONAL EDUCATION IN EGYPT

The nations that made up the Orient considered education essentially a practical enterprise. Wherever higher or professional education flourished, it had two distinguishing characteristics: It was under the control of priests or professional men, who communicated its skill and content

[24] Maspero, *op. cit.*, p. 401.

[25] *Ibid.*, pp. 283–298.

[26] See Margaret A. Murray, *The Splendour That Was Egypt*, Philosophical Library, New York, 1949, pp. 117–121.

to relatives or social equals and it was informal in that neither curricula, faculties, nor degrees were fixed or recognized. In the Orient and in Egypt, during ancient times, there were neither colleges nor universities as we know them or as they were known from the twelfth century onward, although there were some fairly clear examples of higher and professional education.

The temple school, first of all an elementary and secondary school for the sons of priests and others whose social status qualified them to attend, communicated a variety of scientific and historical lore to its students.[27] It seems important to repeat that though these schools were regularly elementary in their outlook, they were also often higher schools. Where the line was drawn between lower and higher education is not easy to discover, but usually, higher education began when the priest who was the teacher in the temple school started to inculcate in his students those skills and attitudes that were the marks of his calling. Whether along with this professional training, for that is what it was, a scientific and literary education of an advanced kind was also given, must for us, at least, remain a mystery; but if secondary education was really a continuation of fundamentals introduced in elementary schools, one may be justified in assuming that higher education under these auspices was not narrowly vocational or professional. It would be a mistake, however, to think that professional or vocational training was not its primary objective.[28]

Almost without exception the testimony that we have agrees on this point: Professional knowledge was regarded as a kind of trade secret, and this knowledge was guarded carefully so that it seldom passed outside the immediate family circle. Higher education, then, was mainly a family affair. Whether for the priest with his divine mysteries or his knowledge of history and science, or for the physician with his magic potions or secret practices, higher education was entwined with the tradition that in it was knowledge which generated power. A real effort was made, usually successfully, by those who occupied a superior station in life to preserve their position by restricting higher and professional learning to those privileged by birth to know its deepest mysteries. It is reasonable to suppose that these restrictions were modified somewhat with the passing of time, but the generally acknowledged higher professions have maintained, nevertheless, a certain exclusiveness down through ancient, medieval, and modern times.

[27] Maspero, *op. cit.*, pp. 301–311.
[28] See Erman, *Life in Ancient Egypt*, pp. 329–364.

Military and engineering education was not quite as exclusive as education in priestcraft and medicine.[29] Perhaps this was so because Egyptian society seemed to have greater need for these professional skills or because the qualities of mind and body essential in these professions could not be assumed to exist in sufficient number within a small social circle. The architect, for example, enjoyed unusual privileges and was much revered. He, even more than a military leader, might be called by the king to manage the affairs of state. Knowing the high place accorded to architects and engineers, we may find the lack of more precise information on the higher education which prepared them a somewhat surprising omission. Preferences in the military establishment were given only to those who had a good literary and scientific education, and technical training for the art of war was left to the tried and true apprentice system of field training and actual combat. Since qualities of blood and birth did not control admission to the military profession, we may suppose that boys of more humble origins often looked forward to a military career;[30] yet we should not assume that military life offered democratic opportunities either for admission or for advancement.

One more professional pursuit needs brief notice here, that of the scribe. For the historian who tries to give an accurate picture of ancient life without abundant detail, the scribe of Egypt poses a difficult problem. There were, it appears, many grades of scribes. Some were prominent, learned, powerful men, resembling lawyers or judges more than clerks, who sat in on the affairs of state and moved in the privileged circles of society; others were simple secretaries, who knew little more than the art of tracing letters. We have already touched on the education of the latter type; of the former we know almost nothing. We may guess that the superior scribes were educated in some kind of higher school, perhaps in the temple schools, but beyond hazarding this guess, we can only say that many of them were qualified for exalted and exacting positions in government. Possibly some of these superior officials who were called scribes were really not scribes in the occupational sense. Since some positions, we know, bore the title of scribe, the mere fact that an able man filled the position did not mean that he had been or would become a professional scribe. He may have been an engineer, a physician, or a military man, and if he was, his education was of the usual type for any one of these professions. It is entirely possible that

---

[29] See Georg Steindorff and Keith C. Seele, *When Egypt Ruled the East,* University of Chicago Press, Chicago, 1953, pp. 86–91.
[30] See Oldfather, *op. cit.,* vol. I, p. 81; and Maspero, *op. cit.,* pp. 283–298.

when he was appointed to a position of some prominence his title made him a scribe.[31]

Passing from the content of higher learning to some other features, such as faculty, facilities, books, and degrees, we can say only this without going into considerable detail: Teachers were themselves professional men, and they used their homes, their offices, or their places of business, and sometimes the temples as the places where they might communicate their secrets and where youth might be given some opportunity for intellectual formation. They had many manuscripts in literature, history, and science, and these manuscripts formed a kind of base around which professional studies were built. Youth passed from these places of higher education when their learning, skill, and maturity were considered to be sufficient. No formal ceremonies launched the novice into the world of affairs.

Ancient Education in China

The origin of Chinese civilization is uncertain. Whether it was indigenous, whether it came from Central Asia or with the Sumerians from common sources, and similar questions—for example, the special dynasties and imperial periods and their cultural, political, and social impact —must be left for specialists. China was the home of a very old civilization, older perhaps than that of any other land except Egypt and Babylonia. Yet Chinese culture seems to have had very little direct influence on the general current of Western thought or Western education. Although one of the oldest nations of the world, China, if judged by Western standards, made relatively slow progress up the ladder of civilization. Because of its traditions and its geography, ancient China remained isolated from the people and the world around her. And in some respects the China of today has changed remarkably little from what she was more than two thousand years ago. In customs, relationships among the various classes of society, methods of business and labor, the administration of justice, and in the framework of thought, the practices of the Chinese have been stereotyped and until recent years have been practically unchangeable.[32]

Notwithstanding what others may regard as imperfections, the Chinese tend to accept their way of life with unusual complacency. In the past they were suspicious of innovation and opposed what they

---

[31] See *ibid.*, pp. 466–470; and Henri Frankfort, *Kingship and the Gods*, University of Chicago Press, Chicago, 1955, pp. 280–295.

[32] See C. P. Fitzgerald, *China: A Short Cultural History*, Frederick A. Praeger, Inc., New York, 1958.

thought were barbarian invasions of their culture; only a few decades ago did they open their cities to foreigners.

Preserving existing institutions and guarding their traditions were commitments not taken lightly. It may be said that the fundamental purpose of Chinese education was to impress upon each succeeding generation traditional ideals and customs and thus to prepare youth to take its place naturally and easily in the established and largely inflexible social order. Chinese educational work did not aim directly at the development of human abilities; in actual practice its principal preoccupation was to cram the memory with the maxims and usages of the past.

As we have indicated, China had a very ancient educational system. Schools, academies, and colleges could have been found there a thousand years or more before the Christian era.[33] Using age alone as the standard, we might accord to China a singular position in the history of education. But how well was this long period used? For two thousand years educational progress in China was slow and painful. The great wall of China, the largest artificial structure on earth, erected in the third century B.C., is some evidence of the early civilization of that land, and it indicates especially the ability of the people to achieve success in the arts of construction. It points also to a characteristic of the people: their willingness to be isolated, and their unwillingness to change. It is not easy to understand why the inventors of paper, printing, and gunpowder, and the first users of the mariner's compass, chose to remain in nearly complete isolation and in relatively static condition for so many centuries.[34]

Possibly the religious system which flourished contributed to this apparent retardation. There were three: Confucianism, Buddhism, and Taoism.[35] The first was chiefly the cult of the upper classes, of scholars and government officials; Buddhism and Taoism were religions of the masses. Buddhism, introduced into China near the beginning of the Christian era, appears to have been more influential and more socially significant than Taoism, but in time, we are told, some of its strength was dissipated in the practices of idol worship. Taoism, originally permeated with mysticism and in some ways related to primitive Buddhism, is said to have degenerated into a religion of spells and incanta-

---

[33] See P. W. Kuo, *The Chinese System of Public Education,* Teachers College Press, New York, 1915, pp. 7–20.

[34] See Howard S. Galt, *A History of Chinese Educational Institutions,* A. Probsthain, London, 1952.

[35] J. K. Shryock, *The Origin and Development of the State Cult of Confucius,* Appleton-Century-Crofts, Inc., New York, 1932, pp. 117–129.

tions. No one doubts that the power of religion in China was great. But it is not easy to attribute to its influence the long record of China's apparent unwillingness to move forward, or to charge it with immobilizing minds in superstition or steeping them in paralyzing traditions. Nor is it easy to assess religion's relationship to education—that is, to the day-to-day work of schools. And at the same time one must remember that China's greatest teacher was also a great religious leader. This was Confucius (ca. 551–478 B.C.). He was neither a prophet nor a revealer, but a provincial prefect and a philosopher, who directed his attention to social reform.[36] Throughout his career he sought to reestablish and preserve the customs and ideals of the past. He emphasized the virtues of obedience to parents and superiors, of reverence for ancestors, and an imitation of their lives. Strength and vigor were added to his teachings when he reinforced them with his own example. Among the many precepts, proverbs, and sayings that he left to posterity was the Chinese golden rule, "What you do not want done to yourself, do not do to others."

Confucius began to teach in a private school at the age of twenty-two. In time he gathered or attracted disciples and imbued them with his ideals. Apparently his influence had an indelible character, for generations of disciples honored his creed and his code, and he continued to be China's most important teacher long after his death. In this sense a Confucian School was founded and preserved. In his capacity as a schoolmaster, it is claimed, Confucius rejected no pupil with ability and ambition, and he accepted none without these qualities. He is credited with the maxim, "When I have presented one corner of a subject, and the pupil cannot make out the other three, I do not repeat the lesson." It may be fairly doubted, however, that this principle was honored generally in Chinese education. But without attempting to evaluate the practical application of Confucian thought, we can say that Confucius and his followers recognized knowledge, good behavior, fidelity, and uprightness of character as the proper ends of education.[37] These objectives were to be achieved in many ways, no doubt, but the chief means to their attainment was apparently the grading of instruction. Confucian theory, if not practice, seems to have been to organize four levels of education. The first level trained the mind by stimulating reflection and the heart by encouraging practice in virtue. The second level was concerned with correct and fluent speech; the third, with the science of government. The fourth involved practical and theoretical consid-

[36] See Woody, *op. cit.*, pp. 114–116.

[37] See Knight Biggerstaff, *The Earliest Modern Government Schools of China*, Cornell University Press, Ithaca, N. Y., 1961, pp. 18–33.

erations of morals. Although mental training was not omitted, the general purpose of education in the Confucian view was moral development. This purpose, along with other teachings of Confucius, exerted a profound influence upon the Chinese people and their educational doctrines for nearly twenty-five centuries.

Although Confucius erected and standardized traditions in morals and politics, his school of thought was not the only one to claim the allegiance of men's minds. But the complexities of Chinese philosophical and social thought cannot be unraveled in this book. Other features of ancient Chinese education should receive brief notice here.

The family in China had a position of singular importance. Family life was recognized as the basis of all social and civic order; because of its central position the family was venerated. Within the family circle, absolute power was vested in the father. In all matters which concerned the family or any of its members his word was law. The conception of the state as a family, only larger and more widely scattered, made for a ready transfer of the authority which the father had over the family to the emperor, who was empowered to wield absolute authority over his subjects—in this sense, members of his family.

But to return to domestic affairs. Here the relationship between husbands and wives was unenviable. Wives were really a class of slaves. Their position was, of course, consistent with the disdain that the Chinese had for women. Even in infancy the inferiority of a girl to a boy was clear. When a boy was born, there was reason for celebration, and the infant was dressed in the best that the family could provide. With the birth of an infant daughter, there were no very obvious signs of joy, and she was dressed in an indifferent manner. It was conventional for a father, when asked to number the children in his family, to count only the sons.

We have already referred to the educational objective accepted by the Chinese. But it should be understood that this general objective included, or could be made to include, social, political, and literary ends as well. The Chinese made no commitment, however, to anything resembling universal education, and made no effect to provide schools for all the people. Nonetheless, education was encouraged by restricting an enormous civil service system and all positions of power and honor to people who were well educated.[38]

To ensure the promotion of the educated and the advancement of the worthy, the state instituted a system of state examinations, probably around 1100 B.C., which continued in one form or another until the

[38] Chang-tu Hu, *China: Its People, Its Society, Its Culture*, Hraaf Press, New Haven, Conn., 1960, p. 410.

beginning of the T'ang period in A.D. 620. These examinations were administered by a board, which periodically permitted candidates to appear before it.[39] All who chose to present themselves, except the sons of barbers and one or two other classes, were allowed to compete. Depending on the age and ability of the individuals who were successful on the examination, opportunities for further education were offered or appointments to positions in the civil service were made. The ladder to success seems to have been related rather intimately to achievement in learning. Such a system of state examinations was completely organized somewhat late in antiquity, probably not before the Christian era in the Occident; but in a rudimentary form such a system may well have existed from about the time of Confucius.[40]

To attend any school in China was probably a rare privilege. At any rate, going to school for the first time was a great occasion. At about six or seven years of age, the child was ready to enter school. To provide schooling, parents sometimes pooled their resources and employed a teacher. This they were entirely free to do, for the government was concerned neither with the standards of the school nor the qualifications of the teacher. If parents were successful in engaging a teacher who was competent, the children were lucky, for good teachers were not easy to find; they were much in demand, and they usually commanded a good salary. In the absence of any kind of financial assistance from the government, these privately organized schools usually had to be content with whatever quality of teaching they could get. Under such circumstances, education could not have been compulsory, not, at least, in the sense that attendance in a school was required. Yet the educated boy, that is, one with elementary schooling behind him, was not uncommon. If parents were unwilling or unable to procure the services of a schoolmaster, it was possible for boys in some localities to attend schools which were endowed out of the charity of wealthy people. In all of this the state took no active role: there were no public elementary schools, and no public buildings were maintained as schoolhouses, although classes were sometimes held in temples or other public buildings. More often than not, however, school was kept in the home of the schoolmaster or in the room that was provided by some wealthy patron of the school. In the ordinary classroom the furniture consisted of an altar dedicated to Confucius and to the god of knowledge, a desk and chair for the teacher, and desks or stools for pupils. The latter were there

[39] *Ibid.*, 411–412.

[40] See Jên-chi Chang, *Pre-Communist China's Rural School and Community*, Christopher Publishing House, Boston, 1960, pp. 99–108; and Shryock, *op. cit.*, p. 52.

only if the students themselves were able to supply them; if not, they sat on the floor. Such rooms were simply places where the exercises of learning could be carried on; no thought was given to creating an educational environment for the broader and deeper formation of students.[41]

When a boy went to school, he went with much ceremony; his first day, as we have suggested above, was a day to remember, and it was hoped that the memories would be pleasant ones. At this time the school boy was given another name, perhaps to accentuate even more the beginning of a new period of life. The first years of school, however, went to make up an indifferent experience. They contained little to remind the boy of the promise held out on the first day of his educational adventure. He learned to read and write, and he was exposed to some training in computation. For most of the students education did not go beyond these elements. Actual teaching practices took no account of the learner's academic interests, if he had any. Students were expected simply to acquire the basic tools. This was done mainly by rote. Only after the names of the characters of the Chinese alphabet were learned was any effort made to teach the meaning of words. The child's instruction in writing was solely mechanical. The expression of thought was at best a secondary consideration, and ingenuity and resourcefulness, traits which Confucius had praised, seem to have had no place in these schools. Fear, not interest, was the motive which kept the child at his studies. Memory was the chief, perhaps the only, faculty thought to be in need of cultivation.[42]

There was nothing very elevating surrounding the experiences of a school day in this land of custom and iron-bound tradition. Yet the teachers were given considerable respect. Today's readers must find this deferential attitude somewhat surprising, considering that Chinese teachers belonged to a profession which lacked any very seriously applied requirements for admission. The profession was, in fact, open to anyone who chose to enter it. In his work in the classroom the teacher was aided considerably by a generous grant of authority; he assumed the father's place. Discipline was inflexible and severe; no good teacher spared the rod. Any teacher who earned the reputation for moderation in the administration of discipline was considered to be a poor teacher. Aside from his role as a disciplinarian, the teacher was mainly a hearer of lessons.

Accounts of Chinese education are, of course, subject to some

[41] See K. S. Latourette, *The Chinese: Their History and Culture,* The Macmillan Company, New York, 1946, pp. 788–794.

[42] See Robert E. Lewis, *The Educational Conquest of the Far East,* F. H. Revell Company, New York, 1903, pp. 113–117.

variation. China was a large land that could hold diverse practices. It is not unreasonable, therefore, to suppose that changes either in time or setting might require some alteration in the general and brief description we have given of education in that ancient land. As a final word, we might remark that beyond the elementary levels, education in China was not very well organized. We could even accept the statement that there was no organization at all for education on the higher levels. Boys who were able sometimes aspired to more learning than the elementary teacher could give them. They had to satisfy these aspirations, not in high schools and colleges, but through tutorial arrangements with men or older boys who could lay some claim to a scholar's reputation. It is unlikely that many distinctive details of teaching and learning under such conditions could find their way into history. It is entirely possible that tutors opened schools, and it is likely, also, that the needs of government motivated the state to sponsor some special schools. Neither the features of such schools nor the schools themselves, if and when they existed, made a deep imprint on the history of ancient education. Aside from the rich accounts of what may be described as internal history, we find almost no sources that place China in a position of pedagogic influence in the ancient world, although it is undoubtedly correct to believe that selective cultural influence from China ranged more widely in the early societies.

The Foundations of Education among the Jews

Whether one finds the birthplace of Western civilization in Egypt, in Israel, or elsewhere, he cannot possibly overlook the achievements of the Jews, made against considerable obstacles, or the contributions they made to the forming of an educational ideal that gained general acceptance in the West. In the first days of their history, the Jews were little different from other primitive people, and what has been said earlier about education among primitive tribes applies also to them. There appears to be no basis for claiming a precociousness for these people; culture and learning did not come any more naturally or easily for them than for any others. Nor can one avoid the conclusion that the slow interchange of ideas which led to what we may call civilization enabled all early peoples to lay a foundation for culture and learning. Isolation slowed progress; amalgamation speeded the growth of an intellectual life which, in either simple or complex form, permitted men to move slowly out of a primitive stage of existence and prepared them to begin building a better world and a finer life for themselves and their progeny.

As a nomadic people the Jews pursued a pastoral calling. Sometime around 1650 B.C. they wandered into Egypt, where they began to acquire some of the civilization of that country, but where they enjoyed little, if any, freedom.[43] In time they became a subjected people, and, in a state of near slavery, were forced to labor for their Egyptian masters.[44] Moses led them from this bondage in about 1220 B.C., and they settled in the land of Canaan. Here they experimented with various types of social and political organization for nearly a century. This was the period of the judges and kings (1150–586 B.C.), and the time, too, when the kingdom was divided into Judah and Israel. In 721 B.C. the Israelites were swept away by the Assyrians; in 586 B.C. the people of Judah became the captives of the Babylonians. Babylon was reconquered by the Persian Cyrus, who returned the Jews to Jerusalem in 536 B.C., and they remained under Persian protection for the next two centuries. Under Ezra and Nehemiah the Jews revived their earlier cultural and material standards, although this renaissance was relatively brief and ended about the time of Alexander's death in 323 B.C. Thus, after the middle of the sixth century B.C. began a series of suppressions, which lasted through 175 B.C. and included domination by the Persians (538–333 B.C.) and by the Greeks, Egyptians, and Syrians (332–175 B.C). Jewish independence was enjoyed from 175 to 63 B.C., when Rome began to master the Jews. The year A.D. 70 marks the end of a period of continual decline in the fortunes of the Jews; from this date they became a persecuted people without a national home and were forced to wander throughout the world.

With such obstacles constantly confronting them, it is remarkable that the Jews were able to preserve their identity, to say nothing of building a culture which became for centuries a source of religious and moral inspiration and knowledge to many peoples. Among the many symbols that gave meaning to the Jew's life, that which stands out especially is a strong note of monotheism. The Jew gave his undivided allegiance to one God. This belief came in time to be surrounded by a body of law, some of it divinely inspired, which called to the Jew's attention his obligations and duties to God. The law became the central feature of Jewish life and the fundamental motivation for learning.[45]

---

[43] See Max Wurmbrand, *The Jewish People*, Massadah-P. E. C. Press, Jerusalem, 1966, pp. 51–53; and W. M. F. Petrie, *Egypt and Israel*, SPCK, London, 1912, p. 17.

[44] *Ibid.*, pp. 21–40.

[45] The law should not be thought of as being tantamount to statutes. This would be a far too narrow conception of law and would miss the whole point of Jewish law. The law was, rather, an oral tradition which contained and illuminated life's basic ideals. See George Horowitz, *The Spirit of Jewish Law*, Central Book Co., New York, 1953, pp. 660–680; and J. M. P. Smith, *The Origin and History of Hebrew Law*, University of Chicago Press, Chicago, 1931.

INFORMAL EDUCATION AMONG THE JEWS

With the exception of some private schools in the larger towns, all Jewish education during the postexilic period and before the Babylonian captivity was informal. This means that fathers and mothers were charged with the responsibility of giving their offspring a religious and moral education based on the traditions of the people and the law as it was given to them by Moses and interpreted for them by the prophets. The education of children was not an obligation to be taken lightly, for Jehovah had commanded that the law be "taught diligently unto thy children." Apart from instructing children in religion and morals, parents had to prepare them for life in the world and to give them some skill for meeting the multiple demands that a somewhat primitive society might impose. This preparation included physical training as well as an informal apprenticeship for life. How could life be sustained without men who were hunters, herdsmen, and fighters, and women who were skilled in the household arts? And after all of this practical training was accomplished, there was still time for social education, which, it appears, went little beyond games, contests, and dancing. As time passed a regular apprentice system came into existence. Fathers were to teach their sons a trade, and the secrets of the trade were considered to be family property.

Since life among the Jews probably did not require the keeping of records or the rendering of reports, as in Egypt, the art of writing did not command the attention of the Jew.[46] Jewish scribes are usually mentioned in the historical sources relevant to the postexilic period, but such scribes were simple clerks who had neither position nor learning—quite different, as we shall see, from the scribes of a later period. The art they possessed, it is assumed, was borrowed from the Egyptians. Without any great need for writing—the Jewish law was inscribed in the heart—and without ready access to good and inexpensive materials for writing, the art itself was not an important part of education's content during those years when Jewish education was solely in the hands of the family. Without any emphasis on writing—and surely there was little in the way of a written literature—reading was not an essential skill. It seems fairly clear that some members of the society were both learned and literate, although it does not follow necessarily that any attention was given either to reading or to writing in Jewish family education.[47]

[46] See Petrie, *op. cit.*, pp. 31–50.

[47] See Roland de Vaux, *Ancient Israel: Its Life and Institutions,* McGraw-Hill Book Company, New York, 1961.

FORMAL EDUCATION AMONG THE JEWS

Perhaps the claim could be sustained that Jewish education was more effective as a purely family practice than it was when it became more fully institutionalized. There seems to be little question that education's history was longer as a family affair than it was as a school's function. But any attempt to prove such a claim would be so subject to involvements and fine distinctions that the possibility of historical illumination would be remote; and in such an exercise the important point would have to be neglected, namely, that the Jewish family, with schools or without them, never relinquished any of its responsibilities for the education of the young.[48] Jewish schools were established to supplement, not replace, the educational activities of the family.[49]

In the postexilic period, the economic life of the Jew was altered somewhat; in the earlier times he had been a farmer or a shepherd; now he became a craftsman, fisherman, or merchant, and he lived in a town, where the economic environment enabled him to profit from his new endeavor. In a more urban than rural setting a class of scribes, who became the educators of the Jews, came into existence. The new Jewish scribe was different from either the Egyption scribe or the earlier Jewish scribe; in a sense he took the place of the prophets of the old order.

These new scribes became the Jew's first great teachers. They were lawyers, interpreters, and writers, and from them the people of Israel received interpretations of God's law and directions for conforming to it. But they were not ordinary teachers or teachers in an ordinary sense; it is doubtful, for example, that they ever limited their activities to classrooms. Their influence was felt, not in guiding teaching and learning processes, but in setting a pattern and tone for a national intellectual and moral life. Nor were these scribes simple men of common origin. The skill and erudition demanded of one who aspired to the scribal order—and this very likely was the ambition of every Jewish boy —required years of leisure for study and sufficient wealth to ensure the opportunity for leisure. Scribes came from a class and in turn became a class. No other occupation merited the same reverence or prestige as that of the scribe.[50]

To become a scribe a young man had first to secure the necessary leisure; and, if nature's endowment of intelligence was generous, he himself would have to have the drive to study with men who had al-

[48] Eliezer Ebner, *Elementary Education in Ancient Israel*, Block Publishing Co., New York, 1956, pp. 29–37.

[49] Deut. 6:1–9.

[50] Ecclus. 38:24–39.

ready been inducted into the ranks of an intellectual elite. No schools or universities promised the youth that they would start him on his way to success. Here, as elsewhere in early societies, the bases of an apprentice system were in evidence; prospective scribes were taught, guided, and counseled by men who were already members of the guild. Still, this was not a craft guild in which a skill or trade could be perfected under the watchful eyes of a master; rather, it was a kind of association, in which the young could learn from, and be inspired by, those who were already in possession of knowledge. Though communication of knowledge of the law was undoubtedly an important element in such associations, it was through contact, the friction of mind on mind, that understanding and sometimes wisdom were achieved. Yet with all its excellence the scribal order was unable to broaden its scope or extend its vision much beyond the law. The scribes became myopic in their concern for the law and were inclined to be rigorous, casuistic, and narrow in its interpretations.[51] With both strengths and weaknesses, however, the scribes were the intellectual leaders among the Jews and the teachers of a whole people.

Schools for the people receive no notice in the history of Jewish education until about 200 B.C. This omission of record, of course, need not mean that such schools did not exist before; in the absence of information about them, the historian can only suggest that if there was formal or institutionalized education, it may have been carried on in connection with the temples, the shrines, or the synagogues. The synagogue was surely a place of meditation, prayer, and instruction; but the instruction sponsored there was probably an exposition of the law. Though the instruction of children in lesser branches of education must have been considered important, there is no definite evidence that synagogues themselves became what we today would call elementary schools. By about 70 B.C. schools were conducted in or near synagogues, probably simply because other facilities were not available and those of the synagogue were satisfactory. On the other hand, a certain amount and kind of instruction, not necessarily in the formal elements of education, was an essential in the synagogue's general purpose.[52]

Schools for elementary education were common by A.D. 64, when the decree was issued that all Jewish boys had to attend elementary

[51] B. Spiers, *The School System of the Talmud*, Stock, London, 1898, pp. 28–34, 40–54.

[52] See Nathan Drazin, *History of Jewish Education*, Johns Hopkins Press, Baltimore, 1940, pp. 60–80; Fletcher H. Swift, *Education in Ancient Israel*, The Open Court Publishing Company, La Salle, Ill., 1919, pp. 90–91; and Ebner, *op. cit.*, pp. 60–72.

schools. This decree is attributed to Rabbi Joshua ben Gamala. With it we have what is, perhaps, the clearest evidence of formal education among the Jews.[53]

These elementary schools were not in their essentials greatly different from elementary schools in any other place at any other time in educational history: Reading, writing, and simple computation were taught, as were the social and religious inheritances. No subject was approached with greater care than the law, and for this the chief textbooks were Leviticus and Deuteronomy.[54] Advanced instruction, in which a boy might be engaged when about fifteen years of age, was mainly a continuation of the study of the law; but schools for such advanced instruction could hardly ever be found except in a good-sized town.[55]

The curriculum of Jewish schools was definitely conservative. There was no thought of change and no mention made of progress; boys and girls were expected to memorize the code of life and keep it. This code was neither flexible nor ephemeral; it was to be engraved on the hearts and the souls of children. The chief engravers were parents and teachers. To achieve the objectives common to all Jewish education and to employ the means which were available to the schools, teachers had to adopt methods or techniques of instruction as permanent and inflexible as the goals themselves. The content of the curriculum was truth, completely and perfectly recorded by the scribes, and this content was to be mastered with thoroughness and accuracy.

In the Jewish conception of child nature especially, and also in the belief that all knowledge was assembled and just waiting to be known, one may find the central justification for the educational process adopted and approved by the Jews. Children were judged to be "wild things" who had to be tamed. If they were left to themselves, their natural willfulness would prevail, and they would never achieve the self-discipline or docility that perfect subjection to the law demanded.[56] This view of child nature does not, of course, set the Jews apart in any way; it was accepted, seemingly without question, by all early peoples. But what was accepted theoretically may not always have been applied

---

[53] See Abraham Cohen, *Everyman's Talmud*, E. P. Dutton & Co., New York, 1949, pp. 231–238.

[54] Drazin, *op. cit.*, p. 60; and Ebner, *op. cit.*, pp. 38–50.

[55] See S. W. Baron, *A Social and Religious History of the Jews*, Columbia University Press, New York, 1952, vol. II, pp. 88–93.

[56] See Adolphe Lods, *The Prophets and the Rise of Judaism*, K. Paul, Trench, Trubner & Co., Ltd., London, 1955, pp. 301–306.

practically in Jewish child care and education.[57] Jewish children were handled carefully and sternly, but certainly, a way of life which prefaced a Christian conception of man's nature, the severity so common to the time was tempered by the Jewish parent and teacher with some tenderness. Their love for children mitigated, though in no way altered, their sense of duty; parents could and did demand exact conformity to social and religious discipline, but they could do all this without descending to harshness and cruelty.

In the training and education of Jewish girls we may find the main clue to the breadth and vision of these people. In lands around them the conviction had prevailed for centuries and continued to prevail that girls and women were naturally inferior to men and boys. Though fully aware of this traditional degrading of females, the Jews did not accept the concept. It is true that schools, when they were opened, did not admit girls; and in economic, political, and religious activities women were not accorded anything like modern equality; yet certainly motherhood was honored, and Jewish women were the fortunate recipients of respect and reverence. Girls received a careful and thorough domestic training, and in some homes they learned to read and write. A few Jewish women gained great prominence in religion and letters. In no other ancient land were women so fortunate, for in no other land was there this same conception of man or the same understanding of his relationship to one God.[58]

"Fear of the Lord" stands out as the chief motive underlying Jewish life and work. Not only children but all people were admonished and threatened with divine reprisals. This was the unassailable value in life, which permeated emotion, understanding, and the standards of conduct. Fear of the Lord was accepted as the beginning of wisdom. In education this precept was translated to mean that the child was to accept unquestioningly everything taught to him and preserve and transmit inviolably all that he had learned. No other principle could have supported better or served so well the mnemonic methods of instruction that were universally recognized and accepted.[59]

When the basic guiding force in Jewish life was not sufficient to motivate the child in his work, other means were sometimes employed. Punishment of various kinds was a means to stimulate a boy given to sloth; rewards and praise might be used to encourage even greater

[57] See David Daube, *Studies in Biblical Law*, The University Press, Cambridge, England, 1947, pp. 181–183.

[58] See Dagobert D. Runes, *The Hebrew Impact on Western Civilization*, Philosophical Library, New York, 1951, pp. 700–722.

[59] See Horowitz, *op. cit.*, pp. 630–635.

effort from children already bent to their tasks of absorbing the content of their curriculum. In extreme cases, where boys were hardened recalcitrants, the penalty of death could have been imposed.[60] Consistently with the Jew's view of things, however, extreme measures to encourage learning or to exact discipline were resorted to only after more moderate devices had been tried. Reproof and admonition were universally accepted as better motivators than punishment or chastisement.

In the *Talmud* one finds a collection and codification of Jewish religious and legal ordinances, interpretations of the works of the prophets, science, folk tales, ethical and historical teachings, and various kinds of knowledge; but he also finds a fund of fundamental educational ideals. This is to be expected, because a variety of institutions of higher learning—colleges of scribes and some synagogues—had a hand in producing the *Talmud*, a document which had a permanent influence on Jewish education.

Although one would certainly not want to accept uncritically a codification of law and life that was put in written form about the second century A.D. as a faithful and necessarily accurate account of Jewish practices common hundreds of years before, the *Talmud* is, nevertheless, a source of information which must not be overlooked. In it the status of the teacher is clearly enunciated: "The teacher precedes the father; the wise man, the king." In their respect for instruction and for the intermediary whose function it was to teach, the Jews apparently remained constant. For prophets, scribes, and rabbis, as well as for teachers concerned with guiding and directing the most elementary phases of learning, the Jews had nothing but reverence. All these men were teachers; all were doing God's work. And the teachers themselves, whatever their rank on the intellectual or social ladder, were dedicated to their vocation. Teaching was not a function to be performed by just anyone; and if we may judge from the various accounts given of Hebrew teachers, aspiring teachers approached their work with timidity and humility. Their obligation was heavy, and they felt it keenly. One would not venture unhesitatingly upon an occupation dedicated to performing God's work. No little share of the success of Jewish education was due to the high quality of Jewish teaching.[61]

After centuries of near isolation, the Jews' intellectual life was affected by the influx of Greek ideals and language. The new current of thought began to be felt three or four centuries before the birth of Christ. The extent of this influence on Jewish education is not easy to

---

[60] Deut. 21:18–21.
[61] See Cohen, *op. cit.,* pp. 81–90; and Ebner, *op. cit.,* 51–62.

evaluate; scholars voice some question as to the nature of its effect and as to whether the effect was permanent or ephemeral. No one can be certain that the influences moved only in one direction, for the moral ideal in education—undoubtedly the distinctive quality of all education among the Jews—came in time to demand some attention from the Greeks, especially from the Athenians.

Summary

The uncomplicated education of early societies, with constant, unrelenting attention to life's essentials, could continue only so long as men were preoccupied with the things they could not afford to ignore. Had life remained unchanged, education would have remained static too, but life did change, and men could no longer be content to master the arts of simple existence. As their world grew larger and as they passed through upgrading social periods, education—still centered on utility—was directed to keep pace.

Still in a context of practicality, the syllabus of experience was broadened to include skills no less important than, but different from, the ones primitive men had prized. Tilling land, remaining in one geographic location, organizing simple trades, and affirming the worth of a division of labor all made education and training wear a new face. We begin to see it most clearly in Egypt, where, now, classes emerged in the general society, and education was geared to the appropriate tasks of a class and somewhat segregated life. On the upper perimeter of society, some men began to enjoy wealth and leisure. Not having to spend all their waking hours in labor, they could turn their attention toward what was fine, ornamental, enjoyable, and spiritual. And they could think seriously about the route their ancestors had taken through history. The products of this human exertion became themselves objects worthy of study. But they could not be studied seriously without schools.

At some point in history schools were created to supplement the home and society as educational agencies. What a school taught was, on the one hand, relevant to the life of the group it served; on the other, it was something the home or society generally could no longer teach with the same efficiency.

Whether in Egypt, China, or among the Jews, schools arrived as afterthoughts—as supplements—to an educational program believed to be sound. Schools helped and followed, they did not create and lead; and their commission, either broad or narrow, was securely grounded in the peoples' values. By the time we are ready to leave education among the ancient Jews, we see dimensions of education that, while less refined and explicit, are as broad and significant as our own: physical wellbeing, fundamental tools of learning, vocational skill, and moral and religious values.

II

Greek Educational Ideals & Practices

Before the Homeric age—about 850 B.C.—Greeks followed the customs of their ancestors and concentrated on the values associated with primitive life. We know too little about the foundations of Greek history to say whether imported or indigenous ideals motivated the inhabitants of the peninsula toward the better things of life, but in spite of historical mysteries concealing Greek origins, we know about as much about them as they themselves knew. Our purpose, however, is not so much to elaborate the origins of a people, but to find the mainstream of their cultural evolution and the development and form of their educational aspirations.[1] This purpose may, to some extent, be achieved by

[1] The reader interested in the broader backgrounds to Greek history should see F. A. Hooper, *Greek Realities: Life and Thought in Ancient Greece,* Charles

taking the Homeric age as a starting point, for before this the Greeks did very little to merit our special attention.

Even beginning with Homer, it is hazardous to study Greek culture and education with any assumptions about unity: legends and tales overburden oral and written accounts, and certainty is extremely elusive until at least the first Olympiad—the beginning of the Olympian games in 776 B.C. But more dependable records only serve to convince us that to write about the Greeks and assign to them a cultural unity—something possible with the Jews, for example, who were one people sharing common goals and values—is impossible. Ancient Greece was composed of discrete groups whose racial origins can be differentiated, and these tribes, clans, or "city states" (as they came finally to be known) may have had some common traditions and social and cultural goals. So much is readily admitted. But there were also sharp differences, and these differences, more than the similarities, guided the city states along different, even hostile, cultural routes.

In this book we must be interested not in historically inconsequential cultural enclaves but in cultural models whose influence was both lasting and profound. We find these models in Athens and Sparta, Greece's two best-known city states, which represented Ionian and Dorian cultural ideals respectively.

If Sparta and Athens—but especially Athens—are sources from which some present-day cultural ideals are drawn (and debate on this point no longer seems rewarding) then we are justified in looking to Greece for the foundations of Western education. Never totally immunized from the world around them, the Greeks must have learned from others: not everything in their culture was pure invention. But they did create models for mental life and human culture—sometimes by invention, sometimes by imitation, and sometimes by artful combinations of both—and bequeathed them to the West. The Greeks were the first people seriously concerned with and supremely dedicated to human values. Among ancient men, they (especially the Athenians) were vanguard advocates of the arts of thought and of expression.

Life and Education in Sparta

In no ancient land was education given more attention than in Sparta, for there it was appointed to guard the status quo.[2] In consequence of their

---

Scribner's Sons, New York, 1967; and Chester G. Starr, *The Awakening of the Greek Historical Spirit*, Alfred A. Knopf, Inc., New York, 1968.

[2] Kenneth J. Freeman, *Schools of Hellas*, 3d ed., The Macmillan Company, New York, 1922, p. 12.

military prowess and, to some extent, of the accidents of history, Spartan citizens were a master class dominating a majority of the people—mainly noncitizens—who lived in the city state. Some noncitizen Spartan residents could trace their lineage to ancient tribes which had roamed the Spartan plains long before the first Dorians appeared to suppress and subjugate them around 1104 B.C.; others were captives of war. But together, and without reference to background, these noncitizens were forced to serve their masters. Now and then, engaging in the dangerous enterprise of conspiracy, they upset social balances and won short-lived respite from an uninspiring existence. For the most part, however, their opposition led only to greater oppression, so in the end it was better for perioeci (freeborn persons) and helots (slaves or serfs) to stay within the narow boundaries that law and custom prescribed.

In such a system the citizen, with slaves to do all his work, had leisure to embark on the one human "art" that was important: war. By the Spartans, and sometimes by their Athenian neighbors, who now disappoint us, war was recommended as a liberal art. Without taking the time or space to argue the validity of the assertion that the Spartans engaged in liberal arts in preparing for and waging war, one may venture a contradictory claim: No activity in which a Spartan could have engaged was more practical than training for military efficiency.[3] His life, together with the safety of the city state and the perpetuation of Spartan standards of living, was challenged constantly both by the helots, the largest group of subject people in Sparta, and by Sparta's foreign enemies, with whom war was more or less regularly waged. Military efficiency was more than a simple luxury to be afforded in a state whose citizens had leisure to use in this way; it was a necessity to be supported without interruption in order to preserve a way of life which Sparta refused to alter and which indoctrination, training, and education ardently justified.[4]

Personal, intellectual, and moral autonomy were blocked by totalitarianism in its purest form in Sparta. Boys and girls were born and bred to serve the state. Citizenship implied subservience to state goals, and severe penalties—death, ostracism, or at least disgrace—were visited on young people who failed in their patriotic duty to dedicate their energy and their lives to the state's inflexible objectives. Personal

[3] See Thomas Woody, *Life and Education in Early Societies,* The Macmillan Company, New York, 1949, pp. 234–240; Freeman, *op. cit.,* pp. 12–38; and H. I. Marrou, *A History of Education in Antiquity,* Sheed & Ward, Inc., New York, 1956, pp. 15–16.

[4] Plutarch *Lycurgus.* In *Plutarch's Lives,* Loeb Classical Library, Harvard University Press, Cambridge, Mass., 1914–1926, vol. I, pp. 293–297.

thought, interest, and hope were subordinated to the state's good. Sparta became an armed camp. Neither an enemy nor an innovation could easily penetrate the city's borders.

With almost complete freedom from the cares of money making (citizens were supported from land allotted to them and tilled by their slaves), and with no trade or profession to occupy either their time or their thought, Spartans were free to imbibe and practice the accepted mode of life.[5] Although patriotism and obedience were virtues expected of both men and women, the means used to inculcate these and subsidiary virtues were different for boys and girls. A Spartan woman was not considered a man's equal, but neither was she doomed to a role of servitude. Her first duty was to bear strong, healthy children; her second was to show, by example of deed and word, her complete devotion to the state. Wives and mothers did not engage in actual combat on the field of battle, but with moral strength and resolute patriotism they supported their soldier husbands and sons and encouraged them to give, if need be, their last full measure of devotion to the state. So drilled were women in this sacrificial attitude and so high was the premium placed on fortitude that a Spartan mother could tearlessly advise her son, about to leave for the frontier and battle, to come home with his shield or on it.[6]

No school was assigned the role of preparing Spartan girls for their mission in life. Aside from play and exercise which might have been taken with boys in the girl's earlier years, the education of a girl was directed by her mother. But this was not an education in the household arts like that given to the women in every other early society. Spartan women were free from toil; all menial tasks, for that matter, all domestic routine, were the work of slaves. It may be said, then, that the education and training of Spartan girls was carried on informally and somewhat incidentally. There was no doubt, however, as to the objective to be achieved, and mothers and society at large were the Spartan girls' teachers.

The life for which the Spartan boy was prepared demanded that he be a thoroughly trained citizen, which was equivalent to a demand that he be militarily efficient. These boys needed the perseverance which comes from firmly held ideals, but they needed also strength, endurance, cunning, and courage. To these basic qualities was added skill in the use of arms and a thorough knowledge of tactics and strat-

[5] Freeman, *op. cit.*, p. 11.

[6] See Charles A. Forbes, *Greek Physical Education,* Appleton-Century-Crofts, Inc., New York, 1929, pp. 40–44; and H. A. Harris, *Greek Athletes and Athletics,* Indiana University Press, Bloomington, 1966.

egy. Such objectives were too important to be left to chance or treated casually, so Sparta's code gave the training of boys precedence over all else save war itself. There are many ways of characterizing the Spartan system, but its most striking feature was rigidity. Nowhere in Sparta was conservatism more apparent than in the carefully arranged steps enabling a boy to ascend a figurative ladder to citizenship and the life of a soldier.[7]

THE EDUCATION OF BOYS IN SPARTA

There may be some inaccuracy in referring to the regimen approved for Spartan boys as education. Although authorities do not always agree as to whether these people were literate or illiterate, whether they knew Homer, or whether, in fact, they had any music, art, or literature, it may be too exacting a judgment to maintain that their training was entirely devoid of intellectual discipline.[8] Still, the years Spartan boys spent in what we might call schools were years devoted to systematic physical and military training, and no definite extant evidence shows that any attention was given to such elements of education as reading and writing, to say nothing at all of mental culture.[9]

Tradition attributes intellectual keenness and laconic speech to the Lacedaemonians; their emissaries and generals are said to have been impressive men, fortified with skill and courage and knowledge. But music, art, and literature that did not serve the state's practical objectives, that is, that did not stimulate emotions believed to be related to patriotism, found few patrons and sometimes, according to many authorities, were actually outlawed. Spartans were suspicious of both the novel and the complex; they could, and did, ostracize a man or a boy who, after being on official business in a foreign land, returned to Sparta with a knowledge of rhetoric which he did not conceal.[10]

[7] For what still stands as the best single treatment of Spartan social and educational values, see Werner W. Jaeger, *Paideia: The Ideals of Greek Culture,* Oxford University Press, New York, 1945, vol. I, pp. 77–115.

[8] See W. Barclay, *Educational Ideals in the Ancient World,* Collins, London, 1959. pp. 39–51.

[9] Many authors write on this point. Among them, Isocrates (*Panathenaicus,* Loeb Classical Library, Harvard University Press, Cambridge, Mass., 1927–1929, vol. II, pp. 209, 251), who asserted that the Spartans were illiterate; Plutarch (*Lycurgus,* in *op. cit.,* vol. I, p. 257), who claimed the Spartans had just enough literary skill to "serve them;" and J. F. Dobson (*Ancient Education and Its Meaning to Us,* Longmans, Green & Co., Inc., New York, 1932, p. 17) and Forbes (*op. cit.,* pp. 13–16), who take the position that nothing was allowed in education not serving the state's practical goals.

[10] See Charles S. Baldwin, *Ancient Rhetoric and Poetic,* The Macmillan Company, New York, 1924, pp. 18–22; and Freeman, *op. cit.,* p. 21.

Intellectual education was not an objective in the Spartan system. Beyond memorizing the laws of the state, acquiring a sketchy knowledge of Homer, and listening to the tales of heroes, genealogies, and military actions of the past, students were apparently given little training that could be called intellectual. Its place was taken by social and ethical education and, of course, by physical and military training. To posterity the Spartan left few mysteries concerning the hierarchy of objectives he espoused.

To secure the values held to be most desirable, the Spartans, in the sixth century B.C., began to develop a system of training from which they permitted few deviations. Their view of life, as well as of law and education, was given to them, it is said, by Lycurgus and was preserved in *Eunomia*. But this lawgiver may have been either a man or a god—tradition honors both claims—or neither, for there is reason to believe the Spartan system was already in the process of evolution before Lycurgus appeared on the scene, and that the system was adapted to meet problems with which Lycurgus could not have been familiar.[11] Whatever the truth may be on this point, the laws of Lycurgus and the system they ordained prevailed with only minor amendments throughout the city state's history. In connection with the laws of Lycurgus it is probably worth mentioning that they were contained neither in constitutional nor in statutory codification but in oral tradition.[12] This tradition dates from 855 B.C.

The first step in preparing boys for citizenship was taken long before they had attained either physical or mental maturity. Within a few days after the birth of a male child—and after he had been bathed in wine to test his endurance—a council of elders appointed to act in the name of the state inspected the infant. It rested with this council to determine the boy's fate. Should it, in its wisdom, decide that the boy was of sturdy stock, strong and healthy, he was given a chance to live as a member of a citizen household. Any other verdict placed the boy's life in jeopardy, for without the council's approval the child could not be reared for the life of a citizen. He was taken to Mount Taügetos and exposed. There he might be left to die unless the helots or the perioeci rescued him.[13] To be snatched from the jaws of death by exposure was not a reentry to the Spartan citizenship circle; rejection by the council canceled forever a boy's chances of becoming a citizen-soldier.

[11] J. A. Bury, *A History of Greece*, St. Martin's Press, Inc., New York, 1922, p. 135; and Morton Smith, *The Ancient Greeks*, Cornell University Press, Ithaca, N. Y., 1960, pp. 30–31.

[12] Jaeger, *op. cit.*, vol. I, pp. 82–83.

[13] Plutarch *Lycurgus*. In *op. cit.*, vol. I, p. 255.

But the brighter side of the whole affair, if, indeed, it was the brighter side, was approval by the council. From this time until the lad was seven, he was left in the care of his mother and his nurses. But the state had made its claim on him, and this was a claim never to be relinquished.

When the boy reached seven years of age, his father enrolled him in the state training school, and with this matriculation systematic preparation for citizenship began. Even before this, however, the boys had been exposed to military life and to adult ideals. They had accompanied their fathers to *pheiditia,* or military clubs, and had sat on the floor to listen to the pithy speech of their elders or to snatch food from the mess table. In a way, the club was as important to the boys as it was to their fathers. Any Spartan who was unable to contribute his share of the provisions for the club lost his membership and also his rights as a citizen; his son, moreover, lost his opportunity for education in the state system. Maintaining solvency was probably a burden which fell more heavily on the slaves than on the masters, for no Spartan would sacrifice his place as a citizen if his slaves could be made to produce more wealth for him. Wealth for its own sake was not, of course, a motive for the Spartans; all a master wanted was enough to fulfill his obligations as a citizen. One of a Spartan father's obligations was the complete support of his sons through the educational system.[14] There was no such thing as state support of education, although state control was both obvious and inflexible. The obligation to pay for the education of one's sons began when, at seven years of age, they became what we would call "wards of the state."

The little boys who were ushered into what, in many respects, was a new life were not entirely unprepared for the rude regimen that faced them. Their infant years had been, in fact, a kind of preparation for what they were now to meet. And at this point we might inject a word of caution to students who have begun to form an image of the first level of formal training in Sparta: In no way did the Spartan school adumbrate the elite boarding schools of later centuries. The lads were organized into "packs" or classes called either *ilai* or *agelai.* It is usually assumed that each of the *ilai* contained sixty-four boys; the exact composition of the *agelai* is unknown. In these packs the boys were foragers and apprentice fighters. They roamed the countryside to exercise their bodies and to pilfer food for their stomachs. A single garment was allowed each boy; with it and whatever else he could improvise or steal he protected himself from the winter's cold and the summer's heat.

[14] Freeman, *op cit.,* pp. 14–15.

The boy's chief teacher was called a *paidonomos*. He was a citizen of rank and a soldier of repute; under his direction a number of assistants carried on the more immediate supervisory functions in connection with the boys' training. It would not be a distortion of history to associate this principal teacher's office with that of the superintendent of a military academy or a commanding general directing military maneuvers. Or one might think of the position as similar to that of a national minister of education, or, even better, of a director of education and training for all the boys of a country.

The assistants, not the *paidonomos*, came in contact with the boys: They corrected them and flogged them and, it may be supposed, gave them specific instructions as well as general directions. But learning by doing was the principle most often honored. Under the leadership of a boy, by which term we mean someone under twenty, who demonstrated his qualifications for leadership, the pack ventured into the territory surrounding the city state; by being exposed to the basic needs for survival the boys learned what they lived.

Life in the open, dependence on one's self, exercise, fighting, foraging, stealing, killing, these were the constants of the curriculum. Stealing was permitted within certain limits; that is, after reaching a stipulated age, probably ten or eleven, a boy could steal certain things from certain classes of people.[15] Such discriminate pilfering was entirely legal. Because most Spartan property was held in common, one may suspect that what was stolen was taken from noncitizen groups. According to the testimony of Xenophon in his *Anabasis,* the Spartans were the most skillful highwaymen of the time.[16] Killing, like stealing, was, within certain limits, an approved military exercise. One may doubt that young boys just being inducted into the packs sought mortal encounters with helots or slaves, but as they became older and bolder they did seek to apply some of the many tactics they had been taught. Bands of young men not yet inducted into the professional ranks of the soldier—therefore young men who were not yet citizens—bivouacked in the country, and when their leaders gave the word, they ambushed a lone helot simply to gain the experience of slaughter.[17] But this was no crime. The elders had seen to it that war was declared on the helots each year, not for this purpose only; but in such a manner these assassinations were legalized.

From the ages of seven to eighteen the boys of Sparta were oc-

[15] Plutarch *Lycurgus.* In *op. cit.,* vol. I, pp. 257–259.

[16] Xenophon *Anabasis* iv. 6.14. G. Bell & Sons, Ltd., London, 1915.

[17] Plutarch *Lycurgus.* In *op. cit.,* vol. I, p. 291; Isocrates *Panathenaicus.* In *op. cit.,* vol. II, p. 277.

cupied in preparing themselves for the life of a soldier. These years were really devoted to a kind of basic military training.

At seventeen or eighteen the boys became *ephebi* and entered upon a new phase of preparation for the life of a citizen. They were released from their pack schools, took an oath of allegiance to the state, an oath which included a special clause expressing hatred for the state's enemies, and joined new packs. The packs for these older boys tended to be private organizations; that is, they stood somewhere between the military organization itself and the "boarding school" which the young men had just left. A young Spartan with ambition or position recruited as many young men as were willing to join him in his venture. He became the chief. The father of this young chief acted in the capacity of a superintendent for this private army or military unit; over its actions he exercised almost complete authority, and for its accomplishments he felt a good deal of pride and took a great amount of credit. Such private squadrons were in constant competition with one another. They would seek to display their superiority in the gymnasium, on the hunting expedition, in exterminating "enemies" of the state, and in fighting with other squadrons. On appointed days or at a surprise signal, these squads would assemble, fully armed, for the purpose of doing battle with one another. This was no mock warfare, for all of the implements of war known to the day were used to gain victory. For the Spartans these occasions were eagerly anticipated, and memories of them were savored; participants anxiously awaited such jousts in order to demonstrate their skill in the use of arms, their courage and their endurance, and above all, their great devotion to the state.

Apparently no Spartan could conceive of a better way for inducting young men into the ranks of citizens. The system never changed in anything except minor incidentals. All the virtues held to be most desirable, even necessary, for citizenship could be evaluated in such a system. The young man who could meet all of the ordeals with success was judged to be ready to take his position with the elite. Failure was almost too terrible to contemplate, for it meant that the portals of citizenship were closed; the Spartan who was not a citizen was nothing.

At about the age of twenty the period of preparation came to an end. Now the young man took his place in the regular military organization, and, according to some accounts, became a citizen. When a young Spartan became a citizen in a legal sense is a question that remains unanswered, for it is also claimed that he did not achieve the distinction of citizenship until he had spent ten years successfully in military service. In other words, one could accept the age of thirty as the minimum legal age for citizenship. And to all the training, discipline, and hardship that had gone before was now added the requirement that the young man take a wife. How serious and how binding was this requirement? The Spartan who had not proved himself on the field of battle could not hope to occupy a position of any influence in the councils that managed the affairs of state, and the whole Spartan philosophy of life seemed to commend the married state to the young soldier.[18] Nevertheless it appears, if the original accounts of Spartan life can be trusted, that not all Spartan men married, and such an oversight did not either deprive them of any opportunity to become citizens or strip them of the rights and duties of citizenship. Whatever the truth may be, we can at least say that the common practice was for Spartans to spend ten years on active army duty and then to return to become husbands and fathers.

Active duty was followed by a lifetime of service in a ready military reserve. Every Spartan male who was a citizen was always a soldier, either active or ready for action, and to this end the whole system of education or training was directed.

A general evaluation of Spartan education seems unnecessary, for the strengths of the system, as well as the weaknesses, are obvious.[19] But one might add here the evaluation of Aristotle: that as long as the Spartans were the only Greeks who practiced the art of war with diligence they maintained superiority, but when other city states, some of them with broader purposes and therefore broader education and training, turned to the objective of military excellence, the superiority of the Spartans vanished.[20]

Athenian Ideals and Practices

What we, as the beneficiaries of models from ancient life, owe to the Spartans can be indicated mainly by pointing to examples of totalitarianism and police states that have plagued mankind down through history. Possibly the Spartans have been judged too harshly; but the original sources, including Xenophon, who was a constant admirer of the Spartan system, do not lead one to a more lenient interpretation. Our inheritance from Athens, though far richer and more human, is not so easy to identify, for this inheritance can hardly be disassociated from our culture as a whole. However, our indebtedness to Athens should motivate us to trace some of her educational and intellectual

[18] Plutarch *Lycurgus.* In *op. cit.,* vol. I, pp. 247–249.

[19] For an analysis of the failures of Spartan education, see Woody, *op. cit.,* pp. 269–272; and Marrou, *op. cit.,* pp. 24–25.

[20] Aristotle *Politics* vii. 13. In *The Works of Aristotle,* Oxford University Press, New York, 1908–1931.

history, in order that we may see these influences more clearly. The task is not without real difficulties. Life and institutions are never quite as simple or as neat as histories sometimes represent them. Besides, man's life in society is subject to change; it is not a static society that we are trying to describe and understand.

Athenians were imaginative, artistic, creative; they tried to organize a citizen society wherein individual freedom to cultivate what may have been distinctive Athenian qualities of mind could be ensured. More basic than this, they had a vision or ideal of community life, and it was to this ideal that every Athenian citizen paid allegiance. The ideal was not merely political, nor was it primarily educational, literary, or religious; it was all of these, and for want of a better word it may be referred to as culture. No society before had held such a view of the community which, though it had practical ends, was concerned mainly with the higher life and was organized with the ultimate purpose of making men more human.

There can be little question that Athens bequeathed to later generations an imperishable heritage of art, literature, and philosophy. On a plane higher than all forms of expression or modes of thought was the Athenians' ideal of culture. They left, moreover, a model of government, which permitted a high degree of freedom for citizens and opportunity for personal and political initiative. More dramatic and somewhat outside the boundaries of culture is the Athenian defeat of the military power of Persia, a triumph which preserved the future of Western civilization. But these are items to be pursued in a broader history. Now we should turn to the Athenian educational ideal; in doing so, however, we should keep in mind that educational objectives and practices are closely connected with an Athenian view of culture. And since this culture was subject to change and to progress, there are different, perhaps nearly discrete, periods of Athenian education to be treated.

AN ATHENIAN EDUCATIONAL IDEAL

Early in the intellectual history of Greece, and for reasons always subject to some debate, a choice was made between mysticism and reason, between religion and philosophy, between theogony and cosmogony. The effect of this choice was to rescue Greece (especially Athens) and eventually the culture of the West, from the tyrannies of mysticism, and to put undoubted confidence in the power and the worth of reason. "Wisdom is better than strength," "Know thyself," "Avoid excess," "It is hard to be virtuous," the wise men said, and so Athenians, through their most influential spokesmen, elected to extol reason, and to search for human values and ideals, by using the qualities of their mind.

With the basic issue (reason is supreme) settled, the Athenians turned to the equally troublesome task of finding means for cultivating reason, and thus of ensuring its perpetuation as a cultural ideal superior to vulgar superstition, dangerous opinion, or the subtleties of Orphic religion. Tradition, too, was subject to some outright rejection, and so the lessons which Homer and Hesiod seemed to teach in their venerated poetry were at least made to undergo careful scrutiny. Cultural theory did not always recommend the works of Homer as acceptable educational guideposts, or endorse them without qualification. Too much in Homer, despite the sentimental attachment which the Greeks had for him, was unphilosophical and out of step with rationalism. To embrace the Homeric tradition without applying rigorous tests of reason was merely substituting the tyranny of tradition for that of superstition. This would not do—but then, neither was it possible to expurgate Homer from Greek life; and so, much of Homer's work remained for centuries to form a kind of foundation from which mental life might spring. While it was possible to pay allegiance to Homer, it was, in a sense, a new Homer who was quoted, for his ancient values were overlaid with philosophical doctrines leading to different metaphysical meanings. Although it may not be wrong to speak of Homer as the "educator" of the Greeks (which in fact we do), it should be understood that as the message of Xenophanes, Heraclitus, and Parmenides became clearer, and more fully embraced by educated Athenians, the triumph of reason over mystery was assured.

Still, to argue that Xenophanes, Heraclitus, and Parmenides (or they, along with the Seven Sages—Solon, Periander, Chilon, Pittacus, Bias, Thales, and Cleobulus) could have changed the attitudes of the Greeks enough to turn them away from myth and legend and toward mental refinement, philosophy, and science, is unconvincing. Immortal thinkers played their part, but in the last analysis the victory of reason over ancient doctrine and dogmatic assumption was due to the Greek spirit which found its fullest satisfaction in an expression of its own rational power.

Translating this philosophy of mind into a cultural doctrine, with means of education to sustain it, meant that Athenians (and possibly most other Greeks, too) would aspire to a kind of citizenship for which they should be broadly educated, refined, sensitive, ethically conscious, civic-minded men.[21]

---

[21] Thucydides *History* . . . ii. 40–41. Translated by Benjamin Jowett, Oxford University Press, New York, 1900. See also R. W. Livingstone, *The Greek Genius and Its Meaning to Us*, Oxford University Press, New York, 1915, p. 141; and Barclay, *op. cit.*, pp. 90–93.

This cultural doctrine—at once an educational ideal—did not spring suddenly and full-grown into Greek life. It evolved through centuries of cultivation, to be seen finally and most distinctly about the middle of the fifth century B.C., and the instruments of education evolved along with it. Now we should want to know some of the educational details associated with cultural doctrine, and to find them we turn to three historical periods in Greek education: early and later Athenian, in this chapter, and Hellenistic, in Chapter IV.

EARLY ATHENIAN EDUCATION

As the educator of Greece, Homer's influence was felt more keenly and had a more permanent and profound effect on Athens than elsewhere, although Sparta and other Greek city states were also steeped in Homeric tradition. To assign Homer pride of place in Greek educational history needs some justification, for he was a primary force in Greek life and thought even though he was neither pedagogue nor schoolmaster.[22] For centuries the epic poems attributed to him were read and memorized in schools (the works of Homer were and are the foundations of classical education), but we would be missing Homer's real genius if we assume that his influence was pervasive simply because his works were known and studied. This study was only a beginning (though necessary) step which led to a total immersion of the Greek mind into values expressed with exquisite artistry. These values were absorbed into men's thinking and living so thoroughly that for two centuries Athenian education was dominated by Homer, and indeed, ideals of life honored and expressed in Homer's epics were accepted and followed as the Athenian rule of life. Athenian values were an admixture of archaic ideals (with which Homer himself was of course familiar) and the embellishments of the poet's imagination. Tradition recommended them, and Homer's art made them appealing.

Among an aristocracy responsible for political and social control in Athens, Homer was well known. Boys knew the heroes of his tales; they knew what these heroes thought and how they spoke; and they knew what they would do if they were faced with the problems of the Athens of their own time. Being a poet rather than a historian, Homer enjoyed certain special privileges. Had he been a historian describing a past that was expected to govern the present and direct the future, his fame very likely would not have been great, and his influence on Greek life would

[22] See T. W. Allen, *Homer: The Origins and the Transmission,* The Clarendon Press, Oxford, 1924; and C. H. Whitman, *Homer and the Heroic Tradition,* Harvard University Press, Cambridge, Mass., 1958.

probably have been negligible. As a poet, however, he framed an ideal and captured the imagination of all who knew his works. Life as it was set forth in the great epics had an appeal which could not be contained in any narrow code of action. Homer did not tell the Greeks how to live, nor did he put words in the mouths of the gods that would dictate a course of individual action. Virtue, in the sense of right action, was not part of his poetic message. Without exceptionally generous interpretations on the part of a reader, moral lessons are not to be found in Homer. Still, it is fair to say that it was the Homeric sense of greatness that gained for Homer the position of educator of the Greeks. The Athenian citizen-aristocrat was primed for glory and heroism; the ideal to which he dedicated himself may be described best by saying that it included all that is contained in the knightly and aristocratic notion of the grand exploit.[23]

The relationship between this ideal and education must be made a little clearer. Homeric values were the accepted goals for life in Athens before the sixth century, and they, like the laws of Lycurgus, were perpetuated in oral tradition. Many Athenians claimed to know Homer's *Iliad* and *Odyssey* by heart. Children learned Homer and gained inspiration from his work in much the same way that Christian children in a later era learned their catechism or Jewish children studied the Jewish law. Schools were not needed to formalize the instruction or to clarify the lessons of this tradition. This was done quite well in the child's daily contacts, and as he grew older he had the same lessons taught to him again by all of life around him.

One must not lose sight of the fact that only the Athenian aristocracy was entitled to this inheritance. Because the few were to be educated in such a fashion, education could be informal. The objectives of education and of life were closely associated and were clear and easy to recognize. Education took no circuitous routes; the boy was to become a citizen, a knight, and a soldier; he was to be a credit to his station in life and to the class from which he came. Skills for making a living were unnecessary—more than this, they were servile and below a young aristocrat's position—and literary accomplishments were accorded no special value. The well-educated citizen of the period before the sixth century B.C. knew his Homer, although he probably could not read. He could count, but quite likely he could not add, subtract, or perform other simple mathematical computations. Few people had any special opportunity to master the skill of writing. Of what real use could these skills have been to the warrior whose mind was set on imitating the

[23] Frederick A. G. Beck, *Greek Education: 450–350 B.C.*, Barnes & Noble, Inc., New York, 1964, pp. 55–66.

heroes of legend and epic? And how could schools have served a society which accepted the values dramatized by Homer?

From the time of Homer to the middle of the sixth century B.C. the chief work of the citizen-aristocrat was soldiering, and the activities preparatory to the life of a citizen were essentially military. In many respects during these years Athens and Sparta were similar, although where Sparta gained her ends by regimentation and strict codes, the Athenians were motivated by a strong sense of duty or dedication to the ideal so vividly depicted in Homer's works. Athens lived on the honor, glory, and ethics of the Homeric model, and this model was influential enough to make unnecessary the prescriptiveness of a Spartan rule of life. It could mold Athenian life as long as Athens was content to conduct her affairs according to an archaic system and to restrict the privileges of citizenship to the members of her aristocracy.

But gradually education drifted away from its preoccupation with military objectives. Perhaps one reason for the shift of interest can be found in the changes which were taking place in military tactics. The citizen-soldier, versatile, skillful, self-reliant, and valorous, was characteristic of the age of Athenian chivalry. Such soldiers were not really needed when military tactics began to accept and emphasize a heavy infantry. The technical qualifications of the Athenian soldier-knight appealed to young aristocrats. No doubt there was a bit of romance about the whole business: this was the life for a citizen; it fulfilled most of his dreams. Could the life and duties and skills of an infantryman have the same attraction for the citizen? What special challenge could be found in the routine but highly effective functions of the infantry soldier? And how could the ideals of Homer's world be served in such a menial capacity? It would be difficult indeed to regard the life and work of such a soldier to be the best, or only, preparation for entering the ranks of the ruling class.

Along with tactical progress in military affairs, the city state was growing commercially. It was not easy any longer, and not always pleasant or gratifying, to live by the rules that had governed men's lives and affairs in the earlier period. Young men of means and position began to see and to respond to enticing opportunities in the economic world of affairs. More than this, the comforts and securities of the aristocracy could not be guaranteed in the new Athens, and military efficiency and knightly ideals were next to useless in the social order that was just coming over the horizon.[24]

[24] See E. A. Havelock, *The Liberal Temper in Greek Politics*, Cape, London, 1957; and William G. Forrest, *The Emergence of Greek Democracy*, Weidenfeld & Nicolson, London, 1966.

Democracy in Athens, however, was only on its way; it had not yet arrived. It was during the years when the aristocratic tradition was having fused to it a number of democratic tendencies that Athens began to encourage schools. A word should be said now about the new ideals that began to shape the foundation for Athenian life and institutions.

THE NEW IDEALS IN EDUCATION

The general picture of Athenian education from the time of Homer to the early sixth century has been described. The reader should be reminded that such an education was conceived in the broadest terms; it could be judged as being the equivalent of life itself. Although broad in the mission that it was to perform, it was narrow in that it bestowed opportunities on very few. The landed aristocracy was entitled to guard and govern; tradition gave it this role. A broad and informal education was directed at preparing gentlemen to exercise the special privileges of their class.

Paternalism was the main operative principle of government, and wealth and position were what made the principle work. How does one prepare himself to govern when these are the conditions which surround him? Mainly, no doubt, by preserving his position of privilege, wealth, and respect. But preparing himself to guard the state was another matter. Possibly it mattered little to the humble shopkeepers, artisans, and peasants whether or not one class of governors was exchanged for another. An aristocracy of wealth and an aristocracy of power may differ greatly on the level of leadership, but for those who are irrevocably committed to a life of doing what they are told, the difference really matters very little. Nevertheless, men will not surrender easily what they value highly. Athenian aristocrats willingly fought to keep what they had; they protected the city state from both foreign and domestic foes. The training which would enable the state's guardians to function well would aim at military excellence, and we have already said that military excellence was closely bound up with the activities of a knight. He had to have strength, courage, and skill in weapons and horsemanship. More than these attributes was an immovable devotion and dedication to the knight's or the aristocrat's code. Strength and skill could be developed, courage and devotion could be inculcated, but without exercises and without challenges these highly prized virtues would surely rust like an unused sword in its scabbard.

How to maintain a high level of efficiency was therefore both a military and an educational question; in a larger sense, it was a social and political question, too. For years sport had been used to keep the citizen-soldier-knight fit. Interest in and devotion to sporting events and contests of all kinds are attested to throughout Athenian history. The Olympian games, perhaps the best known of organized sporting contests, were generously supplemented by less-known, though nonetheless seriously approached, state and local games. All the elements of skill and spirit essential to the knight-soldier were served and perfected by sport. Besides, because sport required leisure, which in turn demanded wealth, competitive games were activities more or less naturally restricted to the aristocracy.

The Athenian people's emphasis on sport might be taken as evidence that they were frivolous, impractical, play-loving, and irresponsible. This would not be a fair characterization of them or of their motives for engaging in sport. But whether or not their addiction to physical competition was born of the highest ideals, their exclusive and fashionable sporting world could not withstand the assaults it had to endure from the changing military picture, the broadening economic opportunities, and the sensitive social philosophy indigenous to the times.

Yet change neither generated a rejection of sport nor relegated it to a lower position in Athenian life. Its practical value was, in a military sense, much less clear, but justifications for bodily excellence to be achieved by sport were quick to appear and were convincing. Where sport had been exclusive because it was expensive in time and money, a new and productive economy opened the doors of leisure to many who previously could not have afforded this luxury. What had been an exclusive preserve for the aristocracy was invaded by persons who by birth, at least, could not be numbered among the elite.[25] Now common merchants had wealth and leisure to engage in most athletic activities, and sport became a popular pastime; in a sense it became democratic. Even paid, professional athletes appeared on the Athenian scene, to the great disgust of citizens who continued to cling to the aristocratic tradition.[26]

It was natural for aristocrats to feel disturbed and displaced by this turn of events. Society was readying itself for democracy, but the aristocracy was unable to accept such a society. Without exclusive privileges, nobility seemed to be less attractive. The major changes in early Athenian education, that is, the new direction away from sport

[25] On the Athenian sporting tradition, see E. Norman Gardiner, *Athletics of the Ancient World*, Oxford University Press, New York, 1930; E. Norman Gardiner, *Greek Athletic Sports and Festivals*, The Macmillan Company, New York, 1910; and Forbes, *op. cit.*

[26] Plato *Laws* vii. 793–794.

and toward intellectual pursuits can be found chiefly in the desire on the part of members of the old aristocracy to protect and preserve their position. They did not have to give up sport, but they felt compelled to find something else which they could reserve for themselves and which would identify them, by its distinctive character, as members of an elite class. If physical prowess was no longer to be the mark of their class, they could turn to intellectual cultivation. And this could be done with relative safety, because the tactics of war no longer depended so much on the varied skills of the individual soldier. What common merchant or artisan could afford the luxury of mental cultivation for its own sake?

Homeric Athenians as a class had been neither illiterate nor unlearned, but they had devoted little attention or energy to mental development. Now, however, the preservation of an aristocracy's identity stood in the balance; this class had all the tools for a successful invasion of the worlds of scientific and spiritual wisdom.

THE ORGANIZATION OF SCHOOLS

Allegiance to the great deed was not so different from devotion to the noble thought. Heroism and courage could be displayed in connection with things of the mind, as in the past they had been demonstrated on the fields of battle. Yet, despite the validity of this new application of time and talent, Athenians could not turn their backs on centuries of respected tradition, and all the physical virtues were obviously part of this tradition. Neither athletics nor competition dropped out of the Athenian system of values. What happened was that the system of values was broadened, allowing for the introduction of new ideals and new practices which could be pursued without interfering with or excluding those already deeply ingrained in Athenian life.

Mental training, a new concept, could now be accepted as a distinctive element in the preparation of an Athenian citizen. Physical development and sport, as we have suggested earlier, were retained as part of an honored Greek ideal, but to them was added a program for intellectual development which included the Athenian literary inheritance. A broader conception of aristocratic education was being realized. It should be observed that the evolution of these ideals and practices proceeded much more slowly than our brief account of them would indicate. At first the new education—that is, the combination of mental and physical training—was as closely associated with the aristocracy as sport had been in former times. But drastic adjustments were made until physical and mental formation was universally regarded in Athens as the kind of education necessary for all free-men.[27]

A definition of the freeman originally restricted this broader concept of education to the Athenian aristocrats. However, with progress on all sides, the new education could not be retained for the few only, because the political definition of the freeman became more liberal. Although Athenian education at this time could hardly be called popular, evidently more and more people were in a position to enjoy its advantages. The demand for education, therefore, contributed to the formalizing of instruction. There is no explanation for the rise of the Athenian school other than one of popular demand for the organization of such an institution. The creation and development of schools is one of Athens' most significant contributions to the history of education.[28]

Before the appearance of the school—and no one knows the exact date of the establishment of the first such institution—the new educational objective was being achieved by means of individual tuition. Families of means could care for their children's education by employing teachers for their private use. Popular desire for education, however, was a serious challenge to this practice, and in time a collective principle won out; schools were organized and made available to the children of freemen. This is not to imply that tutorial arrangements for education were abandoned or that the old aristocracy looked with favor on the practice of distributing more generously what was thought to be an aristocratic education. But whether or not these changes were approved by the few, the picture of the tutor teaching a boy of the privileged class alone in his home was changed to that of Athenian boys leaving their homes in the custody of a pedagogue on the way to schools where teachers were waiting. At this time and for centuries following, educators and philosophers have argued over the advantages and disadvantages of public (collective) and private (tutorial) education. It would appear, however, that the method accepted in Athens at this time gained permanent favor in educational practice.

The studies undertaken by children in these first Athenian schools are shrouded in mystery, for they, like the schools themselves, were in the process of developing. When this education was mainly aristocratic and private, the processes and their expected outcomes were two in number: physical training to develop the body and prepare the youth in athletic skills for competitions; and musical train-

---

[27] Isocrates *Areopagiticus.* In Loeb Classical Library, Harvard University Press, Cambridge, Mass., 1927–1929, vol. II, pp. 131–133; and Plato *Protagoras,* 326.

[28] Beck, *op. cit.,* pp. 72–80; and Freeman, *op. cit.,* pp. 52–70.

ing for spiritual, intellectual, and artistic development. Stress on physical training indicated the Athenian allegiance to Homeric tradition. The first schools, therefore, organized a curriculum which gave generously of its time to physical formation, and evidently there were special teachers for this kind of instruction. Musical training was probably less literary and artistic than we have usually been led to believe. Musical education of the schools of early Athens has been commonly represented as being like musical education in the Hellenistic period, that is, primarily studies in literature and acoustics. Actually the school's name, music school, and the course of instruction therein should be taken a bit more literally. Athenians were music-minded; their amusements and their serious culture required musical ability. Perhaps the music school's first duty during the early period was to prepare boys in vocal and instrumental music. This did not mean that poetry, literature, and possibly some mathematics were ignored completely. But the school was preparing boys for life in their social circle, and life's needs —in music harmony, dancing, choral singing, and accompaniment— could not be ignored. The civilized and educated man was, even in Plato's view, one who could fulfill his social role, and this meant, among other things, that he had to be able to sing, dance, and probably play the lyre.

Literature could hardly have occupied as important a place in these early Athenian schools as it did, for example, in the Hellenistic schools two or three centuries later, because poetry still existed mainly in an oral form. Much of it was Homer committed to memory, though some was from the less-known poets of the age. In any case its purpose, as the Greeks interpreted it, was largely moral. We should probably think it moral in transmitting the permanent ideals of the Greek tradition; the Greeks perhaps thought it moral in the narrower sense of being didactic literature.[29]

The education just described could be given in school or in a series of schools or by a private teacher, without depending too much, if at all, on the conventional literary skills of reading and writing. In time, of course, writing became an important element in Athenian life— all educated men in classical Athens could write—but it is interesting to observe that the skills or tools of learning which all modern education places first in the lists of goals to be achieved were placed last in the Greek system. Schools for reading, writing, and calculating, or lessons in these subjects in existing schools, were slow to come into being in early Athens. This order of learning should not surprise us too much,

[29] F. M. Cornford, *Greek Religious Thought, from Homer to the Age of Alexander,* Dent, London, 1923.

however, if we remember that Athenian boys were not being educated for literary or commercial pursuits. It might be worth remarking here, too, that this somewhat unorthodox order of arranging school subjects did not last beyond the Persian Wars (ca. 479 B.C.), for from about that time onward the three R's became important skills in Athenian life.

It was at about this juncture in the history of education in Athens that the most articulate as well as the most artistic critics of Athenian education spoke out. Their criticisms seem to have been motivated by nostalgia. The aristocratic order, with its educational commitment to the musical rather than the literary and to the athletic rather than the intellectual, was beginning to pass, and its passing was being mourned. Yet those who were criticizing the new education could not have failed to observe that education was not utility-centered; it was still designed for the leisure which only an aristocracy could afford.

One last word needs to be said about these first schools. We have not tried to describe levels of instruction or types of schools, because to do that for the early period would be to engage mainly in guesswork; for later periods such descriptions would have greater validity. But the note that we want to add involves the balance, the near-perfect harmony which has been claimed for the two parts of early Athenian education, the physical and the musical.[30] When, in the earliest years, musical education was preoccupied with music in a narrow sense, there was little occasion for conflict between music and athletics. As time passed however, some critics began to voice their protest against the attention being given to intellectual formation. This was being done, they insisted, at the expense of physical development and bodily beauty and grace. A good deal of hostility developed over the relative importance of musical and physical education as the whole process became more formal, and no real evidence exists of the harmony some historians have found between the two. Aristophanes, a firm friend of the old education and a violent critic of the new, gives us plenty of evidence in *The Clouds* for believing that even in Athens physical and intellectual education made rather strange and uncomfortable bedfellows.[31]

ATHENIAN SOCIETY AS A BACKGROUND FOR EDUCATION

Social organization in aristocratic Athens had its basis mainly in kinship, that is, in families, tribes, and clans. Land was owned either by the family, the tribe, or the clan. Land ownership, subject later to even

[30] E. B. Castle, *Ancient Education and Today*, Penguin Books, Inc., Baltimore, 1961.

[31] Aristophanes *The Clouds* 1009–1014. Translated by B. B. Rogers, Loeb Classical Library, Harvard University Press, Cambridge, Mass., 1924.

greater restrictions, was the mark of an individual's social and political importance.

Throughout most of the period before the Persian Wars, government in Athens was monarchical, although the powers of the king were limited somewhat by a council of nobles and a popular assembly. In the course of time the custom of private property was emphasized and realized, and land ownership drifted gradually from the family and clan into private hands. After the mid-eighth century B.C., the noble-landowner class gained greater strength and brought about a further lessening of the powers of the king, to a point where the monarchy became little more than a symbol. Political affairs in Athens were controlled by the aristocracy, and the state was ruled by nine archons together with the council of the Areopagus. The old popular assembly (ecclesia), to the extent that it still existed, functioned in a largely routine manner. In this aristocratic regime the social classes could be defined as follows: the *eupatridae*, or ruling nobles, whose estates were in the process of growing larger; the *geomoroi*, or smaller landowners, whose property was being absorbed into the holdings of the nobles; and the *demiourgoi*, or artisans. The last two classes, although their members were regarded as free citizens, were without political rights. By the mid-seventh century B.C., Athens became something of a timocracy; that is, property and income now became the chief qualifications for the exercise of civic rights. As a sign of another remarkable change, farmers and artisans now served in military units; however, since the advent of infantry tactics in warfare's methods, no particular glory attached to this service, nor did it bestow any political privileges on those who served. The social structure to which we have made brief reference fostered resentment and dissatisfaction; both became stronger until a climax was reached and reforms had to be initiated. These were achieved in the appointment as lawgiver of Solon (638–559 B.C.), an aristocrat with sympathies for the poor and the politically disenfranchised. Solon's reforms included a cancellation of debts, a freeing of many enslaved people, and a limitation on the amount of land any one individual could own. These reforms tended to give some direction to the first real steps toward democratic or popular government. The old social classifications were retained, but added to them was a fourth class: the *thetes*. An assembly of free but heretofore underprivileged and unrepresented Athenians was created, and a council of four hundred citizens chosen by lot was formed under the direction of Solon. Later, under Cleisthenes (ca. 577 B.C.), all resident freemen, whether native or foreign-born, became citizens, and the council of four hundred was transformed into a council of five hundred members with fifty drawn by lot from each of the ten tribes that were still distinct in Athenian social organization. Athens thus became a fairly well-organized democracy. Under this form of political control she rose to a position of unrivaled leadership among the Ionian states.

At the close of the fourth century B.C., the population estimated for the city state was made up of 21,000 citizens, 10,000 resident aliens, and 120,000 slaves. Because the slaves were committed to all the drudgery of life, Athenian citizens were free to devote their time to civic enterprises. These activities may have included attendance at a public assembly or law court, but they could just as easily have included anything that the citizen undertook to do.[32]

A CHILD'S FIRST YEARS

The birth of a male child was an event of considerable import to an Athenian family. Among other signs of rejoicing, the home was decorated, and an unmistakable air of festivity surrounded the entire household. The birth of a daughter, on the other hand, was not such an event. Whether the child was a boy or girl, its rearing was optional for the father; he had absolute power over its life. If he decided not to keep the infant, he could dispose of it. This was done in any one of a number of ways, there being no prescribed rule governing such early disinheritances. Possibly he would put the baby in an earthenware vessel and leave it either in or near the temple or in some other place in the city where it could be found. Anyone who found such an infant could claim it, care for it, and number it among his slaves. How common was it for Athenian fathers to refuse to accept their own offspring? This is difficult to say, and the answer is not especially important to us. What we should observe in such a custom, especially in considering the relation of the individual to the state, is the parent's authority. The Athenian state, contrary to the practices common in Sparta, did not interfere with, or presume to make, such fundamental decisions for its citizens.

Generally the birth of a child, male or female, was a happy occasion which called for some ritual or feast to pay homage to the gods. The Athenians were not a particularly religious people, but it was the custom to do the gods honor, and the Athenians were very tradition-minded.

---

[32] For discussions of Greek social and economic life, see Hendrik Bolkestein, *Economic Life in Greece's Golden Age*, E. J. Brill, Leiden, 1958; M. Rostovtzeff, *The Social and Economic History of the Hellenistic World*, Oxford University Press, New York, 1941; and A. G. Woodhead, *The Greeks in the West*, Thames and Hudson, London, 1962.

Commonly a festival was arranged after the birth of a child; and on the child's seventh day he was named. Then a sacrifice was offered to the gods, the mother was purified, and gifts were brought to do the youngster even further honor. The child was now an official member of the family, though not in any legal sense a citizen, and he was placed under the care of the gods with whom the family had some special affiliation.

THE STATE AND EDUCATION

In general, one may say that Athenian education was not state-supported, although it is, of course, a fact that five gymnasia—the Academy, Lyceum, Kynosarges, Diogeneion, and Ptolemeion—*were* built and maintained by the city.[33] In addition to the capital and operating costs of the gymnasia, it would appear that their chief teachers, or supervisors, were paid public servants. The support of these establishments is pertinent to our discussion. What was done at a gymnasium was considered not just an important part of Athenian education; it was for many years the essential part, and the physical development promised by gymnastics was, if not the sole, at least the primary goal of secondary education.

Even on other levels, both higher and lower than gymnastics, it would be hard to insist that the city state did not contribute some support; public buildings were often the scene of the schoolmaster's activities, and *paidotribes* (teachers of physical education) were accustomed to using public land and publicly owned equipment. But the point to be emphasized is this: As a rule of tradition, if not of law, the individual was responsible for obtaining his own educational means. Beyond permitting teachers and learners the use of gymnasia, theaters, and temples, public resources were not used to provide the places where instruction or training could take place. And apart from the custom adopted by the city state of supporting the educational ventures of sons of fathers who were killed in battle, the support of education in Athens was an entirely private matter.

Yet we cannot assume that simply because the state does not support education, it is therefore deprived of authority to supervise teaching and learning. Certainly the traditions of Athens could not have argued for stringent supervision over something as personal as physical, mental, and moral preparation. On the other hand, the state looked to its citizens for protection, and during those years when constant dangers

---

[33] See Forbes, *op. cit.,* p. 83.

threatened Athens' way of life, a firm but not inflexible custom came, at least theoretically, into operation: The state was vested with authority to supervise education. However, in actual practice, the state was reluctant to use this authority.

Certain regulations concerning schools in Athens were attributed to Solon.[34] At that time in Athenian history, it is reported, the state enacted regulations concerning the length of the school day, passed laws restricting entry to school premises to authorized persons, framed legislation governing physical competitions, and established regulations pertaining to the age of teachers. There is a hint that something resembling compulsory-attendance laws was passed, but beyond the clearly recognized and ancient custom that a father was to educate his son if he expected support from his son in old age, the details of such legislation, if it existed, are little known. And it could be argued that the state action mentioned above and said to have been initiated by Solon was not really an attempt to control education. Remembering the level of personal morals in Athens, we may easily believe that such legislation was intended to protect the morals of the young.

With respect to the role of the state in Athenian education, the following conclusions seem accurate: The state did not support education; this was an individual matter; the state did, however, have authority to control or supervise education, but this authority was rarely exercised.

The Schools of Athens

Educational practices were not as rigidly adhered to in Athens as in Sparta. It would be a mistake, however, to suppose that in Athens so much freedom of action and thought prevailed that educational practices were in a state of constant flux. Tradition was the main guardian of educational orthodoxy. A system or plan for education that was once generally accepted as customary continued in force as if it had been decreed by the mightiest of kings. During the two centuries before the Persian Wars (479 B.C.), when the school and then a system of schools came into existence in Athens, a plan for education either evolved or was designed. It became the permanent, underlying plan for Athenian education, and in form, at least, there were no major changes throughout the course of Athenian history. The education of the early period gained acceptance as conventional Greek education. It is this Greek education that many writers refer to with admiration; it is this plan for

---

[34] Beck, *op. cit.*, pp. 70–77; Freeman, *op. cit.*, p. 57; and Marrou, *op. cit.*, p. 382.

education that Plato accepts as preliminary to the higher studies for the wisest men of the state.[35]

Conventional Athenian, or Greek, education was not, as we have implied, restricted to the school. There was no intention to allow some of the many sides of potential human culture to remain underdeveloped, but neither was the school or the schoolmaster expected to assume responsibility for the forming of a complete man.

Before a boy was sent to school his education had already begun. The period of home training began at birth and continued until the youngster was about seven years old. This entire period, though by no means invaded by formal instruction, was considered to be exceedingly important, not only to later instruction but to later life as well. These were the years when the foundation of the boy's moral character was laid. One could almost say that these infant years were reserved for moral education. It would not be easy, however, to give the details of the educational work of these first seven years. The child was told innumerable stories, each with a clear-cut moral; he was supervised in his nursery by carefully selected nurses or by his mother. When boys got a little older, perhaps close to seven years of age, a pedagogue became their constant companion and guide. Of course, the poorer families could not afford a pedagogue at all; wealthier families may have had one for each boy in the family; families whose means placed them somewhere between the poor and the rich may have had one pedagogue for all of the boys in the family.[36]

It is not quite accurate to discuss the pedagogue under the general heading of "the schools of Athens." The pedagogue, despite the present connotation of the term, was not a schoolmaster at all. His duty was not to teach letters, although he may have heard lessons, but to inculcate manners and morals. He was the boy's constant companion before he began attending school and during his period of school attendance. In one sense the pedagogue was a member of the family; surely he was being trusted with the family's most precious possession. More accurately, however, he was only a member of the household. In nine cases out of ten he was a slave and a servant; but his role was far greater than his position, for he was a moral master, and as such he occupied an important place in Athenian education.

This pedagogue was usually a man of comparatively old age, unfit for other active work. He was selected to guide a boy because he was

---

[35] Plato *Republic* ii. 376; vii. 521d.

[36] Herodotus viii. 75. In *Herodotus*, Bohn's Classical Library, G. Bell & Sons, Ltd., London, 1886; and for a dissent from the assertion that any family ever had more than one pedagogue see Beck, *op. cit.*, p. 109.

thought to have the qualities for such a role. And the fact that the pedagogue was a slave did not mean necessarily that he was uneducated. Many Athenian slaves were captive people who had enjoyed positions of worth and wealth prior to their captivity. Nevertheless, it was not learning that concerned the pedagogue most, but care. When the boy went to school, the pedagogue walked behind carrying the schoolbooks, musical instruments, or writing tablets. Wherever the boy went, the pedagogue was responsible for his conduct. At home the pedagogue watched the boy's manners, seeing to it that he used his left hand for bread, his right hand for other food, kept silent in the presence of elders, rose from his seat when elders entered, sat erect, etc. For infractions of the manners-morals code the pedagogue might scold or punish, although in punishing he had to be careful that he did not inflict a degrading kind of punishment on a freeborn lad.[37]

THE PRIMARY SCHOOL

The primary school, probably the last of the elementary schools to be developed in Athens, was concerned with teaching the elements of literary education.[38] Reading and writing were clearly part of its curriculum; arithmetic and drawing may have been studied in the primary schools kept by more advanced masters or in schools which arranged a program of studies for more advanced students.

Because education in Athens was really a private affair, the primary schools varied greatly as to standards, teachers, and instructional accommodations. Primary schools, which the children of the poor Athenian citizens attended, were small and inadequate. As often as not, it would seem, the scene of such a school was an unrented shop or a corner in a public building. The schools which attracted the children of wealthy Athenians were usually in separate buildings and were more appropriately appointed. When school was kept in a separate building—and this, of course, would depend on the resources of the schoolmaster—there were usually only two rooms to the building, one for instruction and the other for the pedagogues who waited for their charges.[39]

Materials and tools of instruction were quite limited; the master's techniques were largely routine. As a preliminary to instruction in reading, the names of the letters of the alphabet were taught, after which the pupils were instructed in combining consonants with vowels to pro-

---

[37] Freeman, *op. cit.*, pp. 66–69; and Beck, *op. cit.*, pp. 104–105.
[38] See Plato *Politics* 277e–278a,b.
[39] Woody, *op. cit.*, pp. 300–301.

nounce words. In the next phase the boys learned the forms of letters, perhaps by tracing them, and at this point they may have learned reading and writing by the same process. They were then taught the component parts of a sentence, although it should be noted that Greek grammer was not highly developed and that therefore the scientific approach to grammar, so common to elementary schools of the later centuries, found little place in the early Athenian primary schools. Reading was taught, not because it was a liberal pursuit but because it was useful: By the time this type of school achieved general recognition in Athens, literacy was necessary to success in life.[40]

Still, the extension of literacy did not preface any literary movement. Books were extremely scarce. Boys did not read poetry; they simply committed it to memory. Learning to read may have meant the attainment of some skill in understanding the written word, but in the actual teaching of reading, much more time was devoted to the learning of a few literary pieces by heart than to preparing the boys to enrich their experience through general reading. The reading school produced boys who were able to recite long passages from Homer, Hesiod, Simonides, and the gnomic poets. In addition, they could read public placards and commercial documents. These outcomes were neither higher nor lower than what was expected from such schools.

Writing and reading were learned in the same school. Usually the master instructed his pupils in reading one day and in writing the next. Three styles of writing were common in Athens about this time, and all of them may have been included in the writing syllabus: the formal hand, consisting of separate capital letters, usually taught to children; the cursive hand, examples of which are preserved in Greek papyri; and the short hand, the typical writing technique of copyists, clerks, and scribes. One can be reasonably sure that the first two types of writing were taught in the primary school. There is some doubt, however, that Athenians in a position to send their children to schools would have encouraged them to learn the short hand, which was really the skill of a trade. That such a writing technique became popular in the second century B.C. is not open to any real question, but that it formed a regular part of the early elementary school program is doubtful.

Writing was practiced on wax-coated tablets made of wood; the central panel was surrounded by a flat, raised edge, which served to protect the wax coating of the panel. Several tablets could be fastened together on strings passed through holes bored in the edges. For a

[40] Marrou, *op. cit.*, p. 42.

writing tool the boys had an instrument called a stylus, with a sharp point on one end suitable for making marks and a flat surface on the other to be used for erasing. In the course of time, ink and the reed pen became common implements in the schools.

Pupils just beginning their instruction in writing traced outlined letters made by the teacher.[41] This practice was not abandoned until the boys were capable of writing letters with only the assistance of parallel lines. Letters were written in horizontal and vertical lines so that letters fell beneath one another. No stops or accents were inserted, and there was no space between words. The writing master ruled both vertical and horizontal lines for his pupils. After the boys acquired facility in writing, the master dictated simple words and then passages from the poets to be copied. Various elaborations both in speed and beauty of writing were customary for the more advanced pupils.

In some schools masters were paid to teach their pupils arithmetic. For the most part, this study involved nothing more than simple counting.[42] In Athenian intellectual circles the distinction between arithmetical skill for practical computations and the study of number or quantity and its properties—mathematics in a more proper sense—was made very easily. Possibly the same distinction was not made by people in general or in the elementary school, but this was because little or nothing was known of mathematics in a higher sense. The schoolmaster, who limited his instruction in numbers to counting, did not need to make the distinction. A glance at the mathematical characters the Greeks used, however, will quickly disclose how cumbersome they were; Greek letters were used to do what we do with our common Arabic numerals, and their use involved complexities even greater than those met with in the use of Roman numerals in the Latin schools of the Roman world. It is unlikely that many Athenian schoolboys could either add or subtract. They were taught to count. Not even this was simple, although Athenians counted with their fingers and with their hands.[43] Learning to count from one to one million was the only achievement parents of the day could expect of their sons. The system may have been something like the following: the student held his hand with fingers erect and palms facing outward; by moving his fingers and his hands he could indicate numbers. To put the method in the form of directions: On the left hand, for one, half close the fourth finger only;

[41] Plato *Protagoras* 326.

[42] See Marrou, *op. cit.*, pp. 157–158; and Beck, *op. cit.*, pp. 123–126.

[43] Aristophanes *The Wasps* 656. In Loeb Classical Library, Harvard University Press, Cambridge, Mass., 1924, vol. I, p. 473.

for two, half close the third and fourth fingers only; for three, half close the second, third and fourth fingers; for four, half close the second and third fingers; for five, half close the second finger; for six, half close the third finger; for seven, close the fourth finger; for eight, close the third and fourth fingers; for nine, close the second, third, and fourth fingers. The same operation on the right hand indicated thousands from one to nine. Numbers from ten to ninety were also shown by the left hand: for ten, put the tip of the forefinger at the base of thumb; for twenty, hold the forefinger straight; for thirty, join the tips of forefinger and thumb; for forty, put the thumb behind the knuckle of the forefinger; for fifty, put the thumb in front of the forefinger; for sixty, hold the thumb as in fifty, but bend the forefinger to touch the ball of the thumb; for seventy, rest the forefinger on top of the thumb; for eighty, hold the thumb on the palm; for ninety, close the forefinger completely. The same motions on the right hand were used to show hundreds from 100 to 900. This is not the complete counting system, but it does suggest what the student was expected to learn and something of the challenge that faced him.[44]

For some pupils in some schools the uses of the abacus were taught. The simplest abacus had beads on wires. Ten beads on the top line counted as one each, and added together made ten; the ten beads on the second line counted as ten each, and added together made one hundred; the ten beads on the third line counted one hundred each and added together made one thousand. One may suppose that the use of the abacus was mainly commercial and that practice in its use was not a regular elementary-school exercise.

Drawing and possibly painting completed the primary school program of instruction.[45] Such exercises were part of the curriculum because the Greeks wanted to lay a good foundation for aesthetic judgments. The details of this part of the program seem unnecessary here.

A final word should be added concerning the teachers of these schools. From a glimpse of the teacher's place and status we may obtain a better idea of the value that Athenians placed on their primary schools. There were no qualifications, other than being able to read, which teachers had to meet. For this reason elementary teaching was generally despised and, in addition, was regarded as a servile occupation unworthy of a freeman. Few good teachers were motivated to stay in Athens and conduct primary schools or to come to Athens to open such schools. Many of Athens' elementary teachers turned to teaching

[44] Freeman discusses the counting system and the use of the abacus, *op. cit.*, pp. 104–107.

[45] Aristotle *Politics* viii. 3.1.

because of a lack of other employment rather than because of special fitness for teaching.[46]

PHYSICAL EDUCATION

In early Greece a boy's first somewhat formal preparation for assuming his role as a complete citizen consisted in perfecting physical skills. In the olden days these skills were, as we have already seen, closely associated with the art of war. But later, even without any real need for the skills of the soldier-knight, Athenian boys were encouraged to perfect their bodies and achieve grace and harmonious movement. These were highly prized accomplishments. Nowhere was the influence of the archaic system of values more thoroughly felt than in the area of physical education.

Physical education achieved a regular place in Athenian formal education. It was not simply a program in a school; it rated a school for itself. This was the palaestra. Either following the primary school and preceding the music school, or being conducted simultaneously with the other types of elementary schools, the palaestra concentrated on exercising the body. The school was under the direction of a *paidotribe*. He was supposed to know something about training the body, and some of the more highly qualified *paidotribes* had an elementary knowledge of the art of medicine. He conducted a program which consisted of simple exercises, games, dancing, swimming, wrestling, and throwing the discus and the javelin. The last-named skills were approached in their introductory phases. No building or play yard was set aside for the work of this school; almost any open space would do, and on rare occasions the *paidotribe* took his charges to one of the gymnasia.[47]

Paidotribes were private teachers, who, while earning a living by keeping a palaestra, were preparing for and aspiring to a position in one of the city-operated gymnasia. One may guess, however, that since these men were doing a kind of work which through custom and tradition had won a great deal of admiration, they fared better than others who accepted a teacher's role in elementary education.

THE MUSIC SCHOOL

The music school was also a part of elementary education. During the two centuries before the Persian Wars, the music school was probably

[46] Freeman, *op. cit.*, p. 278; and Marrou, *op. cit.*, pp. 33, 145.
[47] Plato *Protagoras* 325–326.

mainly a place where instrumental and vocal music was taught. The place of music in Greek life must be emphasized if one is to understand why a special school should have been established for teaching music.[48] But as time moved on, need for literary education increased, and the traditional values of Greek life began to give away. Dancing, choruses, accompanied singing, all began to decline in importance. If we look forward several centuries, we shall find the music school without music—music instruction had been converted into an acoustical study—but the recession of music was gradual and slow. In the Athenian education of the old style, the content of the music school was reading, writing (continued from the primary school), poetry, singing, and playing the lyre or oboe.

Some music schools could boast of only one teacher. To him, therefore, fell the task of teaching everything that was to be taught. In better music schools, at least two teachers shared instructional duties: the grammatist and the citharist. The former was the literary master, or more exactly, an elementary teacher of letters. The latter was the choirmaster and the lyre master.

In conventional Athenian education the music school really concluded formal literary and musical education. At about the age of fifteen a boy was excused from further study of letters and music.[49] An Athenian boy had, however, been exposed to a great deal more of the social and literary inheritance than we in the twentieth century think appropriate for elementary schools. His instruction had been both individual and collective; he had copied and composed on wax tablets; and he had memorized a good part of Homer. But this was not all: The poetry of Hesiod, Solon, Alcman, Tyrtaeus, Pindar, Aeschylus, and Euripides was part of him, and the fables of Aesop were as familiar to him as his route home. He had enough skill in singing and playing to adapt himself to the society in which such skills were respected. One is entitled to assume that in the absence of any known criticism of the conventional music school, its work was thorough and complete. The Athenians must have had confidence in it, for before the Persian Wars no other educational level or school tried either to duplicate or to complete the work of the music school.

[48] Plato *Laws* ii. 654.

[49] Plato *Laches* 197a. In Loeb Classical Library, Harvard University Press, Cambridge, Mass., 1914–1952. And Xenophon *Constitution of Lacedaemon* III. 1. In Loeb Classical Library, Harvard University Press, Cambridge, Mass., 1925.

ATHENIAN SECONDARY EDUCATION

It is possible to find a counterpart in modern education for every ancient Athenian school except the gymnasium. To the extent that the gymnasium was a school in the conventional sense—and this could be open to debate—it occupies a unique role in educational history. What has been said about the gymnasium applies to its status during the years before the Persian Wars. There is no question that after the Persian Wars the gymnasia became more and more literary and intellectual and less and less centers of physical training. But in the early period, the three Athenian gymnasia then in existence—the Lyceum, Academy, and Kynosarges—reflected both the aristocratic and the archaic conceptions of Greek education better than any other educational unit. These conceptions, as we have seen, were intimately connected with the ideal of the noble deed. Nobility of action and grace of movement were probably the real objectives of these schools.

Gymnastic training was, of course, securely established in Athenian traditions; when such training was formalized and when it was organized and supervised by state-supported institutions is not easy to say.[50] Surely the Lyceum and the Academy were quite ancient, and the Kynosarges antedated the fifth century B.C. Partly because of their venerable age, these places were prone to reflect aristocratic educational and social ideals. At first the Academy and the Lyceum were open only to freeborn Athenian youth, and the Kynosarges was reserved for the sons of Athenian fathers and foreign-born mothers. No gymnastic training was available in these institutions for boys who did not meet these qualifications. But as we move forward in history toward the Persian Wars and the democratic influences that they released, we see the gymnasia discarding some of their exclusiveness.

We have said that these gymnasia were state-supported institutions.[51] The statement is accurate if we keep in mind that such support applied only to the construction and maintenance of the gymnasium as a physical plant. Activities taking place in the gymnasium were not sponsored and paid for by the city. Even the *gymnasiarch*, the chief teacher or trainer, was not employed by the state. It is true that his position was state-appointed, but it was, in fact, one of honor rather than of employment. His role in controlling and supervising the activities of the gymnasium may not have been very demanding. Under his nominal supervision were a number of gymnasts and paidotribes who

[50] Gardiner, *Athletics of the Ancient World*, p. 41.
[51] Xenophon *Constitutions of Athens* ii. 10.

had actual contact with the boys who came to train in the gymnasium.[52]

In general, the gymnasium was open only to those who were able to pay the fees. The course of instruction occupied two, three, or more years; actually its length depended almost entirely on the boy himself. Boys who were unable to pay but who had some special ability to recommend them could have been selected by the gymnasiarch for gratuitous training. One of the most common recommendations for receiving gratuities of this sort was that the boy had lost his father on the field of battle.

It would appear that Athenian gymnasiarchs were left in their position of honor as long as the gymnasium which they superintended maintained a record of excellence in the many intracity and intercity competitions. To protect his position the gymnasiarch was constantly on the alert for Athenian boys of strength and agility who could contribute to the gymnasium's record. When these boys could not afford the fees, they were trained for nothing.

Considering the social pressures involved—there was no question of legal compulsion—few well-born Athenian boys were willing to place their futures in jeopardy by not attending a gymnasium. As the number of eligible, aspiring Athenian youth increased, the number of gymnasia increased also. There were in all five public gymnasia in Athens, although probably only three were in existence before the Persian Wars. In addition to the three mentioned above, there were the Diogeneion and the Ptolemeion, both public, and several private gymnasia. It might be mentioned, however, that private gymnasia really belong to that period of Athenian educational history when gymnastics were no longer the important content of secondary training. Intellectual formation was the principal objective of these later private gymnasia.[53]

Of the training and kinds of exercises prevalent in the gymnasium during the years before the Persian Wars, little need be said. The elementary physical skills introduced in the palaestra were continued and perfected. Beyond these, such things as riding and driving were practiced. We even hear of some instruction in Athenian law, but there are no detailed accounts of this kind of teaching in the gymnasia of the early period. It is hard, indeed, to think of the gymnasium as a school; perhaps it will be even more difficult to do so when we see something of the physical dimensions of the place.

Possibly there was no typical architecture for the gymnasium. Despite this, we can have a general idea of the gymnasium. It was,

[52] Freeman, *op. cit.*, pp. 224–230; and Woody, *op. cit.*, pp. 311–312.

[53] Freeman, *op. cit.*, p. 125.

first of all, an enclosed stadium with a large playing field, probably about the size of a modern football field, and a race course. The field was surrounded by places for spectators to sit or stand and buildings in which the athletes could rest, exercise, or converse. Rooms for wrestling, bathing, massaging, eating, praying, and just talking, along with gardens, groves, walks, and living quarters for servants and attendants were on the premises. The gymnasium was a unique multipurpose plant with a total area of about 360,000 square feet.[54]

EPHEBIC TRAINING

Ephebic training was the last step on the Athenian educational ladder. We have so far resisted the temptation to speak of the ephebic school, because it is not entirely clear that such training was ever organized into an institution that might properly be called a school. Whether in school or not, there is no doubt that ephebic education was intended to prepare boys for the major responsibilities of citizenship. During certain historical periods, such preparation meant training boys in the art of war; in other and later periods, ephebic education was fairly conventional intellectual training. Thus in later periods it is hardly necessary to speak of ephebic training, for it could not really be distinguished from any other kind of education. Even in the early years of Athenian educational history, ephebic schooling and the so-called "ephebic college" are clothed in considerable mystery.

Some educational historians have credited organized ephebic training with great antiquity; others have claimed that the ephebic system had its origin in the post-Persian War period. Wherever the truth may lie, one can be fairly certain that archaic values were reflected in the ephebic system.[55] One can be confident, too, that the demands made on the citizens for military service required that there be some means available for gaining skill and proficiency in the military arts. As the tendency grew for institutionalizing many things that had been left to individual Athenians, ephebic preparation was probably subjected to some social control. But just when this took place is not known. Neither Plato, Xenophon, nor Isocrates mentions the ephebic college. Aristotle alone paused to describe ephebic training, and he recognized it as the entrance to citizenship.[56]

In Aristotle's time citizenship was open to all Athenian residents

[54] *Ibid.*, pp. 127–130; and Woody, *op. cit.*, pp. 312–315.
[55] Xenophon *Constitutions of Athens* i. 13.
[56] Aristotle *The Constitution of Athens* 42.

born of Athenian parents. The conventional path to citizenship took one through ephebic training. At the age of eighteen or so, the boy applied for it. And this application was no mere formality. His age and parentage were examined by a council or a committee charged with this function. If the candidate was found to be younger than the law required, he was rejected; if his parentage was subject to question, the commission could bring charges against him for falsely claiming the right of citizenship. These charges were heard before the court of the city state, and the verdict was final. It could take one of two courses: A verdict against the boy meant that he would be sold as a slave; a favorable verdict enabled him to enroll in the ephebic course without further obstacle.[57]

Once in the ephebic course, boys received military training. As military science and tactics changed over the years, it is reasonable to assume that the course of training for ephebi changed too. In Aristotle's day this military training was of a year's duration. Then, in public ceremonies, those who were judged successful received the shield and the spear, and at the same time an oath of allegiance—the ephebic oath—was taken. Before Aristotle's time, we are told, the ephebic oath may have been administered to the boys when they enrolled for ephebic training, or the oath taking may even have been deferred until the complete course of three years or so had been finished.[58] Whenever this oath was taken—it was first introduced, tradition says, by Solon—it was always a pledge to honor the laws and traditions of Athens:

> I will never disgrace these sacred arms, nor desert my companions in the ranks. I will fight for the gods and home, both alone and with many. I will transmit my fatherland, not only no less but greater and better than it was transmitted to me. I will obey the magistrates who may at any time be in power. I will observe both the existing laws and those which the people may unanimously make in the future, and if any person seeks to annul the laws or disobey them, I will do my best to prevent him and will defend them both alone and with many. I will honor the religion of my fatherland, and I will call upon the gods [he names them] as my witness.[59]

The ceremonies of the arms and the oath were followed by two years of active service in the Athenian military organization. The period of preparation, which included training in the use of the implements of

[57] *Ibid.*
[58] *Ibid.;* and Woody, *op. cit.*, pp. 318–320.
[59] Quoted in *ibid.*, p. 319.

war and which also may have included some instruction in Athenian law, was over. Now the boys were journeyman citizens, and full citizenship depended upon the soldier's performance and his dedication to the state. Many obstacles faced young men during the two-year period of military service, not the least of which was actual warfare. Young men had to prove that they could uphold the oath they had taken and that they were worthy of citizenship. Even aside from combat and the real trials all brave men face in battle, these two years were most rigorous; discipline was extremely severe, and much physical exertion and skill were demanded of the men in the contests, games, and military maneuvers.

The earlier the period of Athenian history, the greater the likelihood that the soldier-citizens were the men in the military ranks or, at least, the men who would actually be engaged by an enemy in battles or skirmishes. But as armies became larger and as military conditions changed, these soldier-citizens tended more and more to be the officer class. The leaders were the citizens, or prospective citizens; those being led were mercenaries or noncitizen conscripts.

Possibly along with such changes or because of them, the ephebic training usual in the time of Aristotle was modified. This modification may have been due, also, to the declining fortunes of Athenian military power. In any event, ephebic training, instead of emphasizing or giving sole attention to physical and military development, accepted an intellectual function. In time a library was collected for the use of boys in the ephebic course, and with the acceptance of literary and intellectual objectives, ephebic training came to be identified as the ephebic college. It is doubtful that ancient Athens ever really relinquished the practice of ephebic preparation; when citizens no longer needed to be military men or military-minded, the scene of ephebic training shifted from the public gymnasia and the battlefield to the courts, the public arena, the schools, and the libraries.

Later Athenian Education

Beginning around 479 B.C., a date which marks the end of the Persian Wars, Athenian society was subjected to a number of remarkable changes. The success of Athens in defending herself against Persia led her to a position of leadership among Greek city states. It would seem that this advantageous political position was employed to further Athenian economic interests which added to the wealth of an already flourishing economic community. More important to us, however, were the innovations in cultural ideals following this period of Athens' political prominence in the Greek world, for Athens made her great contributions to Western culture *after* her political fortunes among Greek states declined.

As a result of conscription practices employed during the Persian Wars, many noncitizens who had fought for Athens—a civic privilege previously restricted to citizens—asked for the rights they had fought to protect. Their request was granted, and now they became fully accredited members of political society. With all free inhabitants enfranchised, the democratic tendencies that had been felt for as long as a century were now consolidated in practice. But Athenian citizenship meant something more than just being able to cast a vote in determining public policy; at least it indicated, on the one hand, a basic competence to weigh the issues and help shape state action in keeping with moral principle, and on the other, a traditional Athenian sense of justice and equity. Responsible government policy could be framed, it was argued, only by good citizens.

Here, of course, is where education was affected: The old education was both broad in conception, and time-consuming in realization. Twenty or more years were conventionally reserved for preparing an aristocracy to fulfill its leadership role and exert a profound moral influence on the state. And, we remember, schools played relatively insignificant parts in moral formation: Athens herself was literally a big school.

Now the important questions facing education were how to teach men to be good citizens, and how to achieve this objective quickly and without much help from the old-fashioned agencies of moral education such as the theater. The issue Socrates raised in *Protagoras* ("Can men be taught to be good?") was not merely an interesting and artful device for introducing debate, but the central issue in Athenian life.[60] New citizens wanted an education; they wanted to be effective and they wanted to be good; but they could not follow old roads to political virtue because time would not allow this, and the existing schools ill befitted their political and cultural purposes. Schools needed a realignment of purpose and content if they were to be responsible social agencies.

What was done, with the help of Sophists (to the dismay of Socrates, Plato, and Xenophon) was to shorten the school course— as a temporary measure to accommodate adult students—and to depend almost solely on schools to teach men goodness by exposing them to

[60] Plato *Protagoras* 319b.

literature and rhetoric.[61] Traditional individual and social values were in effect sold at discount; skills of oratory became the goals of school learning and were popularly assumed to be equivalent to political virtue. Although in the long run the structure of schooling, inherited from the earlier period, remained largely unchanged, the urgent demand for effective political education imposed new goals, teaching practices, and curricula on later Athenian education.

The same schools remained as symbols or as remnants of an honored but unneeded and unheeded past. Their content was modified only to the degree necessary for making them primarily literary institutions; they became centers for preparing citizens to take advantage of their newly found freedom of political action. Education flourished as never before, because now it was regarded as a means for speeding up a process of social assimilation and of ensuring political autonomy. But the schools of Athens, especially in the first years of this ferment, were capable only of whetting intellectual appetites. They held out hardly any opportunities for higher political training, and they did not make effective speaking the principal outcome of literary training. Something more was needed.

A new education was recommended to produce civic virtue, and in response to this need, the Sophists, a new and different class of teachers, came to Athens. The Sophists, along with the great philosopher–teachers (Plato, Isocrates, Aristotle, and others), now occupied the educational stage in Athens, and the future of education was in their hands.

With the exception of the Sophists, however, philosopher–teachers were uncomfortable with an educational program that could so easily jettison tested and respected cultural traditions. They argued that the new education was dangerous and superficial because it imposed an artificial political culture on *hoi polloi* (the general populace); it confused debating skill with moral and political wisdom. Moral education (that which leads men to a knowledge of the good), they said, cannot be learned in a few short years, if in fact it can be learned in the usual sense at all; and, moreover, assuming that moral wisdom is possible, it can be the possession of only the best minds. Trying to stem the tide of educational democracy, Socrates and Plato resisted what they called "cheap learning," and employed all their artistry in debate to convince their fellow citizens that political virtue and effective speaking were not synonymous. Their counsels of caution, however,

---

[61] Beck, *op. cit.*, pp. 186–187.

went unheeded by Athenian citizens, aristocrats and *hoi polloi* alike, who thought they had found, at long last, the solution to an educational conundrum: a certain means to educate effective and good citizens.

This drastic shift in educational emphasis would not have been possible in Athens except for the greater political freedom now enjoyed by a larger number of citizens and, what is probably more important, a growth of a spirit of individualism which tended to reverse a citizen's position vis-à-vis the state. The old fashion of seeing the world through the medium of his city was rejected by the fifth- and fourth-century Athenian; now he looked at the world directly and considered how it affected him. In religion, he was unwilling to accept the communal attitudes of the supernatural, and instead tried to enter a personal relationship with a supernatural world. He became, in effect, independent of the city, and changed his attitude toward it: now he was a citizen of the world, and the borders of Athens were too confining. Duty to country may conflict with personal ambition; when it does, the former must step aside. Patriotism in the traditional meaning ceased to be the highest virtue; the state was meant to serve the citizen, not the citizen the state, and so an old and unquestioning submission to social and political authority was completely reversed. In this context Sophists became famous, and stationary schoolmasters, generally antagonistic to sophistic pedagogical practice, conducted their schools. Yet Sophists and stationary teachers alike, whatever their theoretical differences, made their schools literary institutions in which they tried to give their students a decent education in order to enable them to function effectively not only in politics and society but, more importantly, as human beings with personal intellectual and moral goals.

What was new in later Athenian education had such far-reaching effects that the pleasant, uncomplicated goals of early Athenian schools became faint memories in the minds of post-Persian War schoolmasters. History opens on a new educational era with new doctrines, new practices, and highly persuasive spokesmen. We will want to listen to the educational theory developed by famous Athenian thinkers and teachers.

Summary

Ancient Greece contained many city states, the most famous of which were Athens and Sparta. Each of the Greek states had some provisions for education or training, but the prevailing educational systems supported or encouraged in Greece tended to follow the practice either of Athens or of Sparta.

Sparta's plan for education was founded on those values which Spartans found most useful to them. The paramount objective of the Spartan education or training system was citizenship. The goal was conceived in a narrow sense; it meant training Spartan boys in military craft. It may be fair to say that Spartans were owned by the state and that in Spartan history we can find some of the best examples of political and educational totalitarianism.

In Athens the goals of education were also expressed by the single term citizenship. But here the term's meaning was somewhat more complex, for the citizen of Athens was not merely a fighter; he was a man too. In this broader conception, the individual was formed in such a way that he knew, revered, and defended the traditions of the state. Such formation was thought to be the development of virtue—or laying the foundations for knightly and aristocratic conduct and eventually for the great deed. For decade after decade, Athenian education was informal. But with schools or without them, the goals of education were preserved with a surprising constancy. Possibly this was because education was quite exclusive; its opportunities were not generously distributed. Even when schools became common in Athens, the honored preferences in education were not greatly disturbed. Despite the adherence and devotion to practices and ideals of the past, Athenian society could not resist change. The most memorable changes took place after the Persian Wars. In earlier years education had been concerned with forming men; now it became concerned with training boys to become effective and successful. To aid in the achievement of this new goal, the Sophists made their way into Athens.

III

Greek Educational Thought

Ancient Greek tradition recommended both persuasive speaking and accompanied singing as important social abilities. In Greek city states where democracy gained a foothold—as in Athens—the greater worth could be assigned oratory, for with skill in oral expression any citizen could command the attention of an audience and by the force of his argument affect public policy. The average citizen, it was assumed, should be capable of delivering a public address; anyone aspiring to a career in politics recognized oratorical ability as indispensable to success. In addition, a judicial system without advocates or lawyers to represent plaintiffs and defendants placed total responsibility on the litigants to argue their own case: a citizen unable to speak convincingly was like a soldier unarmed for battle.[1]

[1] See R. J. Bonner, *Lawyers and Litigants in Ancient Athens*, University of Chicago Press, Chicago, 1927.

Mere facility of expression, however, was insufficient; command of vocabulary was not enough: clarity, content, force, and responsibility were grafted to oratory. So effective speaking, a power to express ideas clearly and persuasively, became an art well worth cultivating. One part of any public address was obviously delivery, which, the teachers of oratory said, depended for perfection on practice, on one hand, and native personal qualities—voice, manner, etc.—on the other. The other, and probably more important, part of public speaking (because mere ornamentation could not be long concealed) was the content of an oration. For judicial proceedings, where two litigants were involved in a dispute over equity, practiced writers could be employed to prepare a speech for the contesting parties and state the facts of the case as seen from one side. Ancient ghost-writers might be countenanced in trials where average citizens were involved in matters having only limited social effects, but for issues of genuine public concern this tactic would never do. The citizen seeking full effectiveness should be capable of writing his own speech, discussing in it vital political and ethical questions and then delivering it with control and conviction. Besides, in the context of policy debates, it would sometimes be necessary for public men to indulge in judicial and deliberative oratory extemporaneously. They needed to speak well, otherwise no one would listen, but it was also imperative that they know what they were talking about. This kind of public speaking required dimensions of thought and expression so far uncultivated in the conventional elementary schools of Athens.

Putting together a program of education with oratorical objectives (the ideal of forming public men) was still a remnant of civic education which could find roots and recommendations in tradition. But it was, nevertheless, sufficiently novel to make ineffective or meaningless the ancient theories justifying civic–military education of the Heroic age. Teachers of earlier days could ignore moral and ethical questions because these were issues handled outside the schoolhouse; it was unnecessary for them to grapple with such things as responsible citizenship because responsibility was formed and tested repeatedly in the exercise of public life. The new age, however, could ill afford such tactics of academic indifference: Prospective public men needed skills, knowledge, and wisdom at their command, and they put their future in the hands of teachers.

Never before had educators been asked to do so much. In a sense, the future of a nation was now their responsibility, for they alone could educate men for political leadership. The better schoolmasters of Athens, recognizing the heavy burden their schools now bore, essayed to state a theory of education for guiding and controlling their work, sometimes probing deeply into previously uncultivated fields of thought which might direct pedagogical processes concerned with teaching public men. But theory, once stated, needed implementation, and so the foremost teachers opened schools, and therein proposed to make their theories work.

The period of later Athenian education, with emphases on individualism and civic education, was willing to accept the elementary schools as they were and to use the foundations they built as intellectual pillars for the higher learning in oratory. Higher learning, a notable omission from the pages of earlier Greek educational history, made its bid for attention: Both in theory and practice, higher learning became an Athenian preoccupation. The Sophists, Plato, and Isocrates became the principal architects of educational theory, and their attitudes and pedagogical doctrines affected teaching and learning for centuries to come.[2]

The Sophists

So much has been written about the Sophists in histories of philosophy, politics, and education—and so little that is entirely dependable—that we wonder what can be added here.[3] No group of teachers has ever suffered more from bad publicity, and in many a contemporary vocabulary the word "sophist" expresses opprobrium. Conventional opinion, along with some respected testimony, often reveals the Sophists as ignorant, evil, pretentious, greedy men who came to Athens to beguile and exploit a gullible people and lead them along fraudulent pathways to what they thought would be knowledge and political wisdom.[4] This serious indictment comes almost entirely from their enemies, who boast Plato as their most vocal spokesman. The Sophists were probably never so bad as their critics said; and there is plenty of evidence, moreover, that Plato and his colleagues were capable of arguing from a platform of vested interest.

Despite Plato's uncompromising attitudes and his convincing and artful condemnations, the Sophists must not be dismissed as inconse-

[2] See Edward J. Power, *Evolution of Educational Doctrine,* Appleton-Century-Crofts, Inc., New York, 1969, pp. 3–13.

[3] See E. A. Havelock, *The Liberal Temper in Greek Politics,* Cape, London, 1957; M. Untersteiner, *The Sophists,* Blackwell, Oxford, 1954; Werner W. Jaeger, *Paideia: The Ideals of Greek Culture,* Oxford University Press, New York, 1945, vol. I, pp. 298–321; and Frederick A. G. Beck, *Greek Education: 450–350 B.C.,* Barnes & Noble, Inc., New York, 1964, pp. 147–187.

[4] For example, see Isocrates *Antidosis.* In Loeb Classical Library, Harvard University Press, Cambridge, Mass., 1927–1929, vol. II, p. 235.

quential figures in the history of education. Although it is true that
their standing as political and speculative philosophers is not high (for
their accomplishments in these fields are unimpressive), as teachers
they cleared avenues for educational progress and were responsible for
organizing the first secondary schools with literary and intellectual
purposes. It was they who took the boys from the gymnasium and
put them into classrooms.

After the Persian Wars the Sophists attracted a great deal of attention in Athens, but they were known throughout Greece as well.
In answering the question as to why they attracted attention we are led
nearer the explanation of their important role in education's long history. First, they contracted with their students to teach whatever the
students needed for success in life. In their teaching they employed
what has been called the simultaneous method. Second, because their
fees for teaching were often high, they found it necessary to advertise,
and their publicity releases usually tended to exaggerate their talents.
Finally, the Sophists attracted attention by attempting to accelerate
education in Athens to the point where it could reach the level of
contemporary Athenian culture. Before examining these points in
greater detail, we might explain that the Sophists did not form a co-
hesive school with a defined doctrine; a Sophist was an independent
teacher. Although we may think of him as a member of a community
of teachers, generally he did not acknowledge any such membership.[5]

The motives which operated on individual Sophists and led them
to offer their services as teachers must remain forever unknown to us.
We may assume that some were deeply dedicated to the work they
sought to perform; others may have been interested only in the income
to be derived from their teaching. We have been led to believe that
every Sophist taught for fees and that he tried to teach several students
at one time because such a technique was more profitable. We have also
been told that taking fees for instruction was a striking innovation and
that it was out of keeping with Athenian practices. It is said that
because the Sophists charged for their instruction and because their
fees were extraordinarily high, they were despised in Athens and in
many other Greek city states. If the Sophists were the objects of derision
in Athens one wonders why they were so successful and so popular
there. The point is this: Since no one knows definitely what the Sophists'
reception was in Athens, we may assume that they were welcome and
that their services were much in demand. In any case their practice
of taking fees for teaching was nothing new in Athens, although their

[5] Kenneth J. Freeman, in *Schools of Hellas,* 3d ed., The Macmillan Company, New
York, 1922, pp. 157–209, has an illuminating discussion of the Sophists.

custom of demanding payment in advance may have been both novel and unorthodox. Athenians had for dozens of decades been accustomed to paying their teachers for services rendered: they paid elementary teachers and, without objection, paid *paidotribes* and gymnasts. The innovation in educational practices introduced by the Sophists was to contract with students for a course of instruction which may have lasted as long as three years. Such practical agreements between students and their Sophist–teachers, though not altogether orthodox procedure in Athens, were nevertheless accepted without noticeable objection from the general population.

The fees that Sophists charged were high when the demand for their instruction was great and low when they were in need of students. It would seem that by resorting to such business practices the Sophists might have disclosed some superficiality in their approach to learning; what they had to offer was worth whatever the traffic would bear. In a society with a long tradition for appreciating value, such a cavalier attitude stimulated statements of reproach.[6] But such reprimands went largely unnoticed by the Sophists' clients, because it was in the new Athens that sophistry flourished—where men wanted the knowledge the Sophists claimed to have—and not in archaic Athens where men valued the traditional ways of thought.

Besides being accused of fraud in their teaching (that is, of teaching what they did not know), Sophists were sometimes held in disrepute because they were thought to have enriched themselves in their profession. But no Sophist is known or remembered for financial opulence, so this charge can be discounted. Still, while admitting that Sophists were popular teachers as a group, we should be disinclined to think that any one Sophist taught hundreds of students at one time. A Sophist's class was probably small, only infrequently numbering more than ten or a dozen students.[7] Yet, as we have said, Plato's dislike for the Sophists was shared by some of his countrymen, and this dislike and distrust were generated partly out of the fear that the masses have for men who know too much, partly because of the prejudice which aristocratic Greeks had for persons who worked for pay, partly from the jealousy which people felt who could not afford what the Sophists had to sell, and partly as a result of the disadvantages which some citizens experienced in competition with public men who had benefited from Sophistic education.

[6] As only one example from among many that could be cited, see Isocrates *Against the Sophists.* In *op. cit.,* vol. II, p. 3.

[7] See Power, *op. cit.,* pp. 43–44.

The Sophists moved from place to place in search of students; so-called "stationary teachers"—Plato and Aristotle for example—waited for students to come to them. It is reasonably accurate, therefore, to think of Sophists as wandering teachers. But when they succeeded in contracting with a number of students, they tried to give their lectures and carry on other teaching practices in halls or buildings, and thus there was some expense attached to their instructional program.[8] Taking this expense into account—and the Sophists were always eminently practical men—they usually tried to lecture to a full house. And as the number of teachers increased, they were forced more and more to compete for the students' fees and even to resort to publicity campaigns in order to attract students. Without modern advertising media, they were forced to carry on their recruitment programs in person. The picture so often drawn of the Sophist is of a man moving about the city or from city to city, disputing, arguing, and taking advantage of every opportunity to display his learning, his versatility, and his wit. Too often we stop here and conclude, possibly erroneously, that this was the extent of the Sophists' teaching. It was not uncommon for Sophists to have a few of their students accompany them on such excursions to round up students. On these occasions we get a glimpse of sophistic display. We are less fortunate, however, in that few examples of regular sophistic instruction have been preserved.

We should hardly be surprised to learn that the Sophists would advertise their product or that they would exaggerate their abilities as teachers. Nevertheless, much of the unenviable fame which attaches to sophistry had its origin in the recruitment procedures. And when the masters of the permanent schools began to lose students to the popular Sophists, these masters generated a resentment for their rivals which, though it may not have interfered with the Sophists' schools of the day, found its way into history to label the Sophists scholastic fakes and academic cheats.[9] This is a reputation which they do not entirely deserve.

After the Persian Wars, Athens could boast, among her other claims to respect, of being a cultural center. This was no idle boast, for the Athenians had made real and significant cultural progress. Their traditional vision of culture was near realization. However, culture in Athens, that is, her high level of art and thought, far outran systematic education. The Sophists' chief work was to close this gap between education and

[8] Freeman, *op. cit.*, p. 158.
[9] Plato *Sophist* 222–224.

culture.[10] It was the existence of this gap which brought such a class of wandering scholars to Athens in the first place.

In a very real sense the Sophists responded to demand, at least, to opportunity. They appeared on the Athenian scene in the fifth century B.C. at a time when society was ready for them. At this time in Athens, it will be recalled, a system of elementary schooling extended through the music school. Beyond this there was sport, with training for games of all kinds, but there were no schools for broader and deeper intellectual formation. With cultural progress so far in advance of elementary intellectual education, it is no wonder that Athenians welcomed a class of teachers who promised to disseminate the latest advances in Athenian culture and wisdom. Apparently the belief that Sophists were somehow involved in a democratic or democratizing movement in the city state is in need of revision. Whoever could pay the fees could be instructed by a Sophist, but the Sophists were not elementary teachers (they appeared to have no interest at all in teaching the basic tools of learning), nor were they committed, except theoretically, to educational equality among citizens. Most students who sat at the feet of their Sophist masters were aristocrats who aspired to cultural rather than political advancement. In any case, the Sophists aimed their teaching toward leadership and social success and were indifferent to the untutored common man whose need for a basic civic education was clear.[11]

LEADING SOPHISTS AND THEIR CRITICS

Of all the Sophists who came to Athens, the most famous and probably the most respected was Protagoras (481–411 B.C.). He was, it appears, the first to refer to himself and others like him as Sophists, teachers of wisdom, an occupation that in Greece of his time enjoyed some respect.[12] His name is famous, of course, as the inspiration for Plato's *Protagoras,* the great philosopher's only tribute to the worth of the body of itinerant teachers who invaded Athens. *Antilogies,* Protagoras' book, has been lost, but in it he is known to have contributed to the refinement of the Greek language, and to a development of Greek grammar, making it a suitable vehicle for conveying scientific and philosophical thought. Protagoras is said to have been the first to recognize the genders of nouns and the moods of verbs, but his chief importance lies in the

[10] See H. I. Marrou, *A History of Education in Antiquity,* Sheed & Ward, Inc., New York, 1956, pp. 47–49.

[11] See Plato *Protagoras* 317.

[12] *Ibid.,* 316b, 319a.

introduction of subjectivity to ethical thought and in giving this subjectivity philosophical respectability.

In company with other Sophists, Protagoras doubted the possibility of certainty, and he was a sufficiently schooled historian to give examples to justify his skepticism. Literature was filled with tales and legends—which the Greeks took seriously—of heroes who, choosing what seemed to be a valid alternative, were destroyed not because they were wrong but because there was always another side to what they believed was right and true. If men could not know what ought to be done on an objective level, they must then make their decisions acording to the doctrine that "man is the measure of all things." Knowledge of the good and the true—the reality, in fact, of everything—depends on a man's cognition: what seems useful to him is good, and what is effective is true. This doctrine, of course, led to extreme subjectivism which somehow, at least in teaching and learning, needed justification. Protagoras' justification was the "better argument": The teacher or debater capable of making his view appear the better was in the end right, and much of sophistic education, we are told, centered on preparing skilled debaters who, irrespective of the inherent worth of a proposition, could win an argument.[13] Finally, Protagoras built his teaching technique on the assumption that virtue could be taught—that is, that all men (not just aristocrats) could profit from the effect that instruction has on original nature.

Protagoras' propositions unquestionably contributed to his own fame as a teacher as well as to sophistic pedagogy generally, but when he entered the arena of theological debate he became the object of religious prejudice. He published a theological book by reading it before a selected audience in the house of his friend Euripides, and in this book admitted to agnosticism: "In regard to the gods I cannot know that they exist, nor yet that they do not exist; for many things hinder such knowledge." Such admissions proved to be unlucky for Protagoras: He was charged with impiety and banished from Athens, and his books were not only forbidden to all readers, but were publicly burned whenever found.[14]

Gorgias of Leontini (ca. 483 B.C.), a famous Sicilian orator who served his country as its Athenian ambassador, while in Athens displayed his talent for philosophy and politics. But what interested the Athenians most was his oratorical style: Gorgias wrote a new prose that, with its flourish, rhythm, ornamentation, and figures was highly

---

[13] Plato *Theaetetus* 167a–d; and Beck, *op. cit.*, p. 152.

[14] Freeman, *op. cit.*, p. 230.

appealing and, what is more, was sharply different from the cold, logical speech so common in the schools and assemblies.[15] So Athens adopted him as a teacher and, taking his place alongside Protagoras, he became an important and influential Sophist. Isocrates was his student and, to some extent, we believe, was responsible not only for codifying Gorgias' rhetorical doctrines, but for helping them to enjoy a long life in literary humanism. Plato was Gorgias' principal critic, and since Plato was not disposed to argue with men of little consequence, we may assume that Plato thought his sophistry was both important and dangerous.

We know few details about Gorgias' teaching, although a philosophical skepticism, expressed in his book *On Nature,* unavoidably affected it. In this book Gorgias said: "Nothing exists beyond the senses; if anything existed beyond the senses it would be unknowable, for all knowledge comes from the senses; if anything suprasensual were knowable, it would be uncommunicable, since all communication is through the senses." [16] Thus Gorgias shared Protagoras' precarious platform, but refused to allow men to be the measure of what was right or wrong, true or false. Neither relatively nor absolutely can men speak of truth; nor is there any basic conflict between opinion and truth. There are varieties of opinion: some are expressed crudely and are unconvincing; others, embellished with skillful rhetoric, are eminently persuasive. The objective of all education—set in this context of irrationality—was to teach the art of persuasion or, if needed, of deception. A well-educated person, then, is one capable of using language eloquently, of adapting speech to the needs of an occasion, and of unerring timing for making an argument at the right moment. Although Gorgias does not himself countenance nihilism, he admits that teachers are powerless to control the employment of the art they teach. They should like to see their students win men's souls by persuasion, and to practice the highest human achievement—speech—responsibly, but Gorgias has no safeguards to offer, because he, unlike Protagoras, is convinced that without knowledge of virtue it is futile to engage in teaching men to be virtuous.

Plato, who would not allow such dangerous doctrines to go unchallenged, reserved a special artistry of scorn for Gorgias. Furthermore, in his famous dialogue *Gorgias,*[17] Plato tried not only to put rhetoric in its proper perspective, but to strip Gorgias of a reputation for teaching excellence (which, however, Gorgias retained to the end of his life, at the almost unbelievable age of 109).

[15] See Kathleen Freeman, *Ancilla to the Pre-Socratic Philosophers,* Blackwell, Oxford, 1956, p. 138.

[16] Untersteiner, *op. cit.,* pp. 145–146.

[17] Plato *Gorgias* 459c.

Hippias of Elias (ca. 443 B.C.), another well-known Sophist, enjoyed a reputation for intellectual versatility and wisdom. Among his accomplishments was a reputed mastery of astronomy, arithmetic, geometry, literature, politics, and music; in addition, he was an envoy of his government, an orator, and an historian. According to the legend he was an expert craftsman who could make, among other things, his own clothing and personal ornaments. Hippias boasted, moreover, of his ability to deliver before the Athenian assembly an extemporaneous speech on any subject.[18]

In his educational theory Hippias abruptly departs from the skepticism of Protagoras and Gorgias to embrace a philosophic position wherein knowledge of all things is possible to a man of talent. Learning may not be easy, and Hippias admits this much, but its goal is an understanding of nature's laws enabling men first to know them and then to act in a socially suitable way. Amid all the mysteries of nature are clues to dependable knowledge. Translated into a school's curriculum, these are: physics (giving men a knowledge of the nature of things), letters (equipping men to understand words and use them well), mathematics (a fundamental foundation for scientific study), and ethics (a means for understanding the concept of justice). Hippias' educational formula, less rhetorically oriented than Gorgias', and one recommending broad knowledge as the best guarantee of virtuous action, acknowledged the worth of effective speaking without allowing speech to dominate education. If history accurately reflects Hippias' theories of teaching and learning, and if his own accomplishments are not grossly exaggerated, his brand of sophistry had praiseworthy elements which should be immune to acid criticism from sophistic detractors.

Other Sophists—Prodicus, Antiphon, Thrasymachus, along with names obliterated by time—conducted schools in Athens staying generally within the broad boundaries of educational purpose marked out at the one extreme by Gorgias, and at the other by Hippias.

How acceptable were sophistic doctrines to Athenians, and what was the reaction they stimulated from pedagogical competitors? A few Athenians were uncertain of the direction of their glib oratory, and others were disturbed by their claims and their promises. Some Athenians, especially those of aristocratic backgrounds, believed the Sophists were undermining an established way of life. Despite the distrust of their elders, students with aristocratic backgrounds were the ones who flocked to the Sophists and sat at their feet.

[18] See Beck, *op. cit.*, pp. 183–186.

Xenophon, the soldier, aristocrat, and historian, uttered a common criticism of the Sophists in his *Memorabilia*. In a discussion between Socrates and Antiphon, the former says: "Those who offer it [wisdom] to all comers for money are known as Sophists, prostitutors of wisdom, but we think that he who makes a friend of one whom he knows to be gifted by nature, and teaches him all the good he can, fulfills the duty of a citizen and a gentleman." [19]

Isocrates, in the *Antidosis*, questions the basic merits of sophistic instruction.

> Some say that the profession of the Sophist is nothing but sham and chicane, maintaining that no kind of education has ever been discovered which can improve a man's ability to speak, or his capacity for handling affairs, and that those who excel in these respects owe their superiority to natural gifts; while others acknowledge that men who take this training are more able, but complain that they are corrupted and demoralized by it, alleging that when they gain the power to do so, they scheme to get other people's property. [20]

Isocrates, a wealthy man at the time the *Antidosis* was written, was especially sensitive to sophistic arguments that might be used to deprive him of some of his property. When he was called upon to fit out a ship for the military purposes of the city state, he went to court to prove that he did not have the wealth to accept such an invitation. In *Antidosis* Isocrates used every device that he knew to explain his position in society as well as his educational views. It is by such defensive arguments that the place of the Sophist is brought up for analysis. In addition to the *Antidosis*, Isocrates speaks of the Sophists in his *Against the Sophists*, an oration that was intended specifically as an advertisement for his school. In it he goes to great pains to show that he is not another Sophist; he wants the people of Athens to know what the opportunities for education are in his school. He criticizes the Sophists in this way:

> More than that, although they set themselves up as masters and dispensers of goods so precious, they are not ashamed of asking for them a price of three of four minae. Why, if they were to sell any other commodity for so trifling a fraction of its worth, they would not deny their folly; nevertheless, although they set so insignificant a price on the sole stock of virtue and happiness, they pretend to wisdom, and assume the right to instruct the rest of the world. Furthermore, although

---

[19] Xenophon *Memorabilia*. In Loeb Classical Library, Harvard University Press, Cambridge, Mass., 1923, vol. IV, p. 7.

[20] Isocrates *Antidosis*. In *op. cit.*, vol. II, pp. 297–299.

they say they do not want money, and speak contemptuously of wealth as "filthy lucre," they hold their hands out for trifling gain and promise to make their disciples all but immortal.[21]

Isocrates is especially bitter toward the Sophists' policy of demanding the fees for their teaching in advance. He felt that they were exaggerating their abilities when they claimed to be able to sell wisdom to any who could buy it. His conception of formal education was that it makes students more skillful and resourceful in discovering the nature of things. It teaches them, he would hold, to take from dependable sources that information or knowledge that they would otherwise obtain only in haphazard fashion. Yet formal education is powerless to shape into successful debaters or excellent writers men who are without natural aptitude. Education can lead such men to some self-improvement, and it can open up a number of intellectual avenues for them, but it cannot remake their natural capacities.[22]

The Sophists' method of teaching—often criticized for the novelties that it contained—was held up to ridicule by Aristophanes in the dialogue between Euripides and Aeschylus in *The Frogs*.[23] Later, in *The Clouds*, Pheidippides, whose father has been attracted to sophistic theories of justice to the extent of arguing his creditors out of their due, beats his father. The father protests that the son is lacking in filial duty and respect. Pheidippides, who had been trained well in equivocation, a mark of many Sophists, offers to debate the question with his father and boasts: "I mean to say, we argue up or down—Take which you like —It comes to the same end." [24]

It would appear that Plato had a special dislike for Sophists who taught disputation without ethical considerations. More importantly, he was critical of them for trying to teach students virtue without first offering them a fundamental intellectual education. The consequence of such superficial teaching would appear to have been a marked preference for teaching verbal tricks rather than concentrating upon soundly argued philosophical inquiry. Such emphases resulted in an interest in contest and strife for its own sake rather than the determination of the truth and the cultivation of a vision of wisdom.

Aristotle objected to the sophistic technique of giving precise, unequivocal answers to any questions that were asked them. Such methods, according to the Aristotelian view, actually interfered with the

[21] Isocrates *Against the Sophists*. In *op. cit.*, vol. II, p. 165.

[22] *Ibid.*, p. 173.

[23] Aristophanes, *Plays*, E. P. Dutton & Co., Inc., New York, 1922, p. 52.

[24] *Ibid.*, p. 167.

promotion of scholarship and the development of clear and incisive thinking.

Many modern writers find the Sophists less worthy of censure. It would seem to be a fair judgment that the Sophists were popular not only because there was a need for instruction in the fields of knowledge in which they claimed skill and for training in the arts of rhetoric and disputation, in which they were expert, but also because they fulfilled a role that society had actually created for them. In fulfilling this role they pushed back the boundaries of formal education and laid the foundations for secondary schooling. Finally, Plato, Aristotle, and others rose to meet the sophistic challenge, and in their refutations of sophistic thought and practice important and lasting contributions were made to the methods of inquiry and to the content of our philosophic inheritance. If the Sophists had done nothing more than stimulate rebuttal by thinkers and philosophers, their contributions to later generations, though largely negative, would have been extremely worthwhile.

Socrates (469–399 B.C.)

If one is discussing philosophy or education, it is unlikely that the origins of either discipline will receive much attention before the name of Socrates is mentioned. His reputation has not suffered from wear; the excellence of his thought and the effectiveness of his teaching methods are everywhere the objects of praise. He enjoys the peculiar advantage, not shared by his most illustrious pupil, Plato, of not having recorded his thoughts for posterity. In this way Socrates gained enviable immunity from criticism. Despite almost phenomenal popularity from the time of his death, Socrates, it should be remembered, was condemned to die because of the content and the manner of his teaching. This was the published charge: "Socrates is guilty of crime in refusing to recognize the gods acknowledged by the state, and importing strange divinities of his own; he is further guilty of corrupting the young." [25] There is evidence that the charge against him was trumped up and that the real reasons were personal; the enemies of Socrates used drastic means to secure their revenge.

In any event, the substance of the litigation concerned the effect that Socrates' teaching was having on the youth of Athens. This was a remarkable, if not an unbelievable, accusation. There was little in the demeanor of the Athenian citizen of that day to suggest that Athenians were fearful of the influence teachers might have on youth. The city

[25] *The History of Xenophon,* translated by H. G. Dakyns, The Tandy-Thomas Company, New York, 1909, vol. III, p. 231.

was full of Sophists, many of whom had poor, if not bad, reputations for personal morality. The charge against Socrates, therefore, had many earmarks of vindictiveness. It is of course true that his constant questioning irritated many people and embarrassed others. His "gadfly" tactics may have led to his being called a revolutionary at a time when the people of Athens were tired of all kinds of disturbances. Besides this, Socrates was no democrat; he defended the doctrine of "aristocracy of ability" in a city state where the disillusionment with oligarchy was nearly complete. He criticized democracy and appeared to be opposed to its principles and its practices. Such stands did not make him popular among those who were committed to the democratic experiment.[26] Besides, Socrates was accused of being an atheist—of not believing in the Greek gods and goddesses—at a time when atheism was a popular, though not entirely an orthodox, view in Athens. But the important point would seem to be that Socrates was put to death not because of what he taught but because he refused to acknowledge the right of his accusers to dictate to him. He declined to recant or to admit that his investigations were without solid foundation or that they led to heterodoxy. In this way he provided succeeding generations with a moving example of the importance of freedom of thought and freedom of inquiry; Socrates died as a martyr to both.[27]

Ends are often more auspicious than beginnings. Socrates was born of poor parents. He learned to read and write, probably from a primary schoolmaster, and thereafter, instead of attending the elementary schools in Athens—the palaestra and the music school—he followed the trade of his sculptor father. No doubt his apprenticeship in this trade was completed with the attainment of sufficient skill to place him among the masters of the guild, although there is neither testimony nor evidence to document this belief. In time, either because of other interests or because he just tired of his trade, Socrates turned away from sculpture and became a teacher.

Because he embraced the teaching occupation, Socrates was called a Sophist by some of his contemporaries. It is possible that in the Athens of his day he was so regarded, but if Socrates was a Sophist, he was not an ordinary one. He did not seek students; they sought him. His teaching involved no fees, no contracts, no lecture halls, no advertising campaigns, no promises of success. He did share the sophistic interest for preparing leaders for politics and society, though not according to any formula, and for accelerating education to the point where it would

[26] See William G. Forrest, *The Emergence of Greek Democracy*, Weidenfeld & Nicolson, London, 1966.

[27] See Plato's *Apology*.

more nearly approximate Athenian culture. One would probably not be wrong in thinking of Socrates as a fairly important figure in the origin and development of secondary education.

Socrates was no spirit; he was a man. And the reader may be wondering how Socrates supported himself, his wife, Xantippe, and his family without an income from his trade as a sculptor or from his art as a teacher. Evidently he was not a good provider, and one can sympathize with his poor wife. His income was small and irregular; its source was the patronage of people who encouraged Socrates to lead a life of inquiry and dialectic.

Patrons of the arts are not usually pure philanthropists. Their altruism is tempered with a desire for value received; in other words, they sensibly support a man whose capacity for making valuable social and intellectual contributions is recognized. What did Socrates' patrons see in him? And what of the generations of students and scholars who followed Socrates? Did they find merit in his views? How did Socrates invigorate and enrich thought and learning?

An evaluation of Socrates must always remain somewhat tentative. He wrote nothing. Plato, Xenophon, and others who have left accounts of Socrates' life and thought were among his closest admirers. From Plato we have obtained almost everything we know about Socratic thought; to Xenophon we are indebted for most of the details of his life. In Plato's works it is hardly possible to see where Socratic thought stops and where Platonic thought begins. And Plato was under no obligation to make any such distinction in his writing. In fact we may with reason ask whether or not Plato in his dialogues was merely using Socrates as a literary device. It seems entirely possible that Socrates may never have held the views attributed to him by Plato, or that he may be credited with insights and interpretations which were beyond his interests or his abilities. There is no reason for anyone to go out of his way to tarnish his reputation; yet one should know that a great deal of myth and legend attaches to the name of Socrates.

Despite myth and legend, an educational history must try to deal, at least briefly, with the products of Socratic thought and method. Before the time of Socrates, Athenians had avoided searching analyses of man's nature or speculations on the principles governing his conduct. Pre-Socratic speculations had usually centered on nature, with the result that early Greek philosophy was really physics. Why the Greeks avoided a study of man is hard to say. They may have, as some claim, thought that such speculations belonged to the practical order (the illiberal) rather than to the theoretical order (the liberal). For this claim to have much validity one would have to maintain that pre-Socratic distinctions on such matters were clearly drawn and that the allegiances of the time definitely committed the Athenian Greeks to the doctrine of liberal pursuits. These conclusions would not be easy to accept. In any event, the presumption remains that ethical theorizing was stimulated greatly by the activities of Socrates. One aspect, then, of Socratic thought was ethical, and since this thought had some relevance to educational theory, we must give attention here to its ethical content. In addition to this, we must know something about the method of Socrates. It seems to have been novel; and for centuries it has been praised as teaching's most effective technique. We should understand both the method and the principles on which it rests.

SOCRATIC THOUGHT AND METHOD

The breadth of Socrates' interest is difficult to measure exactly. Clearly he was interested mainly, if not only, in man and his actions. He was surely concerned with ethics, and basic to ethical principles are values or evaluations of worth. It was these values or goods that really commanded Socrates' attention: justice, temperance, courage, gratitude, and friendship. He never wearied of discussing topics related to any of these values. And apparently Socrates was never fully satisfied that he or his colleagues completely understood the meaning of these virtues. It was this prying, inquiring attitude that led Socrates into difficulty and eventually to prison and execution.

If we are to understand Socratic pedagogy, we must see that the dialectical techniques flowed naturally from the Socratic definition of intuition. In the Socratic interpretation as we understand it, achieving knowledge was not a discursive process. Teaching was therefore not a matter of implanting or pouring in. Knowledge, according to the Socratic view, is intuitive; that is, it is already in the mind, and the teacher's mission is simply to bring it out. What better technique than dialectic could be devised to open avenues to free, or let out, this knowledge?

Seeking knowledge, for that matter the entire educational process, was not an end in itself. It is not easy to see Socrates as an ardent defender of the doctrine of liberal studies; on the other hand, he showed no great interest in utilitarian studies. He did, it is true, approve of geometry when it was taught for practical application; astronomy had value too, for with it the seasons could be forecast; and arithmetic was useful for business. Despite Socrates' approval of these subjects, it is clear that he thought much more highly of studies that led one to self-knowledge and to an understanding of, and a tendency to, right action. How, he would ask, could a man be just if he did not know the meaning of justice? And what was just in the eyes of one might not be just in the eyes of another. The central issue was to arrive at clear concepts in the field of ethics. Once these concepts were formed and ideas about the meaning of virtue were clarified, one would have some basis for hoping that men might lead a more orderly and efficient ethical life. For Socrates, no doubt, the job of the thinker, the philosopher—the lover of wisdom—was to clarify, to fix general concepts, to introduce precise thinking into intellectual inquiry; the job of the teacher, or more generally, the mission of education was to bring these discoveries to all men. This knowledge would lead them, Socrates maintained, to a more virtuous life. The identification of knowledge and virtue has for centuries been known as the "Socratic fallacy."

As we have said, the Socratic method followed very naturally and very logically the Socratic conception of knowledge. Socrates never implied that teachers were to convey truth to their students. The teacher's place was to stimulate thought, to encourage investigations, and to challenge students to think for themselves. Moreover, truth was something which Socrates did not claim to have. In the dialogues in which Plato depicts Socrates as being unable to give answers, it is not because Socrates, for pedagogic reasons, does not want to give them, but because he does not know the answers. The Socratic method is essentially a method of probing the unknown. The dialectic was an investigation, a quest for knowledge, and not, as those who try to imitate Socrates sometimes claim, a pedagogic technique.

Finally, it should be mentioned that Socrates was no hearer of lessons. We do not mean to imply that he would have found such educational practices unacceptable; he did not use them simply because, on the level of his teaching, such techniques were not at all appropriate. Although it may be true that Socrates had a lasting influence on secondary education, Plato shows him at work on a much higher plane. In actual fact there is little in the Socratic method that could be used without drastic modification on the lower educational levels. Most modern teachers would be wasting their own and their students' time if they were to confine themselves to the method of Socrates. Socrates himself would probably not have used this method if he had been a teacher in the Greek music school.

Plato (427– or 429–347 B.C.)

Of all who admired Socrates, none did as much as Plato to write an indelible record attesting to the greatness of the man. Plato was Socrates' friend, a more or less constant companion, and his student, and sharing many of the older philosopher's views, he, more than anyone else, preserved Socratic thought for posterity. Plato, however, was much more than a witness to the mental acumen of his illustrious friend. In his own right he was one of the world's foremost philosophers. Coupling philosophical insight with artistry of presentation, Plato's works are without equal in the history of thought. No one doubts Plato's prominence in the history of philosophy, and his place in the history of education should be just as certain and as clear. He was a schoolmaster and a theorist: in his thought and work he organized and promoted a philosophical approach to education, an approach meriting the approbation of scores of educators the world over for more than twenty centuries.[28]

We have relatively incomplete knowledge of Plato's boyhood and his early education. He came from an aristocratic and wealthy family, and quite likely his educational opportunity was the best that wealth and circumstances could provide.[29] He had, moreover, the time and resources to travel and the leisure to study and think. His contacts with Socrates served further to stimulate an already active and extremely able mind. The death of Socrates, under trying circumstances for all his friends and for all who respected truth, was, we are led to believe, a powerful force in shaping Plato's future. It may have been a strong stimulus for Plato to carry on the work of his master. Despite the importance of this tragic event in consolidating Plato's dedication to the search for truth, it should be underlined and emphasized that Plato was much more than a disciple of Socrates. In other words, he did not merely carry Socrates' message to all who would listen; he had an important philosophical message of his own which he disseminated vigorously and artistically.[30] Whatever the long-range effects of Socrates' execution on Plato, its immediate effect was to drive him from Athens. Although there may have been other reasons for his departure, the main one was that Plato's life and liberty were in jeopardy. He remained away from Athens for about a dozen years and then returned to his native city, where he established a school.[31]

[28] Many authors have studied Plato's educational views. See, for example, Power, *op. cit.*, pp. 55–77; Richard Livingstone, *Plato and Modern Education*, Cambridge University Press, London, 1944; R. C. Lodge, *Plato's Theory of Education*, Harper & Row, Publishers, New York, 1947; Beck, *op. cit.*, pp. 199–243; and Marrou, *op. cit.*, pp. 61–78.

[29] See R. S. Bluck, *Plato's Life and Thought*, Routledge & Kegan Paul, Ltd., London, 1949.

[30] See H. F. Cherniss, *The Riddle of the Early Academy*, University of California Press, Berkeley, 1945, pp. 236–238.

[31] *Ibid.;* Freeman, *Schools of Hellas*, p. 180, believes the Academy was conducted first in Plato's home.

The school was called the Academy, because it was located near the Athenian gymnasium of the same name. In this school Plato formulated many of the philosophical positions that have become famous and wrote a number of the philosophical treatises that have had such an impressive influence on political and educational thought down through the ages.[32] Plato was primarily a philosopher, and secondarily a teacher. The reader should resist the inclination to draw a mental picture of Plato as an ordinary schoolmaster. In concert with his disciples, who were also his friends, he tried to refine thought so as to ascertain solutions to the universal problems of mankind. But instead of giving his students the answers to the searching questions, and instead of drawing conclusions of his own about the topics under consideration, Plato tried to lead his students through pertinent thought processes.[33] The exact nature of Plato's teaching techniques is not completely clear to us. It is possible that he employed the method of Socrates, for surely his writings prove that he was a master of dialectic. There are good reasons for believing that Plato had greater interest in developing in his students the methodology of learning than in having them deal with the results of this process. It would appear that Plato did on one occasion lecture in the Academy, but the lecture was not popular, and most of his audience left before he had finished. They were unable to follow him. He preferred to use informal discussion for teaching, and these discussion periods were graced with good humor and, we hear, with refreshments—always imbibed moderately—which contributed, no doubt, to the cordial atmosphere of the school. We have so little dependable information on the daily activities of the school, however, that were it not for the *Republic* and the *Laws*, Plato's great political proposals, it would be difficult to give a very thorough picture of Plato's educational doctrines.

EDUCATIONAL IDEALS

The statement has been made that Platonic thought shows an extraordinary and unnecessary preoccupation with education.[34] It is true that education is given a great deal of attention. However, it would seem that in his concern for politics and the ideal state, Plato had no alternative but to deal in detail with the formation of the citizens of such a state. When we understand Plato's purpose, we realize that his

[32] See H. F. Cherniss, *Aristotle's Criticism of Plato and the Academy*, Johns Hopkins University Press, Baltimore, 1944.

[33] See Cherniss, *The Riddle of the Early Academy*, pp. 130–141.

[34] Jaeger deals with this charge. See *op. cit.*, vol. II, p. 200.

interest in education is not something tangential to his major purpose, but an integral and essential means for its attainment. We may conclude, then, that Plato did not miscalculate education's relevance to politics; history has proved him right time after time. On the other hand, Plato's emphasis on education was not strikingly new. Sparta offered a good example of education's function in the making of a state, and Plato knew the Spartan system thoroughly; Athenian practices in statecraft, though different from those of Sparta, gave the formation of the citizen a central place in all educative activities. Plato, then, should not be regarded as an idealist or a visionary on this important point. It is true that he formed a political ideal and worked out means to attain it by using his imagination, but a number of concrete examples of statecraft could have influenced his thought.

Plato's principal educational objectives did not differ from those accepted in early Athens or, for that matter, from those considered orthodox in Sparta. He aimed at good citizenship. Even Plato's school—attended only by carefully selected students—was a place for preparing citizens. But the identity of objectives did not mean an identity of means, for in the Athens of Plato's time military service was not regarded as the citizen's primary duty as in earlier times. Now competence in civic affairs was given first place. Citizenship was the possession of those who had a proper system of values, profound knowledge and understanding leading to wisdom, and an ideal of service to their fellow men and to the state, and who exemplified leadership in politics and society. Civic ability, therefore, was an outcome of education; it could be achieved as the end product of a process of intellectual formation. There is, nevertheless, a clear preference for the elite to be detected in Plato's choice of those who could be educated, and he, like the Sophists, committed himself to the preparation of citizens who would become leaders.[35]

The first, and for Plato surely the most important, use to which the products of education could be put was service to the state, or more generally service to society. As we have indicated, such a view created an unavoidable preference for the education of leaders. The few, not the many, were favored. Perhaps even this had a solid basis in reality, although much modern democratic thought would try to resist all aristocratic tendencies in education. Nevertheless, Plato's proposed curriculum, though most beneficial in the preparation of leaders, surely had its uses, too, for citizens who were not destined for high position. Yet it is difficult to accept Platonic educational views as the theoretical

[35] Plato *Republic* viii. 558.

foundation either for so-called traditional liberal education—the education of gentlemen—or for popular education in its twentieth-century form.

In connection with popular education, Plato was quite willing that everyone in the state be trained, but he would have made the more advanced levels of education special places for students with unusual talent. With respect to liberal education, we cannot state his position in such clear-cut fashion. This is because the expression, liberal education, is subject to many interpretations. From Plato's time to our own, few educators have agreed on what it is and naturally enough, therefore, on how it is obtained. Plato knew what liberal education meant in his time: It was the education given to a leisure class for the leisurely life they were leading and would continue to lead. Such education did not meet with Plato's approval; a life of useless leisure—useless, at least, in a social sense—could not have had anything to recommend it. Surely the highest virtues to be developed could hardly be squared with fifth-century B.C. practices in education. Yet it is impossible to see Plato as a utilitarian. Fortunately, the practical and the theoretical are not separated by the same dichotomy as the utilitarian and the liberal.

Plato's objective, to put it another way, was universal truth. The sophistic doctrine, "Man is the measure of all things," when put in the hands of the orators who had been trained by the Sophists, was interpreted to mean that "what appears to be true, is true." It is only a short step from this position to the pragmatic doctrine that only results count. Plato, of course, was far from being uninterested in outcomes; he was careful, however, to insist that truth should be based on critical processes whereby false and superficial opinions can be detected and discarded, leaving a core of sound knowledge. Plato's emphasis on truth—a truth that is unique, fixed, and eternal—had important consequences for the curriculum.

STATE CONTROL

There seems to be little doubt that Plato willingly, almost anxiously, accepted the traditional Greek view that a citizen's training should prepare him to act for the public good. The individual counted for very little. Perhaps he was but a tool to be used by the state in the attainment of civic ends. That Plato accepted what was a more or less traditional Greek view—one which made the individual's good regularly subordinate to that of the state—is clear from the ideals portrayed in the *Republic* and the *Laws*.

Plato was not a democrat, even though it is possible to find some democratic tendencies in his writings. The supreme good may not have been the state, but in order that the highest good might be achieved, state unity was essential. Only by careful regulation of individual action and by instilling in all citizens, from birth on, an exacting dedication to the state, could this unity be obtained and preserved. It is unlikely that Plato was a state worshiper. Rather, he saw the state as the most effective instrument that could be devised and employed for leading men to the higher life in the realm of ideas. If there appears to be an inconsistency in the idea that men must be slaves first before they can be free, we must not forget the Christian message that men must first lose their lives in order to find them. The Platonic view on state unity may well be interpreted to mean only that men must sacrifice lesser ends for greater. At any rate, whether Plato's views can be defended or not, it is important to know that the principle of state unity, a unity to be achieved principally by education, was basic to his thought. Once this is understood, the inflexible legalisms in Plato's system are not so likely to drive us away from him.

There are unquestionably a number of paradoxes in Plato's writings, and here, in his emphasis on the rigid control which the state is to exercise over education, we find an important one. For though state authority was to be exercised over these matters, still, free and liberal minds capable of apprehending truth wherever it may be found were to have been the products of such an authoritarian system. To call Plato's view somewhat paradoxical does not mitigate the obviously unnatural relationship between authoritarianism and freedom. Nevertheless, it may well be that this is but another of Plato's predictions of things to come—prophetic anticipations of later educational systems—for throughout a great deal of Western man's history, compulsion rather than freedom has been characteristic of his educational practices.

It is not hard to find examples of Plato's theory regarding state control. Book II of the *Republic* contains many references illustrative of Platonic thought on this point. The *Laws*, too, present the same theme. They attest also to the fact that in half a lifetime Plato had not changed his mind. If anything, he had become more explicit in his views; he seemed to be entirely sure of himself when he wrote in the *Laws* that the state should take an active and controlling role in superintending education.

> There remains the minister of the education of youth, male and female; here, too, the law may well provide that there shall be one such minister, and he must be fifty years old, and have children lawfully begotten, both boys and girls by preference, at any rate, one or the other. He who is elected, and he who is the elector, should consider

that of all the great offices of state this is the greatest; for the first shoot of any plant, if it makes a good start, has the greatest effect in helping it to obtain its mature natural excellence; and this is not only true of plants, but of animals wild and tame, and also of man. Man, as we say, is a tame or civilized animal; nevertheless, he requires proper instruction and a fortunate nature, and then of all animals he becomes the most divine and most civilized; but if he be insufficiently or ill educated he is the most savage of earthly creatures. Wherefore the legislator ought not to allow the education of children to become a secondary or accidental matter. In the first place, he would be rightly provident about them, should begin by taking care that he is elected, who of all the citizens is in every way best; him the legislator shall do his utmost to appoint guardian and superintendent. To this end all the magistrates, with the exception of the council of prytanes, shall go to the temple of Apollo, and elect by ballot him of the guardians of the law who they severally think will be the best superintendent of education. And he who has the greatest number of votes, after he has undergone scrutiny at the hands of all the magistrates who have been his electors, with the exception of the guardians of the law, shall hold office for five years; and in the sixth year let another be chosen in like manner to fill his office.[36]

Thus in the *Laws* Plato provides for a minister of education, whose duty it shall be to manage all the schools of the state. He will dictate the regulations concerning discipline in the schools; all matters pertaining to instruction in the schools and gymnasia will be within the ambit of his authority. Even the "going to school" of boys and girls, by which Plato may have meant school attendance at appropriate ages as well as the rather obvious physical movement to and from school, would be under his control. Finally, the minister of education was to control school buildings and everything that went on within them. While the law was explicit in many of its demands, it was nevertheless true that the minister of education could do many things at his own discretion. No wonder that Plato implored the legislators to look for the best man for this position, to choose the most superior of all. Besides making a judicious selection of ministers of education, the legislators were admonished to create a fabric of law within which ministers of education could be prepared and which would be a guide to them, once selected, in the performance of their duties.

But how can our law sufficiently train the director of education himself; for as yet all has been imperfect, and nothing has been said either clear or satisfactory? Now, as far as possible, the law ought to

[36] Plato *Laws* vi. 766.

omit nothing that concerns him, but to explain everything, that he may be an interpreter and tutor to others.[37]

As a final word on this matter of state control, and in fairness to Plato, it should be said that he had visions of a state wherein law's place would eventually be preempted by widespread culture. Whether a completely and competently educated citizenry would make even the most fundamental law unnecessary is to be doubted; for fundamental law may find an even more secure foundation in oral tradition than it does in statute. But it would seem that Plato did see education as a substitute for regimentation and extremely detailed legal codes.

> If our citizens are well educated, and grow into sensible men, they will easily see their way through all these, as well as other matters which count, such, for example, as marriage, the possession of women, and the procreation of children.
>
> Thus educated, they will invent for themselves any lesser rules which their predecessors have altogether neglected. I mean such things as these: when the young are to be silent before their elders; how they are to show respect for them by standing and making them sit; what honor is due parents; what garments or shoes are to be worn; the mode of dressing the hair; deportment and manners in general.[38]

THE EDUCATION OF BOYS AND GIRLS

Social as well as educational traditions had regularly recommended various kinds of training for girls. Females, however, according to the same tradition, were not thought to be equally capable as boys in mastering the intricacies of education. Accepted Greek practice, whether in Sparta or Athens, placed girls on a different level from boys. In Sparta, as we have seen, some of the games and contests intended especially for little boys were entered by little girls. However, this type of cotraining did not continue for the Spartan girl; by the time she was eleven or twelve years of age she was no longer welcomed to the boys' exercises. The Spartan code, nevertheless, demanded certain competence from the woman; she was to be trained or groomed for motherhood. Yet with all of this attention to important details of female education, there was hardly ever any suggestion that the sexes were equal.

In Athens girls were somewhat less well off than in Sparta. It was the exception, not the rule, to find Athenian girls prepared in much of

[37] *Ibid.,* vii. 809.

[38] Plato *Republic* vii. 425.

anything beyond those domestic arts informally communicated or directed by mothers or domestic servants. With these examples of the treatment of women Plato was thoroughly familiar. In addition, he knew of, and referred to, other approaches to the education of women common to countries outside the Greek world.

But what is important to us here is the recommendation of Plato concerning the education of girls. He proposed that boys and girls be educated in separate elementary and secondary schools.[39] Plato believed that boys and girls should be educated alike, although he probably did not consider a woman to be a man's equal. From the age of six to the time when students entered higher studies, girls were to follow the same educational program as boys, but in their own schools. Had Plato thought that woman's nature was different from man's he would unquestionably have provided for schooling consistent with these natural differences; yet, coeducation was approved in whatever may have been done before children reached the age of six. Advanced or higher studies attracted only the best minds; these higher studies were available to the best minds, regardless of sex.

It seems clear, however, that little explicitly and formally educational could take place before the age of six. At the other end of the scale, so few would have been involved that the matter of coeducation in higher studies could not have had any great effect. Thus Plato was really advocating parallel education, but he was doing so largely for social and moral and not for intellectual reasons. Within this utopian system, however, either a man or a woman with the capacity to do so could rise to the highest position that the state could offer.

ELEMENTARY EDUCATION

Students who came to Plato's school, the Academy, were fortified with the best foundation traditonal Athenian elementary education was able to give them. This small, highly selective school could be very demanding in its entrance requirements. It was really a school for leaders. The remarkable thing about all of this, however, is not that Plato was conscious of the need for solid preparatory education (this could be assumed), but that he was willing, even in his literary utopia, to accept with only a few modifications the pattern of elementary education that had been traditional in Athens. Though no statement in his writings expresses his satisfaction with elementary education, yet by indirection he does give it his approval. At the same time, it should be remarked

[39] Plato *Laws* vii. 804.

that Plato spends little time in discussing the lower levels of education.[40]

From what he does say, it appears that Plato would have made some slight revisions in conventional elementary education. For example, he would have made greater use of educational games and toys during the years of three to six. This learning by play would form part of the preschool preparation. But of even greater significance than mere skill was the inculcation of a love of excellence; the pleasure of excelling was never to be minimized, and a favorable attitude toward it was to be cultivated principally by employing amusement. Plato may not have introduced pleasure and amusement as motives to education; no doubt they were around long before his time. He did, however, recognize the multiple uses to which they could be put. Despite this, there is no suggestion at all that Plato shared the illusions of later educators who were unwilling to regard education as a demanding discipline or to give it due respect. Even though details of educational theory and technique may not be totally ignored (and Plato did not ignore them), he wrote that "the most important point of education is right training in the nursery." [41] This may not sound highly philosophical, or, indeed, Platonic, yet it is Plato speaking.

With the end of the nursery period—about the age of three—Plato proposed that the children receive further preparation for formal education. It should be noted that the Greeks had always considered the years before seven a period in which the child was preparing for schooling. All that Plato was adding were a few details with respect to his preparation. We may follow his thought with his own words:

> Up to the age of three years, whether of boy or girl, if a person strictly carries out our previous regulations and makes them a principal aim, he will do much for the advantage of the young creatures. But at three, four, five, and even six years the childish nature will require sports; now is the time to get rid of self-will in him, punishing him, but not so as to disgrace him. We were saying about slaves, that we ought neither to add insult to punishment so as to anger them, nor yet to leave them unpunished lest they become self-willed; and a like rule is to be observed in the case of the freeborn. Children at that age have certain natural modes of amusement, which they find out for themselves when they meet. And all the children who are between the ages of three and six ought to meet at the temples of the villages, the several families of a village uniting on one spot. The nurses are to see that the children behave properly and orderly,—they themselves and all their

[40] Plato *Republic* ii, iii; *Laws* vii.
[41] *Ibid.*, i. 643.

companies are to be under the control of twelve matrons, one for each company, who are annually selected to inspect them from the women previously mentioned, (i.e. the women who have authority over marriage), whom the guardians of the law appoint.[42]

Education proper began when the child was seven. And following the traditions of Athens, this education was to consist of gymnastics for the body and music for the soul. We have discussed these components of Athenian education in Chapter II; here we shall try to indicate the principal changes that Plato wanted to adopt. At the same time, we should not forget that this traditional Athenian elementary education of which we speak was classical education in its original form, and that by accepting it, although dictating some revisions, Plato strengthened classical education's claim to man's allegiance.

The basic literary skills that we assume were taught to most Athenian boys during their first years in school seem not to have commanded Plato's attention. There would be no good reason for Plato to tamper with reading and writing, the basic elementary instruction of the day. In another area of the elementary school's program—counting—Plato did prescribe some reorientation. Calculation was added, for, as Plato said, all branches of instruction which are a preparation for dialectic should be presented to the mind in childhood. Plato was convinced that everyone who could reason could share in mathematical knowledge, at least, up to a point.[43] There is no evidence that Plato led any city-wide campaign for upgrading the teaching of arithmetic in the Greek schools, but in the *Republic* and in the *Laws* he does suggest a revision and some rethinking of elementary mathematics.

In physical training, too, Plato wanted some changes. He was somewhat disturbed at the unwillingness of his fellow citizens to continue the old tradition of gymnastics for the body and music for the soul. The two had at one time been inseparable. But Plato saw how some men became preoccupied with music to the extent that they grew soft and cowardly; other men pursued gymnastics so exclusively that they became insensitive to culture and were little better than savages. He was concerned especially with the place of dancing and wrestling in Greek schools. But here again Plato shows less concern for the actual skills in the dance or in gymnastics generally than he does for the spirit with which they are taught and practiced and the environment in which they

---

[42] *Ibid.,* vii. 793.

[43] In *Republic* vii. 526b, Plato writes of mathematics as "a something which all arts and sciences and intelligences use in common, and which everyone first has to learn among the elements of education."

are imparted. Plato never objected to excellence in any form. Gymnastic training or any other discipline which aimed at excellence was sure to obtain Plato's approval. But training for superiority was another thing. A boy might wrestle in order to achieve all the values that the sport offered, and Plato would commend him for it, but if he wrestled, not for inherent values but in order to defeat an opponent in a contest, his action would not be entirely meritorious. Plato did not speak out violently against competitive sport, but evidently he did not entirely approve the professionalism that was finding its way into sport.

It is true that Plato's views on elementary instruction and physical training did not mark any sharp break with traditional education in Athens. But in asking for a state-controlled, state-financed system of elementary education, with state-approved teachers, Plato was surely setting himself apart from the past. Despite the theoretical relationship that the state had to education, instruction of the young in Athens had been largely a family affair. Consistent with his ideal of state unity, Plato would have had education on all levels subject to closer control and teachers on all levels recognized as public officers. It would no longer have been possible for an unqualified person to open a school. By taking this stand Plato may have offered teachers their first glimpse of professional status.

There were other departures. Since Plato believed that good music was heaven-born, he advocated the enactment of laws that would have prevented, or at least deterred spontaneity in music. When modes of music change, he said, the state changes with them. This thought may be put another way: Music, according to Plato, was primarily a vehicle for the inculcation of morals, and tested procedures for developing character should not be tampered with. Finally he argued for a strict censorship of literature.

HIGHER EDUCATION

The generalization that Plato accepted traditional Greek elementary education—even though this generalization cannot be applied uncritically—must not be extended to include higher educational levels. What is distinctive in the thought of Plato as it applies to the content of instruction in the schools is to be found in his prescriptions for the curricular organization of secondary and higher education.

Few readers are unaware of the long course of studies through which Plato would have put the best minds. Fifty years is a long time to spend in education. But although we should not ignore this aspect of his program, we should not overemphasize it. The important thing is that the end of such a long and exacting course of study is the attainment of truth. Above all else Plato was interested in truth. And now it should be stated clearly, Plato refused to trust man's senses in this search for truth, because, he said, the senses are deceptive. Searching for truth, moreover, is an occupation for mature men; the dull, the slow-witted, and the young should be excused, for, in addition to its great promise, truth-seeking has elements of danger: opinion may be mistaken for knowledge. We cannot fully appreciate Plato's educational thought unless we understand his determination to expand the boundaries of knowledge. His students were encouraged to be frontier thinkers.

Before the time of the Sophists and Plato the Greeks had made no clear distinction between elementary and secondary education except in physical training. The palaestra was a school for elementary physical education; the gymnasium may at least be called a secondary experience, for it is not easy to refer to it as a school in the ordinary sense of the term. Music was taught on the same level of relevance to life as were reading and writing and counting. The absence of literary secondary education may be somewhat surprising, but in view of the traditions of Athens it is not too difficult to understand.

The Sophists were among the first, if not the first, secondary teachers. Plato followed them and improved on their work; or perhaps it should be said that Plato reacted to the Sophists and perfected what they had begun. He was the first to devise both a theory and a content for secondary education. Once the young minds were exposed to the primary skills of reading, writing, and arithmetic in the initial and formal educational experience, Plato would begin secondary education. This would be at about the child's thirteenth or fourteenth year. Few details concerning such things as school buildings or teachers' qualifications are known to us, nor do we know whether or not Plato spent much time considering these points. Secondary education would be made up of music, literature, and mathematics. Music would be both instrumental and vocal; it had a social as well as a moral value. Literature, with the same limitations and cautions that Plato had previously imposed, would be carried into secondary education. As always, Greek literature, with expurgation or without it, was an artistic articulation of the exploits of a mythical hero. Mathematics was the innovation: numbers, geometry, and arithmetic were in the program.

Judging from Plato's references to the age of students,[44] we have defined for us for the first time the nine-year secondary school. Such a

---

[44] *Ibid.*, vii. 536.

school was of course no stranger to the modern period in educational history (1500 to 1900); its model was classical. Plato's proposals concerning secondary schooling were, perhaps, the first to be made on the level of theory.

As an aristocrat steeped in the traditions of Athens, Plato remembered gymnastics, but even when he was unable to approve the direction taken by the gymnastics of his day he refused to bar them from education. However, since his concern was neither with popular education nor with keeping boys in school who preferred to be elsewhere, he could keep gymnastics as a part of Greek life or culture or of education in the very broadest sense, and at the same time separate them from the school. He could also recognize the possibility of using gymnastics as a device for screening; that is, for discovering the young men most suited for advanced studies.[45]

When the nine-year secondary school curricula were completed, a boy would undertake to fulfill the requirement regarding gymnastics. Plato's view may be given here as it is expressed through the person of Socrates. Socrates is asked at what age young men ought to be inducted into the course of higher studies. He replied:

> At the age when the necessary gymnastics are over: the period whether of two or three years which passes in this sort of training is useless for any other purpose; for sleep and exercise are unpropitious to learning; and the trial of whom is first in gymnastic exercises is one of the most important tests to which our youth are subjected.[46]

After the two- or three-year period of compulsory physical training, the young men returned to their studies. They were now about twenty years old. From among those who had proceeded this far up the educational ladder, the best would be selected for ten additional years of study. Arithmetic, which would sharpen the intellects of the bright and even improve the minds of the dull, geometry, which needed no recommendation to the Greeks, music and astronomy, both approached in their theoretical aspects, were the fundamental subjects of this curriculum. Plato can again speak for himself:

> After that time [after gymnastic training] those who are selected from the class of twenty years old will be promoted to higher honor, and the sciences which they learned without any order in their early education will now be brought together and they will be able to see the natural relationship of them to one another and to true being.[47]

[45] Plato *Laws* vii. 810; *Republic* ii. 377; x. 595.
[46] *Ibid.*, vii. 298.
[47] *Ibid.*

This ten-year course enabled the student to cross the threshold of philo-sophical studies, which involved five additional years of study.

Such was the long course devised by Plato for making a philos-opher. But it was not yet complete. For fifteen years following their formal preparation, the students of philosophy would take an active part in the government of the city. We may go to the *Republic* again for Plato's description of his program.

> And how long is this stage of their lives to last? Fifteen years, I answered; and when they have reached fifty years of age, then let those who still survive and have distinguished themselves in every action of their lives and in every branch of knowledge come at last to their con-summation: the time has now arrived at which they must raise the eye of the soul to the universal light which lightens all things, and behold the absolute good; for that is the pattern according to which they are to order the State and the lives of individuals, and the re-mainder of their own lives also; making philosophy their chief pursuit, but, when their turn comes, toiling also at politics and ruling for the public good, not as though they were performing some heroic action, but simply as a matter of duty; and when they have brought up in each generation others like themselves and left them in their place to be governors of the State, then they will depart to the Islands of the Blest and dwell there; and the city will give them public memorials and sacrifices and honor them, if the Pythian oracle consent, as demi-gods, but if not, as in any case blessed and divine.[48]

PLATO'S INFLUENCE

Before going any further we should say that Plato's plan for higher education was nowhere completely put into practice. In the Academy, where future political philosophers were educated, it was possible for Plato to translate many of his theories into policies and procedures to guide teaching and learning. But regardless of the inner consistency and the general logical structure of the studies in Plato's famous school, the system practiced there was partial and inchoate when compared with the theoretical model provided in the *Republic* and the *Laws*. Plato's was a utopian plan, sincerely proposed, but never fully tested.

Plato's influence as a teacher must have been great, although we cannot call many witnesses to support this assumption. His influence as a molder of later theories and practices seems to be universally recog-nized, and it was quite profound. We cannot claim that Plato's thought

[48] *Ibid.*, vii. 302–303.

has always been predominant in the educational systems and schools of the Western world, but we should be unrealistic not to recognize that in some way Plato has affected all of them by his conviction that the bedrock of education must be truth and that truth may be achieved only as a result of determined effort. This dedication to truth dominated Plato's plan and, translated to school practice, meant that the curriculum should be centered on studies capable of forming good minds: science and mathematics. Wherever the doctrine of discipline is found in education, its best justification can always be traced to Plato. No literary utopia has ever wielded more practical influence than Plato's; yet it remains true that Plato's ideal of the search for truth in education has frequently been rejected in favor of utility-centered curricula and objectives.

Isocrates (436–338 B.C.)

A good deal of the tradition regarding the life of Isocrates must be accepted with caution. The available biographies are, for the most part, late compilations in which it is most difficult to distinguish fact from fiction. All of them must be measured against the standard drawn from Isocrates' autobiographical statements.

Isocrates was born in 436 B.C., five years before the Peloponnesian War. He died in 338 B.C. His father, it is said, was a manufacturer of flutes. This business must have been profitable, for the family, according to Isocrates' own testimony, lived in comfortable circumstances. Isocrates received a good education at the hands of the most prominent teachers Athens could boast.

The details of his formal education are little known; biographers claim that he profited from the established education of Athens as well as from the Sophists, who had only recently arrived in Athens to prepare the Athenians for citizenship and practical success. It has been claimed, too, that Isocrates sampled the teaching and the wisdom of all the renowned Sophists who taught in Athens.

The teachers from whom he is said to have learned most were Gorgias of Leontini, a famous Sophist, and Socrates. From Gorgias Isocrates inherited his ardent and lasting affection for oratory. His indebtedness to Socrates is somewhat more complex. Socrates knew him well and liked him, and, according to the testimony of Plato, Socrates, recognizing Isocrates' brilliant mental qualities, predicted a promising future for him as a philosopher. Whether or not Isocrates would ever become prominent in philosophy, Socrates goes on to say, would be up to the gods and to the ability of "some divine impulses" to lead him.[49]

Either these "divine impulses" were diluted or somehow became confused, for although Isocrates never ignored philosophy, he refused it a place of any special significance in his school. As a matter of fact, he may have regarded the teachers of philosophy as his competitors. He generated an extreme dislike for philosophical professors and denounced them on various occasions. He denounced Plato, too. Actually, Isocrates and Plato were competitors. This need not mean that their views never coincided or that they never realized the possibility of mutual accommodation of ideas, but it does mean that Plato pursued one objective, Isocrates, another. Plato hoped to lead his pupils toward intellectual research and a life that would enable them to search for truth. Isocrates tried to inculcate the principles of practical life; his teaching was meant as a preparation for success in society and politics.[50]

Still, and even admitting the fundamental dichotomy just referred to, Isocrates carried over into his thought and work many of the intellectual, political, and moral positions generally attributed to Socrates. The similarities fail to prove that the teaching of Socrates had a permanent influence on Isocrates. On the other hand, we may suppose that in certain areas of thought and action Isocrates demonstrated tentative affinities with Socratic thought.

1. The *Antidosis,* a treatise in which Isocrates defends and justifies himself to the people of Athens, is strikingly similar to Socrates' defense before these same people. It is considerably more detailed than anything reported for Socrates by either Plato or Xenophon, yet it is constructed in such a way that an indebtedness to Socrates is apparent. The tone of the *Antidosis* alone seems to place Isocrates in an ideological fellowship with Socrates, for both, it appears, were completely, if unfortunately, misunderstood by their contemporaries.

2. Isocrates shared the Socratic aloofness and disdain for public life.

> But I thought as he said these things, and I think now, that they would be of all men the strangest and most perverse who could take offence at being told that I hold myself at the service of Athens in discharging the liturgies and performing any public duty she enjoins, and yet do not ask to have any part in the allotment of the offices nor in the distribution of the gifts she doles out to others, nor in the privilege

[49] The comment is made at the close of Plato's *Phaedrus.*

[50] See Power, *op. cit.,* pp. 32–43; Beck, *op. cit.,* pp. 253–290.

of prosecuting or defending cases in the courts. For I have prescribed this course for myself, not because I am rich or have any false pride, nor because I look down on those who do not live in the same way as I do, but because I love peace and tranquillity, and most of all because I see that men who so live are looked up to both in Athens and in other parts of the world. Moreover, I consider that this kind of life is more agreeable than that of men who are busy with a multitude of things, and that it is, besides, more in keeping with the career to which I have dedicated myself from the first.[51]

3. Isocrates was most critical of Athenian democracy, and his criticism, though it brought no retribution like that inflicted upon Socrates, did not endear him to the democrats of Athens.

And yet how can we praise or tolerate a government which has in the past been the cause of so many evils and which is now year by year ever drifting on from bad to worse? And how can we escape the fear that if we continue to progress after this fashion we may finally run aground on rocks more perilous than those which at that time loomed before us? [52]

4. Isocrates' contempt for some of the Sophists reminds one of Socrates' disdain.

Indeed, who can fail to abhor, yes to contemn, those teachers, in the first place, who devote themselves to disputation, since they pretend to search for truth, but straightway at the beginning of their professions attempt to deceive us with lies.[53]

5. Although Isocrates resided in a borderland between philosophy and politics—he was neither a philosopher nor a statesman in the Platonic sense—and in oratory engaged in a kind of ambivalence that Socrates opposed, he did, nevertheless, share with Socrates an emphasis on ethics. This is evident, of course, only when we keep our eyes on the prudential morality of the Socrates of Xenophon and not the idealistic morality of the Socrates of Plato. But Isocrates did more than just share Socrates' interest in moral philosophy; he added to it an oratorical dimension which is displayed in the following quotation:

There is no institution devised by man which the power of speech has not helped us establish. For this it is which has laid down laws concerning things just and unjust, and things base and honourable; and

[51] Isocrates *Antidosis*. In *op. cit.*, vol. II, pp. 150–151.
[52] Isocrates *Areopagiticus*. In *op. cit.*, vol. II, p. 115.
[53] Isocrates *Against the Sophists*. In *op. cit.*, vol. II, p. 163.

if it were not for these ordinances we should not be able to live with one another. It is by this also that we confute the bad and extol the good. Through this we educate the ignorant and appraise the wise; for the power to speak well is taken as the surest index of a sound understanding, and discourse which is true and lawful and just is the outward image of a good and faithful soul. With this faculty we both contend against others on matters which are open to dispute, and seek light for ourselves on things which are unknown; for the same arguments which we use in persuading others when we speak in public, we employ also when we deliberate in our own thoughts; and, while we call eloquent those who are able to speak before a crowd, we regard as sage those who most skillfully debate their problems in their own minds. And, if there is need to speak in brief summary of this power, we shall find that none of the things which are done with intelligence take place without the help of speech, but that in all our actions as well as in all our thoughts speech is our guide, and is most employed by those who have the most wisdom. Therefore, those who dare to speak with disrespect of educators and teachers of philosophy deserve our opprobrium no less than those who profane the sanctuaries of the gods.[54]

Despite the claims that may be made for Socrates' influence on Isocrates, it should be remembered that sharing ideas need not imply borrowing them. Thinking men may have much in common and still be original. Originality, moreover, is not the only road to intellectual or philosophical glory. It is entirely possible that the most lasting and profound influence that was exerted on the great Attic orator by Socrates was a sobering one which touched his life and thought deeply. It was this influence which may have led Isocrates to try to be a statesman and a philosopher without really committing himself to the extremes of either. He would have shared with Socrates the thought that one good man—a gentleman in the aristocratic meaning of the term—is worth much more than a learned scholar, because the gentleman could be a man of action responding only to the attractions of a single goal, while a scholar could easily become confused in examining the conflicting aims or claims of contending positions. So Isocrates, covering himself with a cloak of neutrality and seeing the dangers which may befall the enthusiastic man of action, tried to compromise. He manifested his philosophical turn of mind by working out certain moralisms; he attempted statesmanship, without ever holding any public office, by issuing political pamphlets from the friendly confines of his study. In his own life these compromises between action and thought were not especially

---

[54] Isocrates *Nicocles.* In *op. cit.,* vol. I, pp. 79–81.

successful. Yet the Isocratic judgment which endorses such compromises became a fairly constant and even a respected tradition in the history of Western culture.[55]

ISOCRATES THE SCHOOLMASTER

Isocrates has been called the most famous schoolmaster of antiquity. Whether or not this claim can be supported is not our special concern here. Certainly, few teachers ever conducted a more stable school—one that was in continuous operation for nearly fifty-five years. Isocrates opened his school in his own home when he was about forty-two years old; he was still teaching when he was ninety-seven. Unfortunately his fame does not shed any light on the levels of education with which he dealt. Was his school a secondary or a higher institution? This question must go unanswered. The whole issue is complicated by the fact that the course in his school lasted for only three or four years. This was too short a period in which to cover a secondary and a higher curriculum, yet Isocrates is always talking about the content and the objectives of both levels.

When Isocrates opened his school, he advertised its existence by preparing a pamphlet to be read by the people of Athens. This was his *Against the Sophists*. The title has more than passing significance. Isocrates was promising the people of Athens that his school would teach them what they needed to know. This promise and the assumptions necessary to make it put Isocrates in the position of having to distinguish his school and his practices both from the Sophists and from the stationary teachers of Athens. The following were the two main points which Isocrates thought important enough to refer to especially:

First: In order to distinguish his school from that of Plato (Plato's school, the Academy, was opened in 387 B.C., and Isocrates began his teaching career in 393 B.C.), Isocrates emphasized the democratic features of his school. They were mainly that the students could come from any walk of life and find the environment of the Isocratic school inviting and friendly, and that what they studied there was to form them in such a way that they could reenter general society, not the society of the elite or of the aristocrats. Here, perhaps, Isocrates was reflecting not only his convictions with respect to the formative function of education but his own social and class inheritance as well. Isocrates, unlike Plato, did not spring from aristocratic or noble blood.

[55] Beck, *op. cit.*, p. 289.

Isocrates attempted to place a democratic aura over or around his school; yet in practice the school fostered a strange kind of democracy. It is true that it was open to all who cared to, and could afford to, attend. But the charges for instruction at the Isocratic school, although one cannot be precise about them, were far from being moderate. Without visible means of support other than the income from the school, Isocrates became one of Athens' richest men.

Instructionally, the Isocratic democratic ideal was supported by the oratorical ideal of good speaking. Isocrates never tired of telling his readers (and, we may suppose, he told his students too) of the great expectations he had for oratory. All the culture and education of antiquity, he said, could be transmitted most effectively by holding firmly to the oratorical idea.[56] Here again Isocrates is calling attention to the essential difference between his school and the schools conducted by the philosophers. Despite this difference, Isocrates maintained that he was teaching true philosophy, and that he himself was an authentic philosopher: not a dreamer, who neglects what is practical and essential, but a man who studies subjects that will enable him to manage domestic and civic affairs. That which is of no immediate use either for speech or for action, Isocrates said, does not deserve the name of philosophy.

Second: If Isocrates was anxious to show the people of Athens that his school was not a mere imitation of Plato's, or a school devoted to an unreal or misunderstood ideal of truth, he was just as anxious for the people to know that he was not another Sophist, or better, because the Sophists enjoyed some respect in Athens, that his school was superior to those conducted by most Sophists. And here the differences seem to be not so much on the level of theory or of essential content but on the level of emphasis and methodology. When Isocrates does not want to be confused with the Sophists, he does not say that he disapproves their objectives. He rebukes them instead for their failures in achieving, or even respecting, these objectives in the practical order. Isocrates had, in fact, much more in common with the Sophists than he had with Plato. Sophists who claimed to teach the exact science of a happy and successful life and who then in practice indulged in captious wordy contests which had no relation to life came under his personal ban, but not for what they said they would do but for what they actually did, or failed to do. Other Sophists promised to teach the art of oratory to anyone who could learn the alphabet; but the "art," in the Sophists' system, consisted in following a few simple rules and in memorizing a few clever catchwords and phrases. Here again Isocrates approved the

[56] Isocrates *Nicocles*. In *op. cit.*, vol. I, pp. 80–83.

objective, although he had piercing denunciations to make respecting the method and also the degree to which the ideal was actually attained.

If one is to judge from the successes enjoyed by the schoolmaster, Isocrates, it may be said that he advertised his school convincingly in his treatise *Against the Sophists*. It may be said also that he remained relatively true to the original definition of his mission; a half-century later in *Antidosis* he is able to refer to and quote from *Against the Sophists* with every evidence that his earlier views had not been changed in any important way.

We know the practices in schoolmastering to which Isocrates objected, and we know his devotion to oratory. We know something less, however, about the actual methods of his school. Like Plato, he was apparently willing to take conventional Greek elementary education as he found it.[57] To the lower level he added both the secondary and the higher. Secondary education was in Isocrates' hands a study of grammar and literature, which, along with a smattering of mathematics, would prepare students for studies in rhetoric.

Isocrates' higher education gave a very special place to rhetoric, it is true, but, according to the famous master himself, in addition to good style and composition, its primary objective was teaching morals. Isocrates' claim for his school and for his kind of education was that it formed the gentleman. This is my definition of the educated man, he says: (1) He is capable of dealing with the ordinary events of life by selecting the right course of action; (2) he is always correct and proper, and he treats everyone with whom he comes in contact with fairness and gentleness; (3) he is always the absolute master of his thought and deed; and (4) he is not spoiled by success.[58]

Isocrates was interested in teaching rhetoric, but he was always aiming at something beyond it. This aim was to be achieved by following the course of studies he proposed. He advised students to study those things that would lead them most directly and most quickly to prudence or practical wisdom. But study alone, Isocrates was quick to see, is not enough; it must be supplemented by practice. And so we find the students debating and deliberating. They wrote and recited their own speeches on topics of contemporary interest or on subjects drawn from history, philosophy, or political science. In all of these speeches style was given constant attention, and to this end models were always readily accessible. The models were the speeches of the great orators and the orations that Isocrates himself had written.

[57] Isocrates *Panathenaicus*. In *op. cit.*, vol. II, p. 389.
[58] *Ibid.*, p. 519.

THE INFLUENCE OF ISOCRATES

In recording the history of thought it is extremely difficult to be precise about influence. The effect that the thought of others had on Isocrates can be guessed at and reported, but the influence that he exerted on later educational theory can be evaluated and communicated only very uncertainly. It may be possible to call him the "father of literary humanism." Certainly he felt a commitment to the culture of the past and held that a principal purpose of education was to transmit this culture. The most excellent as well as the most sublime vehicle to be used for this purpose was oratory. Isocrates may have had a naïve and uncritical attitude toward the past, but he had nothing but respect for the poet's skill in making the past a living experience for the student. All of life's most fundamental experiences could be, and were, according to Isocrates, manifested in the great classics. It was the educated man's conversance with these fundamental experiences and the basic ideas to be drawn from them, joined with cleverness and elegance in expression, that impressed Isocrates most; and whether by coincidence or design, this mark of culture impressed secondary education and secondary educators from Isocrates' time down to the end of the nineteenth century.

Isocrates prized words, although it would be grossly unfair to call him a narrow pedant. Words were vehicles for thought, much of it ethical thought. Distilled in the classical tradition, thought was the content and finally the outcome of humanistic scholarship. No thinker or teacher in the history of education was more influential in giving to secondary education both its content and its form than this most famous schoolmaster of antiquity.

Aristotle (384–322 B.C.)

Aristotle's theory of education, as it has come down to us, does not appear as complete as that of Plato or Isocrates. In the seventh and eighth books of the *Politics,* Aristotle touched on the educational questions which in his time were of most interest: whether education should be public or private and what education's proper function was. It is obvious to anyone who reads the *Politics* that Aristotle was sensitive to the role education should play in a state; yet we have no explicit educational theory from the pen of the great philosopher. He may have produced one—he did promise to do so—that has been lost.

Aristotle, a teacher and a scholar with nearly universal interests, conducted one of Athens' most famous stationary schools, the Lyceum.

This school occupied his time after he had dissolved his association with Plato's Academy. As a scholar, philosopher, and scientist he laid the foundations for, and advanced progress in, a number of academic and scientific fields. Any one of his contributions to human knowledge would be sufficient to win for him a lasting place in the history of thought. Here we are interested in Aristotle as a representative of Greek educational thought, and we may begin by admitting that his role here is subordinate to that of either Plato or Isocrates. Nevertheless, such an assessment leaves plenty of room for Aristotle. What were the principal educational views of this great man? Possibly the one that belongs first is the Aristotelian position that "all art and education aim at filling up nature's deficiencies." [59] The capacities of the individual to be educated—and these would include intellectual, moral, and physical qualities—are the foundations on which all education rests. Added to these more or less natural endowments are the habits that are formed through care and exercise. All else, says Aristotle, is the province of instruction. "We learn some things by habit and some by instruction." [60]

Education's general function is to direct men toward happiness. There may be all kinds and descriptions of happiness, but a utilitarian or materialistic view of happiness never quite seems to fit into the Aristotelian mold. There is also, of course, the question of the meaning of education. And here, one may be sure, Aristotle is thinking of it in its very broadest sense.

The setting for education should be social. Aristotle called into question the common practice among Athenians of caring for the education of their children by hiring tutors for them. Now he agreed with Plato, and incidentally with the Spartans, when he wrote that the education of the young required the special attention of the lawgiver.[61] This lawgiver should concern himself especially with education's public nature and with educational uniformity and opportunity. This would be done, not to control citizens or to deprive them of freedom, but to fit them with the best possible character.

THE EDUCATIONAL INFLUENCE OF ARISTOTLE

It is entirely accurate to assert that Aristotle's reputation in the history of thought rests on credentials only indirectly associated with the theory

[59] Aristotle *Politics* vii. 17.
[60] *Ibid.*, vii. 13.
[61] *Ibid.*, viii. 1.

and practice of education, and to affirm his role as being secondary to Plato's or Isocrates' in building a classical educational tradition that has withstood the erosions of time. Nevertheless, it is important to recognize Aristotle as a spokesman for a cadre of scholars who regularly subordinated educational theory to speculative philosophy. In other words, Aristotle's theory of education, and whatever he had to say about teaching and learning, are always footnotes in a philosophical disquisition; it is always necessary to build Aristotle's educational thought from the rational principles of philosophy which he set down. And in formulating these rational principles he began with metaphysics (the fundamental nature of the universe and of man's nature), moved from there to politics and ethics, and ended up with psychology. With this foundation of rational thought about the nature of the world and man, it was then possible to consider the kind of education that might enable men to develop into sensitive intellectual and moral persons who would always seek happiness.

Aristotle's study of man and the world led him to conclude that the education of men must be controlled so that they would always love the things they should love and hate the things they should hate; and he could find no agency better equipped to exercise this kind of control than the state. Thus, he allowed the state to mold youth according to national objectives by giving it complete control over the agencies of teaching. He assumed, of course, that the state's officers would be guided by reason when they directed the course of education, and that even when in practice this system might not be perfect, it would at least be better than a system wherein the direction of education was left to the judgment of private persons and independent schoolmasters. Aristotle is quite explicit when he assigns education to the state and withdraws it from the domain of private initiative. Moreover, he can bolster his doctrine with some strong arguments:

1. The stability of government depends on education, and the state, which is a political society, has a right to preserve itself.

2. Political societies have but one end—the good of all persons in those societies—and this good can only be advanced and protected by a system of education that honors community of goals and interests.

3. State control of education eliminates the possibilities of differences in educational opportunity, because in a state system the rich and the poor are afforded the same chances for schooling (and with this schooling all classes of persons can contribute to the common good).

4. In order to ensure a common acceptance of moral and social objectives, all citizens of a state must be educated uniformly, and a

guarantee of this degree of uniformity can come only from state control.

Once Aristotle set down the principal foundations for education, he moved on to other important questions (though he always handled them in the same way: as elaborations of philosophical doctrines), such as what should be taught. Here Aristotle was content to accept the traditional subjects of the Greek schools and to acknowledge that after the primary teaching is out of the way and boys are able to read and write, they should move on to gymnastics and music. The former builds good bodies, but it also has a lot to do with forming good moral habits (and Aristotle was devoted to the idea that, in the last analysis, education's principal function was to mold men of character). Music—what we now think of as a component of secondary education—should concentrate on instrumental and vocal music as well as on the literary monuments of ancient Greece. All this was in keeping with tradition as well as with (except for that of the Sophists) current Greek practice.

The content of education bothered Aristotle much less on this level than did the objectives of such teaching. He cared very little whether the boys in the music school knew the authors, and whether they could recite long passages from their works, but he was vitally concerned about the kinds of virtues that were formed in such school environments. He never admitted that knowledge could make men good, and he doubted that direct moral teaching contributed much to the formation of character, so he argued for schools that would ennoble the souls of their students. Yet, he was never very specific about how this might be done. He did say, of course, that education should be liberal rather than practical, that it should be concerned with the genuine vocations of the soul rather than with the appetites of the body, and that it must teach necessary and useful things without vulgarizing the students.

Aristotle was quick to acknowledge that moral virtue—good character—comes not from nature (a person is not born with or without virtue) but from education and habit, so he talked about imitation, emulation, and the grand ideals that could be found among the great orators, generals, and heroes. Still, even when Aristotle admitted that education is a critical item for achieving virtue, he did not mean that virtue can be taught or that it is ever a certain outcome of instruction. He knew that the issue was involved and that even his best answers were far from definitive, so he left the matter somewhat up-in-the-air—confident, no doubt, that future generations would wrestle with it. Thus wedded to philosophy, Aristotle created a scholarly tradition in which education was always understood as a rational enterprise, a handmaiden of philosophy, whose policies and practices were necessarily the products of reason.

If we read Aristotle for ideas about the way education should be organized, about what elementary, secondary, and higher schools should do, and about what they should teach, we shall almost surely be disappointed, for if these topics interested him, he chose not to write about them. He stayed on the levels of theory and philosophic principle and, for the most part, his influence on the education of later generations had to be mined from these. In his own day his educational attitudes were paid scant heed except by the students who enrolled in his Lyceum. Plutarch (A.D. 45–125) in his *On the Education of Children,* followed Aristotle so closely that we sometimes wonder when we are reading Plutarch and when we are rereading Aristotle, and Plutarch's work undoubtedly gave greater currency to Aristotle's educational thought. Yet, apart from Plutarch, some unnamed scholars of Syria and Arabia, and a few schoolmen of the Middle Ages, it would be hard to find anyone of stature in the history of educational philosophy who maintained that he was a faithful follower of Aristotle's educational doctrines.

Xenophon (430–355 B.C.)

There is a vast difference between the intellectual inheritance Plato bequeathed and that left to later generations by Xenophon. The latter could be ignored, and no great harm would be done to the history of educational thought or to the student's understanding of it. Yet Xenophon was not an entirely unimportant man, either for his own day or for our own. He reflects best the essential conservativism of mankind. Plato, Isocrates, and Aristotle were all devoted to reform and progress; they did not disregard the past, it is true, but they were critical thinkers with an eye on the unknown future. Even the Sophists had estimable dynamic qualities to recommend them. Xenophon, however, was willing to look to the past not just for guidance but for control, and without exception his interest in education was to restore and consolidate archaic educational practices in Athens.

Xenophon, a writer of history and biography, neither was nor pretended to be a philosopher. His greatest single literary work was *Memorabilia,* a biographical account of the great Socrates. In educational thought he did little more than praise the accomplishments of the past.[62] His views on education, presented in an interesting fictional

[62] See Beck, *op. cit.,* pp. 244–252.

essay, *Cyropaedia,* tell us about the upbringing of a Persian prince, Cyrus. Beginning with the assumption that of all living things men are most difficult to control, and mustering some evidence to support this assumption from the societies he knew best, Xenophon goes on to praise a plan of education which will give the objective of control pride of place. The model for his educational plan is Persia, for there, he said, the educators had mastered this issue of control. Yet, while Xenophon praised Persia and credited her with having discovered what needs to be done in education, what he recommends reminds us of Sparta and archaic Athens. What may be called his educational theory rested on three points:

1. Education's aim is the common, not the individual, good.
2. Curricula should be centered on military goals.
3. Literary curricula are valueless appendages in formal education.

Nothing in Xenophon's educational views suggests progress or recommends our further study, although on one point, it must be admitted, he showed some independence of thought: contemporary opportunities for the education of females were about right, that is, none at all. An evaluation of Xenophon's educational theory may be coupled with one on his educational pronouncements: Both are interesting but neither commanded the attention of later educators.

Summary

The Sophists came to Athens to offer Athenians an opportunity to pursue literary culture by means of secondary education. The cultural inheritance of Athens was great; the actual accomplishments of the large majority of her citizens were low. The people wanted to improve themselves in order to be closer to the cultural ideal. Thus the Sophists came to Athens because they were invited and because good opportunities for profit and fame awaited them there. The picture of a group of hated Sophists invading Athens to teach an unwilling people what they did not want to learn needs to be redrawn.

Once the Sophist came to Athens, he offered his services to all, that is, to all who could pay the fees that he charged. And he offered to teach whatever his students wanted to learn. He assumed that they would have had an elementary education, although in actual practice few Sophists seem to have worried about the backgrounds of their students. The Sophists' objective was to teach their students how to be successful.

Plato, a stationary teacher in Athens, disapproved of the Sophists. He disliked their methods, and he deplored their purpose. Plato's general educational view was to subordinate everything to truth. He followed this ideal in his own school, the Academy, and he followed it, too, in the plans that he drew for education and presented in literary and artistic form in the *Republic* and the *Laws*. Throughout his long life Plato never ceased to support a kind of education which was predominantly philosophical, scientific, and mathematical.

Standing somewhere between the Sophists and Plato is Isocrates. Here was the most famous schoolmaster of all antiquity, and he, like the Sophists, emphasized eloquence as the goal of formal education, although the oratory he endorsed was somewhat more responsible than that of the Sophists. The Isocratic educational theory was built around the theme that the right word is the sure sign of good thinking. Building on this theme, education became literary or literature-centered, and Isocrates is credited with being the father of literary humanism.

Aristotle and Xenophon fill out the picture of Greek educational theory.

IV

Greek
Education
in Transition

The Hellenistic Era: Its Spirit of Educational Inquiry

In the Hellenistic era the education of Greek antiquity, without good models to follow and without a city state to stabilize it, was formalized and institutionalized and was thus given its historical form. Every effort was made to perpetuate ancient ways of living and learning, but since classical Greece was so far in the past, the classical inheritance was continued the only way possible: through literature in the schools. For the first time in Greek education, the school became the principal agency for perpetuating valued traditions. Yet schools capable of meeting the broad objectives required to do this did not materialize overnight; nor did Hellenistic education suddenly spring into being with fully developed instructional appurtenances. The age of Hellenism matured slowly, often betraying its cultural insecurity and frequently misreading the signposts of classical education. The hope of Hellenistic men, and the commission of their schools alike, was to be true to the past, though in many instances, with both general culture and schooling, failures equalled ambitions. But failures, even if real and important, should not be allowed to conceal success: In general, the principal and lasting contribution of Hellenism was its unalterable commitment to formal education as an instrument for cultural transmission.[1]

The Hellenistic age, unquestionably an important period in the history of education, must be given general historical identification as a preliminary to any elaboration of its educational features. From about the middle of the fourth century B.C., or about the time the Athenians were defeated by Philip of Macedonia in the Battle of Chaeronea (338 B.C.), to A.D. 529, when a few pagan schools were closed in Rome and Athens by government decree, the Hellenistic influence was strong. Some scholars claim that the age lasted almost a thousand years. Although the outlines of Hellenistic influence were never entirely obliterated during this long period of time, the Hellenistic period proper was somewhat shorter. Without altering the date given for the beginning of the period, about the middle of the fourth century B.C., we might move the closing date back to about the end of the second century A.D., at which time the last of the Hellenistic-Roman schools came into existence and after which the Roman genius for educational organization began to appear more clearly. From this point on, though a remarkable fusion of Greek culture and Roman application still remained and though nothing had yet appeared that could be thought of as an autonomous Roman culture, Hellenistic influences were somewhat diluted.

It must be made clear at the outset that the long Hellenistic, or "Greeklike," period was not restricted to Rome in either setting or influence, although without Rome the effects of Hellenistic education probably would have been insignificant, and the classical inheritance undoubtedly would have died a premature and unheralded death.[2]

A popular fault, sometimes shared by educational historians, is to acknowledge Greece and Rome as the original homes of the classical heritage when, in fact, Greece alone should bear this distinction. Yet, Rome was involved, and long before Vergil produced an authentic Latin

[1] See Max Cary, *A History of the Greek World from 323 to 146 B.C.*, Methuen, London, 1951, pp. 180–186; and J. B. Bury, *The Hellenistic Age*, Cambridge University Press, Cambridge, 1923, pp. 40–60.

[2] Moses Hadas, *Hellenistic Culture: Fusion and Diffusion*, Columbia University Press, New York, 1959, pp. 301–311; and Werner W. Jaeger, *Early Christianity and Greek Paideia*, Belknap Press of Harvard University Press, Cambridge, Mass., 1961, pp. 42–46.

literature, displayed a profound interest in absorbing and stabilizing Greek cultural and intellectual traditions. Generally, however, the Roman interested in literature and letters who had both time and talent to study the monuments of antiquity was able to establish intellectual contact with Hellenistic rather than classical Greece. So the sources of his information and inspiration were secondhand, and had themselves been transplanted to the localities, municipalities, and principalities that sprung up around Asia Minor from their Athenian motherhouse. Hellenists regularly made vicarious intellectual pilgrimages to Athens to embrace her traditions and emulate her achievements; the Hellenistic educator mined the treasures of the classical heritage by means of literary study.[3]

Hellenism, following in the footsteps of many cultures that had preceded it, began by living in the past. One of the first cultural objectives that grew out of this examination of the past was the acceptance of an aristocratic character for classical education. This character was securely identified with education in early Athens, and it is a character that classical education, even in contemporary times, has not completely lost.[4] Aristocratic education in classical Greece had never given any amount of thought to perpetuating its kind. Somewhat naïvely, no doubt, it assumed that what was good for the Greek citizen would never really change and that no external supports were needed to maintain these values. This confidence might have been well founded in archaic Athens and in classical Greece, for then the structure of society and the tone of culture supported the kind of education dedicated to the ideal of the heroic deed.[5] But the communities that sprang up outside of Greece, where Hellenism received its greatest impetus, had no such structures of social or cultural traditions to rest on. What they found in classical ways of living could not be left to a living or an oral tradition. Formal communication of these traditional values seemed essential, and to do this job the school became more important than ever before. Moreover, the job seemed to require literary abilities. Not only did the school become important, but the school as a literary agency gained nearly universal recognition. The Greeklike feature remained, of course, for this was the very heart of Hellenism, but it existed in the new era more

[3] See R. R. Bolgar, *The Classical Heritage and Its Beneficiaries,* Cambridge University Press, Cambridge, 1954, pp. 13–44.

[4] Gilbert Highet, *The Classical Tradition,* Oxford University Press, New York, 1949, pp. 100–104; and G. H. Macurdy, *The Quality of Mercy: The Gentler Virtues in Greek Literature,* Yale University Press, New Haven, 1940, pp. 171–174.

[5] See C. H. Whitman, *Homer and the Heroic Tradition,* Harvard University Press, Cambridge, Mass., 1958.

on the level of inspiration than of established fact. Athens founded schools about the sixth century B.C., but these schools were not especially important for communicating the culture of Athens, and they were not truly literary institutions.[6] The chief outcome of Hellenism in the history of education was to commit the school primarily to literary objectives.

Yet this was not an immediate outcome of Hellenism, for the traditions of the past had to do a good deal of unfolding before this came about. The clearest goal of what was then called classical education was superiority in sport. It is true that sport was criticized, even condemned, by philosophers and educational theorists in Athens,[7] but excellence in sport persisted with only slight deemphasis as the true mark of the gentleman right down to the time the first Hellenistic settlement was incorporated. From that time on, however, although the gymnasium remained intact, sport began to decline, and its place was preempted by literary instruction.[8]

This emphasis on literary education was neither precisely Athenian nor traditionally Greek, yet it was the outstanding feature of Hellenistic education. So true is this, that what for the past four hundred years has been called classical education had its more exact model in Hellenistic schools. It is the education that achieved definite form in the two or three centuries preceding the opening of the Christian era. It was the basis for teaching and learning in later Rome, and its fundamental contribution is clear, in spite of Latin features that become apparent when one studies Roman schools. These Latin features were tied to essential features, and these essential features were not distinctly Roman. This, too, was the kind of education that became attractive to the Christians when Christianity reached a stage in its development that seemed to demand an intellectual basis for its creed. And finally, this Hellenistic codification and amalgamation of educational thought and practice was what passed for and still passes for classical education in modern and contemporary times. We need not be critical of this mislabeling; perhaps we should hardly expect that the authentic classical ideal or the educational informalities of early Greek times, with sport as their center and heroism as their most prominent objective, would have made much of

---

[6] See LaRue Van Hook, *Greek Life and Thought,* Columbia University Press, New York, 1937, pp. 12–18; and Martin P. Nilsson, *Die Hellenistische Schule,* C. H. Beck, München, 1955, pp. 71–73.

[7] Plato *Laws* 795–796.

[8] See H. I. Marrou, *A History of Education in Antiquity,* Sheed & Ward, Inc., New York, 1956, pp. 105–106; and M. Rostovtzeff, *The Social and Economic History of the Hellenistic World,* Oxford University Press, New York, 1941, pp. 1505–1506.

an imprint on modern educational practices. Yet the roots of classicism were not found in Hellenism, but in the Greek of antiquity. This is an important point to remember. Hellenism synthesized more than it generated; it symbolized more than it created; but in doing so, this age stood at an intellectual crossroads and accepted, integrated, embodied, and perpetuated the classical tradition. In some respects this age is more important to the history of education than Greek education itself.

If the age was important to education, it is no less true that education was immensely important to the age. Alexander the Great had carved out an empire, and he and his successors carried out a policy of establishing Greek communities throughout the Hellenistic kingdom. The kingdom exercised general administrative control, and though it intended to maintain its ultimate authority, it was always willing to delegate a certain amount of control and responsibility to the cities which it had created or reanimated. It was always made clear, however, that whatever functions these cities performed, they were functions delegated to them. The autonomous city state of Greece could make definite and fundamental policies and, depending on its strength and the opportunities of the day, attempt to carry them out. This the Hellenistic city could not do. Despite appearances of independence and the kingdom's encouragement of the city's assumption of control over machinery for the administration of political life, the city had no real authority.[9] It lacked the legal and the moral power to discipline, not its citizens, but its inhabitants. (The inhabitants of the city were citizens of the kingdom.) The city lacked authority to demand allegiance from the people or the stature to merit it. Whereas the municipal organization in Greece had been of a city-state type, which carried with it the implication of organic character, the Hellenistic urban center was a mere municipality and no real heir to the ancient city state.

The moral and political sterility of the Hellenistic city was a weakness, to be sure, but it was not a total loss. Had the larger political unit —the kingdom—supplied and imposed the moral authority and the fundamental political discipline that classical Greek cities had themselves supplied, the city's position would not have been improved, but at least a norm or a standard of action would have been provided as a guide and control for the lives of the city's people. This, however, the larger political unit did not do, and it did not permit the city to exercise a degree of autonomy necessary to exercise the control itself. At this point the importance of education to the Hellenistic city becomes a

[9] Pierre Jouguet, *Macedonian Imperialism and the Hellenization of the East,* A. A. Knopf, New York, 1928, pp. 411–415; and William W. Tarn, *Hellenistic Civilization,* E. Arnold, London, 1952, pp. 221–225.

little clearer. It would indeed be surprising to find that the interest in education was not rooted in real life. Education became important to the Hellenistic man and to the society he lived in because it alone could supply the moral bases on which individual and social discipline could be built. Could an objective for education be more practical than this?

In time the Hellenistic educational objective grew broader; the citizen of the later period became enamored of the Athenian humanism of the golden age of Pericles, and he began to look toward education to find the key to the building of a complete personality. One can hardly express his desire without becoming poetic, for the idealistic hope for human perfection calls for poetry to capture and convey its thought. It revolves about the commitment to make complete and perfect use of all nature's endowments. This was the fundamental principle behind Hellenistic education. With such high ideals inspiring their educational enterprises, we can hardly understand why these Greeks of the Alexandrian empire missed the mark in accomplishment by so much, unless, of course, their ideals were unrealistic rather than high. They were unrealistic, not in aiming at human perfection, but in assigning to formal education the primary goal of the complete intellectual and cultural improvement of man. This was not the same thing as the "education of the whole man" that our contemporary educators speak of, for Hellenistic schools had few physical and fewer moral commitments. In trying to follow earlier educational practices too closely, Hellenistic educators misinterpreted some of them. They thought classical education had accepted a total cultural commission, whereas, in fact, it had not.[10]

Wherever the Greeks settled, as they spread throughout the Mediterranean world, they met with peoples not Greek in origin; probably the majority of the inhabitants of the Hellenistic cities were not Greek. Though all of them, the Greeks and the non-Greeks alike, could admire and try to absorb the culture of the past, they could never really achieve their ambition simply through the medium of schools. Nevertheless, the idea of perfection and devotion to the Greeklike things of life dominated their thought, inspired their hopes, and consolidated their interest in education.

Educational Theory

Not only was Hellenistic man more interested in the cultural function that schools could perform than any of his ancestors, but he was also

[10] Werner W. Jaeger, *Paideia: The Ideals of Greek Culture,* Oxford University Press, New York, 1945, vol. I, pp. 298–321.

much more interested in creating a theory for education, not as a corollary to political theory, but as a separate or independent doctrine leading to culture. The age, then, among other things produced an educational theory of an easily recognizable kind. Plato, Isocrates, Aristotle, and others of the Greek world proper had not overlooked the significance of education, and in many respects what they had to say about it was superior to any pronouncement made in the Hellenistic age, but they did not single out education for independent analysis and treatment. This was done by Hellenistic philosophers and writers.[11]

Aristippus (ca. 435–350 B.C.), who belongs to the very early fringe of Hellenism, wrote a book entitled *On Education*. Clearchus of Soloi, who lived in the third century B.C., was the author of another book, *On Education*. Theophrastus (ca. 370–286 B.C.), often recognized as a disciple and interpreter of Aristotle, was the author of a work entitled *Of the Education of Kings* and of another called *A Polemical Discussion on the Theory of Eristic Argument*. Aristoxenus, who belongs to the third century B.C., produced a treatise on the *Rules of Pedagogy*. Cleanthes (ca. 331–232 B.C.) is credited with *Of Education, Of Usages, Of Dialectic, Of Moods or Tropes,* and *Of Predicates*. Zeno (ca. 333–261 B.C.) was the author of two works on education, one entitled *Of Greek Education* and the other *A Handbook of Rhetoric*. Cleomenes of the second century B.C. wrote a book *Concerning Pedagogues*. All this activity gives evidence of considerably more professional interest in education than earlier times could exhibit. With this activity and the mixture of good and bad omens in it, the historian gets his first glimpse of a willingness, if not a desire, to separate education and learning from life. Perhaps the separation was implicit in the cultural doctrines and ideals of thinking men of the time. They may have wanted to remove education from the market place, or they may have been unaware of the force that they were creating—a force which lasted several hundred years and which was, unfortunately, especially instrumental in keeping education impotent. This judgment is in no way intended as a criticism of the theories of education proposed at this time or as a denunciation of the techniques and methods of teaching and learning that were only then in the process of evolvement. Singling out education for special theoretical and practical attention was probably inevitable in the context of the times and was in some ways a step forward. The science of educa-

[11] See Diogenes Laertius *Lives of Eminent Philosophers*. In Loeb Classical Library, Harvard University Press, Cambridge, Mass., 1925, Books V, VII, IX; Bruno Snell, *The Discovery of the Mind*, Blackwell, Oxford, 1953, pp. 180–195; and G. H. Clark, *Selections from Hellenistic Philosophy*, Appleton-Century-Crofts, Inc., New York, 1964, pp. 115–140.

tion profited from the literary and theoretical specialization, but the place of education in the life of a growing man—the relationship between learning and life—took a backward step. If Plato and Isocrates generated a dilemma in educational theory and bequeathed it to the educators who followed them, the educators of the Hellenistic age seem in their turn to have created a dilemma with learning on one horn and life on the other.

Hellenistic educational theories were successful in bestowing on formal education an importance that it never had enjoyed before. Men became professional intellectuals because of the value they saw in learning and because of inner motives that are not subject to scientific or historical analysis. But there was an added motive: Accomplished men of letters and learning received special reverence. The cultured mind became a goal worth seeking. The most direct road to culture was formal education.

Both Plato and Aristotle had emphasized the need for state control over education, if the state was to succeed in achieving the highest ends.[12] Neither had made much of a mark on educational practice in Athens: the Greeks went right on leaving education in the hands of the individual.[13] No doubt some control of an indirect and indefinite kind was imposed by custom or tradition, but this was obviously not the kind of public control that the philosophers had written about. In the matter of regulation by the state, Sparta seems to have been the model. In Hellenistic cities, however, education ceased to be a matter reserved exclusively for private initiative—the theories of Plato and Aristotle were now being heeded—and generally speaking, education was subject to the control of the public. State legislation over education became the normal thing. Instead of attributing this practical innovation to Rome, as is so often done, historians should recognize and emphasize its rightful place of origin in Hellenistic Greece.[14]

In may not be too much to maintain that in early Greece not only were girls not educated, but educational theory, apart from Plâto's tongue-in-cheek prospectus, which could have made room for girls, made no plans for their participation in instructional programs. In this transitional age, however, educational opportunity was distributed a good deal more freely than heretofore, and girls as well as boys could

[12] Plato *Republic* 401d–e; Aristotle *Politics* vii. 15.

[13] See Thomas Davidson, *Aristotle and Ancient Educational Ideals*, Charles Scribner's Sons, New York, 1901, pp. 198–203; A. S. Wilkins, *National Education in Greece in the Fourth Century B.C.*, Stechert-Hafner, Inc., New York, 1911, pp. 160–165; and Jaeger, *Ideals of Greek Culture*, vol. III, pp. 197–212.

[14] Rostovtzeff, *op. cit.*, pp. 1059–1061.

attend the schools. Girls were even permitted to go to the palaestra and the gymnasium.[15]

Educational Operations: General Organization

The organization of education in the age that stood between the earlier Greek and the later Roman systems must always remain something of a mystery. This is so because each of the cities, functioning as a free agent in about the only area left for such freedom of action, organized its educational institutions to suit itself. There was no one, unified program. We must trace not one but many discrete systems of educational organization. For reasons we have already discussed, the Hellenistic towns were most anxious to follow their own private plans for education. School models did not come from Greece, but ideals of humanism and liberalism did. Each city was anxious to show its independence, so far as educational structure was concerned, but at the same time it wanted to demonstrate its dedication to the cultural values of Greece.

Largely by default, then, education became a city responsibility. The kingdom, content to leave the cities alone in this area of activity, allowed Hellenists to pay allegiance to individualism. Yet, in spite of the appearance of educational autonomy, some common features are apparent in school practice and curricular content. Although diversity and variety were prized, no city took its freedom in education so seriously as to countenance indifference to the schools wherein the cultural legacy could be transmitted.[16] And these common features illuminate Hellenistic education more than the differences which are found in school organization, the titles of various educational officers, or the special civic relationships that evolved between schools and municipalities.

The general assumption that every Hellenistic city had a gymnasium, if valid, would justify a belief that lines of cultural affinity remained intact between Athens and the Greek world around her. There is, however, much less certainty about the nature of the Hellenistic gymnasium. Possibly the municipalities organized on the fringe of the Greek world were loyal to names and not to essential natures of Greek institutions. In any case, besides the gymnasium, every Hellenistic city seems to have had an ephebeum.[17]

[15] C. Seltman, *Women in Antiquity*, Pan, London, 1959, pp. 18–21.

[16] Rostovtzeff, *op. cit.*, pp. 1084–1095.

[17] Clarence A. Forbes, *Greek Physical Education*, Appleton-Century-Crofts, Inc., New York, 1929, devotes chapter 7 to ephebic institutions in Greek cities and the cities throughout the Hellenistic world.

The ephebic system in Athens had a twofold purpose, military and civic. Its military purpose was to produce soldiers; its civic purpose was to form citizens. This may have been a needed combination at one time in Athenian history, and to some extent the ends that were now sought formally had been obtained informally in the past. But ironically enough, at the point in history when Athens no longer had any special need for citizen-soldiers, because Athens was no longer a free city, the system to produce them was most highly developed. Civic leadership in the political arena was no more needed in Athens, when ephebic training reached its highest point, than a civic army. When autonomy was lost, military training and civic virtue became a mere display. It should be understood that this paradoxical idea-pattern of civic and military education was transplanted from Athens to the Hellenistic towns, where it had as little meaning as it had in Athens.[18]

Unrealistic and unnecessary ephebic training made change inevitable. The changes were made first in Athens, and then the departures from the ephebic ideal began to take shape in the Hellenistic ephebic institutions. Although there were pockets of anachronism or ultraconservatism in the Hellenistic area of influence, where young men went right on following the original curriculum with its strict military and political orientation, the Athenian revisions were usually quite acceptable, and Hellenistic ephebea lost no time in adapting them to their use. New objectives were substituted for the old; civic education aimed not at leadership in public affairs but at the perpetuation of an aristocratic way of life; military training was conveniently redirected toward sport. The glory of the ephebeum was its ability to transform hope into reality; in it the Hellenistic boy could be immersed in Greek culture, and from this immersion ensued an even greater consolidation of the position of the aristocracy. Aristocracy was made the equivalent of civilization, and it was judged that culture, not position or wealth, could distinguish Greeks from the other inhabitants of the city. The distinction was important, for, as Rostovtzeff has shown so clearly in his monumental study of Hellenistic life, the city was a place for many allegiances and many races. Cultural homogeneity for the Greeks was possible only when it was cultivated with extraordinary care.

SCHOOLS OF THE HELLENISTIC WORLD

Apart from the ephebic schools, which along with most gymnasia were maintained at public expense, there was no state system of publicly

[18] A. H. M. Jones, *The Greek City from Alexander to Justinian,* Oxford University Press, New York, 1940, pp. 220–225; and E. R. Bevan, *Hellenism and Christianity,* Books for Librarians Press, Freeport, N.Y., 1967, pp. 202–207.

supported schools in the Hellenistic cities. It was true that all the schools felt the state's influence to some degree, for in this period the injunctions of the philosophers like Plato and Aristotle with respect to state control of education, were beginning to be heeded.[19] Still, in practice, the control fell short of the ideal presented by the philosophers. Of course it was in the general organization of schools that the state made its influence felt most effectively, and not in the day-to-day operation of educational institutions. Perhaps the largest single factor that militated against any greater assumption of authority over education by the city was the fact that schools did not receive regular support from municipal governments. The structure of municipal government was too fragile to permit the kind of revenue vehicles that would have made such support possible. Ephebea were supported to some extent, as were gymnasia, but the support was probably neither generous nor regular, although it very probably did include provision out of the public treasury for the site of such institutions, the buildings, and other necessary physical facilities. As ephebic institutions attuned their objectives more and more to those of Attic ephebea, and as such places began to join in their curricula both sport and literary education, the costs tended to be considerably lower than before. But even in the days when the ephebea were inclined to hew closely to the line of original purpose and when total costs were higher, these costs were borne largely by the young men who attended. This was still the established practice in most Hellenistic cities. In spite of these private contributions, the ephebic school may be considered a state school. Apart from the ephebic school, there were, strictly speaking, no other state schools.

Other schools that existed in these cities were either endowed or instituted by private venture. In either case they were private schools, and from this distance in history the points at which public authority touched them are not especially visible. Most schools in the Hellenistic world were conducted by enterprising masters, who saw an opportunity to make teaching and learning pay, and some of these masters were able to make an especially handsome profit from their endeavors. Profits aside, these private school teachers, most of whom were conducting elementary schools, were seldom accorded much, if any, recognition for the relatively important work they were doing. The fact that their work was socially important and even necessary did not result in any improvement in the teachers' status. The main reason for the low estate of teachers may be found in the generally accepted custom of permitting anyone who wanted to teach to do so; he would need only

[19] See R. W. Livingstone, *Greek Ideals and Modern Life*, Harvard University Press, Cambridge, Mass., 1935, pp. 161–170; Bury, *op. cit.*, pp. 81–83.

to open a school. There were many teachers without any real qualifications for teaching. An occupation which apparently requires no special knowledge or skill would naturally not be held in reverence, and teachers would not be accorded any special social esteem.

Another source of school support, apart from state support and student fees, was the public-spirited, wealthy citizen. From very early classical times down through the Hellenistic period, tradition recommended that men of wealth endow some enterprise of public worth. Some schools were founded or maintained in this way.[20]

School Programs

So far we have tried to see education as it was related to cultural and political life and to understand the role assigned to it in the Hellenistic world. Now we will move from the level of educational theory to practice, and in doing so we will want to know something about the schools that were organized, and what they tried to teach. As we move closer to school practice, however, we will see that its evolution was guided by the fundamental cultural attitudes of the time—all based on classical values—and that later educational theory and practice were deeply affected both by what Hellenistic educational theorists said education should be, and by what Hellenistic schoolmasters did in their classrooms. Both influences make legitimate claims for attention in the history of education, because both affected teaching and learning for the next one thousand years. The most obvious as well as the most lasting effect of Hellenistic education on school programs was a separation of levels of instruction into elementary, secondary, and higher, each with its own subject matter and specialized teachers. Now, for the first time in practical pedagogy the order of learning is paid heed, and school programs begin to wear a new face.[21]

PHYSICAL EDUCATION

A distinctive feature of early Greek education was its attention to physical training—yet this discipline which eventually incorporated drill, health study, and scientific methodology, remained underdevel-

[20] See Marrou, *op. cit.*, pp. 112–115.
[21] Nilsson, *op. cit.*, pp. 47–50.

oped during the classical and early Hellenistic periods and was, in fact, nothing more than athletics.[22] This narrowness, however, had a redeeming feature in the universality of athletic opportunity: Youth of all ages, beginning with childhood and extending through ephebic training, were welcomed to the playgrounds. Once there, they could run and play with few restrictions. Certain types of sport were reserved especially for aristocrats (riding is an example).[23]

Physical education, set in the context of a sporting tradition, was one way of inducting Athenian youth into a life of culture and leisure. In the Hellenistic municipality anything that reflected the life and values of ancient Greece was fervently embraced, and so physical education was enthusiastically invited to become a staple in a broadly gauged educational program. Without exception, Hellenistic towns had an abundance of sporting facilities: Every city, favorably disposed as it was to Greeklike institutions, constructed gymnasia where boys and girls could exercise, play their games, and master a variety of athletic skills that were both prized and praised.[24]

Unquestionably, classical and Hellenistic values justified sport, and educational theory recommended it. But the schools' curricula, for some strange and inexplicable reason, found physical education incompatible with its purposes, and so Hellenistic schools neither conducted nor supervised athletic training or contests. But even with the schoolhouse door closed to it, sport was justified as part of a broad education, and a true citizen of the Hellenistic world counted the social graces and physical benefits derived from athletics to be essential parts of a decent education.

For as long as he was able, the citizen frequented the gymnasium and his private sporting club. When his skill and condition warranted, he competed in the city's athletic contests. He enjoyed the challenges of competition and savored whatever honor was attached to athletic success. In the last analysis, however, the principal motive was a sheer love of sport, and for this good reason the towns were made to resemble a vast playground where various athletic and sporting appetites could be satisfied.

While sport was mainly informal it was, nevertheless, important, and we would be surprised indeed to find the Hellenists indifferent to

[22] E. Norman Gardiner, *Athletics of the Ancient World,* Oxford University Press, New York, 1930, pp. 113–118.

[23] Kenneth J. Freeman, *Schools of Hellas,* 3d ed., The Macmillan Company, New York, 1922, pp. 118–120, 143.

[24] See Forbes, *op. cit.,* pp. 135–139; and Gardiner, *op. cit.,* pp. 132–137.

teaching or coaching in connection with athletic skills. Sport, within the broad limits of Hellenistic cultural theory, had fundamental educational worth, and this worth both justified and recommended instruction. So, without being a school in the strict sense, the playground was unquestionably a place where learning was prized, and where coaches were present who, for a fee, would supervise the acquisition of athletic technique. Although the playground's informal curriculum must have been as varied as Hellenistic sporting interests, certain athletic events were accorded pride of place both on the playground and on the field of serious competition, and to these events children, young men, and adults gave the bulk of their attention. Running, jumping, wrestling, boxing, throwing the discus and javelin—all transplanted from the classical gymnasium—formed the core of sport and were, therefore, the principal components of physical education.[25] The notable exception on this list is swimming, a skill that all classical Greeks evidenced and a majority of Hellenists displayed, too: Both in the classical gymnasium and on the Hellenistic playground, swimming was paid scant heed.

ELEMENTARY EDUCATION

With the advent of Hellenism, the principle of division of labor was applied to formal education in a way not done before. Earlier teachers, we may be certain, recognized the logical order of regular procession from the simple to the complex, and the best educational philosophers had spoken convincingly about an order of studies and about the foundations of knowledge that are required before science and philosophy are encountered on higher school levels. But what a few good teachers may have done and what some philosophers undoubtedly counseled was outside the mainstream of pedagogical practice, for what they were doing in their own schools or what they said ought to be done was, because of education's predominantly elemental character, dispensed from urgent and general application. A terminal elementary school may afford the luxury of being indifferent to the legitimate demands of secondary and higher studies for basic tools of learning; it finds its teaching commission in the most fundamental of life's needs, and when some skills have been communicated it assumes that its work is finished. Without later steps on an educational ladder, and in the absence of any clear commitment to literary teaching, it can

[25] Thomas Woody, *Life and Education in Early Societies*, The Macmillan Company, New York, 1949, pp. 309–313.

ignore—as the Athenian elementary schools did [26]—or leave to chance, the whole business of postelementary school accomplishments.

All this is fairly safe, and such elementary school practices and theories may be condoned in societies wherein schools are not charged with a heavy responsibility for cultural transmission. But Hellenistic schools were so charged: cultural transmission became their sole function, and in order to fulfill it they needed, first, to convert all schools into literary agencies, and second, to arrange the content of education to ensure that by means of literature the classical heritage would be continued in an undiluted form.

This was, to be sure, a huge order for schooling; yet schoolmasters could find some comfort in knowing that their functions were limited mainly to literary goals. No one believed that the total education of a citizen could be the school's responsibility, although every Hellenist dogmatically assumed that education would form the whole man. Physical, moral, and social education were totally divorced from elementary school functions, and this may have been a mistake. But it had the effect of leaving elementary schools to deal with only a relatively small part of what the educated community thought formal schooling should do. As we have seen, physical education, though important, was handled outside the school, and moral education was always too important a matter to be left to teachers. The nurse, the pedagogue, the family itself were moral teachers, and the school's intrusion at this point in teaching was unwelcome if not actually proscribed. In the end, then, of the four parts of elementary education—literary, moral, social, and physical—only one, the literary, was a proper function of the Hellenistic elementary school.

At first, elementary school instruction had some nonliterary features (drawing, instrumental and vocal music, dancing), and to some extent they distort the picture of the school as a pure instrument of literary teaching. But these were things that needed to be taught, and elementary schools—at least temporarily—admitted them to their syllabus. The evolution of drawing as a school subject is imprecise; apparently drawing was more important to the schools of early Greece than in the schools of the Hellenistic world.[27] Still, drawing masters found

[26] Frederick A. G. Beck, *Greek Education: 450–350 B.C.*, Barnes & Noble, Inc., New York, 1964, pp. 80–85; and T. B. L. Webster, *Art and Literature in Fourth Century Athens*, University of London, Athlone Press, London, 1956, pp. 112–118.

[27] See Frederic G. Kenyon, *Books and Readers in Ancient Greece and Rome*, Oxford University Press, New York, 1932, pp. 61–71; and Jaeger, *Ideals of Greek Culture*, II, p. 228.

customers in all Hellenistic centers, and even in higher studies, instruction in drawing was sometimes included. In general, however, the place of drawing in Hellenistic elementary education was tenuous. Its decline was inevitable since, at best, it would be a poor vehicle for perpetuating the classical past—not because draftmanship is unrelated to art, but because classical Greece was almost barren of visual art. Despite this, drawing refused to surrender easily: it was always to be found in some Hellenistic elementary schools, and was always the special skill of at least some elementary teachers.

Music, too, sometimes found a place in the lower school. More commonly music was taught by special masters. Masters, we say, because instrumental and vocal music were not taught by the same teachers. In spite of what would appear to have been a somewhat unrealistic specialization in the teaching of music, music continued to retain a fairly secure position in Hellenistic culture. Music had been so firmly woven into the fabric of Greek life that it would have been strange indeed to find that the Hellenistic age rejected music while retaining such a wholehearted attitude of acceptance toward most Greeklike institutions and the bulk of Greek culture. Though we may doubt that music had a permanent and an important role throughout the Hellenistic age, we may be sure that it retained a role that was always and everywhere superior to that of drawing. Yet it, too, declined. The Hellenistic age was able to retain a general devotion to Greek culture and at the same time allow music to become less important both in education and in life. Literature crowded music out of the school's curriculum; acoustical studies invaded music itself and changed its course. These are the most obvious illustrations of how music began to lose its hold on Hellenistic culture. By the end of the Hellenistic period, music as it was known in Athens of the fifth century B.C. no longer existed.[28]

As traditional concerns of elementary education were gradually lost, the primary school was left with reading, writing, and counting. These subjects were taught with little imagination and with less skill. No thought was given to adapting the materials of instruction to the nature of learning. This was so, no doubt, because the masters knew little of the nature of learning and almost nothing at all about the arts of teaching. As we have said, anyone who could read could teach in these schools. There was no alternative for the child; he had to put up with such teachers.

The teaching of reading began with the alphabet. Here the child's attention was directed at learning names; there was no concern for

[28] Aristophanes *Clouds* 960, 1357; *Wasps* 959, 989; and Plato *Protagoras* 326.

sounds. A great deal of time was spent on learning the alphabet. From the alphabet instruction moved to syllables, and from them to words and then to texts. Recitation was mainly memorization, and writing was taught with the same lack of imagination as reading. In general, children learned to write by copying. Counting completed the elementary school program, and it was conducted according to the same involved counting system that had been common to the schools of Athens.[29]

Elementary schools could be found throughout the Hellenistic world, and all free children were expected to attend such schools. In some cities girls and boys were enrolled together and were engaged in learning the same things. Yet in spite of their fairly vital interest in primary education, Hellenistic cities did not see fit to set aside or construct any special buildings for schools. A school was kept wherever a vacant room could be found. It needed no equipment other than a few chairs or benches on which the children could sit.

Children in the elementary schools that present-day educators approve have no reason to envy the children who attended lower schools in the Hellenistic cities. Instruction was poor, and progress was slow. An elementary school child would probably not be able to write his name after three years in school, and even simple addition would have been beyond the ability of the child who had spent five years there. Another feature may be added to the generally unattractive portrait of life in these schools: children were treated brutally. Corporal punishment was used for both prevention and cure, and fear was the only motivation in which the schools had confidence. Tradition decided what was to be taught; the teacher's ability or inability controlled pedagogic practices. Learning under such conditions must have been both arduous and painful.

SECONDARY EDUCATION

Literary and scientific secondary education developed rather slowly. Both had existed in theory much more than they had in practice in the pre-Hellenistic years. The Athenians, of course, had had a secondary level, but the emphasis on this level (we are thinking of the gymnasium, of course) was on physical rather than literary training. In some other places the emphasis may have been artistic rather than literary. The claim that the secondary school with a definite commitment to literary education had its real beginning in the Hellenistic period may be given

[29] Plato *Laws* 809c–d; Xenophon *Memorabilia* IV. 4.7; Aristophanes *Wasps* 656.

a sympathetic hearing. Prior to this time, the organization of a content for literary studies of the secondary type would have encountered some difficulty. The great Greek classics existed mainly in oral tradition. This oral tradition was part of elementary education, although not necessarily a part of the elementary school's curriculum. The classical willingness to leave to informal transmission the literature and the literary inheritance that were prized so highly may well have worked to retard the development of literature as a school subject. The place of literature in formal education was one of many questions; others involved grammar and science.

Hellenistic teachers accepted the Greek classics as part of the content of secondary education, and in doing so they went one step beyond their classical ancestors. To these studies in literature they added an ever-growing body of scientific and mathematical knowledge. Finally, the science of language—grammar—arose, and this, too, was added to the content of the secondary school.[30] There were, then, three principal curricular areas: literature, science, and grammar. They were not, however, of equal value in the eyes of the Hellenistic man of culture.

Literature   Hellenistic schools made the classics a formal part of secondary school education. Few innovations in the history of education may lay claim to greater permanence than this: from secondary schools that operated before the Christian era down to those being conducted today, classical studies may still be found. And more than this, some of the classics read, studied, and explained then are still being read and studied today.

As we have said, Homer had a solid reputation for being the educator of the Greeks. Not only Athens, but all of the Greek world felt his influence. The Homeric impress on early Greece was unquestionably great, and its influence was not limited to Greece, for the most popular of all of the ancient poets to be accepted in Hellenistic intellectual circles and in the school's literary curriculum was Homer.[31] The preeminent literary works were the *Iliad* and the *Odyssey*. But other epic poets were studied; Hesiod would be an outstanding example. Lyric poets and dramatists were also read and studied. One would surely hesitate to try to draw up a complete list of the literature studied in these schools, for the classical heritage was rich.

[30] T. B. L. Webster, *Hellenistic Poetry and Art*, Methuen, London, 1965, pp. 180–185; and D. L. Clark, *Rhetoric in Greco-Roman Education*, Columbia University Press, New York, 1957, pp. 211–215.

[31] See Beck, *op. cit.*, pp. 55–66; and J. L. Myres, *Homer and His Critics*, Routledge and Kegan Paul, Ltd., London, 1958, pp. 33–35, 66–69.

Although the curriculum with which the teachers of literature had to work had rare quality, the teachers were not disposed, or perhaps were unable, to take full advantage of it. Instead of directing their students in a search for literary taste and appreciation, they turned them toward the superficialities of literary study. Analysis of the text and searching for unusual words or expressions were all preliminary to reading a poem or drama. Sometimes the student hardly had time to read the literature that he was studying.

Grammar It is safe to assume that literature preceded grammar and science in secondary school studies. Literature had existed in a fuller and more complete form for a much longer time than either grammar or science. How far back would one have to go to find the origin of literature in the Greek world? At least as far back as the time of Homer —seven or eight centuries before Christ. Grammar as a body of knowledge about the structure of language was developed in the first century B.C. by Dionysius Thrax of Rhodes.[32] Dionysius produced the first book on the subject, a book that was used as a text and reference in the teaching and study of grammar for centuries. This sixteen-page work was still found in use in the later Middle Ages.

In Dionysius' *Grammar* we have the beginnings of a new subject for secondary schools. From this time on, that is, from about the first century B.C., secondary schools that followed the Hellenistic model included literature and grammar in their curricula. Dionysius defined grammar as the practical knowledge of the usage of writers of poetry and prose. He dealt with accent, letters, syllables, and parts of speech. The book concluded with a brief treatment of the declension of nouns and the conjugation of verbs.[33]

In actual practice in the schools, grammatical study not only included the scientific, abstract, and arid approach to language that had been introduced by Dionysius (which must have turned many a student away from serious study because of the obvious implication that learning and life had little in common), but included an introduction to composition as well. Composition, however, was not stressed in the secondary school, for both oral and written compositions belonged to the sphere of higher education.

Science Science or science study did not begin with the secondary schools of the Hellenistic world. Yet the age did give science a larger

---

[32] Bolgar, *op. cit.*, p. 23.
[33] Dionysius Thrax *Grammar* 7, 8–10, 15–20.

role in formal education than any earlier age had given. Excepting the scientific investigations conducted by men engaged in higher studies or by scholars commissioned for such purposes, scientific study and mathematical study of this period attained a degree of formalization not found in earlier educational history. The Hellenistic age had, of course, the benefit of theoretical justification for treating science as a secondary school subject. Both Plato and Isocrates had agreed that such studies had a great deal of merit for formative and cultural purposes.[34] Such support, coupled with the advances being made in scientific and mathematical knowledge and man's natural curiosity about the world in which he lived, made the inclusion of science in the curriculum almost inevitable. In their ardent desire to be Greeklike, Hellenistic people often did not distinguish between the real nature of Greek institutions and the ideal picture, given by Plato, Isocrates, and Aristotle, of what they ought to have been. By putting science in the secondary school, Hellenistic educators were surely not following classical practice. But this is not too important a point, because classical Greek secondary schools were not literary institutions at all. Science in the secondary school curriculum may or may not have been a sign that Hellenistic people wanted to be better Greeks than the Greeks themselves had been. Without further speculation on these obscure matters, we should touch quickly on what the study of science in these schools entailed. A broad curriculum probably contained geometry, arithmetic, music, and astronomy.[35]

The geometry studied in these schools started and stopped with Euclid, although, in finding justifications for geometric knowledge, Hellenistic science teachers departed from him. He had assumed that geometry should be pursued for its liberal values and for its power of mental discipline; [36] they, however, preferred to handle geometry as a study with practical applications. (In the absence of a versatile computational arithmetic, they were probably right.) Arithmetic in Hellenistic schools differed very little from Greek arithmetic, a fact which helps us to understand why it was studied in the secondary schools. Today we find schoolboys and schoolgirls laboring over their addition, subtraction, multiplication, and division problems, and for the most

[34] See Edward J. Power, *Evolution of Educational Doctrine,* Appleton-Century-Crofts, Inc., New York, 1969, pp. 75–76.

[35] See Marrou, *op. cit.,* pp. 176–185.

[36] Euclid *Elements of Geometry* I. 5. Dover Publications, New York, 1956. See also Thomas L. Heath, *A History of Greek Mathematics,* The Clarendon Press, Oxford, 1921, vol. I; and B. L. Waerden, *Science Awakening,* Oxford University Press, New York, 1961, pp. 91–103.

part they meet these problems in the elementary school. Hellenistic arithmetic study was neither commercial nor practical; it was a study of the theory of numbers—the Greek notation made any other approach most impractical—and far too complicated for elementary school students.

Music was, in a sense, an adjunct of mathematics. In Athens and in other Greek cities from the sixth to the third century b.c., music had probably been an elementary school subject. In what was the generally accepted definition of secondary education, music had no recognized position. Usually school subjects start on a high level and sink. In other words, the normal development has been that subjects are introduced in higher schools, and when a subject becomes generally accepted as a part of organized knowledge, it drops to the secondary school curriculum and from there to the elementary school. Music, at least as far as Hellenistic education is concerned, provides us with the rare example of a subject going up the educational ladder rather than down. Yet it should be pointed out that music itself had changed, or rather, that the subject that was brought to the secondary school was a different kind of music from what had been or even what was then accepted as a cultural tool. This was the kind of music that declined in value as a part of Hellenistic life. The force of this decline was such that both instrumental and vocal music, the kinds of music that had occupied an integral part of Greek life before, declined too. Despite these trends, conventional music did not disappear completely from the schools of the Hellenistic world. Music could still be found in the curriculum of some of the schools of later Rome.

Astronomy, the most popular of the four sciences, had something in common with geometry, for it too could be studied in different ways. When Plato's directions were followed (he said astronomy used by good minds could reveal God's intention in creating the world) students studied astronomy to discover the divine plan. But even when Plato's influence was absent, astronomy had a liberal side: the knowledge compiled in Ptolemy's thirteen books of *Almagestes* could be mastered simply because it was good to know such things. Practically, however, astronomy had two recommendations. First, it enabled men to predict and chart the seasons and to construct dependable calendars. Second, easily and often intentionally confused with astrology, it was used to cast horoscopes—to allow men to draw back the veil of the future, to foretell the events of a person's life, and to answer horary questions. Thus swamped in superstition (probably because it *was* superstion), astronomy-converted-to-astrology maintained an untroubled position of superiority in the schools' science courses.

In the final analysis, however, neither a science course nor any of its parts could break the grip which literature and grammar had on secondary school curricula. Science was difficult, specialized, and a study for the few who wanted to be experts. Students who essayed first and foremost to imbibe of the classical heritage (which actually contained little scientific knowledge) could easily rationalize their rejection of science curricula, for culturally they found science barren, and emotionally they found it unbearable.

HIGHER EDUCATION

We have drawn a general picture of the lower schools that flourished in the Hellenistic world.[37] It would probably be a mistake to maintain that a high degree of uniformity was attained in the various elementary and secondary schools, but certainly there was much more unity of purpose than could be found on the level of higher education. Of course the lower schools had a so-called liberal commitment: They wanted to transmit Greek culture. The same purpose was accepted, though not as an exclusive objective, by some of the schools of higher education. Higher schools that directed their energies at cultural transmission were the schools of rhetoric and philosophy. Almost without exception they were found in every city of any size, although the most illustrious institutions of higher learning flourished in Alexandria, Pergamon, Delphi, Rhodes, Beirut, Antioch, Constantinople, and, of course, Athens. In time, however, if we read the history of these two parts of higher education correctly, both rhetors and philosophers began to show less and less interest in culture and greater and greater interest in building an academic domain of their own in which rhetoric or philosophy became pretty much an end in itself. The other side of higher education—if one side was ostensibly cultural—was professional. The line to be drawn between professional and technical higher education is almost always quite thin, and one hesitates to be too positive on such delicate and elusive matters. Yet the Hellenistic age rejected what we would call technical higher education, and this rejection was intentional, for a critical attitude was current which dogmatically undermined the worth of illiberal studies. At the same time, however, inconsistency accompanied this skeptical spirit: Hellenistic people loved and worshiped the architectural designs of their Greek ancestors, and wanted to emulate their constructionary capabilities. A solid cultural pragmatism should have justified engineering education and a variety of architectural schools, but it did not—so, Hellenists made their way through history

[37] See also Marrou, *op. cit.*, pp. 142–175; and Nilsson, *op. cit.*, pp. 69–81.

without the benefit of special technical institutes or technical curricula in existing higher schools.

Ephebic schools were everywhere, and either because they had drifted away from original purposes or because those original purposes were impossible to achieve, they added cultural studies to the course and taught a higher literature in the gymnasium's auditorium. But this was irregular teaching, offered only when a Hellenistic sophist or some wandering scholar appeared with a prepared lecture, and thus its mark on higher learning was weak and ephemeral. The regular disciplines of higher learning were medical, scientific, rhetorical, and philosophical, all pursued separately in their own institutes and training programs.[38]

Medicine played an important part in Hellenstic life because, being able to afford health care, citizens were anxious to have physicians' skills. Society could support a large number of both public and private doctors, and to educate them several medical schools were established. But the medical school was interested—as rightly it should have been— in the medical arts, and not in general culture; its course consisted of a transmission of conventional medical knowledge, always emphasizing the clinical, and reducing theory to a minimum. The main thing was practice. After a short stay in the classroom, an aspiring physician attached himself to a doctor (who may have had as many as a dozen medical apprentices), accompanying him on his rounds, watching the treatment, and staying with patients throughout the day. When training, or rather this crude internship, was finished, the young doctor was ready to practice his profession. (Internship usually took a long time— Galen interned for eleven years, although he was an exception—but could, with shortcuts, be completed in only six months.) Yet, despite the obvious worth of medical skill, a physician was universally recognized as a technician, and not as a man of culture: His cultural status was always inferior to the rhetor's and the philosopher's, both of whom represented the finest products of Hellenistic higher learning.

Scientific higher learning, evidencing some cultural involvement, stood above medicine, but below rhetoric and philosophy, in Hellenistic priorities. Herein scholars, scientists in the broad sense, applied their talents to a systematic formulation of knowledge—an educational undertaking of great consequence for the future of grammar, rhetoric, medicine, geometry, and many other fields of human knowledge. And these scientists had an institution—the *museum*—wherein they could carry on experiments and dedicate themselves to study.[39] Appointed to

[38] See Rostovtzeff, *op. cit.*, pp. 1088–1094, 1096, 1600.

[39] See D. E. O'Leary, *How Greek Science Passed to the Arabs,* Routledge and Kegan Paul, Ltd., London, 1949, pp. 170–173.

their positions in the museum and supported in their research and study, scholars were relieved of having to use their energy and their time in making a living.

With enviable institutional subsidies and personal endowments (whose source was royalty, state treasuries, and philanthropists), scholars could lose themselves in their work. However, in doing so, they did not always retire from public view. Sometimes they invited the public, or specially interested persons (including students in the higher schools), to the museum or to the library or laboratory connected with it, to witness or to hear of new discoveries or interpretations of a scientific nature. At other times they communicated with the educated community by means of prepared lectures—the ancient equivalent of publication.

In addition to giving scholars facilities for study, the museum, although it was never an authentic advanced school, may have been an inspiration and a prototype for higher education in later centuries. At the very least it showed what capable, dedicated scholars could do in an atmosphere receptive to inquiring minds and wherein liberty and the leisure to pursue knowledge without interruption or interference were ensured.

So Hellenistic higher education was both cultural and professional, and its subject matter had a fourfold division: rhetoric and philosophy represented culture; medicine and science spoke for man's everyday needs. The first two deserve further notice.

Rhetoric   We know of the exceptional interest which educated men in the Hellenistic world had for rhetoric, or oratory, and we recognize their attitude as even more surprising because oratory had become an art without political significance. In ancient Athens, rhetoric flourished as a useful and necessary tool for a citizen engaging in public affairs; its worth was acknowledged even by Plato, who was also its severest critic. Now, however, political activity and responsible public oratory were removed from their natural habitat, because citizens were excluded from any role in forming public policy. Nevertheless, even with its public voice muted, rhetoric was studied as if the political climate of the ancient city state remained intact, and it was studied with exacting care. But on the level of practice (and no ancient rhetor could afford to neglect this part of rhetoric), the old judicial and deliberative oratory, with all its political meaning and significance, was transformed to a safer, politically antiseptic literary oratory. And change did not cease here, for now, still conscious of citizens' political insecurity in a state extremely jealous of its power, rhetors told students which subjects to prepare their speeches on (at least those which were to be read by, as well as to be delivered before, an audience). Thus composition, a long uncultivated side of rhetoric which eventually succeeded in dominating the entire rhetorical syllabus, received new emphasis.

Hellenistic rhetoric had three parts, although each did not receive equal attention: *information, style,* and *delivery.*[40] The content of a speech was important, especially if it was to be read, and so students of rhetoric were expected to know the classics and to be able to cull from them appropriate phrases, names, and references. This, however, was the principal business of the grammarian—the secondary school teacher—and if he had conducted a good school, higher education should be left only to supply refinements to a basic general education. Rhetorical masters preferred to assume the adequacy of secondary schools, for, valid or not, this assumption allowed them to devote meticulous attention, and almost full time, to style and delivery. Style apparently ranked first in importance, and was cultivated by using superior classical models. Delivery, which applied especially to public speaking, meant constant practice in following a long and detailed agenda of rules. As years passed, the agenda became fuller and fuller, because, though new rules could be added, no conscientious teacher of rhetoric would ever leave anything out.

Philosophy   Philosophy, despite being able to claim an entirely authentic record as part of the classical heritage, lacked rhetoric's popular appeal. Most philosophers wanted it this way because, first, they believed that in order to be fully effective teachers, they should have fraternal relationships with their students. Large classes would obviously undermine this pedagogic principle. Second, philosophy was assumed to be a minority culture. Philosophers assumed this because of their conviction that philosophic knowledge was too precious to be shared with any but the most capable students; the ordinary educated person tended to avoid philosophy because of its traditional Platonic affiliations with mathematics and science. Some students simply found philosophy too difficult, although more often than not their rejections were based not on degrees of difficulty—because rhetoric, too, was hard and arid—but on philosophy's apparent indifference to the Hellenistic ideal of culture, which automatically subordinated the content of thought to the power

[40] Clark, *op. cit.,* pp. 140–145; and Webster, *Hellenistic Poetry and Art,* pp. 191–204.

of expression. Under the circumstances it was easy for philosophers to keep their classes small.[41]

In a world where literature and rhetoric held pride of place, a philosopher needed more than ordinary perseverance to be true to his discipline. He needed zeal, devotion, and intense hope to stick with studies which made no guarantee that wisdom was at the end of a long intellectual road. Still, some students were always prepared to make the necessary effort, and their motives for seeking wisdom were undoubtedly sustained by the realization that philosophy, after all, though a less popular branch of higher learning, was as respectable as rhetoric.

A student's first decision was which kind of higher learning to pursue. If he selected philosophy, his second was to decide which philosophical school of thought to follow. The ancient world, we know, boasted varieties of philosophical opinion, all the way from Plato's basic conservativism to the eccentric tactics of the Cynics, who counseled withdrawal from the world and, in a way, wore their philosophy on their sleeves: they refused to wash, wear decent clothes, or cut their hair. Yet, among so many philosophical positions, only four schools of thought stood prominently in Hellenistic higher education, and students made their conversion to philosophy in one of them. These schools, all with headquarters in Athens—Platonic (Academy), Aristotelian (Lyceum), Epicurean (Garden), and Stoical (Poecile)—were distributed generously among Hellenistic cities. They admitted anyone who wanted to sample philosophical study in a brief introductory course, but before they would agree to spend time unravelling the mysteries of their own philosophical classics, a student would have to prove his allegiance not only to philosophy, but to the philosophical doctrines of that school.

We have said that the normal place to study philosophy was the recognized school. From what we have said, however, it might be assumed that departure from custom was impossible. So to keep the record accurate, we should add that philosophers acting independently of any school sometimes taught outside them, and some even established isolated schools. Also wandering philosophers—actually, popular lecturers or preachers—moved from city to city in the manner of Sophists, and taught whatever they could to whomever would listen. These were the *eclectics* who, though not responsible for the invention of eclecticism, took what they liked from various doctrines, and tried to articulate a philosophy of their own.

[41] See Paul E. Moore, *Hellenistic Philosophies*, Princeton University Press, Princeton, N.J., 1923, pp. 300–354; and Clark, *Selections from Hellenistic Philosophy*, pp. 150–250.

In the established schools philosophical teaching began simply enough. Students enrolled and were exposed first, as we have said, to an introductory course. Some students sampled the teaching of several schools in the introductory course before making a decision, and an intellectual commitment, to one. When the decision was made, a regular program of instruction began with the history of philosophy, wherein the strengths and weaknesses of various doctrines were explored. Then followed courses in the school's own doctrines, and now philosophy teaching had two dimensions. First, the doctrines had to be learned to the letter, and every detail the classical philosopher mentioned needed notice and analysis. This side of instruction obviously was overburdened with erudition. The other side was more current, allowing teachers to try to relate the fundamentals of philosophic wisdom to life's realities. Here we see the professor descending from his lofty eminence to apply his school's doctrines to the burning questions of the day and make them speak a language of relevance.

The philosophical curriculum formed by the classics of a school always contained logic, ethics, and physics. But, true to ancient preferences in speculation, Hellenistic philosophers applied their scholarship to ethics. Besides, with ethics as with everything else, their preoccupation was with wisdom more than with truth: They wanted to understand life and guide it, rather than merely codify and understand its secrets. But, somewhere along the road to wisdom, Hellenistic philosophers lost their way. They began to argue with rhetors over the respective values of their different kinds of higher learning, and they began to argue among themselves about the truth of their respective doctrines. They fought and disputed and became most unphilosophical; they descended to polemic, and too frequently took philosophy teaching down the road to polemic with them. In the end both branches of higher learning, each asserting its cultural superiority, were swamped by hostility, debate, and artificiality. At the end of the Hellenistic age, neither philosophy nor rhetoric had a speaking relationship with one another—or even with life.

Summary

Hellenistic education provided classical (early Greek) education with its historical form. Had it not been for the Hellenistic period, it is doubtful that many of the classical views and practices in education would have been preserved. For the most part, what we today call classical education is really Hellenistic education.

The distinctive quality of Hellenistic man was his devotion to Greek culture. Preserving the glory and the traditions of classical Greece seemed more important to him than anything else. For this reason Hellenistic cities were much more conscious of the need for schools than the classical age had been. To some extent education at this time became a municipal concern. Schools were organized on all levels. Even physical education was not ignored. Elementary schools taught what elementary schools usually teach, although in this context we see music slipping out of the school. Secondary education—the grammar school—was totally different from what it had been in classical times. For the first time there was a definite commitment to literary studies, and the secondary school was given the assignment of carrying out this commitment. Higher education was served mainly by schools of rhetoric and philosophy. Of the two, the age prized the former more highly.

V

Roman
Educational
Tradition
& School

Education in Early Rome (800 to 275 B.C.)

It is fairly common to speak of Roman education as an extension of
Hellenistic education. Such a generalization, although it has a good
deal to recommend it, nevertheless errs in a number of important respects. It seems to forget that there was a purely Roman education in
Rome before the onset of Hellenism and long before the literary qualities of classic culture, screened through the values of the Hellenistic
world, could have permeated Rome. The inauguration of education
in Rome coincided with the elemental organization of Roman society.
Rome's education could not have been a mere extension of the education in the Hellenistic world. Yet we cannot deny that Rome was influenced tremendously both by Greek and by Hellenistic educational
thought and practice.

In considering this question of influence, we must not overlook the complexity of man and the social institutions he creates, or try to put the various thoughts and practices of education in a neat chronology. In the context in which we are now working, we must keep two things in mind: We must recognize that Roman education, though possibly not Roman culture in a literary and aesthetic sense, was at one time autonomous, and we must also realize that the major movements in Roman education (movements recorded late in Rome's educational history) had their inspiration in Hellenism or classicism. We shall not, then, overemphasize the original autonomy, but we shall understand that Roman education was never a mere duplication of Greek or Hellenistic education. It could not have been, for it had its own traditions, and usually, considering the Roman mentality and allegiances, there was no other choice but to honor them.[1]

What were these traditions and how did they manifest themselves in education? We are thinking now of a time between the sixth and the fourth centuries B.C.

First of all, the early Romans were a rural people. They lived on the land, and they tilled it themselves. Even the Roman aristocrats were devoted to agricultural and rural pursuits. Their language, their buildings, and their values reflected solid, common origins. They had few illusions about education. There was no talk of liberal education, because it would not have meant anything to anyone. These people were for the most part farmers, and they expected very little from education; all they asked was that it initiate the young into contemporary society, that is, give them an understanding of the Roman way of life. This may not have been as easy a commission as it sounds or as the Roman people thought it, but at least it was less complex than the demand sometimes made upon education by other ancient societies. For example, the Greeks in Athens could ask education to perform the initiatory function and at the same time attempt to attain important cultural and literary objectives. Early Roman life was neither complicated nor pretentious; the traditions were solid and clear; Romans looked not for great or heroic deeds but for easily recognized and fundamental virtues. Society was simple. Education could therefore be simple and clear and still perform a role that was vital and essential. Its principal constituent was custom or tradition, and the typical Roman of the early days never tired of confirming the belief that what was good enough

[1] See Aubrey Gwynn, *Roman Education from Cicero to Quintilian,* Oxford University Press, New York, 1926, pp. 11–21; and Martin L. Clarke, *The Roman Mind,* Cohen and West, London, 1956, pp. 55–58.

for his ancestors was good enough for him and for his successors. This was a view from which Romans were not likely to stray.[2]

Such a philosophy of education—and who would doubt that it was a philosophy, albeit in a somewhat raw form—allows no place to the school. The relationship between theory and practice could be quite close and consistent; schools were not essential and were, therefore, rarely found. The family was the chief educational agency; it was the best, if not the only, school of the early Roman period.[3]

The Greeks, whose cultural and educational development was about two centuries ahead of the Romans in 600 B.C., could have taken a theoretical stand alongside the Romans on this matter of family education; but the Greeks hardly ever put their theory into practice. While emphasizing the importance of the family and its influence on the formation of youth, a Greek father could turn his son over to the care of a nurse or a pedagogue. Greek philosophers could argue about the moral training of children and insist that it was far too important a matter to be left to the schools; they could and did establish it as a family responsibility. Yet, in fact, the family seldom assumed the responsibility. For the Greek such questions were too often just academic. For the Roman family, education was not a matter of theory; it was a natural thing, to be realized in daily life.

While young and immature, children needed a mother's care and guidance. From her they learned what they needed to know first if they were to become worthy Roman citizens: the basic tools of learning (which may have included reading, writing, and elementary computation), and moral values. From this point on we hear almost nothing about the tuition of girls, and thus are led to believe that education became boy-centered. In any case, the father entered the picture, and now both domestic education and the preparation of a son for Roman life were in his hands. And here we come face-to-face with a distinctive technique in all (especially early) Roman education: learning by doing. Boys were schooled in what their fathers did. Fathers and sons were always together cementing a filial relationship, to be sure, but also laying the foundations for their next phase of life as Roman citizens.

The Latin ideal of family education set in a context of practicality was confirmed in daily life as the performance of high duty. With a

[2] See Tom B. Jones, *The Silver-Plated Age*, Coronado Press, Sandoval, N.M., 1962, pp. 23–31; and Donald C. Earl, *The Moral and Political Tradition of Rome*, Cornell University Press, Ithaca, N.Y., 1967, pp. 41–48.

[3] Plutarch *Education of Children* 4; see also András Alföldi, *Early Rome and the Latins*, University of Michigan Press, Ann Arbor, 1965, pp. 115–121.

constancy typical of Roman character, sense of duty knew neither peaks nor valleys in application. Yet emphasizing duty never meant that Roman fathers were prudish about the learning experiences their sons might have. A Roman boy could be seen in the banquet hall, at the gaming table, or at other places where a more sensitively moral people would think a properly mannered boy should not be, but wherever he was, in good surroundings or bad, he was with his father. Paternal instruction and care were not synonymous with austerity and self-denial; education under the auspices of parental masters could be fun, and on occasion even frivolous. But moral excellence and an inculcation of a high sense of duty were its expected outcomes. A father unable to mold his son in these educational objectives found society accepting few excuses for his ineptitude; his stature in the community was directly affected by the impression his son made. No wonder, then, that sense of duty was unwavering: its social reinforcements were too imposing to ignore.[4]

Another side of family education should be seen. It had to do with instilling pride in the family traditions along with the family's good name. Of course, the idea of family was as broad as its physical make-up, and this was very broad. Such a far-reaching concept of family, however, added to, rather than detracted from, the bulk of lore concerning family backgrounds. Here we come very close to the Greek ideal of the noble deed, an ideal that played an important role in early Greek education. In Rome, however, the ideal was far more social than it had ever been in Greece; and this social feature, we may insist, was distinctively Latin. As far as educational practice was concerned, this objective of instilling reverence for the family and its traditions was achieved through example and precept. Every Roman family was eager to build a fine and even enviable family tradition or to add to one already founded. In this respect Roman families were usually quite successful. It becomes apparent, now, how Roman education, in spite of its negligible intellectual content, could have had such an important influence on the essential fabric of Roman society.

EDUCATION AND THE PUBLIC MAN

Even though Roman education in its nascent years was practically oriented, it was spared both non- and anti-intellectualism. The relative

---

[4] Tacitus *Dialogue of the Orators* 28 says of a youth that "whether destined to be a soldier, jurist, or orator, his whole energies should be solely devoted to duty." See Ramsay McMullen, *Enemies of the Roman Order*, Harvard University Press, Cambridge, Mass., 1966, pp. 80–81.

absence of mental training was neither conscious nor planned, it would appear, and its inconspicuousness seems natural enough when we remember that early Roman culture itself was not very intellectual. Nevertheless, the whole of education and culture went beyond the family level. The family was a starting point, but the goal was the attainment of many virtues, one of which was absolute and unquestioning devotion to the community or the state. This high goal, too important to be left to chance or controlled only by a family, was an end to be achieved in public education. Every Roman youth of a good family—a citizen family—should be prepared for public life.[5]

One element in this preparation of a young man for public life was Roman law. Later in Roman history we see the evolution of a body and a philosophy of law and a system of legal education, but throughout most of Rome's early history law meant the laws of the Twelve Tables, and knowledge of the law meant memorizing the edicts. There is no need here for details on the laws of the Twelve Tables. Generally speaking, they were intended to regulate the social intercourse of the two major classes in Roman society, patricians and plebeians. Because these laws could claim to be an integral part of Rome's traditions and because a knowledge of law is an obvious and necessary part of the equipment of a public man, boys who were serious about a public career tried to achieve as complete an understanding as possible of the laws of the Twelve Tables. As to the laws themselves, the time of their origin is indefinite and has been ascribed to various periods from the early fifth century B.C. to the late third century B.C. Traditionally, the Tables were at first ten in number; two were added later. It has been maintained also that the laws were really Greek and that they were borrowed by the Romans. None of these esoteric items need delay us. We are interested in the content of the education of young men who were preparing for public life; the Twelve Tables formed part of that content.[6]

A boy's preparation for public life always remained a father's principal concern, but when he became sixteen, several important changes took place in his training. One was that his father was no longer so much in evidence; another was that his education, despite its lack of formality, assumed some professional dimensions. It all began with a ceremony reminiscent of old tribal initiations. The boy's life of family education and family control was terminating, and celebrating this liberation seemed justified. His toga, which had identified its wearer as a boy,

[5] H. I. Marrou, *A History of Education in Antiquity*, Sheed & Ward, Inc., New York, 1956, pp. 233–234; and Ramsay McMullen, *Soldier and Civilian in the Later Roman Empire*, Harvard University Press, Cambridge, Mass., 1963, pp. 180–185.

[6] Cicero *Laws* II. 23, 59.

was replaced by the *toga virilis*, the symbol of the young man. At long last a citizen and eligible for militiary service, the young man stood at the threshold of public life. Now, in preparation for a public career (for which he was still too young), he would face seasoning and a broadening of his range of experience designed to shape him for political destiny. (As we shall see, seasoning and experience had two more or less formal parts, the first of which took about a year.)

Roman fathers, we have said, never fully relinquished their authority over their sons' education. However, when a son reached this stage of development, common sense normally suggested at least some delegation of teaching and guidance functions. An old friend or relative—a man of public position, sagacity, and experience, who could be a tutor for a young man in the curricula of public life—was called in. Teaching was still learning by doing, although the platform for instruction was manifestly wider than anything the family could offer. As a boy, the candidate for public life followed his father from place to place; as a young man he similarly accompanied the public man who had agreed to take him under his wing.

The details of this public apprenticeship are often obscure: Where did the boy live? Were any expenses involved in his training? These are but two examples of inquiry that indicate how little we know about this kind of education. It is true that one or another historical figure has left an account of what happened to him as he passed through this educational period—Cicero is one—but the accounts can hardly be taken as typical.[7]

The next step in the preparation of the public man was military service. Possibly other societies regarded the attainment of military status as tantamount to citizenship and civic stature, but the Romans apparently did not. A young man became a citizen at sixteen. The Roman boy did not have to wait until his tour of military service was over, as the Athenian youth did, to have citizenship conferred upon him. However, while Athenian citizens were public men in every way that society wanted them to be by virtue of their citizenship, the Roman boy followed a long route toward this objective. One step along the way was military service.[8]

---

[7] Cicero *Laws* I. 13; Cicero *De Amicitia* 1; Pliny *Letters* VIII. 14; and Gwynn, *op. cit.*, pp. 64–65.

[8] See J. Carcopino, *Daily Life in Ancient Rome*, Yale University Press, New Haven, Conn., 1941; Thomas Woody, *Life and Education in Early Societies*, The Macmillan Company, New York, 1949, pp. 520–526; Cicero *Offices* II. 13; and H. E. L. Mellersh, *The Roman Soldier*, Taplinger Publishing Co., New York, 1965.

Although a good deal of information is available on the Roman military system, the details of the discipline of arms as it pertained to public education are not well known. Distinction in military service, especially in war, was the most certain path to greatness and to positions of honor and power in the state, and we may assume that young men pursuing public education were exposed to a period of military service of somewhat indefinite duration, in which they learned warlike ability, physical steadfastness, discipline, unflinching courage, and obedience. With the termination of a tour of military service, a young man was ready to take his place as a public man.

After this preparatory period—long or short, as the case may be— the young Roman was on his own. All his ideals had been shaped in such a way that service to the state belonged among them. But whether or not he became a public man or an exceptionally efficient public servant was up to him as well as to the fickleness of opportunity. In any event, the education we have described led young men up the ladder of public service. We cannot be certain that there were exact counterparts for this Roman practice in other early societies.

One more point ought to be mentioned in connection with education in early Rome. Whether boys were preparing for public life or looking forward only to the care of their own property, they were interested in physical fitness and sport.[9] Of course the Romans liked to think that whatever games or events they participated in had practical worth, and usually their play was useful to them in some way. Still, it would be a mistake to think that the Romans were not sport-minded. Roman children began with the usual games that all youngsters play, and as they grew older they took part in ball games, wrestled, ran, jumped, hunted, and rode horseback. Some of these sports were conducive to the skills needed in military activities, it is true, but we can suppose that sport was sometimes pursued simply for the sheer enjoyment of it.

Swimming was almost as important as walking; every Roman boy or girl knew how to swim. Dancing and music, though chiefly associated with religious cults and funeral processions, could be considered enjoyable in themselves. The Romans, however (and this may be why they are often thought to have forsaken sport), refused to give much public attention to competitive games; for them recreation was mainly a private matter. Despite this firmly held view, certain public games can be traced back to a very early period in Roman history. Sport in Rome was not essentially different from what it was in Greece, although the

[9] W. W. Fowler, *The Roman Festivals of the Period of the Republic*, The Macmillan Company, New York, 1925, pp. 35–40; and Woody, *op. cit.*, pp. 509–513.

Romans had no gymnasia, and in sporting events they would not expose their bodies.

Later Roman Education (275 B.C. to A.D. 300)

Built on the secure foundation of Roman tradition, later Roman education never forgot its past. This means that although the native traditions may have become pretty thoroughly interspersed with Greek influence and Roman innovation, they were still occupying an essential directive function. Romans did not want to betray their past. Yet Rome was in no position either socially or psychologically to escape the cultural influences that were appearing on her borders. Even had she wanted to, she could not afford to ignore them. Of these influences, along with a variety of internal circumstances that pleaded for change and updating, the most pervasive, permanent, and effective emanated from Hellenistic Greece.

It should be remarked here that the Romans were not trying to isolate themselves from the world around them. They were already committed to extending their sphere of authority, and in attempting to do so, they were brought in contact with a variety of cultures, many of which seemed to them to be superior to their own. Rome's political, military, and economic history, however, lies outside the ambit of this book.[10]

Despite an indigenous teaching tradition, Roman education underwent drastic changes, inspired by Greek models. And despite the existence of an autonomous and rural culture in early Rome, before this distinctive culture could be brought into reality and Rome thus extricated from barbarism, all kinds of classical and Hellenistic influences had descended on her.[11]

Perhaps the picture of Hellenistic influences descending on Rome is not as accurate as it should be. What actually happened was that the Roman Empire was being extended. With each new acquisition of territory, Rome met with cultural forces that affected her deeply. Undoubtedly a number of stages of Greek influence could be isolated, but their enumeration and analysis belong to other histories, and we shall content ourselves here with the conclusion that when Greater

[10] See M. Rostovtzeff, *The Social and Economic History of the Roman Empire*, Oxford University Press, New York, 1957, pp. 47–61; Michael Grant, *The World of Rome*, Weidenfeld & Nicolson, London, 1960, pp. 90–97; and Paul Louis, *Ancient Rome at Work*, Barnes & Noble, Inc., New York, 1965, pp. 111–116.

[11] Jones, *op. cit.*, pp. 38–59; Marrou, *op. cit.*, pp. 242–246; Gwynn, *op. cit.*, pp. 46–58; and Glen W. Bowersock, *Augustus and the Greek World*, Clarendon Press, Oxford, 1965, pp. 82–92.

Greece surrendered to Rome at Tarentum in 272 B.C., and when Rome became a bilingual empire with the annexation of Greece and other Macedonian and Asiatic provinces, these outside influences really began to be effective.[12] This is the beginning of a period of adaptation; it marks also the first steps in a Roman adoption of Greek culture.

GREEK INFLUENCE ON ROMAN EDUCATION

Important and interesting as they are, cultural evolutions cannot be traced in this book. We want to deal with only one part of that immense subject—educational evolution. When Greece made her educational conquest of Rome, both the content and the form of Roman education were changed in a number of important respects.

While remembering that Greek influence may always have had some role to play in Roman education, we must look for a really decisive influence. Perhaps we shall find it in the Greek slaves who were brought to Rome and made teachers. The earliest example of this custom is to be found in the teaching of Livius Andronicus, a Greek captured at Tarentum, who was finally emancipated after he had finished teaching his Roman master's children. With his freedom secured, he stayed in Rome and for the next sixty-five years functioned as a teacher and writer.[13]

Now a strange and often contradictory period in Roman education begins, with old customs and traditions, still objects of reverence, overlaid by a new education sought with eagerness and enthusiasm. Greek captives enjoyed an unusual reception in Rome, where now, rather than being treated as slaves, they were escorted to the classroom as teachers without ever having to answer any questions about their qualifications. The Romans wanted teachers of Greek, and were willing to take any they could get. Greeks brought exceptionally high prices in the slave market, yet since supply hardly equalled demand, as a matter of public policy Rome encouraged free Greeks to immigrate and enter the teaching profession in Rome.[14]

Why did the Romans want Greeks for their teachers? First of all,

[12] Theodor Mommsen, *The History of Rome,* Charles Scribner's Sons, New York, 1903, vol. III, p. 136; and Alexander H. McDonald, *Republican Rome,* F. A. Praeger, Inc., New York, 1966, pp. 60–65.

[13] W. C. Lawton, *Introduction to Classical Latin Literature,* Charles Scribner's Sons, New York, 1903, pp. 19–21; Cicero *Brutus* 72.

[14] Gwynn, *op. cit.,* pp. 34–41; A. S. Wilkins, *Roman Education,* Cambridge University Press, New York, 1914, p. 43; Moses Hadas, *History of Latin Literature,* Columbia University Press, New York, 1952, pp. 123–128; and Jones, *op. cit.,* pp. 49–51.

we must remember that Rome could boast of little in the way of a literary tradition. But a more complete answer is to be found in what may be called a Roman educational awakening. Tired of being thought barbarians, Romans wanted, more than anything else, to learn Greek and thus rise to a position of cultural equality with Greece. Yet, even while this motive was clear, some people in Rome wanted nothing whatever to do with Greek-inspired education. Whenever they gained power to do so, they proscribed by law not only the teaching of Greek but the teaching activities of Greeks in Rome as well.[15]

ELEMENTARY EDUCATION

Although Roman education was always affected to a certain degree by Greek teaching models, and in fact a point was finally reached in Roman educational history where the Greek influence became decisive, Rome tried to be loyal to her own past. Rather than let Greek education dominate the whole of Roman instruction, she developed an educational plan wherein her own as well as Greek cultural values could be realized. This plan promoted the founding of schools which while sharing the broad objectives of Greek teaching allowed Latin curricula to flourish. Competing with Roman schools, in which Latin was taught with a commitment to traditional Roman values, eventually were Greek schools delegated to a teaching of the classical Greek heritage.[16] What really came to exist, then, was a dual system of schools—the Latin and the Greek. (In historical focus, the evolution of dual instruction is seen to have been so slow that some Roman education, especially on the fringes of the Empire, may have totally escaped the effects of Greek influences upon it.)

Roman elementary schools, which must have germinated around the seventh century B.C., were reshaped by Greek influence before they could assume a definite and indigenous character. (The ideas that reading and writing were important school subjects prerequisite to formal literary instruction, and that such instruction was vital to the completion of the whole man, came from Greece by various indirect routes.) In the end, even this web of direct and indirect inheritance, woven around elementary education in Rome in order to preserve traditions of supreme cultural value, failed to make elementary schooling popular. Although by the third century A.D. elementary schooling

[15] Gwynn, *op. cit.*, pp. 63–65; and Charles H. Coster, *Late Roman Studies*, Harvard University Press, Cambridge, Mass., 1968, pp. 212–225.

[16] Marrou, *op. cit.*, pp. 255–265; and Pierre Grimal, *The Civilization of Rome*, Simon and Schuster, New York, 1963, pp. 424–428.

was available throughout the Empire,[17] another three hundred years passed before elementary schools were fully integrated with Roman life and society. But by then it was too late—not only for the schools, but for the Roman state.

What were Roman elementary schools like, and what did they teach? First of all we might mention that the term used by the Romans to designate an elementary school was *ludus*. Literally *ludus* meant sport, play, or game, but it would hardly be correct to assume that the boys and girls who attended Roman *ludi* were there to play games. Rome had a proud tradition of elementary literary and reckoning instruction; mothers had taught children their letters and their sums long before elementary education was institutionalized. This was important work, for which the mother was praised in those early years; it was no less important now when the teacher rather than the mother was the *litterator*.

The teacher, the *litterator*, was responsible for teaching reading, writing, and calculation in the school. Moral education, too, formerly the special prerogative of mothers and fathers, now seemed to be in the hands of the pedagogue. We have met the pedagogue before when he accompanied Greek boys to and from school; and now, largely because of the influence of Greece on Rome, we meet him again. If the Roman family had not actually relinquished its responsibility for the moral formation of children, it had at least delegated this important duty to the pedagogue. Whatever his relationship to the family, whether slave, servant, or trusted freeman, the pedagogue had at least a tangential relationship to elementary education, for he was concerned with his charge's manners and morals.

Elementary schooling began when boys and girls were about seven years old and lasted until they were about twelve. (The first elementary schools were ill-equipped: books, maps, handbooks, and most of the pedagogical appurtenances were absent. In the elementary schools of Republican times, however, books are said to have been plentiful.) The site of the school was a porch or a booth, and apparently no great effort was made to isolate the school from the traffic and distractions of everyday life. The discipline of the school was such that the young scholar had better tend to his schoolwork and ignore the outside world. The teacher on his raised platform, and the students surrounding him on the floor, plodded through a school day of reading, writing, and elementary calculation. Neither the teachers' methods nor the content of the subjects

[17] Wilkins, *op. cit.*, p. 43; and Solomon Katz, *The Decline of Rome and the Rise of Mediaeval Europe*, Cornell University Press, Ithaca, N.Y., 1966, pp. 43–51.

themselves were in the nature of good omens for teaching and learning, for the paralyzing effects of past practice (affected only slightly by instructional evolution) were everywhere in evidence. Roman elementary-school teachers were good imitators, but poor innovators.[18]

SECONDARY EDUCATION

Leaving the *ludi magister* and the elementary school, boys and girls privileged by social position to aspire to secondary education enrolled in the school of the *grammaticus*, the custodian of what we might call "general education." [19] Now literature and grammar (the latter a study of language structure) were unfolded before them. In fact, in most essential respects these Roman grammar schools duplicated the grammar teaching of Hellenistic schools. Put most briefly, grammar school education was expected to supply a fund of general knowledge and provide an instructional foundation for any subsequent professional or other higher study.

Secondary schools differed in some ways from the schools with which Roman youths presumably were familiar. As was true on the elementary level, separate school buildings were unavailable for secondary teaching, but special schoolrooms with a clearly academic decor were maintained, and the student, immunized from multiple distractions, was encouraged to study by the mere atmosphere of the place.

The *grammaticus*—the secondary-school teacher—wore a cloak whose attractive ornamentation added some color to the educational setting and made him feel important. (These teachers had to take their compensations where they could find them; they were not well paid.) Actually, both socially and financially, secondary-school teachers could lord it over their elementary-school counterparts, even though when doing so they had to recognize that their income was probably no greater than that of an ordinary tradesman. To add insult to financial insecurity, secondary-school teachers were forced to face the fact of social unacceptance and parental distrust. An old question is framed again: Can society expect to have the services of good, effective, and trustworthy teachers if it refuses to reverence and reward them? Rome ignored the question, took her teachers as she found them, and generally refused to award them distinction and respect.

Such conditions are, of course, always deplorable wherever they are

[18] See Jones, *op. cit.*, p. 43; and F. W. Householder, *Literary Quotation and Allusion in Lucian*, Columbia University Press, New York, 1941, pp. 80–85.

[19] Suetonius *Grammarians* 4–24; and Quintilian *Education of an Orator* I. i. 6–8, 9.

found. Yet it is possible to understand why the Romans may not have thought very much of their elementary-school teachers. They demanded very little from them and, of course, did not ask them to have any academic or scholarly qualifications. Anyone could have been an elementary-school teacher. But could the same be said of the *grammaticus?* Could anyone do what he did? It was not enough for him to know how to read and to be able to compute in whole numbers and fractions. The secondary-school teacher had to know grammar and literature. Any able teacher had to have some kind of academic background, for the content of the grammarian's teaching was something that had to be learned; it did not come from living. There was a certain inconsistency in seeing a Roman parent send his child to school, eager to have the child introduced to learning and culture, prizing them both highly, and yet refusing to value in any proper or realistic manner the work of the *grammaticus.*

We must always remember that there was no such thing as secondary education in Rome before the Greek slave-teachers brought a content to form it. Secondary education in Rome was Greek, and consisted largely of the study of the Greek classics. And if Roman youth were to study Homer and other accepted Greek authors, it is easy to see why schools were established for learning the Greek language.

Yet what appeared at first to be a decisive victory for a secondary education of a Greek type was subject to some cultural and educational annotation. Greek classics were translated into Latin. Livius Andronicus translated the *Odyssey*—in about the year 250 b.c., it is said—to begin a secondary education of a Latin type.[20] Homer's epics were not a national literature for the Romans; yet their hesitation in accepting them as a fixed content for secondary education could be moderated somewhat, because now, at least, the literature was in their own language. If they had had to depend on a national literature for the rise of secondary education, then Roman secondary schools would have been delayed for another century. Yet no one can be sure that this employment of Greek literature translated into Latin retarded the growth of Latin literature. As it was, when Virgil and Horace and other Latin writers appeared on the scene, Roman secondary schools were equipped to handle an authentic Latin literature. Even then, secondary education in Rome did not become exclusively Latin. The dual approach was still accepted, and Greek literature was still studied.

The other side of secondary education—grammar—was a little

[20] Gwynn, *op. cit.*, pp. 34–35; and Frank R. Cowell, *Cicero and the Roman Republic,* Chanticleer Press, New York, 1948, pp. 73–81.

slower than literature in making its Roman debut. Of course literature had a long time advantage over grammar. The former began with Homer; the latter waited for Dionysius Thrax. Dionysius was known in Rome very shortly after his work on grammar appeared, and was still as closely studied in Rome at the time of Virgil and Horace as he had been in the Hellenistic grammar schools. Although the grammar of Dionysius was not studied in Greek—it had been translated into Latin by Varro (116–27 B.C.)—in its essentials it was Greek grammar, and it was not accompanied by any transition to strictly Latin teaching. The great grammatical works of Donatus, Servius, and Priscian followed the grammatical path that Dionysius had blazed. The first textbook on Latin grammar, written by Remmius Palaemon, did not appear until the first century.[21]

When grammar seemed unreal, as it often did, literature made some effort to rescue learning from the pedantry into which grammar led it and to put it in a Roman, lifelike context. This was possible only after Rome had obtained a literary tradition and a literary content of its own, for before this was accomplished the Greek classics that were studied in the original or in translation were the only literature worthy of the name. For understandable reasons the Romans were most anxious to have their own literature. And once they had a literature of their own, they were impatient to study it, that is, to get it into the school's curriculum. So Latin works became part of the secondary school literary study even during the lifetime of their authors. This was an extremely unconventional innovation.

Because the Romans were thus disposed to take their Latin literature where they found it, there was a good deal of variety in the content and quality of the literary pieces studied in the schools. Yet what began as an ephemeral content did not remain in a state of flux. The giants in Roman literature began to assume their proper places, according to their tremendous literary strengths, and in time we find Virgil, Terence, Sallust, and Cicero the accepted and immovable authors of the Latin classics. At this point the evolution of Latin literature came to a halt. And from now on, humanistic education chose to look backward and defended the assumption that the content of these classics could never be improved upon; it could only be imitated.

Literary scholarship and the science of grammar were approached among the Romans much as they had been among the Hellenistic teachers and students. Their content was so little changed that we need

[21] H. Nettleship, *Lectures and Essays* (Second Series), Clarendon Press, Oxford, 1895, pp. 163–165; and William R. Halliday, *The Pagan Background of Early Christianity*, The University Press of Liverpool, Liverpool, 1925, pp. 50–60.

only refer the reader to the previous chapter, where the studies in the Hellenistic grammar schools were discussed.

HIGHER EDUCATION

Later Roman education was, as we have said, two-dimensional. One dimension was Greek, having evolved from Hellenistic cultural assumptions and pedagogic practices, and was accepted as prescriptive in the eastern half of the Roman Empire. The other dimension was Roman—though really a subtype of the Greek since it essayed to cover the same instructional ground, and merely added the study of Latin and Latin literature. (The higher it became, the more heavily it depended on authentic Greek models.) This latter type of Roman education was found in the western provinces, especially in Italy, North Africa, Spain, Gaul, and Britain. Thus, when we talk about Roman higher education, we really have Greek education in mind and, to some extent, are repeating much of what we already know about the higher schools of the Hellenistic age.

A Roman boy, after completing his studies in grammar, could go on to higher schooling and study rhetoric, which was aimed at teaching him how to master the art of oratory. There were rules, methods, and customs firmly entrenched in the rhetorical tradition, and all had to be learned exactly. Once this was done, a long period of practice in speaking began. The custodian of all this activity, and the finest example of Roman higher education—if we accept the common Roman opinion—was the school of rhetoric, presided over by the most illustrious of Latin schoolmasters, the rhetor. For the most part, teachers of rhetoric were independent masters who achieved a reputation for teaching oratory, and because of this reputation attracted students to their schools. The more success they enjoyed, the more elaborate became the setting for their instruction. Some had fine buildings for lecturing and study; most embellished their persons with ornate garments and used them as symbols of their professorships; a few were honored with appointments to high positions in government; one or two had their salaries paid by the state. But with or without these embellishments, even the best schools of rhetoric were not real universities, but independent institutes where a special kind of higher study was pursued.

With the completion of rhetorical study (the boy started his work in the school of rhetoric when he was about fifteen, and was ready to leave when he was about twenty), the formal education of most young Romans came to an end. Now they were ready to enter public life. But if a young man wanted to, he could continue his study of oratory, either with his former master or with a new one, or he could turn to the study of law, medicine, or philosophy. If he chose advanced instruction in oratory, a kind of postgraduate course, the student was treated to an interesting departure from academic rule and ritual, for advanced study in Latin rhetoric made a concession to reality and hoped to find its problems and its questions in the real social and political world. If medicine was the kind of post-rhetorical study the young man wanted, the calendar was again turned back to the Greeks: The student would attach himself to a physician and learn the practical side of medicine from him; for the theory of medicine he would read Galen. Post-rhetorical study in philosophy was occasionally decided on, but, despite the philosophers' claims to intellectual superiority in the Roman scholarly world of the day, philosophy was not a popular study. (For this it had mainly itself to blame, since it was concerned with the mysteries of the universe, and with other problems remote from man's life.) It was the extraordinary young man who chose to turn his back on Roman life and refused to heed the remark of Quintilian that some people who found the study of oratory too difficult became lawyers, while others turned to philosophy.

Rhetoric was indeed the prime study, with law next in importance. (The other higher studies, despite their unavoidable presence in an organized society, were insignificant by comparison.) Yet, when we look for an original feature to Roman higher education, we do not find it in rhetoric, but in law. The Romans created their own original type of higher education with their law schools. Without going into detail here on the Roman science of law or the Roman system of teaching law, we can say that the prospective lawyer always began his study with the grammarians and then turned to rhetoric, because every jurist was expected to know first how to interpret the authors, and then how to speak well. Besides, he had to know his law well enough to be able to cite the legal authorities, had to be aware of precedents of analogy or tradition, and was expected to administer the legal code with an elevated sense of justice, goodness, and order. Practitioners and teachers of law wrote systematic treatments of the elements of Roman law (for example, Gaius' *Institutes*), commentaries on the statutes, and books on legal procedure—books which quickly became classical because, being among the first, they were recognized as authoritative, and the teaching of law could be organized around them. Teachers of law, making full use of the experience they had in studying the poets and the other classical writers, could now devote all their talent to illuminating and interpreting the authors of the law books. These teachers began by working independently. However, as time passed and the law became more complex, and the need for specialists became more evident, they combined their efforts and organized their teaching in schools. It is interesting to note that these schools were not unlike contemporary colleges of law.[22]

DUALISM IN ROMAN EDUCATION:
ADDING TO THE CLASSICAL TRADITION

What began as a commitment to dualism in education—one system of schools for a Latin education and another system of schools for a Greek one—tapered off in time to the point where schools accepted a dual function. One part of this function was achieved by teaching Latin, the other was attained by teaching Greek. Some emphasis should be given to the compromise, because in accepting this dual function Roman schools began what has since been regarded as real classical teaching. In other words, the classical inheritance was contained in and communicated by both Latin and Greek. The man who was fully educated would know both languages and both literatures.[23]

This was an attitude which would come to be associated with classical teaching of a later period; it was not necessarily a natural outgrowth of classical thought, and it was obviously not a part of classical method. As a matter of fact, it is almost impossible to imagine the Hellenistic Greeks using Latin as a cultural instrument. They regarded Latin as inferior, not only because it was inadequate for communicating subtle scientific and philosophical ideas, but because it had no respectable cultural or literary traditions behind it. Only in one area of study had the Greeks accepted Latin; this was in the study of law, but law was hardly ever regarded as a study with cultural value. We know how the Greeks defined the word *barbarian;* their inflexible attitude as to the intrinsic superiority of the Greek language never changed. Bilingual classicism did not originate in Greek lands, and it never had Greek approval.

Rome took the heart of classical education and without changing it in any essential respects, preserved and transmitted this education to later generations. With Rome the classical influences became a glorious and revered heritage. How did this happen?

[22] See H. F. Jalowicz, *Historical Introduction to the Study of Roman Law,* Cambridge University Press, New York, 1952; and O. Schulz, *History of Roman Legal Science,* Clarendon Press, Oxford, 1946.

[23] E. P. Parks, *The Roman Rhetorical Schools as a Preparation for the Courts Under the Early Empire,* The Johns Hopkins Press, Baltimore, 1945; Hadas, *op. cit.,* pp. 141–145; and S. F. Bonner, *Roman Declamation,* University of California Press, Berkeley, 1950.

As Roman political influence was dispersed more and more widely, it became necessary for Roman officials to know many languages. In time most of these officials, who had to be prepared to go anywhere in the service of the Empire, achieved considerable fluency in Greek. There were obviously practical reasons for having Greek taught in the schools. But they were not the only or the real reasons. Romans were moving up in the world. They could look at their magnificent political and military accomplishments with approval. Where did Rome have a peer? Was beaten Greece, a country without military power or political influence, really Rome's equal? The practical-minded Roman could see that Greece was a conquered land, but when the Romans came in contact with the people, it was evident to them that the Greeks had a culture and a view of the world which the Romans could not claim. Even their language was a vehicle which could convey thought far better than the Roman tongue could. This seeming superiority of Greek gave the proud Romans feelings of inferiority with respect to their own language. As far as literature was concerned, they knew there was no argument. What Roman writer had Homer's stature?

If the Romans thought so highly of Greek, why didn't they simply adopt it as their own language? Such a question is too complex to answer here. Of course, it would have been entirely impractical to forsake Latin in favor of Greek. At least half of the Roman Empire was Latin. Romans had many allegiances, one of which was to their own language. Latin was the official language in most of the Empire, and was used in public documents and official proceedings. The public officer, however, who could meet the people in every corner of the Empire and converse with them in their own language was equipped for political effectiveness. This was a clever technique; but the official's linguistic skill was never an acknowledgment that any other language could preempt Latin as Rome's official tongue.

Multilingualism was found infrequently in Rome, but bilingualism was common. Its evolution began with a political or administrative motive and finally became a matter of cultural integration. During a time in Rome, marked out roughly by Cicero's lifetime (106–43 B.C.), this cultural integration was at its climax.[24] The two languages seemed to be entirely natural tools in the hands of an educated man. Cicero could write and speak and think in Greek as easily and as naturally as in Latin. And Cicero's excellence may well represent the apogee of this integration to which we refer. Before Cicero, culture was so tied to Greece that the Greek language was indispensable. Only a fool would

[24] Woody, *op. cit.*, p. 581; and Cowell, *op. cit.*, pp. 129–133.

claim to be an educated man unless he had all the classical tools, and the classical tools were still Greek.

Virgil and Horace changed this attitude. Roman education never ceased to be bilingual, because it was believed that there was something culturally superior about having a second language, and also, perhaps, because the Romans, like us, used another language to help in learning their own. But it was no longer necessary to study Greek literature in Greek and the new Latin literature in Latin. Translations were not necessary either; Latin literature was enough. Greek began to decline.[25]

The decline of Greek is evident after the time of Cicero. The Greek culture that seemed so natural to Cicero became for his successors little more than affectation. But the evidence of a decline does not explain it. Latin was more and more valued as a means of communication, and by the time the Christian Church adopted Latin as its official language, probably sometime in the early third century, the day of Greek had pretty well passed. Greek never recovered its position of superiority.[26]

Rome and the Future of Education

We are prone to yield to the temptation to look for ways in which Rome made original contributions to culture and learning, for generally speaking, we find it hard to separate high historical significance and creativity. Rome, however, was remarkably uncreative. The fact in no way destroys or even minimizes her historical worth. In spite of our categorical statement, we should not make the mistake of insisting that the Romans were never able to create anything. This would be a monstrous claim, and under no circumstances could it be justified. In culturally significant areas, however, though Rome was a great assimilator of culture and a great agent in spreading the culture she absorbed from others, she was not creative.

Rome excelled in administration. As she pushed her military authority into the Alexandrian world, she adopted and adapted. Rome was precocious, and what she learned so quickly and so easily she retained in her national memory. When she turned to other lands to conquer, she spread the culture she had absorbed. Although this appears now to have

[25] M. A. Cary, *A History of Rome Down to the Reign of Constantine*, St. Martin's Press, New York, 1938, p. 14; Joseph Vogt, *The Decline of Rome*, New American Library, New York, 1968, pp. 301–309; and John Dickinson, *Death of a Republic*, The Macmillan Company, New York, 1963, pp. 350–358.

[26] Rostovtzeff, *op. cit.*, pp. 33, 113, 191, 211; and Edward M. Pickman, *The Mind of Latin Christendom*, Oxford University Press, New York, 1937.

been a simple and easily executed policy of Romanization, it was really quite difficult. Even with the genius of Roman organization and executive ability, complete Romanization of "barbarian" lands was impossible. In the sense that success is a relative thing, the Romans succeeded, that is, they won more often than they lost. Yet they were not even successful in having Latin adopted as the general language of communication in all the lands over which their jurisdiction reigned. This goal was never fully achieved, although the Christian Church came closer to establishing Latin as a universal language than imperial Rome ever did.

The Roman schools of which we have spoken above were found in Rome proper. In republican days they were rarely found outside the city of Rome. The Empire enlarged their scope, but the Empire never succeeded or hoped to succeed in establishing a complete system of Roman schools everywhere in imperial Rome. Although the influence of Rome, both political and cultural, was ubiquitous in the Empire, formal education was not. Yet some schools could be found in every part of the Roman world, and by the time educationally minded emperors came into power in Rome, the Empire was ready for their policy of distributing education more generously throughout its extent.

In the early years, the Roman state had what we may call a laissez-faire policy with respect to education. This policy did not change materially until the Empire came into being. Hellenistic Greeks thought they saw the first signs of Rome's barbarism in her apparent indifference to education, but in this matter they read signs poorly. Although Rome had no official policy of providing for education, the state's laxity in establishing schools never meant that the Romans ignored education. If we may depart a little from our main theme here, we can call attention to the cultural blindness of the Hellenistic Greeks and the weakness they shared with many states—and individuals—in interpreting all values in the light of their own and in evaluating all social functions by the part they played in them. Had the Hellenistic world been only a little more alert, it would have seen that classical Greece pursued the same noninterventionist policy in education that republican Rome accepted.

Throughout a great part of Rome's history, she had neither a plan for compulsory education nor a system of schools supported by the state. From time to time a man of some importance and wealth helped establish a school and prevailed upon the public treasury to share some of the cost with him. But a few schools of this type do not make a system nor would they justify the conclusion that the Roman state had entered the business of education. Late in the Republic, the state became more active in encouraging education. Under Augustus education was given even further encouragement: In a decree proclaiming the banishment of all foreigners from Rome, teachers and physicians were made exceptions. Vespasian, though he had banished philosophers from Rome, lent his support to rhetoricians and established a professorship of rhetoric, to which the first appointee was the great Quintilian. Besides, the emperors built libraries and collected books; they subsidized teachers and exempted them from taxation and military service; and finally they endowed chairs of teaching outside Rome and made grants to the various cities and towns to establish schools.

In return for its generosity, the Roman state demanded considerable control over education. When teachers' salaries were paid from the public treasury, the emperor wanted his agents to have a decisive voice in appointing teachers; when teachers of rhetoric and philosophy were awarded honors and money, the emperors wanted them to sacrifice some of their freedom of thought and liberty of expression. Thus public or state assistance to teachers and schools was not an unmixed blessing; control followed the funds. Eventually, because state control over education in Rome moved steadily forward, the state assumed that it could suspend, direct, or completely proscribe all teaching whenever it saw fit. Two emperors, Theodosius and Valentinian, forbade the opening of schools without the state's prior approval, and Justinian issued his notorious edict in A.D. 529, closing the schools of philosophy and law in Athens and all higher schools in Rome, save those engaged in the teaching of law.

Summary

Rome had a teaching tradition of her own. During the early years of Roman education, probably before the third century B.C., the practical orientation of the Romans is clear. Education was organized so young people would be prepared to take their place in society. Since literary achievements were not generally recognized, they found little recognition in the educational program. During this early period the child—usually a boy—was trained or educated first by his mother, next by his father, and then by a relative of position or a public man of trust. Finally he fulfilled his debt of military service to the state. By then he was a citizen, and he was on his way to becoming a public man.

This kind of education changed somewhat when the Greek influence began to invade Rome. The change was not so drastic, however, that it eroded archaic practices. Rather, it added something to the Roman educational model that was not there before. What was added was the Greek school. Thus, side by side, the Roman school and the Greek school enjoyed Roman confidence and patronage.

Finally, the Greek educational influences became so strong and the parallel system of schools so unwieldy that the Romans adopted an educational organization with only one school, which offered both Greek and Latin studies. At first the Greek studies predominated because of the greater reputation of Greek literature. Yet when Latin literature (Virgil, Horace, Cicero) gained status, its school standing equaled Greek literature.

In the later period the Romans took the educational organization and program of the Hellenistic Greeks, adapted them somewhat to their own needs, and continued this type of education in a system of schools that lasted as long as the Roman Empire lived. When the Empire died, the schools died with it.

Rome's chief importance in the history of education is that she preserved Greek and Hellenistic education and spread it throughout the Roman world.

VI

Roman Educational Theory

By about 150 B.C. most educated Romans were bilingual, speaking both Latin and Greek, for the cultural inadequacies of their own national background had convinced them that their vernacular—Latin—was not enough if they wanted to be truly civilized men. Yet, aside from issues of cultural inferiority, always deeply felt by Romans, there was the matter of patriotism to be considered: Should a good Roman citizen be allowed to forget Rome's national past and enthusiastically embrace the Greek cultural inheritance?

By Cicero's time (106–43 B.C.), Roman educators were in a dilemma: On the one hand, they recognized the absolute necessity of depending heavily on the Greek intellectual and literary inheritance; on the other, they were often forced by public policy to jettison outright, or at least to go through the motions of discarding from the schools, everything lacking an authentic Latin character. We know from various sources, for example, of an official and studied opposition to Greek culture, and we know, too, of a special aversion to the study of Greek rhetoric.[1] From time to time, laws were enacted which closed schools of Greek rhetoric and philosophy in Rome, or banished all Greek teachers therefrom. No doubt these laws were seldom enforced with any degree of vigor, yet they are evidence of an official and public attitude toward non-Latin studies. The fact that Latin study without some help and reinforcement from Greek sources—and sometimes from Greek schoolmasters—was impossible, did not trouble the lawmakers. But where the legislator could ignore the obvious and quickly discard the rich Greek scholarly appurtenances, the Roman educator was unavoidably charged with making over Roman education, keeping such Greek implements as were essential but making them appear to be fundamentally and authentically Roman. This was no easy task, but it was a commission the Roman educational theorist could not ignore.

If the course of Roman political history had been different, it would have been possible for Roman educational practice to take its direction from Greek or Hellenistic theory. As it was, however, Roman educational theory was required to strike out on its own and, by careful concealment of what was really Greek in origin and elaboration, to make Roman pedagogy appear as a product of Roman national life. This strange anomaly of history can neither fully explain nor justify the rationale of Roman pedagogic theory, nor can it account for the undoubted genius of Cicero and Quintilian, the principal spokesmen for the oratorical code in Roman teaching. It can, however, tell how Roman educational theory got its start.

With this beginning, Roman educational theory could move forward to truly remarkable heights, motivated first by Cicero's reasoned doubt that everything the Greeks had said about a decent education had immediate application to a Roman citizen, and second by the idealistic visions of Cicero and Quintilian to set a direction for education wherein the highest type of personal culture could be guaranteed.

Once Romans understood that everything the Greek theorists had said was not above doubt, and, moreover, that many of their theories lacked a clearly practical ring, they could become excited about a philosophy of education that appeared to be a product of their own reasoning. And many Roman writers, from Cicero to Vitruvius to

[1] See Aubrey Gwynn, *Roman Education from Cicero to Quintilian,* Oxford University Press, New York, 1926, pp. 59–69.

Quintilian, including Sextus Empiricus, Varro, Verrius Flaccus, Pliny the Elder, Palaemon, Aulus Gellius, Marcus Aurelius, and the two Senecas, grappled with various sides of educational theory. Yet, the standards of excellence for educational theory in Rome, and for educational practice outside of Rome for the next 1,500 years, were set not by the ephemeral Latin writers, who now and then took pedagogical theory for their subject, but by the giants of Roman education theory: Cicero and Quintilian.[2] For insights into later educational practice and the theory guiding it, more than for an elaboration or description of a Roman system, we turn now to an examination of their principal educational views and attitudes.

Marcus Tullius Cicero (106–43 B.C.)

Marcus Tullius Cicero exerted a greater influence upon Roman education during the latter part of the Republic than any other man of his time. He was Rome's leading orator and statesman. He was exceptionally proficient both in rhetoric and philosophy, and wrote much on those subjects as well as on politics and education. Cicero was not an educator. Even his educational writings did not express the point of view of an expert in the subject, but sprang from a knowledge of the fundamental place that education must occupy in society and of the demands that society makes on educated men. Thus *De Oratore* (The Orator), in which most of his educational views are to be found, is an expression of the ideas of an educated man about the purposes and methods of a system of education through which he himself had passed; it is an expression, moreover, of his convictions as to education's practical results. His writings on education are often in the nature of reflections, and they should not be taken as descriptive accounts of the conduct of the schools during this period of Roman history.

Cicero was the son of a Roman knight. His family was relatively new. In Rome he received an excellent education in Greek rhetoric and was also well educated in law. At seventeen he served in the army. He became a pleader in the courts at twenty-five, but ill health forced him to retire from this line of work for two years. During this period of inactivity he studied philosophy in Rhodes and Athens, then returned to Rome and resumed his legal career. He became the greatest of Roman orators and one of the outstanding writers of the golden age of Roman literature. His influence is felt even today.

De Oratore, published in 55 B.C., contained the basic principles

[2] See William M. Smail, *Quintilian on Education,* Oxford University Press, New York, 1938, pp. xxviii–xxx.

which Cicero felt were necessary for an orator's education. He distinguished between technical training and general education, or liberal culture. He insisted that the orator needed a broad, well-rounded, and general education in the liberal arts as a basis for the higher professional education of oratory. This liberal education was also considered necessary for success in professional and public life.

The branches of study that he included in this well-rounded education were grammar, literature, logic, geometry, astronomy, music, physics, history, civil law, philosophy, and rhetoric. Cicero claimed that philosophy gave substance to rhetoric. He was the first Roman theorist to endorse history as a valuable study, especially national history. He wrote that "if an orator knew not history, he remained always a child." A well-rounded education should be supplemented with wide experience, upon which the orator could always draw. In addition, it was Cicero's constant claim that the purpose of study was for usefulness in public and private life and not for knowledge alone.[3]

DE ORATORE

Compared to Cicero's other writings on education (*De Inventione, Partitiones Oratoriae, De Officiis, Brutus,* and *Hortensius*), *De Oratore* is the most complete and contains the fundamentals of his doctrine; in addition, among his many dialogues, it had the most profound and permanent influence on Western culture.

We have already said in a general way that Cicero wanted, or felt compelled, to reform Roman education. Reform was dictated by the adamant attitudes influential Romans had formed about the Greek heritage in their schools and culture. But this was only part of the story, for Cicero had ideas of his own about education, distilled from his own schooling, private study, and public life in the courts, and he was sincerely interested in upgrading the educational programs of Rome. The fact that his interest (like Quintilian's) extended only to the upper classes should not detract from its genuineness. This was a public motive; besides he had personal reasons for writing *De Oratore.*

After an interlude of political exile from Rome, Cicero wanted to employ a fairly safe vehicle for bringing his name again into public view. Education was a public issue of consequence and always worthy of a Roman citizen's attention, but it was neither a burning political issue nor an especially dangerous one. Cicero could satisfy his ambitions for the time being with a polished essay on education and not jeopardize

[3] Cicero *De Oratore* I. 45–73.

his recent political reinstatement in Rome . In addition, a new dialogue on education could give him an opportunity to correct and improve upon an educational tract of his youth, a work he called "schoolboy notes," *De Inventione*. Finally, Cicero's son, ten years old when *De Oratore* was published, and a nephew a year older, were at a stage in their intellectual development where a carefully reasoned guide to their future schooling could be useful. Thus in *De Oratore* we find Cicero proceeding from mixed motives—some clearly personal and practical, others infected with an idealism worthy of his genius.[4]

Following ancient traditions in educational writing, Cicero almost ignored the child's first years—a huge difference from Quintilian's approach—to tackle the problem of schooling when the student is ready for rhetoric and literature. What has taken place before is important, to be sure, but it is mainly a parental duty. Cicero wanted, at one and the same time, to show his allegiance to Rome's teaching tradition (by confirming the precedents of parental responsibility for elementary teaching), and to absolve himself from treating of the details of primary education. Besides, in the *Partitiones Oratoriae* he had already said as much as he thought needed to be said about infant education. Yet, in neglecting to go into detail about the child's early education, Cicero may have misread a major change in Roman life: many parents, now too busy to direct the elementary education of their children, were employing instead teachers or tutors. Cicero himself followed this practice with his own son and nephew.[5]

Since *De Oratore* was planned as an essay on oratory (it is by no means a manual or a handbook), its principal concern is with the teaching of rhetoric. It sets high goals for oratorical education. But it is, and does, far more, for ultimately it is a manifesto and guide for the formation of a public man whose culture is both broad and noble. Following Cicero's program, the boy begins his serious postelementary study with the liberal arts: literature, rhetoric, philosophy, mathematics, music, astronomy, geometry. The list of the arts given by Cicero reminds us of the seven arts later codified by Cassiodorus.[6] Varro, in his *Disciplinae*, added medicine and architecture; and Vitruvius, writing for future architects, supplemented the list with drawing, optics, history, and law. But all the lists had literature—or grammar, as it was commonly

[4] R. R. Bolgar, *The Classical Heritage and Its Beneficiaries*, Cambridge University Press, Cambridge, 1954, pp. 30–32.

[5] Gwynn, *op. cit.*, p. 80.

[6] See Cassiodorus Senator, *An Introduction to Divine and Human Readings*, translated, with an introduction and notes, by Leslie Webber Jones, Columbia University Press, New York, 1946.

called—and rhetoric as part of a fairly regular curriculum of studies. The fact that Cicero embraced the conventional arts is not the critical point: *when* and *how* the arts were to be taught is the instruction which puts Cicero in a class by himself.

The product of a good education is, according to Cicero, the true orator—the public man capable of thinking, speaking, and acting in a praiseworthy way. In order to become a true orator, one needs a broad preparation which, because of its breadth, is the most difficult of all formal learning. An orator must speak well, and thus must know how to use not merely his voice, breath, tongue, but (especially at a time when the law of gesture still dominated public speaking) his whole body. Too, his memory must be improved by exercise, for the assumption is constant that every prospective orator not only will be endowed with excellent native speaking talent, but will already have a growing stock of examples and illustrations ready for use.

The studies Cicero envisions for the future orator are numerous and detailed, since "No man can be an orator possessed of every praise-worthy accomplishment unless he knows everything important and all liberal arts." [7] Poets and historians are singled out for special attention, although all writers in the arts and sciences must be studied with care. Law and political philosophy must also be studied, for no public man can speak convincingly without certain knowledge of both. Cicero goes out of his way to endorse the content of learning, which in the end is what is distilled into the matter of a speech, but affirms that form is important, too. The ancient dictum, sometimes attributed to Socrates, that "All men are sufficiently eloquent in that which they understand," is rejected by Cicero and replaced by his advice that polished expression is a separate accomplishment to be cultivated by the future orator.

With this Ciceronian emphasis on eloquence, which comes from a special study of the subject and is not naturally attached to an intellectual mastery of any field of knowledge, we come face-to-face with Cicero's theory of rhetoric. Stripped of its erudite technicalities (which, in any case, were never so abundant as in Quintilian's pedagogical work), we find *De Oratore* saying that the duties of the secondary-school teacher are "to comment on the poets, to teach history, to explain the meaning of words, to impart correct accent and delivery." [8] The first part of the admonition is directed at both the authors to be studied, and the teacher's interpretation of them; the last part, "to impart correct accent and delivery," is the work of a professor of eloquence, the expert

[7] Cicero *De Oratore* I. 6.

[8] *Ibid.*, I. 187.

in teaching rhetoric. Whether there were two teachers, or only one, should make no matter—and we are led to believe that in Cicero's time the Romans were content to allow the distinction between grammatical and rhetorical teaching to be blurred—for Cicero is less concerned with the specialization of teachers than he is with their special functions in the classroom. In any case, secondary schools must handle both branches of education considered essential by Cicero: knowledge and eloquence.

When their secondary-school work was concluded, students should be ready for more advanced teaching—especially in rhetoric but also in philosophy, history, and law—and for practical experience in the courts and in public life. Taking a leaf from the book of his own educational experience, Cicero counsels learning by doing. But only up to a point, he says, for though experience in the courts can never really be substituted for in the classroom, men do not become good speakers merely by speaking (although by speaking badly they surely become bad speakers).[9] One avenue to good speaking, in addition to the techniques about platform performance, which can be taught, is extensive writing. Cicero is on record as saying that writing is the best "teacher" of oratory; even the orator called upon to speak without notice is able to reproduce the character of what was written previously, and whatever he says, regardless of its shortcomings, will be better than if nothing had been written. And finally, Cicero recommends imitation of the best models as another way to achieve excellence in oratory.[10]

When Cicero handled the question of the choice of authors, he touched also on the language—Greek or Latin—to be preferred in study. The Greek authors were judged best, although there is the faint hope, in Cicero's comments, that Latin literature might some day be qualified to take its place alongside the Greek, or even preempt it. The same thing could be said about language: Cicero liked Latin and paid allegiance to it (no true Roman could do otherwise), but he nevertheless preferred Greek to Latin as a medium for instruction. In Cicero's writings there is the implication that these preferences are forced upon him by the current state of Latin literary culture; Quintilian, on the other hand, seems to see a metaphysical superiority in Greek language and literature.[11] If we can suppose that Cicero left slightly ajar the door of culture to allow Latin's admission at some future time, we can also believe that Quintilian used all his artistry to close the door tightly.

[9] *Ibid.*, I. 33.

[10] *Ibid.*, II. 22.

[11] See Edward J. Power, *Evolution of Educational Doctrine,* Appleton-Century-Crofts, Inc., New York, 1969, pp. 94–95.

The foregoing issues were important to Cicero, and he never neglected them, but he was always anxious, as in Book III of *De Oratore,* to involve himself in the theory and technique of rhetoric. We have already noticed his willingness to admit practical experience to rhetoric's broad course, but we are always aware that more must be added. Cicero was convinced that existing schools of rhetoric were inadequate and that they often did more harm than good. Their teachers taught an academic rhetoric, were themselves without experience as public speakers, and were preoccupied with the tricks of debate. This type of rhetorical teaching, Cicero said, should be replaced by a more responsible oratory, one aimed at important public issues. In other words, deliberative and judicial oratory should be given pride of place, and epideictic oratory should have a clearly subordinate role.

On this level of choice of oratorical type, Cicero remained true to his own plan and always advocated responsible speech on issues of public significance. He was, thus, ready to jettison the purely literary oration which had been inherited in Rome from the Hellenistic cities. But in discarding the literary oration as a type of rhetoric, Cicero never meant to expurgate the techniques of oratory or the technicalities of rhetoric from higher education. For the most part, these mechanics of oratory were of Greek invention and Cicero, although often appearing to be uneasy in discussing them, is surely content to retain them. So in the end, Cicero's reform of rhetoric was not predicated on eliminating an arsenal of rules and technicalities, but on assigning to rhetoric a higher public purpose, and providing literary models for embellishing that purpose. The polished orator was, to his mind, always the best example of the educated man.

Still, this is only part of the Ciceronian educational code; what remains allows us to think of the orator as both a philosopher and a civilized, cultured human being. Cicero, we see now, wanted education to produce more than just a good speaker or a deep thinker. He wanted to unify both. In a way, he revives the old arguments between Plato and Isocrates when he considers the reciprocal arrangements between philosophy and rhetoric not only in formal learning but in practical life as well. Perhaps Isocrates and Plato were promoting incompatible goals in their own day, although it would seem that their refusal to find a compromise rested not on essential points but on their own vested interests.[12] Cicero was freed from such dilemmas, for he had no established school to protect. Looking forward to the best in education, he called for accommodations between philosophy and oratory: If one

[12] *Ibid.,* pp. 75–77.

wants to call the philosopher, "who instructs us fully in things and words, an orator," he is satisfied; or if one prefers to consider the orator, who represents "wisdom united with eloquence, a philosopher," he will not quibble over names.[13] The fully educated person, Cicero avers, is at once more than a philosopher or an orator. To educate such a person, he wrote, the lesson of his dialogue should be followed: "No man has ever become a great orator unless he has combined a training in rhetoric with all other branches of knowledge," [14] and "No one can hope to be an orator in the true sense of the word unless he has acquired knowledge of all the sciences and all the great problems of life." [15]

This is a huge order for teaching and learning, for at the very least the ideal orator would be not only a master of eloquence, but also a master of ethics, psychology, history, law, military and naval science, medicine, and the natural sciences. Cicero is duplicating the Hellenistic ideal of universal culture, and he may be asking for too much from the busy citizen who must also involve himself in life. At any rate, the educational task as Cicero describes it early in *De Oratore* is really too great to be handled completely in one book on the subject, so Cicero decides to treat of those subjects which are of immediate value for judicial and deliberative oratory: history, law, and philosophy.[16] And here there is a guarded assumption that the essential elements of liberal education falling outside these studies have been taught in the lower schools.

History, which had a special value for Cicero (as it had for all Romans) was given an enviable position in Roman schools, but it was never taught as a separate subject. It was really attached to, and in a sense was intended to illuminate, literature. Its accomplishments along these lines, however, were hardly noteworthy, and Cicero was keenly aware of this. He changed the thrust of history teaching and, without divorcing it from literature entirely, gave it both a pragmatic and a nationalistic orientation: "To be ignorant of what happened before you were born, is to live the life of a child forever. For what is man's life, unless woven into the life of our ancestors by the memory of past deeds?" [17] This is high praise indeed, but what Cicero really means is that history, in addition to linking us with the past, is an inexhaustible storehouse of rhetorical illustration. "The first rule of history," Cicero maintained in *De Oratore*, "is to say nothing wilfully false; the second,

[13] Cicero *De Oratore* III. 19–35.
[14] *Ibid.*, II. 5.
[15] *Ibid.*, I. 20–21, 72.
[16] *Ibid.*, I. 21.
[17] Cicero *The Orator* 120.

wilfully to suppress no truth." [18] He wanted emphasized in all history teaching an accurate knowledge of chronology (in which Roman schoolboys were then deficient), historical insights into the standards of public morality, and the historical influences of great personalities. These should form the core of history, Cicero says, and they must be taught without too much attention to literary ornamentation.[19]

Because an orator will almost inevitiably have a public position, he must be well-versed in law. This is a subject with which all Romans should have felt at home and Cicero, we should think, would have an entirely clear position. In a way he disappoints us, for, although in *De Oratore* he appears to favor an extensive study of public and private law as complementary to the ideal education he recommends, there is a suggestion that law and oratory may be separate sciences, each with its own special clientele.[20] In any case, Cicero's future orator must know *some* law, and he should aim not merely at presenting issues in the courts but at sharpening a judicial demeanor, and thus at an upgrading of the administration of public law.

Finally, philosophy enters the curriculum, for the true orator can never be devoid of wisdom. Cicero rejects the primitive standard—"An abundance of matter will give abundance of words—" [21] to state his own principle: "The choice of words, their proper place, and rhythm is easily learnt, or can be picked up without any teaching. But the matter of oratory presents a vast field, which the Greeks have neglected and have thereby been the cause of making our young men ignorant even in their knowledge." [22] The function of philosophy is to correct the defects in an orator's education; its aim is to instill wisdom. Philosophical study must consist of reading the best philosophers; Cicero recommends Plato, Aristotle, Chrysippus, Themistocles, Pericles, Theramenes, Gorgias, Thrasymachus, and Isocrates.[23] But philosophy is not merely a matter of reviving the arguments and counterarguments of the ancients. Rather, in Cicero's program, it is a means for getting the orator involved in life's deepest problems and of giving him a foundation from which he may make eloquent pronouncements about the burning issues of the day.

Cicero's educational program was composed mainly of five studies: literature, rhetoric, history, law, and philosophy. Coupling them with

[18] Cicero *De Oratore* II. 62–64.
[19] *Ibid.*
[20] *Ibid.*, I. 166–203, 234–255.
[21] *Ibid.*, III. 125.
[22] *Ibid.*, III. 93.
[23] *Ibid.*, III. 59.

experience in the practical necessities of life in a careful, dedicated way should produce Cicero's perfectly educated human being, "the cultured orator. Grant me that such a man is also a philosopher, and the controversy is at an end." [24]

Marcus Fabius Quintilianus (A.D. 35–97)

Quintilian was born in Calagurris in Spain about A.D. 35. He was educated as a public man in Rome and returned to his native Spain when he was about twenty-five years old. In Spain he practiced the arts of oratory. About the year 68 he was invited to return to Rome, where he acted as a pleader in the courts and as a teacher of rhetoric, and in both activities enjoyed more than usual success. In A.D. 76, when Vespasian arranged for teachers of rhetoric to receive salaries from the public treasury, Quintilian became a public teacher. He retired from teaching about the year 88, and devoted himself to study and writing. In A.D. 96 he published his famous book on the education of an orator, *Institutio Oratoria* (*Education of an Orator*). Quintilian was able to write from his eminent position as Rome's most cultured and successful teacher with more than twenty years' experience. His theories on education were responsible for setting the pattern that Latin grammar schools followed for centuries.

Institutio Oratoria consists of twelve books. The greater part of the work is a technical discussion of rhetoric and the role that rhetoric should occupy in secondary and higher education. The goal of this kind of education was the making of an orator, a public man, and Quintilian's treatise was intended to give direction to schools and schoolmasters for educating young men for oratory. Book I and Book II are devoted to details of educational methods, content, and organization of schools. Books III through VII are concerned with the study of the rhetorical device of invention. Books VIII through XI contain Quintilian's views on elocution, memory, and pronunciation. Book X contains what is probably the first formal list of "great books." Book XII turns its attention to the orator himself and asks what kind of person he should be and what moral stature he should have. Considering both the breadth and the attention to detail of Quintilian's *Institutes* it is not surprising that this work came to be the final and standard book on the theory and practice of Roman oratory, and that it is universally recognized as the most elaborate and most complete treatise on Roman education ever written.[25]

[24] *Ibid.*, III. 142–143.
[25] Bolgar, *op. cit.*, p. 346; Smail, *op. cit.*, pp. lii–lv.

EDUCATION OF AN ORATOR

After twenty years of teaching, and not yet an old man, Quintilian retired from his post as public professor of Latin rhetoric and looked forward to a life of enjoyment and leisure. But his greatest accomplishment was yet to come. Friends convinced him to write an educational guide or handbook which they might use in directing the education of their own children. Quintilian accepted this friendly commission and performed it with unusual care—aware, no doubt, that his own two sons might also benefit from what he had to say. (We see here a parallel between Quintilian's motives for involving himself in the theory of education, and Cicero's. For Cicero, too, had members of his own family in mind when he wrote *De Oratore.*) Quintilian wrote for two years, and at the end of that time was able to show the finished work, *Education of an Orator*, to his friends. They must have been impressed, as we are, at the breadth of this opus, which is rather more than a simple guide to the education of children. It purports to be, and to a great extent is, a discussion of the multiple issues surrounding teaching and learning from a child's birth to his final formation as an accomplished orator.[26]

QUINTILIAN'S THEORY OF TEACHING

Quintilian begins his discourse with preliminary studies—those most appropriately followed at home. The customs of Roman education, having by now been reformed from archaic practices assigning to mothers the role of infant teaching, allowed parents the alternative of delegating infant education and training to domestic nurses. Thus the nurse, or governess, was a teacher during the most critical period of formation, and it was with her qualifications that Quintilian concerned himself. Nurses were of course freed from literary teaching, which was the principal avenue to intellectual culture, but they were in an ideal position for laying the foundations for it: Throughout Quintilian's theory of education, the acquisition of moral virtue always precedes intellectual development.

Quintilian refused to write any justification for a parental abdication from the responsibilities of moral teaching. He goes into great detail in his emphasis on the role of the nurse, but he is also fully aware of parental qualifications and responsibilities for shaping a child's character. Because Quintilian's recommendations on this point are incomplete, we are left with the precise knowledge only that he wanted to emphasize parental responsibility: Parents might not themselves become

[26] Quintilian *Institutio Oratoria*, preface, 4–9.

pedagogues, but they were always charged with superintending the educational process.

Obviously it is too much to suppose that parents will always be with their children. Nurses, too, must allow time for free play. There are, then, periods when children are left to themselves. Yet, according to Quintilian, these free hours, reserved supposedly for leisure and recreation, are often as formative as the hours spent in learning the intellectual lessons of the schoolmaster or the moral lessons of the pedagogue. During these times of freedom, children must not be left unguarded or unguided. Here, for the first time in the history of educational theory, attention is called to the guidance of informal learning where the principal tools of learning are a child's companions.

We should pause to note Quintilian's silence on the subject of girls. Our references to his comments on children are to boys. Indeed, the whole of *Education of an Orator* is devoted to boys. In ignoring girls, Quintilian both confirms a precedent, and sets a course that is to be honored almost without question for the next thousand years.

At this point, Quintilian wants parents and nurses to assess the qualifications of a boy's companions. Just what the guardians of youth were to seek in playmates is unclear, but Quintilian's recommendation is clear: The informal activities of boys are to be supervised and watched with unusual diligence. Not to do so is to run the risk of having the good work of the home jeopardized on the playground; to supervise them carefully is to guarantee a strengthening of home-instilled character through life's daily contacts. Some educators before Quintilian may have seen the importance of informal education, but none before him had with so much precision set the theoretical foundation for the environment of moral education.

The place of parents and nurses in handling the education of the young belongs under the general heading of early home training, and this is two-sided. One side is moral (and Quintilian wants to lay this foundation carefully), and the other is intellectual. We can understand Quintilian's determination to combine these two sides when we recall his educational aim: the perfect orator. He tells us this about the orator: "the first essential for such an one is that he should be a good man, and consequently we demand of him not merely the possession of exceptional gifts of speech, but of all the excellences of character as well." [27]

In our study of Greek education we listened to spokesmen praising moral education, and by now we understand something of both the order and the meaning of character education. Isocrates had argued that men are good after they have come to appreciate their intuitions of

[27] *Ibid.*, I. i. 9.

virtue; but Plato rejected Isocrates' argument to maintain that knowledge of virtue was an outcome of long and profound study. Quintilian seems to stand with Isocrates, and at the same time tends to discredit the Platonic version of philosophy:"For I will not admit that the principles of upright and honorable living should, as some have held, be regarded as the peculiar concern of philosophy." [28] Isocrates' influence on Quintilian is in fact so great that we find him repeating the counsel of the most famous schoolmaster of antiquity with his assertion that the ideal orator is the only person who can make an authentic claim to the title of philosopher. Before education in oratory starts, Quintilian says, young men should have their habits in the art of right living; and these habits come more from practice than from learning.

In establishing perfect oratory as the aim of an educational program, Quintilian sometimes is thought to have aimed too high. Undoubtedly the goal he has in mind is difficult of attainment, but perfect eloquence, though seldom attained, is not beyond the reach of a human intellect. He justified his high goal this way: "Those whose aspirations are highest, will attain to greater heights than those who abandon themselves to premature despair of ever reaching the goal and halt at the very foot of the ascent." [29]

Quintilian attaches special meaning to levels of aspiration, and he does not want his thought here to remain hidden away in theory. The ideal of excellence must be communicated to boys from their earliest years; parents and nurses, if they are good teachers, will never permit boys to forget their need to excel. In that part of the discourse dealing with early home training, Quintilian pleads with fathers to entertain high hopes for their sons at all times, for these hopes will serve as inspirations to exert extraordinary care in planning and directing educational programs. It is Quintilian's considered view that boys are always capable of mastering the various arts involved in oratory. What is lacking is care, not capacity. Thus Plato's assertions respecting an aristocracy of ability are rejected, and in their place Quintilian preaches a doctrine of optimism: Most boys are quick to reason and ready to learn; curiosity and willingness to learn are instinctive qualities of youth, and boys always show promise of many accomplishments until faulty pedagogy gets in the way.

By Quintilian's time the conventions of Roman society, which dictated that the initial responsibility for good teaching rested with nurses

[28] *Ibid.*, I. i. 10.
[29] *Ibid.*, I. i. 20.

and parents, may have given the nurse pride of place. Quintilian is on sure ground when he recognizes the nurse as the first person a child hears, and that because children are both imitative and impressionable they retain best what they learn first. Good impressions, although appearing to have a certain permanence, are less durable than bad ones, and Quintilian strengthens his argument by affirming that although what is good readily deteriorates, no one can convert vice into virtue.[30] And what appears to be true on the level of character-building is also true of correctness and incorrectness in styles of speaking. Quintilian refused to allow any boy to become accustomed, even in his earliest years, to an incorrect style or manner of speech which in later years would have to be unlearned. His assumption is clear: Relearning is more difficult than learning. And he is prepared to justify a common Roman practice whereby good teachers regularly charged double fees for teaching students who had studied their first lessons with inferior masters.

After reading Quintilian, we know that nurses are to be well-educated. We know, too, of his conviction that parents should be as highly educated as possible—and he is thinking not only of fathers, but of mothers as well. How Roman fathers might have obtained their education is fairly clear, for in the Roman system there was a dense network of schools open to boys. But the education of women was another matter, and this question would involve not only mothers but nurses, too. It is plainly impossible to represent Quintilian as a champion for the education of women, yet he was fully aware of the role that mothers played in the early moral education of their children, and he wanted to endorse this role without at the same time becoming involved in any liberal movement for upgrading the educational opportunities for Roman girls.

Quintilian set as his goal the education of a perfect orator. Without becoming swamped in detail, we can try to delineate the general recommendations he made to achieve such a high goal. The first book of *Education of an Orator* begins with preliminary education (preliminary to the school of rhetoric), treating of infant education in the home, moral teaching under the direct supervision of nurses and parents, and the teaching duties of the grammar master. With the latter the boy is introduced to formal schooling. Quintilian repeats what he has said about the qualifications of home teachers, and then moves on to discuss the duties and qualifications of the grammar master, the introduc-

[30] *Ibid.*, I. i. 5.

tion of lessons in Greek, the teaching of the alphabet and handwriting, and the organization of lessons for strengthening the memory.

Throughout the twelve books, and usually as a corollary to the subject matter under analysis, methods of teaching are recommended, explained, and evaluated. Quintilian is determined to outline methods of teaching enabling students to master the art of oratory, understand the laws of rhetoric, and develop a general competence for elevating their powers of eloquence. In treating of these items he tries to avoid the normal outcomes of textbook study, especially of textbooks on rhetoric, which, in aiming at completeness, actually ended up by impairing or crippling the nobler elements of style. He looked for balance in rhetorical study, opposed outright expurgation of codes of rhetoric, and voted for detail in learning (though detail was not the obsession with Quintilian that it was with so many of his confreres). Formal study was to come alive, and the barren and unbearable elements of pedantic instruction were to be avoided. Quintilian's goal is high, and his conception of rhetoric's place in the educational process is broad; and as this conception is translated into a book with twelve parts, we come face to face with an effective demonstration of everything potentially useful in the education of an orator.

Before moving on to a closer examination of Quintilian's recommendations concerning methods of teaching, we should take notice of his attitude toward two important aspects of education: the beginning school age, and the relative merits of public and private teaching. Age seven had been accepted, almost without question, as the time for beginning schooling; Quintilian was prepared to modify this dogmatic assumption and allow students to study when they are ready. He meant that there is no point in waiting for any certain magic age before beginning teaching: "Though the knowledge absorbed in the previous years may mean but little, yet the boy will be learning something more advanced during that year, in which he would otherwise have been occupied with something more elementary." [31] Quintilian's justification for this attitude is simple and straightforward: The early years of literary education are almost exclusively involved in mnemonic teaching, and the memory of youth is exceptionally retentive.[32]

After disposing of the matter of the beginning school age, Quintilian turns to another assumption dominating education: Public education is a threat to the morals of youth and, moreover, is unable to offer

[31] *Ibid.,* I. i. 18.
[32] *Ibid.,* I. i. 19.

high-quality learning. He takes a long time to answer this objection, but in the end satisfies himself, although possibly not his readers, that neither the morals of youth nor the quality of learning is in jeopardy in the public school. As a matter of fact, he thinks, boys might be better off in public schools than under the guidance of a private master.[33]

QUINTILIAN'S THEORY OF LEARNING

Consistent with his general message in *Education of an Orator*, Quintilian always stresses the prime object of education (to create or encourage mental activity), and throughout it we find references to sharpening intelligence, native powers, and capacities.[34] Another emphasis in his theory—one now almost universally adopted in methodology—is the need for accommodating the content of education to the intellectual abilities and interests of students. In other words, the individual differences among students are relevant both to methods and to objectives of teaching. He appears also to recommend teaching techniques based on the hypothesis that nurture can correct nature.[35] To some degree Quintilian was a follower of Isocrates, who had built his theory of teaching on a foundation of natural ability. But Quintilian moved past Isocrates in maintaining that training and education could modify the weaknesses of nature. The faculties of memory, imagination, and sense perception, he wrote, could be improved by study even when in their original state they were inferior.[36]

Care, we know, was with Quintilian an educational watchword, and he enjoined teachers to proceed through learning step-by-step, "making haste slowly," leaving out nothing. Neither he nor his ancient predecessors ever told anyone that learning was easy; they understood it to be a long and difficult ordeal which, in addition to assimilating masses of information, involved the whole matter of learning how to learn. A theory of learning, he said, containing a principal commitment to fostering mental activity, has two dimensions—formation and information—and both are grounded on the foundation of early education. As learning proceeds up the educational ladder, the techniques of drill, repetition, and stimulation must be employed. Drill is a way of reinforcing knowledge, and it is basic to formation because discipline is necessarily involved. Stimulation has its source partly in

[33] *Ibid.*, I. ii. 4–5, 10, 12, 16–20.

[34] *Ibid.*, I. i. 1–3; iii. 1–3, 10–11; ix. 26–27; II. iv. 6–8; viii. 1–5; xix. 1–3; III. ii. 1; XII. i. 19.

[35] *Ibid.*, II. xix. 1–3; XII. i. 19.

[36] *Ibid.*, I. x. 34–49.

the teacher's scholarly example and partly in the student's joy in learning.

Learning is indeed hard work, and Quintilian is willing to help the student find time for some leisure and amusement. Yet, even when he does, he is not forgetting that education is a full-time occupation: games, he wrote, are a ready mirror for the character of those who play. But, in addition, because serious learning is hard work, vigor and zeal for study may be regained by allowing students intervals of rest, and periods of recreation, wherein they may be distracted from their school work. Quintilian also allows for long holidays from work, although he cautions teachers to administer their various prescriptions of work and play with more than ordinary care.

Quintilian couples relaxation and play with an enlightened attitude toward corporal punishment, and thus reveals one of the humane features of his school. He wanted to avoid all physical punishment, a view inspired partly by his belief that flogging—a common practice at the time—was fit only for slaves. A student who is insensitive to a teacher's stimulation and who refuses to respond to reproof is only hardened by beatings, and made less receptive to the values of education. While these warnings were undoubtedly offered sincerely and have a high degree of validity, they are somewhat beside the point when we see Quintilian's whole argument: He is convinced that any imposition of force in education is unnecessary when teachers are qualified. Good teachers will understand the genuine motives of education, and they will know that competition, commendation, attraction to the teacher's person, and interest in learning itself are more effective motives than any kind of physical chastisement. Good order in the classroom was an instrument, not an end, of learning, and Quintilian, knowing that children under the control of teachers were almost helpless and easily victimized, refused to endorse any school practice allowing masters an unlimited disciplinary authority over their persons.[37]

Quintilian succeeded, where others before him had failed, in opening new frontiers for educational technique, and, despite the fact that his recommendations did not find their way at once into school practice, they became the foundations on which modern pedagogical technique could be built. Most of what is now an approved part of teaching practice caught his notice. Teachers were told to study the psychology of their pupils; to learn and then apply fundamental principles to teaching and learning. They were directed to look more deeply into motivations for learning, and to do something more than tell the student that what they were teaching was important for him to learn.

[37] *Ibid.,* I. iii. 8.

Quintilian greatly respected the motives generated by the process of learning itself, and among them the one that most caught his fancy was competition. Although competition was hardly new even to the pedagogy of Quintilian's day, he was the first educational philosopher to support it with a psychological rationale, and to establish it as an educational technique of unassailable worth. And competition in the hands of Quintilian's schoolmaster was always supplemented with safe-guards allowing for either a proper matching of competitors of equal capacity, or a competition by an individual student against his own record of achievement. After the competitions were over, and when the reports of achievement were in the teacher's hands, commendations should be distributed to all pupils, both to superior students and to those whose accomplishments were only average. Where praise is con-cerned, there is no frugality in Quintilian's theory.

In a prominent place, standing alongside competition and com-mendation, we find repetition, and Quintilian never tired of reaffirming its importance or advocating its constant employment. Yet, he knew how deadening needless repetition could be, and how pointless it was to continue to teach students things they already knew. So the point of individual differences comes up again: Allow for different kinds of teaching for students of varying levels of intellectual maturity and achievement in learning.

At this point something should be said about the qualities Quin-tilian sought in good teachers. (Although he is explicit only when he writes about the qualifications for teachers of rhetoric, we may assume his intention of applying them to all other teachers as well.) Character comes first, and in Book II, where the topic is the teacher of rhetoric, this special emphasis is justified: "The reason which leads me to deal with this subject in this portion of my work is not that I regard charac-ter as a matter of indifference where others teachers are concerned (I have already shown how important I think it in the preceding book), but that the age to which the pupil has now attained makes the men-tion of this point especially necessary." [38]

Boys came to the teacher of rhetoric in their early adolescence, and remained in his custody until they were young men; thus it was especially important for the teacher's character to be impeccable and, in addition, for him to have a unique talent for shaping character in young men of bold spirit. The teacher should set a superior example of personal self-control, but he should also be able to govern the be-havior of the young men by strict discipline. From what we know of Quintilian's attitudes toward discipline, we may assume that the disci-

[38] *Ibid.*, II. ii. 2.

plinary prescription recommended equal parts of severity and moderation. But there is more.

> [The teacher's] instruction must be free from affectation, his demands on his class continuous, but not extravagant. He must be ready to answer questions and put them unasked to those who sit silent. In praising the recitations of his pupils he must be neither grudging nor over-generous: the former quality will give them distaste for work, while the latter will produce a complacent self-satisfaction. In correcting faults he must avoid sarcasm and above all abuse: for teachers whose rebukes seem to imply positive dislike discourage industry. He should declaim daily himself, and what is more, without stint, that his class may take his utterances home with them.[39]

The eloquent man, upon becoming a teacher, attains prominence in the profession only when he mixes prudence and judgment and a broad knowledge of teaching techniques with oratorical ability. And even then he must be willing to go down to the student's level if he is to be effective: A rapid walker walking with a small child will reduce his pace, and give the child his hand, to keep from walking too fast for his young companion.[40] Quintilian uses this analogy to illustrate how teachers must maintain close intellectual contacts with their students if they are to teach effectively.

Teachers today regularly assess the ability of their pupils as a part of the whole teaching process, but the teachers of Quintilian's time had few dependable tools for making such assessments. What they had were mainly mnemotechniques, even the best of which lacked sophistication. According to Quintilian, the first and the surest sign of ability was a good memory, so he counseled his readers to test the memories of their students to find the differences in ability among them. Although we should like to amend Quintilian's solemn advice today, at that time neither Quintilian nor anyone else could gainsay the importance of a good memory, for in an age when neither aids to memory nor general compilations of knowledge were available in anthologies to replace the well-filled memory, a highly retentive memory had an extraordinary academic appeal. Scholars carried their bibliographies in their minds, and orators kept their examples and illustrations in their memories. These conditions of learning always supported Quintilian's statements on memory.

Second only to memory as an index of ability was facility in imitation. Most ancient educators—Quintilian among them—and their fol-

[39] *Ibid.*, II. ii. 5–8.
[40] *Ibid.*, II. iii. 7–8.

lowers regarded imitation as the essential element of classical teaching, and they were determined to honor the traditions of the past. Despite our current doubts about the universal efficacy of imitation as a teaching technique, we should admit that, in good hands, imitation was a useful technique for reaching the goals of learning prized by ancient educators. In bad hands, however, the result was narrow and pedantic instruction. Still, we should not be too quick to condemn Quintilian on the score of inadequacy, for when he recommended imitation of the best models, Greek and Latin literature was both extensive and readily available.

But even with so much literary excellence at the schoolmaster's disposal, Quintilian is content to recommend an almost exclusive study of Cicero. This may be a limitation or a shortcoming in Quintilian's theory, but neither Cicero nor any other writer was to be merely copied. The good authors were used as guides, and a student's mind was attuned to the models selected. Properly used, Quintilian tells us, imitation is a technique enabling students to grasp and assimilate grand ideas, effective methods of learning and speaking, and meaningful sentiments. Imitation meant, first, reading literary models to absorb the ideas they contained and, second, rereading them to notice how these ideas were presented with force, appeal, logic, and eloquence.[41]

Following Cicero, Quintilian agrees that writing is a preparation for speaking, so he has a good deal to say about the way students should learn to write. He is always ready to remind students that good writing is a necessary preliminary to superior oratory, and that the ability to write well results only from learning and practice. He tells students to begin with a draft, and to think of it as an outline to be filled out, finished, and polished. He instructs them, moreover, to be tentative at every stage of their writing—to use the eraser as freely as the pen.

Every aspiring writer, if he heeds Quintilian's advice, will realize that good writing is the end of a long process of rewriting: "Write quickly," Quintilian says, "and you will never write well; write well and you will soon write quickly."[42] Because students more often than not do not start out with the conviction that everything they write must be revised if it is to be superior, the difficult task of inculcating an attitude of self-criticism is an important duty of the teacher. At first, teachers must show their students where their essays need improvement, and give them necessary directions for revision. But since teachers will not always be correcting orations, the student must aim toward

[41] *Ibid.*, I. iii. 1; IX. i. 30; ii. 35; X. i. 3; ii. 1.
[42] *Ibid.*, X. iii. 10.

cultivating his own powers of literary criticism, and learn to set standards for his own compositions. The student who is never fully satisfied with the quality of his essays will be ready to welcome outside criticism. (Such criticism should concentrate on elements of writing often ignored even by good authors: use of words, clearness of expression, mechanics of style.) The point Quintilian is determined to make is simple: Good writing is an outcome of learning, and if this goal is ever to be reached, students must be humble and docile, and willing to listen to the teacher's advice.

Still, writing is more than a skill or a mechanical technique. It presumes clear and fundamental thought. And, since thinking is the bedrock of Quintilian's theory of learning, he is prepared to tell us to think, for we learn to think better the same way we improve our other human abilities: by thinking.[43]

Admonitions are added for the student who may despair of ever reaching the high goals set by Quintilian. Despair is foolish, he says, for if a student is talented, healthy, capable, and ambitious, and is lucky enough to have dedicated teachers, a respectable record of achievement is possible even though he may not rank first in his class. An awareness of the relationship between achievement and capacity is important here, and students should be able to find satisfaction in whatever level of success they enjoy, providing they have used their capacities to their limit. The fundamental object here is not an accumulation of knowledge but a development of intellectual capacities. While the latter inevitably vary from person to person, we are prepared to admit that Quintilian's goal for human learning was realistic as well as high.

QUINTILIAN'S CURRICULUM

In Quintilian's writings the foundations of learning husbanded in primary schools—reading and writing—are taken for granted. The more important curricular questions begin with the grammar school, where the grammarian is assigned two duties: teaching the art of speaking correctly, and introducing students to interpretations of the poets. But since neither correct speech nor literary study are merely mechanical, the theory of writing and the art of reading must be added. Then comes criticism, whose principles must be learned and applied to reading and writing, music, geometry, and philosophy. The latter is expected to impregnate grammar study with knowledge.

---

[43] *Ibid.*, X.

Two sides of grammar study proper are clearly delineated by Quintilian: the learning of the structure of language (with which the reader is already all too familiar), and the assimilation of knowledge through reading (reading, that is, which is guided by the needs of superior oratory). Reading was always the most dependable way of getting knowledge, but it properly included, in addition to material carefully selected to store the mind with information, such aspects as rhythm in breathing, cultivating a sense of timing, and training in rate, animation, modulation, and correct sentence order. Both sides of grammar were essential and, although grammar was but a preliminary study, Quintilian never meant to treat it as an inferior subject. He praised it as a branch of knowledge necessary in youth—as a foundation for rhetoric—and pleasant in old age:

> The elementary stages of the teaching of literature (grammar) must not therefore be despised as trivial. It is of course an easy task to point out the difference between vowels and consonants, and to subdivide the latter into semivowels and mutes. But as the pupil gradually approaches the inner shrine of the sacred place, he will come to realize the intricacy of the subject, an intricacy calculated not merely to sharpen the wits of a boy, but to exercise even the most profound knowledge and erudition.[44]

Before we leave the grammar school and close the book on the functions of its teachers, something should be said about Quintilian's attitude toward music and geometry. Quintilian begins by registering his doubt about any need to justify music's curricular standing, and then goes into great detail to do what he thinks unnecessary. He parades the wisdom of ancient educators and philosophers, and the conventions of mankind, to assert the value that music has for forming the body and ennobling the soul. The disciplinary value of music is one argument, but there is another, Quintilian thinks—and he wants to be complete in his presentation. Instrumental and vocal music were useful to the future orator: both could contribute to refining his mode of expression, developing vocal patterns, lending rhythm to gesture, and adding to grace and harmony in speech and movement. This should have been enough to clinch the matter, but Quintilian refuses to leave any loose ends. When he studied classical education, he found a good model in the Athenian music school, and tried to follow it. Such schools had stressed the literary side of musical education, and in doing so had given the prospective orator, or public man, a broad foundation of

---

[44] *Ibid.*, I. iv. 6–7.

general information. So for its informational value, in addition to other recommendations for it, Quintilian assigns music a prominent place in the curriculum.

Classical schools tended to avoid mathematical studies, especially on the lower levels of schooling, for what seemed then to be good reasons (the lack of a flexible and adaptable notation), but in reading the record of these ancient schools Quintilian found geometry, and raised it to the level of a liberal study.[45] He could be convincing when he wrote "no mathematics, no orator," but at the same time, when he was putting various subjects in the curriculum, he could pay geometry only scant heed. Mathematical studies were not especially prominent among the curricular entries endorsed by this great Roman, and when geometry found its way into the school it was justified not for its liberalizing or disciplinary values, but because it was useful in developing logical skills and a knowledge of numbers and symbols.

The curriculum of the grammar school—the custodian of secondary education—is fixed; what remains in Quintilian's curricular plan pertains to higher education, a domain presided over by the teacher of rhetoric. Teachers of rhetoric must begin their teaching where teachers of grammar stop, and care must be exercised to keep the boundaries between grammar and rhetoric clear and precise.[46] The total thrust of rhetoric is to teach students a theory of eloquence, and how to be eloquent in practice. Thus, though we find the objectives of higher learning stated simply and clearly, beneath the surface, and partly concealed by Quintilian's skill as a writer, is a vast network of rhetorical theory and rule awaiting mastery. We can make only passing reference to Quintilian's directives to teachers of rhetoric, for in *Education of an Orator* he uses the greater part of nine books to elaborate on them. And even then it is doubtful that he added much to the science of Latin and Greek rhetoric: he took both as he found them, and tried merely to supply a pedagogy for teaching the rules and regulations of rhetoric.

In addition to his recitation of rule and regulation, a task undertaken with the utmost seriousness, Quintilian appended recommendations regarding those orators and historians that students should read.[47] Criteria for selection come easily: Only the best writers should be read, and among the best Quintilian preferred those recognized for their transparency of style and lucidity of expression. Livy was better than

[45] *Ibid.,* I. x. 33–37.
[46] *Ibid.,* II. i. 4–8.
[47] *Ibid.,* X. i. 72–82.

Sallust, he said, although Cicero was always given pride of place—and teachers should choose all their literary models only after testing their similarity to Cicero's writings.[48]

Quintilian's general concept of education is the same as Cicero's; both maintained that the aim of education is to produce the orator. In Cicero Quintilian honored Rome's greatest orator and education's best model. The education described by Quintilian is a formal and institutionalized process. Instruction was to be given in school, preferably in public schools, and the content of this kind of education was to be largely grammatical and rhetorical.

According to Quintilian, the orator should be a good man. He should be a master of the liberal arts and skillful in the art of speaking. The public interest should be his special interest and he should seek to serve it at all times. The orator was defined as "a good man skilled in speaking."

The following is a summary of the main educational ideas expressed by Quintilian: He believed that the great object of instruction was to create or stimulate the student's mental activity. Teaching had to be accommodated to the ability of the student. Quintilian recognized the fact of individual differences, and he advised teachers to adjust their methods and the forms of study according to the special qualities of the students. Knowledge could not be acquired easily, and it could hardly be acquired at all unless the process of acquisition was logical. Education's main function was to correct the weak points of nature. Quintilian never tired of advising that the first years of life were the foundational years and therefore the most important. During these early years, he said, all kinds of mental work must take the form of amusement. Young children learn with ease, and the whole course of their education will be determined by what is done in their infant years. Therefore the very best teachers should be assigned to the education of the young. On this lower level especially, but perhaps on all levels as well, a variety of subjects should be taught simultaneously and not in succession. Variety in study, this great Roman teacher argued, promoted activity; and the capacity of the young for congenial work, he wrote, is very large. At the same time, since relaxation and amusement are necessary, periods for play and rest are essential. During these noninstructional periods a great deal can be learned about the child by observing him. Quintilian always advised against corporal punishment. He felt that it disgraced the student and that it did not lead him toward greater performance. The true motives for good work are competition,

[48] *Ibid.*, X. i. 105.

commendation, affection for the teacher, and interest aroused by the subject itself. These were the things that were to be attended to, not fear and punishment. The usual child, Quintilian maintained, is eager for knowledge; he is intelligent and curious about the world in which he lives. It is the fault of the teacher if he loses this interest or this curiosity. Public education (by which Quintilian meant education in common) is better than private education (by which he meant tutorial arrangements), and large classes of students stimulate both teachers and students to do better work. The best teachers, he said, prefer to teach large groups of students. In such public teaching the students learn from one another and develop friendships which are lifelong.

Quintilian cautioned teachers about overteaching, about needlessly intervening between the student and his studies. He noted that attainment is always lower than the goal aimed at, and for this reason he advised all educators to set their goals very high. As far as teachers themselves were concerned, he wrote: Ability and learning are desirable on all levels; teachers must be strictly moral; they must be friendly, clear, patient, generous, and ready to give praise.

The surest sign of a child's ability is the power of his memory. The next is his power of imitation. Quintilian advised that students be spurred on by praise, for success delighted them, and failure made them lose their drive for learning. The student must be made to realize that revision of written work is every bit as important to the excellence of the final copy as the initial steps in writing.

Finally, we may say a word about the curriculum Quintilian proposed for the schools that would educate orators. Since this curriculum is not novel, we need only say that it would consist of the following: (elementary) correct speech, writing, reading, Greek grammar, Latin grammar; (secondary) correct speaking, literature and literary criticism, astronomy, philosophy, geometry, music; (higher) literature, history, composition, rhetoric, logic, ethics.

Summary

The foremost Roman educational thinkers were Cicero (106–43 B.C.) and Quintilian (A.D. 35–97). Both acknowledged the importance of the public man, and both tried to promote an educational program wherein public men could be prepared. This, in the terminology of the day, was the education of an orator.

In his great book *De Oratore*, Cicero laid a foundation for an orator's liberal education by stressing the significance of broad and dependable knowledge that must form the context of any speech. Rhetoric, or oratory, the ability to speak well, was paid heed in Cicero's plan, but it was always built on the bedrock of extensive and profound knowledge.

Taking Cicero as his guide, Quintilian broadened educational theory and practice in his incomparable *Education of an Orator* by proposing a plan of teaching beginning with the birth of a boy and continuing until he was an accomplished orator. Quintilian tried always to be complete and accurate both in his accounts of educational purpose, and in his recommendations about teaching methods.

Both *De Oratore* and *Education of an Orator* and their authors had a decisive impact on later educational priorities of content and purpose. Cassiodorus reread Quintilian and used him as a guide for rebuilding a Christian school syllabus; medieval rhetoric knew no greater master than Cicero; and all of Humanism watered at the educational springs that were opened by Cicero and Quintilian.

PART II

Christian &
Medieval
Education

M uch of the heritage of the ancient world held a number of attractions for many Christians, who, in addition to being aware of them, frequently were anxious to incorporate them into their own way of life. What is more, in order to be an effective force in a society that was strongly Roman and pagan, Christians were almost compelled to pay heed to educational plans which for so long had guided the formation of the citizen. Christians, then, unable to ignore the world in which they lived—assuming they wanted to—may have understood fully the dictum that anyone who refuses to be part of society can have no role in shaping it. Their faith, understandably highly important to them, was one thing; the society of ancient Rome with all its appurtenances for learning was quite another.

Whenever they sought the balance of compromise, Christians had to be certain that doctrinal concessions were never made. The first Christians began by assuming certain things about education. First, they asserted that morals and faith were not the business of the school, but of the home and the Church. Second, techniques of learning—such things as style and form and the correct use of language—were the principal business of schools. Finally, whenever schools taught the literature of the pagans, which in the nature of their type of learning they could hardly avoid doing, proper safeguards should be erected to eliminate, or at least minimize, dangers to morals and faith. Not all of this, to be sure, was universal opinion within the infant Christian community, but it was the compromise position most often expressed and embraced. Using the balanced doctrines of compromise, then, Christians tried to resolve the educational dilemma of their age.

Christian educational compromises, whether redundant or progressive, were regularly subject to debate. And it was these debates, usually engaged in by the best-known of the Fathers, which produced the first theoretical statements on the meaning, purpose, content, and techniques of Christian learning. Strangely, Christians refused to believe in the solution which would have directed them to create schools of their own, although in the first centuries of the Christian period they did establish institutes—places without any real literary character—wherein the elements of Christian doctrine were taught to various classes of Christian people.

With the decline of the Roman Empire, the schools belonging to it fell into disrepair, and the long heritage of ancient learning was put in jeopardy. Whether or not Christians were concerned about the security of the classics and the classical heritage is not, in this context, a central question. They *were*, however, vitally concerned about the practical necessity for literary knowledge, on behalf of both the liturgy and the government of the Church, and so they tried to revive learning. First, it was important to know what was worth knowing, and when this decision was made, to organize such knowledge and to elaborate a pedagogy to accompany it. The first achievement was mainly the work of Cassiodorus; the second, the service to learning of the famous Alcuin.

Having been blessed with fairly stable foundations both for the selection of the subject matter of schools and for the methods of teaching these subjects, it was possible for medieval schoolmen to advance beyond the humble beginnings of their Christian predecessors. In doing so they elevated intellectual goals to a high place in the schools (as witnessed in Scholasticism), produced reasoned justifications for these goals in a theory of education that for the first time admitted the classics to the schools without prejudice, and organized various schools, including the great medieval universities, wherein their highly prized intellectual goals could be realized.

VII

Early Christian Education

The Meaning of Christian Education

For the first four hundred years of the Christian era, and in fact for many centuries to follow, a Christian school—that is, a school integrating doctrines of the Christian faith with literary culture—was unknown to Rome. Christian boys and girls therefore attended either the secular schools (some Christians were teachers in Roman or other classical schools) or special Christian "schools." What the secular schools taught, of course, had nothing whatever to do with Christian education. And in the Christian "schools" (if we may call them that), prospective Christians were prepared only for entrance into the Church. These institutes for religious conversion consciously ignored literary and linguistic objectives—now clearly accepted in conventional schools—and instead merely communicated articles of faith, and stimulated feelings of religious devotion.

Why was the Christian Church either indifferent to or opposed to ordinary literary education and to the institutions charged with perpetuating it? Why did the Church refuse to establish her own schools, but at the same time evidence a reasonably sanguine attitude with respect to the fortunes of Christian education? One reason was that she did not want her own schools, either because she did not believe that schools for literary culture were important, or because she had neither the time, energy, nor skill to superintend them. The Church's mission was phrased in supraschool and supraeducational terms and, moreover, was documented by divine authority. Literary education wore a face of sheer ornamentation when compared to fundamental Christian goals, because only salvation counted. And the business of salvation was urgent, because most Christians sincerely believed that the last judgment was imminent. Naturally, then, things of the soul were superior to things of the mind. Still, teaching a common core of Christian belief was imperative to the stability and future of the infant Church, and so foundations slowly but surely were laid for a basic Christian education.

But where and by whom was this Christian teaching done? First and foremost, the child's Christian formation was a parental responsibility. The apostolic message is clear on this point. It is unnecessary to refer to anything more than the admonitions of St. Paul to convince the reader that this was the general Christian position.[1] The family was the first and possibly the best instrument for inculcating Christian education, and it was the natural place for moral and religious teaching to begin. In Roman lands (and of course the Church made some of its greatest progress in areas where the jurisdiction of Rome was felt) this Christian view of parental responsibility was accepted without question as being the only reasonable way to prepare a family for life in the world. Romans, though by this time committed to schools, still continued to accept their traditions on an intellectual level long after they had discarded them in practice, and the Roman tradition of family education had some effect in solidifying the early Christian view. But it should not be thought that Christians simply adopted a Roman way of doing things. The Christian family was the center of the Christian educational structure because it was natural for the family to have this position and because at this time the family was the most effective instrument available to promote Christian education. The Christian practice had something more to it than Roman tradition. Yet it may be overgenerous

[1] See Eph. 6:4; Col. 3:21.

to Christian beginnings to maintain that religious familial education was without precedent. The Jewish model for family education looms much too large to be ignored here; and it was a model that was very apparent to the Christians. The Christian practice was not, however, a mere duplication of firmly established Jewish practices either. There is a noticeable element of autonomy about Christian education in parental hands.

Christian education started and continued with the family, even when parental training was supplemented in important ways. Very early it became clear that in addition to being formed with a Christian mind and Christian heart, a child was to be prepared for Church membership. To be a member of the Christian Church one had to know something of its rules and rituals, and neophytes had to be inducted formally into the Holy Church. The induction was the sacrament of baptism; the preparation for the sacrament was catechumenal instruction. With baptism, this phase of Christian instruction came to an end. In fact, the so-called catechumenal school had a relatively short life. Its importance to the early Church under persecution cannot be overemphasized, it is true, but the time came quite soon when Christianity's foothold was so sure that it was possible to dispense with the more or less formal catechumenal teaching. There is no very clear evidence that the catechumenal school lasted much beyond the end of the second century. There was, however, no end to religious training.

Was catechumenal instruction an example of purely Christian education, separated from secular training, or was this instruction part of the work of a Christian school? By this time in educational history we have a right to restrict the name "school" to those institutions in which a literary training was given or to institutions which made use of literary skills in pushing back intellectual horizons. The catechumenal endeavors had no interest whatever in literary education, and if they did not actually reject the literary inheritance that was so eagerly accepted in contemporary culture, it may have been because they were indifferent to it. The luxury of indifference was something later Christianity could not afford.[2] But in its earliest years Christianity was not even aware of the relevance of culture to the Christian's mission. It is possible to make the claim that catechumenal instruction was a mere extension of Christian education and that it did not contain the germ or the prototype of later Christian schools. Despite this claim, it must be acknowledged

[2] See R. R. Bolgar, *The Classical Heritage and Its Beneficiaries,* Cambridge University Press, Cambridge, 1954, pp. 45–46; and William R. Halliday, *The Pagan Background of Early Christianity,* The University Press of Liverpool, Ltd., Liverpool, 1925, pp. 129–134.

that this catechumenal instruction evolved into highly developed and extremely efficient religious education. The course, in its final and finished form, lasted about three years. To guide the teachers who conducted the course, a theory of religious instruction was produced whose architects were teachers, deacons, priests, and bishops. This theory remained in vogue for several centuries; in a rather disguised form some of the elements attached thereto may be found even today.

We remarked above that Christians' indifference to culture became a luxury which they could not afford. With growth and expansion the Christian Church had to face all kinds of new problems. The natural development of the Church, its preaching and teaching, and its continued permeation of all life made imperative the establishment of an intellectual foundation for its creed.[3] As Christianity became more and more an intellectual religion, education became more and more an important adjunct. By the early sixth century the church was ready to embrace the school as an ancillary agency for a Christian's salvation.

The Dilemma of Christian Education

When Christians were prepared to ignore literary culture and discount its relevance to a Christian way of life, they could concentrate on moral and religious objectives and seek to extend their faith without countenancing any compromise between the classics and religion. If the Christian world was to be an entirely new world, the classical legacy could be paid scant heed. But, though new in some important respects, the Christians' world was in many ways a continuation of ancient social and political, as well as cultural, values. So, taking Christianity at full face value, the majority of early Christians in fact entertained ambivalent feelings about Roman society and its intellectual conventions. Unquestionably they resented paganism and wanted it destroyed, yet they sensed that in destroying paganism they would be annihilating the civilization they knew, liked, and hoped to preserve. They wanted to be Christians, but they wanted, too, to practice their Christianity amid the usual cultural conventions of Roman life.[4]

Christians both accepted and rejected pagan literature, which as a basis for grammar teaching and rhetorical accomplishment was the

---

[3] Werner W. Jaeger, *Early Christianity and Greek Paideia,* The Belknap Press of Harvard University Press, Cambridge, Mass., 1961, pp. 86–102; and Edwin Hatch, *The Influence of Greek Ideas on Christianity,* Harper and Row, Publishers, New York, 1957, pp. 118–131.

[4] R. P. C. Hanson, *Tradition in the Early Church,* SCM Press, Ltd., London, 1962, pp. 42–53; and Harald Hagendahl, *Latin Fathers and the Classics,* Almquist & Wiksell, Stockholm, 1958, pp. 398–402.

staple subject matter of the schools. Their ambivalence of attachment and rejection is understandable: Pagan literature appeared to be essential as a foundation for a decent education, and it was a national heritage; yet jettisoning pagan cultural ideals was imperative to a full Christian profession of faith. Thus Christians were caught in a cultural dilemma: Entertaining an almost unshakable devotion to literature, they kindled an intense hatred for all pagan practices and beliefs. They upheld the value of grammar and rhetoric, studied authors with whom they disagreed, and resented Julian's decree forbidding Christian teachers to lecture on the classics, but at the same time tried to decontaminate the classics—to defuse them of fundamental moral significance.[5] This latter task was a hard one, and compromises were seldom easy to find. Total rejection was always possible, and was sometimes recommended, but this would mean, in a way, the destruction of an existing civilization. Few were willing to go so far. This ambivalence, or dilemma, was characteristic of the educated (though not necessarily scholarly) Christian, and it affected Christian leaders and thinkers as well. The question demanding an answer was how to effect a compromise wherein numerous traits of paganism, apparently essential to any degree of culture, should be preserved, although paganism itself would be purged.

Eastern Christians were less deeply affected by the issue so important to Christians in the West. They appeared more willing to separate learning from faith, or at least to keep the realms of reason and faith distinct. And some Eastern Christians found little difficulty in studying the classics and speculating on ancient philosophy while expressing complete allegiance to Christian doctrine. Christian scholars of the East show in their writings that for them the dilemma of the West was not a burning issue of the day.

But is this an accurate appraisal of Eastern Christianity's approach to pagan learning? Of course we cannot know what the average Eastern Christian thought on this question (if indeed he thought about it at all), but among the spokesmen of the East the apparent hostility between classical learning and Christian faith, so evident in the West, was minimized. Most Eastern Christians had been educated in a cultural climate filled with pagan learning, and they were able to distinguish between the style and method of classical education and the basic, sometimes un-Christian, values it represented. Reconciling the irreconcilable was, they saw, a useless exercise—there was no way to make the

[5] M. L. W. Laistner, *Christianity and Pagan Culture in the Late Roman Empire,* Cornell University Press, Ithaca, N. Y., 1951, pp. 59–61; and P. A. Micklem, *The Secular and the Sacred,* Hodder and Stoughton, London, 1948, pp. 221–225.

classics speak a language of Christian faith or doctrine—but it was still possible to affirm the worth of at least parts of the classical legacy. They refused to spend their time denouncing the classics. Even had they elected to try, could Eastern Christians have purged themselves of their personal intellectual inheritances? By their acknowledgment of pagan learning (what may be called "classical education") they never meant to embrace the whole of its philosophy or its polytheism. In other words, Eastern Christians talked and wrote like educated pagans, and used all the appurtenances of pagan learning—to have done otherwise would have meant cutting themselves off from a large part of existing civilization—without surrendering to the cultural ideals of paganism. Their rejections were important, for without them we should have plenty of reason to doubt the basic orthodoxy of Eastern Christianity. As it was, Eastern Christians were under constant surveillance by their more sensitive and generally less learned Western brothers. Sensitive, we say, not only because certain Western Christians made a career of sniffing for heresies, but because they share the human tendency to fear things that are not fully understood.

As a missionary religion, Christianity was guided by a certain cultural pragmatism that allowed it to speak to potential converts in the West in a less sophisticated language than in the East. Eastern Christians, therefore, used their traditions as they found them, and regularly endorsed the classics as a necessary foundation to a religion that could be approached by intellectual avenues. The West, with a lower threshold of cultural awareness, and an almost natural Christian distrust of the classics, chose to make its appeal on the level of faith, dispensing, at least for the time, with tools of learning. Learning, therefore, began by being an ornament which the Christian might or might not have. In any case, the assumption was clear: Learning was unnecessary to faith. What was not quite so clear was that learning might, in fact, be dangerous to faith.[6]

After about three hundred years—or about A.D. 300—Western Christians became vitally concerned with their cultural-religious conflicts, sometimes showed signs of being about ready to bury them, and as a minimum response endeavored to do something about them. Christian doctrine had matured to a point where codification was essential, and if this codification could have permanence, and could command intellectual respect and assent, its prospects would be better. At this point

---

[6] G. L. Ellspermann, *The Attitude of the Early Latin Christian Writers Toward Pagan Learning and Literature*, Catholic University of America Press, Washington, D. C., 1949, pp. 81–93; and Charles N. Cochrane, *Christianity and Classical Culture*, Oxford University Press, New York, 1944, pp. 501–518.

skill in grammar and facility in rhetoric became important, for truth should always be dressed in the finest garments. Schooling appeared to be imperative, so without creating any real schools of her own, and without publishing any general endorsement of classical learning or admitting any affection for its appurtenances, the Church decided to make greater use of the conventional school system. Christian attendance in pagan schools—by now a common practice—was not the question at issue. Something far more important was at stake: Should Christians seek to intellectualize Christian doctrine, and should they use philosophy and literature to build rational foundations for faith? If grammar and rhetoric were allowed to enter into the Christian code, would this not open the door to a fundamental paganism which might eventually destroy Christianity? Even with the familiar subjects of classical education, ambivalance was still in evidence. The course of Christian educational action that in the end was followed was one of uneasy compromise.[7]

Generally speaking, Christians used conventional schools, but they used them with premonitions of danger and with protests that true Christian wisdom was being sacrificed to the gods of pagan learning. Christians were regularly cautioned about the dangers that lurked in such schools, and they were encouraged to make their own Christian education—that broad education given by the family—so strong that the pagan literature and the pagan learning could not undermine it. With these cautions and warnings in mind, Christians continued to accept and use the classical schools.

It is a wonder that they were able to do so in view of the continuing hostility to what was called pagan learning. Thus, at least on the theoretical level, the dilemma remained unresolved. St. Basil (fourth century A.D.), although at one time a friend of learning, was able to write in his later years that he was spending all his time with the scriptures and with other similarly motivated writings. To his old teachers, the classics, he could say: "If ever I learned anything from you, I have forgotten it." [8] This was the man who earlier had written the well-known essay, *On the Reading of the Profane Authors*, for the guidance of Christians in their use of heathen authors. If this essay is read correctly,

[7] Edward K. Rand, *The Founders of the Middle Ages*, Harvard University Press, Cambridge, Mass., 1928, pp. 31–45; and Maude A. Huttman, *The Establishment of Christianity and the Proscription of Paganism*, Columbia University Press, New York, 1914, pp. 77–91.

[8] St. Basil, *Letters and Select Works*. In Philip Schaff (ed.), *A Select Library of Nicene and Post-Nicene Fathers of the Christian Church*, 2d ser., The Christian Literature Publishing Company, New York, 1895, vol. VIII, p. 322. See also George L. Prestige, *St. Basil the Great and Apollinaris of Laodocea*, SPCK, London, 1956.

it turns out to be advice to well-advanced students on how to avoid the dangers in such authors, advice which is quite different from a general endorsement of them. And this is the same man who, to confound the picture even more, had written to the celebrated Sophist, Libanius: "What fruits do they not gather, who spend even a short time with you?" [9] So St. Basil's ambivalence added fuel to the fire of discontent and confusion that still burned in the West. Western Church Fathers were ready to display even greater hostility toward classical schools and education than any Eastern divine had shown. Tertullian, Tatian, Augustine, and Jerome certainly did not seek any alliance between Christianity and Greek learning. Tertullian expressed the most uncompromising view. He had little or no confidence in reason, and he claimed that Greek learning—especially philosophy, "which really treated nothing"—was only a network of contradictions. He would have nothing to do with anything but faith: "With our faith, we desire no further belief. For this is our palmary faith, that there is nothing which we ought to believe besides." [10]

It is fair to claim that Tertullian is not the best representative of the Christian position, for his orthodoxy may be questioned. Yet his view was only a little more extreme than the general view of the time. St. Augustine (354–430) in his *Letters* [11] and St. Jerome in reporting his dreams [12] took the same stand. Even Pope Gregory the Great at the end of the sixth century opposed liberal culture and considered it dangerous and unnecessary. Although Jerome's and Gregory's positions on this question, though not the same, were quite consistent, Augustine sometimes followed Ambrose in seeing that pagan learning and the forming of Christian character were complementary. In his *Of Christian Doctrine*, Augustine was able to praise the liberal arts and write introductions to them, and he seemed to suggest that all the arts be integrated in the crown of all studies, theology. But in his *Retractions*, where he again discussed the question of the arts, Augustine was not so sure of the value of arts and the power of theology to integrate them. He concluded that he had gone too far in praising them and withdrew some of

[9] St. Basil, *Letters and Select Works*. In Schaff, *op. cit.*, vol. VIII, p. 325; and Ernest F. Morison, *St. Basil and His Rule: A Study in Early Monasticism*, H. Frowde, New York, 1912.

[10] *The Writings of Q. S. F. Tertullianus*, translated by Peter Holmes, T. & T. Clark, Edinburgh, 1870, vol. II, p. 10.

[11] *Letters of St. Augustine*, translated by J. G. Cunningham, T. & T. Clark, Edinburgh, 1875, vol. II, pp. 192–193; and Jerome *Lettera a Leta*, Editrice Ciranna, Siracusa, 1959, pp. 3–46.

[12] F. A. Wright, *Selected Letters of Saint Jerome*, Loeb Classical Library, Harvard University Press, Cambridge, Mass., 1933, vol. XVI, p. 127.

his previous endorsement in a charming and pithy statement: "Many saintly men know them [the arts] not, and some who know them are not saintly men." [13] This goes pretty far, but it does not go far enough to take away all the props that stood under classical learning.

There is another side to the question, the side that sees a closer correspondence between learning in pagan hands and Christian truth. It is not the partially humanistic position of a St. Jerome, who could see the classics and their literary implements as necessary instruments for Christians. It is, rather, a recognition that truth is truth wherever it is found, whether in philosophical dialogues or in scriptural commentaries. We do not find such a view expressed too often, and it is doubtful that any Western Church Father shared it. But we should know that the liberal attitude existed. We find it expressed best in a delightful dialogue called *Octavius*, written by Minucius Felix. E. K. Rand has called this work "the first monument—or at least one of the first monuments—of Christian Latin literature." [14] *Octavius* is a report of a conversation between two friends, one a Christian and one a pagan. The latter claims to be an orthodox Epicurean. The conversation begins with a number of charges which the pagan makes against the Christians' practices and beliefs. He goes on to become involved in a philosophical monologue that appeals for its authority to Epicureanism and skepticism alike. Finally, he concludes his diatribe. Now it is is the Christian's turn. Being a gentleman, he presents his case for the Christians with courtesy and care. He does not say everything that can be said, but only enough. He does not argue or even recognize his friend as a philosophical adversary. He uses reason to show why there must be one God and that He is the God whom the Christians adore. But this is all incidental to the main point, the Christian's conclusion of the discussion: "I have set forth the opinions of well-nigh all the philosophers of more conspicuous renown, who denote the one God with diverse names. One might well conclude that either Christians today are philosophers, or the philosophers of old were Christians." [15]

What is the answer? Where did the early Christians stand on the educational question? Was there one Christian answer? We can be certain only that there was no one answer and no official stand taken by the Church. The relationship between learning and Christianity was an open question. And it was not answered on the level of theory, although on the practical level the children of Christians and Christian teachers

---

[13] In Rand, *op. cit.*, p. 228. See also Matteo da Ferrara, *The Life of St. Jerome*, St. Anthony Guild Press, Paterson, N. J., 1949, pp. 1–58.

[14] Rand, *op. cit.*, p. 43.

[15] *Ibid.*, p. 47.

could be found in most of the pagan schools spread over the Roman Empire. It is impossible to find the connection between the views expressed by various Church Fathers and the actual educational practices of the day.

CHRISTIANS IN CLASSICAL SCHOOLS

Possibly the real reason why educational theory and practice were so far apart in the early years of Christianity was that the theoretical expressions were directed not at learning in the schools, which was a preliminary kind of training, but at the formation of an intellectual life, which was something quite beyond and different from school learning. At any rate, there were Christian teachers and students in the classical schools. It may be interesting to see what they were exposed to and how they got along.

We can hardly believe that the Church was opposed to learning as such. Back in the years of the early Church, it became more and more apparent that some learning was an essential tool for the faithful. But how to get the pagan skills without getting pagan impiety and immorality along with them was the big question. Children in the pagan schools began with their letters, then moved on to reading and writing, and, if they went beyond the primary school, continued with the study of grammar and literature. Literature contained myths involving the gods and poetry that was unquestionably out of keeping with Christian morals. But there was no law that children should remain away from such schools, although there were canons which enjoined bishops and priests from spending their time with the profane authors. In this matter the law is stricter for the cleric than for the layman—and understandably so. The Church wanted clerics to be attending to their business and not engaging in literary pursuits. The determination of the Christian, as this objective was illuminated for him by the Church, was to superimpose religious truths on humanistic education.

A Christian adult could be a teacher in pagan schools almost as easily as a Christian youngster could attend such schools. A general injunction advised teachers who were able to do so without depriving themselves of their livelihood to give up teaching the secular sciences. This was a mild and tolerant proviso, and the view it expressed was to become more rather than less tolerant as time passed.

By the year 362 there were Christian teachers on all of the educational levels. This does not mean that teaching became a primary objective for Christians, but only that the Church's attitude was sufficiently relaxed to allow Christians to become teachers, and that the non-Christian attitude was sufficiently tolerant to allow Christians the freedom of pagan schools. The date 362 is one to remember. It was in that year that the Emperor Julian became concerned about Christian teachers occupying the important professorships in the pagan schools. He decreed that all teachers would have to be approved. He was especially interested in their morality, and by morality he meant that teachers who taught the classical poets would have to believe in the gods. To teach the poets and not to believe in the gods was, according to Julian, a kind of fraud and therefore immoral. This ban did not remain in force for any great length of time; after two years the order was rescinded. Christians went back to the schools.

In the meantime Christians had reacted to Julian's measure. They refused to be deprived of a literary inheritance or to be excluded from the art of teaching. They began to experiment with a school that had a real religious mission and whose content was derived from Christian sources. Such experimental schools were probably not immediately successful; actually they had too little opportunity to develop. Nevertheless, in their unfinished state, these schools that were organized as a result of the Julian edict were the first Christian schools.[16]

Although the Church could accommodate to classical education, and Christian teachers could teach and Christian students could be taught without too much evidence of discrimination, the Christian teacher let pass few opportunities for giving the Christian message. This teaching of the Gospel was done unofficially as an aside or as a bonus. Perhaps one of the conditions that the Church laid down for teachers who were to teach in pagan schools was that they seize every occasion to strengthen Christian beliefs. Yet in spite of this, formal education, especially on the highest levels, was apparently not affected to any extent by the teachings of Christianity. Christians and pagans got along well; there are many accounts of Christians having studied under pagans and of pagans having studied under Christians, and as far as we can judge, religion did not intrude on the highest studies. The Church seemed content to emphasize Christian education in the traditional sense and leave the pagan schools relatively undisturbed. Even when Christians were in the majority, they do not seem to have made any exceptional efforts to introduce Christian teaching into the schools' syllabus. All of this would suggest that the Christian influence on the school was slight.

[16] Bolgar, *op. cit.*, pp. 47–48; and Edward M. Pickman, *The Mind of Latin Christendom*, Oxford University Press, New York, 1937, pp. 373–391.

Laying the Foundations for a Christian Educational Tradition

Questions of origin are usually interesting to historians and to students of history, but they are often quite complex. We usually wonder where to begin. Christianity itself and Christian education present no such problem. They began with Christ; no other origin was possible. Of course the historical setting which antedated Christianity could not be ignored, but the explicit Christian mission was independent of this historical background. Christ's teaching was directed at the salvation of souls and the institution of a new order or a new ethos. Justice was the basis of the old law; charity was the basis of the Christian code. In a real sense Christ and his disciples were revolutionaries. We should not be surprised, then, that the established order treated them as subversive men. The fundamental Christian doctrine could not be separated from Christian educational views. Early Christianity showed little interest in formal schooling—we have seen some of the reasons for this [17]—but there were educational positions implicit in Christian doctrine that were waiting to be made explicit.

Christ himself was a teacher. Some would maintain that He was the world's greatest teacher; others would reserve this honor for Socrates. There is no sure way of demonstrating which was the greater teacher, that is, which was the better pedagogue, and we are forced into this neutral position if we think of teaching only in the sense of communication and formation—a high type of schoolmastering. In the broader sense of teaching—influencing, reforming, capturing men's minds and loyalties—Christ had no equal. In a way, the comparison of Christ and Socrates as teachers is a comparison that misses the greatness of both and betrays, besides, a lack of understanding of the missions that each set out to accomplish. Christ was no schoolmaster, although He was called rabbi, and Socrates never claimed divinity. Only on the level of methodology is there a possibility of comparison; yet we should know that methodological similarities mean very little and methodological differences may mean even less.

Despite the fact that Christ was not a schoolmaster, He was the originator of the Christian educational tradition. What He inaugurated was carried on by His apostles. We are not, of course, dealing with specific educational doctrines or practices; obviously neither Christ nor His apostles were educational philosophers or thinkers in any professional or limited sense. Nevertheless, an educational theory was implicit

[17] Geraldine Hodgson, *Primitive Christian Education*, T. & T. Clark, Edinburgh, 1906, p. 222; and Henry Chadwick, *Early Christian Thought and the Classical Tradition*, Oxford University Press, New York, 1966, pp. 39–55.

in the body of Christian doctrine—the same theory that is still in the process of being developed and understood—and it belonged to the tradition that was begun by Christ and was preserved by the apostles and by the Christian church that Christ founded. It is important for us to see how Christianity resolved the educational issues that faced it, issues which were both theoretical and practical. Here the question of where to begin is somewhat more difficult to answer. One could look to the Church Fathers and other Christian writers, but there were many such writers of varying importance. Yet we can isolate the early Christians who were most responsible for shaping the Christian educational tradition. They were: Clement of Alexandria (ca. 150–215), Origen (ca. 185–254), Jerome (331–420), Ambrose (340–397), Chrysostom (344–407), and Augustine (354–430).

CLEMENT OF ALEXANDRIA

Not all scholars believe that Clement of Alexandria was the first Christian to deal with educational theory. Such a claim has been made for St. Justin Martyr (ca. 100–165) who, it is said, was the first to develop a Christian theory of thought.[18] In addition to this, in his *Apologies*, Justin was supposed to have explained Christian thought to the pagan world.[19] Despite what may have been unusually successful efforts on Justin's part to explain the reasonableness of Christianity to the pagan world, it is hard to see why one should make claims for him in the realm of educational theory. Admittedly, it is not easy to isolate educational theory at any time, and in this period it was even more difficult, but Justin was surely not alone in trying to explain Christian beliefs to the pagans. This was a preoccupation of many Christian writers and it had nothing to do with the formulation of Christian educational theory. In this field Clement was a pioneer.

Clement of Alexandria was one of the first Christian thinkers to be really aware of a theory of education. We mean, of course, a theory of education in a formal and general sense, for, broadly conceived, Christianity itself might be understood as a theory of education. In recognizing and attempting to develop a theory of education more fully, Clement was somewhat different from his Christian associates. He was different in two ways mainly: He showed some understanding of the need for learning itself, and he was cognizant of the role intellectual culture could and should have in spreading and consolidating the Christian

[18] Jaeger, *op. cit.*, pp. 28–29.

[19] J. E. Sandys, *A History of Classical Scholarship*, Cambridge University Press, New York, 1906, vol. I, p. 332; and Chadwick, *op. cit.*, pp. 28–37.

message. While no one seemed to give a second thought to his interest in learning purely as a human ability, his apparent championing of the cause of liberal culture as a handmaiden of higher Christian thought and action came in for a good deal of criticism. Whether or not this phrase was used in his own time, his contemporaries were prone to look upon him as a "liberal Christian." Still, his so-called liberalism could not have been especially flagrant or offensive, for in many localities for many centuries Clement was called a saint. Popes Clement VIII and Benedict XIV, however, found reasons for excluding his name from the Roman Martyrology. Here we are interested in his educational ideas and his place in educational history and not in the claims made for or against him in the matter of his having been a saint.

In general, it seems safe to say, no one really disagrees with the conclusion that Clement was a great teacher or that the plan for his school in Alexandria was a noble one; or that his support of liberal culture in the Church was good; or that in seeing Christianity in its relation to the whole field of human thought he was traveling the road of orthodoxy. Nevertheless, he has been charged with gnosticism and heresy, an indictment which we have the commission neither to prove nor to disprove. But in his own day, when Christianity was viewed as a progressive doctrine, Clement's views may have been a bit too conservative. The Christians of the early centuries fully expected the Savior to return for a final accounting of mankind within a few short years. For the most part they saw no good reason, at least no compelling reason, to firm up their faith or their basic beliefs with intellectualism. They saw no need for theology in a formal sense, less need for philosophy, and no need at all for using pagan literature or any models from pagan learning, represented best in grammar and rhetoric, to convey or strengthen Christian doctrines. In addition, they found it difficult or impossible to distinguish between the arts and sciences of the pagans and the pagan view of life. In passing through pagan hands, or in coming from pagan minds, all of these things were tarnished. Even if the early Christians had thought that pagan literature had utility for Christianity, they would have avoided using it. In this sense some early Christians were progressive. They turned their backs on the past; they felt that they did not need the past; and they were understandably suspicious of any of their brethren who showed signs of conservatism. Clement was the object of some of these suspicions, as were others with whom Clement may have found some intellectual fellowship. His fame as a teacher may have created more fears concerning his complete orthodoxy than it allayed. But whatever his values, they were less subject to criticism in his own time—probably because of the inevitable lag in communication and the unsettled and generally unorganized state of Catholic orthodoxy—than they were two or three centuries later. But with all of this Clement could count himself fortunate, although he did not recognize his good fortune, for had he lived during the time of Gregory the Great or later and held the same so-called liberal views, his influence might have been stifled and his place in history denied him.

Clement was not born into the Christian religion. Although accounts of his life differ, the Alexandrian teacher became, it appears, a Christian in his early adult years. Perhaps he experienced an intellectual conversion; if he did, little account of it is left in his writings. Apparently he found little or nothing painful about the religious experience which brought him to accept the Christian doctrine; and possibly he had to give up little from his former actions and beliefs in order to participate fully in the Christian Church. A life of leisure and learning were the most obvious features of his pre-Christian life. He became in turn, then, a Christian, a priest, and finally the most famous of teachers for his place and time.

It would be a mistake to think of Clement as an academician in any narrow sense. It is true that his fame is that of a teacher, and the institution with which history most closely associates him was a catechetical school. Yet Clement was not only a teacher; he was a pastor and, in his later years, a writer. His school, which was left in his care by Pantaenus, was hardly a school in the ordinary modern sense. More like the Academy of Plato or the Lyceum of Aristotle, it was a well-appointed home with a good, possibly an excellent, library, which the youth of Alexandria who came from good families might attend. It bears in historical writing the name of catechetical school, though it was considerably more than the usual run of catechetical schools of that or any period. Christian doctrine was explained, the scriptures were prominent in all of the teachings, and a wide range of learning was undertaken. Nevertheless, the boys who had the good fortune to attend the school were not always Christians, and those who were did not, for the most part, have any vocation for or interest in catechizing. In other words, the school was a kind of study club in which young men approached Christian teachings for personal reasons, either religious or liberal. The impression that this school over which Clement presided was a Christian teachers' institute represents a narrow and inaccurate view.

There are three areas, then, in which to carry out an investigation of Clement's place in the history of educational theory: the nature and objectives of the school he conducted, his work as a teacher, and his writings. Of his school's nature we have probably said enough, except to add that during Clement's stewardship it was not subject to ecclesiastical control. It was independent of this kind of supervision for several reasons. Clement's work was well known and admired in Alexandria. His appeal to the more highly placed people of the city was recognized by the men who occupied the episcopal chair in Alexandria. The bishops of the city during the period of Clement's educational activity there were favorably disposed to a cultural approach to Christian teaching. Possibly, also, Clement's activities were not clearly understood, so that what at later times and in other places was to be represented as a real dichotomy, that is, liberal learning versus Christian beliefs, did not attract attention. Possibly Clement's stature was unassailable. Whatever the reasons for the freedom of the school, it was independent while Clement remained in charge of it. When he relinquished his head-mastership because he was forced to leave the city, the school passed to the management of Origen, under whom it was controlled by the authorities of the Church.

Of Clement's work as a teacher, only a little· is known with any accuracy, and most of our impressions of his ability must be inferred from his fame as a schoolmaster. Enduring fame as a teacher—not merely the accolades of a few satisfied students—is the honor history has given Clement. Clement's academic morality and his stature as a scholar have been the objects of severe criticism,[20] but no one has challenged his place as a great, perhaps the greatest, of early Christian teachers. He is represented as a mild, thorough, learned man. While little fame attaches to his originality in scholarship and less distinction to his literary ability, as a teacher he was well prepared to direct and guide students on intellectual adventures. He was both widely read and broadly educated, and his life was devoted completely to learning. This devotion may have been the real source of his success with students, whom he no doubt inspired by his example and who are said to have shown many evidences of the excellence of their education. Apart from whatever fine qualities the man may have had as a learned and inspiring teacher, it may be that the bold course he charted for his school was the real source of his fame. He aimed at no less than a synthesis of knowledge and faith—of reason and revelation. In its earliest years Christianity was not a doctrine which had great appeal to the learned or the sophisticated. There was even some antagonism to learning among Christians; the classics, for example, with their false gods and their immoral tales were often proscribed and pagan thinkers were subject

[20] See R. B. Tollington, *Clement of Alexandria, A Study in Christian Liberalism,* Williams and Norgate, London, 1914, vol. I, pp. 108–118; and Eric F. Osborn, *The Philosophy of Clement of Alexandria,* Cambridge University Press, New York, 1957, pp. 160–170.

to condemnation and the vehicles of their thought to ridicule. Still, here was Clement—not alone, to be sure, but in a minority—who with mildness but firmness retained and defended his background of learning in the classics when he entered the Church and went on to seek a reconciliation in his teaching between the world of ideas and the world of faith.

Clement may not have been an iconoclast, though there was a stubborn independence about him, but he was no starry-eyed intellectual either. Any portrait of him which neglects his acceptance of scripture as the final authoity would be unjust. He did not put reason on one stool and faith on another and abstract from both in order to put something new on a third stool. Rather, he tried to move the two stools so close together that both could be used to support any weight that fell on either. Analogies, however, are often either dangerous or unsatisfactory, for here one might assume from the image used that Clement regarded revelation and reason as equals. He did not. Not for a moment did he show any doubt as to the superiority of revelation. On the other hand, he showed no inclination to discount the worth of reason and the outcomes of its employment. Where much of early Christian educational theory was anti-intellectual, Clement went out of his way to defend the role of reason. By this we do not imply that he was interested in glorifying Greek learning or even secular learning, for Clement gives us many examples of his apprehensiveness concerning the real or spurious knowledge then available to man. Nor was it expurgation that he was working for, but something far more significant than taking an editor's pencil and striking out whatever was offensive to Christianity. He was defending reason, and in doing so he was saying that revelation could be made more meaningful by using reason to explain it. In addition, all human knowledge, being the product of reason, could and should lead man closer to God. Clement was not undertaking a defense of secular knowledge, for if he is understood correctly, he is saying that there is no such thing as secular knowledge. On the other hand, Clement was no rationalist either, though he did defend reason against numerous castigations by many early Christians.

As a writer, Clement leaves a picture which is somewhat less precise than that left by the oral tradition which portrays his role and success as a teacher. The liberal thought claimed for him in his instruction shows through rather dimly in his writings. He wrote toward the end of his life, preparing his writings for publication in the twilight of his career. Always his pronouncements were mild and noncontroversial, and possibly this feature became even more evident in his writing. Bold conclusions and straightforward demands for reform are characteristic of youth, not old age. By the time Clement was ready to write, he may have become even more moderate in his manner of expression than he had been in earlier years. It may have been, also, that his published works were delivered originally in the classroom, where mind in contact with mind brought greater clarity in purpose and greater unity of meaning.

Then, too, it must be acknowledged that Clement was not a polished writer of prose. Either he cared little for style, or he did not have the skill of an accomplished writer. His work is ponderous. His thought is usually simpler than his words. It is not that his eloquence conceals commonplace ideas, because Clement is hardly an eloquent writer. He seemed to try to find and adopt the most difficult manner of presentation for an idea. He carried into his compositions the intentional verbosity of many of his classical predecessors, and at times he came perilously close to being unintelligible. It has been said that Clement was not repudiated as a heretic in the fifth and sixth centuries because he was not understood.[21] And as if his unintelligibility was not enough to discourage many readers, he added to their confusion by filling his works with quotations from a variety of sources, usually the Bible, and he did not use sources well.

There was, of course, no good reason why Clement should not have proceeded in this way, because it was a style that was both accepted and approved in his time. Still, it must have caused hearers and readers a good deal of difficulty. He is hard to follow. But since sources extant in Clement's library were neither generally known nor generally accessible, by the generous employment of quotations Clement was really doing his readers a favor. Yet the modern reader cannot help but wish that Clement had made use of footnotes. His purpose would have been served just as well, and he would have spared the reader the agony of following his thought through a maze of quotations and interjections. Too often the quotations seem to obscure rather than to illuminate Clement's thought. He tried, apparently, to cultivate intentional obscurity. At least he wrote for those who were among the intellectual initiate, and he tried to write in such a way that comprehension would not come easily. He may have confused obscurity with profundity; he may have written as he did hoping to contribute to the expansion of the reader's mind and not merely to fill it; or, fearing criticism if he put his thought too clearly, he may have resorted to obscurity as a protective measure. It is more likely, however, though

---

[21] Edgar J. Goodspeed, *A History of Early Christian Literature,* University of Chicago Press, Chicago, 1942, pp. 16–31; and M. C. Strachey, *The Fathers Without Theology,* W. Kimber, London, 1957, pp. 81–92.

we may try to pick our way through the alternatives mentioned above, that this excellent teacher was simply a poor writer.

And this brings us to the difference between classroom teaching and academic writing. It raises, too, the problem of the degree of responsibility a writer must assume over and against that of a teacher. The teacher's audience is limited, and he knows something about his pupils. If they raise questions or objections, the teacher is there to explain, elucidate, or defend his views. The relationship between the teacher and the learner is important; it is and must be one of superior to inferior, for the teacher must know, or he cannot teach, and the student must be seeking knowledge, or he would not be under the tutelage of the teacher.[22] This is not true of the author. He does not know his readers, and they do not know him. He can assume little background for judgment or evaluation. The writer expresses himself and must rest his case and his reputation on what he has written. Emendations cannot be made easily, if at all; critics must be heard to be answered. The author, then, in Clement's view, needs both greater courage and greater confidence than the teacher. He is unable to avoid responsibility for what he has written; he must have confidence in his convictions and the courage to express them. Yet, as Clement wrote, he did "not imagine that any composition [could] be so fortunate as that no one [would] speak against it." He continued with considerable self-assurance:

> But that is to be regarded as in accordance with reason, which nobody speaks against, with reason. And that course of action and choice is to be approved, not which is faultless, but which no one rationally finds fault with. For it does not follow, that if man accomplishes anything not purposely, he does it through force of circumstances. But he will do it, managing it by wisdom divinely given, and in accommodation to circumstances. For it is not he who has virtue that needs the way to virtue any more than he that is strong needs recovery.[23]

What he seems to be saying here, and this is a good example of his indirectness, is that the author who is reasonable and careful has nothing to fear from critics who are also reasonable and careful. Perfection need not be demanded, only prudence and care.

[22] William Fairweather, *Origen and Greek Patristic Theology,* Charles Scribner's Sons, New York, 1901, pp. 10–15; and Maurice F. Wiles, *The Christian Fathers,* J. B. Lippincott Company, Philadelphia, 1966, pp. 177–183.

[23] Clement of Alexandria, *The Writings of Clement of Alexandria,* in *The Ante-Nicene Christian Library.* Translated by Alexander Roberts and James Donaldson, T. & T. Clark, Edinburgh, 1870, vol. I, p. 359.

One more point concerning Clement's writing should be touched on—the reason for his having written at all. From his tone one gathers that he preferred not to write, but that he felt some obligation to do so because of the message he had for others who wanted to know more about Christianity. But apart from what may have been missionary zeal, there was another and quite prosaic reason: His memory was dimming with the passing years, and he recorded his thoughts in order to have something on which to rely when his memory failed even more. What we are reading when we read some of Clement's works, especially *Stromateis*, are his lecture notes, organized a bit and perhaps enlarged somewhat, but his notes nevertheless. This statement does not seem to apply to *Paidagogos* and surely not to *Protreptikos*, perhaps the most charming of his writings and a work which represents Clement at his very best.

These three works must be studied especially to discover Clement's theory of education: *Protreptikos* (*An Exhortation to the Greeks*), *Paidagogos* (*The Instructor or Tutor*), and *Stromateis* (*Miscellanies*). Clement, is is said, planned these three books as a trilogy on Christian education. Certainly no one who has read the books could think that Clement was writing a theory or philosophy of education in any formal sense; his theory is incidental to other main ideas, particularly to his exposition of Christian doctrine. Moreover, educational theory was more practical in Clement's day than in ours, and the subjects with which he might deal quite appropriately seem rather foreign to modern educational theory. The big questions of Clement's day revolved about the *what* of education. There was no dispute about the *why*, and it was still much too early to think in scientific terms about the *how*. Why, of course, is the question of why man should be educated. For the Christian in Clement's time, the answer was obvious. The eternal view was dominant; educational objectives were all made to subserve man's final end. No Christian thinker from the early Christian period to the beginning of the modern era ever pretended to question this conclusion. But if no consideration was given to the possibility of a variety of educational objectives, both temporal and eternal, primary and secondary, the question of *what* should be taught became more acute. It is with this question that Clement deals, and, of course, it is an important and recurring question in the history of education. The question of content was central in Christian educational theory from the time of Clement to the time of Hugh of St. Victor. And from this central question flowed a number of additional significant questions: for example, the whole matter of whether education was to be made available to everyone or only to a few, and whether those privileged to obtain the advantages of education were to be clerics and prospective clerics only or laymen. But much of this is anticipatory both of Clement's views and of the views of others from the early Christian period through the Middle Ages.

What is considered to be the first work in Clement's trilogy on Christian education is *An Exhortation to the Greeks*. It has usually been evaluated as a rhetorical plea to the Greeks to look at Christianity more closely; it is surely not an apologetic work. The two later works, it has been suggested, are the ones that really deal with educational questions. No doubt both *The Instructor* (or, as it has been rendered, *Christ, the Educator of Children*) and *Miscellanies* have a great deal of educational import in them, but many people believe that the basis of Clement's educational theory is really found in the *Exhortation*. Let us examine this plea to the Greeks more carefully.

Clement is obviously not assuming the role of an educational theorist in any limited sense. His object is to call to the attention of the Greeks the beliefs they had so long accepted and to point out to them the wisdom of looking at these beliefs a little more critically. He does not say that they are or have been ignorant, but he does say that the "extremes of ignorance are atheism and superstition, from which we must endeavor to keep." [24] He is suggesting that they strip themselves of superstitious beliefs and look at the gods they have honored. He recommends that they observe honestly and carefully and then in all candor arrive at a reasonable conclusion. Reason is the human ability on which man must depend, and for reason to be effective it must be informed. Clement puts it this way:

> Then, he that is uninstructed in the word, has ignorance as the excuse of his error; but as for him into whose ears instruction has been poured, and who deliberately maintains his incredulity in his soul, the wiser he appears to be, the more harm will his understanding do him; for he has his own sense as his accuser for not having chosen the best part. For man has been otherwise constituted by nature, so as to have fellowship with God. As, then, we do not compel the horse to plough, or the bull to hunt, but set each animal to that for which it is by nature fitted; so, placing our finger on what is man's peculiar and distinguishing characteristic above other creatures, we invite him—born, as he is, for the contemplation of heaven, and being, as he is, a truly heavenly plant—to the knowledge of God, counseling him to furnish himself with sufficient provision for eternity, namely piety. Practice husbandry, we say, if you are a husbandman; but while you till your fields, know God. . . . Your means and substance you squander on ignorance, even

[24] *Ibid.* vol. II, p. 34.

as you throw away your lives to death, having found no other end of your vain hope than this. Not only unable to pity yourselves, you are incapable even of yielding to the persuasions of those who commiserate you; enslaved as you are to evil custom, and, clinging to it voluntarily till your last breath, you are hurried to destruction: "because light is come to the world, and men have loved the darkness rather than the light." [25]

Then Clement exposes the Greeks to a little of the basic Christian doctrine, not apparently to convince them of the truth of these beliefs or to defend the Christian point of view, but simply to give them some information on which to ponder. Neither the Greeks nor other readers are led to believe that reason as it is represented in classical philosophy and literature is the sure or steady road to faith and salvation. Clement admits that some of the non-Christian philosophers had glimmerings of truth; and he charges that many of the pagans had devised pernicious, evil systems of philosophy and had disseminated literature that both injured and ignored morality. He says, though his language is somewhat equivocal, that the learning of the classical sages cannot be accepted as a beacon for truth:

> Wherefore, since the Word Himself has come to us from heaven, we need not, I reckon, go any more in search of human learning to Athens and the rest of Greece, and to Ionia. For if we have as our teacher Him that filled the universe with His holy energies in creation, salvation, beneficence, legislation, prophecy, teaching, we have the Teacher from whom all instruction comes; and the whole world, with Athens and Greece, has already become the domain of the Word.[26]

This passage would be easy to misinterpret. It would not be entirely fair to Clement to take him at his word here, for he really does not mean what he seems to say, and the context of the quotation is actually broader than *An Exhortation to the Greeks* itself. Clement does not mean to say that learning is unimportant and that the Greeks have nothing which the Christian learner might seek. He is saying that the human learning of Greece—the search for ultimate causes—is no longer necessary, for the First Cause Himself has already given man the information he needs on this essential level. But he does not say that Christ is going to give, or has given, man all of the information and instruction he needs in every avenue of human activity. He means that with God-given ultimate answers, man needs to search no longer for

[25] *Ibid.*, vol. II, p. 92.
[26] *Ibid.*, vol. II, p. 100.

these hidden, basic truths. He implies elsewhere, though he does not say it here, that there are many kinds of questions, not all of them of ultimate concern, and that man must try to use the reason God has given him to understand the world. In this way man will come, Clement maintains, to a fuller and more complete knowledge of God.

If the three works mentioned above are a trilogy on Christian education, then the first, *An Exhortation to the Greeks,* is really the foundation for the trilogy. In it Clement demonstrates his meaning better than he explains it. He is asking the Greeks, as he would ask all men, to use their reason. Reason is man's supreme endowment, and its cultivation leads to human truth, which in turn gives man a larger vision of divine truth. Had not reason's place been established by Clement here, both the *Paidagogos* and the *Stomateis* would surely lead many readers to wrong conclusions. This trilogy must be studied as a unit, for it has an internal unity, and each part rests somewhat on every other part. Having established reason as the foundation for human development in the first treatise of the so-called trilogy, in the other works Clement is able to go directly to the points he wishes to discuss—moral training in *Paidagogos* and a variety of intellectual matters in *Stromateis*—without stopping each time to remind his readers that he is willing to pay allegiance to man's intellectual abilities. It is on man's rational nature that Clement's theory of education rests. Without this foundation Clement becomes a mere eclectic or a pious tinkerer in Christian pedagogy.

In *Paidagogos* Clement displays remarkable breadth of vision, because he treats that part of human formation without which an educational theory would be inadequate or incomplete. *Paidagogos* is not simply a sermon on the moral formation of youth. To consider it as such would not recognize its special distinction or recommend it to the attention of readers interested in the formative years of Christian educational theory. An assertion of the importance of character formation in the molding of men has unquestioned value. But this is not the same thing as integrating moral and intellectual formation and ascribing to each its proper role in man's life as he moves toward his ultimate destiny.

Paidagogos is made up of three books. Book I contains thirteen chapters, Book II, twelve, and Book III, twelve. The first book is of the greatest value to us, though Books II and III were probably especially valuable at the time they were written. For example, they treat of subjects from conduct or manner in eating to bodily exercises for the sake of health. Today they have a puerile character, but Clement's advice concerning deportment at the public bath was not superfluous or puerile when it was given. It is axiomatic that the past should not be judged by the present.

In Clement's view, Christ is both the example and the teacher. There is no suggestion at all that one is superior to the other. In *Paidagogos* Clement is dealing only with morality or the inculcation of virtue. He is not ignoring learning and intellectual virtue, but in this work he is simply not considering Christ's wisdom and knowledge.

Moral formation is far too important a subject to be left to schools. There are many reasons for this opinion: School life is deferred to a time when many of the child's most basic moral habits have already been formed; moral education is too broad a responsibility for the school, which has the child under its care for only a relatively brief time; moral formation cannot be solely a function of the school, because there are too many experiences over which the school has, and can have, no control, that are instrumental in shaping character. Clement's discussion of moral education is not intended for schoolmasters. It is a fine piece of pedagogical writing that is intended to have universal appeal. It is directed toward all Christians, whether they are parents, teachers, or merchants, for all of them, when it comes to moral formation, are teachers of the young. But even taking into account the universality of its message, we must conclude that Clement's treatise probably had greater meaning for teachers of his day than of our own. Schools were both schools and homes then. Christian teachers often accepted very young students and cared for them from their late infant years until they were ready to stand alone in the world. Clement's own school, while never a nursery, was a place for living as well as a place for learning, and it was, according to his own pedagogical creed, a place for moral as well as intellectual formation.

Stromateis, a book which critics say was written before *Paidagogos,* has a character that is hard to describe. Some parts of the *Miscellanies,* it appears, have been lost. However, of those which remain only a few of the 193 chapters in the eight books have a direct bearing on educational theory, although all of them are really concerned with mental culture. The difference to be noted, though, is that some of the chapters take up the problem of intellectual formation in and for itself, while others contain only the content which students of that day might have used for intellectual cultivation. More than any of Clement's other works, *Stromateis* has a lecture-note character; notwithstanding Clement's caution that he has only hinted at some things and left other things out altogether, the reader of *Stromateis* may be pardoned if he concludes that Clement often left out too much.

Stromateis, as we mentioned above, is made up of eight books, comprising in all 193 chapters, some of which are very short. No one book, let alone the entire work, displays the kind of unity that would enable one to summarize either its purpose or its contents. It is surprising, indeed, and somewhat disappointing, that in the work which Clement reserved for a discussion and analysis of intellectual education, he is at his worst as far as style and design are concerned.

Clement's educational thought is not elaborate; nowhere does it wander very far from fundamentals. In his *Stromateis* it is possible to find the foundation for all subsequent Christian schools and educational systems. Clement's contributions notwithstanding, it may be observed that the fundamental issue with which he dealt still continues to be an issue in Christian schools and in Christian educational theory. Although Clement did not have to raise the question in this way, it is possible to interpret him as asking: What is the primary function of a school? Admittedly this is a somewhat narrower problem than the one with which Clement dealt, but it was surely, though implicitly, contained in the larger one which faced him. We have stated above that the problem which vexed Christian thinkers involved the relative position and worth of reason and revelation.

No Christian disputed the preeminence of revelation, but some in accepting revelation degraded reason to the point where intellectual effort was both useless and dangerous. Instead of leading man to virtue and salvation, it was often maintained that cultivation of reason would lead to eternal destruction. Clement, in a moderate, perhaps oversanguine manner, expressed the view this way:

> Some, who think themselves naturally gifted, do not wish to touch either philosophy or logic; nay more, they do not wish to learn natural science. They demand bare faith alone, as if they wished, without bestowing any care on the vine, straightway to gather clusters from the first. Now the Lord is figuratively described as the vine, from which, with pains and the art of husbandry, according to the word, the fruit is to be gathered.[27]

ORIGEN (ca. 185–254)

Clement set the pace. He was the first but by no means the last to work toward a reconciliation or a compromise between classical and secular learning and Christianity. He was followed in this work by Origen. It is not easy to see how Origen surpassed his teacher, Clement, al-

---

[27] *Ibid.*, vol. II, p. 379. See also Titus Flavius Clemens, *Christ the Educator*, translated by Simon P. Wood, Fathers of the Church, Inc., New York, 1954.

though such a claim is made with monotonous regularity. As a matter of fact, Origen and Clement had somewhat different interests, and to compare the two men is not altogether fair. Clement was a teacher and an educational thinker; Origen was a scholar.

Origen cultivated fields that had been only explored by Clement and others. He was interested in teaching and writing; he was attracted to secular and divine subjects; and he had the instincts of a scholar. There is a story, apparently authentic, to the effect that Origen owned an exceptionally fine library, one that may have been left to him by his father, who was a teacher of rhetoric, and that he sold the library for an annuity that amounted to about ten cents a day for the rest of his life. If this seems an unusual act for a scholar, it must be remembered that Origen was seeking leisure and freedom from economic cares, both of which are indispensable to the man who wants to lead the life of a scholar and devote his best energies to learning. Yet giving up a library would be sacrificing the scholar's most valuable tool. But Origen apparently arranged to sell his books and have them too, for the agreement that brought him the annuity also permitted him to use the collection of books and manuscripts that formerly had been his property. If we have established Origen as a man of learning and common sense, we have done him simple justice. We have yet, however, to establish him as an outstanding figure in the history of educational thought.

He was one of the most famous of the early Christian teachers. The Alexandrian Catechetical School was never better known or more influential than when Origen was its master. When he was forced to leave Alexandria, the stature of the school diminished at once. The testimony of his own time, that is, of fellow teachers and students, plus his acknowledged influence on later generations would be enough to justify his reputation. But many of his writings are extant and bring his thought directly to us.

Briefly, what was the educational position of Origen? Following the lead of Clement, although without any acknowledgment of indebtedness, Origen continued to seek a means for bringing sacred and secular subjects closer together. It seems unlikely that Origen respected secular subjects for what they were or that he saw secular knowledge as an end in itself; he probably regarded secular subjects as mere means for understanding or confirming Christian beliefs. St. Jerome expressed this opinion of Origen's position when he wrote of his genius and praised his spirit and his skill. Students, he said, came to Origen in large numbers for instruction in all subjects including secular literature. "These he received in the hope that through the instrumentality of secular literature, he might establish them in the faith of Christ." [28] In other words, secular subjects had value only insofar as they could advance or illuminate the Christian cause.

Origen himself seems to confirm Jerome's view in a letter to Gregory "Thaumaturgus," who, along with his brother, was one of Origen's most prized students at the school in Caesarea. In this letter Origen urged young Gregory to devote all his strength to the Christian cause. This devotion might, in part, be shown by extracting "from the philosophy of the Greeks what may serve as a course of study or a preparation for Christianity, and from geometry and astronomy what will serve to explain the sacred Scriptures, in order that all that the sons of the philosophers are wont to say about geometry, and music, grammar, rhetoric and astronomy, as fellow helpers to philosophy, we may say about philosophy itself in relation to Christianity." [29] Origen's advice is an express recognition of the value of secular subjects and secular learning but only as instruments to a more sublime goal. In spite of this evidence, some scholars maintain that Origen freed Christian education from its narrowness and opened to it all of the prospects of liberal culture. But if Origen was not an unwavering friend of liberal learning, he was certainly not an uncompromising enemy. By the time Origen finished his work Christian education had made considerable progress, and it had left behind the untenable stand that secular subjects were to be avoided altogether.

As a last word on Origen, we may say that he seemed to have a deeper understanding of the nature of education than most of his predecessors or his contemporaries. He tried to inculcate in his students motives for learning that were not based on fear. His school was a workshop in which character and mind were formed. And as a general evaluation we may add that he was an excellent example to help disprove the shibboleth that scholars always make poor teachers.

ST. JEROME (331–420)

A certain contradiction between the actions and the expressed attitude of Jerome had a good deal to do with the reception Christians were to give classical learning. We have seen that various points of view,

[28] Jerome, "Lives of Illustrious Men," in *A Select Library of Nicene and Post-Nicene Fathers of the Christian Church*, 2d ser., vol. III, p. 349. See also Chadwick, *op. cit.*, pp. 100–112; René Cadiou, *Origen: His Life at Alexandria*, B. Herder Book Co., St. Louis, Mo., 1944, pp. 222–231; and Harry F. Robins, *If This Be Heresy: A Study of Milton and Origen*, University of Illinois Press, Urbana, 1963, pp. 180–184.

[29] *Ante-Nicene Christian Library*, vol. X, p. 388.

some expressed in extreme form, either commended Greek learning or condemned it. The Christian was often not able to say exactly where he stood on the matter. Should he turn his back on all secular learning? Should he accept pagan learning as an instrument? Should secular knowledge be accepted as valid and valuable for Christians? Christians looked toward their leaders for guidance. How much help was Jerome to them?

It seems unnecessary for us to concern ourselves here with the details of Jerome's life or even of his career, although we must not overlook the fact that he was a great Christian scholar. The *Vulgate* alone attests his scholarship, although Jerome's Biblical commentaries and his *Lives of Great Men* are added evidence. Jerome was a scholar, and he provided an excellent example of scholarly competence for his fellow Christians to emulate. Even when he was experiencing the trials of the ascetic life in mountain caves or on desert sands, Jerome continued his studies. He could arrange, it seems, to have his library with him wherever he went.

Often, however, Jerome did one thing while he preached another; he was a scholar but he did not endorse classical scholarship for his companions in Christianity. True, he became a schoolmaster for a few years to found and conduct a boys' school in Bethlehem. But the most lasting impression that Jerome created, though not necessarily the most effective, was that scholarship should be feared and learning avoided. When Jerome was on the desert, having deserted civilization to find salvation, he had a dream which he reported vividly.

> I could not altogether give up my library, which I had collected at Rome with much zeal and much labor. And so, poor wretch, I would fast in preparation for reading Tully. After the long vigil of the night, after the tears which the remembrance of my past sins drew from the depth of my heart, I would take Plautus in hand. If I ever recovered my senses and tried to read the prophets, their uncouth style rubbed me the wrong way; and because with my blind eyes I saw not the light, I deemed it the fault not of my eyes, but of the sun. While thus the old serpent was beguiling me, one day, about the middle of Lent, a fever flooded me to the very marrow and wracked my weary body. Pausing not—incredible as it may sound—it so fed on my hapless limbs that I could scarce cleave to my bones. Meanwhile they made ready for my obsequies. The vital heat of my soul, of my breast, in a tiny spot, was still tepid—when, of a sudden, I was caught up in the spirit and haled before the judgment seat of God. Blinded by its light and by the brightness of those who stood about it, I fell prostrate to the earth, not daring to look up. When the voice asked me concerning my

condition, I replied that I was a Christian. "Thou liest," answered he that sat upon the throne. "Thou art a Ciceronian, not a Christian; for where thy treasure is, there shall thy heart be also." [30]

If this is not a hostile attitude toward pagan learning and scholarly excellence, it is at least a warning that such learning does not have a high place on a hierarchical scale of Christian objectives. Did Christians accept the implications contained in Jerome's dream and leave Cicero alone? Perhaps they did not go quite that far. Yet it can hardly be argued that Jerome's words would lead Christian minds toward learning or the intellectual life. Still, there was this example of refusing to repudiate learning, so what really did he mean? Jerome's counsel and example confused many Christian minds, but he meant to convey the idea that a good scholar must turn to the classics for an education in style while studiously ignoring their content. The former was good and useful for every educated Christian; the latter was dangerous and should be overlooked. While this may have been realistic advice to the advanced student capable of separating the form of good writing from the matter, or the story, it was, for the most part, a formula unacceptable for teaching schoolboys.

Another point might be mentioned before we move on. Jerome expressed his principal views on education in his many letters. In them we find that he had something to say about the education of Christian girls. In doing so he shaped much of the policy on women's education for the next thousand years. His advice on the education of girls may be found mainly in two letters, one addressed to the noble mother, Laeta, concerning the education of her daughter, Paula, the other to Gaudentius, advising him about the education of his daughter, Pacatula.[31] In general, the girls' education was to be pointed toward Christian service, and was to be almost entirely religious. There were, nevertheless, some tools that Jerome would have the Christian girl use and she could learn their use best by following this prescription:

> Have letters made for her, of boxwood or ivory, and let them be called by their names. Let her play with them, and let the play be part of her instruction. She must not only get the right order of the letters and memorize them in a song, but now and then mix the alphabet, last with the middle and middle with first, so that she may tell them by sight as well as by hearing. But when she begins with trembling hands

---

[30] *Selected Letters of Saint Jerome*, translated by F. A. Wright, Loeb Classical Library, Harvard University Press, Cambridge, Mass., 1923, vol. XVI, pp. 125–127.

[31] *Ibid.*, vol. XVI, pp. 363–365.

to draw the pen through the wax, either let her elder's hand guide her tender finger joints, or let the letters be graven on the slate, that the marks she traces be confined within the edges of these furrows and not stray outside. Let her learn to join syllable to syllable by the inducement of a prize—something very acceptable to that tender age. She should have companions in her task of learning, whose accomplishments she may envy and whose praises may spur her sense of shame. Don't scold her if she is slow, but arouse her ambition by praise so that she may delight at victory and smart at defeat. Above all, don't allow her to hate her studies, lest the bitterness of them, acquired in childhood, may last to her mature years.[32]

Jerome was certainly aware of approved techniques in teaching and of the psychological principles that supported such techniques. Even so, we can call him an educator only in a rather tangential way.

ST. AMBROSE (340–397)

The position of St. Ambrose in the history of education is not as clear as that of Jerome or Clement. He was not a teacher, except in the episcopal sense, and he was not engaged in building a theory of education. Yet his name ought to be mentioned in any general account of the evolution of Christian education, because he committed himself to a definite acceptance of scholarly content and form for Christian literature. The old indecisiveness with regard to classical scholarship and its intellectual standards, an indecisiveness that left the individual Christian in a quandary, was resolved by Ambrose. Christians could still hear a certain amount of declaiming against learning and arguments that intellectual formation was an obstacle to salvation. Nevertheless, the works of Ambrose, principally *The Duties of the Clergy* and his works on theology, originated a Christian educational tradition or at least reinforced the tradition started by Clement, with exemplary Christian determination. Even more than any of his predecessors, Ambrose accepted and supported the full utilization of man's mind and the intellectual instruments the ages had refined. The eminence of St. Ambrose, who was a great bishop of Milan and a powerful theologian, forestalled criticism. His reputation was not adversely affected by his stand in favor of intellectualism or by the fact that he was himself a thorough Greek and Latin scholar. St. Ambrose stands at the historical gateway to the Middle Ages as one of the principal inspirational sources for the intellectual energy of that era.

[32] *Ibid.*, vol. XVI, pp. 345–347.

ST. JOHN CHRYSOSTOM (344–407)

Along with Clement of Alexandria and Origen, St. John Chrysostom, a Church Father of the East, reacted to the educational questions of the day. The most important question that the Christians had formulated concerning education was: What, if any, use could be made of classical learning ? Except for St. Ambrose, the Western Fathers were unsure of classical learning, and the fact that they did not always proscribe it testifies to their prudence rather than to their willingness to accept the content of pagan culture. Of course, the mere use of the vehicles of classical learning did not imply any acceptance of the culture itself. Some, however, did not understand this; and others, understanding it, still saw danger in any employment of pagan learning. But the Fathers of the East, who had been closer to the classical culture and who often had been nurtured on it, were able to see ways of using classical litera-ture and all of the implements of classical learning without allowing the non-Christian spirit that permeated them to cloud Christian thought. Some of the Fathers of the West did not have this advantage of fa-miliarity with the classics, although it would not be fair to say that the opponents of the use of the classics were the Fathers who were most ignorant of them. We have already said enough about this problem. In a way though, it is this same problem that alerts us to the work and influence of St. John Chrysostom.

He advised parents to see to the Christian education of their chil-dren. This meant to him, as it had to earlier Christians, that parents were responsible for the moral and religious formation of their off-spring. He told parents that this was their first duty, and as the times did not make possible any ready delegation of this function, one that had to be fulfilled personally. Certain elements in education could be delegated, and Chrysostom had no intention of turning parents into schoolmasters; but the parent who sent his son or daughter to the schools to be trained in the skills of learning had to be sure that the school would not undermine the moral and religious foundation already laid. This important responsibility was placed squarely on the shoulders of parents. Was it really possible for parents to know what the dangers were that lurked before their children in the schools of the day? St. John seemed to be convinced that parents who could direct the Christian education of their children would be equal to the task of detecting and evaluating dangers in formal instruction.

Instead of firing a broadside at the classical schools of the day or declaring them out of bounds with a sweeping condemnation, Chrys-ostom wrote:

If you have masters among you who can answer for the virtue of your children, I should be very far from advocating your sending them to a monastery; on the contrary, I should insist upon their remaining where they are. But if no one can give such a guarantee, you ought not to send children to schools where they will learn vice before they learn science and where in acquiring learning of relatively small value they will lose what is far more precious—their integrity of soul. . . . Are we then to give up literature? you will exclaim. I do not say that; but I do say that we must not kill souls. . . .

When the foundations of a building are sapped we should seek rather for architects to reconstruct the whole edifice, than for artists to adorn the walls. . . . In fact, the choice lies between two alternatives: a liberal education which you may get by sending your children to the public schools, or the salvation of their souls which you secure by sending them to the monks. Which is to gain the day, science or the soul? If you can unite both advantages, do so by all means; but if not, choose the more precious.[33]

Chrysostom undertook a more systematic treatment of educational questions than any of the other Church Fathers, and came closer to being an educational thinker than any of his contemporaries. It has been claimed, and with good reason, that he produced the finest educational treatises of the period. They were scattered among his many works (722 are credited to him) and remained uncollected until John Evelyn translated them and grouped them together in one volume called the *Golden Book of St. John Chrysostom*.[34] The most complete of St. John's single works on education was *Concerning the Education of Children.*

In his various writings on education Chrysostom touched on most of the educational topics that are today considered to be of greatest significance. He concerned himself with theories of child development and child psychology; he dealt with home training and with certain aspects of vocational guidance; he treated the problem of cultivation of the senses and the powers of observation; he was interested in incentives for particular goals as well as general questions of motivation. To this catalogue of broad interests must be added his theory and method of sex instruction. In brief, the idea was to prepare young men and women for marriage. This instruction was to begin early and was

[33] Quoted in Hodgson, *op. cit.,* p. 223; and see M. L. W. Laistner, *Christianity and Pagan Culture in the Late Roman Empire,* Cornell University Press, Ithaca, N. Y., 1951. (This volume contains an English translation of St. John Chrysostom's Address, "Vainglory and The Right Way for Parents to Bring Up Their Children.")

[34] William Upcott (ed.), *The Miscellaneous Writings of John Evelyn,* Henry Colburn, London, 1825.

to continue over a long period of time. Little was left to chance, for Chrysostom could see no sense in neglecting to prepare for one of life's most important vocations, and the training was approached with meticulous care.

Chrysostom was an effective champion of Christian education. All his writings and all the provisions he would make for education had Christ at their center. The world and everything in it could be used to educate young people, but young people should always be educated toward Christian wisdom. In his own words Chrysostom reflects this view very clearly: "This is the very sum and top of all wisdom, that he be not taken up with impertinent and childish vanities. Teach him therefore that riches avail nothing, worldly glory nothing, power nothing, nothing death, nothing this present life. Thus he shall indeed become a wise man." [35]

ST. AUGUSTINE (354–430)

In the history of the Church St. Augustine has few equals. He was a powerful ecclesiastic in his own time, and his disciplined and astute mind was a source of intellectual inspiration for many centuries. The impression he made on theology and philosophy was significant. Augustine is generally recognized as the father of early Christian philosophy. Yet despite his renown in philosophy and theology, we must pass over these areas of thought to ask: Where does Augustine stand in the history of education?

To begin with, we find fairly orthodox educational attitudes reflected in Augustine—orthodox, at least, for Western Church Fathers. He had been thoroughly schooled in the classics, although it appears that while his accomplishments were outstanding in Latin they were only a little more than ordinary in Greek. In spite of this generally acknowledged excellence in classical learning, Augustine's judgment about the place of the classics in the education of Christians is somewhat equivocal. It is only fair to say, however, that he was neither more nor less indecisive on this question than most of his eminent contemporaries. Augustine would probably have supported the stand that the classics and all of pagan learning could be used, with proper precautions, as instruments of Christianity, even though he several times made some strong statements which indicated that he might place a severe limit on the value of the classics and their use by Christians. On occa-

[35] *Ibid.*, p. 136; and see C. Baur, *John Chrysostom and His Time*, Newman Press, Westminster, Md., 1959; and William R. W. Stephens, *Saint Chrysostom, His Life and Times*, J. Murray, London, 1872.

sion, in the heat of controversy or in dealing with particular problems, he denied the worth of most, if not all, secular knowledge. But these polemics are probably not typical of his general attitude.

If the following excerpt from Augustine's *On Christian Doctrine* may be accepted as representative of his position, then he apparently conceived of knowledge as arranged on a hierarchical scale. Some kinds of knowledge were more valuable and therefore more desirable than others.

> Moreover, if those who are called philosophers, and especially the Platonists, have aught that is true and in harmony with our Faith, we are not only not to shrink from it but to claim it for our own use from those who have unlawful possession of it. For, as the Egyptians had not only the idols and heavy burdens which the people of Israel hated and fled from, but also vessels and ornaments of gold and silver and garments, which the same people when going out of Egypt, appropriated to themselves, designing them for better use, not doing this on their own authority, but by the command of God, the Egyptians themselves, in their ignorance, providing them with things which they themselves were not making good use of; in the same way all branches of heathen learning have not only false and superstitious fancies and heavy burdens of unnecessary toil, which every one of us, when going out under the leadership of Christ from the fellowship of the heathen, ought to abhor and avoid; but they contain also liberal instruction which is better adapted to the use of the truth, and some truths in regard even to the worship of one God are found among them. Now these are, so to speak, their gold and silver, which they did not create themselves, but dug out of the mines of God's Providence, which are everywhere scattered abroad and are perversely and unlawfully prostituted to the worship of devils. These, therefore, the Christian, when he separates himself from the miserable fellowship of these men, ought to take away from them and devote to their proper use in preaching the Gospel. Their garments, also, that is, human institutions such as are adapted to their intercourse with men, which is indispensable in this life, we must take and turn to Christian use.[36]

Although it may be said that all Augustine's writings have educational implications—for what philosophical and theological works do not?—those that are of especial interest to the educational historian are: *Confessions, The City of God, On Christian Doctrine, Catechizing the*

---

[36] *A Select Library of Nicene and Post-Nicene Fathers of the Christian Church,* 1st ser., vol. II, p. 554. See also Ellspermann, *op. cit.,* pp. 142–181; Bolgar, *op. cit.,* pp. 45–58; and Eugene Kevane, *Augustine the Educator,* Newman Press, Westminster, Md., 1964, pp. 93–108.

Uninstructed, and *De Magistro.* In most of his writings we find sections that deal with the liberal arts, for in spite of some serious reservations, Augustine was still deeply interested in liberal learning.

The *Confessions* are autobiographical and include many comments on Augustine's own education as well as unusually fine insights into psychological problems, especially problems of learning. *The City of God* is an expression of a philosophy of life and as such is basic to a Christian philosophy of education. Although this work is primarily inspirational, its instrumental value should not be discounted completely. In *On Christian Doctrine* we find Augustine explaining how scriptural study should be approached and also how rhetoric, philosophy, and classical literature might be used in conjunction with divine studies and for the end of divine studies. *Catechizing the Uninstructed* was intended to be a guide for teachers who directed the religious instruction of those about to enter the Church. This work has been interpreted as a guide to the program of the so-called catechumenal schools, but by the time Augustine appeared on the scene the catechumenal school was rarely found and had not been in general use for more than a century. This work was effective, nevertheless, for though catechumenal schools were hard to find, religious instruction was still given, and the Church was very much interested in converting people who were still outside the Christian communion. Augustine's own conversion may have contained experiences which he felt could be useful in illuminating the whole matter of instruction for religious neophytes. But we must remember, too, that Augustine was the bishop of Hippo, and had a definite obligation to direct the religious education of those who had just embraced Christianity. Finally, there is *De Magistro.* This work voices general ideas about the teacher and teaching, and deals with the fundamental conceptions which make up an ideal of the instructor's art. It is well worth studying but not with the expectation of finding a full exposition of a philosophy of education. It was never intended to be anything other than what it is: a discourse on the authority and general function of the teacher. Augustine's *De Magistro* has often been regarded as anticipatory of the *De Magistro* of St. Thomas Aquinas.

Before we leave St. Augustine, we should admit the difficulty of weighing the significance of his educational influence. On the one hand, he seemed to stimulate learning both by his excellent scholarly example and by precept; on the other, he cautioned against the excesses of intellectual activity. There is little wonder, then, that the Christian writers of the day were somewhat confused. They found it hard to discover just what the Christian's position should be with respect to classical or pagan learning. The relative unwillingness to accept or to pursue secular knowledge was due primarily to the Christians' lack of trust in the intellect. They took the following words of St. Augustine as a warning to them to beware of too much intellectual activity, and generations of Christians who followed Augustine did not easily forget or ignore his caution:

> Accordingly, I think that it is well to warn studious and able young men, who fear God and are seeking for happiness of life, not to venture heedlessly upon the pursuit of the branches of learning that are in vogue beyond the pale of the Church of Christ, as if these could secure for them the happiness they seek; but soberly and carefully to discriminate among them. . . . But for the sake of the necessities of this life, we must not neglect arrangements of men that enable us to carry on intercourse with those around us. I think, however, that there is nothing useful in the other branches of learning that are found among the heathen, except information about objects, either past or present, that relate to the bodily senses, in which are included also the sciences of reason and of number. And in regard to all these we must hold by the maxim, "Not too much of anything." [37]

Some commentators maintain that Augustine was instrumental in retarding scholarship and freedom of activity in learning. There may be some truth in this accusation, for he was surely devoted to authority and discipline and to the Church's primary teaching function. Other scholars insist that he helped to construct an intellectual framework for Christian thought and educational activity that lasted almost to modern times. There may be some truth in this claim also, for it is not hard to identify the influence of Augustine in both the early and the late Middle Ages. Yet, these generalizations leave us somewhat in the dark on Augustine's position vis-à-vis a pagan literary inheritance. He could and did separate this inheritance into definable parts, keeping some for Christian educational use and discarding others. The principle of selection achieved respectability with him; that is, Christians should appropriate for their own use the classical treasures they wanted. They could take parts without taking the whole. This was Augustine's compromise; it was simple and manageable and it had profound effects on the future of Christian education. In addition, he told his contemporaries to employ the principle of selection by compiling summaries of the classics. Thus students could go to these summaries and safely study

[37] St. Augustine, *Works*, vol. IX, *Of Christian Doctrine*, T. & T. Clark, Edinburgh, 1875, Book II, chap. 26; St. Augustine, *On Christian Doctrine*, Liberal Arts Press, New York, 1958; and J. M. Flood, *The Mind and Heart of Augustine*, Academy Guild Press, Fresno, Calif., 1960, pp. 75–81.

the wisdom of the ancients without at the same time being exposed to the dangerous elements in their thought. For the teaching of grammar and rhetoric, he advised the preparation of textbooks which should contain the rules of good writing; and for models he recommended, not the classics, but the Scriptures. Augustine proved the classics redundant for teaching grammar and rhetoric, although even in accomplishing so much he was unwilling to break with the past. Some borrowing from the classics was, Augustine thought, still necessary if the foundations were to be properly laid for philosophical and theological study, but the amount borrowed could be severely circumscribed. This was the Augustinian compromise, and his best advice to teachers.[38]

The First Christian Schools

We have already expressed the doubt that the first organized efforts by Christians to instruct either the faithful or those persons aspiring to Church membership could be called scholastic. Christian schools with a formal, literary-centered curriculum were slow in coming. We have already explored a number of reasons for the delay. In any event, the monastic school seems to have been the first Christian school.

There was Christian-centered instruction before the monastic school appeared, but little of this instruction went beyond religious teaching. Though the monastic school was primarily religious in purpose, its curriculum was not always made up exclusively of a religious content; in other words, it often fulfilled the first requirement of what we now call a school—an institution with a literary curriculum and with literary objectives. These early efforts to consolidate and spread the Christian faith are worth examining. They were directed mainly in catechumenal, catechetical, and cathedral or episcopal centers of teaching.

CATECHUMENAL SCHOOLS

Catechumenal instruction was intended to prepare a prospective Christian for the sacrament of baptism. We know little about the begin-

---

[38] See Rand, *op. cit.*, 251–258; Bolgar, *op. cit.*, pp. 35–36, 50–54, 57–58; St. Augustine, *De Magistro*, translated by F. E. Tourscher, Villanova College, Villanova, 1924, pp. 14–98; Gerald Bonner, *St. Augustine of Hippo: Life and Controversies*, Westminster Press, Philadelphia, 1963; Peter R. L. Brown, *Augustine of Hippo: A Biography*, Faber, London, 1967; H. I. Marrou, *St. Augustine and His Influence Through the Ages*, Harper Torchbooks, New York, 1957; and Herbert A. Deane, *The Political and Social Ideas of St. Augustine*, Columbia University Press, New York, 1963.

ning of such instruction, but we may assume that in the early Church
some preparation was always needed as an essential preliminary to
baptism. In the most general sense, then, catechumenal instruction
began with the Church itself and lasted until infant baptism became
common—about the ninth century. But in a more specific sense, the
catechumenal school belongs to the first two centuries of the Christian
era. Thereafter, though religious instruction continued and became
much more thorough and more carefully graded, the catechumenal
school did not keep its institutional form. It may be argued that the
catechumenal school did for non-Christians what the Christian family
did for its younger members; that is, it inducted them into a Christian
moral climate and a Christian way of thinking and indoctrinated them
with Christianity's basic precepts. The reason why the catechumenal
school did not last much beyond the second century is to be found
mainly in its principal objective. There was a social environment which
assumed much of the educational work that the school had done in
earlier years.[39]

The catechumenal schools were conducted by Christians known
for their steadfastness and their allegiance to the Christian religion.
Teachers in such schools did not need the qualifications of schoolmasters, for the instruction given probably never went outside the realm
of Christian history, doctrine, and practice. In the catechumenate's most
infant years the teachers or leaders were clerics, usually bishops or
priests. But this was only natural, considering that the Church was just
getting started. Shortly thereafter the guidance of prospective Christians was entrusted to minor clerics or to laymen. Although the bishops
began to delegate this important work, they continued to show great
interest in it and to supervise it with considerable care.[40] The course of
instruction was probably neither detailed nor extensive, but the time
required to pass through the course was long. Possibly three or five
years elapsed before a candidate was baptized, and thus finished his
course in the catechumenal school.

A final word may be appended concerning teaching technique employed in these schools where Church doctrine was learned and over-
learned following a pedagogy of question-and-answer. This approved
and apparently effective catechetical technique outlived the schools
responsible for producing it: for centuries, religious catechisms were

[39] See Edward J. Power, *Evolution of Educational Doctrine*, Appleton-Century-
Crofts, Inc., New York, 1969, pp. 122–128; and John E. L. Oulton, *Alexandrian
Christianity*, Westminster Press, Philadelphia, 1954, pp. 400–425.

[40] Hanson, *op. cit.*, pp. 81–105; and Carlton J. H. Hayes, *Christianity and Western
Civilization*, Stanford University Press, Stanford, Calif., 1954, pp. 10–62.

written to accommodate the question-and-answer techniques of religious instruction.

CATECHETICAL SCHOOLS

If catechumenal centers of teaching were not the first authentic Christian schools, then catechetical schools may lay claim to such a distinction. The fame of the Alexandrian catechetical school under the mastership first of Clement and then of Origen ought to satisfy any skeptic. If this is not enough, then the catechetical schools of Caesarea, Antioch, Edessa, Nisibis, and Rome may be cited. There is no doubt that they were outstanding centers of learning. But were they Christian schools?

First of all, the teachers in the schools just mentioned had no commission to teach Christian doctrine as had the teachers in the catechumenal schools. It is curious but true that the Christian leaders of this period saw fit to appoint teachers to communicate elementary points of Christian doctrine to the uninitiated, but saw no similar need to commission teachers to teach Christian doctrine on higher levels. The teachers in catechetical schools of the type that flourished in Alexandria may have been Christians, but they were not in any full sense Christian teachers. Usually they were laymen who taught on their own responsibility and authority. The Church could, of course, interdict their schools but otherwise could exercise no authority over them. And it was the unusual catechetical school that made any attempt to integrate religious and secular knowledge. The well-known catechetical schools were of a type that emphasized secular knowledge. It was the main, if not the only, constituent of the curriculum and the principal reason for the school's existence. Such schools were the pagan schools all over again, except that Christians taught in them and that in some schools a course of religious instruction was added for those who wanted it. Perhaps it was only in this additional instruction that these schools differed from pagan schools, for we know that Christians had been teaching in the pagan schools all along. If these schools were the best representatives of catechetical instruction, it may be necessary for us to revise what is often a first impression in the history of education: that catechetical schools were authentic Christian schools. But there were other types of catechetical schools.

As more Christians began to show enthusiasm for secular knowledge, because compromises between faith and pagan culture were either sensed or effected, schools arose as a natural consequence of demand. Occasionally a Christian qualified to teach and, trying to make a living in this way, simply opened a school and thus liberalized educational opportunity. Yet this is only part of a picture completed by a number of inchoate institutions, conveniently classified as catechetical schools, intended to continue the religious formation of a Christian convert in his postbaptism years. In these places clerical and lay Christians offered courses of instruction devoted entirely to Christian doctrine, and differing from catechumenates only in the level of their teaching and (also, of course) in the fact that their students were professed Christians. Catechetical teaching centers were most prominent and influential in the early Christian period. Although their written history is sketchy, we may be confident in saying that their tenure was impermanent and their teachers were denied any lasting notice on the educational record.

Another catechetical school, one acting as a minor seminary and giving basic instruction and guidance to boys aspiring to holy orders, offered a course preparatory to the training supervised in episcopal residences. Catechetical schools of this type could not have been popular, for clerical training, almost entirely nonacademic, followed a route marked out by traditional apprenticeship practices. Moreover, the regular Roman schools were available for literary teaching, and their classical course was superior to anything which temporary and preparatory Christian institutes could offer.

Neither catechetical schools as places for secular education and fairly advanced learning, nor as institutes for religious instruction and formation of practicing Christians, nor as preparatory schools for boys aspiring to the Christian priesthood, filled all the requirements of a Christian school. The first type mentioned here, however, interests us most. It was an academically centered school promising the most for the future of Christian education and schooling, even though this promise was not fulfilled until a time well after the catechetical schools had passed out of existence. We return again to Alexandria, where the most famous catechetical school of all was conducted and where Origen, its famous master, began his teaching career.

Under Clement, the Alexandrian school was nonintegrated; that is, its masters were Christians, but the main content of its curriculum was secular. Religious studies were "extras" or almost on the same level as the extracurricular activities of the schools of the mid-twentieth century. This was hardly a Christian school in the most complete meaning of the term. Yet when Origen gained control and became its chief teacher, the content of studies was divided. Under this new leadership the Alexandrian catechetical school became a school for advanced theo-

logical studies [41] as well as a school for the study of mathematics, literature, and philosophy. The latter studies, which could perhaps be called
liberal, were pursued on a secondary level of teaching; the religious
studies were accomplished on the level of higher education. So there
were actually two schools, one for secular knowledge and another, separate from the first, for higher, specifically religious studies. What this
type of educational organization might have produced if it had been
cultivated is hard to say.

Catechetical schools were impermanent fixtures in the Christian
educational system; they disappeared rather quickly. There were different reasons for their disappearance just as there were different types
of schools. The catechetical school with an academic orientation depended too much on a few men to sustain it. When these men died or
were otherwise prevented from maintaining an association with the
school, the school either declined or disappeared. There was insufficient
interest in the kind of learning these catechetical schools offered to keep
them alive, vital, and permanent. Even the Church Fathers who expressed interest in education in their writings and in their sermons
made no effort to create or preserve catechetical schools committed to
clear-cut academic objectives.[42]

Catechetical schools for advanced instruction in catechism disappeared when religious teaching of this type became a definite function
of the Church. Such teaching had always been the Church's responsibility, but the Church saw fit to delegate the actual teaching to trusted
Christians. When the Church distributed this commission less freely,
the catechetical teachers decreased in number. This did not happen,
however, until other types of Christian schools had appeared on the
scene.

Finally, the few ecclesiastical catechetical schools disappeared when
the training of future clerics was regularized. The kind of education
that this type of catechetical school purported to give was offered in
an educational adjunct, or annex, to the cathedral or episcopal school.
But this was a development some distance in the future, as we shall
see shortly. The basic reason for the anemic career of schools of this
type was that what they proposed to do was done in part by the pagan
schools—the teaching of elementary literary skills—and in part by the

---

[41] See Tollington, *op. cit.*, vol. 1, pp. 213–223; and Oulton, *op. cit.*, pp. 114–128.

[42] Alvin Lamson, *The Church of the First Three Centuries*, Walker, Wise and
Company, Boston, 1860, pp. 12–22; and Gordon L. Keyes, *Christian Faith and the
Interpretation of History: A Study of St. Augustine's Philosophy of History*, Univer-
sity of Nebraska Press, Lincoln, 1966.

clerical apprenticeship system. In other words, there was no real need for such schools during most of the early Christian period.

CATHEDRAL SCHOOLS AND EPISCOPAL SCHOOLS

In the time of the early Church, boys who had some aspiration to clerical life were educated in the regular, pagan schools and were then apprenticed to a bishop. They learned to be priests by living and working with the bishop. He taught them what he thought they needed to know and what experience had taught him, and when he felt that they were ready, he ordained them. This informally organized training led to the formation of the cathedral school. Actually, it was not a school in any complete sense of the word. However, as time went on, the bishops may have offered the young men attached to them a more formalized course of instruction or one more highly specialized in doctrine and theology. The bishop was still the teacher, and because the teaching was done in or near the cathedral, the name cathedral school came into common use. Probably the bishops engaged in this kind of instruction never thought they had organized a school.

Apprenticeship training built on a foundation of classical education could lead a young man to holy orders. A continuance of classical education beyond elementary studies was not thought to be necessary; in fact, it was sometimes studiously avoided by clerics themselves, who had known the Church to proscribe clerical use of the classics. But some elements of learning were essential, and in the absence of any Christian schools on the lower educational levels, the classical or the pagan schools were about the only places where these tools of learning could be obtained. As long as they were available, the pagan schools were used. But the whole climate of education changed when the Roman political and social system collapsed, for the classical school collapsed with it.

Now a new dimension was added to clerical education. Boys who were to become priests went to the bishop when they were mere lads seven or eight years old, and they took their complete education from him or from the teachers he appointed, in what was called the episcopal school. From the teaching of the most elementary skills of learning through the classics and through specialized training in theology, the whole gamut was the work of the episcopal school. The chief and sometimes the only teacher in such a school was the bishop himself.[43] The

---

[43] See Francis P. Cassidy, *Molders of the Medieval Mind*, B. Herder Book Company, St. Louis, Mo., 1944; and Henry O. Taylor, *The Classical Heritage of the Middle Ages*, F. Ungar Publishing Company, New York, 1957.

episcopal school was a real Christian school, although what we have called the cathedral school was not. But the episcopal school did not arrive on the educational scene until the early sixth century.

PARISH SCHOOLS

With the spread of Christianity, the Church's organization expanded also. Urban centers had their cathedral churches and their bishops to care for Christian souls, but now with parishes in the rural areas, the need for priests became greater and ordained priests were encouraged to perpetuate their class. In the Church's need for priests and in the relatively barbaric environment surrounding rural parishes, parish schools were born. Classical schools had not penetrated the rural areas, and even the most elementary schools in the Roman system were scarcely found in every village. The parish school was a village school conducted by the parish priest mainly with the object of giving an early education to boys who might become priests. These schools were, of course, only elementary, but they were the first step in a system which seemed to extend all the way up to the episcopal school. By assuming responsibility for the elements of literacy, parish schools relieved episcopal schools of some responsibility for teaching their students how to read and write. In a real sense the parish schools were an extension of the educational idea which brought episcopal schools into existence.

The origin of parish schools is far from clear. Little is said of them either in the historical accounts of the early Church or in official Church documents. It is usually assumed, probably with reason, that parish schools were more or less regularly found after the fifth century, and that from that time on one of the important functions of the pastor of the parish was to supervise education in his parish, or if need be, to accept the duties of a teacher.[44]

MONASTIC SCHOOLS

Monastic schools, making an appearance in the fourth century, were the first Christian schools. Their religious purposes were entirely clear, but they had literary objectives intended to supplement and complement moral and religious formation. Yet, despite the schools' definite literary aims, the classics were neglected. More than this, determined efforts were made to forget them.

Both Eastern and Western monasticism began by placing little

[44] See Hodgson, *op. cit.*, pp. 225–237; and Jean Decarreaux, *Monks and Civilization*, Doubleday, Garden City, New York, 1964, pp. 360–372.

value on learning. Most early monks, we know, were not ordained priests, a fact allowing them to regard learning—even mere literacy—as an obstacle to holiness. Eastern monks, trying to escape from the world (and certainly their monastic ideal allowed them this luxury), never attached any educational functions to their monasticism. Inducting novices into monastic life followed prescribed formulas, and even among Eastern monastic groups had a bookish side, although literacy was perhaps unnecessary. In any case, every monk was expected to know several Psalms and some Epistles; anyone unable to read had to learn them by heart.

But what may have been acceptable in the early centuries of Eastern monasticism did not always remain acceptable. St. Basil's *Rule,* for example, required that young boys who were admitted to the monastery be taught to read. Nothing was said about a thorough education since none was needed, but literacy seems to have been an unavoidable minimum. St. Jerome, too, although his views on education and its relationship to monastic life belong to the West, prescribed a completely ascetic education—one intended for girls who were to become nuns—for Paula and Pacatula.[45] Even the great Chrysostom had advised parents to send their children to the desert for their education. He thought a ten-year stay would do them good.[46] Whether or not Chrysostom expected that boys so educated would become monks is not the point to be considered here; at least they would have been under the direction and guidance of monks, and their education would have been a monastic one to the degree that it would have been useless for boys who were to return to the world. It may have been that Chrysostom had in mind what many Eastern rules had prescribed: that no boy was to be admitted to the monastic internship who was not committed to a life in the monastery. He came, in time, to acknowledge the imprudence of sending a boy away from the world in order to learn to live in it. As a result of his changed view, he endorsed family religious training (a practice that in actual fact was associated with all Christian education) and secular and literary education in the classical schools.

In general, Eastern monasticism did not engage in education because it did not have to. The relatively high standards and the fairly general distribution of education in the East absolved the monasteries from engaging in work for which they had not been designed in the first place.

What we have said of Eastern monasticism and its general unawareness of education and educational problems cannot be said of

---

[45] *Selected Letters of Saint Jerome, op. cit.,* vol. XVI, pp. 363–365.

[46] See Laistner, *op. cit.,* pp. 130–131.

Western monasticism. Almost from the beginning, the monasteries of the West accepted the elements of learning as essentials to the full monastic life. Monks did not have to be learned and not many of them were, but they had to be able to read. The same was true of the convents; rules for religious women were very nearly uniform in their demand that all the nuns were to learn to read. If the ability to read was important for women, it was obviously more important in this day and age for men. Many rules that preceded the *Rule* of St. Benedict (ca. 525) had emphasized the importance of studying the written word, but the *Rule* of St. Benedict consolidated the practice and gave reading an unassailable place in the monk's life and duty. The Benedictine *Rule* did not, as other Western rules before it did not, assume that boys would come to the monastery already educated. Therefore it was necessary to have a system of education for young men who applied for admission to the monastery. In spite of the exclusiveness of most early monastic schools—they were intended specifically for novices and often the admission of any others was prohibited—these schools were both Christian institutions and schools in a proper sense. And more than this, during the dark years that were about to envelop Europe, the monasteries, largely because of their educational features, were true homes for Christian culture.

Summary

The first Christians showed relatively little interest in establishing systems of schools that would continue the classical literary tradition. There were two principal reasons for this lack of interest. One was that Christians felt they had no real need for such an intellectual inheritance, and even if they had felt the need there would have been no reason for them to establish such schools, because a well-established system of classical schools was already in operation. The other was that the educational goals they sought to achieve were of such a nature that they could be obtained more satisfactorily in a family plan for education. Christian education meant family education. The values of the Christian life and the moral habits to sustain these values were to be communicated in the home. Thus those Christians who chose to turn their backs on classical learning could do so without endangering the kind of human formation they considered most valuable. And the Christians who decided to imbibe the classical tradition could do so without creating any special schools under Christian auspices.

It would be a mistake to think that Christians were not aware of classical or pagan learning. They were very much aware of it. Few of them, however, were inclined to embrace it. Yet many Christians did see the need for a substantial intellectual foundation for their faith. While the dangers of learning were often emphasized, the values of learning were regularly, if not popularly, promoted. Christianity found itself in a dilemma in regard to the classics and generally in regard to the content of the pagan schools. Time saw a slow but gradual resolution of this dilemma.

The resolution was not attained without painful effort. Yet throughout most of the early Christian period, it was entirely usual to find both Christian teachers and Christian students in the classical schools. At the same time, Christian thinkers and teachers gave their views on the educational questions of the day, and in so doing they laid the foundations for a Christian theory of education. The most prominent of these figures were: Clement of Alexandria (ca. 150–215), Origen (ca. 185–254), Jerome (331–420), Ambrose (340–397), Chrysostom (344–407), and Augustine (354–430).

Although a system of Christian schools was not to be found during the early Christian period, some Christian institutions were operated which came close to being schools with specifically religious objectives. These were the catechumenal, catechetical (of three types), and cathedral institutions.

After the Roman system of schools had pretty well collapsed, Christians organized parish and episcopal schools. The first true Christian school, created around the fourth century, was the monastic school.

VIII

The Development of Christian Educational Doctrine

The Collapse of the Classical System

Slowly but surely the Christian movement proceeded through the Roman Empire and spread beyond it whenever missionaries found the means to carry the gospel of Christ that far. By the time of Constantine's reign (306–337) the Christian strength, although by no means overwhelming, was remarkable. In 313 the decree of Milan promulgated by Constantine had ended the persecution of Christians and had extended to them the civil rights enjoyed by followers of other religions or of no religion. At the same time Constantine showed great interest in education, and the schools on all levels and almost everywhere in the Empire flourished under the emperor's favor. This was especially true of higher studies in Constantinople, where scholars were encouraged in their studies and rewarded generously for their work. Almost everywhere teachers were attracted to the schools with the lure of high salaries and privileges and immunities that were hard to find elsewhere.

During this time Christian teachers in even greater numbers than before found their way into the schools. Unfortunately, educational prosperity of this magnitude was not permanent. The edict of 362, to which reference has already been made, was published by Julian.[1] From this point on the classical school, which continued to be the school of the Empire, was in a state of flux. It enjoyed periods of prosperity but also had to endure long periods when the professed interest in education was not too evident in practice. These schools were pulled in two directions as occasional attempts were made to reform them. The Christians, understandably enough, were never completely satisfied with them. On the other hand, a number of influential people in Rome had a nostalgic yearning for the pagan-centered classical schools of years past. Julian, representing this position, made one last desperate effort to revive pagan culture. He failed; yet classical schools surely did not disappear when Julian's scheme proved unsuccessful.[2] Classical schools never disappeared completely, as the modern and contemporary educational eras can attest.

Students of the history of education, when meeting the subject of early Christian education immediately after having studied the chapter in their textbook treating of Roman education, often assume that the Roman schools simply disappeared from the face of the earth and that a new educational order came into being. They have not been told how the Roman schools were disposed of. Possibly they have an erroneous impression that the Christian school conquered the classical school and in doing so was left in command of the educational field. We have seen that there was no Christian school worthy of the name until about the fourth century, and that this monastic school had neither the will nor the strength to engage in any struggle for survival. The classical school system of Rome had begun to decline before Christianity received its tremendous boon in the edict of Constantine. The collapse began in the outskirts of the Empire.

---

[1] R. R. Bolgar, *The Classical Heritage and Its Beneficiaries*, Cambridge University Press, New York, 1954, pp. 47–48; and Alice Gardner, *Julian, Philosopher and Emperor, and the Last Struggle of Paganism Against Christianity*, G. P. Putnam's Sons, New York, 1895, pp. 158–161.

[2] H. I. Marrou, *A History of Education in Antiquity*, Sheed & Ward, Inc., New York, 1956, pp. 323–324; T. R. Glover, *Life and Letters in the Fourth Century*, Cambridge University Press, New York, 1901, pp. 150–153; and Giuseppe Ricciotti, *Julian the Apostate*, Bruce Publishing Company, Milwaukee, Wis., 1960, pp. 141–147.

One established policy of the Empire, it will be recalled, was the support and control of education. Although the efforts of the state were partial, possibly even sporadic, the policy of the Roman state was clear. This policy led to the decline of private schools and private tutors. Either private masters found it hard to compete with the state schools, or they were motivated for financial or other reasons to become part of the public system. There is no question here of educational doctrines or purposes or of theories of curriculum; public schools were just as classical as private schools had been. But in tying themselves to the Roman political system, the schools became utterly dependent on that political system. It was their life's blood; when it died, they died with it.

The branches died and fell away long before the trunk was afflicted. The Anglo-Saxons had shattered Roman Britain by the early fifth century. Its political system was replaced in violence and its educational system became a vacuum of barbarism. But the fifth century was late in the history of educational collapse. In Gaul decay had begun in the third century, and by the early fifth century Roman dominion over Gaul was a thing of the past. Perhaps decay is the wrong word, since it connotes internal weakness or rot. Although the Gallic schools may have been weak, it is far more significant that Germanic barbarians crossed the Rhine River in 276 and that from then on Gaul became an insecure appendage of the Roman system. What happened in Gaul and Britain happened also in the other continental outposts of Roman influence. There were exceptions, for example, Africa. Here the Roman influence remained fairly secure for another two centuries and then was challenged by the Arabic invasions: another kind of barbarism from another source. Italy was the last great stronghold of the Roman system and thus of classical education. Classical education on all levels was found in the Italian cities, and some of the cities—Milan, Ravenna, Pavia, and, of course, Rome—were great university towns for a hundred and fifty years after the Roman system had collapsed in Britain and three hundred years after it had started to collapse in Gaul. The force of the early barbaric invasions had not been great enough to push all the way into Italy and disrupt an established way of life. Italy's time was yet to come. By about the middle of the sixth century the Lombards swarmed down on Italy and laid waste almost all of the culture that stood before them. The political system was destroyed; the social system was badly disrupted; culture and learning were given little or no chance. For a hundred years or more—it was close to the end of the seventh century before a revival of culture was seen—Italy was subjected to the same fate that had been visited on Gaul and Britain. The great traditions, social, political, cultural, and intellectual, were buried by the barbaric hordes from the north. When they finished overrunning the country, Italy was intellectually barren. The educational slate was not wiped clean, but there remained only dim outlines of past vitality, excellence, and glory.

What was left to take the place of the classical school? There were few Christian schools, and of them the most important was the monastic school. The educational problem that faced the few surviving schools and the newly created Christian schools was the problem of what to teach. The old hostilities to pagan literature still existed. Some of these hostile attitudes never actually left the Christian school or what by now can be called Christian education. But this is not a point of history, although some historical dimensions may be involved. There stood the monastic school, but it, too, was insecure. What was it to teach, and to whom? We have already touched on the first point; [3] with respect to the latter, it is fairly clear that many monastic schools could not or would not accept children of the world; that is, they could not accept students who had not committed themselves to the life of religion. This ban had its origin in the canons of the Council of Chalcedon and apparently remained in full force for some time.[4] Christians were required to face once more the problem that had faced them so often before, the problem of content for their schools.

Continuing and Consolidating the Christian Tradition

By the time the Middle Ages were ready for the universities, a fairly definite theory of education had been worked out, and Christians were quite certain what schools ought to teach.[5] But these decisions were the final result of a long and sometimes painful process of educational evolution. Our object is to try to establish some of the foundations of a teaching tradition that culminated in the medieval university.

BOETHIUS (ca. 480–525)

Too often Boethius is just a name in the history of thought. One writer may say that he was the last of the ancients, another that he was the first of the Scholastics, a third that he was both. We should not like to

---

[3] See also M. L. W. Laistner, *Thought and Letters in Western Europe, A.D. 500–900*, The Dial Press, Inc., New York, 1957, pp. 21–37.

[4] Marrou, *op. cit.*, pp. 337, 341.

[5] See Daniel D. McGarry, *The Metalogicon of John of Salisbury*, University of California Press, Berkeley, 1955; and Hugo of St. Victor, *Didascalicon: A Medieval Guide to the Arts*, translated, with an introduction and notes, by Jerome Taylor, Columbia University Press, New York, 1961.

believe that the only claim for the man is based on authority, for surely his relevance to history should be made clear, or his name should be dropped from the catalogue of famous men who helped shape our intellectual inheritance. Is it not possible that Boethius, like Martianus Capella (ca. fifth century), has been given far more credit than he deserves? Or has Capella's significance been overstated?

Martianus Capella, along with Cassiodorus and Boethius, is said to have been responsible for what the Middle Ages knew about the liberal arts. Since knowledge of the liberal arts was pretty well disseminated in that period, this is saying a great deal. The claim made for Capella contains much truth. Nevertheless, it is hard to evaluate his position in the history of education. His work, *The Marriage of Philology and Mercury,* was written in Carthage in North Africa in the early fifth century. Cole has called it the most successful textbook ever written.[6] Yet despite this claim, even despite Capella's tremendous popularity in later years, we may wonder if it is accurate to refer to this book as a text. It was either allegory or fiction.

According to the story, Mercury decides to take a wife, and after surveying the field, selects Philology. At the wedding Mercury presents his bride with a number of appropriate gifts, the most elaborate of which was introduced by Apollo. He brings forward seven maid servants; as each is introduced she steps forward, is described, and then goes on to explain herself. The seven maids are the seven liberal arts, by now—or by Capella—reduced from eleven or nine to seven. Thus the encyclopedia of the arts, for this is what the *Marriage* was, had nine books: one for each of the arts—grammar, rhetoric, dialectic, arithmetic, geometry, astronomy, and music—plus two introductory books. Capella's book was not the only means that later ages had for understanding the nature and function of the arts that classical culture had seemed to prize so highly, but it was a very popular source of information. So in a way Capella's book was a textbook, for it contained many of the things that students of later times, especially of the Middle Ages, studied. The trivium and the quadrivium were there, although Capella did not introduce into his description of them the fine distinctions later thinkers were prepared to make.

Boethius must share the stage with Capella. Even if Capella's part is a big one, the principal actor is still Boethius. He, like Capella, transmitted culture, but he did even more: he placed the content of this culture in a Christian frame of reference, and he made it intellectually and doctrinally palatable for Christians.

[6] P. R. Cole, *Later Roman Education,* Teachers College Press, New York, 1909, p. 16.

Here was a man of good standing, who married well and became an important political figure. But he fell into the pitfalls of politics, spent his last years in prison, and was executed for political crimes. The great work that came from Boethius' pen in his most mature years and the one which had a lasting and profound influence on European thought structure was the *Consolation of Philosophy*. As Rand has said, this was prison literature.[7] Even so, in general estimation it seemed to stand above Capella's *Marriage of Philology and Mercury* and Cassiodorus' *Divine and Human Readings*. It was more generally accepted than the former because of the reputation that Boethius had for being a Christian saint, and it was more thorough and satisfying than the latter because much of Cassiodorus' work is simply based on the *Consolation*. Professor Patch gives high praise to Boethius' book:

> The work was quoted verbatim in almost every connection, and, it is perhaps fair to say, thousands of times, if we may judge by the instances that have been listed. From casual reference and extensive borrowing, Boethius is everywhere recognized as an authority, fully as eminent as one of the Church Fathers, but more versatile than most of them. . . . One must call the roll of practically everyone of account in the Middle Ages if one is to include those who showed indebtedness to him.[8]

The *Consolation of Philosophy* was one of those books that no educated man left unread. It was, probably to a greater extent than Capella's fictional account of the arts, the textbook of the Middle Ages and, though unconventional, one of the most successful of all time. But Boethius wrote much beside the *Consolation*. He was engaged in scholarly endeavors long before he fell victim to political chicanery. He wrote some pastoral poetry; he prepared an arithmetic book based on the earlier work of Nichomachus; and he began a tremendous project which involved translations of and commentaries on both Plato and Aristotle. His commentaries on Porphyry's *Isagoge*, an *Introduction to the Categories of Aristotle*, brought logic up to a point where Christians could begin to regard it more favorably. Eventually they adopted it as an instrument for building their own intellectual system. Boethius offered, in addition to writings on philosophy and education, treatises

[7] Edward K. Rand, *The Founders of the Middle Ages*, Harvard University Press, Cambridge, Mass., 1928, p. 159; and John A. Langford, *Prison Books and Their Authors*, W. Tegg, London, 1861, pp. 5-25.

[8] Howard R. Patch, *The Tradition of Boethius*, Oxford University Press, New York, 1935, p. 24; and Boethius, *The Consolation of Philosophy*, translated by W. V. Cooper, J. M. Dent and Company, London, 1940.

on theology and music and many commentaries on the works of classical authors. If we find difficulty in accepting Boethius as the first of the Scholastics we can at least call him the schoolmaster of the Middle Ages in the same sense that we called Homer the schoolmaster of the Greeks.[9] Students who look to Boethius for solutions to practical educational problems—problems such as Quintilian tried to solve—will look in vain. Boethius' importance does not lie here.

It is worth the risk of repetition to emphasize the significance of Boethius. He was an inspiration to Christians in that he could integrate a tremendous wealth of classical learning and pagan philosophy with a healthy and apparently orthodox Christian faith. He led the early Middle Ages to the doorstep of philosophy, and, although the times were anything but encouraging for building intellectual foundations, provided budding Christian philosophers with a content and a terminology, and with the inspiration for moving ahead. More than this, he constructed a bridge between the classical years, with their high culture and their profound accomplishments in the arts, and the Christian Middle Ages, with their spirituality and their motivations for reconstructing the social order. The material for the bridge which Boethius built was the content of education, mainly the arts and, as they came to be known, the seven liberal arts.

ST. BENEDICT (ca. 480–546)

A contemporary of Boethius and a builder with him of Christian tradition: this is an apt characterization of St. Benedict. Yet it does not begin to tell the whole story. St. Benedict, it is said, was not much affected by learning or art, and his biographer has described him as one who was "sagely ignorant and wisely uneducated." [10] How unlike Boethius he must have been! The really important question, however, is hardly whether or not St. Benedict was learned, but whether or not the liberal arts had a place in the monasteries his religious rule brought into existence.

One conclusion might be that in following the monastic traditions with their usual hostility toward classical learning, the Benedictine monasteries turned their backs on the liberal arts.[11] Yet we know that

[9] See Helen M. Barrett, *Boethius: Some Aspects of His Times and Work,* Cambridge University Press, New York, 1940, pp. 160–179.

[10] Rand, *op. cit.,* p. 239; and T. F. Lindsay, *Saint Benedict, His Life and Work,* Burns, Oates, London, 1949, pp. 73–81.

[11] Edward C. Butler, *Benedictine Monachism,* Speculum Historiae, Cambridge, Mass., 1961, pp. 331–338; and John Chapman, *Saint Benedict and the Sixth Century,* Sheed & Ward, Inc., New York, 1929, pp. 187–193.

Christianity had now developed to the point where the written word was indispensable to it. There are not too many steps between this emphasis on the written word and a definitive Christian literature and the liberal knowledge to subserve it. In the *Rule* of St. Benedict a certain amount of sacred reading was prescribed.

There are some other alternatives. It is likely that liberal studies did find a place in Western monasticism; otherwise how is it possible to explain the learning that emanated from many of the monastic houses of Europe? Or it may have been that the secular schools were expected to provide the learning preparatory to sacred studies or to higher schools of theology. Benedict himself had attended a classical school which purported to offer studies in the liberal arts.

If the liberal arts were given a place in the Benedictine system, this place was usually well concealed. However, we do consider the monastic schools the first Christian schools in the proper sense, and we know that they evolved from an elementary to a higher stage. It may well be a mistake to look at the first monastery in order to find what we have really no right to expect for several centuries yet to come. We shall probably be making extravagant claims if we think that St. Benedict contributed to Christian culture and education in the same way that Boethius did, or that Boethius influenced the education of every peasant in the early or the later Middle Ages, or that the monastic schools were such a great force in education that they caused it to be widely and generously distributed. Benedict's contribution was that he laid the foundation for the Christian institutions in which Christian thought could revitalize and redirect classical culture. Here was the opportunity to breathe a Christian soul into pagan literature. From an educational point of view, the monasteries of the sixth century are of much less importance than those of the ninth and tenth centuries. Yet the later monasteries could not have reached their importance had it not been for the monastic beginnings of the West in the sixth century.

In a way, the cultural demeanor of Boethius and the Christian rusticity of Benedict are both mutually hostile and complementary. Although modern historians may have taken too literally the self-acknowledged ignorance, or preference for ignorance, of men like Benedict, it is safe to assume that Benedict would have had some reservations about the direction of Boethius' learning. We must admit that the monastic ideal was originally frankly hostile to culture. On the other hand, we cannot ignore the Benedictine definition of the monastery as "a school for the service of God." The complementary role of monasticism was to be found, therefore, in the preservation of culture in the monasteries when it most needed to be rescued from oblivion, and in the monks' cultivation of the intellectual inheritance when they found a place for the liberal arts in their system.

Most of the strength of the secular schools had been lost by the sixth century. It is not likely that Benedict or his immediate followers had any thought of building on the educational foundation of the secular schools, nor is it likely that they thought of the monastery as a step on the educational ladder. We have already seen how the monastic schools had to provide for the most elementary literary training of their novices, if they preferred to have them literate. They would have avoided teaching even these fundamentals if the public schools, the educational remnants of the Roman system, had been available to do the job.

Thus Benedict's contribution to the intellectual development, or redevelopment, of the West is to be discovered, apart from its relevance to spiritual improvement, in the type of monastery that he founded and the rule that he devised for it. It became the principal agency for the preservation and advancement of learning and culture during the period from the sixth to the twelfth century. Cultural foundations are constructed from many things: Eminent writers and thinkers are two elements to which must be added, now, the monasteries wherein elementary learning was preserved and communicated.

CASSIODORUS (ca. 480–575)

There are different opinions as to the date of Cassiodorus' birth. Some scholars think he was born as early as 480; others move the date forward as far as 490 or 491. Research seems to bring agreement on the fact that Cassiodorus died when he was ninety-five years old, but it cannot clear up the uncertainty about the exact date of his birth or death.[12]

Flavius Magnus Aurelius Cassiodorus Senator[13] was born into a distinguished family, whose male members had held important and powerful positions in the service of rulers, and Cassiodorus followed in the footsteps of his illustrious forbears.[14] After being educated in

---

[12] The word Senator is part of Cassiodorus' real name and is not a title, as is so often assumed. See Cassiodorus Senator, Flavius Magnus Aurelius, *An Introduction to Divine and Human Readings,* translated, with an introduction and notes, by Leslie Webber Jones, Columbia University Press, New York, 1946, p. 4.

[13] *Ibid.*

[14] Rand says, "Next to Boethius, Cassiodorus was the most important figure at the court of Theodoric" (*op. cit.,* p. 240). Cassiodorus was destined to a historical subordination to Boethius, and considering the work of the two men, the judgment of history may have been right.

rhetoric and philosophy—not an unusual education for a young man of his class—Cassiodorus began his public life as an assessor.[15] This was only the first step up a ladder of public service that was to take him almost to the top. At the end of his public career he held the highest office that the state had available for citizens without royal blood.

His official duties kept him in touch with letters, and he, like Boethius, coupled his public duties with scholarly interests and accomplishments. Yet not until Cassiodorus left the public service did his life assume a dimension that was to have a great effect on the learning and culture of succeeding generations. While still an important public official he wrote a *Chronicon*, an abstract of the history of the world from the Flood down to his own day,[16] and the *Gothic History* in twelve books. Neither work would stand too searching a critique, but they had, nevertheless, a certain respectability, and for that day and age were certainly nothing to be ashamed of. In addition to being a writer of books, Cassiodorus was, as so many other public figures often were, an inveterate writer of letters. These letters, both public and personal, showing an unusual sense for the historical, were preserved by Cassiodorus himself. Toward the close of his public career his literary interests assumed a definite religious orientation, displayed first of all in a treatise in twelve books entitled *On the Soul*. The author himself seems to have regarded *On the Soul* as a philosophical work, but it is really a book on religion. It may be considered a sign of things to come during the last part of Cassiodorus' life; it shows his continuous interest in religion.

Some time earlier, probably in the 520s or 530s, Cassiodorus had proposed the establishment of a theological school in Rome. The plan did not come to realization, although it appears that Pope Agapetus favored the idea of creating a school in which the liberal arts would have been taught as preliminaries to sacred learning. Thus theological and scriptural learning would have been given a new and more formal place in the mind and life of reason. Agapetus died in 536, and the plan was given up, but Cassiodorus did not forget the need that Christianity had for a higher type of divine learning.[17] In place of a

---

[15] Edward J. Power, *Evolution of Educational Doctrine,* Appleton-Century-Crofts, Inc., New York, 1969, p. 137.

[16] Cassiodorus Senator, *op. cit.,* p. 12.

[17] It is claimed that the idea for the higher type of Christian school came to Cassiodorus from the Jewish theological schools with which he came in contact when he was in Constantinople. His own testimony ought to be interesting here. In the preface to *An Introduction to Divine and Human Readings* he wrote: "Perceiving that the schools were swarming with students because of a great longing for secular letters (a great part of mankind believed that through these schools it attained

school he founded a monastery, in fact, two monasteries, on his own ancestral estates. They may not have been monasteries in the then conventional sense, because one of their chief objectives was scriptural study, and in the context of the day such an objective was somewhat foreign to the monastic ideal.

Was Cassiodorus a monk when he founded the monasteries or did he ever become a monk? Since it was not at all unusual for a layman to found a monastery in those days, commentators who argue that the founder of the double monastery at Scyllaceum must have been a monk have a rather weak case. But he may have entered the order, either when he founded the monasteries or later. Some authorities maintain positively that he was a monk; others are just as sure that he was not.[18]

We move on now to the matter of Cassiodorus' influence on the Middle Ages. Did this influence have its source in his own writings or was it to be found in the monasteries that he brought into existence? If in the latter, what was the relationship between the monasteries of Cassiodorus and those of St. Benedict? Besides these two questions that need answers are others: What were the effects of Cassiodorus' monastic enterprises on the general monastic ideal? In other words, where did the monasteries go from there? Did they continue to be spiritual hermitages, or did they take on the appearance of spiritual houses with important educational and intellectual functions to perform? What was Cassiodorus' attitude toward the liberal arts? Was he a follower of St. Augustine, or did he advocate a certain independence for the arts? Finally, what did the book, *An Introduction to Divine and Human Readings*, for which he is so famous, contain? Have its value and significance been given an inflated estimation?

Postponing the question of influence on the culture of the Middle Ages, we may begin by examining the matter of Cassiodorus' relationship to St. Benedict. First of all, there is no evidence to suggest that Cassiodorus adopted the Benedictine plan. The general idea of monasticism was well known, and there were a number of special monastic

worldly wisdom), I was, I confess, extremely sorry that the Divine Scriptures had no public teachers, since worldly authors were rich in instruction beyond doubt most distinguished. I strove with the most holy Agapetus, bishop of the city of Rome, to collect subscriptions and to have Christian rather than secular schools receive professors in the city of Rome, just as the custom is said to have existed for a long time at Alexandria and is said even now to be zealously cultivated by the Hebrews in Nisibis, a city of the Syrians, that thereby the soul might obtain eternal salvation and the tongue of the faithful might be adorned with a holy and completely faultless eloquence." (Cassiodorus Senator, *op. cit.*, p. 67.)

[18] *Ibid.*, p. 24; and Jean Leclerq, *The Love of Learning and the Desire for God*, New American Library of World Literature, New York, 1962, p. 28.

plans that may have been followed. Besides, St. Benedict's famous Monte Cassino was not yet solidly established or generally known at the time Cassiodorus began his foundations. It must be remembered that Cassiodorus and Benedict were contemporaries, a fact which may explain why scholars have been unable to find obvious threads of influence running between them. In any case, according to L. W. Jones, "there is no doubt whatever that the pains taken by Cassiodorus for the instruction of his monks distinguish his monastery quite clearly from Benedictine foundations." [19] Even though we may want to accept this point of view, we should not forget that there were clear and definite differences between monasticism of the East and monasticism of the West. While the monks of the East could be holy and illiterate and no one would despise the ignorant monk, Western monasticism was never completely oblivious of the Christian literary tradition that was being built and of the need to perpetuate it.[20] In other words, the Christian religion was becoming more and more a literary, if not an intellectual, creed, and Western monasticism was completely aware of its character. The monks of the West seemed to need simple skills of literacy, although they may not have needed or wanted the skills and motivations for scholarship. In spite of a necessary and natural affinity that the work of St. Benedict had for the monastic foundations of Cassiodorus, the latter made some fairly sharp departures from monastic conventions.

Cassiodorus has been called the "father" of literary monasticism. This is a wonderful tribute and we have no wish to deprive him of it. Yet we are not quite sure what this literary monasticism was that Cassiodorus fathered. As far as the practice of reading and writing was concerned, it would be impossible to claim that either was introduced to monastic life by Cassiodorus. St. Pacomius had prescribed both reading and writing as a daily practice for the monks who lived under his rule, and St. Pacomius died in 346. In addition, copyists working in the monasteries followed the rule he had devised, and there were copyists in other monasteries too. St. Jerome's monastic experiences did not foreclose literary endeavor or scholarly accomplishment. Still, there is really little reason to doubt that, though literary monasticism may have preceded Cassiodorus (if we mean by that simple reading and writing), he brought about an innovation in emphasis. In the two monasteries

---

[19] Cassiodorus Senator, *op. cit.*, p. 23. See also Rembert Sorg, *Towards a Benedictine Theology of Manual Labor,* Benedictine Orient, Lisle, Ill., 1951, pp. 36–81.

[20] See Donald Matthew, *The Norman Monasteries and Their English Possessions,* Oxford University Press, New York, 1963, pp. 12–16; and Lowrie J. Daly, *Benedictine Monasticism, Its Formation and Development Through the Twelfth Century,* Sheed & Ward, Inc., New York, 1965, pp. 377–381.

that he founded, writing and study were regular and important parts of the discipline of the monastery.

Literary monasticism as it appeared in the monasteries of Cassiodorus was more than mere copying. There was a scriptorium in the monastery, a place where monks copied the scriptures and the writings of the Fathers, and where, on occasion and perhaps with special permission, they would also copy the classics. Today we would think of the scriptorium as a printing shop or a small publishing plant. In connection with it, of course, there was necessarily a library supplying the copyist's material, and sometimes his inspiration. This scriptorium, a well-organized and important part of the monastery, enabled monks to support themselves by preparing manuscripts instead of toiling in the fields.

Despite the importance attached to copying manuscripts and the ancillary skills accompanying copying (bookbinding, illuminating, minuscule, ink manufacture, papermaking), literary monasticism had another dimension. It was, as Cassiodorus envisioned it, a scholarly approach to scriptural and theological study. Perhaps this phase of literary monasticism was underdeveloped in the monasteries of Cassiodorus, but that it was there at all or merely provided for, indicates Cassiodorus' insight into the problems of his day as they impinged on the Church, and also into the problems that the Church might expect to face in succeeding ages.

At this point it is natural to ask the question: Was Cassiodorus' interest confined to divine studies only? What was his attitude toward the liberal arts?

The surprising thing about Cassiodorus is not that he was engrossed with divine learning, but that he was as liberal as he was. After all, he was a product of his age, and this age, as we have seen, was somewhat unsure of its attitude toward classical learning. Classical authors were tolerated, but generally speaking, it was safer and more popular to avoid them. The praises of the arts that we find here and there in the writings of Cassiodorus, though genuine, are somewhat reserved; and understandably so, for Cassiodorus, along with St. Augustine and most of the Western Church Fathers, was sincere in his conviction that the arts were simply aids to the study of theology. All liberal culture and all profane science were assumed to be hidden in scripture or derived from it. With this view—one which actually made scientific and cultural studies unnecessary—the surprising thing is not that profane knowledge was neglected but that it was studied at all. This was the general position taken at the time, and it was representative of the age. There is no reason to believe that Cassiodorus rejected this position. Yet he could act like a scholar at times, and evidence some scholarly habits and interests. He would neither encourage nor forbid the reading of the classical authors, but he did encourage—possibly even prescribed—the reading of the Bible for the monks in his monasteries. This in itself was remarkable.

Introduction to Divine and Human Readings   In the preface to this work Cassiodorus explained his motives for writing a guide to divine and human literature and, in a manner of speaking, an educational syllabus for the intellectually inclined monks of his monasteries. After referring to his abortive plan for a Christian school of higher studies in Rome,[21] he goes on to say:

> But my ardent desire could in no way have been fulfilled because of the struggles that seethed and raged excessively in the Italian realm, inasmuch as a peaceful affair has no place in anxious times, I was driven by divine charity to this device, namely, in the place of a teacher to prepare for you under the Lord's guidance these introductory books, through which, in my opinion, the unbroken line of the Divine Scriptures and the compendious knowledge of secular letters might with the Lord's beneficence be related—books not at all fluent, perhaps, since in them is found, not studied eloquence, but indispensable narration; to be sure, they are extremely useful, since through them one learns the indicated origin of both the salvation of the soul and secular knowledge. In them I commit to you, not my own learning, but the words of men of former times, which it is right to praise and glorious to proclaim for future generations, for whatever is said about men of former times by way of praise of the Lord is not considered hateful display. Add to this the fact that one is pleased with a venerable teacher if one consults him frequently; moreover, whenever one desires to have recourse to such teachers, one will find no harshness in them.[22]

This then is his purpose: to instruct his monks in what ought to be studied. The work is divided into two books. Book I is concerned with *Divine Letters* and is arranged into thirty-three chapters. Despite the promise implicit in the book's title, this is hardly a compendium of divine learning. In print, Book I is not more than seventy-five pages long.

In Book I Cassiodorus describes the contents of the nine codices which make up the Old and New Testaments. He names the chief scriptural commentators. He discusses the various methods of understanding

---

[21] Cassiodorus Senator, *op. cit.*, p. 67.

[22] *Ibid.*, pp. 67–68.

the scriptures and adds a caution that editors, commentators, and scribes should be conservative in their handling of sacred texts. He devotes one chapter to the cosmographers—those who explained the nature of the world—and one to ecclesiastical commentators. Then he urges his monks to pursue learning and cultivate it, not for its own sake, but as a means toward better knowledge of the scriptures. This is how Cassiodorus phrases his advice in Book I, Chapter 27:

> We have decided that you ought to be cautioned about this matter too: since we can understand much in sacred literature as well as in the most learned interpreters through figures of speech, much through definitions, much through the art of grammar, much through the art of rhetoric, much through dialectics, much through the science of arithmetic, much through music, much through the science of geometry, much through astronomy, it is not unprofitable in the book which follows to touch briefly upon the elements of instruction laid down by secular teachers, that is, upon the arts and sciences, together with their divisions, in order that those who have acquired knowledge of this sort may have a brief review and those who perhaps have been unable to read widely may learn something from the compendious discussion. Beyond any doubt knowledge of these matters, as it seemed to our Fathers, is useful and not to be avoided, since one finds this knowledge diffused everywhere in sacred literature, as it were in the origin of universal and perfect wisdom. When these matters have been restored to sacred literature and taught in connection with it, our capacity for understanding will be helped in every way.[23]

Monks in the monastery who by reason of lack of intellectual capacity were unable to profit from the studies Cassiodorus outlined in *Divine Letters* should, according to the instructions contained in the volume, turn to manuscripts written on the subjects of farming and gardening. Cassiodorus notes that he had stocked such manuscripts in the libraries collected for the two monasteries. He does not, however, dwell on this phase but returns quickly to literary matters. The monks are encouraged to copy the manuscripts in their libraries, and they are admonished to copy them with care. His interest in the work of the copying monk may be seen in the following passage:

> I admit that among those of your tasks which require physical effort that of the scribe, if he writes correctly, appeals most to me. . . . Happy his design, praiseworthy his zeal, to preach to men with the hand alone, to open tongues with fingers, to give salvation silently to

[23] *Ibid.*, p. 127.

mortals, and to fight against illicit temptations of the devil with pen
and ink. Every word of the Lord written by the scribes is a wound inflicted on Satan. And so, though seated in one spot, with the dissemination of his work he travels through different provinces. . . . A sight
glorious to those who contemplate it carefully.[24]

From here our author turns to orthographical rules for the monk-
scribe to follow and then to bookbinding. The latter is treated briefly
but with more than usual care. Finally, there are instructions on the use
of mechanical devices that were provided for the monastic scriptoria,
a brief discourse on medical works, an admonition to the abbot and the
monks to be honorable and faithful, and a prayer. So ends Book I of
Divine and Human Readings.[25]

Book I held pride of place, for it, according to Cassiodorus and
many of his contemporaries, discussed the essential components of all
knowledge. Yet Cassiodorus did not stop with Book I. His investigation
of secular knowledge, though by no means implying the enthusiasm of
an advocate, suggests at least a more liberal attitude than many of his
Christian contemporaries expressed.[26] Because he was fundamentally
conservative and strictly orthodox, both Christians of his own day and
those who later followed him invested him with trust. Thus they opened
Book II, *Secular Letters,* expecting formulas to pick a way through the
labyrinth of liberal knowledge. What did they find?

They found a preface, seven chapters containing brief accounts of
the seven liberal arts (grammar, rhetoric, dialectic, arithmetic, geometry, music, and astronomy), and a conclusion. In all, the second book
is only about sixty-eight printed pages long.

Cassiodorus' elaboration of secular letters is neither more nor less
original than his divine letters. He was indebted, as most writers are, to
many authors preceding him; and though he may have tried to follow
them faithfully, he sometimes failed. In spite of whatever shortcoming
this second book may have had, it was unquestionably a chief source
consulted by medieval teachers when they wanted to know something
about the liberal arts. They seldom sampled the authors of whom Cassiodorus spoke as follows:

> And, moreover, we shall not fail to reveal the authors, both Greek
> and Latin, whose explanations of the matters which we discuss have
> become famous, in order that those who desire to read zealously may

[24] *Ibid.,* p. 133.
[25] *Ibid.,* p. 141.
[26] See Laistner, *op. cit.,* pp. 59–63.

more lucidly understand the words of the ancients after having first been introduced to them in abridged form.[27]

We have already heard a good deal of the relation of liberal learning to education. Throughout most of history this topic seems never to have lost its freshness. But in spite of all the interest, it is sometimes said that before Cassiodorus the number of the liberal arts was never clearly recognized. Cassiodorus is thought to have fixed the number at seven, possibly because he echoed the ancient claim of mystical significance for this number. This is how the claim was set forth in the beginning of Book II:

> One surely ought to know that the Sacred Scripture frequently expresses by means of this number [seven] whatever it desires to be understood as continuous and perpetual, as David, for example, says, "Seven times a day I have given praise to thee," though he elsewhere vows, "I will bless the Lord at all times; his praise shall be always in my mouth," and Solomon says, "Wisdom hath built herself a house, she hath hewn her out seven pillars." In Exodus as well the Lord said to Moses, "Thou shalt make seven lamps, and shalt set them to give light over against it." Revelation constantly mentions this number in various applications. And this number leads us to that eternity which can have no end: with justice, then, it is always used whenever perpetuity is indicated.[28]

As a final point with reference to Book II, this question may be raised: Was Cassiodorus' *Secular Letters* used as he had intended it to be used? Did he look forward to the time when it would be followed by learned men and used as a textbook by students who were intent upon probing the world's secrets? Neither Book I nor Book II was ever intended for the learned; their language alone is enough to suggest a less ambitious purpose. The treatise taken as a whole was a literary prescription for the monks at Vivarium and Castellum, and not a tool for the schools or the universities. Of course, Cassiodorus had no control whatever over the use that later ages made of *Introduction to Divine and Human Readings*. Let us turn to that question now: What was the influence of Cassiodorus on the culture and the education of the Middle Ages?

Cassiodorus did not introduce to the monastery either the scriptorium or the study of the scriptures. They had been established before his time. But Cassiodorus did succeed in integrating the work of copy-

[27] Cassiodorus Senator, *op. cit.*, p. 145.

[28] *Ibid.*, p. 144.

ing manuscripts with daily monastic life and in transforming the monastery into something resembling a theological school. This was a remarkable service. His systematic approach to literary or scholarly monasticism had important consequences.

Cassiodorus spoke an educational language the Middle Ages could understand, and his recommendations for learning were satisfying to teachers wanting to keep educational priorities straight. Although documenting every claim for Cassiodorus' perennial influence would prove impossible, there were four areas where this influence appeared quite definite: (1) *Introduction to Divine and Human Readings*, especially Book II, which contains the outline for the seven liberal arts, was used as a bibliographical guide for several centuries. In it librarians, masters, and students found inspiration and guidance for their work. (2) Book II took its place alongside the works of Martianus Capella, Boethius, Priscian, and Donatus as one of the important schoolbooks of the early Middle Ages. It made no difference whatever that Cassiodorus' manual had not been intended as anything more than a guide for the monks' study. (3) Because Cassiodorus made a commitment to literary monasticism, both his monasteries and others were encouraged to collect selections of the Church Fathers and the ancient Latin authors. Monastic libraries became depositories for early medieval culture. The fact that they performed the function of preservation when no other agency was prepared or inclined to do so should hold all of Western culture in their debt. (4) Cassiodorus hoped to improve, not merely describe, traditional educational practice. The thing that counted most on the level of pedagogy was his ability to offer a reasonable alternative to the oratorical system of Quintilian, long revered as the only avenue to a decent education. Quite correctly, Cassiodorus recognized his world as different from Quintilian's; while preserving much of Quintilian's content, he sought to reconstruct it along lines that would be practical to the Christian of the age. This meant, for one thing, that studied eloquence, the goal of Quintilian's program, should be replaced by a goal whose educational significance men of Cassiodorus' century could grasp: an ability to think clearly in private, and a reasoned skill for managing the problems of the age. In addition, it meant a deemphasis on specialization: Rhetoric or oratory, no longer a kingpin, was, in Cassiodorus' plan, along with the other arts—especially arithmetic and geometry—a basic subject in general education. Evenness among the arts was restored, and this alone was an important forward step. But of equal significance was Cassiodorus' ability to take the linguistic discipline inherited from the Roman schools and Quintilian, and put it within a

Christian theoretical educational framework having meaning for his time.[29]

GREGORY THE GREAT (540–604)

Again we meet a question that has faced us so often before. Now it is Pope Gregory (590–604) who weighs the merits and demerits of the education of the past; it is the Church's highest officer who gives his views on classical education. Here was a man whose education comprised the secular as well as the divine arts, and who was in turn a political official, a monk, an ecclesiastical officer, a papal emissary, and a pope. Gregory was in a position of authority; his stand on the question of the content and purposes of education was bound to make a great impression on Western and on Christian minds. It would be reasonable to suppose that Gregory's influence was great enough to last for centuries. What direction did this influence take?

It is evident that Gregory was interested in education as well as in church organization, administration, and discipline. But he did not show any sympathy for the education of the past. He was willing, it seems, to turn his back on the past, to reject the heritage of Greece, to repudiate the foundations of his own education, and to start anew. More exactly, Gregory was committed to a practical Christian education that would find its ultimate goal in eternity and its most fundamental curricula in Christian doctrine and morals. We must not forget that Gregory would have permitted the liberal arts to remain, though in a subordinate position and only to the extent that they might be useful instruments for understanding the scriptures and the commentaries on them. The liberal arts became stepchildren who were not really loved or wanted but were being put up with. In a real sense, moreover, these arts could no longer be very liberal.

Although Gregory has his apologists with reference to his stand on the liberal arts, we cannot overlook his often-quoted utterance to Bishop Desiderius of Vienne: "For the same lips cannot sound the praises of Jupiter and the praises of Christ." [30]

Christian bishops were expected to be engaged in something more important than teaching grammar and conducting discussions and seminars on the classics, and Gregory was, in one sense, simply re-

---

[29] Power, *op. cit.*, pp. 144–146; R. E. Swartwout, *The Monastic Craftsman*, W. Heffer and Sons, Ltd., Cambridge, 1932, pp. 121–127; and Paul Abelson, *The Seven Liberal Arts*, Teachers College Press, New York, 1906.

[30] St. Gregory *Epistle* xi. 54. In Minge, *Patrologia Latina*, LXXVII, 1171c.

minding one of the shepherds of souls of this higher duty. Yet, in putting classical learning out of bounds, as he appears to do in his disciplinary letter to Desiderius, he misreads even fundamental Christian educational needs. Since boys in Rome already spoke Latin, the language now necessary to Church services, bishops in Gregory's Rome were absolved from teaching it. But in Gaul, Latin was not a vernacular tongue. So we may assume that if Desiderious, a bishop in Gaul, did not hold Latin grammar classes, then boys there aspiring to the priesthood would be ignorant of that vital language. Gregory judged the Christian world by Roman standards (a dangerous enterprise for so practical a man), and warned his clergy away from both languages and classical teaching. This cautionary measure was of immense practical significance to the Christian community: If bishops could not prepare their successors, who would? Gregory is no mere monk speaking. Just what apology can bring classical learning back within bounds and make it a worthy objective for Christian people? The answer to this question is far from clear. Gregory was not given to looseness of speech; he usually said what he meant. The conclusion seems unavoidable: Liberal learning and the Christian ideal were separated by an impassable gulf. Is there not evidence of this gulf in the following quotation from Gregory?

> Wherefore I have scorned to observe all art of style, in which pupils are drilled in schools of the outer training. For, as the tenor of the present letter makes evident, I shun not the collision of M's; I avoid not the disorder of barbarisms; I despise a conformity to constructions and moods and cases of prepositions. For I deem it exceedingly inept to fetter the words of the Heavenly Oracle to the rules of Donatus.[31]

In Pope Gregory we find official recognition of a new kind of education, a Christian education. It is one that goes far beyond the earlier conceptions of Christian education to which reference has already been made. It included home training and moral formation on the most elementary levels, but it rejected any accommodation of the Christian view of life or goal to the secular schools and the classical education that made up their curricula. Finally, though it did not create the institution for this new education, Gregory's plan came to be a clear endorsement of the monastic school. In other ways and at other places he had already given his unqualified approval to monasticism of a Benedictine type. With Gregory's educational plan, the past loses much

---

[31] This passage is from Gregory's prefatory letter to his moral exposition of the Book of Job (Minge, *Patrologia Latina*, LXXV, 516b).

of its significance for Christian schools. Gregory was no humanist, and he held no brief for humanism.[32]

It was in this setting, where a practical Christian education received praise and encouragement, that the *Introduction* of Cassiodorus and the *Etymologies* of Isidore of Seville achieved their great fame and exerted their most pervasive influence. Though Gregory and Cassiodorus could not have agreed on all points of educational theory, Gregory's program for educational reform did create a climate wherein Cassiodorus' brand of Christian humanism, in which the arts were made subservient to divine learning, could take root and grow.

ISIDORE OF SEVILLE (560–636)

On the important educational questions of the age, Isidore stood about halfway between Cassiodorus and Gregory the Great. He was less liberal (and possibly even less learned) than Cassiodorus, and only slightly less critical of classical and secular learning than Gregory. Without exception, he wrote, Christians are forbidden to read the lies of the poets. He could be dogmatic in his assertions even when he wrote without the voice of authority to support him.[33]

Isidore's impact on educational theory was unimpressive. He added nothing new, although by his work he endorsed the tone and the ideals already set. He wrote a voluminous thesaurus, or encyclopedia, purporting to contain all worthwhile knowledge: *Etymologies*. This book became a standard reference and text from the seventh through the eleventh century, and as such its worth is difficult to overestimate and almost unhistorical to depreciate.

Isidore was credited with being the most learned man of his time, and he may have been. Yet such credit is an index of the general retrogression in learning of his time, and praise for his scholarship reflects how great the intellectual darkness must have been to make Isidore appear so brilliant. His writings, though they attest to the fact that Isidore knew the Father's writings and selective classical authors (he copied verbatim from some), disclose a mind quite capable of accepting the conclusions and directions of authority unquestioningly in all areas of knowledge, even when authority should not intrude.

Isidore's *Etymologies*, because it was such a popular schoolbook,

---

[32] See F. Holmes Dudden, *Gregory the Great*, Longmans, Green and Company, Ltd., London, 1905, vol. II, pp. 16–21; and John W. C. Wand, *The Latin Doctors*, Morehouse-Gorham, New York, 1948, pp. 72–87.

[33] Ernest Brehaut, *An Encyclopedist of the Dark Ages*, Burt Franklin, New York, 1964, pp. 181–204.

warrants our further attention. It is divided into twenty books, which treat the following topics: grammar, rhetoric, logic, arithmetic, geometry, astronomy, music, medicine, law, time, books of the Bible, laws and worship of the Church, God, angels and believers, the Church and the sects, languages, races, empires, warfare, citizenship, kinship, alphabetical lists of words, men, monsters, animals, the universe, the earth, buildings, fields, stones, metals, agriculture, war, games, sports, ships, clothing, food, drink, and utensils. The variety of topics in the work is intriguing and its breadth is imposing.[34] The remarkable thing about this schoolbook was that its contents were remote from life.

Irrelevant quality, however, appeared to make no matter. Perhaps it was impossible for education to reject the past, as Gregory counseled, and give its undivided attention to the practical matter of teaching for salvation. But it was possible, apparently, to insulate education from life and make it virtually meaningless. We have seen how Hellenistic grammarians and rhetors devitalized their learning, and we see Christians of the early Middle Ages repeating the ancients' mistakes. If formal education must have an indebtedness to the past, if it is impossible to concentrate only on divine learning, then secular learning must be stripped of significance. Secular learning's lack of significance and relevance to life's real problems is well demonstrated in its organization and presentation in Isidore's book.

Despite the limitations of Isidore's "textbook" and the valid criticisms that can be made of the book's contents and the author's methods, Isidore was capable of making a positive contribution to the education of his age. As Bishop of Seville, with authority over schools, monasteries, churches, and clergy, he upgraded the quality of the Spanish priest by adamantly prohibiting the ordination of illiterate men. So, in addition to being the author of a nearly universal textbook for the early Middle Ages, he was a spiritual leader who improved the quality of clerical education. Andrew West writes of him:

> Isidore stands last on the list, closing the development of Christian school learning in the midst of a barbarism that was extinguishing not only learning but civilized society in Western Europe. The darkness that followed his time for over a century was profound and almost universal. Rome itself had become barbarian, and only in distant Britain and Ireland was the lamp of learning kept lighted, not to shine again on the Continent until brought thither by the hand of Alcuin.[35]

[34] *Ibid.*, pp. 260–270.

[35] Andrew F. West, *Alcuin and the Rise of the Christian Schools*, Charles Scribner's Sons, New York, 1892, p. 27.

Irish Education (600 to 900)

With cultural frameworks disintegrating and schools falling into disuse, learning was put in jeopardy on the Continent. Amid this cultural and educational rubble (it is a sheer waste of time to try to disprove the historical authenticity of the Dark Ages) stood one European exception: Ireland. For reasons that are sometimes obscure, learning enjoyed fairly enthusiastic cultivation there.

Ireland was never part of the Roman Empire, and its education, therefore, was not directly affected by what was happening to the Empire in the early sixth century or by the erosions that had been wasting it for three hundred years before. On the other hand, standing as it did on the fringe of the classically oriented world, Ireland was in a position to absorb some of the main components of ancient learning, though what passed for classical culture in Ireland was only a reasonable facsimile rather than the real thing. The Irish, of course, were guiltless of cultural fraud in assimilating what they could of a classical legacy and ignoring what was useless or too difficult. By recognizing some classical learning as necessary in a syllabus of Christian education, but at the same time understanding that it was unrelated to their day-to-day life, they could segregate classical instructional appurtenances and continue to use them as antiseptic instruments of learning. So for the first time we find a cultural theory that is content to use parts of ancient learning without trying to recapitulate any aspects of the culture they represented. The classics stood as a way of learning, not as a way of life, and so from this time forward in the history of education, contact with classical culture was limited by the one-sided and often unsatisfactory means of book learning.[36]

The precise state of culture during pre-Christian times in Ireland is difficult to determine. There seems to have been a Celtic literature, and there were Celtic scholars—bards or druids—who conducted schools that preserved and cultivated the Irish literary inheritance. And there was a native script—ogam or ogham—a peculiar invention of the Gael and found only where he had his settlements. If Ireland was barbaric, it was so only in the original and strictest meaning of the word. All the evidences of culture, a native literary tradition, a written literature, schools and teachers, scholars and higher schools, could be found in Ireland before Christian scholars migrated there from a Continental envi-

---

[36] Bolgar, *op. cit.*, pp. 92–95; Ludwig Bieler, *Ireland, Harbinger of the Middle Ages,* Oxford University Press, New York, 1963, pp. 135–145; and John C. Dickinson, *Monastic Life in Medieval England,* A. & C. Black, London, 1961, pp. 40–63.

ronment that was neither conducive nor friendly to learning. Perhaps these scholars did not come in great numbers, but it is said that they came before the time of St. Patrick.[37]

In spite of the existence of Irish scholarship and culture before Ireland was Christianized, we can be certain that the Irish became the schoolmasters of the West and that they molded the connecting link in the chain of learning only after the advent of the Christian period in Ireland. Irish schools, of course, were not the sole factor in preserving learning for later ages, though they played a leading role. The school that rates first place in this consideration was the monastic school. It may be added, in fairness to the excellence of pre-Christian Irish culture, that there was no real need for the schools of the pre-Christian period to engage in any principal mission of preserving culture. Evidently the cultural commitment to progress was so clear that little or no attention was given to preserving the past.

We have seen something of the monastic schools on the Continent, but Irish monasticism and Irish monastic schools were somewhat different from their Continental counterparts. What were the chief features of these Irish monastic schools, the schools in which the culture of the West was kept alive for two or more centuries?

Before answering this question we should mention that monastic schools in Ireland did not replace the bardic schools which antedated them. In actual fact, there was a dual system of education in Ireland: the lay or bardic schools formed one part, the monastic schools the other. Early in the period when this dualism was current in Irish education, perhaps in the seventh century or late in the sixth, the lay schools assumed a responsibility for instruction in military science, law, and general literature. The first two were professional curricula; the last was what one might call a curriculum of general or liberal education that became a professional curriculum when used as a preparatory school by young men who were looking forward to admission to a religious community. Incidentally, this was a common professional use. But whether these schools were exclusively devoted to higher studies, leaving lower education to the monastic schools, or whether they provided opportunity for elementary and secondary education is a point that is obscure and cannot be answered here. At any rate, monastic schools were interested in elementary and secondary education, and

---

[37] James J. Auchmuty, *Irish Education*, Hodges, Figgs & Co., Dublin, 1937, pp. 7–18; and Giles Constable, *Monastic Tithes, from Their Origins to the Twelfth Century*, Cambridge University Press, New York, 1964, pp. 272–281.

they rarely went into the professional areas, except for studies in theology.[38]

Late in the seventh century the value of the bardic schools was questioned (for what specific reasons is doubtful), and they were nearly eliminated from the Irish educational scene. The number of such schools was drastically reduced, by what was called a reform in Irish education, to a half-dozen or so bardic or lay schools. And with this suppression we have, it would seem, the first signs of some decay in Irish scholarship and cultural values. It may be true that the destruction of the Irish educational system was due to invasion and a physical wrecking of the means for education, but it is hard to believe that the suppression of bardic schools was not a sign of internal decay or at least of lessening interest in the kind of education these schools offered. It was also an indication of a shift away from cultural values once quite firmly held. Yet the reduction in the number of bardic schools did little or nothing to tarnish the reputation these schools had for unmatched quality. The teachers were laymen who were following in the footsteps of fathers, grandfathers, and great-grandfathers. Teaching in the Irish bardic school was a family vocation passed on from generation to generation, an intellectual inheritance that was kept vital as it was bequeathed from one generation in a family to the next. That such a practice was followed should not surprise us too much, for we are familiar with it in many of the trades and crafts. Yet it is a tradition rarely met in the history of education.

But to return to the monastic school: First, it has been thought that education in Ireland was purely an ecclesiastical affair. We have seen that such an idea is erroneous, for much of Irish education, especially professional education, was in the hands of laymen. It has been intimated, also, that Irish monastic schools were narrow religious institutions which, though they may have cultivated a kind of catechetical learning, left the elements of general culture completely alone. This criticism, too, is erroneous, although the Irish embrace of the classics was not bred of love. Their education, always subordinated to Christian objectives, was faced with an extraordinary problem: Latin, a language necessary to religious liturgy, lay outside Irish cultural traditions, was difficult to teach, and (granting cultural disaffinity) was almost impossible to learn by employing the usual instruments of pedagogy. The ancient grammars, we must remember, although frequently available

[38] Hugh Graham, *The Early Irish Monastic Schools*, The Talbot Press, Ltd., Dublin, 1923, pp. 108–123; and K. Humphreys, *The Book Provisions of the Medieval Friars*, Erasmus Booksellers, Amsterdam, 1964, pp. 133–151.

to Irish masters, had not been written as handbooks for students unfamiliar with Latin. All ancient grammarians assumed that students could speak and write Latin and Greek, and, beginning with this assumption, they proceeded to philosophize about their subject. So, despite their titles, the grammar textbooks imported to the Irish schools were virtually useless.[39] Faced with this pedagogical problem, Irish teachers took the classics, or fragments of them, and tried to teach students a Latin vocabulary and syntax which was impossible to obtain from the grammar handbooks alone. As instruments for language teaching, the classics retained a fairly secure place in Irish schools, and thus a teaching tradition was perpetuated whereby contacts with the classical world and its ideas were maintained solely through literature. The crude pedagogy of the Irish in teaching Latin was eventually refined by the amendments and innovations of Bede and Alcuin.

The monastic school handled the elementary and secondary levels of education, which are often thought to be the most important to an individual's formation. Under the most favorable circumstances, then, lay and monastic schools complemented each other, for the lay schools built on the foundation that the monastic school had laid. The most distinctive feature of the Irish monastic school, however, was that it was principally, though not entirely, a school for externs; that is, monastic schools were in the business of education, not only for the preparation of boys who were seeking the clerical life, but for all children who came to them. The monastic school was a school in a proper sense; it was not, as on the Continent, merely a necessary but perhaps unwanted adjunct to the monastery, and it was common to find laymen teaching in them (although we know nothing of working conditions or professional status), nor was it extraordinary to find monks studying in the lay schools. Girls, apparently, were included in opportunities for education, although little is known of the details of their studies. And foreign students, if not actually recruited, were at least welcomed to the Irish schools.

It was these Irish monastic schools that brought about a new flowering of the culture of antiquity as interpreted through Christian eyes. Science, too, though of course without experimental or observational techniques, had a place in the curriculum. In short, the monastic school in Ireland became a preserve for the seven liberal arts. Despite its protection of the liberal arts and a certain relative breadth in the curricu-

[39] See C. S. Baldwin, *Medieval Rhetoric and Poetic*, The Macmillan Company, New York, 1928, pp. 16–21; and G. L. Hurst, *An Outline of the History of Christian Literature*, The Macmillan Company, New York, 1926, pp. 146–151.

lum, the aim of the Irish monastic school was frankly linguistic and religious.

Besides supporting schools that grew out of Irish monasticism, the monasteries themselves acknowledged a literary ideal which had, as we already know, the emphatic endorsement of Cassiodorus. In nearly every monastery in Ireland there was a scriptorium and a library.

Within the borders of Ireland flourished the "school of the West." The Irish cultivated and preserved learning until the end of the eighth century, when the Danes invaded the Emerald Isle and, with a special fury directed at instruments of literature and religion, destroyed thousands of manuscripts by fire or water. But by this time Ireland had been able to perform a work of transmission. The culture that had first of all been imported to Ireland was returned to the Continent by Irish monks and scholars, and though in itself this was not enough to produce a renaissance, it was the basic material out of which the renaissance of the ninth century was fashioned. Ireland had been the university of the Western world in the seventh and eighth centuries.

The Moslems and Learning in the West

Learning and culture in Continental Europe declined to the point of near extinction. The decline must be understood, for it is relevant to a number of later historical developments. That a revival was possible at all was due to the ability of the people in other lands to communicate their learning effectively when Continental Europe was ready to accept it. Thus we may say that Continental Europe's cultural revival was possible because in a number of places outside the Continent culture did not decline. But this is not the whole story. We cannot neglect the truly important preservative function that the monasteries on the Continent performed, and we should not try to inisist that there were neither cultured nor educated men on the Continent during the three-hundred-year period following the sixth century. We have already seen something of two of three important factors that contributed to the renaissance of the ninth century: monasticism on the Continent of Europe and the Irish reservoir of learning and culture. The third was Moslem learning.

These Moslems, sometimes called Arabs, were the followers of Mohammed (569–632); they accepted the religious doctrines that he preached and the holy book he left for them, the Koran. The religious doctrine and the Arabic language were central elements in a culture that included music, science, architecture, literature, and philosophy.

This culture, which may be called Arabic civilization, was picked up by the Mohammedans as they moved their conquering armies westward from Arabia all the way to northern Africa and across the Mediterranean to southern Spain. If these Arabs were barbarians, they were surely something more than mere barbaric collectors. They did not carry culture as a veneer but used it to good advantage, not only to themselves but indirectly to the advantage of all the Western world. What significance did Arabic arts and learning have for Western education?

In the first place, the Moslems appear at a time when classical learning was in danger of being lost in the West. They took the philosophy and science of the Greeks and grafted them to their own ideas as well as to ideas borrowed from others, especially from India and China. The Moslems were anything but provincial, and though they were selective, they did not reject anything that might be of value to them. They were philosophical and scientific scholars. But in another way the Moslems performed a service of nearly inestimable value: They preserved the writings of the Greek scholars and thinkers—of Aristotle, Euclid, Galen, Ptolemy, to mention only a few of the authors for whom the Moslem scholarly community showed special reverence. Even though the hazards of multiple translation canceled out some of their worth, it is fair to say that during the first years of the later medieval period most of what Europe knew of the classics was known through Arabic preservation, translation, or transmission. The Arabs were responsible for reintroducing the learning of antiquity to Western Europe, but they did more: the Arabic notation and algebra were their contribution and invention respectively. The former served to make arithmetic a standard school subject, for before the advent of the Arabic notation, as we have seen, arithmetic was really a theory of numbers rather than an art of computation, since neither Greek nor Roman numerals had the flexibility necessary for an elementary arithmetic. With the possible exception of elementary-school children, who generally find no joy in doing the fundamental operations and who often resist the attainment of skill in arithmetic technique, the peoples of the Western world stand indebted to the Moslem for his notation.[40]

In the practical arts, Moslems were both skillful and imaginative. Among the many practical achievements credited to them, one stands out especially because of its relation to learning: the manufacture of

[40] Ira M. Lapidus, *Muslim Cities in the Later Middle Ages,* Harvard University Press, Cambridge, Mass., 1967, pp. 112–115; and Bertold Spuler, *The Muslim World,* E. J. Brill, Leiden, 1960.

paper. This art the Arab learned from the Chinese, and his perfection of it was a tremendous achievement and a great contribution to the cause of learning and cultural progress.

There is one last area in which the influence of the Arab was productive of results, not in that he created something new but rather in that he stimulated Christians to be more creative. This creativity was displayed particularly in the field of theology. The religion of Mohammed was a challenge to Christianity, and Moslem scholars furnished persistent, pertinent, and often effective opposition to Christian theologians. In order to defend Christian doctrines and Christian theology, to give them greater strength in the face of Moslem assaults, Christian theologians perfected and elaborated their own system. As a result of the Moslem threat, real theological scholarship arose, possibly for the first time. It may even be possible to argue that the principal impetus for the establishment of the Christian university of the medieval period was given by the challenge of Mohammedanism. If this is an extravagant claim, we can at least say that the Mohammedan ideological threat was one of many contributing factors in the creation of the greatest of medieval institutions, the university.[41]

Modifying Educational Thought and Reviving Educational Interest

We come now to a revival of learning—to be followed by two others, both of which were stronger—encouraged by Charles the Great (768–814) and guided by Alcuin (ca. 735–804). This first renaissance, a vital step in the evolution of modern education, prepared the ground for the renaissances of the twelfth and fourteenth centuries. This revival of learning was nurtured by sources to which reference has already been made: monasticism, Irish learning, and Moslem culture. These must be considered indispensable wellsprings even when we admit that the leadership of Charlemagne and Alcuin exercised the most direct force in bringing a revival of learning to fruition. Nor can we forget that other men and institutions continued the work they started.

At this point we should make some mention of Christian scholarship in England in the seventh and eighth centuries. England's role in the revival that was generated in the late eighth and early ninth cen-

[41] See F. J. C. Hearnshaw, *Mediaeval Contributions to Modern Civilization*, George G. Harrap & Co., Ltd., London, 1921, pp. 107–148; E. M. Hulme, *The Middle Ages*, Holt, Rinehart and Winston, Inc., New York, 1929, pp. 214–237; and Bayard Dodge, *Muslim Education in Medieval Times*, Middle East Institute, Washington, D. C., 1962, pp. 3–98.

turies may not be easy to assess, and we can make only the general claim that England was a cultural bridge between Ireland and the court of Charlemagne. The finest products of English scholarship were Alcuin of York (even though much of Alcuin's formal education had been obtained in Ireland) and the Venerable Bede (ca. 673–735). The former, perhaps not as great an ornament of English learning as Bede, was, nevertheless, the man who rekindled the flame of liberal learning on the Continent of Europe.[42]

Before we turn to the renaissance of the ninth century, we should mention a few points that belong to its antecedent years. Royal patronage of education enjoyed its finest hour in the court of Charles the Great, but other princes in other places had anticipated him. Partly because of this royal interest (superficial though it often was), and partly for reasons of practical necessity, the Church—especially its monastic foundations—reexamined educational assumptions and became uneasy with the stringent prescriptions of Gregory the Great. Guided more by fact and reason than by authority, and superintended by the balanced views of Alcuin and others like him, ecclesiastically controlled education left the door ajar to more liberal policies and practices. One clear evidence of liberalization was the admission, for the first time, of the seven liberal arts to cathedral and episcopal school curricula. Echoes from the past, reminding teachers that praise of classical poets and Christ could not be sung by the same voice, were paid less heed.

Chivalry, too, belonged to this genre, and it continued for some time to be an important instrument for personal education. The grades of training, from page through squire to knight, involved education; yet it is impossible to assume that chivalry, as an educational force, had broad educational effects, for few young people were affected by it, and training under its auspices seldom had any literary orientation.

Finally, the education of women should be mentioned. The seventh and eighth centuries failed to provide much opportunity for their training, nor was the renaissance of the ninth century any more interested in the subject. The kind of education women of this period received lacked any signs of uniqueness; it was simply domestic training and applied uniformly to both ordinary and unusual women.

[42] M. L. W. Laistner, *Bede as a Classical and Patristic Scholar*, Royal Historical Society, London, 1933, pp. 69–94; Alexander H. Thompson, *Bede: His Life, Times, and Writings*, Russell & Russell, New York, 1966, pp. 198–206; The Venerable Bede, *The Ecclesiastical History of the English Nation*, J. M. Dent & Sons, Ltd., London, 1954; and W. Levison, *England and the Continent in the Eighth Century*, Oxford University Press, New York, 1946, pp. 70–81.

CHARLES THE GREAT (CHARLEMAGNE)

Learning in eighth- and ninth-century Europe was uneven, often hidden, somewhat unpopular, and in general (to use a physiological term) sick, but it was not dead. Reservoirs of literary and linguistic culture, buried away in the monasteries, could be mined; Irish and English syllabi were available for import to the Continent; and Moslem learning, standing at the fringe of the Frankish Empire, was susceptible of appropriation. Ingenuity rather than creativity is the distinctive feature of the ninth-century renaissance, and this quality best describes the person of Charlemagne. It was left to him to ignite the lamp of learning whose ancient flame had been extinguished in preceding centuries by political discord and decay, by Christian indifference and animosity, and by the natural hostilities of competing cultural inheritances. Who was this man Charlemagne?

Charles the Great has historical credentials as a leader of rare quality. A soldier and a king, he was also an organizer and administrator of considerably more than ordinary ability, and apparently he had humanitarian instincts as well.[43] He promoted cultural and educational projects, and on this part of his work our interest centers. Before 800 Charles was the king of the Franks and the Lombards; after 800, the year he was crowned as the successor to the ancient Roman emperors of the West, Charles was recognized as the ruler of the Continental German-Roman world. He had all the authority he needed to establish or restore learning and culture to a place of importance. But, what is more important, under Charles Europe enjoyed a period of peace, and in such an environment of relative tranquility the arts and sciences had a greater opportunity to flourish than before. To credit Charlemagne with having created conditions favorable to learning is to tell only part of the story of the Carolingian contribution to educational history. Charles himself took an active interest in education and literary culture. He wanted greater and better opportunity for the education of children, and he demanded improvement in the standards that governed the education of the clergy. This latter demand led to liturgical and literary advancement in the Church and in ecclesiastical circles.

It is possible to discover something of Charlemagne's attitude toward education by seeing what he did for the education of his own children and what course he followed in developing his own mind, by examining the provisions he made for education in his own court,

---

[43] Douglas Woodruff, *Charlemagne*, P. Davies, Ltd., London, 1934, pp. 141–143; and Donald A. Bullough, *The Age of Charlemagne*, Elek Books, London, 1965, pp. 201–210.

and by understanding what he did to stimulate education in his empire.

Charlemagne's attitude toward the education of his own children is reported as follows by his biographer:

> The plan that he adopted for his children's education was, first of all, to have both boys and girls instructed in the liberal arts, to which he also turned his own attention. As soon as their years admitted, in accordance with the customs of the Franks, the boys had to learn horsemanship, and to practice war and the chase, and the girls to familiarize themselves with cloth making, and to handle the distaff and spindle, that they might not grow indolent through idleness, and he fostered in them every virtuous sentiment.[44]

Of his own education, we can say that he liked to listen to music and that a good deal of his leisure was taken up by having readers read to him. The works of St. Augustine are said to have been his favorite literature. He spoke both Latin and German, and, according to some authorities, was fairly well versed in Greek. In addition, he was a patron of the arts and sciences, supporting scholars who worked in these fields; besides he reformed Frankish law and improved the Frankish language.

Some of this work of scholarship and of legal and linguistic reform was carried on at the court of Charlemagne. Here Charles was not only the patron but a student as well. He was not, so it is said, too great or powerful in his own eyes to sit at the feet of a humble scholar. Although Charles may not have been able to write, he encouraged the writer-scholars of his court, and the literary output therefrom was noteworthy both in quality and quantity.

The patronage of scholars and schooling was common in royal courts before and during the time of Charlemagne, but both were advanced considerably as a result of his interest in education and culture. Palace or court schools in the Frankish Empire, following the example of the king's court, became important educational forces. They provided opportunity for learning, of course, but they also gave leadership and example to the monastic schools and other schools on the Continent.

Although what has been said up to this point about Charles and his educational interests is not without relevance to the cause of education or learning in general, we can point to a more direct and perhaps more effective way Charles had for stimulating revival. He issued edicts, de-

[44] Einhard, *Life of Charlemagne*, University of Michigan Press, Ann Arbor, 1960, pp. 3–74; and E. S. Duckett, *Alcuin, Friend of Charlemagne*, The Macmillan Company, New York, 1951.

crees, or capitularies—letters of advice—which called on secular and ecclesiastical officials to promote education. Besides this, his appointments of bishops and abbots as well as of secular officials were consistent with the high value he attached to competent education.

In 787 Charlemagne issued the following capitulary to all abbots and bishops of Frankland, in which they were encouraged to promote learning and teaching in the religious communities subject to them:

> During recent years we have often received letters from different monasteries, informing us that at their sacred services the brethren offered up prayers on our behalf, and we have observed that the thoughts contained in these letters, though in themselves most just, were expressed in uncouth language, and while pious devotion dictated the sentiments, the unlettered tongue was unable to express them aright. Hence there has arisen in our minds the fear lest, if the skill to write correctly were thus lacking, so too would the power of rightly comprehending the Sacred Scriptures be far from fitting, and we all know that if verbal errors be dangerous, errors of the understanding are much more so. We exhort you, therefore, not only not to neglect the study of letters, but to apply yourselves thereto with perseverance and with that humility which is well pleasing to God, so that you may be able to penetrate with greater ease and certainty the mysteries of the Holy Scriptures. For, as these contain images, tropes, and similar figures, it is impossible to doubt that the reader will arrive far more readily at the spiritual sense, according as he is better instructed in learning. Let, therefore, there be chosen for this work men who are both able and willing to learn, and who are desirous of instructing others, and let them apply themselves to the work with a zeal equaling the earnestness with which we recommend it to them. It is our wish that you may be what it behooves the soldiers of the Church to be— religious in heart, learned in discourse and eloquent in speech.[45]

In 802 Charlemagne was responsible for the issuance of another capitulary which, though perhaps somewhat less well known than the one of 787, may have had a much greater effect on bringing about a revival of general learning. In it a practice invented about four hundred years earlier was revived and reinforced with imperial authority: it directed parish priests to instruct children in the elements of learning. Charlemagne's minister of education, Theodulf, prepared an order that read, in part, as follows:

[45] Quoted in J. Bass Mullinger, *The Schools of Charles the Great and the Restoration of Education in the Ninth Century*, Stechert-Hafner, Inc., New York, 1932, pp. 97–99; and see Bullough, *op. cit.*, pp. 42–45.

Let the priests keep schools in the villages and towns, and if any of the faithful wish to give his little ones to learning they ought willingly to receive them and teach them gratuitously, remembering what has been written: "They that are learned shall shine as the brightness of the firmament; and they that instruct many to justice, as stars for all eternity." And let them exact no price from the children for their teaching, nor receive anything from them save what the parents may offer voluntarily and from affection.[46]

Example and edict were unquestionably instrumental in upgrading education, and to Charles' credit he supplied both. But he did even more. He wanted a great teacher who could grace his palace school, and thus influence all teaching in the Empire. To secure the services of such a teacher, he turned to Italy and invited a famous scholar, Peter of Pisa, to cross the Alps. Peter's credentials as a classical scholar were faultless, and he proved to be a great ornament in Charles' palace school—but neither classical scholarship nor ornamentation were really what Charles wanted, nor were they the essentials of educational reform. A practical and competent elementary education in Latin was the most pressing need and, as it turned out, one that Peter was either unwilling or unable to fulfill. Peter was dismissed, and Alcuin of York was appointed as his replacement.[47]

ALCUIN

The educational work of Alcuin was incipient and premonitory, and the outcome was greater than the plan. This is a fair, though not an especially flattering, introduction for the new master of Charlemagne's palace school. Andrew F. West's evaluation, which may be taken also as an introduction to our study of the man, is even more severe:

> While he must be refused all the credit that belongs to a courageous mind which advances beyond what has been known, he must yet be highly esteemed for the invaluable service he rendered as a transmitter and conserver of the learning that was in danger of perishing, and as the restorer and propagator of this learning in a great empire, after it had been extinct for generations.[48]

[46] Quoted in Patrick J. McCormick and Francis P. Cassidy, *History of Education,* The Catholic Education Press, Washington, D. C., 1953, p. 222; and see Stewart C. Easton, *The Era of Charlemagne,* Van Nostrand Co., Princeton, N. J., 1961, pp. 180–183.

[47] Harold Lamb, *Charlemagne: The Legend and the Man,* Doubleday, Garden City, N. Y., 1954, pp. 66–69; and Bolgar, *op. cit.,* pp. 106–117.

[48] West, *op. cit.,* p. 90.

Alcuin, educated at the cathedral school of York, a famous school founded by Egbert, the Archbishop of York, in 732,[49] remained at York as a student and master until 782. In that year he left York at the invitation of Charlemagne and with the permission of the Archbishop of York, and became the master of the palace school at Aachen. Besides being the schoolmaster of the palace, he became the "schoolmaster" of Frankland and the chief educational adviser to Charles the Great. Thus in the capitularies that are of educational import and are rightly attributed to the Emperor, we see the hand of Alcuin.

The reputation of Alcuin was such that Charles was, first of all, anxious to have him associated with his court, and, second, more than willing to listen to the advice that Alcuin could give on educational practices and on the need for a revival of learning. The palace school Alcuin was called upon to manage was already in operation when he arrived at the court and had apparently been conducted for several years, but during all of those years it was probably little more than an elementary school, and not an institution that could have added anything to the illustrious name of Charles the Great. Alcuin made it a school in the full sense of the word. In addition to this, the court of Charles gained the reputation of being something of an intellectual center. No doubt there was an element of display in all this; having a fine school in a royal court was something like having an unexcelled stable of horses. Yet in spite of a natural inclination toward royal ostentation, Charles was genuinely interested in education, proof of which is his support of the school and of Alcuin himself. Alcuin remained at the court of Charles for about fourteen years. He returned to York after retiring from the mastership of the court school, but was recalled by Charles to quell a theological controversy, and then, though only a deacon and not a monk, was appointed abbot of the monastery at Tours.

Alcuin made six principal contributions to education. He (1) recognized that a competent elementary education was a first, and necessary, step toward educational reform; (2) imported a discipline of study, an elementary syllabus, and a pedagogy for teaching Latin and other basic and practical subjects; (3) prepared Latin grammar textbooks and readers to enable students to learn an accurate, functional Latin; (4) improved elementary teaching and popularized it, extending its scope to fresh subjects and developing techniques for attaining greater teaching efficiency; (5) cultivated a closer relationship between liberal learning and spiritual knowledge; and (6) wrote a number of fairly worthwhile books on education that affected the educational con-

---

[49] Mullinger, *op. cit.*, pp. 49–52.

sciousness of his age.[50] It may be remarked at the outset that as a writer on educational subjects Alcuin was rarely original. He was an able compiler and adapter and, at times, a literal transcriber of the works of others. West wrote that Alcuin "adds nothing to the sum of learning, either by invention or by recovery of what has been lost. What he does is to reproduce or adapt from earlier authors such parts of their writings as could be appreciated by the age in which he lived." [51] However, it may take some special insight or ability to understand what one's own age will appreciate, and Alcuin should be given credit for having had this ability. If he was not an original or highly illuminating writer, neither was he an original thinker and philosopher. He may have been nothing more than a grammarian. But labels are of relatively little significance to us now, and surely a grammarian could have been a broad and profound man or even a frontier thinker. The source of the charge that Alciun was not a philosopher may be found in the fact that he never identified himself with a philosophical school; he was neither a Platonist nor an Aristotelian. But this is slender evidence on which to base a charge that he did not have a philosophical mind. A better source for such a claim is that Alcuin, generally speaking, did not deal with philosophical questions or treat questions in an approved and appropriate philosophical manner.

We have said that Alcuin followed other older and respected writers. Who were they? In his theological works he followed Augustine, Jerome, Ambrose, and Gregory the Great. His principal sources were Latin; apparently he did not know Greek. For his educational writings he depended mainly on Isidore, Bede, and Cassiodorus. He knew something of Boethius but used him only indirectly. Martianus Capella is never mentioned in any of Alcuin's writings. We might here point out the tendency of medieval writers to exaggerate the acquirements of the teachers among them who had good reputations for scholarship. We might remark, too, that later, even modern, writers have often accepted these exaggerations and added to them. Of course it is unfair to judge every age by our own, but it is also unhistorical to magnify a very slender acquaintance with a branch of learning into a mastery of the subject. Alcuin was a great man in his day not because he could pick the minds of earlier scholars—an achievement of which most clever

---

[50] Power, *op. cit.*, pp. 160–161; E. M. Wilmot-Buxton, *Alcuin*, P. J. Kenedy & Sons, New York, 1922, pp. 64–84; C. J. Gaskoin, *Alcuin, His Life and His Works*, Russell & Russell, New York, 1966; and G. F. Browne, *Alcuin of York*, J. Murray, London, 1908.

[51] West, *op. cit.*, p. 90. See also L. Wallach, *Alcuin and Charlemagne: Studies in Carolingian History and Literature*, Cornell University Press, Ithaca, N. Y., 1959.

persons are capable—but because he correctly assessed the current and imperative needs of education and adopted a pedagogy aimed at fundamental, if elemental, goals of learning. His preoccupation was with the teaching of an accurate Latin, and on this score his success equalled his ambitions.[52]

The following are the writings of Alcuin that have the greatest relevance to educational history: *On the Virtues and Vices* and *On the Nature of the Soul* (really theological works, although they do have some educational implications); *On Grammar, On Orthography, On Rhetoric and the Virtues, On Dialectics* (here Alcuin dealt with a technique that, like most Christian writers, he feared); *Disputation with Pepin, De Cursu et Saltu Lunae ac Bissexto* (a treatise on astronomy); *On the Seven Arts, A Disputation for Boys,* and *Propositions of Alcuin.*

The most important of the works listed above is *On Grammar.* It is divided into two parts. The first part is a general discussion of ends and methods in education, and deals also with the duty of the student, or his obligation as a Christian to study the liberal arts. The second part of the treatise is an exposition of grammar proper. According to West, ". . . Whatever is excellent in any way in his Grammar ought to be credited to Donatus, whom Alcuin follows. Isidore also furnishes him many a definition, but wherever this happens the treatise is apt to be childish." [53]

How did Alcuin cultivate a closer relationship between the liberal arts and divine learning? This is an accomplishment for which we have already given him credit.

From the Western Church Fathers to Alcuin it is almost impossible to find an acceptance of the liberal arts for what they were in themselves or a commitment to them in anything that might be called a Christian theory of learning. Although the liberal arts were used for one reason or another throughout the early Middle Ages, they were always regarded as instruments of temporary value that might be used to advance divine learning. There was the suggestion, at times the clear announcement, that the arts would one day lose even this element of usefulness, and some Christians may have hopefully anticipated the time when a semblance of the arts might be dispensed with. Alcuin, however, demurred from going so far.

For Alcuin the arts were seven in number. What earlier writers on the arts had usually advanced as conjecture Alcuin accepted as indis-

[52] See W. S. Howell, *The Rhetoric of Alcuin and Charlemagne,* Princeton University Press, Princeton, N. J., 1941; and C. H. Beeson, *A Primer of Medieval Latin,* University of Chicago Press, Chicago, 1925, pp. 155–159.

[53] West, *op. cit.,* p. 101; and Wallach, *op. cit.,* pp. 51–56.

putable fact: The arts were the necessary steps to higher wisdom, and the higher wisdom was always to be found in scriptural studies. The outcome was that what others had regarded as being merely useful to the scriptural investigations and to divine learning, Alcuin considered indispensable. His support gave the liberal arts a new lease on life, and Alcuin, although his ideas on the subject may have been clothed in simple, even childlike, language or rhetoric, emphasized the need Christians had to value their scanty learning and to advance it, not for vulgar ends but for the love of God. For the first time liberal learning could hold up its head without shame, and on the level of theory could take the place prepared for it in the curriculum of the better schools. Alcuin himself saw to it that the liberal arts were not neglected in the monastic schools over which he had either influence or authority.

The Influence of Alcuin   Alcuin was the leader of a movement that had lasting effects on the history of education. At this point we are interested in the impression he made on the minds of intellectual leaders who followed and continued to cultivate the soil he had tilled. Of many names that might be mentioned, four are especially important in the context of this book. They are Rabanus Maurus, John the Scot (Erigena), Alfred the Great, and Gerbert.

Rabanus (also Hrabanus) Maurus (776–856), a student of Alcuin and later head of the monastic school at Fulda, the abbot of Fulda, and the archbishop of Mainz, carried on the work that Alcuin had begun and in some ways improved on it. The scene of his teaching and personal influence was Germany, although as a result of his writings—and he was a prolific writer—his influence went far beyond the German boundaries. He was called the first teacher of Germany, and his students were to occupy important civil and ecclesiastical positions in that country. Of the many books that Rabanus wrote, the one of most interest to the educational historian is *On the Instruction of the Clergy.* In this book Rabanus counseled—some would say prescribed—an educational syllabus for clerical students. The syllabus was to be built around the liberal arts and included the following: ". . . the unadulterated truth of history, the derivative modes of speech, the mystical sense of words, the advantages growing out of the separate branches of knowledge, the integrity of life that manifests itself in good morals, delicacy and good taste in oral discourse, penetration in the explanation of doctrine, the different kinds of medicine, and the various forms of disease." [54] Rabanus goes on to say that anyone who is unfamiliar with all this

[54] Quoted in F. V. N. Painter, *Great Pedagogical Essays,* American Book Company, 1905, p. 160.

is not really able to care for his own welfare and is, therefore, obviously unable to care for that of others.

John the Scot (Johannes Scotus Erigena, ca. 810–ca. 877), although his system of thought was condemned by Church authorities, broke ground for reason. He may have been, as he is sometimes called, the first Scholastic. In any event, Erigena was a liberal, who based his intellectual position on the thesis that authority emanates from reason, not reason from authority, and that reason needs no authority to support it. This was a bold position. Regardless of its acceptability or orthodoxy, it blazed a trail that led some scholars and some teachers into profitable but unexplored intellectual territory. Erigena initiated a spirit of inquiry, which is an essential, even though at times unpopular, spirit in the advancement of the cause of learning and culture.

Alfred the Great (848–900), the king of Wessex, made his court a center of teaching and learning. He helped to build feelings of pride in Anglo-Saxons. And in order to give these embryonic national feelings an opportunity to motivate productive effort, he build monasteries, sponsored scholars, supported translations of important books, and encouraged court schools. He was a friend of learning, and he initiated an attitude toward learning and culture that the British have never really lost.

Finally, there was Gerbert (ca. 950–1003), or as he is also known, Pope Sylvester II (993–1003). He was a teacher, a scholar, and a builder of libraries. He saw the liberal arts and sciences in the same light in which Alcuin had seen them, and he reinforced the traditions that had their clearest support in the work and theories of Alcuin. As a scholar-pope and the most learned man of the tenth century, Gerbert contributed immeasurably to the consolidation of liberal or secular learning in the Christian educational and intellectual structure.

Summary

When the political structure of Rome collapsed, the schools collapsed with it. Over a period of years the Roman state had shown greater interest in education and had come to exert greater control over it. The support of schools was partly, at least, a state problem. Thus the schools became dependent on the state, and the state's role in education tended to drive out private-venture teachers. The result was that when the state lost its force, the schools, too, found their energies depleted. With the Roman schools gone, nothing was left to take their place. The decline in the fortunes of the Roman Empire, noticeable first on the outskirts of the Empire, began to set in as early as the second century. The movement of decline continued until the sixth century, when Italy, the last stronghold of the Empire, was overrun. For at least the next hundred years the stature of culture and learning on the Continent was low. The classical-Roman system of education had generally made it unnecessary for Christians to create their own schools. Now, however, they were forced to establish them or do without. The large question that faced them when they began organizing schools was: What content should make up the school's syllabus? This was not a novel question but was, nevertheless, a question that was now being asked in a novel context. To continue and to expand what might be called the infant traditions of Christian education, a content for the schools had to be supplied. This was done first by Boethius and then by Cassiodorus and Isidore of Seville. Boethius' *Consolation of Philosophy,* Cassiodorus' *Introduction to Divine and Human Readings,* and Isidore's *Etymologies* were used for hundreds of years as textbooks in the schools.

The goals of Christian education were refined by Gregory the Great. St. Benedict, the father of Western monasticism, provided the institution—the monastery—which education used as a vehicle during the early Middle Ages. In Ireland, especially, the monastic establishments made extraordinary contributions to education and culture. Ireland, moreover, performed the additional function of preserving a great deal of the West's intellectual inheritance.

The Moslems absorbed, clarified, and preserved learning. The West learned from them, no doubt, but the West was also challenged by them. The values of the Christian West stood in peril before the intellectual and ideological assaults of the Mohammedans. Learning and culture, a total intellectual system, became indispensable weapons for the Christians in their contest with Mohammedanism.

A revival of learning in Europe was initiated and guided by Charles the Great and Alcuin. Charles, the king, and Alcuin, the teacher and scholar, succeeded in creating an accurate, practical elementary education, and distributed it generously among the people.

IX

$\mathscr{M}$edieval Education

The voices of Charlemagne and Alcuin were heard in Europe until the advent of the stronger revivals of learning in the eleventh and twelfth centuries.[1] Pockets of ignorance were inevitable in so large an empire, where, in some regions, reform was either unknown or rejected, but new leaders followed in the wake of the old and added their own enthusiasms for education and scholarship. Bruno, for example, a brother of Otto the Great (an illustrious successor to Charlemagne), kept the renaissance of Charles alive. We might even claim that Bruno was as active in the interests of education as his famous ancestor, Char-

[1] See Charles Homer Haskins, *The Renaissance of the Twelfth Century*, Harvard University Press, Cambridge, Mass., 1927, pp. 3–29.

lemagne, had been, for he restored the palace school to a position of excellence equal to its former high estate, searched for and collected classical texts, supported capable scholars and teachers, and encouraged the higher clergy to enlist in the cause of educational reform. Peaks and valleys of enthusiasm and support are apparent from the death of Charles to the beginning of the eleventh century, but through all vicissitudes the basic renaissance policy of Charlemagne was kept intact.

Loyalty to quality education was always a good omen, and the fact that this loyalty was evidenced in royal policy, better still, but the avenue separating policy from practice was long, treacherous, and troublesome. With the best intentions supporting it, even enlightened educational policy must face social, cultural, political, and economic realities. And these realities were in ferment. A quest for culture, a demand for learning, were balanced by the pragmatism of political disorder and unrest, a pragmatism leading eventually to the Empire's dismemberment and the rise of national states. Besides suffering from internal disorder, parts of Western Europe were under attack from invaders more or less regularly from the eighth through the tenth century— from the Norsemen, the Moors, and the Magyars. Not until the eleventh century, with external threats eliminated and internal ferment placated, could Europe face the future with feelings of relative security to boast the end of the Dark Ages and invest its resources in intellectual quickening. The year 1000 marks roughly the time when the European world of learning began to wear a new face.[2]

A new image—one constructed from the remnants of Roman culture —became the chief work of the schools, and so to understand the medieval educational awakening, we should try, as it were, to enter these schools.

Medieval Schools

The medieval age knew a variety of schools, inheriting some from the past and inventing others to fill special needs. From the most elementary to the highest (the universities, the special ornament of medieval education), however, schools were expected to weld together secular and sacred studies, and thus prepare men for eternal life.[3]

[2] See R. L. Poole, *Illustrations of the History of Medieval Thought and Learning,* 2d ed., The Macmillan Company, New York, 1940, pp. 95–98.

[3] John of Salisbury, *The Metalogicon of John of Salisbury,* translated, with an introduction and notes, by Daniel D. McGarry, University of California Press, Berkeley, 1955, pp. 272–274; and Daniel D. McGarry, "The Educational Theory in the *Metalogicon* of John of Salisbury," *Speculum,* XXIII (1948), 659–675.

THE MEDIEVAL MONASTIC SCHOOL

The medieval monastic school achieved a higher educational status than any of its predecessors, with the possible exception of the Irish monastic school.[4] Its impetus for development came largely from ecclesiastical laws and royal proclamations, beginning probably with Charlemagne, for the monasteries were basically conservative and anticlassical and were always suspicious of anything capable of eroding their spiritual functions.[5] Despite these natural antagonisms, however, almost from the beginning of Western monasticism certain literary features were attached to it. While most monks had ill-concealed anxieties about learning, nearly every monastery was compelled by circumstances to organize schools wherein religious novices could be prepared for the duties of religious life. This could be done, however, without any clear commitment to broad learning, and frequently with a minimum of emphasis on literary curricula. But even with these reservations and qualifications, the monasteries assumed a certain scholastic character. And it was this character which was the foundation on which medieval monastic schools were built.

Being authentic schools, medieval monastic schools had regular teachers (some of whom were not monks), a conventional and fairly broad course of studies which included the seven liberal arts, and, in progressive monasteries, of which there were few, professional curricula of law and medicine.[6]

Although their intrinsic worth was minimized, the arts formed the core of the curriculum because monastic teachers chose to follow Alcuin's practice of making them indispensable steppingstones to Christian wisdom. Old classifications were perpetuated: The trivium consisted of grammar, rhetoric, and logic; the quadrivium of arithmetic, music, geometry, and astronomy. Though all the arts were taught in the school, they were studied unevenly. Grammar had pride of place. When a boy studied grammar, he concentrated on mastering the Latin language and then, when he was ready for them, he read some carefully selected Latin authors.[7]

[4] Haskins, *op. cit.*, pp. 35–47; and Hugh Graham, *The Early Irish Monastic Schools,* The Talbot Press, Dublin, 1923, pp. 15–50.

[5] See Frederick B. Artz, *The Mind of the Middle Ages,* Alfred A. Knopf, Inc., New York, 1953, pp. 71–73; and Edward J. Power, *Evolution of Educational Doctrine,* Appleton-Century-Crofts, Inc., New York, 1969, pp. 152–153.

[6] *Ibid.*, pp. 203–204; Paul Abelson, *The Seven Liberal Arts,* Teachers College Press, New York, 1906; and Haskins, *op. cit.*, pp. 191–222.

[7] R. R. Bolgar, *The Classical Heritage and Its Beneficiaries,* Cambridge University Press, Cambridge, 1954, pp. 124–125; and James W. Thompson, *The Medieval Library,* University of Chicago Press, Chicago, 1939, p. 31.

Grammar aimed at linguistic competence, and any pedagogical technique which may have broadened it (as later medieval teachers did) into a dialectical exercise was strictly ignored. By studying grammar, a student learned how to write acceptable Latin according to a preferred ancient style, but he was for the most part unaware of the stories the classical authors told or the deeper, more human meanings the classics contained. Latin grammar, Alcuin had said, was a product of reason—he even hinted it was a divine language—and so should be studied following the approved authorities on the subject.[8] And now, what better sources did monastic teachers have than Donatus and Priscian?[9] They used both: the former for elementary study, the latter for a somewhat more advanced treatment of the subject. Occasionally they introduced the treatises (at least those parts dealing with grammar) of Martianus Capella,[10] Augustine,[11] Boethius,[12] Cassiodorus,[13] Isidore,[14] Alcuin,[15] and Rabanus Maurus,[16] for further elaboration of grammatical usage. In one or two instances the commentaries on grammar, and on the arts generally, by these writers may have been illuminating and well worth the student's time, but it is hard to see how the works of Cassiodorus, Isidore, or Alcuin could have added much to the student's store of grammatical information or understanding after he had studied Donatus, Priscian, and Boethius.

With a foundation in language study, students went on to literature. They studied the Latin classics, especially Virgil, and the better Christian writers. The Greek classics went almost totally unnoticed in the educational syllabus of the medieval monastic school, for, though these schools had some liberal sentiments with respect to what could be studied with profit by Christians, they were evidently not yet liberal enough to admit to their curricula a literature so clearly pagan in

[8] Alcuin *De Grammatica;* and J. H. Baxter and C. Johnson, *Medieval Latin Word-Lists from British and Irish Sources,* Oxford University Press, London, 1934, pp. 18–28.

[9] Priscianus Caesariensis *Institutiones Grammaticae;* and Aelius Donatus *Ars Major* and *Ars Minor.*

[10] Martianus Capella *De Nuptiis Mercurii et Philologiae.*

[11] St. Augustine, *On Christian Doctrine,* Liberal Arts Press, New York, 1958.

[12] Boethius, *Consolation of Philosophy,* translated by W. V. Cooper, J. M. Dent and Company, London, 1940.

[13] Cassiodorus Senator, *An Introduction to Divine and Human Readings,* translated, with an introduction and notes, by Leslie Webber Jones, Columbia University Press, New York, 1946.

[14] Isidore *Etymologiae.*

[15] Alcuin *De Grammatica.*

[16] Rabanus Maurus *De Clericorum Institutione.*

origin. Besides, the Greek language was pretty much a mystery to early medieval scholars, so the less said about it now the better.

The other arts were studied too, as we have said, but were always subordinated to grammar. Dialectic, once part of the trivium, was too dangerous for a Christian school. Even its most ardent exponent, Plato, was aware of its potential hazards and had reserved it as a study, or an intellectual exercise, for highly educated people. So in the hands of monastic teachers dialectic was transformed to logic, and under their auspices became an arsenal of rules for correct thinking. As such, it maintained an intimate affinity with grammar without really being an independent subject. In early medieval monastic schools logic, still "toned down," was treated as a branch of grammar. But both logic and logicians proved to be aggressive, and logic came, in time, to dominate the curriculum of monastic schools. The texts used for logic teaching were Boethius' translation of the *Categories,* Aristotle's *De Interpretatione,* and Porphyry's *Isagoge.*

Rhetoric was studied by using Boethius' works on rhetoric,[17] and sometimes the text of Fortunatianus was a supplement, as were fragmentary rhetorical works of Cicero and Quintilian. Yet here the ancient authorities were of little help, for they had preached a rhetorical doctrine aimed at educating an orator for the public platform, whereas monastic masters were geared to teaching a practical prose writing skill most useful in the composition of letters and of civil and ecclesiastical documents. Thus at least one of the arts was discouraged from living in the past.

The quadrivium—formed of subjects Plato said belonged to higher studies—had secondary-school status slightly below the trivium, and the standard texts on these subjects were already several hundred years old. Still, these old texts remained in vogue; the ancient authorities were respected even in the case of arithmetic, which had undergone drastic technical metamorphoses since the introduction of the Arabic notation. Despite arithmetic's updating, the most popular text was Boethius'. And music, perhaps the most highly developed course in the monastic quadrivium, essayed in theory to be true to its past, but in practice concentrated almost exclusively on perfecting a solemn and spiritually oriented harmony and repertoire. Geometry and astronomy had practical values which monastic teachers never overlooked, and from ancient authorities they extracted information enabling them to compute a liturgical calendar, on the one hand, and, on the other, to measure plots of land and determine the capacity of granaries. The

[17] See C. S. Baldwin, *Medieval Rhetoric and Poetic,* The Macmillan Company, New York, 1928, pp. 52–53; and Haskins, *op. cit.,* pp. 116–117.

liberal values of geometry, praised by Euclid, were ignored, and the subject was studied as if arithmetic had never been invented. Plato had thought that astronomy might contain the key to the secrets of the physical world, and so had endowed it with an intense speculative quality. But the medieval world already had its answers—far better, it thought, than any astronomy might divulge—regarding the composition of the universe, and so monastic teachers were perfectly content to handle astronomy as an instrumental subject. This, then, was the monastic school's curriculum—no doubt fuller in some schools than in others, but a staple in all until the advent of the medieval university and its appropriation of certain subjects formerly cultivated in monastic schools.[18]

At this point we might with advantage say something about the Church's interest in education. By seeing the Church's position clearly, we can more easily understand the academic interest of the monastic school. We may be tempted to attribute the Church's interest in learning to the influence of Charlemagne and to find in the renaissance of the ninth century the impetus for her first valid efforts in the cause of more generously distributed education. Such a temptation should be resisted. We have seen how the early Church understood Christian education and how literacy and a degree of learning became essential to Catholic Christianity.[19] We cannot find proof that the Church supported education and sponsored schools to any great extent before the medieval years, but that was because the Church was simply not in the business of education in any formal or literary sense. We may therefore wonder why she so often bears the brunt of criticisms directed at the educational inadequacies of the early Middle Ages. By 1000, however, the Church's educational policy had been formulated, and this policy exhibited a zeal for learning that in time was felt on all levels of education from the elementary schools through the universities. Except in very sparsely settled districts, a boy would not have had very far to go to find a school where he could learn to read and write, become better versed in religion, and learn the Latin language. To say that the years from 1000 to 1200 enjoyed all the advantages of popular education would be saying far too much. Nevertheless, education must have been generally available, for it is evident from tradesmen's accounts that

[18] Bolgar, *op. cit.*, pp. 117–129; John Lawson, *Mediaeval Education*, Routledge and Kegan Paul, Ltd., London, 1968, pp. 24–27; Charles Homer Haskins, *Studies in the History of Medieval Science*, Harvard University Press, Cambridge, Mass., 1929; and L. J. Paetow, *Battle of the Seven Liberal Arts*, University of California Press, Berkeley, 1914.

[19] See H. I. Marrou, *A History of Education in Antiquity*, Sheed & Ward, Inc., New York, 1956, pp. 330–339; and Power, *op. cit.*, pp. 147–154.

the tradesmen of this period had greater literary skill than their counterparts who lived in the period from 1300 to 1500.

Not all this opportunity for education came as a consequence of the Church's efforts, although much of it was due to her leadership. Since few of the schools of the time were independent of the Church, we can believe that the church-related schools took the important and deciding direction in education. As early as the tenth century the ecclesiastical laws of England had taken a stand in support of broader and better educational opportunity. The responsibility of the clergy in the process of education may be seen in the following excerpt from an ecclesiastical decree:

> Priests ought always to have schools for schoolteachers in their houses, and if any of the faithful wish to give his little ones learning they ought willingly to receive them and teach them gratuitously, remembering what has been written: "They that are learned shall shine as the brightness of the firmament, and they that instruct many to justice, as stars for all eternity." But they ought not to expect anything from their relatives except what they wish to do of their own accord.[20]

It may have been that the church legislation went even beyond this to require priests and clergymen generally to direct the training of young men in the manual arts and crafts.

Somewhat later, in 1179, the Third Council of Lateran formalized in its decrees what had been the Church's attitude toward education for about two hundred years:

> The Church of God, being, like a good and tender mother, obliged to provide for the spiritual and corporal wants of the poor, is desirous of procuring for children destitute of pecuniary resources the means of learning to read and of advancing in the study of letters, and ordains that every cathedral church shall have a master who will instruct gratis the ecclesiastical students of that church and the poor scholars, and that a grant be assigned him which, by suffering for his maintenance, will thus open the door of the school to studious youths. A free school shall be reopened in the other churches and monasteries. . . . No one may exact any remuneration, either for the license to teach, or for the exercise of teaching, even if his right be based on custom; and the license to keep a school shall not be refused to any person who can demonstrate his capacity for it. Offenders shall be deprived of their ecclesiastical living, for it is meet that, in the Church of God, he who

[20] A. F. Leach, *Educational Charters and Documents*, Cambridge University Press, New York, 1911, p. 37.

hinders the progress of the churches by selling, from cupidity, the permission to teach, should be himself deprived of the fruit of his labor.[21]

Later councils recognized and renewed the decrees of the Third Lateran Council, which, though hardly a constitution for church-supported popular education, were certainly important stimulants in the cause of greater educational opportunity.

Thus the Church's educational policy was born. Now for the first time the Church entered the field of education, not merely to superintend the preparation of future clerics, but to provide opportunity on a much broader base to all who wanted to study secular subjects. Secular learning was still pretty much what it had been before, but Christian theories of education were in the process of becoming considerably more mature. Because of this policy there arose in Europe educational institutions and schools attached to religious institutions that were to play an important role in European education for centuries to come.

CATHEDRAL SCHOOLS

We have already seen how cathedral or episcopal schools were attached to the Church in the early Christian period,[22] and we have understood that they were not schools in any very strict meaning of the term. In the beginning, at least, they were agencies for apprenticeship; the bishop was the master and he trained the young men who came to him to be priests. In time, of course, these centers for the training of priests came to have an instructional character and began to admit literary subjects to their curricula. Even then the bishop continued to be the chief, if not the sole, teacher at the place. By the ninth century these cathedral schools (which were really the forerunners of modern diocesan seminaries) accepted the seven liberal arts, or some of them, as subjects to be included in a course of studies for the intellectual formation of prospective priests. No doubt the cathedral schools of this early period varied in quality, and they must have varied considerably in curricula, just as today's schools may vary in the standards of excellence they achieve and maintain. Not every ninth-century cathedral school saw the need for the liberal arts, and almost all cathedral schools kept them in what was considered to be their place.

From 1200 and for three centuries thereafter the cathedral schools played an increasingly important role in spreading educational oppor-

[21] G. D. Mansi, *Collectio amplissima Conciliorum*, vol. XXII, p. 227.

[22] See also Poole, *op. cit.*, pp. 95–100; and Haskins, *The Renaissance of the Twelfth Century*, pp. 97–104.

tunity throughout Europe. There were great numbers of cathedral churches and collegiate churches to which schools were attached. The former were bishop's churches—in a sense the headquarters of a diocese —to which many priests were usually assigned. These priests were organized into chapters and lived under a rule, or canon. Hence they were called *canons*. Each chapter had a dean (the chapter's superior), a precentor (the cleric in charge of cathedral music), a treasurer, and a schoolmaster (called a *scholasticus*, or chancellor). The chancellor, we should say, was more than an ordinary schoolmaster, for he exercised a general supervisory function over all collegiate or cathedral church educational involvements. Apart from cathedrals there were great churches with large congregations which, as a consequence, had chapters or colleges of canons assigned to them who also engaged in teaching.

Cathedral and collegiate school curricula were narrow or broad, depending on the chapter's clerical talent for teaching. Some such schools stayed safely on the level of elementary teaching while others embraced the seven arts and bravely approached the portals of higher learning. A general evaluation of these church schools is barely possible because of wide ranges in purpose and quality among them; yet they were the principal centers for teaching the liberal arts during the eleventh, twelfth, and thirteenth centuries. When eleventh-century monastic schools showed a lessening interest in secular teaching, cathedral and collegiate schools took up the slack to assume educational and scholarly responsibilities formerly handled by monastic institutions.

The greatest cathedrals had schools with more or less complete curricula, including theological courses, or institutes, presided over by the chancellor himself. Large and important cathedrals created and supported schools offering students a number of enviable opportunities for study which could advance them all the way through the subjects of their quadrivium of arithmetic, geometry, music, and astronomy. Of course, cathedral schools of this stature also offered divinity courses leading to clerical ordination. The smaller cathedral and collegiate schools taught a trivium of grammar, rhetoric, and logic, and thus put themselves at the center of medieval secondary education. Besides their literary curricula, these smaller places frequently maintained song schools where boys trained for church choirs and prepared to take an active part in liturgical services. Whether or not song schools were exclusively music institutes or sometimes were engaged in elementary teaching is not known. In any case, their ancillary relationship to cathedral and collegiate-type education is certain.

Monasticism might point to Bec and Cluny and praise these centers for the part they played in a moral and intellectual quickening. The cathedral schools had their finest examples in the institutions of Chartres and Laon, both famous classical centers renowned throughout Europe for the quality of their instruction and for the great scholars assembled in their chapters. And in this connection the educational historian hesitates to mention the name of Chartres and its famous school without mentioning also the names of John of Salisbury and Bernard of Chartres, important spokesmen for medieval pedagogy.[23]

COURT SCHOOLS

We have seen some of the features of monastic and cathedral schools and are ready to acknowledge their importance as centers for an evolving intellectual culture. Along with the municipal schools located in the greater cities, they provided a foundation on which the universities could be built. However, court schools shared some of the responsibility for education, and deserve some credit for providing a higher quality of educational opportunity. Indeed, court schools are recognized as the secular contribution to a blossoming medieval intellectual life.

The court (or palace) school was an old institution that as early as the ninth century began to exert an important influence on education, so when we meet it again we know we have not discovered a new school. For centuries, civil government—and royal courts were government seats—had been keenly aware of its need for literate scribes and clerks to perform routine, though important, administrative functions. Nobles, moreover (for somewhat different reasons), also sought to improve their minds through literature, and to master the fundamental literary skills. Besides these various motives for learning, courts were highly competitive, and when educational resources became something the courts could compete about, each court tried to surpass the others. The larger, wealthier courts usually excelled because of their greater resources, but smaller courts never surrendered without trying. Often pride alone led important princes to found schools in their courts and to patronize promising scholars. But a patron's motives did not impede scholars, poets, physicians, and scientists from utilizing a patronage to good advantage. Entourages of princes could on occasion become enclaves for intellectual ferment.

[23] McGarry, *op. cit.*, pp. 670–675; W. W. Williams, *Monastic Studies,* Manchester University Press, Manchester, 1938, pp. 15–30; L. J. Paetow, *Guide to the Study of Medieval History*, Mediaeval Academy of America, Cambridge, Mass., 1931, pp. 474–483; and Henry Daniel-Rops, *Bernard of Clairvoux,* Hawthorn Books, New York, 1964, pp. 123–141.

As a matter of routine, countless courts maintained elementary schools for noble children—and also, perhaps, for the training of clerks and other civil servants. Yet, at best, court schools were exclusive establishments with an extremely limited and select clientele; no historian has ever argued that they accelerated the evolution of popular elementary education. In the great courts and apart from conventional practice, advanced curricula were sometimes organized for students of medicine, theology, and science. One illustration of this is the court school of Henry II, king of England from 1154 to 1189.[24]

There was yet another kind of education in which courts were interested, and another school they sustained: a school for knights, for chivalry was an institution characteristic of the age of feudalism. Knights were mounted troops who provided the lord or overlord with military power, and he, in return, endowed them with estates called *fiefs*. When chivalry was in flower, the knight was a public figure whose importance could not be gainsaid.

How did a young man become a knight? At this point education enters the picture, with a regular training program leading through the stages of page and squire to knight. Although the arts were relatively neglected in the formation of this versatile cavalryman, we must avoid the harsh judgment that knights were crude, rude, and uneducated. They had important social responsibilities, in addition to their military functions; were always the pride of their societies; and normally reflected an image of courage and competence. Although they were not scholars, they nevertheless had what we might call a general education and belonged, no doubt, above their contemporaries, rather in a class by themselves. The ideal knight was commissioned, according to the chivalric code, "to protect the Church, to fight against treachery, to reverence the priesthood, to defend the poor from injustice, to keep peace in his own province, to shed his blood for his brethren, and if necessary, to lay down his life." Courage, loyalty, allegiance, fidelity, manners, and generosity, in addition to horsemanship and skill in the implements of combat, were highly prized virtues and accomplishments for any knight; their inculcation and development could not be left to chance.[25]

In spite of the high esteem which chivalry enjoyed among medieval men, knighthood's contribution to intellectual culture was minor and often incidental. Chivalry was a cult of courtesy, not of intellect. Still, the best knights were both strong in mind and body; they had

[24] Bolgar, *op. cit.*, p. 243; and W. S. Davis, *Life on a Mediaeval Barony*, Harper and Row, Publishers, New York, 1923, pp. 114–123.

[25] See Leon Gautier, *Chivalry*, Barnes & Noble, Inc., New York, 1965, pp. 212–218,

been told throughout their entire careers to listen to good and true men, and we may assume that they took this advice seriously. Some knights are represented to us as philosophers and theologians, and these representations, even when obviously overdrawn, often contain elements of truth. According to the then contemporary standards, knights were educated men without being scholars or linguists. Perhaps their effect on medieval intellectual culture should be stated negatively by saying that they did nothing to retard the evolution and distribution of education's advantages. However, in one way they made a definite (though indirect) intellectual contribution: The lore of knighthood became subject matter for a poetry and literature of chivalry. So in addition to requiring from poets a few romantic verses that might, at opportune times, be quoted to ladies of quality, knights provided literary men with attractive subjects about which to compose epic and romance.

The courts must be given due credit for much of this. They offered, besides, a kind of education which fitted the nobles and their ladies to manage their estates, and in this respect gave practical knowledge a new lease on life. For, lodged amid the classics and their appurtenances, the status of practical learning was in jeopardy.

PRIVATE SCHOOLS

Throughout the history of education, private-venture schools always managed to flourish. Some of history's most famous schools were privately organized, controlled, and supported: Plato's Academy and Aristotle's Lyceum are outstanding examples. Although the medieval period had nothing to compare with the institutes of Plato and Aristotle, it, too, could and did encourage, or at least permit, private venture in education.

The opposite of the medieval private-venture school, and the schools most nearly resembling what we today call public schools, were church schools. But church schools, we know, were far from universal, and even at their best were unable to satisfy the medieval demand for learning. An enterprising person with teaching ability could open his own school and thus make a good living, or, demurring from founding a school, could offer his services as a tutor. Either way, students could be taught reading and writing and, sometimes, the elements of grammar and literature. These private schools, or tutorial arrangements, while almost always strictly elementary and commercially oriented, warrant our attention because they performed two useful services to learning: they contributed to a fairly high degree of literacy among the population of medieval Europe, and they opened the school-room door to girls, an unconventional action for most medieval schools.[26]

MUNICIPAL SCHOOLS

Beginning in about the twelfth century, an important new emphasis was added to European education. Hitherto the tools of learning had been normally reserved for the clergy. The keeping of accounts or the computation of simple problems required the literate hand of a cleric, an obviously cumbersome and inefficient arrangement both for laymen and clerics. The growth of city life, the development of the medieval free town, the increasing importance of guilds, the expansion of commercial enterprises—all these motivated laymen to seek some of the advantages which literacy could give them. There are no signs that any concerted efforts were made to wrest control of education from the Church; on the other hand, there is no evidence that the Church wanted its lay members to remain illiterate and uneducated. Generally speaking, the chancellor was the church officer through whom all educational questions had to pass and from whom all decisions relative to education came. Nevertheless, lay participation in the educational establishment was just beginning to emerge, and a strengthening of the lay hand would not necessarily mean the proportionate weakening of ecclesiastical control. Yet in the long run this was the result, even though no one may have meant to bring it about. In its simplest terms, lay participation in the affairs of education meant that ordinary men and sometimes women wanted to be able to read and write. The Church and the church schools had never actually denied this skill to them at any time in the past; they had simply not had the facilities or the resources to give people what they wanted. And now such schools were not nearly plentiful enough to fulfill the demands of a public newly awakened to the values of literacy. So the schools that came into being were, at least at first, supplemental to the church schools already in operation.

According to the legal climate of the day, it was in the power of the church authorities to proscribe these new ventures in education, for no school could operate and no private teacher could instruct without the Church's permission. Although there is no evidence to support any conclusion that the Church either opposed or forbade, as a matter

[26] Helen Waddell, *The Wandering Scholars*, Constable & Co., Ltd., London, 1927, pp. 116–121; and Pearl Kibre, *Scholarly Privileges in the Middle Ages*, Mediaeval Academy of America, Cambridge, Mass., 1962, pp. 87–91, 131–138.

of policy, the establishment of these supplemental educational institutions, namely, the town schools, it is true that individual chancellors did at times outlaw lay-inspired educational ventures. Such procedures, however, were exceptional, for the Church had no reason to oppose the creation of broader and better opportunities for the education of the people. The new schools came to aid, not to replace, the cathedral, monastic, and parish schools that the Church was sponsoring.

Because of the Church's authority even over the schools that were established by towns, the municipal school movement cannot be considered the beginning of public control over public education. The initiative for municipal schools, it is true, did not come from the Church; yet, although lay officers had some authority over these schools, the Church's fundamental control over education, which had been exercised for about five hundred years, was not eroded in any way by the rise of municipal schools.

The Kinds of Town Schools   A variety of interest is reflected in the kinds of schools established under municipal auspices. This variety would seem to be evidence that the town school movement had broad support, that is, support from the common people who would benefit from such schools. Regular Latin grammar schools (secondary schools) were established in and by the towns; reading-and-writing schools (elementary schools) were opened; private-venture schools were permitted.[27]

Municipal Latin grammar schools were intended mainly for the sons of merchants and shopkeepers, but this was their only distinction from the Latin schools which the Church had controlled for years. In methods of instruction, in curriculum, possibly even in general objectives, these schools were patterned after the church schools of the same type. This would seem to be some evidence to support the view that the municipal school movement did not intend educational reform. If we are surprised that the town fathers saw no need to make their schools different from the church Latin grammar schools, we must remember that these men really did not feel competent to consider questions relative to the internal functioning of an educational institution. In the absence of any sign of liberalization in church educational policy, town fathers, to be on the safe side, merely imitated already existing

[27] Haskins, *The Renaissance of the Twelfth Century*, pp. 62–67; Waddell, *op. cit.*, pp. 130–136; Lawson, *op. cit.*, pp. 31–37; and A. O. Norton, *Readings in the History of Education: Medieval Universities*, Harvard University Press, Cambridge, Mass., 1909.

Latin grammar schools. Such an attitude could not inspire educational reform, nor did it generate any efforts to wrest control over education from the Church.

If town fathers refused to remake secondary schools or to bring their purposes closer to the needs of life in society, they did, at least, see an imperative need for creating schools where the common people could learn to read and write. By now, as we have said, the common people were anxious to have literary skill, but of course the grammar schools were out of reach and, moreover, almost useless as agencies of rudimentary teaching. So, in the long run, the town schools that counted most were reading-and-writing schools conducting their instruction in the vernacular and offering the elements of learning to almost anyone who wanted them.

At first these town schools were regarded as supplements to parish education, for the parish school, we know, had a fairly long history of vernacular teaching. But parish schools, despite their appearance, were never public schools in any full sense, and were actually unable to satisfy the people's appetites for elementary teaching. In addition, parish schools depended almost entirely on the goodwill and resources of a pastor, and were good or bad, popular or unpopular, liberal or conservative, according to the pastor's whim. At best they were of uneven quality. Among ecclesiastical educational priorities they were regularly subordinated to grammar schools. Perhaps the real significance of the parish school is the proof it offers that ecclesiastics were not totally indifferent to vernacular elementary teaching. In any case, with or without educational merit, parish elementary education and parish schools were constants in medieval education. Town schools, however, soon surpassed them in quality and popularity.

Some towns, particularly in France and Germany, broke with tradition, opened elementary schools for girls, and devised a curriculum based on the vernacular—adding, now and then, some rudimentary instruction in Latin. Other towns, ringing the same tree of educational reform, anticipated contemporary coeducation by encouraging public and private schools to open their doors to boys and girls. This extraordinary and unconventional practice met with strong opposition, however, and was suppressed, when it could not be eliminated any other way, by civil or ecclesiastic legislation.[28]

The road that town schools traveled was not entirely free from hazards. Perhaps clashes between town and church authorities were inevi-

[28] Leach, *op. cit.*, pp. 51–63.

table, because the lines of authority on many educational issues were so thinly drawn and so poorly defined, and the positions of superiority that church officers assumed often appeared arbitrary and indefensible. Varying interpretations of imprecisely defined roles resulted in charges and countercharges that one side or the other was intruding on rightful authority or infringing upon legitimate rights. In German states, especially, bitter struggles occurred between town officers and the chancellor of a diocese over the control of teaching or the support of schools, and sometimes these controversies lasted for decades. When compromises were agreed to, opponents usually recognized the right of towns to found schools and to make the necessary provisions for their support but retained the right of teaching for the Church. This should have meant that priests or Church-appointed teachers would be in charge of instruction, and in grammar schools this was very likely the case; but churchmen, lacking interest in elementary teaching, seldom insisted on doing anything more than superintend elementary schools.

Town schools on all levels undoubtedly contributed to a heightening of interest in education, and this alone was worth almost any effort. We may also want to believe that such educational tensions as existed between town and Church officers were a good omen for educational quality, because quality thrives on competition; but we could as easily conclude that these struggles for educational power distracted leaders and helped them to ignore their reasons for supporting schools in the first place.

As a final word on municipal schools, we can say that they broke ground for the great medieval universities.[29] Some scholars believe that their contribution was a definitive one, but again proof is difficult. In large cities great municipal schools arose, and in a somewhat forced evolution no effort was spared to have the finest schools manned by the most erudite teachers. Their schools' excellence was a matter of municipal pride, and this pride, coupled with the real desire for educational quality and unexcelled opportunities for learning, may have led towns to support schools so generously that they could induce Europe's best scholars to teach in them. Such unusual teaching positions motivated teachers to form guilds and to offer their services to the town making the most attractive offer. If this is what happened—and we are led to believe that it was—then some of the seeds that germinated to become medieval universities were planted in municipal schools.

[29] Charles Homer Haskins, *The Rise of Universities*, Holt, Rinehart and Winston, Inc., New York, 1923, pp. 119–126; and Pearl Kibre, *The Nations in the Mediaeval Universities*, Mediaeval Academy of America, Cambridge, Mass., 1948, pp. 31–38.

GUILD SCHOOLS

Guilds were associations of persons who joined together to advance the interests they had in common. In the medieval age there were guilds of all kinds, not even excluding guilds of teachers and students, who came in time to form the educational corporations that we recognize in history as the universities. It is not with these regular educational guilds that we are concerned here, however, but with guilds that were formed among craftsmen and merchants. Although no guild except the scholars' guild was organized with the primary purpose of looking out for the literary education of its members or of those who came to it for training, on the other hand no guild of any kind or description was indifferent to education. One of the central values to be protected by the guild was the quality of the commodities its members produced, and this protection was always achieved most effectively by the careful training of prospective guild members. The theory was that it was easier to prevent poor craftsmanship than to correct it. It must be admitted that every guild was vitally concerned with education in a broad sense. The steps a boy would take in preparing himself for the craft he had chosen, passing from apprentice and journeyman to master, need not detain us here. The guild prescribed the steps involved and superintended the quality of the training. The purpose in all of this was obviously to produce good craftsmen and in so doing to protect the guild's reputation and safeguard the public interest.

There are other, and probably more direct, ways in which guilds became associated with education. One way was through the philanthropy they extended either to schools or schoolmasters; some guilds became benefactors to schools and, without attempting to control them, contributed generously toward their support. Another way in which the guilds made an impression on medieval education was in the schools they created for their own members and their families. Guild membership included apprentices, of course, and many of these apprentices were young boys to whom the masters had a definite and legal educational responsibility. Articles of indenture—the contract which bound an apprentice to his master—required the master to provide food, clothing, and shelter for the boy, to care for him and treat him well, and to teach him his craft and all things belonging to it. This latter came to mean literacy, for after the twelfth century no master could have been efficient and illiterate. Then, too, the guild was often disposed to provide educational opportunity for the children of guild members. Guilds created schools, usually of the elementary type, and employed schoolmasters to conduct the school. Often the school-master was a priest, possibly the guild's chaplain.

Although there was no suggestion at all in the guild school move-ment that it represented any kind of threat to ecclesiastical control over education, the guilds' schools provide us with still another exam-ple of lay participation in the enterprise of medieval education. But this point has no real relevance to the guild schools or their influence. Their greatest significance lay in the fact that through them the oppor-tunities for education in the medieval years were considerably broad-ened.[30]

CHANTRY SCHOOLS

A chantry was an endowment for masses. The endowment supported the priest who was to sing the masses, and it also supported a chapel or a special altar in a cathedral or parish church in which the masses might be offered. The endowment was assigned to the chantry priest. In addition to saying masses for the dead and possibly some other prayers, the endowment usually required the priest to perform certain works of charity, among which was regularly included the teaching of poor children. Thus we have the chantry school, usually an elementary school, but one that could on occasion rise to the challenge of preparing a gifted boy for higher studies. The chantry school could trace its origin to philanthropy, and it benefited from charity more than any other school.[31] It was most popular in England, where there were more than three hundred chantry schools at the time of the Revolt and Reforma-tion. They could be found on the Continent too, although they were not especially popular there. Some other charitable schools of the time, though they may have made but a slight mark on history, were never-theless custodians of important educational opportunities of their own day.

Scholasticism

Scholasticism was a great intellectual effort by medieval Christians to integrate medieval Christianity, the values of a feudalistic society, and an abundance of newly discovered classical material that promised to serve the requirements of an expanding secular social culture. At the

[30] A. F. Leach, *Schools of Medieval England,* Methuen & Co., Ltd., London, 1915, pp. 71–75; and Lawson, *op. cit.,* pp. 12–14.

[31] See C. H. Cook, *Mediaeval Chantries and Chantry Chapels,* Phoenix House, London, 1947, pp. 132–138.

intellectual level Scholasticism was successful, for, in the end, it allowed medieval men of letters to retain their traditional preferences and, moreover, permitted their old institutions to survive. But for all its worth to medieval culture, Scholasticism was merely a temporary solution which could not have produced cultural or intellectual formulas for a world that lay beyond the reach of medieval thought. The fourteenth century brought the Renaissance, and with it the influence of Scholasticism began to wane.

While it lasted, Scholasticism was vital and urgently human, yet it failed directly to penetrate the lives of the people, affecting only the schools and the professions. We should be interested in knowing its impress on education.[32]

Classical sources, we know, were available in Europe for several centuries before the advent of the Scholastic age. But we know, also, that they were either fragmentary, partially ignored, discredited, or useless, because so few competent scholars were available to mine their treasures. With Alcuin's emphasis on an up-to-date pedagogy for teaching an accurate Latin, the ground was broken for a cultivation of classical material and, as time passed, men came more and more to be attracted by ancient literary monuments.[33] Then, too, these monuments became more plentiful. Thus when we reach the twelfth century we find a medieval scholarly world quite aware of the classical authors and temperamentally prepared to exploit their worth. With little classical information at hand, there should not have been any urgent need for organizing it; but the Scholastic period is marked by an abundance of classical sources containing information—particularly that information that had come to light during the preceding two hundred years—which, medievalists thought, should have an organization imposed on it. Starting, then, with classical knowledge, Scholasticism endeavored to organize the whole of human knowledge, and in so doing make the whole and all its parts compatible with spiritually dominated a priori assumptions.

The point had been reached, it was assumed, where searching the past for additional knowledge would be of doubtful value. So Scholastics took what they had, organized it (or, as we have said, tried to), and then turned to a task more attractive to them: applying their knowledge to the current problems of the day.

[32] H. O. Taylor, *The Medieval Mind,* The Macmillan Company, New York, 1930; Haskins, *The Renaissance of the Twelfth Century,* pp. 351–356; and David Knowles, *The Evolution of Medieval Thought,* Alfred A. Knopf, Inc., New York, 1962, pp. 153–171.

[33] Power, *op. cit.,* pp. 158–159; and L. J. Paetow, *The Arts Course at Medieval Universities,* University of California Press, Berkeley, 1910.

Application of this knowledge, when so much of it was pagan, posed a rather difficult question. Classical values were centered on man, and, never ignoring entirely the prescription that "Man is the measure of all things," aimed at personal ambition and success. Christian values, however, directed men to live outside themselves—to replace committed ambition with altruism and sacrifice. Faced with this issue, and recognizing its relevance, Scholasticism essayed to produce a new configuration wherein the Christian world would not be the old pagan world all over again with new religious emphases added, but would represent a distinctive, unbeholden intellectual climate. All in all, the plan was more ambitious than any of its means.

To begin with, classical ideas excavated from the ancient legacy were still potentially disruptive of Christian ideals, and as the number of these ideas multiplied the danger appeared to increase. It was always possible, of course, to discard selected elements from classical culture while retaining those parts that seemed useful. This was the old technique recommended by Augustine and followed for centuries by Christian scholars bent on perpetuating a compromise between the classical and the Christian. But by now, since so much of the classical heritage had invaded the Christians' realms of thought, this simple process of outright rejection was not easy to use effectively. Scholastics wanted to purify knowledge, and to achieve their goal a more complicated process than jettisoning what they disliked was involved. The technique of purification invented depended on logic, making it a Christian tool, and in the end converted the *Organon* of Aristotle to Scholasticism's own purposes.

They began with a determination to maintain intact the teachings of the Church, and employed all the formulas of logic to make reason, as well as the corpus of classical knowledge, reinforce the doctrines of their faith. In some fields of knowledge this purpose was achieved more easily than in others, for logic could be a servant to theology by explaining rational connections between the several parts of dogma, and it could produce, by clever dialectic, artful distinction, and prudent synthesis, a philosophy consistent with theological doctrine. In the broad field of literature, however, a field through which medieval minds liked to roam, logic's task was more complicated. What should Christians do with the literary references to the gods, to sensual love, and to lascivious tales which obviously ran counter to their conceptions of morality? Again they called upon logic, and, artfully using it for reading, they succeeded in introducing a way of "exposing," or interpreting, texts which should not only render them harmless but should make them handmaidens to Christian moral teaching. This idea—proposed first, perhaps, by Hugh (sometimes called Hugo) of St. Victor—was perfected in the hands of his more erudite followers. More scientific logicians and better classical scholars, they would henceforth allow all classical literature a place in the Christian school. The invention of Hugh of St. Victor (explained more fully later) involved the employment of logic in interpreting a text's inner meaning.[34] When this technique was used faultlessly, nothing in the classical literary inheritance could be judged anti-Christian, and, moreover, every classic was utilized to strengthen the edifice of dogma.

With logic tamed, Scholasticism could turn to grammar. Here the object was neither to perpetuate the old methods of teaching the subject nor to sustain the ancient authorities (mainly Donatus and Priscian), but to introduce dialectic, or logical analysis, to grammar. Traditionally, grammatical rules were drawn up by studying the best authors; classical usage was the standard, and in order to attain grammatical competence, students should maintain constant contact with the best authors. In such a system, the classics could not be ignored. Scholastic grammar, however, changed this picture by sending students not to the classical authors or the old authorities, but to a grammar, constructed by reason, wherein the parts of speech could be justified, and their interrelationship explained, by logic.

The assumption made by Alexander of Villedieu, the most famous of scholastic grammarians and the inventor of dialectical grammar, in his pioneering *Doctrinale,* was that the Latin language was created by a rational being. Usage should count for almost nothing in a language with such logical and reasonable credentials, so the traditional dependence on classical authors to authenticate the rules of grammar was eliminated, and language was thus freed from the bonds that had made it subservient to literature. The cultural confidence accompanying a Scholastic's freedom, at long last, from classical Latin enabled him to approach the classics without feelings of inferiority. He could read them without the same admiration of his ancestors, and know that their real worth was concealed beneath a terminology that he could unravel and a construction that he could elucidate with his tools of dialectical grammar.

In rhetoric, Scholasticism's reorganization was less far-reaching. It centered on supplying a technical vocabulary for theology and philosophy, and it raised letter-writing to a technique of true rhetorical rank. The old rules of rhetoric could be used, and were used with a

---

[34] Hugo of St. Victor, *Didascalicon: A Medieval Guide to the Arts.* Translated, with an introduction and notes, by Jerome Taylor, Columbia University Press, New York, 1961, III. viii. 92.

vengeance, to help construct a theology and a philosophy, and to set a style for practical ecclesiastical and civil correspondence. Yet this was done without much dependence on classical ideas, for in none of these areas were the classics of much help.[35] The rules of rhetoric had to be followed, so much was clear, but in following them the scholar paid scant heed to their pagan origin or the legacy they represented. Again, he could assert his intellectual independence from the past.

Yet, even independent of the past, the Scholastic age considered the past of some importance. A wealth of philosophical, legal, medical, and literary knowledge should not be summarily ignored, and Scholastics refused to ignore it. In part, their refusal was predicated on a confidence they had in the new logic, grammar, and rhetoric to decontaminate ancient literature. Despite their distorted quality, classical sources were popularized in anthologies of various kinds and were made available to the schools. Still, with so much of worth, what should be taught? This was a problem for educational theorists, and we shall see shortly how they organized studies for the schools.

Philosophy, law, and medicine, however, belonged to the specialties and generally awaited the attention of scholars rather than schoolmasters. Classical legal monuments—the *Code*, the *Institutes*, and the *Digest*—needed an application of principle to topics of relevance in medieval society which Roman jurists had not covered. Accursius, in his *Glossa Ordinaria*, undertook the task of accommodating Justinian law to medieval conditions, but this was slow work for him and his successors, and even by using their best weapon, logic, they were unable to complete the job during the Scholastic period.

Medicine was easier for the Scholastic. He took Galen's medical learning (probably because Galen had adopted the Aristotelian theory of a soul's dominance over the body) and made it authoritative and prescriptive. Yet in following this course of action Scholastic medicine, caught in the trap of the past, reveled in a philosophy of medicine and was unable to make any new inroads on medical science or practice.

Reorganization and application of ancient philosophy were developments that followed similar movements in fields of general knowledge and literature. The delay was due mainly to the fact that ancient philosophical works did not make their appearance in medieval Europe until the beginning of the thirteenth century. Despite its late start, the Scholastic philosophical synthesis moved rapidly, became the most permanent feature of Scholasticism, and produced the most famous think-

[35] See Baldwin, *op. cit.*, pp. 91–103.

ers of the age. The achievements of Scholastic philosophers are too well known to be described here, but the principal exponents of Scholastic philosophic thought are worth brief notice.

PETER ABELARD (1079–1142)

Perhaps one of the most famous teachers of the medieval age, if not, in fact, the most famous, was Peter Abelard. His life and especially his association with Héloïse has made him the subject of debate, discussion, and dramatic presentation by academicians and nonacademicians alike. As a teacher he attracted students from all over Europe; as a scholar he tackled the question that the age thought most important, the question of universals. Abelard's method of presenting philosophical questions, illustrated in his well-known *Sic et Non* (Yes and No), was adopted by other writers and scholars of the later medieval period. In its most refined form, it is often thought to be *the* philosophical method itself. This may be too strong a statement, however, for Abelard simply arranged theological issues in two classes, affirmative and negative, and then found authorities to support both sides. The Scholastic method is represented more adequately by the work of Peter Lombard.[36]

One great achievement of Abelard, for which he should be remembered in the history of thought and education, was the emphasis that he put on reason as the avenue to truth. The rationalism of Abelard was possibly too extreme, but from his time forward, in the Scholastic movement and outside it, no one could be an advocate of education without at the same time being a champion of reason.

There are few educational theories or techniques of teaching that can be attributed to Abelard, yet his name continues to be illustrious in the history of education. Why is he remembered? First, as a brilliant teacher, Abelard stimulated dialectical studies. His teaching had considerable effect in popularizing the study of theology, and in his hands it gained an eminence that twelfth- and thirteenth-century literary and scientific studies could not match. Abelard's approach gave theological study a more objective basis in formal education. In spite of his contribution of a method to theological study, Abelard himself had no special reputation as a theologian. Second, Abelard's influence, through the unmatched radiance of his teaching, was great enough to promote the popularity of higher education. The University of Paris owed a

---

[36] Albert V. Murray, *Abelard and St. Bernard: A Study in Twelfth Century "Modernism,"* Barnes & Noble, Inc., New York, 1967, pp. 140–143; and R. B. Lloyd, *Peter Abelard: The Orthodox Rebel*, Latimer House, London, 1947, pp. 230–235.

great deal to him, for because of his presence Paris became a prominent center of higher learning.[37] Somewhat less directly other European universities stood in his debt.

PETER LOMBARD (ca. 1100–1164)

Though the work of Peter Lombard lacked the dramatic appeal of Abelard's brilliant arguing, its influence may have been almost as great. Where Abelard provided this age of intellectual quickening with the inspiration for scholarship, Peter Lombard provided it with the method. In organizing and presenting the views of the authorities on crucial topics, he employed a method that was accepted in future times as distinctive of Scholasticism. This system is seen at its best in Peter's work in his *Four Books of Sentences*, a treatise that set the tone in theological and philosophical studies for years to come. The treatise was divided into topics; each topic, in turn, was set forth simply and clearly; the solution or conclusion to any question involved in the topic was offered, and the authorities supporting such a conclusion were cited along with the chief reasons for their support. Finally, the author presented a summary, restating the problem or the topic and repeating the conclusion.[38] Because this method became so firmly attached to Scholasticism, it could not escape having an effect on education everywhere in medieval Europe.

ALBERT THE GREAT (1193–1280)

Albert, the teacher of the famous Thomas Aquinas, broke ground for St. Thomas by using the philosophy of Aristotle as a foundation for his own system of thought. He was, in addition, a botanist and a geographer, who prepared practical books and manuals for the schools. It was as a philosopher, however, that he made his mark on educational thought, and it is for his pioneer work in relating Greek philosophy to Christian thought that the history of education reveres him.[39]

ST. THOMAS AQUINAS (1225–1274)

St. Thomas occupies a monumental position in the history of philosophy and theology. The world has known few minds that were the equal of

[37] J. G. Compayré, *Abelard and the Origin and Early History of the Universities*, Charles Scribner's Sons, New York, 1893, pp. 89–91.

[38] Joannes Duns Scotus, *Philosophical Writings*, edited and translated by Allan Walter, Nelson, Edinburgh, 1962, pp. 76–81.

[39] See S. M. Albert, *Albert the Great*, Blackfriars Publications, Oxford, 1948; and H. C. Scheeben, *Albertus Magnus*, J. P. Bachem, Köln, 1955.

his. He was educated by the Benedictines at their famous Italian monastery, Monte Cassino, at the University of Paris, and at the great Dominican house of studies in Cologne. Albert the Great was his principal teacher at the two latter institutions. St. Thomas joined the Friars Preachers, the Dominicans, and became their most famous scholar. He taught at the University of Paris and at Rome. Thus it can be said that as a living teacher he helped shape the minds and the thoughts of students, and that because of the permanent influence of his work and thought, he is still the great teacher in Catholic schools. In addition to this, although it would not be accurate to say that so-called Thomistic philosophy is the official philosophy of the Catholic Church, nevertheless, the philosophy of St. Thomas has a privileged position in all Catholic colleges and universities as well as in ecclesiastical institutions.

The impact of St. Thomas on Christian scholarship is unmistakable. His work permeated all Catholic educational thinking, and in his own day his leadership continued the emphasis that Abelard had given to reason as a means for attaining truth. Yet St. Thomas was not an educational philosopher in any professional sense. In spite of his *De Magistro* (The Teacher), in which the place of the teacher in the educational process is discussed along with that of the principal agent in the process, the student, we should look in vain for a systematic and explicitly stated educational theory. St. Thomas accepted the prevailing educational theory, and though he may have sharpened it at certain points, he did not go beyond it.[40] This in no way dims the glorious memory or the scholarly luster of the patron of all Catholic schools. The great monument to St. Thomas' prolific scholarship, a living monument, is the *Summa Theologica.*

What position, then, does the educational historian set aside for St. Thomas? Though he was a teacher and apparently a very effective one, his fame rests not on his ability as a master but on his contributions as a scholar. Yet one must not forget that St. Thomas established the pattern for philosophical studies that was generally accepted for centuries, a pattern still considered valid among many philosophers who are Catholics. Moreover, by his separation of issues for scholarly investigation and his artful use of logic, rational distinction, and assumption, he established the Scholastic method as an almost unassailable technique for arriving at truth.

[40] Robert W. Schmidt, *The Domain of Logic According to St. Thomas Aquinas,* Bartinus Nijhoff, The Hague, 1966, pp. 247–283; W. J. Townsend, *The Great Schoolmen of the Middle Ages,* Hodder and Stoughton, Ltd., London, 1881; Mary H. Mayer, *The Philosophy of Teaching of St. Thomas Aquinas,* The Bruce Publishing Company, Milwaukee, Wis., 1929; and John E. McCormick, *St. Thomas and the Life of Learning,* Marquette University Press, Milwaukee, Wis., 1937.

Medieval Educational Theory

We have seen that medieval educators were indebted to the ancients on a number of points, but we have seen also that medieval educational practice and theory differed considerably from what it had been in antiquity. The chief difference is to be found in the answer to the question: For whom was medieval education intended? It was intended mainly for clerics. Since classical education had known no priesthood and had set its objectives for laymen, the influence of ancient educational theory on medieval educational theory could not have been direct. We must wait for the Renaissance before we see again the direct application of ancient educational theory. Besides the difference between those who were to be educated in the two periods, another important distinction was made: Whereas ancient educational theory had provided for the education of citizens of this world, medieval education and the theory behind it were unquestionably otherworldly. Despite the generally high rates of literacy among the people of medieval Europe and the more and more generous opportunities for training in the arts of utility in the later years of the Middle Ages, the emphasis in education was definitely clerical. It aimed to equip men for their journey to heaven rather than for their exploration of the ways of this world.

During the Middle Ages a number of works appeared that were concerned primarily with the education of clergymen. Chief among them were the treatises by Cassiodorus,[41] Isidore of Seville,[42] Rabanus Mauras,[43] Thierry of Chartres,[44] Hugh of St. Victor,[45] Conrad of Hirschau,[46] and John of Salisbury.[47] All these authors wrote before the thirteenth century. The effect of their work was cumulative in pointing medieval educational theory in one direction, the direction that has already been indicated, and for a number of good reasons the direction was not changed.

In the sixth century, Cassiodorus, an able and versatile figure, composed his *Introduction to Divine and Human Readings.* Anyone who has read the work of Cassiodorus might hesitate at first to assign to it a place of importance in the history of educational theory or to think

---

[41] Cassiodorus Senator, *An Introduction to Divine and Human Readings, op. cit.*

[42] Isidore *Etymologiae.*

[43] Rabanus Maurus *De Clericorum Institutione.*

[44] Thierry of Chartres *Heptateuchon.*

[45] Hugo of St. Victor *Didascalicon de Studio Legendi.*

[46] Conrad of Hirschau *Dialogus super Auctores sive Didascalon.*

[47] John of Salisbury *Metalogicon.*

of it as a charter for medieval learning. Yet this is the precise role that it fulfilled. For three hundred years after the *Introduction* appeared there was really no other justification for the study of the arts than the one it presented. Beside this, the work contained the basic elements necessary for the construction of a theory of education. It dealt with the questions of who was to be educated, why education was necessary, and what was to be used as a means in the educational process. It must be admitted that the theory of Cassiodorus had not been refined, and much of the content in the *Introduction* was certainly not original. Cassiodorus' fame comes in part from the fact that he was the first to present the material, but it comes, too, from the fact that he was successful in adapting the theories, plans, and curricula of the past to the needs of the Christian era. There was no question of simple transfer. Although on the level of theory, transfer could have been made with a fair amount of ease, on the level of practice it would have been simply impossible to apply the answers of the ancients, without considerable revision, to the educational questions that were being asked by Christians. It should be pointed out that the question of application here would not have been nearly so difficult if the educational theory of Cassiodorus and those who followed him had been somewhat less limited in its scope, that is, if laymen had been considered as well as clerics. Whether or not the work of Cassiodorus was entirely satisfactory is a question we need not attempt to answer. It was, at least, acceptable, and it commenced a Christian tradition in learning, perhaps even a Christian theory of education, that was continued throughout the medieval years and possibly longer.

Isidore, the archbishop of Seville, appeared on the scene in the seventh century. He was devoted to the promotion of clerical education, on which subject he composed several works. The most important of his writings, *Etymologies,* was a concise encyclopedia of universal knowledge that, if it did nothing else, attested to Isidore's familiarity with about 150 authors from whom he took extensive quotations. In *Etymologies* he discussed the seven liberal arts, in their capacity as useful instruments for advancing the cause of divine learning. As far as educational theory is concerned, Isidore apparently followed, repeated, and reinforced the position that had been taken by Cassiodorus. *Etymologies* became the standard reference book for the Middle Ages and, though often defective, was nevertheless instructive and generally useful.

Rabanus Maurus appeared in the ninth century. This is the man who had studied under Alcuin and had learned from Alcuin that the seven liberal arts were not just useful instruments for studying divine subjects but that they were indispensable. Rabanus, who was a famous schoolmaster in his own right, subsequently abbot of Fulda, and finally archbishop of Mainz, was in a position to make his views on education felt. These views were probably considerably more liberal than those of a Cassiodorus or an Isidore, although they certainly belonged to the tradition that these men had either begun or continued. It may be argued, however, that Rabanus was as much indebted to the Carolingian renaissance and to Alcuin as he was to older theorists, when he composed his *On the Instruction of the Clergy.* In this work he discussed secular learning and divine learning separately. His liberal outlook may be seen in his view that grammar was to include literature, a part of grammar that had been sacrificed by many an early medieval teacher in the interest of studying the structure of language without distractions. Of course this academic method had had the effect of separating grammar, or language, from life itself. Rabanus praised logic as an instrument to be used in the search for truth; he regarded arithmetic as a practical as well as a disciplinary subject; he maintained that geometry had something divine about it, that astronomy was practical, first of all, but was ornamental too, and that music should be appreciated for its importance to life in general as well as for its place in the proper performance of Christian church services. There is no doubt that Rabanus was willing to take the seven liberal arts and use them. But use them for what? His work, after all, was a prescription for the education of clerics. A prescription of this type was badly needed, but it did have the effect of reasserting the importance of clerical education at the expense of education for the layman. As a schoolman and a leader of schoolmen, Rabanus may be considered an even more important figure than Alcuin. From the ninth through the twelfth century he dominated the educational thinking of central Europe, and because of his vital role in the education of that region he has been often called the teacher of Germany.

The works of Cassiodorus, Isidore, and Rabanus had the effect of stimulating educational thought. By the twelfth century scholars were ready to speculate about education, and from this time it is possible to speak in a proper sense of educational theory. The twelfth century has been called the golden age of medieval educational speculation. In the course of this century four important works on educational theory appeared, written by Thierry of Chartres, Hugh (or Hugo) of St. Victor, Conrad of Hirschau, and John of Salisbury.

Thierry of Chartres was a teacher both at the University of Paris and at the famous school at Chartres, where he succeeded his brother, Bernard of Chartres, as chancellor. His influence on the school at

Chartres must have been great. His work on education is regarded by many as especially important; certainly it was the largest work up to that time devoted to the subject of education, and filled two large manuscript volumes. The title of the work was *Heptateuchon* or *A Library of the Seven Liberal Arts*. In this work Thierry took up each of the arts, pointed to its significance, and dealt with the way it was to be employed in practice. The place of the arts in education was surely becoming recognized; yet there is no reason to believe that Thierry modified the clerical frame of reference in which these arts were to be taught and studied.

In the same century Hugh of St. Victor (1096–1141) wrote a prospectus for the education of clerics. He entitled his treatise *Didascalicon de Studio Legendi* or *The Pursuit of Learning*. Once again we meet the division of knowledge or learning into the secular and the divine. But we find in Hugh of St. Victor an inclination to emphasize the unity of knowledge, and this emphasis, it must be admitted, had not been especially apparent in educational theory before this time. As a first step in bringing about a unification of knowledge, Hugh placed all organized learning under the heading of philosophy. Under this general heading he tried to coordinate the various branches of knowledge; or, in the terminology of contemporary education, he tried to integrate knowledge. Although we can hardly make a definitive evaluation of his work, we can say that Hugh of St. Victor was dealing with vital pedagogical questions and with questions necessary to any theory of education. His work is so easily recognized as the production of a man interested in educational theory that he is sometimes called the only educational theorist that the Middle Ages ever produced. Although this must be an exaggerated claim, it serves, nevertheless, to emphasize the stature of Hugh of St. Victor as an educational thinker. In spite of taking fairly advanced pedagogical positions in his thought, he gives little or no attention to the education of laymen, and we can hardly assume that he meant to include them or their educational problems in his treatise.

His frame of reference is clerical education, but it is a clerical education freed from some of its old limitations and based almost solely on reading. Hugh begins with the assumption, later inflated into an article of educational faith, that the classics are filled with all knowledge. The problem for education is to organize all this knowledge under appropriate headings—a task Hugh, along with other twelfth-century educators, undertakes—and to provide instructions on reading in order to grasp the fundamental meaning of what the best authors have written. Up to Hugh's time, students were directed to read, expose, or interpret texts in two ways: according to letter (a grammatical reconstruction to observe the author's uses of, or departures from, grammatical conventions), and according to sense (following the story as the author unfolds it on the pages of his book).[48] Both techniques for reading fulfilled their purposes, and Hugh found no fault with either, but they left untouched the real purpose of reading at all: What did the author mean? What meaning and significance did the book convey, and how did its contents fit into the totality of knowledge?

To the ancient techniques of textual exposition Hugh added a third which, while possibly not original with him, had never before been emphasized in this connection: A book should be read for inner meaning, and not just for what the author seemed to say in his narrative, or for the grammatical illumination and reinforcement he could give. Thus, Hugh recommended an interpretation of texts employing allegory. With allegory as an instrument, well-advanced students could go beyond the author's obvious meaning to one which he himself may not have intended and may not even have been aware of. It was a meaning imposed by divine design—well-hidden, it is true, but possible to elaborate by means of allegorical interpretation. What Hugh really meant to say was that everything in the classics conformed to Christian belief and value; proper reading was the key, not to christianizing the classics, because this was unnecessary, but to a correct understanding of them.[49] Now, according to Hugh's progressive doctrine, every classic was open to a Christian's perusal and was capable, properly interpreted, of further reinforcing the Christian intellectual edifice. The schoolhouse door to classical study was now wide open—provided, of course, that the classics were read and studied properly.

Another of the great twelfth-century educational works was the *Dialogue on Authors* or *Dialogus super Auctores sive Didascalon* by Conrad of Hirschau. This work was prepared while Conrad was teaching at the Cluniac Benedictine Abbey school of Hirschau in Germany. It contains lists and discussions of the authors to be read and studied in the monastic course of grammatical and rhetorical studies. It is thus directed at the education of clerics, although in his treatment Conrad includes standard classical (pagan) works as well as those by Christian writers.

The most famous and perhaps the most effective of the twelfth-century educational theorists was the illustrious humanist, John of Salis-

---

[48] Bolgar, *op. cit.*, pp. 216–217.

[49] Hugo of St. Victor, *op. cit.*, III. xi. 94. See also Jerome Taylor, *The Origin and Early Life of Hugh of St. Victor: An Evaluation of the Tradition*, The Mediaeval Institute, University of Notre Dame, Notre Dame, Ind., 1957.

bury. John has still an excellent reputation for many things in the scholarly arena. In educational theory, his important work is *Metalogicon*, which, as John himself says, is a defense of logical studies. But the title should not be taken too literally; though John is defending logical studies, which include logic, he is by no means elevating logic in the school's syllabus at the expense of the humanistic studies to which he was so completely devoted. *Metalogicon* consists of four books.[50] The purpose of the work is to refute the arguments of those who would curtail the trivium (grammar, logic, rhetoric) and give additional attention to the science-oriented quadrivium (arithmetic, geometry, music, astronomy). It is more than a defense of the trivium; it is an attempt to enhance the position of the studies belonging to the trivium and to cast from them certain appearances of inferiority. In spite of his humanism, we cannot discover that John distinguishes himself from other theorists of his day by giving attention to the education of laymen.

It is true that during this period no one gave much attention to formulating a theory that would make room for the education of laymen. One must not forget, however, that there were some works of a theoretical nature that centered their attention upon laymen and their training. The most outstanding were *On the Education of Noble Children* by Vincent of Beauvais, a Dominican friar, and Egidio Colonna's *On the Governance of Rulers*. Both of these works seem to anticipate Rennaisance educational theory, and it would be easy to transfer them to that period and not incur too much criticism for having done so. In both works the authors discuss the cultivation of literary tastes, natural science, ethics, economics, political science, and philosophy, with the intention of making the subjects available to the lay student. They bring up for consideration such things as marriage instruction, religion's place in the education of laymen, moral training, and physical and military training. Finally, and this should come as something of a surprise, they discuss the education of girls. Both writers say a good deal about the domestic training that girls need; but the important thing is not that they do or do not resolve the question of how women should be educated, but that they bring it up at all. It is true that Vincent touches on the education of girls only in an appendix. Yet the mere fact that girls' mental development was discussed ought to change some conceptions of what medieval education was all about. The surprising thing is not that it was indebted somewhat to classical education but that it was as liberal as it was, since its general objective was the preparation of clerics. We have not intended to give the impression that

[50] See John of Salisbury *Metalogicon, op. cit.*

opportunity for laymen in education was entirely lacking from the fifth to the twelfth centuries, only that their education was underemphasized during this period, in spite of the attention that it had received in the Carolingian revival. Laymen had to wait for the Renaissance of the fourteenth century before much attention was given to the theory that supported educational opportunities for them.

The Medieval University

The universities constitute the greatest achievement of the Middle Ages in the sphere of the intellect. "Their organization and their tradition," says Rashdall, "their studies and their exercises affected the progress and intellectual development of Europe more powerfully or (perhaps it should be said) more exclusively, than any schools in all likelihood will ever do again." [51] These universities were the products of what was highest and best in the Middle Ages, and their rise and growth is necessarily bound up with all the history and the contributions of the times.

During the twelfth century a great educational revival—an intellectual quickening—manifested itself in Western Europe. For some time men of learning had been available as teachers, but now students from all over Europe flocked to them, and the teacher and the scholar became important men. There was a new enthusiasm for logic and philosophy, prompted no doubt by the greater respectability that the arts had achieved, and a more thoroughgoing and productive approach to theology. A scholastic fever began to spread all over Europe; even those who did not live and work in the academic community were affected by it. Some men were willing to make extraordinary sacrifices of home and family, wealth and possessions in order to pursue knowledge. Both young and old were motivated to participate in this fascinating exercise, and they did not stop with one teacher or one school. By the time they had absorbed the intellectual offerings of one school, they were ready to move on to the next, where they hoped that new horizons would be opened for them. John of Salisbury, for example, followed the route to learning that was taken by so many of his contemporaries, a route which took him from school to school and from teacher to teacher. One of his teachers was the famous Abelard, the most fascinating and brilliant academic figure of the time, who did a great deal in the way of starting students up the path of learning. As more and more great teachers began to appear, students began to crowd into the old schools,

[51] Hastings Rashdall, *Universities of Europe in the Middle Ages,* new ed., Oxford University Press, New York, 1936, vol. I, p. 512.

and as the process of learning received greater refinement the age of the universities began.

New thought was finding its way into the intellectual structure of the university. It came from Constantinople, Syria, Sicily, and Spain. In all these places more texts of the ancient sciences and philosophy had been kept than in the West. The Byzantines had kept the old manuscripts in the original Greek; the Saracens had translated them into Arabic. The Saracens had also a considerable inheritance from the Orient. All of this ancient learning was now rapidly becoming available to the Western scholar, especially through Spain, which was the center of the translation of ancient texts into Latin. Aristotle's works, *Physics*, *Metaphysics*, and *On the Soul*, were now available to all who could read and understand Latin. Greek mathematical, medical, and philosophical works were introduced to Europe by Arabic scholars, and it was not long before they found their way into the curricula of the schools. We can hardly overemphasize the magnitude of the enrichment brought to teaching and learning. Men gained new knowledge, new material for individual reflection, and new stimuli for thought and progress.

The desire for higher learning and the determination to push back the boundaries of knowledge form only a part of the picture which eventually became the medieval university. The universal dominion of the Catholic Church had by this time created a spiritual European commonwealth. The scholarly tendencies of the universities and the efforts at association made by their masters would probably have resulted in nothing of great consequence had it not been for the friendly cooperation accorded the universities by ecclesiastical authorities. From the beginning the papacy gave them protection and aid. One after another, the popes gave the universities their most cordial support and, in addition, published bulls chartering universities and establishing or confirming certain privileges for the institutions or their masters.[52]

As early as the eleventh century the Church had formulated a policy on education, as a result of which some famous and successful monastic, cathedral, and collegiate schools developed. In time several of these schools became the *studia generalia* (what we today would call universities), and students flocked to them from all parts of Latin Christendom. Popes, bishops, and abbots sponsored schools and promoted and fostered scholarship in them. The intellectual revival of the twelfth century and the rise of the medieval universities took place under the watchful eye of the Church.

[52] See J. G. Compayré, *op. cit.*, p. 36.

But the Church was not alone; influential schools were founded and patronized by imperial authority. The emperors of Germany, the kings of France, and other princes often undertook to establish universities in their own areas. Besides the growing favor of Scholastic philosophy, the reputation of individual teachers, and the actions of imperial and ecclesiastical authorities in founding and supporting schools, there were other reasons why the universities flourished. Men now began to attach great significance to the subjects that interested them most and that were most essential to their welfare as members of society. With this new interest in secular subjects, a demand arose both for breadth and for specialization in educational institutions. The curriculum could no longer be mainly clerically centered, and even the clerical students began to show greater interest in specialization than ever before. Thus we find that the universities came to offer studies in four faculties: arts, law, medicine, and theology. It should be said that few of the medieval universities offered all these curricula, although all of them did offer arts. Rather they specialized in one of the so-called superior faculties: law, medicine, or theology. In order to be recognized as a *studium generale* (a university) a school would have to have at least one of the superior faculties in addition to the inferior faculty of arts. This specialization drew vast numbers of students to noted centers of study: Salerno for the study of medicine, Bologna for law, and Paris for theology.

ORGANIZATION OF UNIVERSITIES DURING THE MIDDLE AGES

During the Middle Ages there was a great movement toward association; everywhere guilds of various kinds were formed. There were guilds of burghers in the same town, guilds of men engaged in the same crafts, guilds of journeymen, of merchants, of actors and artists, of soldiers, even religious guilds. The medieval universities, too, were formed on the same basis and were an expression of the same movement. They were guilds of masters, or students, or both: associations of men of like mind, purpose, interests and responsibilities, united and organized to defend their common interests and to secure recognition of definite rights and privileges which belonged to them as corporate bodies. The relationship and similarity between universities and guilds, especially craft guilds, is generally recognized in the system of apprenticeship, leading in both to the stage of journeyman or candidacy for mastership, and culminating in the granting of the license to teach or practice the craft after a final examination before the masters of the association and the presentation of a masterpiece.[53] The name university, *universitas*, meant a corporate body of persons, usually a guild, and what we call a university, the *studium generale* or simply *studium* or *schola*, was only one kind of *universitas*.[54]

In the pages that follow, our attention will center upon the University of Paris. The reason for this is that Paris was the most renowned university of the Middle Ages and the model upon which most of the others were organized.[55] We read in the charters of other universities [56] the provision that they should follow in their organization the model of Paris. Hence, what is said about Paris is true, with little modification, of the universities that followed her. Bologna, too, became something of a model, and those *studia generalia* that did not follow Paris tended to follow Bologna. In fact, the Middle Ages produced two different types of university organization: the masters' university, like that of Paris, and the students' university, like that of Bologna. In the former type the masters controlled the school; in the latter type the students were in complete charge of all academic policies. The first was the only type found in England and Germany; the second was found more generally in Italy, Spain, and southern France. Since Oxford and Cambridge, though similar to Paris, differed in some important points, these, too, will be given some special consideration here.

THE NATIONS

Before or after students gathered at a center of learning they grouped themselves according to the nations from which they came. Youths from foreign parts found themselves among strangers and subject to

[53] Lynn Thorndike, *University Records and Life in the Middle Ages*, Columbia University Press, New York, 1944, pp. 290.

[54] See Lowrie J. Daly, *The Medieval University*, Sheed & Ward, Inc., New York, 1961, pp. 111–117.

[55] Nathan Schachner, *The Medieval Universities*, J. B. Lippincott Company, Philadelphia, 1938, p. 56.

[56] For example, in the charter of Heidelberg, issued October, 1386, by Rupert I, Count Palatine of the Rhine, it is decreed "that the University of Heidelberg shall be ruled, disposed, and regulated according to the modes and manners accustomed to be observed in the University of Paris." The Papal bull of 1385 (Urban VI), which had approved the foundation of the university, had specifically enjoined that it be modeled closely after that of Paris. (Frederick A. Ogg, *A Source Book of Mediaeval History*, American Book Company, New York, 1907, p. 346.) All the German universities followed the model of Paris. (See Friedrich Paulsen, *The German Universities: Their Character and Historical Development*, The Macmillan Company, New York, 1895, pp. 146 ff.)

various impositions. Out of necessity they formed themselves into associations for mutual protection. The English students at Paris, for instance, would form a kind of club, as would students from other foreign countries. In time these "clubs" amalgamated into larger and more formal organizations called "nations." [57] Each nation elected one or more councilors or proctors who were entrusted with the interests of the student body and were the official spokesmen for their fellows of the nation. Other officers were the receptor, or treasurer, and a number of outside beadles, who were general assistants, messengers, and heralds. A council of proctors or procurators of the nations represented the student body collectively.[58] The number of nations varied at the different universities and even at the same place at different times. At Bologna, about 1219, there were two distinct *universitates*, although closely allied, the *citramontane* (or cisalpine) and the *ultramontane* (or transalpine) universities, each made up a number of nations, three in the first and fourteen in the second.[59] At Paris there were four nations—the French, the Normans, the Picards, and the English. Orleans had nine nations—France, Germany, Lorraine, Burgundy, Champagne, Normandy, Touraine, Guyenne, and Scotland. Nations were often subdivided into tribes; the French nation at Paris had five such tribes— Paris, Sens, Rheims, Tours, and Bourges.[60]

In the early years of the medieval universities, the nations were organizations or guilds of students, and at the student universities they continued along these lines. But at Paris and at many other masters' universities, the nations came to be composed of masters. Although this may have changed the internal functioning of the nation somewhat, its external image was not altered. Each of the four nations at Paris continued to have its own hall and its own rights and privileges as a corporate body. It had its own seal distinct from that of the university, its common purse, its patron saint, and its masses.[61]

UNIVERSITY ADMINISTRATION

The general administration of the university varied also according to the place. In the south, at Bologna and the universities modeled after

[57] See Pearl Kibre, *op. cit.*, pp. 112–139.

[58] Rashdall, *op. cit.*, vol. I, p. 311.

[59] Pearl Kibre, *Scholarly Privileges in the Middle Ages,* Mediaeval Academy of America, Cambridge, Mass., 1962, pp. 183–191; 261–285.

[60] Robert Goulet, *Compendium Universitatis Parisiensis,* Toussains Denis, Paris, 1517. English translation by Robert B. Burke, University of Pennsylvania Press, Philadelphia, 1929, pp. 37–45.

[61] Rashdall, *op. cit.*, vol. I, pp. 315–320; and Knowles, *op. cit.*, pp. 172–184.

the organization there, the control of university affairs was in the hands of a student council. The guild of students constituted the university. The students determined the fees to be collected, the salaries to be paid to the professors, the conditions preceding and leading to graduation, the time when lectures should begin and end, and all matters of a similar nature.[62] The position of the professor was not an enviable one. Indeed, professors were granted little more than the status of covenanted servants. In the northern universities the control was in the hands of the masters, and the guild of masters made up the university. The explanation of this peculiar variation in administration lies in the constituency of the schools. The bulk of those attending Bologna were law students who had completed the arts course—very likely at some other school—many of whom were well along in years and well able to administer their own affairs. In the northern universities, on the other hand, the great majority of students were quite young and still in the arts course.

At any rate, whichever type of organization had control, whether that of students or teachers, it had to oversee the university's relations with the town and ecclesiastical authorities and to deal with questions of fees, rents, conduct, and discipline. The universities, when finally they received their charters and formal legal rights, received them from the Church or from the state. Thus the charters were either papal or royal. With such charters scholars and masters enjoyed immunity from civil jurisdiction and were answerable for their behavior only to fellow members.[63] As we shall see, even the jurisdiction of local ecclesiastical authorities was gradually curtailed to the point of becoming mainly honorary. Medieval universities were free from all outside control. The University of Bologna, for instance, by the statutes of 1317 had complete civil jurisdiction over its members. By 1411 it had criminal jurisdiction over them as well.

The administration of purely scholastic matters was by faculties. Originally the term "faculty" meant a subject of study, but gradually it came to designate a body of professors in a given subject, and it is in this sense that the word is used here. Eventually four distinct faculties developed: arts, law, medicine, and theology. A student had to complete the course in arts before he could advance to any of the other faculties. The arts course was an expansion of the trivium and quadrivium. Not every university had all four faculties; in fact, such inclusiveness may have been unusual. All, of course, had a faculty of arts. Law as a university subject developed at Bologna and included both civil

[62] Schachner, *op. cit.*, pp. 147–159.
[63] Goulet, *op. cit.*, pp. 51–52.

and canon or church law. Medicine as a subject for study in higher education originated at Salerno and Montpellier, while theology began at Paris. Bologna added the medicine and theology faculties in the fourteenth century; Montpellier added law in the thirteenth century; Paris added canon law gradually to its arts and theology faculties and in the course of time acquired medicine also. Each superior faculty—law, medicine, theology—elected a dean for its own internal administration and academic leadership, and this dean represented the faculty in the university councils. The faculty of arts, however, although this special example is from Paris, was made up of the four nations, each of which had its own councilor or proctor (sometimes even called rector) to represent it in university affairs.

While the importance of the faculties varied at the different universities, in the government of each university the faculty of arts was apt to be the strongest, because it was the largest (having the greatest number of students), and especially because a student had to become a master of arts before he could proceed to further study. When he received the mastership, he was required at many of the schools to take an oath to obey the decrees of the faculty of arts. Consequently that faculty was usually able to control the university.[64] Each nation, moreover, had its own vote at congregations of the entire university. Thus the arts faculty had four votes to one each for the other faculties.

The deans of the faculties, together with the council of the nations, usually elected a rector, who was the head of the whole university. In the south of Europe the rector was frequently a student. At Paris the rector of the faculty of arts, elected by the four nations, was also recognized as the rector of the whole university.[65] By about 1300 the faculties of law and medicine had become subject to the rector of the four nations, and about 1350 the faculty of theology came under his jurisdiction also.[66]

The position of rector at Paris became one of great honor, magnificence, and power. A man's elevation to the post was celebrated by a solemn procession, in which even the communities of religious orders of the neighborhood joined. The rector had supreme jurisdiction, extending to all schools, officers, and trades of the university. He was held in great honor and esteem, was called into the councils of the king, and in procession walked side by side with the Bishop of Paris as his peer.[67]

[64] See Dana C. Munro, *The Middle Ages, 395–1272*, Appleton-Century-Crofts, Inc., New York, 1922, p. 369.

[65] Goulet, *op. cit.*, p. 40.

[66] Rashdall, *op. cit.*, vol. I, p. 325.

[67] Goulet, *op. cit.*, pp. 77–82.

He was custodian of the treasury and the archives and controlled the Pré-aux-Clercs (Meadow of the clerks). He gave letters of scholarship to masters and students, conferred on them the privileges of the gown, and received from them in return the oath of perpetual obedience. He was addressed as *Amplissime Rector,* or *Vestra Amplitudo.* However, his term of office was short, a new rector being chosen four times a year. The rector's revenue came from the sale of parchment, over which he had a monopoly.[68]

The Church had its representative at the university in the chancellor, the representative of the local ecclesiastical authority. The Church was considered to have the first right in education and for many years had possessed a monopoly in it. The right was derived from the pastoral office, the commission by the Savior to "teach all nations," and by her superior dignity. The right to teach, then, was in the beginning granted by the Church to the university, or at least was recognized by the Church when the right was granted by the emperor or some other civil authority. Canon law had previously asserted the principle of church control over education. In the gradual evolution from lower schools to universities, the right of conferring degrees was given to that member of the chapter who had for long been an ex officio director of education, the chancellor. At Bologna by a bull of 1219 of Pope Honorius II, all promotions to degrees were conditioned upon the consent of the archdeacon, who in that chapter ranked next to the bishop.[69] Thus, for a time the chancellor was the real head of the university, and possessed the sole right to grant the license to teach, or the degree. Gradually, however, the chancellor's powers passed into the hands of the rector, and the former's position in the university became largely honorary.

The office of chancellor was originally purely ecclesiastical, being that of secretary of the cathedral chapter in a diocese. Since the secretary had to be a man of learning, it was natural for the bishop to designate the chancellor as the director of education in the cathedral school. He had long claimed the responsibility for the selection of teachers for the schools of the diocese, and when the universities came into existence, he tried to extend his control over them as well. At Paris, the teachers or masters in the university's first years sought a teacher's license from the chancellor of Notre Dame. Up to the beginning of the twelfth century, his control over the university was nearly absolute. Not only did he dispense licenses, but he was also the students' civil and religious judge, and he wielded even the power of excommunica-

[68] *Ibid.,* pp. 44–53.
[69] Rashdall, *op. cit.,* vol. I, p. 223.

tion.[70] It was not unusual for some chancellors to abuse their great powers, and as the universities grew stronger, their officers were not always willing to accept the sometimes arbitrary directions of the chancellor. In the inevitable dispute between the university and the chancellor, appeals were sometimes made to Rome. It came to be a papal policy to decide such disputes in favor of the university, and thus the independence of the university was gained at the expense of a limitation on the chancellor's powers. Gradually the chancellor's tyranny was broken down. Innocent III in 1208 authorized the teachers to be represented by a syndic; in 1209 he bestowed upon them the right to take oaths to observe such rules as they deemed proper and useful to impose upon themselves as a body. Most important, in 1213 he restricted the judicial powers of the chancellor of Notre Dame by forbidding him to refuse the degree to anyone who had been recommended by the masters. This amounted to granting the university its first charter. In 1219 Pope Honorius III forbade the chancellor to excommunicate masters and students in a body without the authorization of the Holy See.[71]

Another very important circumstance that restricted the chancellor at Paris was the possibility that the masters and their students might obtain their licenses by crossing the Seine to its left bank outside of Notre Dame's jurisdiction and within that of the cathedral (later on the abbey) of Ste. Geneviève, which had its own chancellor.[72] In 1216 a school was opened under the jurisdiction of the chancellor of Ste. Geneviève. The chancellor of Notre Dame regarded this as a violation of his rights and refused to regard as valid any degree or license signed by the chancellor of Ste. Geneviève. Upon appeal to the Holy See by the masters, Pope Honorius III ordered that any licentiate of the chancellor of Ste. Geneviève be admitted to teach upon the same footing with the licentiate of the chancellor of Notre Dame. Thus the chancellor of Notre Dame could not absolutely monopolize the power of conferring degrees to teach or practice, since what he refused might be obtained, by crossing the Seine, from the chancellor appointed by the abbot of Ste. Geneviève. In this way the University of Paris came to function under two distinct chancellors.

Inasmuch as all scholars were considered clerics, and the chancellor was the representative of Church authority, it was his office also to try scholars and any laymen subject to the university and "to sever

[70] *Ibid.*, pp. 304–312.

[71] Charles Thurot, *De L'organisation de l'enseignement dans l'Université de Paris,* Dezobry, E. Magdeleine et Cie, Paris, 1850, p. 12.

[72] Rashdall, *op. cit.*, vol. I, pp. 340–341.

from the University wandering, rebellious, forward, and incorrigible scholars, also to restore the penitent and free scholars and masters from the hands of violence." [73]

The chancellor at Oxford had a somewhat unique position. By the papal ordinance of 1214, the bishop of Lincoln was empowered to appoint a chancellor over the scholars at Oxford. Since Oxford did not have a cathedral, there was no cathedral chancellor at hand, and the chancellor of Lincoln was too far away to play an effective role in university affairs. Although the chancellor technically was the bishop's representative at the university, he was not, as the chancellor of Notre Dame was, an outsider, but came to be a real officer of the university. He was, in fact, elected by the masters from among their own number,[74] although this election had to be confirmed by the bishop. His office combined the duties which at Paris would have been assigned to the chancellor and the rector. Deriving his authority from the bishop, he had jurisdiction in trials, and could enforce his decisions by excommunication or deprivation of magisterial license, or by imprisonment in the king's prison or the prison of the town. He had the authority to supervise the schools also. As he moved up to the position of head of the university, he gradually became more and more independent of the bishop, yet retained his episcopally derived authority. The chancellor at some other schools, notably Montpellier, had a similar position.

THE COLLEGES OF MEDIEVAL UNIVERSITIES

At many of the universities, *hospitia,* or halls, were set up to provide food and lodging for students, usually the poor students. Ordinarily these halls were endowed and provided their facilities gratis or at very moderate cost. In the beginning, at least, the students in the halls managed their own affairs, that is, they took care of all the activities that had to do with the house, hall, or hospice in which they lived. This place was also called a college. It should be noted that the name college for such a hall did not imply that any instruction was conducted there. At first the colleges had no interest in giving instruction to the university students who lived within their walls, and certainly no facilities to do so. Eventually, however, instruction was introduced on a tutorial basis, especially for students who were preparing for their final examinations; this, in time, expanded to the point where in the early modern university all of the instruction at a university was given in the colleges.

[73] Goulet, *op. cit.,* p. 60.
[74] Rashdall, *op. cit.,* vol. I, pp. 41–42.

The most noted of the colleges of the Middle Ages was one that gives us a good example of this type of academic institution—the Sorbonne, founded by Robert of Sorbon about 1257. This was a building where the students roomed and had their meals and where they were under the charge of a master. Probably because this college was for very young boys, the students recited their lessons to the master, dined in common, and formed a compact body. The number of scholars at the Sorbonne was restricted to sixteen; in order to be admitted, a scholar had to have the academic objective of theological study. This type of academic foundation suited so well the needs of the time that elsewhere others followed the example of Robert, and endowed colleges were soon established in the leading universities of Europe. It may be mentioned that by 1500 there were seventy-nine *studia generalia* (universities) in all of Europe.

The primary object of these first colleges was simply to afford scholars shelter and protection. The college derived from a hostel in which certain licensed masters used to keep students at moderate terms, offering freedom from extortion and a residence where quiet could be ensured and some discipline maintained. The college principal conducted the students to the lecture hall of the university professor and led them back to the college in a body. Gradually, with the aid of assistants, he came to superintend their studies, started disputations, occasionally heard scholars recite, and thus profitably filled that part of the day that was not taken up in attending lectures. Recognizing that this passing back and forth from the college to the lecture hall took up a good deal of time and often led to some disorder, the principals, or masters, as soon as students in a college became numerous enough, began to give private lectures. Somewhat later these lectures were given official recognition in the university, and eventually they replaced the university lectures entirely. As the colleges increased in number and size, they superseded the university at some places, notably at Oxford and Cambridge, where they took over most of the teaching and disciplinary functions that had previously been the work of the university. Indeed, the colleges became the university and the university became a kind of academic superstructure.

METHODS OF TEACHING

The chief methods employed in teaching and learning at the medieval universities were lectures, repetitions, and disputations. Lectures were of two types, ordinary and extraordinary. The ordinary lecture was given by a master on the subject of one of the texts that had been selected for presentation. Extraordinary lectures were given by masters or advanced students on subjects that may have been of general interest; or they may have been special explanations or interpretations of the text that had been dictated in the ordinary lecture. The ordinary lecture, it should be understood, was usually nothing more than a dictation. The master read from his text, and the students copied. This was one of the ways the age hit upon for providing prospective teachers with some of the tools of their art. Printing with movable type had not yet been developed, but both students and teachers needed texts with which to do their work; thus, the technique of the medieval lecture, where the master simply conducted an exercise in dictation. It should be said that in some of the universities the masters' guild legislated that the ordinary lecture could be nothing more or other than an exercise in dictation. Yet at the same time other guilds permitted their masters to "gloss" the text, or make commentaries or interpretations of it as a supplement to the matter that was dictated. It may well be true, however, that commentaries, interpretations, and explanations were usually reserved for the extraordinary lecture.

The repetition may have been a detailed discussion of a course of lectures that had been given. If so, the master who had delivered the lectures in the first place would assemble his students and give them every opportunity to probe those avenues of thought that had stimulated their intellectual curiosity. Here, with the friction of mind on mind, teaching and learning was at its very best. On the other hand, there was no guarantee at all that the repetition would take this form, and it could have been nothing more or less than a rereading of the lecture that had been given before. Under such circumstances the students would have the opportunity to check their text for inaccuracies or for incompleteness, but such an experience could hardly have been highly stimulating.

The disputation method has been given a good deal of attention. It was surely one of the university's important exercises in learning. Disputations came to be regular techniques in the university because they provided opportunities for clearing up difficulties that masters and students may have faced in their studies. Such exercises also provided students with practice in dialectic, and it would be hard to say which was thought to be the more important, explanation or skillful arguing. Two methods were employed in conducting disputations. One person might take up a thesis and examine both sides of it, that is, argue one side and then the other and finally try to come to some conclusion. Or two persons, scholars or masters, might engage in debate, one taking one side of the thesis presented for discussion and the other, the other.

Normally, such formal disputations and their theses were publicized well in advance, in order that those who attended could be prepared to ask questions or offer arguments from the floor. Even outside the university, usually in ecclesiastical circles and sometimes in the pulpit, the form of the disputation was adopted. Medieval man was about as interested as his Hellenistic ancestor had been in disputing or listening to disputes. In addition to the disputations that formed a regular part of the university's instructional process, a master might organize disputations for his own classes. These would not be given university or public recognition but would merely be ways which a master might devise to enrich the educational experience of the students under him. Of course skill in disputation was considered to be important. The student who took a degree from a medieval university had to furnish evidence that he had taken part in a certain number of disputations, usually six.

STUDENTS AND TEACHERS

Student life at the medieval university is not easy to describe in general. Some students came to the university with plenty of money to care for their wants; others came with meager or limited funds and had to supplement their resources by begging or by seeking scholarships. There is no evidence to indicate that many, or any, of the medieval university students worked their way through school by productive labor.

They lived in the houses that the university and town authorities approved, and they took their meals at local taverns. When they were not engaged in their studies—and they found many good reasons for not studying all the time—the students looked for fun. Often they had to make their own amusement, and this sometimes led to trouble. Many of the most serious disputes, to say nothing of armed conflicts, between town and gown arose out of the exaggerations of sport in which the students sometimes engaged.

Perhaps the most unusual characteristic of the medieval student was his willingness to move from university to university. There were no academic obstacles to such transfers; all that was necessary was physical movement from one place to another. The student would move when his favorite teacher moved or when he believed that some other university held out greater prospects for academic adventure.

The medieval master, who could be called professor or doctor, was first of all a member of a teaching guild. As a member of the guild he had a voice in all the details and policies that surrounded the conduct of academic affairs. He was admitted to the guild, not by the rector of the university or by a faculty dean, but by the masters who were already established members. He earned his income from student fees paid directly to him. The rates for teaching were set by the guild, and the individual teacher could neither raise nor lower them if he wanted to retain his membership in the guild. Most of the masters were clerics as were the students, for the medieval intellectual world did not offer many impressive invitations to laymen. Incidentally, present-day academic costumes are derived from the clerical dress of the medieval masters.

Despite the definite clerical orientation of the university, medieval universities played a significant role in the development of European culture and education. The university had a direct and most pervasive influence on education. It sent out large numbers of fairly well-equipped teachers at a time when they were badly needed, and it compelled the lower schools to improve their quality in order that their students might enter university studies. Most significant of all, the university performed a great service for mankind by placing the administration of human affairs in the hands of educated men. It is easy to detect the quickened pace of social and scientific progress and of human freedom after the university became a securely established institution. Modern and contemporary institutions of higher learning clearly owe a great deal to their medieval forbears.

Summary

The schools of the Middle Ages were more solidly founded than the Christian schools of earlier periods. The monastic school, the first Christian school, was still in evidence, and by this time it had broadened its curriculum to include the liberal arts. Cathedral and collegiate schools were important educational centers from 1200 to 1500. Court schools tried to perform the dual function of educating the sons and daughters of nobles and of training some young men for clerical positions in civil government. Courtly training included the steps which led selected young men to knighthood. Municipal schools were founded to supplement the educational opportunity offered in church schools. For the most part, these schools were identical with church schools in all respects save their sponsorship. In some parts of Europe chantry schools were quite popular; and in England, especially, they made a deep impression on elementary education. Finally, there were guild schools. These schools were intended mainly for the sons and daughters of guild members and for apprentices or others for whom masters had a legal responsibility.

It was during this period that Scholasticism arose and produced a large body of critical thinkers and an impressive array of scholarly works. Abelard, Peter Lombard, Albert the Great, and Thomas Aquinas were among the brightest stars of the period.

In the realm of educational theory the names of Thierry of Chartres, Hugh of St. Victor, Conrad of Hirschau, and John of Salisbury were most prominent. Medieval educational theory remained within a rather narrow framework of educational thought; in its view, education was intended mainly for clerics, and its purpose was largely otherworldly.

Of all the educational works for which the medieval years are most famous, the universities attract the greatest attention. The foundations for modern higher education were laid in these universities.

PART III

The Development *of* Modern Education

A t the close of the medieval period the world of learning and of scholarship began to wear new faces. Altered motives relative to life and education capitalized on new theories which, while more progressive and material, were also more human. Yet, although educators looked forward to a better life, they also looked back to the ancient literatures for inspiration and guides to the so-called "new learning." The best Renaissance schoolmasters tried to excavate from classical mines treasures of pedagogical knowledge which could upgrade educational technique and broaden the moral and intellectual lives of their students.

In forging a new, or different, theory of education, dedicated humanists left their readers with a variety of paradoxes. Although education was to be primarily a preparation for the world, and not for eternal life, in the end, humanistic educational theory and practice both centered on moral formation—the building of character. And, while every humanist talked about educational reform and counseled a rejection of all medieval school practices, probably only two schools and only two schoolmasters (Guarino and Vittorino) succeeded in bringing new life to learning. Even in the hands of the great Erasmus, the most competent of the humanistic educators, Renaissance education proved that moving educational theory from the library to the classroom can be a very slow process indeed.

Erasmus wrote a theory of education that was given a great deal of attention by Catholic and Protestant schoolmasters alike. Luther may have disliked some of the classics, but in his recommendations relative to the study of ancient languages he was remarkably clearheaded: A careful study of the origins of Christianity, essential at least for clergymen, would make a knowledge of the ancient and classical tongues imperative. Still, a scholarly dedication to the classics was, at best, a distraction for a Christian gentleman, so Luther's educational lieutenant, Melanchthon, recommended a narrowing of the classical curriculum. Both Sturm, speaking for Protestant schoolmen, and the Jesuits, representing Catholic humanistic education, narrowed the curriculum even more by mobilizing the classical legacy to support their own religious objectives.

The evolution of educational thought and practice accelerated considerably after the Renaissance, especially after the codification of Erasmus' theory of *pietas et litterata*. The key to this acceleration was profound and serious doubt about the validity of the doctrine that all knowledge of consequence is contained in classical literature. So much had been claimed for the classical heritage as a staple in the school course that its rejection was almost inevitable.

To begin with, the Realists, and especially their great spokesman, Comenius, aiming at using evidences from the world as materials for curricula, invented new methods to attend the new curricula. Then Locke essayed to set the principles for such real, or empirical, approaches to learning. When his recommendations proved inadequate, or when they missed the point of genuine educational reform, the naturalists, led by Rousseau, abandoned the old compromises and proposed a completely new, and negative, theory of education. What they allowed to go untouched on the level of method was handled for naturalism by Pestalozzi.

The business of education had for centuries been speculated about, formed, and reformed, but it was still mainly an art practiced according to the intuitions of good schoolmasters. Then Herbart said that education could be scientific, and that dependable knowledge could be obtained about the important human work of teaching and learning. In his hands a science of education was developed. At about the same time the nations of the West, now conscious of their nationalism, undertook to create school systems of their own, which they expected would always be responsive to public policy. In this mission national states both succeeded and failed; their histories of education are filled with examples of both positive and negative results.

X

The Classic Renaissance & Education

The Renaissance

The intellectual quickening of the twelfth century outlived the medieval assumptions and ambitions responsible for producing it. Its effects on learning probably were less dramatic in the fourteenth century than in the thirteenth, because (in a manner of speaking) the thirteenth had so much further to go. Yet they were entirely evident, and in fact culminated in the Classic Renaissance. It is not too much to say that the renaissances of the twelfth and fourteenth centuries were fed by the same intellectual and cultural theories, although the latter renaissance found it impossible to accept the dogmatic assumptions and doctrinal limitations of the Medieval age. (It could, however, create a dogmatism of its own.) In any case, the great Renaissance of the fourteenth century was not a reorientation, but the end result of a slow cultural process that had been going on for centuries. Similarities between the two ages are omnipresent, and we would be plainly wrong in believing that the thirteenth and fourteenth centuries represented two distinct cultures.[1]

The Renaissance was a number of things: It was a renewal of contacts with classical Greece and Rome; it was an emphasis on humanness; it was a collecting of manuscripts, and a criticism and dissemination of their contents; in part, it was a studied disregard for the centuries that had intervened between the close of the classical period and the onset of the Renaissance (1350); and finally, it was a heightening of the spirit of individualism among men.

In spite of the fact that contacts with classicism had never been completely lost during the medieval period, the Renaissance can be rightly called a movement which had as its central preoccupation the reestablishing of closer and firmer contacts with the classical past. It might be pointed out that the medieval interest in the classical period had been practical in nature. Both Latin and Greek were used in some church services; ancient architecture was used for many churches and public buildings of the medieval world. We note, of course, that the medievalist had added something to classical culture and remolded it, but even with such additions or modifications, an authentic classicism had continued to exist during the medieval period. Classical writers—Virgil, Caesar, Cicero—were fairly well known and generally cherished; Aristotle was used by the medieval Scholastics in constructing a philosophical system that was entirely Christian in its orientation. Aristotle's influence on medieval philosophy was incontrovertible, even though the system of thought that evolved from medieval speculations about the world and man was quite different from the philosophy which Aristotle had proposed. When medieval scholars turned their attention to scientific investigations, crude as they were, they found that in this area, too, classical scientific thought had furnished a basis for their own conclusions about the world. Yet when the Christians of the Renaissance turned to the classics, they did so not so much because they wanted to confirm what they already believed about the universe or themselves,

---

[1] R. R. Bolgar, *The Classical Heritage and Its Beneficiaries*, Cambridge University Press, New York, 1954, pp. 265–268; P. O. Kristeller, *Renaissance Thought: The Classics, Scholastic, and Humanistic Strains*, Harper and Row, Publishers, New York, 1965, vol. I, pp. 151–157; Georges Duby, *Foundations of a New Humanism, 1280–1440*, World Book Publishing Co., Cleveland, 1966; and Gerald G. Walsh, *Medieval Humanism*, The Macmillan Company, New York, 1942.

but because they found their form beautiful and their content provocative.[2]

The Renaissance mind looked both forward and backward. It looked backward for inspiration; it looked forward to the time when a better life would be available to men who had used their talents to produce such a better world. The idea of progress was no more foreign to the Renaissance than was the idea that life could be a good deal more humanly enjoyable than it was. The place that education could occupy in such a world view was by no means insignificant.

RENAISSANCE EDUCATIONAL THEORY

We have noted the principal outlines of medieval educational theory and have seen how it affected medieval schools. Theory's role in education is normally one of supplying a rationale for schools and school practice, and, consciously or unconsciously, educational theories are dominated by a society's basic values. The theory sustaining Renaissance education, we feel certain, reflected the changes taking place in life and society. It should therefore be somewhat different from the directive theory of medieval education. Let us see whether this is true.

Some historians appear to believe that Renaissance educational theory was a bequest from classical educational philosophers. Both in theory and practice, they assume, Renaissance education was revolutionary—a dramatic leap back over a thousand years to feed on the classical doctrines responsible for classical pedagogy—and that these doctrines were adopted as governing agents for fourteenth- and fifteenth-century education, which on a day-to-day level took the ancient Greek and Hellenistic schools for its models. Proof of the revolutionary nature of Renaissance education, they aver, is found in the endless allusions and quotations which humanistic authors incorporate in their educational works. When we sample these works we are quickly convinced that they did, in fact, depend rather heavily on their classical predecessors. However, this borrowing was a part of conventional scholarship, and taking it alone we should be forced to acknowledge that medieval educational writers knew their classical sources about as well as their humanistic counterparts did. Vincent of Beauvais' *On the*

---

[2] See Gilbert Highet, *The Classical Tradition*, Oxford University Press, New York, 1949, pp. 77–81; W. K. Ferguson, *The Renaissance in Historical Thought*, Houghton Mifflin Co., Boston, 1948, pp. 112–115; and E. Panofsky, *Renaissance and Renascences in Western Art*, Almquist & Wiksell, Stockholm, Sweden, 1960, pp. 93–108.

Education of Noble Children, a medieval book anticipatory of Renaissance educational theory, serves as a quick illustration: In the fifty-one chapters Vincent writes, he includes over nine hundred quotations (most are from scripture, the Church Fathers, and Scholastic authors), about one-third of which are authentically classical. No one who has read Vincent could be convinced that his appetite for classical selections betrayed any revolutionary predispositions.[3]

Another interpretation is preferred: The educational theory and practice of the Renaissance were really the end products of a long evolutionary process. Herewith, medieval theory is not indicted as a cultural interloper—nor is its pedagogy, which evidently often agrees with the theory and practice of ancient education, summarily and totally rejected. Medieval education becomes, in this interpretation, a direct descendant of ancient education, and Renaissance education a direct descendant of the medieval.

The point can be made in yet another way: The precedents for Renaissance educational theory and practice were present either implicitly or explicitly in medieval education, and it was entirely unnecessary for the humanistic educator to find a way to ignore the educational impact of a thousand years. Although their protestations in no way changed the facts of history, this did not, of course, prevent humanistic theorists from denying their intellectual and cultural ancestors.

Probably the chief influence of classicism on an educational theory maturing in the Renaissance was on the education of laymen. Medieval teaching programs had been less than generous in their provisions for this. In centering its attention on the clergy, medieval educational theory had to rewrite much of its ancient legacy, for (at least in theory) classical education was open to anyone who could profit from it. Humanistic educators, however, could take the prescriptions of antiquity and apply them more directly because they were interested principally in the education of laymen.[4]

Although we may want to give emphasis to the new direction taken by humanistic education (the education of laymen for citizen-

[3] See Asztrik Gábriel, *The Educational Ideals of Vincent of Beauvais,* Mediaeval Institute, University of Notre Dame, Notre Dame, Ind., 1956; and Arpad Steiner, "Guillaume Perrault and Vincent of Beauvais," *Speculum,* vol. 8, pp. 51–58, 1933.

[4] Daniel D. McGarry, "Renaissance Educational Theory," *Historical Bulletin,* vol. 32, pp. 195–209, May, 1954; John Addington Symonds, *Renaissance in Italy: The Revival of Learning,* Henry Holt and Co., New York, 1920, pp. 16–26; R. K. Kelso, *The Doctrine of the English Gentleman in the Sixteenth Century,* University of Illinois Press, Urbana, 1929; and George C. Brauer, *The Education of a Gentleman, Theories of Gentlemanly Education in England, 1660–1775,* Oxford University Press, New York, 1959.

ship), we are forced to recognize that the curriculum of Renaissance schools was little different from what it had been before. Some historians have criticized the new education for its reluctance to give to its wider group of students the freedom in style and content that, they say, had been afforded clerical students in medieval education, but since this freedom alleged for medieval education is mainly myth, the criticism should not be taken seriously. The essentials of teaching and learning in both periods were nearly identical, in spite of the differences in clientele and goals.[5] The reform characteristic of humanistic education was directed not so much toward what was to be taught, as toward who would be taught, and why.

Despite the general validity of our conclusion that humanistic educational theory was concerned with the education of all men for citizenship, we should not forget that a number of specific issues faced educators and theorists that were not on this high level. One issue had to do with the control of education: Should educational control be vested in the Church or in the state? Of course, there was no possibility of settling this question by going back to the ancients, who had not been faced with this particular choice. The problem the ancients had to settle was the question of state or individual control of education. One may recall that Athens generally favored the individualistic approach, while Rome tended to be more collectivistic in its outlook. It is hard, of course, to generalize about Rome, for, though the Romans may never have lost their inclination to regard the collective good and the welfare of the state as superior to the individual good, there is not much evidence that ancient Rome ever had a full-fledged state system of schools.[6] Thus the humanists of the fourteenth century had no ready ancient model to follow, even if they had wanted one. As for models from their own time, it can be said that they were familiar both with church schools and with schools, such as the municipal schools and some universities, that had a public character. One looks in vain for a definitive position that favored either state or church control of education. There were, however, a number of middle positions. If we must draw a conclusion here, we can say unequivocally only that humanistic educational theory supported the view that laymen with genuine skills for teaching and scholarship ought to replace clergymen as teachers,

---

[5] See John Edwin Sandys, *Harvard Lectures on the Revival of Learning*, Cambridge University Press, New York, 1905, pp. 33–39; and Joseph A. Mazzeo, *Renaissance and Revolution: The Remaking of European Thought*, Pantheon Books, New York, 1966, pp. 298–303.

[6] See H. I. Marrou, *A History of Education in Antiquity*, Sheed & Ward, Inc., New York, 1956, pp. 296–297.

that the Church ought not to dominate education, and that there ought to be plenty of room for institutions not directly controlled or sponsored by the Church.

Humanistic theorists did not spend all their time on this question. There were many others. One was: What value ought to be attached to the classics? While it is no doubt true that the classics were never completely lost, their original purpose was changed by a number of Christian and medieval teachers. They were used exclusively as means or as handmaidens in religious teaching. For the humanists, many of whom had nothing against religious knowledge or religious teaching, this was a misuse of the classics. They saw that they were of far greater value than mere steppingstones to something else. In discussing this question, we must consider the position of the Scholastic method, which had risen to fame and prominence, not to say power, during the medieval years. We need be in no doubt as to the position taken by the humanists. They maintained that the classics were superior in content to any other literature that might be put into the school's program, and that no other content could inspire youth to develop their God-given capacities in the way that the classics could. They saw in the classics not only literary and intellectual inspiration, but moral inspiration as well. Nowhere else, they said, could one find better directions for the building of character than in the classics. Students were advised to study Plato, Aristotle, Plutarch, Seneca, and many other ancient authors in order to find the best ways of forming character. The humanistic approval of the ethical emphases that they detected in the classics may go a long way toward explaining the unrelenting attention most theorists of this era gave to character education when they wrote tracts or treatises on educational theory.[7]

Besides giving inspiration for intellectual formation and directions for building character, the classics were supposed to contain genuine scientific worth; that is, they not only were supposed to contain scientific information of merit but were expected to generate in students a real scientific interest. Although this all may have been true in theory, in practice it would have been hard to find much evidence of natural or physical science in Renaissance education. So taken up were the humanists with the desire to know man that they found little or no time to pursue nature. They were true followers of Quintilian, who, though he said "No mathematics, no orator" and meant it, could find no

[7] See J. E. Mason, Gentlefolk in the Making, University of Pennsylvania Press, Philadelphia, 1935, pp. 44–71; and J. Simon, Education and Society in Tudor England, Cambridge University Press, New York, 1966.

time for science in the educational program that he constructed. Although we may understand that the humanists did not find the supreme value of the classics in ornamentation, it is difficult for us to see the precise point where ornamentation stopped and other values became prominent.

The humanistic educators asked and attempted to answer many other important questions. For example, they concerned themselves with the problem of aim. Should education aim at knowledge or at style? We cannot discover that they resolved this issue or that any of the views they presented contributed to the solution of another problem related to it, namely: Is the end of education discipline or utility? It is of course a fact that the humanists gave more attention to the education of women than their immediate predecessors had; it is quite another thing, however, to claim that this attention led to actual educational opportunities for women that were noticeably richer than they had been before. And, considering the humanist's veneration of the past, we may find it somewhat surprising when he refused to give more attention to physical education in the school's program. On the level of theory, physical development was undoubtedly important; humanists could see the interdependence of mind and body, and could understand and appreciate the ancient educators' interest in physical formation. Yet, it must be repeated, except for a few examples furnished by exceptional schoolmasters (Vittorino was one), humanists were quite willing to leave physical education to the schoolboys' periods of free play and recreation. The same generalization would apply to music, dancing, and drawing—though, we should point out, the humanist was always ready to defend the value of these things. Music, often thought to be an appropriate skill for women, was believed to be an instrument capable of leading them closer to an appreciation of life's finer things. But we cannot attempt to write a very elaborate history of women's educational opportunities at this time; the task would be frustrating and perhaps futile.[8]

Almost universal agreement is apparent on the point that early humanists refused to endow the vernacular with worth. They considered it a vulgar tongue and evidently shared the general prejudice against it. Perhaps the distinction should be made between a language to be used for culture and one to be used for everyday speech. The

[8] R. K. Kelso, *Doctrine for the Lady of the Renaissance,* University of Illinois Press, Urbana, 1956, pp. 81–88; and M. A. Cannon, *The Education of Women During the Renaissance,* The Catholic University of America Press, Washington, D. C., 1916, pp. 17–25.

language for culture—the Sunday language, so to speak—was Latin, then clearly established as the language of learning, and no doubt it had to be. The various vernacular languages were employed as universally as they are today for common speech and ordinary communication, but the weaknesses of a vernacular were real enough, and more than mere prejudice kept the speech of the people from becoming the language of learning in the fourteenth century. Of course, the Latin prized so highly was not the living medieval Latin, but the classical Latin of Cicero's time, and it became the model in both language and literary teaching. But to return to the vernacular for a last word about its major weakness: It contained neither the vocabulary nor the structure necessary to a medium of communication employed as an instrument of learning. As the native languages developed—and some developed more rapidly than others, English being especially tardy in its development—they came to occupy a place of greater prominence in the schools, and especially in the higher schools. We should state quite clearly that prejudice alone did not exclude the vernacular languages from halls of learning, but their own deprivations.[9]

Later, no doubt, the inertia of tradition or preferences for the medium already in use tended to block the progress of the vernacular as a tool in learning. Whether or not the vernacular should be used in the schools was never a matter for debate in the early Renaissance; it is not until the fifteenth century that we witness the beginning of the struggle between the vernacular and Latin in the field of education. And it is safe to say that when the vernacular turned the tables on Latin and became the popular medium for all communication and instruction, its popularity was not due to a new and more pervasive feeling against Latin. There were other reasons. Chief among them was the growing nationalism demanding not only a national language but a national literature as well.

Humanists did not avoid history. They did, it is true, take a relatively dim view of the thousand years that separated the Renaissance from the classical period and were usually willing to ignore them. This attitude toward the past did not mean that the Renaissance was antihistorical. As a matter of fact, the humanist had a better sense of history than his older medieval brother, and had the humanist theorist had his way entirely, he would have insisted that history occupy an important, even a central place in the school's instructional program. In addition to glorifying ancient civilization, history could be expected to uphold sentiments of patriotism as well as to present literary and artistic

[9] See Douglas Bush, *The Renaissance and English Humanism,* The University of Toronto Press, Toronto, 1941, pp. 98–111.

values. There may have been some good reasons for the decided preference that the humanists had for Roman classical history. The great
national heroes about whom the Romans wrote were real historical figures; the heroes of Greek literature had reality only in the imaginations
of the authors. For all their cultural idealism, the humanists were
realists too.

What was to be done with pagan literature—the classics? This was
surely not a new question. It had given educational thinkers and writers a good deal of trouble for some centuries. From the time of Alexander the Great to the time of Alcuin of York there was always some
doubt as to just where the classics should stand in Christian culture.[10]
By the time the humanistic movement attained maturity, no one doubted
the merit of the classics as instruments of study, and few humanists
expressed any fears with respect to the impression the classical authors
might have on the formation of Christian minds. Christian humanism
had come a long way in a short time. There was still a kind of pagan
humanism, of course, which, while emphasizing the intellectual values
in the classics, refused to acknowledge the authenticity of the Christian
message or the Christian mission.

We come now to the chief weak points in the humanistic movement as it applied to education. They need not be discussed in detail,
but they ought to be mentioned. In the organization of schools, in building a systematic curriculum, in psychological and methodological approaches to teaching, the humanists were weak almost to the point of
negligence. With all their concern for education, with a revolutionary
or at least a liberal outlook toward education, the humanists seemed to
be unable to see that order and discipline in the schools were essential
to any degree of excellence. If we maintain that the theory of the
humanists represented progress in education, then we should admit
that the humanists were almost unbelievably weak in transferring their
theories to the schools in which teachers were teaching and students
were learning.

Humanistic Schools and Schoolmasters

Humanism, often another name for the Renaissance, exerted an influence on many of man's activities. The effects of humanism were felt
deeply in the schools. We turn now to study the evolution of humanistic
education in Europe.

[10] See Edward K. Rand, *The Founders of the Middle Ages,* Harvard University
Press, Cambridge, Mass., 1928.

HUMANISTIC EDUCATION IN ITALY

One aspect of the Renaissance in Italy was the attention it paid to a revival of learning. As a matter of fact, so important was this phase of humanism in Italy that it is not uncommon to think of the revival of learning as having been the Renaissance itself. Of course, the Renaissance was more than this, but it was notably a general reawakening to the importance of learning, and it became a movement motivated by a passionate desire to recapture ancient Greek and Roman literature, learning, and culture. Perhaps it was natural for the interest in the classics to be generated in Italy, for the Italians were certainly aware of the glories of their past, if they were not in fact conversant with the things that had contributed to that glory.

Given the ideal, the stuff out of which the ideal could be constructed could be obtained. In Italy, the great revival of learning had as its fore-runners two important names in the history of literature and in the history of thought: Dante Alighieri (1264–1321) and Francesco Petrarch (1304–1374). We cannot, of course, think of Dante as a schoolman or a schoolmaster or claim that he has a part in educational history.[11] But the historian experiences very little difficulty in presenting Dante as a figure who by the spirit of his writings contributed to the humanistic move-ment and the educational awakening that accompanied it. The fact that he was the first layman since Boethius to gain a reputation in literature and to be recognized as one of the most learned men of his day was in it-self important to humanism. And finally Dante showed that a broad cul-ture could be conveyed by the vernacular as well as by classical lan-guages. The ultimate importance of Dante's use of Italian cannot be overstressed, as we consider the broad sweep of educational history. Yet we must admit that the vernacular was not esteemed by confirmed Italian humanists and that little use was made of it for some time, except, of course, as a medium of informal communication among the unlearned and unlettered.

The fact that Dante's *Divine Comedy* was not written in Latin but in Italian did very little to stimulate interest in vernacular languages. Dante did, however, generate interest in the classical past because in his great work he quoted from and referred to the classical authors hundreds of times.

Petrarch's importance as a forerunner of humanistic education is a little easier to recognize. He took the steps that other humanists were to follow in emphasizing the significance of classical language and liter-

[11] See Hans Baron, *The Crisis of the Early Italian Renaissance*, Princeton University Press, Princeton, N. J., 1966, pp. 207–209.

ature as a basis for all education. As a scholar, he made many of the classical works available to students. He was responsible for the establishment of a center for humanistic or classical studies at the University of Padua, and for a long time it was from Padua that the inspiration for continuing the humanistic movement came. From this university Petrarch set out on his journeys in search of classical manuscripts. He and his colleagues left few stones unturned, few libraries untouched, in their efforts to collect classical manuscripts.

But for all their importance, these Petrarchian services to humanism tell only part of the story. He could insist on Greek and Latin as the only suitable languages for literature (a doctrine which proved to be as much a curse as a blessing to the future of education), and advise his students to close their Aristotle and open their Cicero (which tended to make humanism philosophically barren), and at the same time by his own great effort popularize the classics and the many literary forms they represented. Petrarch liked the classics, and by the sheer force of his scholarship he generated a love and respect for them among his countrymen too.[12] Pedagogically, he reintroduced the technique of imitation and made it, again, entirely respectable. What he recommended, however, was not the linguistic exactitude aimed at by the humanistic teachers a century later, which gave the technique a bad name, but a written and oral expression which utilized classical style and ideas as guides. Petrarch refused to say "Write like Cicero," but he did say that good writing and speaking could be achieved by using the best models for developing a personal style not unlike the style of classical authors. The ancients, in Petrarch's educational code, were masters not only of the art of writing but of the art of living as well; this was the point that interested him most, and he was able, because of his work and reputation, to impregnate humanism with this idealism. Petrarch was a first-rate scholar reverencing ideas, and he was, moreover, an orthodox Christian seeking salvation. In the end he became the apologist for humanism by showing how salvation must come through the practice of human virtue, by trusting morality more than theology, and by emphasizing the importance of living well temporally. These lessons, Petrarch maintained, were taught thoroughly by the ancient writers, especially Cicero. So he nailed his educational flag to the mast of classical literature.[13]

---

[12] Pierre de Nolhac, *Pétrarque et L'Humanisme*, H. Champion, Paris, 1907, pp. 11–15; Sandys, *op. cit.*, pp. 37–41; and Ernest H. Wilkins, *Life of Petrarch*, University of Chicago Press, Chicago, 1961.

[13] See Walter Rüegg, *Cicero und der Humanismus*, Rheinverlag, Zürich, 1946, pp. 32–35.

We might mention, at this point, the status of Greek in the program of humanistic education. The Greek language had not been completely forgotten in Europe during the Middle Ages. It is unthinkable that the knowledge of Greek could have been stamped out completely all over Europe. Yet it is true that few people knew very much about the language or were able to read or write it with any skill. One of the major points of emphasis in this reawakening and revival was the value of reading the Greek classics in the original. It was not enough to capture their humanness in translation; it was necessary, too, to taste their sweetness and observe their beauty in the original. The attitudes on this point were so contagious that Greek was subject to a rather significant revival on the Continent. The man who played a central role in this revival, both in the stimulation of interest in Greek and in the development of skill to use it, was Emmanuel Chrysoloras (1350–1413). In 1397 Chrysoloras, who had come to Italy as a diplomat, accepted the chair of Greek at the University of Florence. With him the revival of Greek in Italy really began, and with him, too, humanistic education has its inception.[14]

With this preparation the humanists of Italy were ready to enter the educational arena proper. The first to do so was Peter Paul Vergerius (1370–1445), the author of a work entitled *On Noble Character and Liberal Studies*.[15] The work of Vergerius is usually recognized as the first example of humanistic educational theory.[16] In it Vergerius advocated the teaching of Latin literature as part of liberal education; and he directed the attention of educators to the needs that certain noble laymen had for learning. His work was considered to be entirely orthodox by Church authorities. There is evidence, moreover, that Vergerius was familiar with a number of classical authors; Plato, Cicero, Aristotle were all known to him in one form or another. He could not have known the classical educational writers very completely because the bulk of their works had not yet been unearthed.

Whether or not Vergerius knew any of the ancient authorities on education, his own views were worth a good deal to the teachers of his day. It is claimed that the greatest teacher of the Renaissance, Vittorino de Feltre, was indebted to Vergerius.[17] In his work on *Liberal Studies*, a treatise that was intended as a practical guide for the education of Ubertino, the son of Francesco Carrara, the lord of Padua, Vergerius

[14] Bolgar, *op. cit.*, pp. 268–271.

[15] William H. Woodward, *Vittorino da Feltre and Other Humanist Educators*, Cambridge University Press, New York, 1905, pp. 98–118.

[16] *Ibid.*, pp. 14–15.

[17] A. Gambara, *Vittorino da Feltre*, G. B. Paravia, Turin, 1964, p. 61.

touched on the following topics that then, as now, had considerable relevance to education and educators: the training of children in manners, motivation for study, the relation of capacity to accomplishment, rewards and punishment for success and failure, and the interest of the teacher in the student as a person and not merely as a learning machine. It should not be overlooked that this work was intended to guide the education of a young prince, and though its precepts might well have been applicable to children who were not of noble birth, the context in which it was offered would seem to have somewhat limited its influence.

The work of Vergerius appeared about 1393. Within a quarter of a century later, work had been done and discoveries had been made in connection with the ancient educational writers that had important consequences for humanistic educational theory. In 1411, Guarino da Verona translated Plutarch's *On the Education of Children*.[18] Having Plutarch's work in their hands in usable form, the theorists were now in closer touch with antiquity. It has been suggested that over the years the accomplishment of Guarino and the effects of Plutarch's work cannot be overestimated. Such a claim, however, might be in itself an example of overestimation. Of considerably more import than the translation of *On the Education of Children* was the discovery of a complete text of Quintilian's *Institutes of Oratory*. Poggio, a man renowned for his ability to ferret out old manuscripts, found the *Institutes* at the Swiss monastery of St. Gall in 1416. A few years later Cicero's *The Orator* was found at Lodi.

Thus, men who were interested in dealing with education on the level of theory had available to them four of the most important theoretical works on education ever written: *The Republic* of Plato, *Politics* of Aristotle, *The Orator* of Cicero, and Quintilian's *Institutes of Oratory*. From a study of these authors and from a study of the ancient forms of education, humanistic theorists were able to construct a theory of education which made possible a new order of schools. The greatest and the best known of these schools was conducted by a man who was, and is, acclaimed as the foremost schoolmaster of the Renaissance,[19] Vittorino da Feltre. Before we turn to the work of Vittorino, it might be well to review the theoretical contributions of some of Vittorino's contemporaries and in this review provide the reader with some sense of direction in following humanistic educational practices. The educators to whom we turn now are: Leonardo Bruni D'Arezzo (1369–1444),

[18] See Katharine M. Westaway, *The Educational Theory of Plutarch*, University of London Press, Ltd., London, 1922, p. 14.

[19] Woodward, *op. cit.*, p. 92.

Aeneas Sylvius Piccolomini—later Pope Pius II (1405–1464), Leone Battista Alberti (1404–1472), Battista Guarino (1434–1513), Mapheus Vegius (1405–1458), Matteo Palmieri (1406–1475), and Baldassare Castiglione (1478–1529).[20]

Leonardo Bruni D'Arezzo   Bruni was the author of a tract entitled *On Studies and Letters*. This tract, really a letter, was addressed to Baptista Malatesta, a lady who had some reputation for learning. In the letter, he wrote: "The foundation of all true learning must be laid in the sound and thorough knowledge of Latin: which implies study marked by a broad spirit, accurate scholarship, and careful attention to details." [21] This advice, it must be remembered, is being given to a lady not for her own guidance, because that was unnecessary, and not as a general pattern for the education of women, because Bruni refused to be so narrow in his outlook, but as a general pedagogical doctrine mined, he thought, from the teaching theories of the ancients. Written for a woman, *On Studies and Letters* avoids details of rhetoric, but describes the new method of teaching demonstrated for the humanists by Chrysoloras in his Florentine studium and spread by Vergerius, who, in *De Ingenuis Moribus*, emphasized, as had classical education, the formation of character rather than the acquisition of knowledge. Medieval education, we know, despite its otherworldly features, had given knowledge pride of place in the schools and had thus separated itself from authentic classical goals. But the humanists could return to these goals and try to mold character in schools by emphasizing the traditional appurtenances of classical scholarship. In other words, Bruni tried to show his readers how a return to the classics could build character. He begins with some general recommendations on reading, and then turns to method itself. Teachers, he says, should use the classics not for the ideas they contain, or for a general tone of good writing, but to unearth the smallest literary techniques used by the giants of literature. Students should search the classics for vocabulary, figures, and ornaments of style; they should resist any temptation to develop their own style by using classical writing as a starting point; and they should know and notice everything contained in the classics.[22]

Petrarch had recommended imitation of good authors, and Bruni follows suit. But where Petrarch wanted style, understanding, and even wisdom for the student of the classics, Bruni was content with literary

[20] See *ibid.*, and William H. Woodward, *Studies in Education During the Age of the Renaissance, 1400–1600*, Cambridge University Press, New York, 1924.

[21] Woodward, *Vittorino da Feltre and Other Humanist Educators*, p. 124.

[22] *Ibid.*, p. 128.

and linguistic exactitude. If everything in the classics was to be noticed, and if, in writing and speaking, students were to use only approved classical words and forms, then some additional help was needed for them. The notebook, the storehouse for materials of good writing, became for the first time an indispensable instrument in formal education. A full notebook was, Bruni assumed, the certain road to literary excellence and the undoubted equivalent of a decent education. He left to others the difficult task of showing the theoretical connection between painstaking analysis, attention to linguistic minutiae, and a studied, frozen eloquence, and praiseworthy character. Being unable himself to make the connection did not, however, deter him, and most humanistic educators as well, from setting education's goal as good character, and using purely literary means to achieve it. Sound or unsound, Bruni's attitude grafted itself to humanism and became the principal emphasis and distinctive feature of humanistic educational theory and practice.

Aeneas Sylvius Piccolomini Sylvius prepared a set of directions for the education of boys, although the immediate motive for his book was to guide the formation of Ladislas, the youthful king of Bohemia. The tract, a handbook on the education of noble children but useful even for the son of a shopkeeper wanting to attain nobility of character, appeared about 1450, and because of its fortuitous timing ably incorporated a variety of classical pedagogical advice taken directly from the books of the best classical theorists. While Sylvius' stature in educational thought falls short of real eminence, and his *On the Liberal Education of Boys* puts him on common ground with run-of-the-mill humanists, he deserves our attention here because, when he became Pope Pius II, his humanistic allegiances infected the methods and curricula of Church schools.[23]

The tract begins with a more or less conventional introduction to educational speculation and goes out of its way to prove what then needed no proof—a humanistic indebtedness to classical theory:

> In addressing ourselves to the question of the education of a boy in whom we are interested, we must first of all satisfy ourselves that he is endowed by Nature with a good and teachable disposition. Now this is a gift, not an acquirement; although a gift which has not been sparingly granted. For, as Quintilian rightly says, if flying is instinctive with birds, or galloping with horses, so an eager and forward temper is

---

[23] Pius II, *De Liberorum Educatione*, translated with an introduction by Brother J. S. Nelson, The Catholic University of America Press, Washington, D. C., 1940.

the natural mark of a child. The educator, therefore, is generally entitled to assume a native bent towards mental activity on the part of his charges, although, to be productive of real progress, this innate energy needs to be developed by methodical training and experience; nature, training, practice—these seem to be the three factors of all education.[24]

We have said that these were more or less conventional views of the humanistic educators of this time, and we might also point out that they are still considered to be entirely sound. Perhaps Sylvius made no mark on history for the views that he expressed above. However, in another part of this tract he looks at the opposition which, he must have suspected, came from some churchmen who did not take too kindly to the new emphasis in teaching and learning.

> Now I meet an objection. You will be confronted by the opposition of the shallow Churchmen. "Why waste precious time in studying such sources of corruption as the pagan poets?" They will quote Cicero, Plato, Jerome, and Boethius, and will cry out for the banishment of the very names of the ancient poets from the soil of your country. To this your answer can only be: "If this tirade indeed represents the serious opinion of my people, I can but shake off the dust from my feet and bid farewell to a land shrouded in darkness so appalling." Happily, however, there are in Hungary not a few to whom the poets of antiquity are a precious possession. You will have no difficulty in quoting classical precedent for honouring them as they deserve. Nay the Fathers themselves, Jerome, Augustine, Cyprian, did not hesitate to draw illustrations from heathen poetry and so sanctioned its study. Further, if we are to reject the great writers of antiquity for the errors they contain, how shall we treat the masters of theology? From them proceed heresies. Shall we, then, expel them and their writings, as once the Romans banished doctors because they made mistakes? [25]

This was a strong defense for the classics and the extensive use that the humanists made or hoped to make of them in education. And it was an important defense, too, although it must be admitted that the classics were not in an especially precarious position. The stand that Sylvius took with respect to the classics was given even more stature once he became pope. It would, indeed, be hazardous to make extravagant claims for this man or for the impress he had on educational thought. On the other hand, both his work and his influence stabilized the classics as primary instruments for sound Christian learning.

[24] Woodward, *Vittorino da Feltre and Other Humanist Educators*, p. 136.
[25] *Ibid.*, pp. 149–150.

Leone Battista Alberti   Alberti was a many-sided, accomplished man. He was a painter, a poet, a philosopher, a musician, and an architect. On at least one occasion he turned his attention to education and wrote a short work entitled *On the Care of the Family*, a treatise made up of four books, each of which deals with a different aspect of family life and education.[26] In part, the views of Alberti are the usual ones that have been attached to Christian education for centuries: He writes of the respective positions of parents and children in the family circle, of the role that the home must play in the moral formation of youth, of the central place of religion, and of the fulfillment of God's plan as the overriding ideal in man's life. On these points Alberti is not original, although the reemphasis that he gave them was remarkable, considering the direction that Italian humanism was often inclined to take. But Alberti did not stop here. He underlined the worth of letters both in forming character and in making the mind keener and more colorful. Besides, he encouraged parents to see that their children learned the vernacular well and that they could use it fluently for all the purposes to which the classical languages might otherwise be put. At this point Alberti departs from some of the more rigid humanists of the day; few of them would even admit that there was such a thing as the vernacular, to say nothing of using it widely.

What Alberti had to say about the family in his *Della Famiglia*, however, and his ardent recommendation that merchant-class family life and education use the classics as the bedrock of formation, put him in a class by himself. Most humanists, preoccupied with the education of noblemen, forgot the class from which they themselves had sprung, but Alberti preached a humanism of the good life which at its best could take the son of a merchant, make him feel at home with the classics, and produce a businessman who was at once a gentleman. In theory, at least, humanistic education begins to penetrate the life of the people.[27]

Battista Guarino   Battista's short treatise *Concerning the Order and Method to Be Observed in Teaching and Reading the Classical Authors* was written for Maffeo Gambara.[28] The recipient of this humanistic tract on education has no particular place in the history of education. Nor, for that mattter, does Battista himself, except that he recorded, so

[26] Woodward, *Studies in Education During the Age of the Renaissance, 1400–1600*, pp. 48–64.

[27] See George Santayana, *Two Renaissance Educators: Alberti and Piccolomini*, Meador Publishing Company, Boston, 1930.

[28] Woodward, *Vittorino da Feltre and Other Humanist Educators*, pp. 160–178.

he says, the views of his famous father, Guarino of Verona (a student of Chrysoloras'), who with Vergerius was largely responsible for giving humanistic education its original momentum, and who, along with Vittorino, conducted one of two famous humanistic schools wherein the excellence of the classics was unblunted by literary and linguistic minutiae.

In addition to perpetuating his father's memory, Battista's purpose in writing this tract was, as the title suggests, to guide students in their private reading and to give masters in search of techniques for classical teaching some definite principles of method to follow. He emphasizes the latter. By the classics Battista meant both Greek and Latin letters, and in his view the outcome of their study should be a thoroughly satisfactory training in literature and scholarship. Most of what he has to say is not novel, although he is often more precise than his contemporaries about what should happen inside the schoolrooom.

Reading and composition should be taught together. Beginning students should read the easy authors and write their compositions using the classical tales as models; advanced students should read the orators and historians and write broad compositions based on what they have read. In their reading, students were expected to distinguish between style-and-method and information, and were told to keep a notebook ready for recording details coming to their attention. These details were to be a reservoir on which every intending writer could draw. Battista, endorsing a love of detail, restates his father's undoubted preference for the technique of imitation. Analytically reading the authors and consulting them in connection with composition could unquestionably contribute to good writing, but unless notebooks were filled, an assimilation of classical thought would prove impossible. In Battista's pedagogy, the notebook and everything related to it become an unassailable teaching method.[29]

Within its humanistic frame of reference, aside from a few elaborations and amendments, the tract is both conventional and orthodox. The nature of the child, the skill of the master, the importance of proper content, the attention to moral formation—all of these are treated as earlier humanists and classical theorists had treated them. Only in one passage, early in the work, where Battista compares the master to the father, are his views especially interesting, if not distinctive. He wrote:

> In the choice of a Master we ought to remember that his position should carry with it something of the authority of the father: for unless respect be paid to the man and to his office regard will not be had to

[29] *Ibid.*, p. 173.

his words. Our forefathers were certainly right in basing the relation of teacher and pupil on the foundation of filial reverence on the one part and fatherly affection on the other. Thus the instinct of Alexander of Macedon was a sound one which led him to say that, whilst he owed to his father Philip the gift of life, he owed to his tutor Aristotle an equal debt, namely, the knowledge to use it.[30]

There is no reason to doubt the sincerity of this author when he reflects convictions as to the importance of the teacher. These were views that had been expressed in Western educational thought at least as early as Plato, and the classical writers on education were obviously sincere when they agreed with him. Yet it must be fairly clear to the reader by this time that theory and practice hardly ever went along hand-in-hand. While the theorists extolled the virtues of great masters and pointed to the need for skilled and virtuous teachers of the young, the people who were in charge of selecting masters—parents, guardians, or public officials—went right on taking anybody they could get. This was especially true on the lower levels of education. The most surprising thing about the humanist educators of the fourteenth and fifteenth centuries is that they either did not recognize this separation of theory and practice when they saw it, or did not consider the separation to be really important. At any rate, we need give neither special blame nor special praise to the work or the influence of Battista on this point, although we are led to suppose that in his father's school no such dichotomies were allowed to interfere with quality teaching and learning.

Mapheus Vegius   The work of the Augustinian monk Vegius, *On the Education of Boys and Their Moral Culture,* is the longest and, many think, the most important of the humanistic treatises on education. In Vegius' approach to the classics, the study of which he never tired of recommending, these writings held positive values for Christians.

A question has been raised concerning the lack of originality in this work of Vegius. It is no doubt quite accurate to claim that for many of his views he was indebted to classical writers. But need this be a serious criticism? He was a thorough investigator and reporter of the classical ideas on education.[31]

Vegius' book is divided into six parts. The first three parts deal with the place of parents and teachers in the total educational process; the

---

[30] *Ibid.,* p. 162.
[31] See Vincent J. Horkan, *Educational Theories and Principles of Maffeo Vegio,* The Catholic University of America Press, Washington, D. C., 1953.

last three deal with students in their relationship to God, to their fellow men, and to themselves. Although his work is directed principally toward the education of boys, Vegius does touch on the education of girls, and for them he prescribes a training in household duties.

In a succinct statement on the worth of knowledge, Vegius sums up what may have been the usual humanistic attitude toward it:

> May the youth of happy disposition seize knowledge and dedicate himself to it, since it has in view great benefits. . . . He receives the best guidance how one may live a modest, earnest, and pious life, how one should love parents and fatherland, reverence God, and avoid evil and despise sensuality. . . . Knowledge furnishes youth the greatest pleasure; knowledge of the changes of fate, of times and peoples and their history has something alluring. The doctrines that it offers us, are not merely of great moral influence, but conduce also to prudent judgments, to ripe reflection upon the mastery over the tasks of life. Scientific studies furnish relief and refreshment in those countless difficulties of which human life is full, and they cause us to forget them. In misfortune of any sort whatever they furnish strong protection; they are themselves a support to riches and fortune, in consequence of the extraordinary esteem and worth which science contributes. Finally, knowledge is an ornament of mankind.[32]

Vegius' formulation of the objectives of education is both interesting and enlightening. It is easy to see his Christian outlook. He wrote that the ends of education ought to be such that a youth would reverence God, love his parents, be respectful toward strangers, regard the aged, not disdain youth, be friendly with his equals, never swear or lie or slander, be true to friends, courteous to women, gentle to servants, and good to everybody.[33] These are worthy, though not scholarly, objectives. It should be pointed out, however, that some of the means to obtain these ends would have been the usual literary means that were so much emphasized in humanistic educational practices.

Matteo Palmieri   Palmieri, a close friend of Alberti, wrote a work in dialogue form entitled *Concerning the Method of Ruling the Household and the State*. At first glance this may not appear to have any relevance to educational theory. We find, however, that in this work Palmieri discusses in four books the education of a boy from childhood to manhood and the virtues that would enable him to manage the household and conduct the affairs of the state. So this author deals with

[32] *Ibid.*, p. 119.

[33] *Ibid.*, pp. 119–120.

two kinds of education, domestic and civic, and expects that such education will produce a scholarly man of affairs.

Palmieri himself was a diplomat and a highly skilled and polished man. It is reported that he was sent to the king of Naples as an emissary from Florence. After hearing Palmieri discourse in Latin, Spanish, and Italian, the king is said to have remarked: "What must the Medici be, if this be but a simple citizen-trader of Florence!" [34]

Baldassare Castiglione   *The Courtier,* Castiglione's celebrated work on education, came rather late in the humanistic period and tended to reflect rather than to form humanistic educational thought.[35] Thus *The Courtier* was in a position to exert considerable influence on education after the Renaissance. Although written in the sixteenth century, this work of Castiglione's represented the best in fifteenth-century manners and morals, so that those who followed its dictates could be confident that they would be both learned and cultured. It should be mentioned, too, that the prescription laid down in *Il Cortegiano* was for men and women alike. It is clear, however, that this work was never intended to guide the education of the common man. The title betrays the emphasis; the men and women to be educated were the members of the court or, at least, those who traveled in polite society. The educational doctrine, to be followed by ladies and gentlemen, was a doctrine of courtesy applied to education.

It is only fair to say that the best in humanistic educational theory was broader and more valid than the theories we find in Castiglione, although many of the positions taken in *The Courtier* are entirely responsible and acceptable. Yet in the main Castiglione was reflecting the educational thought of humanism; Renaissance educational theory did emphasize the education of laymen for their role in life. Castiglione narrowed this objective somewhat, but even in a narrower context it is still an outgrowth of orthodox humanistic theory.[36]

Vittorino da Feltre (1378–1446)   The humanists we have already mentioned played important roles in the evolution of educational thought and practice during this period. Their impact was considerable; yet compared with the influence of Vittorino da Feltre, it was relatively weak. Vittorino made no mark on the history of education as a

---

[34] Woodward, *Studies in Education During the Age of the Renaissance, 1400–1600,* p. 66.

[35] Baldassare Castiglione, *The Book of the Courtier,* translated by L. E. Opdycke, Charles Scribner's Sons, New York, 1903.

[36] Brauer, *op. cit.,* pp. 39–41.

theorist. He wrote nothing that could be called a book, although some of his letters have been the subject of careful study. It was as a schoolmaster that Vittorino achieved everlasting fame. One often reads the statement that Vittorino was the most famous schoolmaster of the Renaissance, and there may be only a little extravagance in the claim that he was the greatest teacher of modern times. Both statements are fairly easy to make and almost impossible either to prove or disprove. We make reference to them here simply to indicate that Vittorino was an educator of unquestioned stature and that we can learn much from him.

Little is known of Vittorino's early life. In 1396 he entered the University of Padua as a student. This is an important date in the history of learning, for it was in 1396 that the *studium* of Florence invited Emmanuel Chrysoloras, who was then a professor of Greek in Constantinople, to accept the chair of Greek letters. Thus Chrysoloras became the first professor of the Greek tongue in the West, and to this incident it is possible to relate much that took place in the revival of learning in Europe. At Padua Vittorino was influenced by the spirit of Petrarch, which was still strong although the poet had died in 1376. Vittorino studied under Giovanni Conversino da Ravenna, who had been a close friend and student of Petrarch. He must have breathed in some of the spirit and the restless quest for learning that had motivated Petrarch and his followers.[37]

Neither the details of Vittorino's life nor the course that he pursued at the University of Padua is entirely clear. He began, of course, with the faculty of arts and took his degree in arts. From there he went on, it appears, to one of the higher faculties, although to which one is something of a mystery.

He remained at or near the University of Padua for about twenty years. For a short period of time he was a member of the university faculty in the position of master of rhetoric. It is reported, however, that he could not continue in that position because he felt that the discipline of the students was so bad that learning was impossible. Vittorino was a dedicated teacher who became uneasy when students refused what he had to offer; he may not have remained a member of the faculty for more than a year. Both before and after this academic experience he acted as a tutor to university students and conducted a private school for students who were preparing for the university. Thus Vittorino's career as a schoolmaster began early, but it was not at Padua or in Venice, where he also kept a school, but in Mantua that he

[37] See Gambara, *op. cit.;* and Woodward, *Vittorino da Feltre and Other Humanist Educators,* pp. 26–27.

achieved his great reputation as the finest schoolmaster the Renaissance ever produced.

In 1423 Vittorino received an invitation from the lord of Mantua, Gianfrancesco Gonzaga, to conduct a court school for the children of the Gonzaga family and for the children of the nobles of his court. It was quite unnecessary to seek a man of Vittorino's caliber if the lord of Mantua was interested only in a school; a man with less talent might have been an entirely satisfactory schoolmaster. However, it was usual at that time for rich and influential families to make every effort to consolidate their position and ensure their power. Some families employed painters, sculptors, or architects, thus becoming patrons of the arts whose fame could be spread throughout the country. Since learning and letters were highly prized at the time Gonzaga was looking for a schoolmaster, he decided to secure a man of letters as a teacher, and thus, in addition to providing instruction for the children, he could embellish his own position as a patron of the arts. And who was to say that there could not be justifiable pride or glory in being the patron of and the sponsor for the most reputable school in the region? So much for the motives that may have influenced the lord of Mantua.

Vittorino accepted the invitation extended to him. His teaching career at Mantua began in 1423 and ended with his death in 1446. While he was there he established and perfected what Woodward has called the first great school of the Renaissance.[38]

Vittorino shared the prevalent views on education. When he differed from other humanists on the level of theory it was only in degree, although it is obvious that he was much more of a practical schoolmaster than any of the humanistic theorists whom we have touched on above. He was unquestionably familiar with Quintilian's *Institutes of Oratory* and used it as a partial guide for his own educational plans. He knew Cicero's *The Orator* as well. It would be a mistake, therefore, to think of Vittorino as an educator who stood outside the humanistic tradition in learning. Yet it is well worth our while to look more closely at the ideal that motivated his work. Vittorino brought with him to Mantua a desire to combine the spirit of the Christian life with the educational apparatus of classical literature. He sought to achieve a genuine integration of the two.

In addition to the Gonzaga children in Vittorino's Mantuan school, other children from the vicinity were admitted, although they were always from the so-called "better" families. Compared to modern schools, the one conducted by Vittorino would be called small. Its en-

[38] *Ibid.,* p. 92.

rollment probably never went beyond forty students, who ranged in age from six to twenty-seven. But before the reader reacts unfavorably to this great range in age, it should be said that Vittorino had a number of assistants, perhaps as many as fifteen, to help him conduct the school.

The site of the school was a villa. It was turned over to Vittorino by the Duke of Mantua and was called "Pleasant House." Like a typical humanist, Vittorino favored an educational setting that was devoid of gloom; he wanted his school to be bright and cheerful, and probably "Pleasant House" was really a house of delight.

The spirit of the school also sounds delightful. First of all, Vittorino considered himself the father of his students, and in a sense he was; the children who attended the school lived there. It was their home and Vittorino's home too. In addition to instructing his charges, he was responsible for their moral formation and their physical welfare. His highest desire, as far as cultural development was concerned, was to create in his students a genuine love of learning.[39] When he was successful in doing this a great part of his task was accomplished.

Though history and ethics formed an important part of the program, the curriculum of the school at Mantua was basically a curriculum of the seven liberal arts. In content the arts were essentially the same as they had been in the medieval period, although Vittorino introduced some change in emphasis. He was conservative also in his teaching of Latin. Imbued as he was with the spirit of humanism and recognizing the requirements of learning, Vittorino continued to make Latin the language of the school. Greek was taught, but probably never on a very advanced level, and could not have been Latin's rival. Perhaps the only time the vernacular was used was when the children were at play.

One of the things that Vittorino attempted to avoid was routine, and apparently he was fairly successful in doing so. The first part of the school day—the total school day lasted about eight hours—was set aside for group instruction and lecturing; the second part of the day was reserved for individual work. Attention to the individual student and his special learning problems was perhaps the distinctive feature of Vittorino's technique. There is an account given by Prendilacqua, an assistant to Vittorino, which tells us that "Vitttorino, now well advanced in years, would of a winter's morning come early, candle in one hand and book in the other, arouse a pupil in whose progress he was especially interested: he would leave him time to dress, waiting patiently till he

[39] *Ibid.*, p. 34.

was ready: then he would hand him the book, and encourage him with grave and earnest words to high endeavor." [40] This, the testimony of one of Vittorino's most successful lieutenants, creates a wonderful picture of the great teacher's dedication to the intellectual welfare of his students.

In class, or with group instruction, the technique employed consisted partly of dictation of texts, notes, and translations and partly of oral questioning. The practice of recitation and declamation varied the monotony of the class lecture. Vittorino insisted upon the importance of variety in all of the periods set aside for instruction. There was only one routine exercise—reading aloud. Memorization was as important as recitation. But the outstanding feature of Vittorino's work, to which reference has already been made, was careful individual work. Since the school was amply staffed, the teachers were able to devote time to gaining an intimate knowledge of the tastes, capacity, and industry of each student. Vittorino's readiness to adapt the content of instruction and the techniques used to the students' needs and interests explains in great part the unique success of the school. He had an unaffected pride in his work as a teacher, a keen interest in the progress of each of his students, and, added to this, an unusual insight into the teaching art itself.

Vittorino's fame rests solely on his reputation as a schoolmaster. No one has yet made any claims for his scholarship or for his literary ability. He left no documents explaining either his educational theory or his educational techniques. Yet in actual methods of instruction, so far as our sources enable us to draw any conclusion, we find a definite contrast between those of Vittorino and those of the medieval schools. His attitude toward learning seems fresh and attractive; his school, we are told, was bright and cheerful; his relations with the children in the school were excellent; and he had great hopes for knowledge, which, he believed, could be a great instrument for improving society and for bettering the life and character of the individual man. These are points of emphasis, it is true, but they sharply distinguish the school of Vittorino from the typical school, or better, from the usual medieval attitude toward learning. These distinctions in Vittorino's school are due partly to the influence that humanism had on him; its glow affected him as it affected his age. But in addition to his humanistic approach, Vittorino had an undoubted genius for teaching; he had a swift intuition of the right method to be used in his art.[41]

[40] *Ibid.*, p. 62.
[41] *Ibid.*, p. 63.

HUMANISM IN NORTHERN EUROPE

The spirit of humanism in the north of Europe was somewhat different from what it was in the south; social rather than individual objectives seeemed to dominate its outlook in the north. We shall be interested to see whether or not this difference between the two types of humanism was reflected in the application of humanism to education. In northern Europe a number of important educators belonged to the humanistic camp: in France Guillaume Budé and Peter Ramus; in England, Colet, Elyot, and More; in the Netherlands, the Brethren of the Common Life. Erasmus and Vives cannot really be claimed by any one country, although Vives was a Spaniard by birth, and Erasmus was Dutch. In Germany, Agricola, Reuchlin, Wessell, and Wimpheling were important humanists. Of all these northern humanists, the chief figures for the historian of education were Vives and Erasmus. Before we examine their thought, a word may be said about the less important humanists of this region.

The Humanists of France   Guillaume Budé (1467–1540) wrote a book on education entitled *On the Education of a Prince.* This book expressed orthodox humanistic views on education and directed the greater part of its attention to the formation of the noble child. Still it was different. It was the first humanistic treatise on education to be written in French. Though itself written in the vernacular, the book advocated the study of the classical languages as the most effective means for obtaining a complete education. Budé was especially critical of the University of Paris, which at this time had well-established faculties of philosophy and theology but gave too little attention, so Budé thought, to letters. It would be somewhat unfair to compare Budé's influence with that of Vives or Erasmus; nevertheless, Bude's book did have some effect in that it broke ground for humanistic education in France because of its combination of good pedagogical advice and good scholarship.[42]

Peter Ramus (1515–1574) and François Rabelais (1483–1553) were lesser French humanists. Ramus came rather late in the period, and by his time the direction of humanism was pretty well set. His contribution was mainly that he prepared textbooks with the humanistic content of the seven liberal arts and that he advocated a reform of educational methodology. Ramus' views on the spirit and method of teaching called for a rejection of medieval methods, a freeing of educa-

[42] Woodward, *Studies in Education During the Age of the Renaissance, 1400–1600,* pp. 127–139.

tion from the tight grasp of the past, and a broadening of academic horizons on all educational levels. The textbooks Ramus wrote for students became extremely popular; some even crossed the Atlantic to be used in American colonial schools.[43]

Rabelais, a persistent critic of education, set actual teaching conditions, whose defects he exaggerated, against what may have been an authentic humanistic educational ideal. Predictably, he employed his special skill in satire to underscore the compromises that had been made between humanism's original ambitions and its practical achievements. He hoped for an educational program that could cut its way through ancient and modern knowledge, save time, and yet develop the whole man—a man of character, culture, and judgment, capable of acting forthrightly and effectively in contemporary society. Instead, he found schools dedicated to the rules of ancient grammar and rhetoric, tired and unable to grasp the meaning of character and culture, and at best qualified to produce narrow textbook scholars. His book *Pantagruel and Gargantua,* famous for its caustic rhetoric and biting satire, derides humanistic education for not producing the perfect gentleman, and he tries in a somewhat fantastic way to reform education by showing his readers how, after all, supermen can be educated. Yet, Rabelais' prescription should not be taken seriously (he himself did not take it so), although his strong negativism was no doubt instrumental in generating some hard thinking about schools and education which a century hence could bear some good fruit.[44]

The Humanists in England The English humanists were Thomas Linacre (1460–1524), William Grocyn (1466–1519), William Latimer (1460–1545), John Colet (1467–1519), Thomas More (1478–1535), Thomas Elyot (1490–1546), and Roger Ascham (1515–1568). These men, somewhat more practical in their approach to education than most of their counterparts on the Continent, were more inclined to work with educational questions on the level of teaching and learning. Some were schoolmasters or headmasters, and others were authors of schoolbooks.[45]

The central figure of English humanism was Thomas More. After studying under Colet, Grocyn, and Linacre at Oxford, More rose to prominence in public life in England. In addition, he was recognized

[43] See E. P. Graves, *Petrus Ramus and the Educational Reformation of the Sixteenth Century,* Cambridge University Press, New York, 1912, p. 25.

[44] See John C. Powys, *Rabelais: His Life,* Philosophical Library, New York, 1951, pp. 411–412.

[45] See Frederic Seebohm, *The Oxford Reformers: John Colet, Erasmus, and Thomas More,* E. P. Dutton & Co., New York, 1929; and William E. Campbell, *Erasmus, Tyndale, and More,* Eyre & Spottiswoode, London, 1949.

as an important colleague by the leading humanists of Europe. More's *Utopia*, one of the first English contributions to Renaissance literature, gave English writing an additional significance and distinction. More, while not an educator in any narrow sense, had a consuming love of learning, and gave every evidence of understanding the pedagogical steps leading to its attainment. He is, moreover, recognized as the chief inspiration for humanism in England.[46]

One could not think of English humanists, especially in education, without coming sooner or later to Thomas Elyot and his *The Boke Named the Governour*. (In this, the first book on education to be written in English, the word "educate" is used for the first time.) If at the outset of this book we do not expect too much from Elyot, we shall not be disappointed: He treats of the proper education for boys who in later life are likely to occupy responsible positions in government, and generally in public life. This, then, seems but another handbook for the education of an elite. However, after endorsing the usual humanistic content for the schools, Elyot departs somewhat from the old traditions by proposing that students give more attention to physical education and the social sciences.[47] Elyot treated of another relatively unconventional topic, the education of women, in a book called *Defense of Good Women*. He also made a surprising and most significant contribution to English education by compiling a Latin-English dictionary.

Later in the evolution of English humanism, Roger Ascham appeared on the scene.[48] A professional scholar who at one time had tutored Princess Elizabeth of England, Ascham belongs in this present company of English humanists partly because of his book *The Scholemaster*. Few books of the period have been criticized more than this one on the score of lack of originality, but special merit is not attached only for originality, and perhaps it was impossible for Ascham to be bright and fresh on educational matters that humanists had been talking and writing about for more than two centuries. He repeated an abundance of previously advanced opinions, it is true, but apparently he found fresh ground to cultivate when he advocated a practical humanism which on the pedagogical level could employ English as

[46] Ernest E. Reynolds, *Thomas More and Erasmus*, Fordham University Press, New York, 1965, pp. 123–125.

[47] S. E. Lehmberg, *Sir Thomas Elyot, Tudor Humanist*, University of Texas Press, Austin, 1960; and Thomas Elyot, *The Boke Named the Governour*, Kegan Paul, Trench, Trubner & Co., London, 1883.

[48] Lawrence V. Ryan, *Roger Ascham*, Stanford University Press, Stanford, Calif., 1963; and Roger Ascham, *The Scholemaster*, edited by D. C. Whimster, Methuen & Co., Ltd., London, 1934.

a starting point for the teaching of Latin and Greek.[49] Even his *Scholemaster*, with its much digested classical materials, must have done a great deal to spread humanist ideas.

If indeed More was the central figure in English humanism, he must share that place of honor with Colet when we come down to the level of education. No less than orthodox humanists, Colet accepted the edict that education must aim at character building. But, where too many humanists had simply taken for granted the dictum that good literature and grand classical ideas inevitably produce prudent, conscientious, and cultured gentlemen, Colet could make the theoretical connection between literature and character and, at least to his own satisfaction, prove that broad grammatical skill was essential not just to competent scholarship but to broad and human piety as well.

Beginning with an assumption—which had gone unchallenged for two hundred years—that the content of the classics had hidden treasures capable of forming good men, it was easy to defend the next step: These moral data must be harvested, and their meaning elaborated. But why should all the classics be included in this syllabus of moral education? Why not select the best and ignore the rest? Here is Colet's answer, and basically it becomes a charter for inductive grammar: Language is a body of phenomena whose laws can be ascertained by a study of the facts.

So in stating his principle of education, and in clarifying the connection between literature and character, Colet says that all classical writing must be cautiously examined before any opinion touching its meaning can be given.[50] Nothing can be left out; everything must be noticed and analyzed. Thus a scientific study of language, an elegant Latin style, was justified as against medieval grammatical speculation and the guesses of Petrarch, for the methods and conclusions of grammarians served, in the last analysis, as the only sure guides to interpretation. The meaning of a classic was dependent upon a grammarian's skill.

Colet tried to put these ideas into practice in St. Paul's school, founded in 1512.[51] The curriculum was organized to teach students how to write and speak the Latin of Cicero; notebooks were in constant use;

[49] *Ibid.*, p. 101.

[50] See P. Albert Duhamel, "The Oxford Lectures of John Colet: An Essay in Defining the English Renaissance," *Journal of the History of Ideas*, vol. XIV, no. 4, pp. 439–510, October, 1953; and Percy S. Allen, *Erasmus' Services to Learning*, Oxford University Press, New York, 1925, pp. 1–20.

[51] Robert P. Adams, *The Better Part of Valor: More, Erasmus, Colet, and Vives, on Humanism, War, and Peace, 1496–1535*, University of Washington Press, Seattle, 1962, p. 259.

repetition and imitation, conventional humanist techniques, were everywhere in evidence. Yet, humanist though he was, Colet stopped short of depending solely on classical authors and allowed his students to read some of the better Christian writers. Perhaps he was not entirely confident of the assumption he began by making, or possibly his clientele would not have taken kindly to a jettisoning of Christian literature. In any case, Colet's brave beginning was left unfinished until Erasmus appeared to give "the theory of morality through literature" its final codification.

The Brethren and the German Humanists   The spread of humanism from Italy and France to the Teutonic world was comparatively slow, perhaps because Germany had not had any strong connection with the classical past. Although by the end of the sixteenth century most of the German universities had been reorganized along humanistic lines, it was not the universities that were most responsible for the growth and spread of humanism in Germany. The real source for humanism here was a community of teachers, thinkers, and religious that had been founded by Gerhard Groot (1340–1384) and was known as the Brethren of the Common Life.[52]

Groot's chief aim was to bring about a reform in the Church.[53] In his opinion the surest and quickest way to reach this end was to train young men, and thus the chief occupation of the Brethren was education. The curriculum of the schools conducted by the Brethren included pagan or classical as well as Christian literature. Grammar, rhetoric, logic, mathematics, and philosophy, subjects all common to the curriculum of some medieval schools, were studied too. The most important of the schools opened by the Brethren were at Deventer, Zwolle, and Münster. From these schools came young men with a good education and with a new and somewhat clearer picture of the role of religion and the mission of the Catholic Church. A few of the schools produced young men with truly great minds. One such pupil, who was educated at the school of Zwolle, became the most famous educator of Transalpine Europe, Alexander Hegius (1433–1498).[54]

Though a leading humanist of the late fifteenth century and a serious student of the ancients, Hegius was, like Vives, a believer in the worth of the vernacular. He was also a leader of the movement to introduce new and better materials for instruction into the schools,

[52] Albert Hyma, *The Brethren of the Common Life*, Eerdmans, Grand Rapids, Mich., 1950, p. 116.

[53] *Ibid.*

[54] *Ibid.*, p. 118.

recognizing, for example, that the textbooks of the schools were badly in need of revision.

During the time that Hegius was its rector, the school at Deventer was one of the chief centers of the German Renaissance. An indication of the strength of this intellectual movement may be seen in the 450 classical works that were printed by the Deventer presses before 1500.[55] By the beginning of the sixteenth century hardly a school could be found in the Netherlands and Germany that had not been influenced by Deventer, Zwolle, and Münster. Under the leadership of the scholars and teachers sent out from these three schools, practically all of the larger schools of Western Germany were reorganized and reformed. The thought and practice of Groot and his followers were spread throughout the land. Hyma writes that even "modern education perpetuates the best features of the reformed education of Groot and [John] Cele and the Brethren of the Common Life." [56] Hegius himself was something more than a scholar and a teacher. In the spirit of his broad humanism, coupled with a deep sense of the truth of Christianity, he influenced several thousand students to carry out the Brethren's reform plans in schools, churches, and monasteries.[57] He is another figure that may be added to the list, a growing list, of Christian humanists.

A few other German humanists, all of whom came under the influence of the Brethren of the Common Life, were Rudolph Agricola (1443–1485), Johann Wessell (1420–1489), Jacob Wimpheling (1450–1528), and Jacob Reuchlin (1455–1552).

Rudolph Agricola was born near Groningen and, under the tutelage of the Brethren, revealed special capacities in the classical languages. He studied at Louvain, where he obtained his master's degree, and at the Universities of Paris and Ferrara. His connections with Reuchlin led him to develop a strong conviction that the Hebrew language was essential in humanistic education as an instrument for scriptural studies. He translated Greek classics into Latin and wrote a number of letters in which he expressed many of his educational views. Agricola's most famous pedagogical work was *On the Regulation of Study*. It had great influence on German education.

Jacob Wimpheling, a product of the University of Heidelberg, a distinguished priest and scholar, was rector of the Heidelberg *studium* in 1482. Wimpheling's most important work may have been the education of a large number of humanistic teachers. He wrote several textbooks and speculated on educational theory. His *Guide to German*

[55] *Ibid.*, p. 121.

[56] *Ibid.*, p. 126.

[57] *Ibid.*, p. 120.

Youth, a book which discusses many practical considerations in education, was the first pedagogical treatise in German. As a result of it, we are told, he received the merited title "Teacher of Germany." In the work *Adolescentia* (Youth), he expounded his views on the relationship between the classics and moral and religious formation.

> Of what use are all of the books of the world, the most learned writings, the profoundest researchers, if they only minister to the vainglory of their authors, and do not or cannot advance the good of mankind? . . . What profits all our learning, if our character be not correspondingly noble, or our industry without piety, or our knowing without love of our neighbour, or our wisdom without humility, or our studying if we were not kind and charitable? [58]

He urged the city authorities at Strassburg to begin a school in which education according to humanistic ideals would be offered. Interestingly enough, he was listened to, and the city fathers founded a school that a generation or so later was to be presided over by the great John Sturm.

Jacob Reuchlin, a layman, taught at the University of Heidelberg, where he was an exceptional scholar in Latin, Greek, and Hebrew. Perhaps his greatest scholarly achievement was to bring out a Hebrew grammar and dictionary. Throughout his career he advocated greater tolerance for all people, especially the Jews.

Erasmus

Desiderius Erasmus, who was born in 1469 and died in 1536, was a complex, many-sided, talented man. Although Erasmus is sometimes regarded as an enemy of the Catholic Church, this view is susceptible of some revision. It is, of course, understandable that his allegiance to the Church might be suspected, for he was a regular and often bitter critic of the extravagances churchmen frequently condoned or engaged in. An Augustinian monk, Erasmus found life in the monastery so oppressive that he spent as little time there as possible, left whenever he could, and usually neglected to let his superiors know his plans or get their permission for his travels.[59]

Largely self-educated, although he had attended the schools of the

---

[58] Quoted in P. J. Marique, *History of Christian Education,* Fordham University Press, New York, 1924–1932, vol. II, p. 56.

[59] See John J. Mangan, *Life, Character and Influence of Desiderius Erasmus of Rotterdam,* The Macmillan Company, New York, 1927; and Albert Hyma, *Erasmus and the Humanists,* F. S. Crofts & Co., New York, 1930, pp. 45–51.

Brethren of the Common Life, the University of Paris, and for brief interludes the Louvain and Cambridge (where, he says, he learned nothing of consequence), Erasmus became the greatest scholar of his age. No doubt he shared an egotism common among humanists, but more significantly, Erasmus was determined to make the values of humanism penetrate society. Thus, as a good humanist, Erasmus hoped to refine taste, purify morals, correct ecclesiastical abuses, and promote unity, peace, and harmony in European society. These praiseworthy objectives should all, Erasmus believed, be dependent on Christian wisdom, and so his mission, which was also the mission of education, was to lay the groundwork for learning and living that should be productive of wisdom. At this point, Erasmus made the conventional humanistic assumption: The classics contain a wisdom worth having, and men must find the proper means for assimilating it.[60]

Classical educational theorists supplied Erasmus with his basic educational views, but whereas the ordinary humanist showed a definite inclination to adopt the form rather than the spirit of Quintilian, Cicero, Plutarch, and even Petrarch, Erasmus was inspired by their words. This vision of classical theory compelled him to criticize current educational practice, which he could do with a satirism equal or superior to Rabelais'. Moreover, it provided him with a solid foundation for going beyond the ancient masters to complete the theory they had so bravely begun, and his up-to-date methods deeply affected the teaching of the classics. His justification for language study was usually balanced and sane, for he considered Latin and Greek to be means to an end rather than ends in themselves. (One of his personal scholarly goals was to master Greek, and in this connection his success was considerable.) He also encouraged the study of both language and literature as the principal avenues to character formation. With perfect linguistic skills, men could come in direct contact with the work of their ancient predecessors and, so Erasmus (and others) argued, learn from the great things those men had thought and written.

Erasmus' services to education—services that remained dynamic for four hundred years—may be given a threefold classification. (1) He wrote two exceptionally perceptive and worthwhile books elaborating a pedagogy for teaching the classics, *The Right Method of Instruction* and *The Liberal Education of Boys*, wherein he showed more clearly than ever before how the technique of imitation should be used. (2) He prepared textbooks and models (in other words, materials of, and guides to, instruction) which could be followed by teachers and

---

[60] William H. Woodward, *Desiderius Erasmus, Concerning the Aim and Method of Education*, Cambridge University Press, New York, 1904, p. 164.

students as they tried to read and study their way through mountains of classical literature. (3) He developed a theory of humanistic education wherein the connection so long sought between classical knowledge and style and a sound moral character was finally made.

Before turning to a close examination of *The Right Method of Instruction* and *The Liberal Education of Boys,* we might say a word about three earlier writings of Erasmus which may be classified either as minor educational works or as writings that were incidentally educational. They are *The Manual of the Christian Knight, The Education of the Christian Prince,* and *On Christian Matrimony.* The first is an inspirational and practical work, intended to guide the Christian knight to God. *The Education of the Christian Prince,* written in 1516, appeared only three years after *The Prince* of Machiavelli. Perhaps this work of Erasmus, more than any of his others, would give him the name of a humanistic educator; few educational theorists of this time wanted to neglect an opportunity to write something about the education of a young nobleman. More significantly, *The Prince* of Erasmus is almost exactly opposite in tone and direction to that of Machiavelli. For Erasmus the highest principle of action is not expediency, and the prince is not, like Machiavelli's prince, totally emancipated from the Christian ethic.

The most progressive people of the humanistic period considered a limited monarchy the best form of government. Erasmus shared this view and expressed it in *The Prince.* He believed that the limited monarch was best able to promise good government and therefore to lay the foundation for a more productive, orderly, and effective society. Yet we can detect democratic signs in this work by Erasmus, although we cannot say that it is a genuine charter for political democracy. The prince and his consort are expected to live both in harmony and in contact with their people. There is no charter for aloofness; they should be of the people. Laws are said to serve no other purpose than the welfare of the people; government should be conducted according to law and not allowed to follow the whims of individuals. In other words, Erasmus stood for a government of law and not of men. Such a political environment would provide men with the opportunity to build good lives for themselves and for their families; they could live with a sense of honor and dignity, and their pride would reflect itself in the progress and stability of the nation. Crime should be fought, Erasmus advised, not in a spirit of vindictiveness, not with the idea of punishment foremost in the society that had been injured, but by preventive economic and political and social measures. Still within the context of the preparation of a Christian prince, Erasmus advocated the abolishment of artificial class distinctions. There was no question at all in Erasmus' mind that there are natural distinctions in society among men; what he opposed were unnatural distinctions maintained, even encouraged, by law and custom.

Erasmus expressed the opinion that government should take an active part in the economic development of a country. Perhaps he saw more clearly than any of the other humanists the relationship that exists between economics, on the one side, and a strong and healthy society on the other. He showed special interest in the reform of agriculture, and even went so far as to advocate the government's assistance in the development of a nation's agricultural potential. His measures would have included a reform of the land policy as well as a new and more progressive program of conservation and road building. These unusually advanced social and economic positions would hardly allow us to call Erasmus a conservative. Finally, he took an unequivocal stand against war. The Christian prince, he said, should know that few wars have solved anything and that a war should never be fought unless it is absolutely necessary for the defense of human rights. So much for the syllabus prepared for the prince. It may be remarked that this work by Erasmus was almost completely forgotten by European political thinkers, while the work of Machiavelli became a classic.

On Christian Matrimony, written in 1526, was intended to guide and reform the Christian society in Europe. It was designed to do for the common man what *The Education of the Christian Prince* was to do for the nobles. The chapter that is of greatest interest to the educational historian is the one dealing with the education of girls, a subject either not mentioned at all by the humanists, or else treated in a perfunctory way. Perhaps Erasmus discussed the subject because there was no logical way to avoid it. How could he write on matrimony without saying something about the woman's preparation for it? Few humanists, Erasmus included, thought that women had sufficient intellectual maturity to be educable, yet Erasmus certainly did not approve of crude inequality in the treatment of women. Possibly the best summary of this chapter would be to say that Erasmus wanted girls educated in such a way that they would be good Christian women who could become loyal and effective wives and mothers. Today's reader may find this position something less than acceptable, but he should remember that even on this point Erasmus was many decades, if not centuries, ahead of his time.

The two chief works that Erasmus prepared for the guidance of educators were *The Right Method of Instruction* and *The Liberal Education of Boys.* In the first, Erasmus is concerned primarily with the right method of instruction to be used in teaching the classics, in interpreting the authors, and in teaching the techniques of composition. It would be difficult to find an educational theorist in the history of thought who attached greater importance to the methods of instruction than Erasmus. Of course, he considered methods something more than mere techniques involved in directing learning activities; he included the choice of material as well as the means employed in imparting it as part of the methodological problem. And he insisted that with the right methods of instruction, boys who under ordinary conditions would be little more than acceptable in their accomplishments in Latin and Greek could rise to creditable standards of scholarship. He even went a little beyond this when he promised that boys of average intelligence could look forward with greater hope for achievement in higher learning if their education on the lower levels was reinforced by the correct methods of instruction. The care devoted to the child's early years in learning was considered by Erasmus to be most important. In this respect Erasmus was following the thinking of Quintilian, who never tired of emphasizing the care that ought to be devoted to the early education of children.

Erasmus was no "mere theorist"—to use a somewhat denigrating phrase—when he wrote of methods. He did not neglect the fact that a technique has meaning only when it is put in the context of all the things that teachers do in directing learning. A method is a tool to be used in guiding and directing the learning activities of children in classrooms and laboratories, and has very little meaning outside this context. Thus Erasmus was on solid ground when he proposed that teachers be trained in a systematic manner especially for their work. He went beyond this: He wrote that churchmen and statesmen alike had a duty to see that teachers were available to educate the youth of a country. This, he maintained, was an obligation and responsibility of a superior order.

Although Erasmus' *The Right Method of Instruction* is an educational document of unusual quality and one that influenced educators throughout much of the modern period, his most mature work on an educational subject was *The Liberal Education of Boys*. Taking these two works together, however, we find that they form a coherent and thoroughly humanistic theory of education. Both works are full of a genuine sensitivity to the need for good teachers; both recognize their responsibilities; and both are definitely superior to the educational writings of the earlier humanists.

In *The Liberal Education of Boys* Erasmus deals with the aim of education. Education's objective, in his view, is to lead men toward knowledge, honesty, and independent judgment. If this is a hierarchy, if, in other words, independent judgment is higher in the scale of educational values than knowledge, then Erasmus is really saying that the essential purpose of education is to lead the individual toward autonomy, both intellectual and moral. Or, to put it in another way, sound education is the essential condition of real wisdom.

The versatility of Erasmus is not too difficult to demonstrate. We have seen that he was a follower of Quintilian. When he touched on wisdom he stepped into the tradition of Aristotle, but his Aristotelian praise of wisdom is combined with the Christian ideal of man. He did not forget Plato. There is evidently a similarity between the view that Erasmus expressed on man's need for education and Plato's words on the same subject. Erasmus put it this way: "It is beyond dispute that man not instructed through reason in philosophy and sound learning is a creature lower than a brute, seeing that there is no beast more wild or more harmful than a man who is driven hither and thither by ambition or desire, anger or envy, or lawless temper." [61] According to Erasmus, it is reason that enables men to unite in a community and to remain therein without destructive dissension. Individual differences were recognized and thoroughly understood by this great humanist. Such differences were found only in achievement; or, as Erasmus would say, they were found according to the degree of a man's participation in the achievements of culture.

Where did Erasmus stand on the questions relative to freedom and authority? We could make a reasonably strong case against Erasmus to the effect that he defied and denied all authority. Yet in spite of the strength of our contention, it would not be valid. Erasmus did not oppose authority, although he did deplore its invasion into areas where it did not belong. He would have considered the misuse of the Church's authority, or of churchmen's authority, as offensive as the misuse of an authority based on the ancient authors. Of course, all that Erasmus was really saying (and it was something that needed saying) was that the will of man does not make truth. He was an ardent and courageous enemy of voluntarism.

To turn now to some clear educational issues: We have seen that Erasmus was something of a reformer, that he would have added a good deal to education, and that he would have removed many things from it. Perhaps he opposed nothing with more vigor than the generally cruel discipline that was associated with most of the schools of the day. He deplored the existence of the cruel schoolmaster:

[61] *Ibid.*, p. 186.

A poor master, we are prepared to find, relies almost wholly upon fear of punishment as the motive to work. To frighten one entire class is easier than to teach one boy properly; for the latter is, and always must be, a task as serious as it is honorable. . . . Do schoolmasters consider how many earnest, studious natures have been by treatment of this type—the hangman type—crushed into indifference? [62]

Of course, if teachers were to achieve the best results without the rod as a chief tool for instruction, they needed to have far more insight into child nature than most teachers of Erasmus' time were able to boast.

Even though Erasmus' views may not have been entirely original, they were not simply borrowed and then communicated without considerable analysis and modification. On the point of individual progress he said that three conditions determine the progress that a child in school will make. They are nature, training, and practice. By nature Erasmus meant innate capacity for achievement and a natural motivation to attain excellence. By training he meant the instruction and guidance that the student would be able to obtain; the more skillful and careful this instruction and guidance, the better for the student involved. By practice he intended a free exercise by the student of that capacity which nature had implanted and which instruction had shaped, directed, and polished. "Nature without skill training must be imperfect, and practice without the method which training supplies leads to hopeless confusion." [63]

Method, then, may count for more than most humanists had realized, and because most humanists, we know, were not good methodologists, Erasmus wanted to set the record straight. Again, we are brought face-to-face with the technique of imitation. How does Erasmus want us to use it, and how did he build on the citadels of pedagogy which earlier humanists had tentatively constructed? It was good, of course, to affirm the worth of the classics, but it was even better to be able to write like the classical authors. But did this mean to draw a certain literary idealism from them, or to copy them? For Erasmus, good writing was itself a praiseworthy thing, and writing like the ancients had written was simply a means to that end. Thus the spirit, vigor, and style of the classics should be followed as guides to good writing, and whenever appropriate, classical examples, even quotes, should be used to contribute to eloquence. To tell the schoolboy to write using Cicero as his model was good advice only as long as the teacher meant that

[62] *Ibid.*, pp. 205–206.
[63] *Ibid.*, p. 191.

Cicero's ideas, his clarity of expression, his style, and his eloquence were worthy literary ideals to aim for. Good writing should not be a shallow mimicry, or a literal transcription of the best authors. This latter, Erasmus thought, might result in good penmanship, but it could not pass muster as decent education.

Still, imitation stands on the level of worthy aspiration, and it must be brought into the classroom if it is to have pedagogical significance. Imitation, according to Erasmus, has two sides: one has to do with words, phrases, the arrangement of material, and the excerption of re-usable themes; the other is concerned with ideas—understanding them, and illustrating them in written discourse following an eloquent and convincing style. Perhaps this much could have been said about imitation by most humanists from the time of Vergerius, but Erasmus is not finished. Now he takes us to the teaching models he prepared, and for which we have given him credit, *De Copia Verborum et Rerum*,[64] and *Adagia*, wherein imitation is made manageable. The student begins to read his classic, notebook in hand, and as he reads he puts in the notebook (under proper headings which Erasmus has supplied) words, phrases, and ideas which come to his attention. The whole purpose of reading, and not reading just some of the classics but all of them, is to transform the ying and the yang of Latin and Greek literature into a series of notes that can be preserved and, when needed in writing, repeated.

Without a notebook, imitation would not have amounted to much; with it, however, humanists following Erasmus' program of instruction could almost copy the epics, dramas, and histories of classical authors, maintaining substantial identity in details, an accuracy of general form, the speech, the imagery, the situations and characters of ancient literary sources—in a word, could mine the classical treasuries—and use these prototypes in their own literary endeavors. Classifying, analyzing, recording, and memorizing were all part of imitation, and it was this method almost alone that allowed the classical heritage to become an integral part of European thought.

So far Erasmus has told us how to use the classics, but he has yet to tell us why, when the aim of education is the man of character, classical literature should dominate the curriculum. Colet, we know, had made some progress in proposing an acceptable theory; Erasmus was to go even further, and in the end his theory, whatever rejections

[64] Desiderius Erasmus, *On Copia of Words and Ideas*, translated with an introduction by D. B. King and H. D. Rix, Marquette University Press, Milwaukee, Wis., 1963.

we might impose or interdictions we might make, was embraced as the fundamental theoretical justification for Christian humanism—for moral formation through literature—for the next four centuries.

Erasmus' theory that literature can indeed make good men was based on two arguments: First, much of Christian culture was based on Greek ideas—the Church Fathers themselves had used elements of pagan thought to construct rational foundations for their theology. Second, a careful study of the best classical writings would prove that the moral ideas in the classics were sufficiently similar to a Christian morality to be capable of enhancing virtue.[65] If this second argument was unconvincing as it stood, Erasmus could add another: The diligent effort and determined discipline necessary for success in classical study (perhaps an outcome of exhaustive linguistic scholarship) generated virtue. So, both from their content and the arduous discipline essential to their mastery, classical curricula were securely on the side of moral virtue. Now, at long last, the humanist's curriculum had its charter for the highest educational goal, moral virtue.

The theory, now complete, needed, Erasmus thought, some technical guides to make it effective and to protect it from turning out students who would be faultless linguists and erudite literary scholars but insincere Christians. To ensure his theory's proper use, he recommended first that students, prior to beginning their study of the classics, be given a sound moral training at home. With this foundation laid in the home, the student would be immunized from any possible pagan contamination; but more importantly, he would have inherited the bedrock of morality on which further education in virtue could build. Second, since some pieces of classical literature were too advanced for schoolboys and might therefore mislead them, the classics chosen for the curriculum should be carefully selected, and the more dangerous ones excluded. He did not mean, of course, that they should never be read, because this ran counter to his preference for using the whole of classical literature for complete scholarship and true wisdom—but there was no point in being in too much of a hurry to make a good scholar. Third, because even the best classics contained passages which were either offensive to Christians or patently immoral, Erasmus had to find a way to make them acceptable. He decided to borrow the medieval technique, one made popular by Hugh of St. Victor, of allegorical interpretation. With it, at least the major difficulties could either be explained away or (better yet) made to conform to a Christian system of values.

[65] M. A. Phillips, *Erasmus and the Northern Renaissance*, Hodder & Stoughton, London, 1949, pp. 141–143; and Allen, *Erasmus' Services to Learning*, p. 17.

Finally, mainly because of Erasmus' unhappy experience with Scholastic philosophy and Scholastic philosophers, and, moreover, because he believed that philosophy was fundamentally anticlassical, he advised schoolmasters to expurgate any formal study of philosophy from the curriculum.[66]

Selection, however, became the principal technique for implementing Erasmus' theory, and when the other safeguards were forgotten or fell into disuse, it remained as a main force dominating the curriculum of sixteenth- through nineteenth-century European schools. Erasmus' place in educational history is fortified by the extended influence he had on the curriculum of secondary education. Both John Sturm and the Jesuits listened to him, and, through them and others, Erasmus dominated the pattern of modern education.

Our brief discussion of the educational work of Erasmus may be summarized by pointing to the principal positions that he took:

1. He recognized the worth of physical education, as any good humanist would almost certainly have to do, but he did not give much attention to it in any school program with which he dealt, and this, too, was a typical attitude among the humanists.

2. He acknowledged the rights of the middle class for educational opportunity, and he was generally unwilling to think in terms of a "class to be educated."

3. He understood and respected the individual differences and special talents among children, but he would not have authorized any onesidedness in their education or their training. He prized and proposed the well-rounded, generally educated, culturally competent individual.

4. He maintained that formal education should begin at an early age, but he did not become any more definite about the exact time. No doubt, following all educators since the time of Homer, as well as his own observations of child nature, he would have thought a child should begin formal schooling at the age of seven or thereabouts.

5. The curriculum that Erasmus devised or approved was mainly classical. Yet it had a range that would have surprised the present-day pragmatist. In it, language was emphasized as a tool, a door to experience, Erasmus said, rather than a barrier to shut it out. For the first time in about a thousand years of educational history, we find an edu-

---

[66] Woodward, *Desiderius Erasmus, Concerning the Aim and Method of Education,* p. 165; see also, Percy S. Allen, *The Age of Erasmus,* The Clarendon Press, Oxford, 1914, p. 222.

cator who is unwilling to endorse the separation between language and life and between learning and life that had become evident as early as the Hellenistic period.[67]

6. Erasmus was very liberal-minded when it came to understanding the possibilities of adding to the body of man's knowledge. The door of the school was never closed to any subject. The curriculum was open to all legitimate areas of experience, and the schoolroom was a forum in which all questions could be raised and discussed. Erasmus' *Latin Conversations*, a work intended for school use, brought up and discussed many subjects that even the teacher of the twentieth century might hesitate to introduce.

7. Despite his liberalism, that is, his willingness to admit non-classical curricula to the schools, he proposed and clarified a theory of education and a pedagogical method aimed directly at the classics. Thus, he kept the classics in an immovable position in the school's syllabus, and showed teachers how to use them to achieve the highest goal of humanistic education, moral virtue.

Juan Luis Vives (1492–1540)

Juan Luis Vives began his scholarly career as a Scholastic and converted to humanism under the influence of Erasmus. The Spanish-born Vives receives our attention not only because of his practical accomplishments in pedagogy—where, taking the notebook techniques and topical headings of Erasmus, he tried to apply them especially to Latin language teaching—but because he was one of the most original of humanistic thinkers. Having been the tutor to Princess Mary of England, a certain luster attaches to his name, and this temporary teaching assignment is sometimes allowed to overshadow far more significant achievements.

Vives put humanistic education on the road to realism without himself being an authentic realist. By "realism" we mean an educational theory wherein the worth of knowledge is found in its use and not in ornamentation. The humanists, of course, had said all along that classical knowledge was eminently useful in making good men, but their promises were so seldom matched by the practical results of teaching, with classical teaching too often being nothing more than ostentatious pedantry, that their protestations began to fall on deaf ears. Vives hoped, following Erasmus' charter of moral virtue through literature, to transform humanistic education from the artificial level of literary excellence to a human and practical level of social signifi-

[67] See *ibid.*, pp. 179–181; and Allen, *Erasmus' Services to Learning*, pp. 2–15.

cance.[68] Such compromises between humanism and realism were not easy to effect, and we must think of Vives as a realist in a relative sense: He was more realistic in his expectations for teaching than, say, Castiglione, Colet, or Budé—that is, more willing to put into the school's curriculum instruments capable of furnishing students with skill in daily living. He justified useful knowledge and, very possibly, thought of schooling as an interlude providing students with an opportunity to learn something very well and to learn to do something very well. On another side, one anticipating a science of education, Vives was more of a realist than any of his contemporaries: He tried to elaborate the essentials of method, and endeavored to find their psychological bases in child nature.

Ignoring the old debate aimed at choosing between Erasmus and Vives as the superior humanist educator, a debate which has always been fruitless because its terms are wrong, we can say that Vives reminds us much more of modern-day educators than does Erasmus, although he shared with Erasmus the humanistic determination to make character the end of education, and he perhaps surpassed Erasmus in upgrading the pedagogical means to achieve this. Beginning with Vives, however, we see a progressive decline in humanistic preferences and educational goals as the machinery of teaching and learning is brought up for inspection and much-needed improvement. So Vives stands at the end of an old era with strong allegiances to the doctrines of Erasmus, and at the beginning of a new one using a language of educational reform marking the awkward beginnings of a science of pedagogy.[69]

Vives, moreover, was something of a pioneer in a number of important educational and social areas; his *De Anima* (*Concerning the Soul*) explored the relationship between learning and psychology. His work in breaking ground in this area is so well thought of that Vives is often called the father of educational psychology. His *De Subventione Pauperum* (*On Poor Relief*) is a vivid illustration of Vives' interest in the plight of the poor and of social problems in general. *On the Instruction of Christian Women* is an early, though by no means the earliest, treatment of the education of women. Because of this work and because of his commission as tutor to the Princess Mary, Vives has often been thought of as the chief mover for greater opportunities for the education of women. The perspective of history suggests to us

[68] Juan Luis Vives, *Vives: On Education*, a translation of the *De Tradendis Disciplinis* by Foster Watson, Cambridge University Press, 1913, p. 300.

[69] Roberto Weiss, *Humanism in England During the Fifteenth Century*, B. Blackwell, Oxford, 1957, pp. 96–99.

that the role of Vives in the education of women has been overemphasized. His work, *On a Plan of Studies for Youth* and *Concerning the Teaching of the Arts*, contains the best evidence of his humanism. The latter is unquestionably his most complete as well as his most mature work on education.[70]

Without going into the details of his *Plan of Studies for Youth*, the following summary may be made of Vives' educational theory:

1. He emphasized the role that parents should take in the education of their children. Vives, along with his humanistic contemporaries, gave more attention to the school and literary education than was common, say, in the medieval period, but he remembered that the child is first of all a responsibility of the parent. He insisted, moreover, that the basic foundation of education considered in its broadest sense is most securely laid in the home during the child's earliest years.

2. He thought that children should be sent to school when they were about seven years of age. Here Vives agrees with the usual humanistic and classical view of the right age to begin formal education. It may be noted, however, that nothing in his view suggests the kindergarten or any other kind of institutional training that might be considered preelementary.

3. Vives preferred, as most humanists did, that boys be educated in public schools where there were many boys rather than in private schools which were in reality mere tutorial arrangements. However, if the tutorial system was to be used, Vives admonished parents and others responsible for the education of youth to be certain that more than one student was under the direction of a master. He proposed that at least one companion be provided for every tutored student. Vives' reasons for this position were not, as is often supposed, that the student's morals would be more secure if he attended his lessons with a companion, but that he would enjoy greater opportunities for learning with a companion or in a group.

4. Vives willingly endorsed the inclusion of sport, drama, entertainment, and recreation in the educational program.

5. Instruction was to be adapted to the individual. Of course, Vives did not envision broad commitments to public or universal education, or he could not have taken such an unequivocal stand on this point. Yet within the context in which he operated, he insisted that the students be taught according to their ability to learn. Who could dispute the validity of this position? In order to assure the practical application of the stand he took in theory, he advised that every boy be studied

[70] Juan Luis Vives, *op. cit.*, p. 325.

by his teachers for at least two months before instruction was to begin. How could teachers adapt learning procedures to the needs of the students unless they knew their students thoroughly?

6. Vives advocated the public support of education. That is, he regarded education as a public enterprise and thought that the public ought to pay for it. He saw, too, that opportunity in education was bound to be limited if such opportunity had to be provided by private means alone.

7. In keeping with a completely orthodox humanistic view of education, Vives supported the notion that the environment in which teaching and learning take place should be pleasant and generally conducive to learning.

8. He took a firm stand on the value of the classics. He would never have left them out of the school's curriculum. Yet he did reject the absurd imitation of the classics that so many teachers were prone to insist on. Although Vives thought the classics important, he advised teaching the vernacular in the schools and using it as a means for introducing students to Latin.

9. Vives gave his complete support to studies in history and the natural sciences.

10. When he spoke of the education of women, Vives suggested for them a careful study of the vernacular, Latin, religion, and moral precepts. The development of good conduct was much emphasized as was training for the care of children and household management. No mathematics, science, or politics appeared in the school's syllabus for girls. Yet Vives did not agree with the educators of his day in thinking of the education of women in terms of the finishing-school.

Summary

The Renaissance was a renewal of interest in the past. It was an attempt to capture the goals and practices of the classical period, but above all it sought to regain the spirit, the humanism, of classical antiquity. In education this meant not so much a turning away from the practices and theories of the medieval years as an attempt to give them a new direction. The new direction was influenced greatly by the great Roman educator, Quintilian. The curricula and methods of the schools remained much as they had been before, although the humanists did emphasize the education of laymen for citizenship. This change was at least a partial rejection of the medieval plan, which had called for a clerical monopoly of education and a preoccupation with otherworldly objectives for education. Besides this, humanistic educational writers dealt with such issues as the control of education, the value of the classics, the relative claims of knowledge and style, the education of women, the place of physical education, and the use of the vernacular in school.

In the south of Europe the prominent theorists of the humanistic age were Vergerius, Bruni, Piccolomini, Alberti, Guarino, Vegius, and Castiglione. For all their humanism, they showed unusual interest in the education of noble children and a remarkable lack of interest in the education of the common man.

The great schoolmaster of the Renaissance was Vittorino da Feltre. Although in its curriculum his school reflected orthodox humanism, Vittorino, with the intuition of genius, organized and conducted a school that was unique in the method and spirit of instruction.

Erasmus and Vives, in the north of Europe, offered educational views that were somewhat more mature than those of their southern counterparts. The theories of these men and the practices they advanced exerted greater influence on later modern education than those of any other humanistic theorists.

XI

Religious
Reforms &
Education

We cannot hope for a basic understanding of the great Religious Revolt without at least being aware of ferment in European society for a hundred years before Luther. Fifteenth-century Europe was in a state of flux, trying to adapt to unaccustomed modernity brought about mainly by inventions such as movable type for printing, and by the opening of new scientific and geographic worlds. If European society did not exactly wear a new face, at least it had great aspirations for changing its old one. Traditionally, the Renaissance has been interpreted as a dramatic leap back over a thousand years, although a more contemporary scholarly estimate sees the Renaissance as having evolved from its antecedent medieval civilization.[1] If the argument is sound that the Renaissance evolved from the Middle Ages, the argument that the Religious Revolt was as much a reaction to, as an outcome of, the Renaissance may also be sound. In any case, the fifteenth century differed from the centuries preceding it mainly in its featuring of new political and social orders wherein human individuality and personal objectives found freer expression.

To give all the credit to the Italian humanists for the achievements and great moments of the Renaissance is to go too far. We might even suggest that their formalism and preoccupation with imitation tended to slow rather than to foster the free play of individual character and natural feeling. In Italy the first signs of humanism were found, and there too the humanistic movement achieved its initial form. In Italy, as well as in southern Europe, humanism was usually aristocratic and individualistic in its economic, social, and educational aims. But as the ideals of the humanistic movement spread north, the movement became more religious, moral, and social. Education in the north of Europe, especially in the hands of the Brethren, Erasmus, and Vives, was understood to be a means for social and moral reform and not merely a means for personal improvement and the individual pursuit of culture. To put it another way: The humanism of the Renaissance in southern Europe was intellectual and patrician; in northern Europe it made its appeal to the masses through religious and emotional means. In both the north and the south of Europe the scholars of humanism were somewhat opposed to Scholastic philosophy and its formalistic methods, and in both places the humanists were opposed to authoritarianism. This opposition to authoritarianism, especially in the north, sometimes took the form of protests against the doctrines and practices of the Catholic Church. Often there were demands for a return to simple, uncomplicated, nonritualistic devotions.

The protests did not mean, of course, that humanism bred paganism, for there is no sign of paganism in simple demands for reform; but it did breed a questioning attitude concerning the complexities of Catholic Christian doctrine, and it stimulated ideals of greater religious freedom. Perhaps these outcomes were unavoidable. The conditions of study and thought have been revolutionized by a considerable increase in the number of universities, many of which were intended to promote the humanistic modes of thought, by inventions associated with print-

[1] See R. R. Bolgar, *The Classical Heritage and Its Beneficiaries*, Cambridge University Press, New York, 1954, pp. 239–240; and Herman von Gelder, *The Two Reformations in the Sixteenth Century: A Study of the Religious Aspects and Consequences of Renaissance and Humanism*, M. Nijhoff, The Hague, 1964, pp. 22–31.

ing, by the appearance of the lay scholar, and by the rise of studies that had little direct connection with theology or philosophy. The growing antagonism between Scholastics and humanists was at first little more than a matter of competition for university positions, but gradually humanistic thought sought to refashion the mind of the Church in accordance with the naturalistic standards of classical virtue, laying more emphasis on the natural goodness of man than on his fallen nature. The general revulsion from ascetic ideals was strongly aided by the new ventures of travel and geographic discovery and the pursuit of commercial profit. The spirit of human gratification was found in some of the works of the ancient writers, and this spirit found fertile soil for growth in some humanistic centers.

There was also a general laxity within the Catholic Church itself. This, together with the other conditions present in the society of the time, precipitated the revolt. The more sensitive observers of the day could probably see it coming. The signs were clear: The authority of the pope had been weakened; a great part of the clergy had been caught up in a spirit of worldliness; Scholastic philosophy and theology had lost some of their earlier strength, vitality, and meaningfulness; and serious disorders were evident in political life. To many contemporaries the later fifteenth-century popes seemed intent upon three objects—the consolidation of their political power in central Europe, the continuance of their artistic and literary patronage, and the maintenance of the papal Curia and its financial system. These and other interests resulted in the identification of the papacy with one nation, Italy. Thus the nepotism, worldly life, unscrupulous state policy, and scandal-giving appointments furnished just enough fuel to keep the fire of discontent burning, and it warmed agitators to the task of seeking reforms in the Church. At the same time they were pursuing their own selfish ends, which included the secularization of property and the suppression or elimination of ecclesiastical jurisdiction.

On the eve of the Revolt, then, the papacy, though still in principle accepted as the divinely founded spiritual head of Christendom, had ceased to exercise any real leadership in Europe. Italianized in sentiment and policy, it exerted political power in central Italy and was active as a secular state; but in the world at large, where changing conditions of life and thought were bringing serious religious and intellectual problems up for solution, it was ineffectual. Throughout the entire church organization, office had come to suggest profit rather than duty, and the papacy was losing touch with the people and with the churches in the national states. The Catholic Church was not prepared for the revolt that swept over it. In all of the areas of its activity there was perplexity and confusion. A wealth of inflammatory religious material had been for years in the process of laying a foundation for revolt; the fuse for a huge explosion was set; all it needed was the final spark to set it off. This spark was supplied, and the fuse was ignited at Wittenberg.[2]

Martin Luther (1483–1546)

The leading figure in the rebellion against the Catholic Church was Martin Luther, the son of a lower-middle-class miner. Born in Eisleben, Luther began his early schooling at Mansfield, where, we may assume, he took his primary education before he went to Magdeburg to study under the Brethren of the Common Life. It is said that he went to school in Eisenach also, but we know little or nothing of this experience. In fact, little is known of his life or his schooling on the preuniversity levels, other than the places where he attended school.[3] At eighteen he began his university studies at Erfurt, a university of two thousand students that was then recognized as one of Germany's finest. In the university he pursued the usual studies of liberal arts and philosophy and studied under masters who had good reputations for scholarship. By 1505 Luther was ready to take his master's degree in arts. At almost the same time he began the study of law, a scholastic interest prompted mainly by his father; yet it was not a lasting interest, for almost immediately he abandoned it and turned to the monastic life. An unusual event helped to bring about this rather abrupt change in plans. While riding back to Erfurt after a visit to his home, Luther encountered a violent storm. The danger seemed so great that he was certain his life was in peril. Calling upon St. Anne for help, he vowed that if his life were spared he would become a monk. This episode was said by Luther to have happened in July of 1505. He entered the Augustinian monastery at Erfurt on July 17, 1505.[4]

Luther's progress in the monastic community was rapid—almost too rapid, for on April 3, 1507, only a year and eight months after he entered the monastery, and barely nine months after his religious profession, he was ordained a priest. After ordination he undertook formal theological studies, which he completed in about eighteen

[2] See Philip Hughes, *A Popular History of the Reformation*, Hanover House, Garden City, New York, 1957, pp. 11–13.

[3] Richard Friedenthal, *Luther: Sein Leben und Seine Zeit*, Piper, München, 1967, pp. 15–30.

[4] *Ibid.*

months. In the fall of 1508 he was transferred to Wittenberg, where the Augustinians had a house, as a lecturer on the ethics of Aristotle. At the same time he continued studies for a higher degree in theology. Before the year was out, Luther returned to Erfurt to lecture on theology in the house of studies of his own order. In 1510, while at Erfurt, he was assigned the duty of going to Rome, accompanied by a companion, to represent the Augustinian Hermits on an ecclesiastical matter. He returned in 1511 and was again sent to Wittenberg, where he was given a variety of assignments and where, in 1512, he obtained his degree as doctor of theology. The next year he was appointed professor of theology at the University of Wittenberg.[5]

The gifted Luther betrayed no sign in 1513 that he would become a religious outcast by 1517. His duties at the university, and the demands for his time in his office of subprior of the religious community, kept him busy. Sometimes they took him outside the monastery and into the affairs of the world, and there he found it difficult to fulfill all the religious observances required by the rule of religion. This experience apparently disturbed him greatly, and he began to have doubts about the depth of his religious vocation. Frustrations and tensions led him into extremes of mortification and penance, and in the end, ignoring the rules of monastic life and the counsel of his spiritual advisors, he chose to rely on his own strength, upon penance, and upon faith. Eventually faith alone became for him the hallmark of personal salvation, and it was this conviction that he later advanced as a doctrine for the salvation of mankind. The intercession of the Church, her officers, and her sacraments all became totally unnecessary. But when, on October 31, 1517, Luther nailed his ninety-five theses to the church door at Wittenberg, precipitating the great Revolt, his "faith alone" doctrine was not among them, for at that time he was attacking only ecclesiastical abuse.[6]

Although our present interest in Luther is educational, not religious, we must remember that Luther was a religious reformer whose educational expressions are always subsumed to religious statements. We find his educational theory in sermons and religious tracts but not in pedagogical monuments. Yet, despite what may appear to have been indifference to educational questions, Luther was keenly sensitive to educational theory in general, and to humanistic promises and practices in particular. He could avoid any preoccupation with a theory for

[5] *Ibid.*

[6] Heinrich Boehmer, *Road to Reformation*, Muhlenberg Press, Philadelphia, 1946, pp. 77–79.

schools and teaching, and at the same time display a clearheaded attitude toward it. Luther constructed only a framework for education, and left it for others to work out the details.

Organizational patterns for schools were deeply affected. In Germany before the Revolt, schools were conducted and for the most part owned by the Catholic Church; little educational opportunity was offered outside church-related institutions. At the time of the Revolt, church-owned assets, including church and school buildings, were confiscated, not by the new religion, but by princes, nobles, and state officers. Some school buildings were destroyed, others were converted to a variety of uses. In the nature of things the new religion had few resources at its disposal to offer better, or even replace old, educational opportunities. The bulk of education and the the means to offer it lay in ruin in the wake of the Protestant Revolt.

This was physical ruin, and schools could be rebuilt; in time the ruins were changed into wonderful school plants, but this reconstruction was hardly the work of religious revolt or reform. It came, rather, from the impact of nationalism on education, an impact that was not felt until the eighteenth century. In addition to the physical destruction that was visited upon the means of education, a kind of spiritual destruction accompanied the new religious message. Faith alone was needed for salvation. The seed of faith may grow as rapidly and flower as generously in the unlearned as in the learned. What man really needs learning? Besides, the clerical profession, one that had been sought after by many because of the attractive opportunities it offered, was dried up. The clergymen of the Protestants could not look forward to many, if any, of the advantages that clergymen enjoyed in the old order. The clerical orientation in education, one that had been strong up to this point in European educational history, was fast disappearing. Formal education was losing many of the motivations previously supporting it. Luther was faced with imposing educational problems.

One of his first statements on education—it is said to be the first Revolt document on education—was "A Letter to the Mayors and Aldermen of All Cities of Germany in Behalf of Christian Schools." The officials to whom Luther addressed this letter were reminded of their duty to build schools, to replace those that had been destroyed, to assemble libraries, and generally to assume responsibility for education. In the "Letter" Luther expressed a strong conviction of the spiritual benefits to be derived from education, especially in enabling men to understand the scriptures. Education also provided a strong foundation for civil authority.

Luther's theory of education was based on his love of God and his allegiance to Germany; both required—the former for worship, and the latter for prosperity—the presence of educated men. The Bible, he said, should do most to inculcate piety, but whether in German or in Latin, the Bible was removed from the languages God had apparently chosen for its first writing: Greek and Hebrew. If God had thought these languages worthy of scriptural use, then men, too, must accept them as worthy of study in order to know more fully the divine message they conveyed.[7] The humanists had regularly advocated the study of ancient languages; reading the scriptures was, for them, more than a pleasant pastime. Thus, it was easy for Luther to look with favor on this side of humanistic educational doctrine. Language study (but for mentally qualified youth only) received his endorsement, as did the study of humanistically oriented rhetoric. With religious ritual for the most part jettisoned, Luther's revival needed effective preachers to spread the message of religious reform. Medieval sermon books were of no help, nor was medieval homiletic technique, so classical rhetoric (the artful use of the spoken word), as modernized by Erasmus and other humanists, was pressed into service. This ancient model was embraced without the compromises or the anxieties that had plagued Catholic Christians for many centuries.

Religion had clear educational requirements—Luther was quick to point them out, although evidence is lacking that at this time those requirements bespoke popularizing or universalizing educational opportunity—and so did secular society. Italian humanism had succeeded in applying the rational techniques of classical study to business and civic administration; shortly before Luther's time this type of study was imported to Germany. Latin was used, of course, for it was the language of affairs; so in order to produce a class of men capable of serving the good German secular society, Luther once again found humanistic education appealing. His "Sermon on the Duty of Sending Children to School," delivered in 1530, is an educational *credo*.[8] In this "Sermon" we have an example of Luther's honest concern not only for the education of children but also for the dignity of the teacher and the respect that should be given him.

Where were your supply of preachers, jurists, and physicians, if the arts of grammar and rhetoric had no existence? These are the foundation, out of which they all flow. I tell you, in a word, that a

---

[7] Martin Luther, *Pädagogische Schriften*, F. Schoningh, Paderborn, 1957, pp. 102–110.

[8] Frederick Eby, *Early Protestant Educators*, McGraw-Hill Book Company, New York, 1931, pp. 142 ff.

diligent, devoted schoolteacher, preceptor, or any person, no matter what his title, who faithfully trains and teaches boys, can never receive adequate reward, and no money is sufficient to pay the debt you owe him; so, too, said the pagan, Aristotle. Yet we treat them with contempt, as if they were of no account whatever; and, all the time, we profess to be Christians. For my part, if I were, or were compelled, to leave off preaching and to enter some other vocation, I know not an office that would please me better than that of schoolmaster, or teacher of boys. For, I am convinced, next to preaching this is the most useful, and greatly the best labor in all the world. . . . My friend, nowhere on earth can you find a higher virtue than is displayed by the stranger, who takes your children and gives them a faithful training, a labor which parents very seldom perform, even for their own offspring.[9]

In addition to expressing his sincere respect for education in this tract, Luther took occasion to point to the two principal reasons why education should be supported. In fact, he divided the "Sermon" into two parts. The first part dealt with the spiritual benefits to be derived from sending children to school; the second part dealt with the temporal benefits. In the first part, Luther was pleading with parents under his general religious jurisdiction to send their bright boys to schools where they could be prepared for the Christian ministry. At this point Luther emphasized the need for the study of the classical languages and for other ancient languages in order that the study of scripture might be promoted. This emphasis led him to endorse Latin schools at the expense of schools then being conducted in the vernacular. In spite of Luther's hope that the Bible in the vernacular could be put in the hands of all the German people, the vernacular schools did not receive a great deal of support from him. In the second part of the "Sermon" Luther pointed to the good that well-educated boys and young men could do for the state. "A Sermon on the Duty of Sending Children to School" was intended to be chiefly an admonition to parents and others in charge of children to select the most gifted children and educate them in schools for the elite.

The moving force behind Lutheran education was not Luther but Philip Melanchthon.[10] Luther himself looked at education through the eyes of a preacher and with the mind of a religious reformer. Melanchthon, on the other hand, was an educator by profession and was anxious to act as Luther's educational lieutenant. Luther was willing, it appears,

---

[9] Quoted in *ibid.*, pp. 144–145.

[10] Bolgar, *op. cit.*, pp. 344–345; and G. M. Bruce, *Luther as an Educator*, Augsburg Publishing House, Minneapolis, Minn., 1928, pp. 71–73.

to endorse and promote the views and methods of the Protestant humanist, Melanchthon.[11]

Because the Scholastic universities depended on the philosophy of Aristotle, Luther distrusted the content and methods of the studies. He believed that in them the authority of Aristotle superseded the authority of the scriptures. This attitude stemmed in part from the fact that whereas Luther considered Greek and Hebrew to be essential for the furtherance of biblical studies, the old universities emphasized the study of Greek in order that Aristotle might be understood more exactly. This was, to Luther's way of thinking, a perversion of studies, and he attacked at one and the same time the authority of Aristotle and the authority of the Church, which he believed relied too heavily on the philosophy of Aristotle. By the time Luther appeared on the stage of history, Scholasticism had seen its best days. It had been declining in importance for about a century, and Luther did all that he could to hasten its demise.[12]

Luther turned away from Scholasticism to humanism, at least to Melanchthon's kind of humanism. According to this way of thinking, education should provide suitable preparation for the study of the scriptures. Both Luther and Melanchthon supported the theory that the Bible and the catechism—the Lutheran catechism—should have a central place in the syllabus of every school. Yet they willingly included rhetoric and dialectic, for this was an age of controversy, in which effective writing and speaking were important, as were history, natural science, vocal and instrumental music mainly for church use, and gymnastics. History was especially emphasized for the sake of studying moral truth and social institutions. The study of nature was intended to give the students some slight insight into the goodness and greatness of God. Gymnastics were considered to be of value both to the body and to the soul as a means of driving away all care and melancholy from the heart.[13]

---

[11] C. L. Manschreck, *Melanchthon, the Quiet Reformer*, Abingdon Press, New York, 1958, p. 118.

[12] See Jacques Maritain, *Three Reformers: Luther, Descartes, Rousseau*, Charles Scribner's Sons, New York, 1929, pp. 10–25; and F. E. Cranz, *An Essay on the Development of Luther's Thought on Justice, Law, and Society*, Harvard University Press, Cambridge, Mass., 1959, pp. 171–178.

[13] F. V. N. Painter, *Luther on Education*, Concordia Publishing House, St. Louis, 1928, pp. 198 ff.; and Frederick Eby, *op. cit.*, pp. 41–43. One example may be enough to show how definite some of Luther's views were on education. We find him saying this: "But, you say again, if we shall and must have schools, what is the use to teach Latin, Greek, Hebrew, and the other liberal arts? Is it not enough

On the subject of method, Luther seemed to be mildly anticipatory of the educational realism of the seventeenth century. He suggested that the natural activity of the child be utilized in learning; he tended to oppose any methods that would repress child nature. It is not easy to be sure just where Luther stood on some of these points, for, as we have already said, he was not accustomed to deal with educational questions in terms of school practices and techniques. In the same vein we may suggest that he advocated the use of concrete examples in teaching and that he thought that the grammatical approach to the teaching of languages was somewhat unnatural.

In its first years Protestantism contributed little to a higher education. For reasons that we have already discussed, the universities in Lutheran Germany were seriously depopulated. It was not until the University of Halle was founded in 1694 that higher education took a new lease on life, but this new lease had only a tangential relationship to the Protestant Revolt.[14]

Philip Melanchthon (1497–1560)

Philip Melanchthon's early academic career followed fairly conventional Scholastic patterns. First studying logic and Scholastic philosophy, he took his master's degree in arts at Tübingen and then began to lecture on grammar and rhetoric.[15] During this teaching interlude his interest in humanistic study was whetted and he became, as a result of self-education, a thorough advocate of humanism. His classes concentrated on the classical authors, although patristic and contemporary writers were also in the approved program of studies, because he favored them, and in his teaching he emphasized the values of ancient usage and discarded the Scholastic practice of teaching grammar as a branch of logic.

At this time Luther's religious reform was just beginning, and he saw the need for securing support for his ideas. Luther and Melanchthon became friendly, and eventually the former enlisted the latter in the ranks of his religious crusade. Melanchthon, professor of Greek at Wittenberg, at Luther's suggestion was offered the professorship

to teach the Scriptures, which are necessary to salvation, in the mother tongue? To which I answer: I know, alas! that we Germans must always remain irrational brutes, as we are deservedly called by surrounding nations." (Painter, *op. cit.*, p. 183.)

[14] See V. W. C. Hamlyn, *The Universities of Europe at the Period of the Reformation*, G. Shrimpton, Oxford, 1876, pp. 212–217.

[15] Manschreck, *op. cit.*, p. 49.

in theology as well. With this joint appointment, working in both Greek and theology, Melanchthon had ample opportunity to test the validity of the assumption that classical studies were useful to theology. His academic experience confirmed this assumption in a number of ways. He became, in fact, a Christian humanist, and began to see learning in a new light: The purpose of education is to give the student a comprehensive and integrated meaning of the world. In order, however, to achieve this high purpose, the curriculum must concentrate on language study, which makes an essential contribution to understanding, and at the same time subordinate its content and goals to religious objectives.[16]

Subordination of more or less conventional humanistic curricula to religion was the key to Melanchthon's solution. Apart from this, he stands on fairly common ground with earlier humanists who, in their affirmations of humanism, were usually content to say that eloquence alone was a worthy outcome of such study, or that personal development itself was worth the effort of determined classical scholarship. Almost to a man they refused to find, or even to look for, a goal for scholarship outside scholarship itself. Parting company with humanistic ornamentation, Melanchthon was clearly practical: The goal of classical study was to produce a confirmed Christian who could write, speak, and think clearly about the important questions of the day.

Humanism was thus brought down to a level where its commission in educational terms was no longer to produce a few great men, but to educate the entire Christian community by offering basic wisdom which, Melanchthon thought, could surely be excavated from the classics. A narrow concentration on any one part of classical knowledge was unnecessary, perhaps dangerous, for wisdom is not found in specialization, Melanchthon wrote, but in the generality of good literature.[17] Still, exposing students to a whole body of undifferentiated classical literature could be hazardous, and Melanchthon sensed this, too. The classics were full of pagan thought which the older humanists had decontaminated by emphasizing language and style over content, but Melanchthon refused to follow their course. He decided instead,

---

[16] Philip Melanchthon, *Melanchthon on Christian Doctrine*, translated and edited by C. L. Manschreck, Oxford University Press, New York, 1965, pp. 340–347; E. C. Helmreich, *Religious Education in German Schools: An Historical Approach*, Harvard University Press, Cambridge, Mass., 1959, pp. 290–297; and Robert C. Worley, *Preaching and Teaching in the Earliest Church*, Westminster Press, Philadelphia, 1967, pp. 181–183.

[17] Karl Hartfelder, *Philip Melanchthon als Praeceptor Germaniae*, A. Hoffmann and Company, Berlin, 1889, pp. 71–72; and Henry C. Barnard, *German Teachers and Educators*, Brown and Gross, Hartford, Conn., 1878, p. 195.

following perhaps the advice of Erasmus, to select those classics that could be read with impunity by the youthful Christian.

When Melanchthon employed selection the list of acceptable classical authors shrunk, and in the hands of his followers the list was abbreviated even more. Squared against Christian Protestant sensitivity and fundamental moral convictions, the whole of classical literature could not pass muster; everything seeming to conflict with Christian belief was abandoned. Thus in theory Melanchthon was broad and liberal, and allowed humanistic education to believe in itself; in practice, however, his humanism was extremely limiting and was dominated by attitudes of caution and doctrines of religious faith. Melanchthon succeeded in demonstrating once again the great distance separating the library (the home of theory) from the classroom (the home of practice).

This circumscribed humanistic curricula, however, linked later Christian schools, both Protestant and Catholic, with the theory of Erasmus, and allowed them to follow a classical course while at the same time guarding their religious convictions from the eroding effects of pagan ideas. With Melanchthon the theory of fifteenth-century humanistic education is complete. Its aim—to produce a thorough, well-instructed, reasonably versatile Christian—separated it somewhat from Petrarchian and Erasmian humanism, but its content, even expurgated and excerpted, contained enough of the classical heritage to keep Christian humanism alive for several centuries to follow.

Melanchthon's Christian humanism, combining three educational positions—(1) the medieval, for its comprehensive meaning, (2) the humanistic, for its attention to language, and (3) the Protestant, for its unwavering love of God—was embraced by the most distinguished of Protestant schoolmen, John Sturm.

John Sturm (1507–1589)

Despite their obvious interest in education, Luther and Melanchthon were destined by the force of circumstances and their own careers to remain on the level of theory. They added the final touches to humanistic educational theory by saying again, as Erasmus had said, that education should form a man of character, but they interpreted the meaning of character in less expansive terms than Erasmus, and were determined to subordinate whatever elements of classical knowledge they selected for the school's syllabus to the interests, tests, and goals of denominational religion.

A contemporary of Luther and Melanchthon and the greatest of

Protestant schoolmen, John Sturm, took this theory of Protestant humanistic education and gave it pedagogical form.[18] Under his supervision, secondary education achieved status superior to lower or higher education—it was better to be a well-instructed and sincere Christian than to be a learned scholar—while retaining an exclusively classical content centered on the Latin authors. Other leading Protestants, especially Luther and Melanchthon, had recognized the worth of classical learning, and tried to maintain this learning in a position of relative importance, although definitely subordinate to the new religious doctrines. In other words, the theory of the Protestant movement as it touched education turned back the calendar to the time in educational history when the liberal arts and the classics were regarded as useful instruments for divine studies—adding the thought, however, that the totality of human experience could be enriched by studying the patterns of ancient culture with scrupulous attention to detail.

Sturm, however, refused to follow this educational doctrine to the letter. Religious and moral principles drawn from Christian sources, not from the classics, should be taught first and then, whenever possible, should be supported by selected material from the classics.[19] Sturm came close to denying both old and recent interpretations that the classics contained moral wisdom; moral wisdom, he thought, had an independent status. The teacher's first duty was to inculcate piety, and when this was done he could turn to teaching the arts of expression. Since Latin was the learned language of the time, the arts of expression meant a detailed study of Latin, but in Sturm's school Latin was stripped of its artistic and "divine" qualities and taught merely as a means of communication.[20]

John Sturm, a scholar and a teacher, had received the best education his age could boast. Elementary studies were made available to him in the court school; he spent three years with the famous Brethren of the Common Life; and he concluded his formal education by spending five years at the recently established and humanistically oriented University of Louvain. He spent a short time on the faculty of the University of Paris, and in 1537 was invited to become rector of the Gymnasium at Strassburg. He accepted the position tendered by the town fathers and remained at the school for forty-five years.

[18] See S. S. Laurie, *Studies in the History of Educational Opinion from the Renaissance*, Cambridge University Press, New York, 1903, chapter 3.

[19] Johann Sturm, *De Literarum Ludis Recte Aperiendis*, Strassburg, 1538, p. 104.

[20] C. Schmidt, *La vie et les travaux de Jean Sturm*, Strassburg, 1855, pp. 285–299; and James E. Russell, *German Higher Schools: The History, Organization, and Method of Secondary Education in Germany*, Longmans, Green and Company, New York, 1899, pp. 300–307.

When Sturm arrived in Strassburg to assume his duties as rector, he found the town conducting three Latin schools. Although these schools were operating according to the humanistic plan for such schools laid down by Melanchthon, they were not as effective as the town fathers thought they should be or as efficient in their methods and precise in their aims as Sturm wanted them to be. His first step, therefore, was to reorganize the three schools by consolidating them into one school. This was but the initial step in a long-range plan that Sturm had for secondary education. He spelled out his plan in a book entitled *The Best Mode of Opening an Institution of Learning.* This book was not intended to be anything more than a guide for Sturm and for his teachers in opening and conducting the Gymnasium at Strassburg. It was very detailed and touched on every phase of the school's operation. Not only was it detailed, it was also final. Once Sturm decided on the direction that his school would take and the means that should be used in it, he was unwilling to allow any deviation from the plan. Throughout Sturm's long association with the school in Strassburg there were remarkably few changes in its structure. Perhaps the main change from the original plan was the substitution of a nine-year program for the ten-year course that had been originally projected. It was as a nine-year school that the classical Gymnasium became the supreme model for all modern secondary education. In addition to drawing up the formal plan for the conduct of an institution of learning, Sturm often wrote letters to the teachers in the school, giving them directions and advice.[21]

What was Sturm's goal for this brand of classical education? What were the chief means for achieving it? The goal of teaching, Sturm asserted, was threefold: piety, knowledge, and the art of speaking. Piety belonged to the province of moral and religious instruction and was husbanded in regularly held and carefully supervised classes in religious teaching. "Knowledge and purity and elegance of diction should become the aim of scholarship, and toward its attainment both teachers and pupils should sedulously bend their every effort."[22]

The remainder of the aim of Sturm's classical teaching, with piety already accounted for, was knowledge and eloquence. To achieve these objectives would not be easy, nor would the time consumed in their pursuit be short. Assuming the effort, then, what were the means? Sturm was convinced that only through Latin study should knowledge

[21] Johann Sturm, *Epistolae Classicae*, Strassburg, 1565, pp. 220, 275.

[22] Barnard, *op. cit.*, p. 195; see also Charles B. Eavey, *History of Christian Education*, Moody Press, Chicago, 1965, pp. 380–383.

and eloquence be achieved, so he built the curriculum around Latin, complaining only that it could not be studied from the first without the aid of German. The Latin he liked, the only Latin allowed in the school, was pure Ciceronian Latin. This Protestant schoolmaster, more than any other schoolmaster of his time, advocated a return to Latin eloquence, and with this emphasis Sturm established a standard of excellence for education that dominated secondary schools for centuries.

The curriculum Sturm organized aimed directly at the realization of the superior goal of oral and written eloquence. He refused to allow vernacular teaching. Greek and Latin language and literature formed the core of all studies; the scriptures were read in Greek and Latin; and the teaching of logic involved a thorough knowledge of Latin. Neither mathematics, geography, history, nor science was taught. The school's curriculum was narrow and the goals precise; yet this curriculum, although narrower than anything Melanchthon would have approved, was carefully organized and graded. Each class had its authors (Cicero, Jerome, Virgil, St. Paul, Horace, Homer, and Sallust), and the accomplishments of a lower grade were the foundations on which the next higher grade built. In other words, the grades were tightly integrated, and students were promoted from one grade to another when their achievement warranted such promotion, although the actual movement from grade to grade was made only once a year. In a grade, excellence in achievement was rewarded by premiums and prizes of various kinds; students were made to see that diligence in study could bring enviable distinction and honor. Scholarship alone might be good, but its extraneous fruits might be even better.

The success of Sturm's school plan was extraordinary, and with success came fame and imitation. All over Europe and in America, too, Sturm's brand of secondary education was adopted with enthusiasm. This fame and status, an undoubted historical fact, must occasion some surprise, for Sturm's plan was neither ambitious nor novel, except that it narrowed classical literary curricula to safe selections and concentrated on the teaching of pure idiomatic Latin. Both novelties, of course, were fundamentally a service to religion, rather than a service to learning, and this, in the last analysis, is what may have spelled success for the plan. Here at last was a school program with respectable content confirmed by learning's best traditions, narrow enough to be managed, precise and moderate enough in its goals and expectations to be capable of realizing them, and safely anchored in the harbor of religious orthodoxy.[23]

[23] Laurie, *op. cit.*, chapter 3.

Other Developments in Protestant Education

Standing behind Luther, Melanchthon, and Sturm as educational reformers in the Protestant tradition were such men as John Bugenhagen (1485–1558), John Brenz (1499–1570), Valentin Trotzendorf (1490–1556), Ulrich Zwingli (1484–1534), John Calvin (1509–1564), and Mathurin Cordier (1479–1564). In general they accepted the basic religious doctrines of the Revolt and at the same time saw the need for revising or reorganizing the existing system of education in order that it might serve the ends of religious reform more explicitly. Bugenhagen, for example, achieved considerable repute as an organizer of schools in northern Germany. In addition to the Latin schools which formed a part of the system he created, he became interested in the schools in German for certain children of the lower and middle classes. Despite the general indifference of Luther and Melanchthon to vernacular schools, Bugenhagen forged ahead with his plans for them and to some extent succeeded. At least, the vernacular school became somewhat better known as a result of his work.[24] Brenz and Trotzendorf were minor figures, who organized schools in various parts of Germany and tried to introduce more practical teaching methods in them.

Neither Zwingli nor Calvin emerged as an ardent spokesman for educational reform, and it would be impossible to inscribe the name of either on any short list of great educators; yet the Calvinistic religious persuasion had a remarkable and lasting effect on educational attitudes. In both Europe and America (but especially in colonial America), where Calvinism made inroads its doctrines represented a world view and a theory of man's nature that unavoidably permeated social and educational thought. If we think only of the American colonial college and its allegiance to theistic higher education, we must be impressed by Calvinism's ability to influence the direction and purpose of education. But in this respect higher education did not stand alone, for the lower schools, too, were shaped according to denominational predispositions. The curriculum, the textbooks, school discipline, and educational purpose were all interpreted according to a fixed Calvinist policy, and the schools were made to pay heed to denominational purpose and need. Perhaps for a century in English America's first years, formal education had no better friend and constant supporter than the Calvinist creed.

Zwingli was a religious reformer who approached his task with all the zeal of a Luther but with a far more practical attitude. He made

[24] Walter M. Ruccius, *John Bugenhagen Pomeranus*, The United Lutheran Publishing House, Philadelphia, 1916, p. 75.

haste slowly and in the end had severed all connections with the Catholic Church. He turned almost at once to the improvement of schools, and instead of talking about the need for better schools that might provide a steady supply of ministers for the churches, he saw to it that these schools were established. Moreover, he saw to it that they were closely supervised and that they held to their original aim. Their purpose was, of course, to teach a greater knowledge of God, for the schools were really professional divinity schools. The curriculum of these schools, in addition to the religious studies, which were central, was largely humanistic. Most of Zwingli's views and attitudes on education may be found in his *Christian Education of Youth*, which appeared in 1523.

This work of Zwingli's adds very little to the body of knowledge about education; even in his own time it was not thought of as a forward-looking document. Perhaps it did not have to be. In any event the educational career of Zwingli was interrupted by an untimely death, and his work was carried on by John Calvin. Calvin did not alter the educational plan that had been proposed by his predecessor. Schools and colleges were established on the basis of Protestant religious doctrines and humanistic educational theories. Though Calvin is remembered as a great religious organizer rather than as an educator, he did have a short career as a teacher when he taught for Sturm in Strassburg. His greatest impact on the world of the mind was made by his *Institutes of the Christian Religion*. It was in this work that the Calvinistic doctrine of predestination was clearly set forth.[25]

The tendency among sixteenth-century Protestant schoolmen was, as we have said, to use humanistic paradigms for clear and rather narrow religious purposes. Begun by Melanchthon, this trend was further amplified by Sturm, and even more by the Frenchman Mathurin Cordier.[26] Cordier spent a lifetime teaching Latin, and during this long career as a teacher he emphasized (1) a correct Latin stripped of linguistic novelties attached to it by its close association with vernaculars, (2) a prudent selection and grading of materials of instruction in order to serve the ends of moral teaching, on the one hand, and to accommodate student learning capacity, on the other, and (3) an

---

[25] See Jean Calvin, *Institutes of the Christian Religion*, edited by John T. McNeill and translated by Ford L. Battles, Westminster Press, Philadelphia, 1960; Jean Horace Rilliet, *Zwingli, Third Man of the Reformation*, Westminster Press, Philadelphia, 1964; Robert C. Walton, *Zwingli's Theocracy*, Toronto University Press, Toronto, 1967; and John T. McNeill, *The History and Character of Calvinism*, Oxford University Press, New York, 1954.

[26] Mathurin Cordier, *Colloquiorum Scholasticorum Libri IV*, Stephanus, Geneva, 1564, Book I, par. 30.

outright sermonizing whereby students were exposed, over and over again, to copybook maxims of morality. Cordier's *Selections from Cicero, Familiar Letters,* and *Latin Colloquies* are object lessons in how to teach a correct Latin as a language for contemporary use—especially for necessary correspondence—without any dependence on the classics themselves and without paying tribute to the age that produced them.

Cordier's pedagogy was based on the assumption that fluency in Latin was plainly the equivalent of a decent education. Working from this assumption, he constructed a school curriculum, aiming directly at linguistic skill, wherein grammar textbooks replaced literary models for language teaching, and into which classical literature was admitted cautiously, carefully selected and expurgated, only when it suited his own ideas of propriety.

Erasmus, Melanchthon, and Sturm set higher standards for teaching and learning than did Cordier, and because they did they were less frequently followed than Cordier, whose practical influence on school curricula, through his narrower vision of education and his dry textbooks for the schools, must be seen as the real representative of a kind of humanism that won a place for itself in Western secondary education. As we move forward in time from Erasmus, we see, along with a better organized pedagogy (itself important), a progressive departure from the traditional corpus of humanism. Ideas, style, and grand thoughts are sold at discount to be replaced by a narrow Latin eloquence comfortably situated as a medium for religion and morals. Cordier's teaching exemplifies the final stage of deterioration in humanistic zeal; but it exemplifies, too, a kind of education which religiously-minded teachers of the sixteenth and seventeenth centuries were willing to embrace.[27]

Apart from men and theories of education, what can be said about the general impact of Protestantism on school learning? First of all, municipal schools, regularly organized in large European cities from the early years of the medieval period, were allowed to wear a new face. For decades these schools had taken all their scholastic cues from Church schools. Now, however, being less impressed by such schools, they set a course of their own, admitted the vernacular as a subject of study, and occasionally even allowed girls to study in the same classrooms as boys. It made relatively little difference that the spokesmen for Protestant education should not have looked with favor on these departures, for the spirit of Protestantism was taken as a charter of independence for town schools. And while this independence seldom

[27] Mathurin Cordier, *Maturinus Corderius's School Colloquies*, J. Read, London, 1719, pp. 312–320.

affected the quality of learning in the schools, it undoubtedly put the schools in a more favorable position vis-à-vis the town treasury, and permitted them to depend heavily on public financial support. Many of these municipal schools became free schools; yet, it should be remembered, they were not truly public schools, for their doors were open usually only to the sons and daughters of the so-called "better" classes. Remembering this artificial exclusiveness, we should be extremely reluctant to cite these schools as precursors of free public education.

In England the Revolt, led by Henry VIII, took its toll of schools and colleges. Both in Britain and Ireland the monasteries had had exceptionally close ties with education and for many years had offered the greatest opportunity for schooling. England's break with the Roman Catholic Church led to the abolishment of these monastic institutions and to a confiscation of their property. In addition, the chantries, which had been so popular in England for many years, were closed; their bequests were claimed by the crown; and the chantry schools that were conducted in connection with them were cast into oblivion. Nobles had for some years conducted schools at their palaces, and bishops and other ecclesiastical dignitaries had secured schoolmasters to teach selected students. The court school or the palace school, which dated at least from the time of Charles the Great, was swept away by the tide of Henry's religious revolt. It is easy to see why Henry should not have allowed the ecclesiastical schools to continue to operate, but it is almost impossible to understand why the schools connected with the courts should have disappeared too. Perhaps Henry was attempting to make a clean break with the past, although the essentials of Henry's proposed reforms in religion did not argue for a clean break. At any rate, the instructions that were given in religion following the English Revolt were quite generally given in English, and the tools of such instruction were catechisms and primers also written in English. This move had some indirect consequences for education, in assuming that the vernacular should be given a principal position as a language of instruction. Though this is by no means an innovation, it is, however, a significant emphasis.

The funds confiscated from schools and religious houses and the property taken over by the crown were used in any way the king wanted to use them. When the spirit moved him he endowed some schools and colleges. Latin schools and the especially favored colleges of Oxford and Cambridge received most of these endowments. How large the endowments were is not as important as the fact that the action taken by the monarch in supporting schools and colleges established a precedent for further state or royal patronage of education. And in the context of these times in Henry's England, the schools and colleges lost some of their independence every time they accepted a favor or grant from the king. On the level of higher education, Scholasticism was ushered out and humanism was given free entrance. Grammar and literature, good humanistic subjects, took the place of dialectics as the most prominent study in the curriculum. On the lower levels, where there was little disposition to leave such matters as the determination of school policy and the selection of schoolbooks to the teachers of the local schools, the state began to assume an important role in shaping educational policy. In time, especially under Elizabeth, not even the universities were exempt from state surveillance; the crown exercised strict supervision over all of the schools and licensed or accredited the teachers who taught in them. It was during this period, too, that the great English public schools came into existence. These were the schools that achieved such enviable reputations for preparing young Englishmen for public life.[28] Despite the excellence that these and other English schools attained in later years, the period of revolt was a time when both in quality and in quantity education in England deteriorated. Many of the schools and colleges were forced to close; educational opportunities for everyone, but especially for women, declined sharply.

Catholic Reforms and Education

The Church attempted in a number of ways to bring about the reforms that were recognized now as necessary. Most of these, of course, had to do with the religious side of revolt and reformation, but from a strictly educational point of view, two reforms had special significance. One was the legislation of the Council of Trent (1545–1563), the other was the creation of the Society of Jesus. Not only did the Council of Trent deal with matters of doctrine which were of a superior order, it dealt also with the matter of discipline and routine in church-related education. Most especially this point of reform touched on the education of

---

[28] Nine "great public schools" were recognized by the Clarendon Commission of 1864. They were Winchester, Eton, St. Paul's, Shrewsbury, Westminster, Rugby, Harrow, Merchant Taylors', and Charterhouse. See K. Charton, *Education in Renaissance England,* Cambridge University Press, New York, 1965; C. McMahon, *Education in Fifteenth Century England,* The Johns Hopkins Press, Baltimore, 1947; R. Weiss, *Humanism in England in the Fifteenth Century,* The Clarendon Press, Oxford, 1957; and D. Bush, *The Renaissance and English Humanism,* University of Toronto Press, Toronto, 1939.

the clergy. Discipline for the education of the clergy was reestablished, and it was decreed that every diocese should have its own seminary for the preparation of priests. Codes were written regarding the qualifications of teachers in these seminaries. Thus, all over the world the education of priests and the standards required of prospective clergymen became more or less uniform. The Council also admonished bishops and pastors to give greater encouragement and support to the parish schools. In a word, the Council of Trent gave its complete endorsement of the revival and revitalization of Catholic education. It supported the idea that free schools should be opened for the poor and that colleges should be made more accessible, and it rejected the notion that the Catholic Church had anything to fear from education or learning.[29]

THE SOCIETY OF JESUS

The Council of Trent was a specific Catholic reaction to the Protestant Revolt. A renewal of interest in education and the management of schools was a reaction shared by many of the existing religious orders; and two new religious groups, the Jesuits and the Ursulines, appeared on the scene to promote Catholic causes generally and to advance the fortunes of Catholic education. These two new groups, it should be emphasized, were only two among many that labored in the field of Catholic education, but by their work they achieved a reputation for effective teaching and merited the praise of the educational world.

The Ursulines, the first teaching order of women established in the Church, were founded by St. Angela Merici in 1535. Long before she entered the religious life, St. Angela displayed a vital interest in education. She conducted a school for girls in her home when she was only twenty-two years old. When she was sixty-two, St. Angela, with the help of twelve companions, founded the Ursulines. This community of religious women was followed by many other orders and communities that have done important educational work down through the years.

Religious associations of men were generated in this age also, and they, too, turned their energies to the work of educational and religious reform. Among these religious communities, then only recently formed, were the Oratory of Divine Love, the Theatines, the Capuchins, and the Jesuits.

Throughout the history of education, probably no group of teach-

[29] See Hughes, *op. cit.*, pp. 155–159.

ers has gained greater fame than the Jesuits. The Sophists may be more widely known, but we cannot claim for the Sophists either the uniformity or educational practice or the devotion to purpose that was distinctive of the Jesuits. The Society of Jesus, moreover, was carefully and closely organized; this, of course, could not be said of the Sophists. Many other religious orders within the Catholic Church performed outstanding services for the development of Catholic education, and lay groups of Catholics and individual masters were often exceptionally successful in conducting schools of high quality in an environment of traditional Catholicism.[30] Yet for all the excellence that may be claimed, for example, for the Brethren of the Common Life, the Jesuits occupy a unique position. No one should assume that they have not had their detractors over the centuries—both within and without the Church— but even their enemies have found it difficult to ignore the successes of the Society of Jesus during the three centuries following the Revolt. It was in the sixteenth, seventeenth, and eighteenth centuries that the educational reputation of the Jesuits was established.

Before entering upon a detailed discussion of their work, particularly of their method of study, a word should be said in general about the reasons for their phenomenal success. Why could their work extract almost universal acclaim from Europe? Why did they succeed so marvelously where others had failed so miserably? The first reason is that the Jesuits had a dedicated group of teachers. They had been carefully educated over many years; they were trained to teach with the same careful attention that had been directed at forming their minds; and they were motivated by the zeal which their society generated. This does not indict the character, devotion, mind, or skill of the other teachers of these or preceding centuries. It would be both unhistorical and unflattering to maintain that the Jesuits were so good and so successful because other teachers were so bad. The second reason for the success of the Jesuits was that they developed a uniform plan for education. We shall have something more to say later about the *Ratio Studiorum,* the plan to which all Jesuit schools conformed. The plan included certain educational practices that today are taken for granted, for example, the grading of students and an organization of the curriculum to fit their ages and maturity. No Jesuit school neglected these steps. Finally, the Jesuits engaged in gratuitous teaching. The Jesuit institutions of Europe were founded with endowments of sufficient size and scope to enable them to conduct schools and charge nothing at all for the instruction that was given. Fees could have been charged, and sometimes

[30] *Ibid.*

were charged, for food and lodging, but no charges were made for the actual costs incurred by teaching.[31]

St. Ignatius of Loyola (1491–1556), a Spanish nobleman and soldier, was the founder of the Society of Jesus. Ignatius' military career was interrupted in 1521 when he was wounded at the siege of Pampelona. While recuperating from his wounds his mind turned to religion, and he decided after much mature thought to become a soldier in the army of Christ. His original intention seems to have been to become a missionary in order to combat the influence of the Mohammedans. When he had recovered his strength, he went to Jerusalem with a small band of followers (the Society was not yet formed), where he hoped to convert the Mohammedans, or at least to blunt their effectiveness. Within a relatively short period of time he realized that neither he nor his followers had the missionary skill or the fundamental religious education to accomplish their purpose. Ignatius returned to Europe and began to prepare himself for the work to which he was now dedicated. Among other schools, he studied at the University of Paris. This period devoted to study must have lasted about six years, for in 1534 Ignatius and a few loyal followers formed a society. This was not yet the Society of Jesus, but it was the germ of what was to come. In 1540 the Society of Jesus was duly organized and recognized by Pope Paul III. At that time the membership of the newly formed society was limited to sixty, but this was a restriction that was removed within three years.

The objectives of the Society of Jesus were all based on the central idea of strengthening and spreading the influence of the Church. The Jesuits became the pope's special task force, and they vowed to go anywhere and do anything to protect the life of the Church. Yet in actual practice their principal work embraced or came to embrace three things: preaching, confession, and education.[32]

Jesuit Schools Protestant schoolmen were not the only ones capable of setting definite limits on classical study. The Jesuits followed, and contributed to, the trend we have observed taking place, a trend restricting humanism to language study and equating the broader outcomes of learning with religious piety. In a Catholic educational setting, the Jesuits were master organizers who could build a progressive curriculum, carefully selecting the authors to be read and interpreting them rhetorically, studying literature for its transfer values to composition,

---

[31] See Allan P. Farrell, *The Jesuit Code of Liberal Education*, The Bruce Publishing Company, Milwaukee, Wis., 1938, pp. 162–165.

[32] See Robert Schwickerath, *Jesuit Education: Its History and Principles*, B. Herder Book Company, St. Louis, 1904, p. 107.

and teaching classical Latin from specially prepared grammar text-books. Although Jesuit educational humanism is too big a subject for a quick summary,[33] we can, with its principal emphasis clear, turn to some of its details.

Generally speaking, the Jesuits were not interested in and did not engage in elementary education. Whether this was due to the circumstances of the time, to the increasing popularity of secondary education as a result of Sturm's influence on it, or to a natural desire on the part of the Jesuits to use their talents on educational levels where they could be expected to do the most good is not entirely clear. The Jesuit tradition would lead one to believe that the last interpretation is the most valid. At any rate, the Jesuits opened elementary schools only when they found such a procedure unavoidable, and they relinquished the schools for children at the earliest opportunity. Jesuit teachers were hardly ever found in elementary classrooms. Yet when they were in missionary countries, for example, during the colonial years of North America, they never hesitated to do what needed to be done.[34]

The Jesuit system of education was highly organized and intimately related to the fundamental foundations of a religious society. No thought was given to any plan for teaching that did not assume that Jesuits would be the teachers. In other words, laymen did not figure prominently, or at all, in the Jesuit system of education. This emphasis on the society's teaching function was entirely natural and was in no way restricted to the Society of Jesus. Other religious orders made no provisions for lay teachers in their schools either, but simply followed the medieval practices that were based on the concept of a clerical monopoly in education. The principal roles in teaching, among the Jesuits and other orders or congregations, were assigned to clerical teachers. Surely one of the reasons why the Jesuits were as successful as they were was that they had a devoted body of teachers; the dedication that the Society demanded could hardly ever be found outside the ranks of the Jesuits.

The schools of the Jesuits were humanistic schools. They took the content of Christian humanism, organized it carefully, and presented it according to the best teaching techniques they could devise or discover. Consistent with the humanism of Europe, this meant an emphasis on Latin. So far as the place of Latin in the school was concerned, there

[33] St. Ignatius of Loyola, *Ratio Studiorum*, in Edward A. Fitzpatrick (ed.), *St. Ignatius and the Ratio Studiorum*, McGraw-Hill Book Company, New York, 1933, pp. 20–32.

[34] See Thomas Hughes, *History of the Society of Jesus in North America*, Longmans, Green and Company, New York, 1907–1917, 3 vols., I, pp. 325–329.

would be little to choose between Sturm's Gymnasium and the schools of the Jesuits. In the teaching of Latin grammar and Latin literature, the Jesuits sought to achieve, as Sturm had, knowledge and eloquence. In their teaching methods they used a practice revived from Hellenistic pedagogy, the practice of prelection. Although prelection in the hands of Jesuit teachers became an important technique and, in the evaluations made of Jesuit pedagogy, their most significant contribution to method, it is easy to overestimate its importance. The great fame that attaches to Jesuit education could hardly be attributed to prelection, a technique in teaching that was in regular use at least sixteen or seventeen centuries before the Jesuits appeared on the stage of history. Not prelection alone, but prelection carefully organized and integrated with other techniques, such as the technique of repetition and the wise use of prizes, rewards, and premiums, brought the Jesuits their great fame as schoolmasters.[35]

The early years of modern education under other schoolmasters were harsh years from the point of view of discipline. The earlier lament of St. Augustine could be applied again. (He had said that if he were given the choice between death and returning to the primary school, he would choose the former.) The educated opinion of the day chose to accept the view that a schoolmaster who taught without severity was simply worthless. Into an educational world that honored this attitude almost without question, the Jesuits introduced their code of mild discipline. They tried to avoid chastising the students put under their care, and if a boy could not be led they refused to drive him. Young men who did not fit into the practices of the Jesuit schools were released. They were not beaten and forced to conform in either an intellectual or a physical sense.

After the time of Comenius the educational world was to hear a great deal about the advantages that could be gained for learning if classes were very large. Yet from the beginning and throughout most of their history, the Jesuits kept their classes small. They were also rather selective, for they believed that their efforts were better spent in teaching bright boys than in teaching the average or the slow. With the policy of gratuitous teaching, economic obstacles hardly ever stood in the way of the education of a talented youth in a Jesuit secondary school or college.

The Ratio Studiorum   The heart of Jesuit pedagogy is to be found in the *Ratio Studiorum*. This is the instrument that guided Jesuit schools and Jesuit teaching and brought fame to both.

[35] Farrell, *op. cit.*, pp. 173–177.

On December 8, 1584, a board of six Jesuits was convened by the Jesuit General and commissioned to examine the record of Jesuit schools and to make recommendations concerning the future course and philosophy of Jesuit education. This board continued to meet for about two years, examining all the evidence that it could gather from the forty-odd years of Jesuit educational history. In the summer of 1586 this board was ready with its report and recommendations. They constituted the first draft of the *Ratio Studiorum*. This first draft was offered as nothing more than a point of departure; it was sent to all the Jesuit provincials with instructions that it be examined and discussed. As a result of the discussions in the provinces, certain recommendations for revisions of the draft or criticisms of it were to be made within a six-month period. These were to be sent to Rome, to the Jesuit General, where they would be examined and where some of them would be incorporated in a new document: This document, the second draft of the *Ratio*, appeared with the force of law late in 1586.[36]

The 1586 edition of the *Ratio* dealt with the following general topics: the organization of the curriculum and a separation of the humanities from philosophy and theology; the selection of teachers for the courses in the humanities; the establishment of standards for the selection of grammar texts; the consideration of the place of Greek in the curriculum; the invention of exercises and methods for stimulating study, and for studying Latin and Greek; and finally the determination of policies with regard to promotions, vacations, discipline, and the inculcation of piety.[37] Though the *Ratio* was to be followed by Jesuit teachers and had an unquestioned official status in Jesuit schools, the document was not regarded as definitive. In other words, it was to be a growing, evolving document that would change as time and new ideas required. Yet it was not to be so flexible that Jesuit schools in different countries could conduct substantially different educational programs or even follow a course that was locally attractive, and still claim to be within its boundaries. The *Ratio* changed a great deal over the years, and the changes, for the most part, came from the schools or were inspired by them. It was a successful educational instrument because it was realistic; it was a philosophy and practice for education that came from the hands of teachers. And, though it had undoubtedly a long-range flexibility, the *Ratio* had also what might be called a short-term rigidity. The total nature of the *Ratio* was demonstrated to some extent in an appeal that came from the German Jesuit schools to permit the addition of a course in German history to the curriculum. The ap-

[36] *Ibid.*, pp. 201–217.
[37] *Ibid.*, pp. 228–235.

peal was not regarded with favor. In refusing to permit the addition of a course that seemed to be good for certain schools in certain areas, the Jesuit authorities were simply applying a basic principle in their theory of education. A well-known Jesuit scholar has put it this way: ". . . for the principle animating the Jesuit system was not so much the communication of information from many fields of knowledge as the formation of intellectual habits and literary expression." [38]

A new edition of the *Ratio* appeared in 1591, incorporating the lessons learned from the use of earlier editions. Although the 1591 edition was binding on Jesuit schools, it was not intended to be the final document codifying Jesuit pedagogy. It was expected and planned that another and possibly a definitive edition would follow the one which appeared in 1591. In 1599 the third edition of the *Ratio Studiorum* was ready.

The third edition was the product of approximately a half century's work. The first thirty or more years were spent in gathering, testing, adapting, and experimenting. The reports from the schools, the impressions gleaned from visiting schools, and the actual teaching experiences in the classroom played a large role in giving final form to the *Ratio*. But there were other important influences too: Nadal's 1551 plan for Messina, Ignatius' fourth part of the *Constitutions*, the *Ordo Studiorum* of Nadal, and *De Ratione* of Ledesma. These were works that stood out especially as the Jesuit educational tradition was being shaped. The final ten or fifteen years of this half century of preparation were spent in sorting, revising, and codifying everything that had been gathered or learned during the earlier period.

Though we cannot make an extensive analysis of the Jesuit *Ratio Studiorum* here, we think it important to give a brief summary of its essential points. The section in the document of 1599 that dealt with the administration of schools was clearer than that in the earlier editions. It defined the offices in education and set the limits of responsibility for school officers. In methodology, the most elaborately developed section in this edition, a twofold aim was achieved: helping the new teacher adjust to the system and perpetuating educational policies and practices that guaranteed universally high quality in the schools. The section on curriculum concerned itself with the relative importance of the humanities, philosophy, and theology in the order of studies. The basis of all studies was formed out of the classical languages and literature. This, of course, was in line with what was then accepted as a theory of cultural transmission. Mathematics and science were given a subordinate position as mere adjuncts to philosophy, and the vernacu-

[38] *Ibid.*, p. 249.

lar, though its use was not forbidden, was given only slight attention. Both Latin and Greek were taught, though Greek had a position in the curriculum inferior to that of Latin. Its relative unimportance followed the orthodox humanistic tradition. Spiritual growth among the students was given high priority on the Jesuit scale of educational values, yet very few classes in religion found their way into the curriculum.

The section on discipline was remarkable for its moderation, considering the standards of discipline common to that day. The Jesuits looked not to corporal punishment or to fear for good order. Good example, the hope for honor, and the fear of blame were the motives that dominated the policies on discipline.

Remarkable unity was established through a definite declaration of aims, the centering of all studies around the classics, the use of uniform texts and techniques in the classroom, uniform entrance and promotion requirements, and the consistent insistence on attainment of eloquence in both oral and written work, regardless of the matter studied. Purpose and organization stand out in the Jesuit system. According to Allan Farrell, "In the last analysis, that which made the Jesuits the schoolmasters of Europe for nearly two centuries was organization." [39]

The Jesuit system of education was interrupted when the Society, due largely to religious politics and national pressure, was suppressed by Pope Clement in 1773. At that time the Society had 865 schools. After forty-one years, in 1814, the Society of Jesus was restored. In 1820 a general congregation of the Order requested a modernization of the *Ratio* and suggested that such a modernization adopt the pattern followed when the *Ratio* was born. A committee was appointed to begin the work in 1830; by 1832 it had completed its task of adapting and revising the *Ratio* of 1599. The new edition ushered in few changes, the only noticeable alterations being in curriculum. In the nineteenth century it was not so possible to reach agreement on curricular questions as it had been in the sixteenth century. Yet the changes in curriculum, or the liberalization of Jesuit policies toward it, did destroy the essential unity which the older orders of study had possessed. The new edition was directive rather than mandatory; at least, this was the official position until 1853, when another attempt was made to revise the *Ratio*. Neither this attempt nor the one made in 1906 was successful. The status of the *Ratio* was explained as follows by a Jesuit historian: "Only by a decree of a General Congregation of the Order is this sanction possible. Such a decree, however, was not passed; consequently, the revised *Ratio* has not the force of law in the Society, but is merely to be considered as a regulation of the General. So much liberty is left

[39] *Ibid.*, p. 191.

to Provincials that the teaching in Jesuit colleges can be adapted to the educational needs of all countries." [40]

When it seemed impossible to draw up a new *Ratio* that would be binding on all Jesuit schools everywhere in the world, a kind of compromise was effected. Each province was to draw up its own course of study, based, as far as possible, on the previous editions of the *Ratio* and the educational traditions of the Society, and submit it for approval. This compromise has lasted to contemporary times, and while it allows the Jesuits to continue many of their fine pedagogical practices in schools of the modern age, they operate their schools without the unity that they once enjoyed from the guidance and direction of the *Ratio Studiorum*.

Summary

The Protestant Revolt and the Catholic Reformation had important consequences for education. Neither was an educational movement in any narrow sense, yet both were movements that looked to education for the fulfillment of their ideals.

Protestantism, as evidenced by heresy and schism, had been brewed in Europe before the time of Luther, although Luther was the religious leader who gave it its most definite and lasting form. The new religious doctrine that Luther preached needed the support of education, and many of Luther's sermons and letters attest his interest in the schools. In spite of Luther's interest in the education of the people, his program never provided the breadth of educational opportunity that was available in the years that just preceded the Lutheran movement. Often the education of the common man was badly neglected, and schools with a program in the vernacular were never really supported.

Protestant leaders in education—and followers of Luther—were Philip Melanchthon and John Sturm. To Melanchthon goes the credit for being an organizer and administrator of schools in many Protestant lands. These schools, however, were always Latin schools for students of the elite. Sturm was a schoolmaster, the greatest of Protestant schoolmasters and quite possibly the greatest schoolmaster the modern age produced. He organized and conducted the Gymnasium at Strassburg, which formed the model and provided the tone for all modern secondary education.

Catholic reforms which touched on education were led by religious orders and congregations, both for men and women, and by the great Council of Trent. The Council breathed new life into Catholic action and discipline. All the religious orders showed a renewed interest in education and tried to reorganize and reestablish it on a sounder basis. To the Society of Jesus, however, goes the chief credit for leading a Catholic educational renaissance.

---

[40] Schwickerath, *op. cit.,* p. 198.

The Jesuits became the best known schoolmasters of Europe. They developed the famous *Ratio Studiorum,* a guide to their aims and practices, and were more successful than other groups of teachers because they organized their educational program and devised their educational method with greater care. In addition, the Jesuit schools could count on a dedicated group of teachers, a uniform method of instruction in the hands of carefully trained Jesuit schoolmasters, and the best students of the land, for Jesuit schools were free schools, and economic obstacles never stood in the way of talent that needed to be developed in them.

XII

Realism
in Education
in The Seventeenth
Century

The first schools, whenever they were founded, were expected to perform a useful service by doing what could no longer be done easily without them. Originally the school was an extension of the home (an idea still current), and the organized experiences it offered were practical, as the day-to-day home training and education had been practical. So far we have followed the evolution of schools, the codification of teaching theories to guide them, and an elaboration of various pedagogic means, all intended to guide and guard the fluctuating aims of formal learning. We have noticed how, as the centuries passed, schools discarded their practical or utility-centered goals, and how they became preoccupied with literary and linguistic excellence. We have also seen how even these objectives were subjected to scrutiny and reappraisal, and how a literary syllabus judged adequate in one genre was discarded as being useless or dangerous in another. We have detected, too, a regular tendency to separate life from learning, and to make the curriculum of the school an arsenal of rules and literary codes into which matters concerned with real life could not be expected to penetrate.[1]

Predictably, this process of educational evolution was marked by unevenness. Only from time to time did a school, such as Vittorino's or Guarino's in the Renaissance period, or a theory, such as Erasmus', try to bring life and learning back into a single focus, to make the whole business worthwhile from a human point of view. Medieval education (another illustration) prided itself on its practical orientation, for its ultimate dual purpose was to interpret the world of man along distinctly Christian lines, and to preserve the society of which it was a part. Its great ornament, Scholasticism, while succeeding at an intellectual level, and practical enough for the initiated few, had almost no contact with common men, and never directly influenced their lives.[2]

Humanism, basically a conservative theory, at least as it began, because it sought to revive ancient values of life and education, proved in the last analysis to be unmanageable unless much of its content, and therefore its genius, was pared away. When this paring was done, as it was by later humanists who were also deeply committed to religion, the result was a dry-as-dust school program aiming at only a small part of classical excellence, Latin eloquence.[3]

In the end Scholasticism, humanism, and Christian humanism, despite their long life and decided impact on school learning, all must be counted as failures. Together and separately they succeeded only in driving schools toward further isolation from life, and made learning an antiseptic exercise largely ignoring personal aspirations or society's legitimate needs. Each of these academic theories always had enough fundamental pragmatism in it to keep it alive, but too little, as it turned out, to make its pedagogy stand the hard test of life's persistent realities.

The seventeenth century, the threshold of the modern age, was ready for another approach to learning. Unwilling, as it turned out, to discard as useless everything that was part of traditional educational programs, its leaders tried, nevertheless, to construct a paradigm that would fulfill keenly-felt human aspirations. This paradigm was realism,

[1] See Edward J. Power, *Evolution of Educational Doctrine*, Appleton-Century-Crofts, Inc., New York, 1969, pp. 392–394.
[2] See R. R. Bolgar, *The Classical Heritage and Its Beneficiaries*, Cambridge University Press, New York, 1954, pp. 243–245.
[3] P. O. Kristeller, *Renaissance Thought: The Classics, Scholastic, and Humanistic Strains*, Harper and Row, Publishers, New York, 1965, vol. I, pp. 95–98.

a way of thinking and acting that permeated not just education—
although its effects on education were deep and far-reaching—but all of
life.

Realism

When scholars dogmatically assumed—as they had for centuries—that
all knowledge was hidden in classical texts, their principal concern was
one of devising literary and linguistic techniques sufficient to possess
this knowledge. And this preoccupation was justified by every tome
on educational theory. But if educational theory could be made to stand
still, knowledge could not: More careful observation of man, of nature,
and of social institutions produced knowledge calling into question
many of the old assumptions. As methods for obtaining verifiable
knowledge improved, a large body of scientific knowledge became
available and stood, almost as a hostile culture, challenging the old
theories of life mined from ancient authorities.

The list of scientific innovators of this age is long and impressive.
The principal names are Descartes, Galileo, Newton, Stevin (inventor
of decimal fractions), Gilbert, Harvey, Torricelli, Boyle, and Kremer
(mathematical geographer). Working along new lines, these great talents revolutionized mathematics, astronomy, mechanics, instrumenta-
tion (thermometer, telescope, microscope, micrometer, thermoscope,
barometer, air pump, pendulum clock), geography, biology, and medicine. No longer content to take the word of traditional authority, they
sought to find out for themselves how nature's laws worked and how
they affected men.[4]

These scientific achievements, monumental as they were in themselves, opened new avenues between knowledge and social progress in
a world made suddenly so much larger by discovery and exploration.
Social amelioration, now more possible than ever before, had its prospects set forth in a number of literary utopias: Campanella's *The City
of the Sun*, Andreä's *Christian City*, and Francis Bacon's *New Atlantis*
were the ones most often read, but there were dozens of others. Methods
of finding dependable knowledge were tested anew, and the older, less
valid techniques were discarded whenever they were found wanting.
School practices were reexamined, and determined efforts were made to
channel the findings of an awakened science into the schoolroom by
means of revised curricula, on the one hand, and a reformed pedagogy
which should exploit natural learning processes, on the other. Such fer-

[4] See Alistair C. Crombie, *Medieval and Early Modern Science*, Doubleday, Garden
City, New York, 1959, vol. II.

ment was a good omen for education and it was capable of affecting existing schools. Yet, despite its implicit endorsement of broader educational opportunity for the mass of mankind, the realist movement was only prophetically anticipatory of the cause for popular education.

In the hands of scientists, social reformers, and educators, realism took different forms or affirmed different emphases. On a strictly educational level, realism was either socially, humanistically, or psychologically oriented. But whatever the orientation, each emphasis found common ground in the doctrine that learning must come to grips with data as they surface in contemporary society. What is taught in the school's curriculum must be valid and, moreover, must have meaning and be capable of practical application; pedagogical techniques should be based on the clearest principles of human learning. With this much agreed to, realists turned to the question of which data are most relevant for inclusion in a school's teaching program, and which techniques of teaching are most efficient for producing the goals of a decent education.

Humanistic realism, while not ignoring an abundance of scientifically validated knowledge, and in fact agreeing to add it to the curriculum, retained an allegiance to much of past educational practice by asserting that only by being able to use language flawlessly would men be successful in capitalizing on their scientific discoveries. Science might be the key to producing dependable knowledge, but language was still the means of communicating it. Thus a humanistic realist like John Milton (1608–1674) could praise the progress of the scientists, endorse their preferences for inductive over deductive methods, and applaud the new mathematics and the new astronomy, but at the same time insist on a school program with language and literature at its heart, because these subjects were the bedrock for intelligent discourse among learned men.[5] Milton was anxious to ride the bandwagon of scientific progress, but neither he nor any of his humanistically oriented colleagues was willing to be its driver.

Social realism sought both language and literary skills and scientific knowledge, but its chief proponents were anxious most of all for social reform. Social reform, they averred, could be generated best not by studying the textbooks, or even by experimenting in the laboratory, but by coming directly into contact with society's institutions, learning how they operated, and, whenever necessary, endeavoring to reform them. Since social realists could find little susceptible of curricular cod-

---

[5] John Milton, *Milton on Education*, edited by O. M. Ainsworth, Cornell University Press, Ithaca, N. Y., 1928; and H. F. Fletcher, *The Intellectual Development of John Milton*, 2 vols., University of Illinois Press, Urbana, 1956 and 1961.

ification in the institutions, they advised their students to use society itself as their school.[6]

Realism with a psychological emphasis turned out to be the most productive type. As its leading spokesman, it could point to Comenius, who refused to think about what should be eliminated from the school's curriculum, but instead tried to find a way for teaching all worthwhile knowledge—scientific, literary, and social—most effectively.[7] This purpose led him to consider not only the psychological bases of learning but the physiological bases as well, and finally to produce a plan for education that explained how the fundamentals of universal wisdom could be taught to everyone by using a method of education that begins on the sensory level.[8]

Irrespective of emphases, realism contributed to a many-sided educational revolution. Its greatest names are John Amos Comenius and John Locke, but before we go to them we should illustrate how other realists—namely Bacon, Descartes, and Ratke—blazed a trail for the great spokesmen to follow.

FRANCIS BACON (1561–1626)

Finding the origin of a seventeenth-century scientific quickening is an almost impossible task. Although it is popularly associated with Sir Isaac Newton (1642–1727) and the appearance, in 1687, of his famous *Principia*, we should prefer to explain the scientific awakening as an outcome of realism.[9] In this connection, as an exponent of realism, Francis Bacon becomes a highly significant historical figure, although he was neither an educational theorist nor a schoolmaster. He belongs, rather, to a class of practical scientists determined to convert the secrets of nature to the advantage of mankind.

In the history of education Bacon will be remembered first for the respectability with which he endowed induction as a means of obtain-

---

[6] See George N. Clark, *Science and Social Welfare in the Age of Newton,* The Clarendon Press, Oxford, 1949, pp. 76–84.

[7] J. E. Sadler, *Comenius and the Concept of Universal Education,* Barnes & Noble, Inc., New York, 1966, pp. 26–31.

[8] M. W. Keatinge, *Comenius,* McGraw-Hill Book Company, New York, 1931, pp. 109–116. This book is a reprint, in a slightly shortened form, of *The Great Didactic of John Amos Comenius,* Adam and Charles Black, London, 1896.

[9] See Gerd Buchdahl, *The Image of Newton and Locke in the Age of Reason,* Sheed and Ward, Inc., New York, 1961; Isaac Newton, *Newton's Philosophy of Nature: Selections from His Writings,* edited with notes by H. S. Thayer, Hafner Publishing Company, New York, 1953; Edward N. da Costa Andrade, *Sir Isaac Newton,* Collins, London, 1954; and Arthur E. Bell, *Newtonian Science,* E. Arnold, London, 1961.

ing verifiable knowledge, and next for his unqualified assertion that knowledge should be used.[10] No one more than Bacon popularized the idea of equating knowledge and power: "Human knowledge and human power meet in one." A friend of education without being a teacher himself, and a promoter of science while lacking the credentials of a first-rate scientist, Bacon exerted a strong influence on realism and helped usher in the modern age.

Bacon's principal writings most often mentioned in intellectual histories are *Novum Organum*, *New Atlantis*, and *The Advancement of Learning*. In the first, Bacon idealized induction as a way of pushing back boundaries of knowledge—not (as with deduction) as a way of reworking and trying to squeeze new meaning out of things already known. While Bacon cannot be credited with the invention of induction, it is only fair to allot him considerable credit for its popularization at a time when deduction and syllogistic thinking were common in all classrooms. Although Bacon's preference was entirely clear, deduction was not summarily rejected: it was good mental exercise, Bacon agreed, and could be used in the schools when more important employments were already cared for.[11]

In *New Atlantis* Bacon shows us, as all utopian writings hope to, how men can lead ideal lives providing they follow certain social, political, and intellectual patterns. Making use of inductive techniques and emphasizing, moreover, the usefulness of knowledge, *New Atlantis* displays a utopian community where inhabitants cooperate not only in discovering knowledge important to their lives but also in applying it in a harmonious, democratic way.[12]

Although Bacon's isolation from pedagogy was obvious (an abundance of evidence supports the fact that he seldom spoke the language of education), his long-range influence on schools and learning was considerable. Along with other realists of his age, he emphasized man's need for knowing the real, physical world in which he lived, and for having methods of converting that knowledge to useful social purposes. In praising knowledge for use Bacon was, in effect, telling future gen-

---

[10] Francis Bacon, *The Advancement of Learning, and Novum Organum*, rev. ed., John Wiley & Sons, Inc., New York, 1944, pp. 280–281; S. H. Mellone, *The Dawn of Modern Thought*, Oxford University Press, New York, 1930, pp. 16–21; and James G. Crowther, *Francis Bacon, the First Statesman of Science*, Cresset Press, London, 1960, pp. 291–295.

[11] Bacon, *op. cit.*, pp. 180–185; and see Benjamin Farrington, *Francis Bacon, Philosopher of Industrial Science*, H. Schuman, New York, 1949, pp. 79–85.

[12] Francis Bacon, *The Advancement of Learning and New Atlantis*, Oxford University Press, New York, 1906; and see Paolo Rossi, *Francis Bacon: From Magic to Science*, University of Chicago Press, Chicago, 1968.

erations of teachers and students to follow a plan of teaching that would allow them to be more versatile, more effective members of society.[13]

RENÉ DESCARTES (1596–1650)

Like Bacon, Descartes eschewed both educational theory and the classroom; he was not especially interested in, nor attracted to, distinctively pedagogical issues. Philosophically, Descartes portrays a complex combination of idealism and realism. His "Cogito ergo sum" (I think, therefore I am) and his ontological argument for the existence of God—"I am able to think of God, a perfect being, because God has implanted the idea"—put him on common ground with fairly orthodox idealism.[14] His realism, however, was also orthodox; he affirmed positively the reality of the external physical world, a world that men could know if they devised proper means. Descartes' means were highly scientific, depending on tested methods wherein mathematics was given pride of place.[15]

Although Descartes' theory of knowledge frequently sustained various forms of rationalism, its effects on realistic pedagogy should not for that reason be discounted. Rationalism began with an idea, and in the froth and foam of mental processes gave the idea meaning, sometimes without ever testing it against the data of sense-knowledge or day-to-day experience. This was not what Bacon wanted, nor was it a practice a realist like Comenius could approve, but it did point to one highly important element in the education of men: the power of the human mind. So realists could accept Descartes' affirmation of mental power, and count it a plank in their educational theory, and then use their own pedagogical devices to perfect this power of mind. Neither Comenius nor his erudite follower John Locke was concerned so much with what was used to form and perfect man's mental processes as with the outcome of the process itself. They liked useful curricula, it is true, and they used them whenever possible. But they could also embrace

[13] Bacon, *The Advancement of Learning and New Atlantis*, pp. 260–263; and Karl R. Wallace, *Francis Bacon on the Nature of Man*, University of Illinois Press, Urbana, 1967, pp. 101–107.

[14] René Descartes, *Descartes' Philosophical Writings*, selected and translated by Norman Kemp Smith, The Macmillan Company, New York, 1952, p. 81; and see Jacques Maritain, *Three Reformers: Luther, Descartes, Rousseau*, Charles Scribner's Sons, New York, 1928.

[15] René Descartes, *Discourse on Method*, translated with an introduction by Laurence J. Lafleur, Liberal Arts Press, New York, 1960; and Albert G. A. Balz, *Descartes and the Modern Mind*, Yale University Press, New Haven, Conn., 1952, pp. 470–476.

school subjects whose chief merit was in mental discipline, because they believed that such studies could contribute to the making of strong minds.[16]

The goal uppermost in Descartes' system of thought was certainty, and in this context his philosophy affected education. He was impressed with mathematics as a principal means for obtaining positive knowledge about the mechanisms of nature, and he was no less impressed with the power of human minds to construct a mathematical apparatus and use it to achieve certitude. Descartes tilled the subsoil of educational reform. The precision and certitude made evident in mathematics were transferred to all human problems, and realist educators were quick to see great educational promise in their emancipation from the humanistic and Scholastic theories of the past. In capitalizing on positivism, however, education was made to take a precarious path between realism and rationalism, and in negotiating this narrow pathway the hopes and promises of educators often fell short of their genuine aspirations.

WOLFGANG RATKE (ALSO RATICH) (1571–1635)

It would be a very liberal interpretation of the meaning of the term "science" that would permit its use in connection with the work of Ratke. But to some extent Ratke's work does represent a development in the same direction that the exact sciences were taking. Advocating the use of the vernacular in formal education, a recommendation by no means original with him, he gave attention to what he called the "natural" method of learning. Following the natural rules of learning, some of which were faintly implied in his work, students might be expected to be able to learn twice as much in half the time. This, of course, opened the door to pansophic emphases in education that were added by Comenius and others, but in the work of Ratke the motivating force was not encyclopedic knowledge—something that he approved—but natural learning. To develop this natural method of learning was the motivating purpose behind all of Ratke's endeavors. Thus he began, somewhat awkwardly, it is true, the development of an educational method which in its more polished phases is associated with the names of Comenius, Locke, Rousseau, Pestalozzi, Froebel, and Herbart.[17]

[16] See Walter B. Kolesnik, *Mental Discipline in Modern Education,* University of Wisconsin Press, Madison, 1958, pp. 111–118; and M. L. Cuff, *The Educational Theory of John Locke,* The Catholic Education Press, Washington, D. C., 1923, pp. 41–55.

[17] John W. Adamson, *Pioneers of Modern Education,* Cambridge University Press, New York, 1905, p. 105.

Ratke was one of the most unusual men ever to concern himself with education. Apart from all else, the thing that stands out about the man and his work is that he hoped to keep his methodology secret. Almost from the beginning, his work had something mysterious about it. The contradiction in his methods (for how could educational reforms really be brought about if the reformer refused to put his means for reform in the public domain?) revealed a basic and perhaps an indelible contradiction in the man. Born at Wilster in Holstein, Ratke attended the Hamburg Gymnasium and afterward studied philosophy at Rostock, a university of some repute. He pursued a theological course, for he had long aspired to the Lutheran ministry, but a speech impediment forced him to turn to some other type of social work. Perhaps his interest in education was developed quite naturally, or possibly it was a kind of second choice. At any rate, Ratke undoubtedly possessed admirable tools for the trade of a teacher, and was especially well schooled in languages. He was a linguist who spoke and wrote with considerable facility in Hebrew, Arabic, Latin, Greek, and German.[18]

Ratke made his first appearance on the educational scene when he proposed to Prince Moritz of Orange a new method of teaching, a method which he claimed to have invented. In general terms—and this is the only way in which Ratke ever discussed his novel method—his proposition to the prince claimed that (1) the languages—Hebrew, Greek, Latin, and others—could be taught to young and old more effectively and in a shorter time than ever before; (2) a school could be established in which all the arts and sciences could be taught more effectively than ever before; (3) a single language could be adopted in the principality, a measure which would facilitate the administration of civil affairs; and (4) a single religion could be accepted, a simple procedure which would promote domestic and spiritual peace and tranquility.[19]

The prince was apparently not convinced that Ratke could perform up to the level of his promises, and he showed little or no interest in the universal method of instruction that Ratke claimed to have at his command. The most important part of this method, at least at this time, was the provision that all instruction would begin with the vernacular and would move upward and onward from there. Since this idea was not cogent enough to secure employment for Ratke, he took his method and left Orange. We meet him again in the city of Frankfort, where he

[18] K. Seiler, *Das Pädagogische System W. Ratkes,* Erlangen, 1931, pp. 17–28.

[19] Henry Barnard, *German Teachers and Educators,* Brown and Gross, Hartford, Conn., 1878, p. 67.

presented himself to the city fathers and offered to use his universal method in the city's schools. This was about 1612. Before anything could come of the proposition, although it has been said that some money was given to him by the city as a retainer and that an offer was made to provide his venture with the physical facilities that were needed, Ratke left Frankfort and went to Augsburg. Apparently the city of Augsburg had invited Ratke to establish a school there, although in actual fact we know nothing of the way he spent his time in Augsburg. He returned to Frankfort in 1617. Again he approached the city fathers and asked them to appoint an agent to whom he might explain his educational plan. The city council did appoint such an agent, with whom Ratke had several meetings. Eventually the agent made his report to the council, and the council, in turn, informed Ratke that he had its permission to apply elsewhere for an educational position.[20]

Ratke's big chance was not long in coming. In 1618 he was invited by Ludwig von Anhalt Köthen to undertake the work of educational reform in his principality. On April 10, 1816, Ratke arrived in Köthen to begin the work that he had promised the prince he would do. Special buildings, assistants, printing presses, and all the things that Ratke had requested for his work were either ready and waiting for him or were soon put at his disposal. Ratke was apparently given a free hand in bringing his schools into existence. He was, moreover, given every assistance in setting up a school that was to operate as a training school for teachers in his method. As an interesting sidelight, it might be mentioned that the prince was so confident of the work that Ratke could do that he promulgated a miniature compulsory-attendance law. If Ratke's method was any good, the prince was not going to have it wasted.

The schools that Ratke established were six-class schools. The first three classes—perhaps the first three years—were conducted in the vernacular, and the vernacular language was included in the curriculum as a subject of instruction. Beginning with the fourth class, Latin was introduced. From then on it was the main subject of instruction, although Greek was introduced in the sixth class.

The actual workings of Ratke's schools are little known. There is no question but that he ran into some difficulty, for in October of 1619, about a year and a half after coming to Köthen, he was imprisoned by the prince. He remained in prison until about the middle of 1620 and was released only after he had signed a declaration that he had "claimed

[20] R. H. Quick, *Educational Reformers,* D. Appleton & Company, Inc., New York, 1897, pp. 103–118.

and promised more than he knew or could bring to pass." [21] Whether or not the real reasons for Ratke's fall from favor can be found in the educational plans and practices he espoused cannot be answered definitely here. It may be suggested, however, that the reasons were not wholly educational. Ratke was a strong, uncompromising Lutheran; the principality in which he was working was committed unequivocally to the Calvinistic Reformed Church. The religion taught in Ratke's school was, in doctrine and form, the religion in which he himself believed. This was a kind of arrogance that the citizens of the place, to say nothing of the prince, would not long accept. It was hinted, also, that the discipline of the school was somewhat less rigid than the citizens of that time and place thought they had a right to expect, and they complained that too much time was wasted on recreation. In addition, they opposed the speed which was one of the cornerstones of Ratke's educational plan. He had, after all, promised to do twice as much as had normally been done in only half the time. Speed was of the essence. This commitment to speed, however, led, it is said, to passing students too quickly from one level of instruction to another without being certain that they were ready to take the step up. There were complaints, possibly rumors, that the students did not write well.

After his bitter experience in Köthen, Ratke wandered around Europe. It seems unlikely that he ever again obtained a favorable position as a teacher or director of education. Nonetheless, he was a fairly good publicity agent for his own cause. He spread the word that he really did have a secret method of teaching, one that was far more successful than anything yet invented; but he refused to let anyone know what this method was. Even the great Comenius wrote to him, asking for some of the details of the method, but to no avail. Perhaps it was not as secret as he thought. From his actual teaching experiences and from the emphasis which he made in pedagogy, we can reconstruct fairly well his principles of teaching. The recommendations which Ratke made, or implied that he would make, may be inferred from his general outlook.

1. A natural method of learning should be followed. Though Ratke nowhere spells out what this natural method is, we should not be too severe with him for what is apparently only an oversight. He had an intuition that there was a natural method of learning, but he was unable to go much beyond this. Much of modern pedagogical thought begins with a similar intuition.

[21] Frederick Eby, *The Development of Modern Education*, 2d ed., Prentice-Hall, Inc., Englewood Cliffs, N. J., 1952, p. 165.

2. Only one thing should be learned at a time.

3. Repetition is necessary for impression. Ratke accepted a principle of learning here, repetition, that has almost always been accorded a position of importance in any hierarchy of learning principles.

4. The natural method of learning that Ratke suggested prompted him to begin all instruction with the vernacular. When the students undertook Latin, they did not study Latin grammar first. Rather, they gained a knowledge of the Latin tongue by reading and speaking, and later learned grammatical structure by its application to what they had read. This innovation in the teaching of a language is certainly a part of the general realistic outlook, and may well have been Ratke's most important contribution to the history of pedagogy.

5. Motivation was to come from the desire or interest of the student to learn something about the subject that was put before him. Ratke was violently opposed to compulsion and harsh methods in teaching, and the discipline in the schools that he managed was always mild. But this refusal of his to accept fear as the most effective motive for learning often led not to praise but to severe criticism of his work.

6. Rote memory was little employed as a technique for learning in Ratke's plan or in the schools that he operated. He aimed at understanding. This, too, is a sound principle, which today is accepted by all teachers.

7. Finally, it may be said, Ratke had such complete confidence in the method he devised that he claimed everything should be taught according to it. Of course, if Ratke did discover a natural method of learning, it would be hard to see why it should not be applied to all learning experiences.[22]

We have suggested above that it is difficult to evaluate the merit or the influence of Ratke's so-called "secret method" or his educational plan. In spite of this, we can say that Ratke broke ground for Comenius and that his most important contribution to the history of education was that he prepared the way for a greater man.

John Amos Comenius (1592–1670)

Accepted customs and social conventions are seldom altered apart from determined efforts to preserve them. Interwoven, as it must be, with all social institutions, education offers an excellent illustration of cultural lag; and in the seventeenth century, despite the advocacy for reform coming from scientists and realists, educational reform was often made

[22] On these points see Quick, op. cit., pp. 109–118.

to mark time. Seventeenth-century European social climate, following centuries of intellectual ferment, social unrest, and multiple illustrations of the inhumanity of men toward men, was unquestionably ready for change—but the nature of this change was defined in the critical areas of religion and politics.

The period of the Reformation saw an attempt by certain devout Christians, angered at the laxity and even worldly arrogance of the Roman Catholic clergy, to branch out on their own in the foundation of religious sects which would provide for their salvation. Salvation, at this time, was not only concerned with the period of life after death, but with the salvation of the earthly dignity of man and with materialistic success leading toward the ultimate, heavenly reward.

Not only were these new religious sects lacking in true, international leadership and organization, they were also subject to the political vagaries of the rulers and princes of the independent states of Europe. The resultant conflicts which arose were, therefore, both political and religious. A Catholic prince was able to secure the assistance of the militant Jesuit order, and with the Jesuits' more unified chain of command and authority, was better able to rout the Protestant forces struggling for recognition and survival in his country. A Protestant ruler, on the other hand, oppressed his Catholic opposition by both political and military action, occasionally securing the assistance of sympathetic, neighboring princes.

The so-called "Religious Peace of Augsburg," in 1555, did little to alleviate the situation. The effect, really, was to legalize these religious divisions by placing final authority for the determination of a state's religion in the hands of the ruler of each state. Under such authority no freedom of religion, as it is known today, existed in many countries.

John Amos Comenius was a Protestant with definite convictions against the claims of the papacy in Rome. To Comenius the only authority for the religious guidance of mankind lay in the interpretation of the Bible, the only true source for the word of God. The pope was the anti-Christ, and the Catholic clergy representatives of a group seeking only secular power. So firmly was Comenius convinced of his stand that he even urged the Jesuits to see the error of their ways and follow him.

The sect to which Comenius belonged was known as the Unitas Fratrum, or Unity of Brethren. The Unity had been in existence since 1467, at which time

> . . . over sixty delegates met in a small village and chose three laymen as candidates for the priesthood. These were ordained by the laying-on of hands by the assembled group. But the youngest of them, having

been chosen by lot the chief among the three, later received an additional ordination to the episcopal office; this ordination was performed by the priest Michael, who possessed Roman Catholic ordination to begin with. . . . Thus originated the most truly national of the Bohemian religious communions—the Unity of Brethren.[23]

With this unorthodox procedure for ordination to the priesthood, the Unity repudiated its belief in the apostolic succession formerly adhered to. The die was cast, and the struggle for survival of this new sect began.

The conflict between Protestant and Catholic forces continued in Bohemia under wavering rule, culminating in the Thirty Years' War, which broke out in 1618. Although the irate Protestants expelled the Jesuits for "all time" from Bohemia at the start of this religious war, the tide of battle turned in 1620 with the defeat of the Czech-Moravian forces at the Battle of White Mountain. Emperor Ferdinand II, with the help of the Jesuits, forced Roman Catholicism upon the entire Czech nation. The nobility had the choice of becoming Catholic or leaving; the peasants had no choice. Comenius, whose aversion to the Catholic Church was well known, was forced into hiding, and later into exile from his native land.

To many who have studied the history of education the name of John Amos Comenius is that of a pioneering educational theorist. He has been called an educational reformer and the father of modern educational theory and practice. His best known work is *The Great Didactic*, in which many of his ideas on education are set forth. Initially he makes proposals for a standardized, thorough, and humane system of teaching and learning. Many stop with this general concept, or view the attempts of Comenius as a chapter of the past containing some "good ideas." A more detailed analysis of this man's work seems warranted out of deference to his influence in the whole field of education.

To know Comenius, we must first understand the basic principles of his philosophy. Although he is thought of primarily as an educator, this aspect of his life and work was really secondary. Primarily, John Amos Comenius was a man of God. His life motivation was to serve God. He realized this ambition when, in 1618, at the age of twenty-four, he was ordained a priest in the Unity of Brethren. He was not lacking in educational experience, however, for he had been teaching at a school of the Unity for two years prior to his ordination.[24]

---

[23] M. Spinka, *John Amos Comenius: That Incomparable Moravian,* University of Chicago Press, Chicago, 1943, p. 10.

[24] F. Kozik, *The Sorrowful and Heroic Life of John Amos Comenius,* State Educational Publishing House, Prague, 1958, p. 21.

In addition to being a religious man and an educator, Comenius was a humanitarian. He had suffered enough under political and religious persecution to know some of the needs of mankind. In his early schooling he had experienced the rigors of the heartless, inefficient methods of the time. To complete his qualities, he was an idealist. The combination of all the above facets of his personality made him a potential force for the good of mankind through education. His travels while in exile added an international approach to his proposals for educational reform. Although his first loyalty was to his own group of Brethren, he continued to work in exile for the betterment of mankind in many countries and unselfishly gave the benefits of his wisdom wherever and whenever he found a receptive ear.

Comenius was born in 1592 in Nivnitz in Moravia. Moravia, located in the center of today's Czechoslovakia, was then, as it is now, in the heart of a troubled sector of Europe. Comenius' early education had been strictly religious. At the age of twelve, after having lost his parents, he lived with an aunt and attended an elementary school for less than two years. The methods in the school were painful and crude. At sixteen he went to a Latin school run by the Unity of Brethren, and there his love for learning was kindled. A nobleman, Count Zerotin, aided the young Comenius in his studies, urging him to continue to the priesthood.

After a brief visit to Amsterdam in 1612, Comenius began to study his life's work, theology, at the University of Heidelberg in 1613. Here he started the ambitious project of a Czech-Latin dictionary, which was to take him forty-four years to complete. In 1616 he obtained a position at a school in Prague, where he taught for two years prior to his ordination in 1618. Almost at once after becoming a priest, Comenius was made pastor of a parish in Fulnek, which was an especially troubled area in the year that marked the beginning of the Thirty Years' War. Fulnek was ravaged in 1620, and Comenius went into hiding. His parishioners and friends were able to hide him for eight years. But in 1628 he gave up his life of concealment and left his native land for the city of Leszno, Poland, which was to be his second home until 1656.

Throughout his life Comenius was a prolific writer. We have already mentioned his long-term work on a Czech-Latin dictionary. In 1612 he wrote *Labyrinth of the World,* in which he chided the pseudo-scholars of the day for their claims to be teaching the seven liberal arts. In 1614 he wrote *A Theater of All Things,* a sixteen-volume encyclopedia in Czech. This work, the first of its kind, was written by a twenty-two-year-old university student. Two years later he published

a small but complete Latin grammar, because he was not entirely satisfied with the grammars that were then in use. While in exile, from 1628
to 1631, he wrote *Janua Linguarum Reserata* (*Gate of Tongues Un-
locked*), which made him famous throughout Europe for his shifting
of the approach of Latin instruction from words to things. This book
employed the Baconian principle of an inductive, scientific method of
study and led to the proposal of a lifetime dream, the pansophic college.[25]

Whenever Comenius was in exile, and this was often and for extended periods of time, he never gave up the desire to live in his home
country. His travels throughout Europe included stays in England,
Sweden, and Hungary, where he gave the benefit of his knowledge
and ideas to any who requested them. In England, his close friendship
with Samuel Hartlib was due to the great encouragement Hartlib and
others gave to his pansophic theories. In keeping with his humanitarianism, Comenius yearned for the establishment of a pansophic college
which would be of benefit to the whole world. In such a college the
universal knowledge of the centuries, compiled by the best scholars
of the day, would be amassed for the betterment of mankind. The
breadth of such a task is easy to appreciate. No such dream has ever
been realized. It is little wonder that the troubled era in which Comenius lived did not see its attainment.

With his exile in 1628 Comenius had additional time to spend on
educational reform. The followers of the Unity were widely dispersed,
but Comenius looked forward to the time when they might return to
Moravia and began to prepare the way for them by writing his greatest
treatise on education, *The Great Didactic*. He finished this work about
1632. That it did not make much impression on the educational world
at that time was probably due to the fact that the work was written in
Czech. In 1657 it was translated into Latin, and from that time on it was
somewhat better known. The original Czech manuscript was discovered in Lissa in 1841 and was printed in 1849. The first complete English translation was made in 1896.[26]

Into *The Great Didactic* Comenius poured his soul, with the firm

[25] Keatinge, *op. cit.*, pp. 231–238; and see P. R. Cole, *Alsted, A Neglected Educator*, Collins, Ltd., Sydney, 1910, pp. 17–21; and W. S. Monroe, *Comenius and the
Beginnings of Educational Reform*, Charles Scribner's Sons, New York, 1900, pp.
82–83.

[26] Keatinge, *op. cit.*, p. v.; and see R. F. Young, *Comenius in England, 1641–1642*,
Oxford University Press, New York, 1932; and John Amos Comenius, *De Rerum
Emendatione Consultatio Catholica*, edited by J. Cervenka and V. T. Miskovsila-
Kozakova, Publishing House of the Czechoslovak Academy of Sciences, Prague,
1966.

conviction that all men could be taught all things to make them learned, virtuous, and pious. The firsthand knowledge Comenius had of the crude educational methods of the time, together with his devotion to God's work, demanded of him that he be instrumental in correcting the faulty ways of mankind through an infallible system of teaching and learning. Comenius wrote:

> Didactic signifies the art of teaching. . . . We venture to promise A Great Didactic, that is to say, the whole art of teaching all things to all men, and indeed of teaching them with certainty, so that the result cannot fail to follow; further, of teaching them pleasantly, that is to say, without annoyance or aversion on the part of the teacher or pupil, but rather with the greatest enjoyment for both; further, of teaching them thoroughly, not superficially and showily, but in such a manner as to lead to true knowledge, to gentle morals, and to the deepest piety . . . that we may lay the foundations of the universal art of founding universal schools.[27]

The thoroughgoing character of Comenius' aspirations is apparent from the above quotation. He realized that the proposal of such a method would be met by many doubts or, even worse, would be ignored. Invoking God's help, as he does throughout the work, Comenius appeals in his "Dedicatory Letter" to the leaders of human society—rulers, pastors, and parents—to realize the sacred trust which has been given to mankind in the form of little children. Scripture points to the command of God that elders must be "as little children" to attain salvation. Children must, therefore, be given their rightful place in the world. Children are the future older generation, and great care must be taken of their education in order that the corruptness of mankind may be remedied.

To the persons and agencies concerned, Comenius recommends the use of teaching as an art. Parents, schoolmasters, students, schools, states, churches, and heaven itself, would derive the benefits from this system. The attainment of this ideal through education would, in Comenius' view, provide mankind with knowledge, morals, and piety, so that they would live happily on earth and, ultimately, in heaven.[28]

The purpose of education is logically presented by Comenius in the first chapters of *The Great Didactic*. Scripturally, man is seen to be the most excellent of things created by God. Reason, given to man, permits him to know that there is a life beyond this life and that existence on

[27] John Amos Comenius, *The Great Didactic*, translated by M. W. Keatinge, Adam and Charles Black, London, 1896, in the "Greeting to the Reader."

[28] *Ibid.*, p. 166.

earth is therefore merely preparatory. For life in accordance with God's will man needs erudition, virtue or seemly morals, and religion or piety. These primary aims of life—learning, virtue, and piety—must be attained, and the surest way to attain them is through education.

That man is capable of being educated is evident by the presence of the sense organs, through which the rational soul can perceive everything in the universe. In one of his many analogies Comenius compares the brain, the workshop of thought, to wax, which either receives the impress of a seal or furnishes the material for small images. This comparison is similar to the *tabula rasa* concept later proposed by John Locke. Further analogies between the making of objects from materials and the formation of the intellects of men are used by Comenius to explain the necessity of education. Education is compared to the tools applied to inanimate objects to perfect them. He refers to the adage, "As the twig is bent the tree's inclined," in stressing the necessity for education from the child's most infant years.

Comenius' foresight can be detected in his proposal to educate both boys and girls of all social classes in common schools. The inability of parents to educate and train their children is taken for granted by Comenius, as is the need for wise and generous teachers. All men are formed in the image of God, and according to Comenius all men have a common destiny. The same commonness should apply to education. Although Comenius stresses the universality of education, he does not claim that all men should be taught identically. Only that which concerns man as man should be taught to all, for in later life some things will be of more use to one man and other things to another. Again Comenius returns to his theme: Knowledge, virtue, and piety must be acquired in order to serve God and oneself.

Following the admission that children differ and that education need not be identical for all, Comenius describes the conditions prevalent in the imperfect schools up to and including those of the seventeenth century. Schools, heretofore only for the rich, must be made available to all, and teachers must adopt an approach that will make learning more pleasant. Comenius acknowledges the differences in the intellectual capacities of children, and would have a brighter student assist in the instruction of slower ones. The instructor must recognize individual differences. Following this, the proposal that schools must be run with clocklike precision appears to many to be a contradiction in Comenius' plan.

Having laid the groundwork for the establishment of reformed schools, Comenius outlines, in the last half of *The Great Didactic*, the requirements for the methods he proposes for teaching and learning. A statement of first importance is that the subjects being taught should be geared to the ability and maturity of the students. In addition, examples of the application of what is to be learned should precede the memorization of mere rules, and subjects should be integrated and graduated for more thorough comprehension. Other prime requirements would be readiness and perseverance on the part of the pupil and the proper environment of the school itself. With the realization of these requirements, many of the conditions necessary to the development of wisdom, virtue, and piety are also realized.[29]

Methodology was very important to Comenius. He considered it to be so crucial a factor in teaching that he declared one "right method" should be used for all teaching. This, no doubt, was the natural method of which we heard so much from Ratke. Ideally, one method of teaching applied to every subject would simplify the task of the teacher and make learning somewhat easier for the student. Unfortunately, the hope for achieving such a method is based on invalid assumptions about learning and knowledge.[30] Perhaps Comenius did not really intend to go as far as to say there should be only one method for teaching; perhaps he was only striving for greater organization in teaching during a chaotic period in education's history.

The principles of thoroughness in teaching advanced by Comenius in *The Great Didactic* seem to be quite sound. He admonished teachers to teach only those subjects which would be of some use to students, maintaining that useless subjects could never be defended, and he directed that they be taught without interruption and only after careful preparation or cultivation. Later learning was to be based on previous learning, and subjects linked within and among themselves. Lesson plans were required of all teachers.

Many have questioned the size of classes proposed by Comenius. He seemed to believe not only that large classes were necssary at that time from a social point of view, but that they were also desirable educationally. He wrote that teachers would be more attentive to their work if their classes were large. By large classes he meant possibly as many as two hundred students. Of course, in order that anything at all should be accomplished under such conditions, systematic sectioning of students was required, with key students supervising and tutoring perhaps twenty others.

Utilizing many of the foregoing principles, Comenius explained the application of the senses in learning the sciences. A student must keep

[29] *Ibid.*, p. 168.

[30] See J. Needham, *The Teacher of Nations,* Cambridge University Press, New York, 1942, pp. 71–73.

the eye of his mind pure and see that the object is brought near to it. He must pay attention and proceed from one object to another, using a suitable method. In the matter of learning the arts, the proper use of materials can be acquired only through practice. For the teaching of the arts Comenius prescribed the use of models, and the instructor, he insisted, must teach by demonstration and practice instead of by words alone.

Comenius was never opposed to the languages. He was convinced that they needed to be in the curricula of the schools, but he objected to making the study of language an end in itself. He saw the languages as tools or instruments for learning and communication and was unwilling to isolate them from the real problems of life and living. For this reason he was often critical of the language teaching of his day; he was especially critical of the aridity of language study and of its irrelevancy. In his own system, which he set forth in the textbooks he prepared, words were joined to objects—Comenius was the first to illustrate a Latin-grammar text—and a language was learned only as thoroughly as was considered necessary. In such an academic context the vernacular was given a place of primary importance; Greek, Latin, and Hebrew followed it. Only one language was to be learned at a time.[31]

COMENIUS' LEVELS OF EDUCATION

Proceeding from his understanding of human nature, Comenius outlined a distinct series of schools that was designed to take a student from birth to maturity with the proper organization, gradation, and integration of studies. The first of these four six-year schools was the Mother School, covering a period from birth to the age of six. With the mother as the tutor, the child was to learn by association of things with words. Of course Comenius could see from firsthand experience that few mothers were ready to assume the responsibility for launching their children on their educational careers. Yet whether they were ready or not, they had been starting their children's education for centuries and would continue to do so. Taking a realistic position in the matter, Comenius decided to help mothers prepare themselves. He wrote a book called *The School of Infancy*, in which he tried to give directions to mothers on how to educate their youngsters during the first six years of their lives.[32]

During the second six-year period, boys and girls would attend the

[31] Comenius, *The Great Didactic*, p. 86.

[32] J. A. Comenius, *The School of Infancy*, edited by E. M. Eller, University of North Carolina Press, Chapel Hill, 1956, pp. 21–22.

Vernacular School. Here proficiency would be developed and to some extent perfected in reading and writing the mother tongue, and skill would be developed in counting. Singing was to be taught, as were various hymns and Bible stories. The principles of morality were to be taught by the use of rules and by practice in the art of living. Economics and politics were to be taught on a rather elementary level; that is, they would never go beyond the assumed needs of the students. General world history, covering the creation, fall, and redemption of man, was to be presented, along with geography and topography. At this point in Comenius' educational plans we note the emergence of a "theory of education for life," for here in the Vernacular School the curriculum was to provide opportunities for study of the mechanical arts. This is one way in which Comenius acknowledged the natural differences among students. This level of education, the Vernacular School, was to have been the last formal education for many of the students in it; girls would always cease to pursue formal education at this level, as would boys who lacked real academic interests or abilities.[33] The boys who were anticipating higher studies would proceed to the next level, the Latin School, for a term of six years.

The curriculum of the Latin School was designed to produce grammarians, dialecticians, rhetoricians, arithmeticians, and geometricians, musicians, and astronomers. In addition, the boys were to be physicists, geographers, chronologers, historians, moralists, and finally theologians.[34] Boys who followed such a course of studies in the Latin School would be considered to have a solid foundation upon which their final training in the university could be built. The last level was, of course, the University School, a school which was open to the highly qualified and which, in addition to its teaching function, recognized the university's function in research.[35]

Classes in the Vernacular School were to be held for two hours in the morning and for two hours in the afternoon. Each year of the six would be set aside for a specific class, and each class would have its work assigned to it. It was only after much study and deliberation that Comenius arrived at the right order of study. He tried to determine what the students' previous experiences would permit them to study with the greatest benefits. He decided finally that the grammar class should be held during the first year of the six, to give the students

---

[33] O. H. Lang, *Comenius: His Life and Principles of Education,* E. L. Kellog and Company, New York, 1891, p. 65.

[34] J. A. Comenius, *The Analytical Didactic,* translated by V. Jelinek, University of Chicago Press, Chicago, 1953, pp. 168–169.

[35] Comenius, *The Great Didactic,* p. 412.

further basic foundations. The class in natural philosophy was next, followed by classes in mathematics, ethics, dialectics, and lastly rhetoric. In connection with the work of each of these classes, Comenius decreed that history should be studied, in order that every student might have a thorough knowledge of the events of the world, from ancient times to the present.

Writing on the universal and perfect order of instruction, Comenius attempted to justify his assurance of the future success of his methods by a comparison between the student being taught and a piece of paper on which print is impressed. Originally documents had to be hand-copied by many for distribution to the few. With the invention of the printing press, this situation was changed, and printed materials could be prepared by the few for distribution to the many. Not only would the new system of printing be faster, but it would also be more accurate. Once the type was set, the finished products were identical, and this identity was due to standardization. The analogy drawn by Comenius is easy to understand. The point where it touched education, particularly on the question of a single method, has been the subject of much discussion and, over the years, has led to a great difference of opinion. For his part, Comenius believed so deeply in the good that could be accomplished by the use of his standardized methods that he wanted the world to start using them at once. Their use, he wrote, would assure that "the entire youth of both sexes, none being excepted," would "quickly, pleasantly, and thoroughly, become learned in the sciences, pure in morals, trained to piety, and in this manner instructed in all things necessary for the present and for the future life." [36]

Comenius has been called a realist. He knew that his educational theories were somewhat advanced for the world in which he lived and that they could be applied only with great difficulty. He realized that surprisingly few teachers were prepared in such a way that they could follow his pedagogical advice. Even if qualified teachers were available, Comenius might well ask how the towns and villages were going to support them. Another obvious obstacle was the inability of children on the lower social and economic level to attend school. Usually they had to work at home or in the shops. If these obstacles were not enough, there was the opposition that came from the accepted educational opinion of the day. This opinion found expression among educators and politicians who did not want the world to change; they were entirely content with society as it was, and they wanted to keep it that way.

[36] *Ibid.*, pp. 166–168.

Yet one hope for making some inroads on the established opinion and practice of the time lay in the preparation and distribution of specially prepared textbooks. These were the products of Comenius' work and ideas. If they were used as tools in the schools and used with success, then the application of other more advanced ideas might be looked for with greater hope. Perhaps it was in this area, the preparation of textbooks for the schools, that Comenius made his greatest mark on his own time. Certainly the total effect of the work of Comenius for seventeenth-century educational reform was not great. The majority of the reforms that he advocated were destined to lie dormant, only to be put into effect one by one as men in changing times demanded, and to some extent obtained, educational reform. Free and universal education, open to all and compulsory for all of both sexes, is now a reality in the world's most advanced countries. Comenius' ideas for preschool home training surpass even the most advanced modern ideas of the kindergarten's role in public education. Instruction in the native tongue of the pupil, graded subject matter, psychological adjustment to the maturing student, all are accepted without question in today's school programs. Parents and educators are willing to consider the nature of the child's mind and to correlate thoughts and things. History, geography, drawing, and manual training are now being given without any doubts as to their need or their worth, and schools try to gear their programs to bring life and learning as closely together as possible.

As we said before, the accepted customs of mankind cannot be changed quickly, and Comenius was aware of this. *The Great Didactic* proposed a reform in the field of education that must have appeared to the author, at times, to be little more than a dream. He knew it was possible to realize the fulfillment of this dream in a limited way and in particular localities, but he was enough of a realist to know that his voice was not strong enough to turn the educational tide in favor of the realistic views that he advocated. Nevertheless, in the face of great odds against him, he spoke out for educational reform. His voice was heard—but not until many years later, for it was the nineteenth rather than the seventeenth century that benefited most from Comenius' direct educational recommendations, and in the mid-twentieth century his expressions relative to international education stand out as prophetic anticipations.[37]

[37] N. M. Butler, *The Place of Comenius in the History of Education*, Bardeen, Syracuse, N. Y., 1892, p. 18; and S. S. Laurie, *John Amos Comenius*, Bardeen, Syracuse, N. Y., 1892, pp. 17–19.

Religious Education in the Seventeenth Century

Of all the movements promising to remake modern education, two of the most important attempted to keep religion and education close together. One was the work of the Brothers of the Christian Schools (the Christian Brothers), whose founder, St. John Baptist de la Salle, may be regarded as a pioneer of modern education. The other was Pietism, applied to education by August Hermann Francke.

THE CHRISTIAN BROTHERS

The Institute of the Brothers of the Christian Schools, founded by St. John Baptist de la Salle in 1684, inaugurated a plan for teaching which had its bases in the educational requirements of poor children in seventeenth-century France.[38] The Brothers' schools started as small, local institutions and for thirty or more years were unknown outside three dioceses in central France. During this interlude of scholastic germination, the Brothers reexamined old educational assumptions and concluded that instruction would have to suit the children using their schools. Since they were engaged in teaching poor boys of humble origins, this principle meant that the school's curriculum had to aim at preparing them for life without at the same time merely teaching them a trade. Whether boys who attended the Brothers' schools should be artisans, shopkeepers, or unskilled laborers was not a choice the teachers might make; they were to give their students a basic literary, religious, and moral education which would prove practical whatever their vocation, and the boys would choose what that was to be. When the Brothers' schools multiplied and extended to all of France, and then to other countries, this principle remained intact.

The Educational Accomplishments of the Brothers   The original and fundamental realization behind the work of the Brothers was that educational opportunities necessary for the human development of poor boys were generally denied them. They became concerned, then, first with elementary teaching, and developed a course of instruction broad enough to meet a boy's basic educational needs yet narrow enough to prepare him for the realities of life in society. Considering the realism of this purpose—for they never forgot who their students were—and the remarkable success they had in achieving it, we cannot wonder when John William Adamson, in his *Pioneers of Modern Education*, counts

[38] See W. J. Battersby, *De La Salle, A Pioneer of Modern Education*, Longmans, Green and Company, New York, 1949, p. 41.

the Christian Brothers among the most successful innovators in modern education.[39]

Along with the idea that opportunities for elementary education needed a more generous distribution in seventeenth-century France (in fact, as a necessary corollary to the idea) was the conviction that instruction should be in the vernacular. The Brothers could argue, as others before them had argued, that to take poor boys, whose social and economic horizons were limited to begin with, and feed them an educational diet of Latin grammar and literature, was both socially and educationally inconsistent. And in making their argument, the Brothers became the principal promoters of elementary education in the vernacular for poor boys. Yet, despite the cogency of their position, which seems too obvious to debate, their plan for teaching reform had spirited detractors. For a long time the Catholic hierarchy, who regarded the schools, especially in France, as a training ground for prospective clerics, refused to retreat from its traditional position that Latin should be taught in every school. Its members could not understand, no less approve, any school which as a matter of policy restricted or ignored Latin teaching. So, overcoming such opposition to the vernacular school took all of La Salle's talents of diplomacy and was, in fact, the most serious external challenge to his and his coworkers' reform efforts. Eventually, however, the Brothers convinced the bishops that their schools would do religion no harm and, moreover, that for most boys who came to the Brothers' schools, Latin would always be a useless and mysterious tongue.

One of the first weaknesses La Salle detected when he turned his attention to education and tried to work out a plan for elementary instruction was that the teachers were generally poorly prepared or not prepared at all for the kind of work they had to do in the schools. Some provisions may have been made for the preparation of teachers for higher and secondary schools, but little thought was given to the preparation of teachers for the elementary levels. This led La Salle in 1687 to establish a normal school, a teachers' training college, for the preparation of Brother teachers who were to conduct the schools of the Institute.[40] We have no clear record of any teachers' training school earlier than the one founded by and for the Brothers of the Christian Schools, although such projects were surely speculated about long before this. In 1439 a training center for grammar school masters was proposed at God's House, Cambridge, by William Byngham. Even before

[39] Adamson, *op. cit.*, p. 212.
[40] Edward A. Fitzpatrick, *La Salle, Patron of All Teachers*, The Bruce Publishing Company, Milwaukee, Wis., 1951, pp. 177–181.

this, there are evidences that the formal preparation of elementary school teachers was considered, but apparently no practical outcomes were achieved.

In addition to the regular schools conducted by the Brothers, schools were opened for young people who for one reason or another could not attend the regular schools. These were the Sunday Schools or the Continuation Schools of the Christian Brothers. Such schools did a great deal of good work, but they never became principal considerations in the educational work of the Brothers.

One of the things for which La Salle and the Christian Brothers are remembered is class or group instruction, sometimes called simultaneous instruction. It has not been uncommon to credit La Salle with having founded, discovered, or invented class methods of teaching. Actually, the practice of having one teacher teach several students at the same time is much older than the seventeenth century. It would be difficult, if not impossible, to assign either a date or an inventor to this method of teaching, for it goes back to the beginnings of formal education. But in the hands of the Brothers the method was thoroughly exploited and skillfully employed. The great Comenius was perhaps the most thoroughgoing advocate of simultaneous instruction, but it was the Christian Brothers who were most successful in developing it as a modern educational technique. They used it with skill for a hundred years while teachers in other elementary schools were using the conventional technique of individual instruction, a method which made the teacher a mere hearer of lessons. Without a method such as the Brothers perfected, popular elementary education would never have been possible.[41]

Along with the application of the technique of simultaneous teaching, the Brothers made greater and more effective use of monitors than had been made before or since in the history of education. It should be pointed out, however, that the Brothers never used monitors for instruction, an omission which made their employment of monitors essentially different from the system devised in later years by Joseph Lancaster and Andrew Bell.

The Work and Influence of La Salle   There is little reason to doubt that La Salle was a pioneer of modern education. Yet it was as a man of action, as an organizer and administrator of the Institute's schools, rather than as an elaborator of theories that he made his mark on education. We look for signs of La Salle's influence in deeds rather than in written words; we find them in institutions more than in books.

[41] Battersby, *op. cit.,* p. 165.

During the course of forty or more years in which La Salle was connected with education, there were a number of times when he was called upon to set down his thoughts on paper. These thoughts may be found in his letters and in some of his devotional works, as well as in the *Rule* of the Institute itself. His principal writing with a strict pedagogical character was *Conduct of the Schools,* a document which may be thought of as the *Ratio Studiorum* for the schools of the Brothers. Though the book was extremely useful to the Brothers who later established schools all over the world, its content illustrates the non-literary character of La Salle's educational efforts. It was not until after his death in 1719 that any known printed edition of the *Conduct* appeared, in 1720.[42]

Despite the tardy appearance of the work in printed form, in its essentials it had been in existence from the earliest years, when the Institute was but a small and little-known diocesan association. At Rheims the founder of the Christian Brothers had drawn up a set of directions for the Brothers to follow, and each of the Brother teachers had a manuscript copy. Since the *Conduct* cannot really be separated from the *Rule* of the Institute itself, we may assume that every Brother was especially familiar with the teaching directions that made up the *Conduct.* As the educational work of the Brothers recommended itself to other dioceses, *Conduct of the Schools* grew more detailed in content. The experience of the Brothers at Paris and elsewhere, but especially at Paris, led to a more rapid development of their special teaching technique, and this technique found a definite and permanent expression in a more complete edition of the *Conduct,* prepared by La Salle in 1695. This was still a manuscript edition, privately circulated. Even when the *Conduct* appeared in printed form, it was not given wide circulation. It was and is regarded as a teacher's manual for the Brothers of the Christian Schools to follow. This does not mean, of course, that it is not a pedagogical classic in its own right.

In any event, the *Conduct* is still, as it was in the seventeenth century, a living instrument for guiding teaching. It is not a stereotyped document that does not admit of addition or modification; La Salle himself made many changes in the *Conduct* during his own lifetime. As the educational needs of the world have changed and as we have come to know more and more about the science and art of education, the *Conduct* has been modified by the faithful followers of La Salle.

The 1720 edition of the *Conduct* helps us to picture the schools of the Brothers as they were conducted in the seventeenth century. Its

[42] See Francois de La Fontainerie, *The Conduct of the Schools of Jean Baptiste de la Salle,* McGraw-Hill Book Company, New York, 1935.

contents disclose both the organization of classes in the schools and the course of study pursued. If we try to summarize the contents of the *Conduct* in bold strokes, we might say that the great aim of the Brothers was to teach religion and to inculcate piety in their charges; that a secondary but still important aim was to give boys the kind of educational experience that would be valuable to them in the kind of world they were living in; and finally, that the means to achieve all of this, as grasped by the founder and through him by the Brothers, was the effective use of the simultaneous method for teaching large classes of children.

This technique of simultaneous teaching enabled the Brothers to wield considerably greater educational influence than either the number of Brother teachers or Christian Brothers' schools might suggest. In Western Europe generally, but especially in France, the Brothers became the respected custodians of elementary education, and in France in the eighteenth century were so highly regarded that they escaped the purge visited on religious teachers by advocates of secularism. In the United States the Christian Brothers engaged in secondary teaching (a thrust unusual for them in Europe), taught in a few colleges, and sometimes staffed parish elementary schools. It is fair to admit that the luster of their European school achievements was somewhat dimmed by transplantation in the United States.

PIETISM

How can one convey the meaning of Pietism as it found expression in Germany in the seventeenth century? Perhaps we may call it "realism with a soul." The realist educators were looking for the content of education and the inspiration for it in the real world, the world that could be experimented with, the world to which the inductive method could be applied. The Pietists were realists, too, at least in a way, for they tried to find in the message of Christ the content of education and the inspiration to preserve and extend it. The Pietists made their mark on religious history because of their opposition to authority and externalism and by emphasizing the inner workings of faith and religious feelings. In education, the Pietists, following the lead of the illustrious Francke (1663–1727), tried to subordinate all learning to a vital faith in the principles of Christian life.[43] Some Pietists may have gone so far as to assume that all learning is due to divine illumination. When this

[43] August Hermann Francke, *Pädagogische Schriften*, Beyer, Langensalza, 1885, pp. 17–21.

view was emphasized, that is to say, when it became fairly commonly believed that truth would come to one as a result of inspiration or of intuition rather than by the hard work of discursive learning, the movement began to lose both force and significance. But as long as it remained within the limits of a method that tries to promote efficiency in obtaining natural knowledge and in applying that knowledge for the good of the individual and mankind, Pietism accomplished a great deal of good.

August Hermann Francke was a thoroughgoing exponent of Pietism. Although he may not have been its religious leader, he was without question the greatest of Pietist educators. His fame rests mainly on his achievements in the field of educational opportunity; he opened schools and prepared teachers. He started a small school for the poor in 1695 and later added a boarding school, an orphanage, and an elementary school. In addition, he founded an institute for training teachers about 1700. It is estimated that Francke was directly or indirectly responsible for the creation of about two thousand elementary and secondary schools in Germany.[44] Anyone involved in the creation of so many schools, either directly or remotely, must be given some notice in the history of education.

The central theme dominating Francke's scholastic endeavors puts them on common ground with the techniques of Comenius' realism: All learning should begin with sensory data and experience; its content should be religious, useful, and real. Scientific knowledge was admitted to the curriculum, although it was regularly subordinated to religion and, in any case, was studied as part of a world view in which man's relationship to God was stressed with unrelenting zeal and devotion. The driving force behind pietistic education, as interpreted and applied by Francke, was to make religion a profound and vital reality in the life of every German child; the schools' objectives were distilled from this creed. With such clearly held religious motives, it was hard for any school to follow a conventional humanistic course, or to begin with the classical languages as both Luther and Melanchthon had recommended, although pietistic schools were always able to ratify some of the subjects common in the classical course of studies. But, at best, their relevance to religious piety was imprecise, and, in the end, reading the New Testament in German was praised as a more important accomplishment than studying Greek or Latin literature.

The service Pietism performed for learning is found mainly outside

[44] Koppel S. Pinson, *Pietism as a Factor in the Rise of German Nationalism*, Columbia University Press, New York, 1934, pp. 35–41.

the schoolroom, in a popularization of learning which, as we have said, led to the establishment of schools where German children who heretofore were neglected were now welcomed with enthusiasm. Once in the schools, however, apart from a determined religious zeal and a dedication to the theory that education is piety's best friend, these children were seldom exposed to a teaching program giving the principles of realist pedagogy a chance to operate freely. Yet, by stimulating interest in education, Pietists broke ground for a German system of schools, and thus played a highly significant role in the development of modern education.[45]

Germany was most affected by Francke's educational pietism, but the United States, too, felt his influence. Several of his coreligionists and some of his pedagogical followers came to America and, especially in Pennsylvania and Georgia, established schools following Francke's model.

THE EDUCATION OF GIRLS

Although most humanistic writers on education had given some space in their books to the proper training of girls, what they said must have been either unconvincing or unimportant, because schooling for girls remained well into the modern period one of the least cultivated areas in pedagogy. And neither Protestant nor Catholic educational reformers were especially effective or interested in altering this traditional and conventional lethargy. Unquestionably the Catholic religious orders for women (for example the Ursulines) broadened educational oportunity for girls, but, even at its best, women's education played an indefinite and unimportant role in the total educational picture.

François Fénelon, Bishop of Cambrai (France), redressed this attitude when, in 1687, he published his book *On the Education of Girls*. In this influential book he set forth a principle so simple that we wonder why it had not been made before, or even why its statement was necessary at all. Girls, he wrote, should be educated in a way that will prepare them for their station in life, and the proper vocation of a woman is to be the mother of a family. Fénelon could think of nothing more important than this. Girls should be able to read and write, they should know history, and some should even learn Latin, because this study would discipline their minds. But all should be trained to manage the affairs of a family. Clearly, Fénelon was more interested in a

---

[45] Francke, *op. cit.*, pp. 91–99; Barnard, *op. cit.*, pp. 167–169; and Eby, *op. cit.*, pp. 244–260.

woman's skill in housekeeping and child care than he was in her mental discipline. On direct pedagogical issues he was less prepared to make specific recommendations, yet he approved attention in female education to health, emotional formation, honesty, modesty, and freedom. And he expressed a cautious doubt about the efficacy of direct, formal instruction.

Had others been interested in the subject to which Fénelon addressed himself, he probably would have been heeded less. As it was, however, his attitudes not only filled a vacuum, as it were, but exerted an influence far out of proportion to their essential merit. When schoolmasters finished reading Fénelon's book, they had his doctrine: Girls should be educated—but not the same way boys are, because the minds of girls are different from boys' minds, and the vocation of their lives is totally different from boys' vocations. This doctrine, which had its most explicit codification in Fénelon's book, stood virtually unchallenged for a century after its formulation in *On the Education of Girls*.

John Locke (1632–1704)

Seventeenth-century education began with a tentative preference for realism and ended with a strong attachment to empiricism. The great Comenius, we know, was at once an advocate of realism and a promoter of a reformed pedagogy. Locke played a similar reforming role which, while lacking Comenius' breadth of educational vision, added an empirical dimension to Comenius' realism. Born in Wrington, England, where his father was an attorney, Locke received an excellent education at Westminster School, one of the famous English public schools, and at Christ Church College, Oxford. His penchant for study was extraordinary; he entered Oxford at about age twenty and was still there, working on a studentship, when he was fifty. During this long academic career Locke studied Greek, rhetoric, and ethics, taught a variety of subjects and tutored hundreds of students, and finished his university course with a medical degree.

Locke's place in intellectual history seems secure; his influence on the thought of later centuries was perhaps even greater outside than inside the educational arena. His written works disclose a seminal mind which could range almost effortlessly among the fields of government, philosophy, economics, education, and religion. He liked to think of himself as a philosopher (an opinion shared by other scholars, who sometimes call him the only authentic philosopher England ever produced), and in this estimate he was probably right. *Two Treatises on*

Government, an exercise in political philosophy, is undoubtedly his best-known and most influential book.[46]

LOCKE'S EDUCATIONAL WORKS

Having been directly involved with academic institutions and study throughout most of his life, John Locke's background qualified him to theorize about the problems of teaching and learning, and to express his thoughts to the waiting scholarly community. Oxford was his intellectual home for three decades, and in this university atmosphere his ideas on education were germinated. Yet, he was more than an armchair theorist, for his contacts with students enabled him to see firsthand the learning process in operation. In addition, because he knew that university students would not always be the best subjects for his study and observation, he sought contacts with children—especially the children of Lord Shaftesbury—and observed and recorded their intellectual development with scientific care.

Despite some inconsistency among his philosophical, psychological, and pedagogical writings (a fault not easily or briefly explained), Locke's contributions to educational theory and practice proved to be both valuable and progressive. In Locke's day, teachers were determined to make their students ornaments of erudition: They reverenced all signs of intellectual progress and studiously neglected physical training. Locke had definite notions about this neglect, and expressed his opinion with boldness. Quite possibly his most audacious departure from conventional educational practice was his assertion that the body must be properly trained if the mind is to be strong and good. Today we take this principle for granted, at least on the level of theory, but it took a bold man to say such an unconventional thing in the seventeenth century.

As an educational theorist, Locke's claim for attention rests mainly on *An Essay Concerning Human Understanding,* written in 1689, *Some Thoughts Concerning Education,*[47] published in 1693, and the incomplete and unrevised *Of the Conduct of the Understanding,* which first appeared in the posthumous edition of Locke's works in 1706. This latter short work, composed as a manual of self-instruction for young men, not only is complementary (and in many ways supplementary) to

---

[46] R. I. Aaron, *John Locke,* Oxford University Press, New York, 1937, p. 55; and H. R. Fox Bourne, *The Life of John Locke,* Harper and Row, Publishers, New York, 1876, vol. I, pp. 191–198.

[47] John Locke, *An Essay Concerning Human Understanding,* 28th ed., Tegg and Son, London, 1838; and John Locke, *Some Thoughts Concerning Education,* edited by R. H. Quick, Cambridge University Press, New York, 1934.

Some Thoughts, but also is important to an adequate appraisal of Locke's theory of education. Whereas *Some Thoughts* is mainly concerned with specific directions for physical, moral, and intellectual training, in the *Conduct* and the *Essay* Locke wrestles with the issue of cultivating man's rational element, a fundamental philosophical and psychological problem too important, Locke believed, to be left to schoolmasters. Schoolmasters may, of course, play some part in perfecting reason, but since the process must begin early in a person's life, even before teachers appear on the scene, mothers and fathers are its most important directors, and after them carefully selected tutors. Far from displaying the same undoubted confidence in school learning as Comenius and Francke, Locke preferred the auspices of a tutor. Indeed, for the most part his pedagogical affirmations must be weighed in a tutorial context.[48]

The genesis of *Some Thoughts Concerning Education* is interesting. A friend of John Locke's, Edward Clarke, wanted some advice concerning the education of his son, and realizing that educational questions were often foremost in Locke's mind, sought his help. In answer to Clarke's request, Locke wrote a series of letters. The letters, naturally enough, were written in the style one usually employs in friendly correspondence. A few years later, however, after the contents of the letters became more generally known, Locke's friends convinced him that he should collect the letters and publish them in book form. In the dedication of the printed work, Locke declared that the only thing different from the original letters was their order and a slight refinement in the style, designed to make it less intimate.[49] Locke did not have the time, or did not take the time, to publish his views on education in a carefully organized book on the subject. As a literary work, *Some Thoughts* suffered from its hurried publication; the work as a whole is highly repetitious.

In reviewing Locke's *Some Thoughts Concerning Education,* we must keep in mind: first, that Locke had no thought of writing about the education of ordinary people, since he makes clear that the letters are intended as guides to the education of young gentlemen; and second, that Locke's methods were intended for an individual system of instruction and not for the teaching of large numbers of students in a classroom.[50]

[48] See John W. Adamson (ed.), *The Educational Writings of John Locke,* Cambridge University Press, New York, 1922, pp. 12–13.

[49] B. Rand (ed.), *The Correspondence of John Locke and Edward Clarke,* Harvard University Press, Cambridge, Mass., 1927, p. 27.

[50] Cuff, *op. cit.,* pp. 28–29.

Locke's educational aim is threefold: (1) vigor of body, (2) virtue of the soul, with its manifestations in good breeding and wisdom in conduct, and (3) knowledge, or mental acquirements. Knowledge, the last of the three-point aim, is also subordinate to the two former points.

Keeping Locke's aim before us, let us turn to a closer look at his *Some Thoughts.* Being a medical doctor and, in addition, hampered by a frail constitution, Locke naturally devotes his attention first to the care of the body. Yet he is quick to acknowledge that this attention is only a first step; it should not stop here. In order to fashion the body into a strong and vigorous organism, nature must be given full scope of action: "It seems suitable both to my reason and experience," Locke wrote, "that the tender constitutions of children should have as little done to them as is possible and as the absolute necessity of the case requires." [51] He warns parents against spoiling their child's constitution, claiming that strength of the physical organism can be secured only by accustoming it gradually to the endurance of hardships encountered in the course of life. His main theme is that a person can bear anything to which, from the beginning, he has become habituated. In line with this, Locke advised that children be taught to tolerate temperature change by not dressing too warmly either in summer or winter; to spend as much time as possible in fresh air; to bathe in cold water; and to sleep on hard beds. He insisted, moreover, and at great length, on simplicity and frugality of diet; bread, milk, and gruel would be sufficient nutriment for childhood. Reason must control the appetite, and a child should not be given anything to eat or drink simply because he wants it but only when it is needed for subsistence. He cared nothing about regularity in eating habits, although he was quite sure that children ought to get plenty of sleep on a regular schedule. If this regimen seems disagreeable to human nature, it is not because Locke wanted life to be painful and disagreeable. Rather, he had the sincere conviction that physical hardness was a prerequisite to the attainment of self-denial and self-restraint, both of which would become essential attributes in the life of a gentleman. Locke's own words may be interesting: "Plenty of open air, exercise and sleep, plain diet, no wine or strong drink, and very little or no physic, not too warm or straight clothing, especially the head and feet kept cold, and the feet often used to cold water, and exposed to wet." [52]

Having strengthened and disciplined the body to ensure its obedience to the dictates of the mind, the educator may turn to the next

[51] *Ibid.*, pp. 15–16.
[52] Locke, *Some Thoughts Concerning Education,* p. 26.

task, which is to set the mind in right order. In the refinement of the mind, Locke attaches far more importance to the formation of virtuous habits and even of those social qualities which go by the name of "good breeding" than to the mere inculcation of knowledge. In Locke's view, a sound mind need not mean necessarily a well-informed mind. A pupil may be well schooled in language, philosophy, and literature, and yet be badly educated. Character, virtue, wisdom, and breeding are the marks of a sound mind; learning is secondary.

Locke discovered all virtue and moral power in the achievement of the ideal: " . . . that a man is able to deny himself his own desires, cross his own inclinations, and purely follow what reason directs as best, though the appetite lean the other way." [53] A multiplicity of rules and principles of good behavior does not produce right conduct. The fewer the regulations that children must learn, the better, says Locke. Once habits are settled, they tend to operate naturally, and therefore no precious time should be wasted. From infancy a child must be made to realize that there are things he may and may not do and things he may and may not have. Locke does not argue for the breaking of children's spirits by excessive rigor in discipline. He would have the child at ease and free. The perfect solution in raising children is to allow them freedom but at the same time to direct them away from those things they naturally crave toward those things which are somewhat less attractive to them.

Most expedient in the formation of good habit and virtue is the early recognition of parental authority. In the early years of the child's life the motives for this recognition would stem from awe and fear. These sources of motivation ought to change as the child grows older. Yet for holding children on the road to duty, rewards and punishment are unavoidable, although pains and pleasures of the body are not what Locke has in mind; in fact he rejects them. "Esteem and disgrace are, of all others, the most powerful incentives to the mind, when once it is brought to relish them. If you can once get into children the love of credit and apprehension of shame and disgrace, you have put into them the true principle which will constantly work and incline them to the right." [54] Constant reference to parental authority may ensure good behavior when the child is young; but unless the reason is carefully guided from the earliest years, the child may wander from duty and virtue when he has left home and school. A calm insistence on what has

[53] *Ibid.*, p. 27.
[54] *Ibid.*, p. 39.

been determined as proper to reason, once implanted in the child's mind, will expand in power as he progresses.[55]

Example is an excellent teacher of virtue. A child more readily comprehends what he sees in others than what he hears, and therefore those about him should be careful in their actions. This brings out the need of proper environment. Locke opposed public education and favored private or tutorial arrangements, arguing that in a public school teachers exert less influence on the character of a child than fellow students do:

> For let the master's industry and skill be ever so great, it is impossible that he should have 50 or a 100 scholars under his eye any longer than they are in school together; nor can it be expected that he should instruct them successfully in anything but their books; the forming of their minds and manner requiring a constant attention and particular application to every single boy, which is impossible in a numerous flock, and would be wholly in vain, when the lad was left to himself, or the great prevailing infections of his fellows the greatest part of the four-and-twenty hours.[56]

It can be put in another way: Locke wanted children to remain at home under the care of their parents as long as possible, for he believed it foolish to sacrifice virtue for a little Greek and Latin.

If we turn to consider the special virtues that Locke held to be most necessary for young gentlemen, we see that he emphasized the social virtues and the social side of virtue. He recognized the supernatural sanction of virtues by referring them to God, "the independent Being, Author, and Maker of all things, from whom we receive all our good, who loves us, and gives us all things.[57] Locke seemed to regard this reference to God as sufficient to establish a religious basis for morality. This is a slim foundation compared with the one that he constructs for rational, social, and utilitarian virtue. On the level of theory he does take into account divine ratification of virtue, but on the level of practice he is content to accept something less: This is natural virtue.[58] He values breeding, good breeding, and everything included in that expression, as the best and surest sign of a gentleman. With all its limitations and its misplaced emphases, Locke's theory is really one of moral education. He is quite definite in placing moral formation above intellectual formation in the hierarchy of educational purposes.

[55] Cuff, *op. cit.*, pp. 21–23.
[56] Locke, *Some Thoughts Concerning Education*, p. 53.
[57] *Ibid.*, p. 116.
[58] *Ibid.*, p. 115.

At any rate, Locke places his discussion of intellectual education last in *Some Thoughts*. The outstanding feature of his discussion of this phase of education is his almost total disapproval of the prevailing system in regard to both matter and method. He thought contemporary education out-of-date, and directed his most pointed criticism at the classical languages which continued to dominate the curriculum of the schools. Without totally rejecting the cultural, aesthetic, or intellectual values of Greek and Latin literature for a gentleman, he questioned the inordinate emphasis usually given Latin and Greek grammar, rhetoric, and literature, which, he declared, would be of little practical use to the man of affairs.[59]

Although Locke sought moral training before intellectual formation, he never counseled delay in teaching the usual tools of learning. As soon as a child begins to talk, the teaching of reading should begin. The start should be in the nature of play, and a few letters should be introduced at a time until the child has command of the entire alphabet. Letters should then be turned into syllables and before long into words, although the whole process should be like a game. When the child begins to read he should be given simple, pleasant books, such as Aesop's *Fables;* when facility increases, Bible stories may be added. Reading should be followed by writing.

In all schooling, the mother tongue should be given first attention. Locke was fairly sure that the weaknesses of the vernacular—especially English—were due to the overcrowding of the curriculum with the classical languages. He would have brought greater prominence and respectability to the vernacular by having gentlemen carry on their oral and written discourse in the vernacular language. Once the vernacular was securely learned, another language might be undertaken, and in the usual course of events this would be rather early in the child's educational career. The second language for English youngsters, who seemed to be Locke's only concern, might be French, and it should be started early, as we have said, because in early life children's organs of speech are very pliant, so that the formation of sounds is relatively easy for them. After French, Latin could be introduced. The method of instruction for all foreign languages would be the same—conversational. A child would never be troubled, if Locke had his way, with the grammar of a language until he had developed the facility to speak it. And then grammar would be a subject of study only for those students who wanted to make a critical study of the language. Normally, grammatical studies would not be undertaken until the student was quite mature. If

[59] Cuff, *op. cit.*, pp. 29–30.

it appeared that a young man's business might in later years require a foreign language of him, then Locke would have him learn the grammar of that language.

Locke spoke out against the practice, then common, of having children compose themes and verses in Latin on topics with which they were almost totally unfamiliar. He was no less critical of the practice of forcing children to learn long passages by heart, for he was convinced that memorization served no useful cultural or educational purpose. Greek, save for the student aspiring the scholarship in the classics (which, however, could be a useful occupation), was accorded no standing in the currculum.[60]

In addition to vernacular-language study, the curriculum should include arithmetic, geometry, and history, all of some consequence to a gentleman engaged in business affairs. Obviously Locke's gentleman was not modeled after the Renaissance courtier who was free to lead a life of leisure and for whom any test of utility had relatively little meaning. The latter's schooling could be, and often was, merely ornamental, but Locke's gentleman should always be first a useful man. For this reason he praised arithmetic as "the easiest and consequently the first sort of abstract reasoning, which the mind commonly bears or accustoms itself to. Hardly anything in life and business can be done without it. A man cannot have too much of it or have it too perfectly." [61] Arithmetic teaching, according to Locke's prescription (although he carefully avoids going into detail on the techniques involved), should begin with counting, and then proceed to addition and subtraction. After mastering these elemental mathematical functions, students encountered geography, where they learned about latitude, longitude, and meridians, and finally moved on to astronomy. All these subjects were taught gradually, following religiously the principles that simple relations must precede complex ones and that the purpose of all teaching is to illuminate, not confuse, understanding. Once students have some arithmetic, geography, and astronomy, geometry may be introduced; perhaps the first six books of Euclid should be enough. In any case, Locke refused to recommend advanced mathematical study for any student unless the student himself showed unusual interest in, and facility for, the subject. In other words (and not only with mathematics, but all studies), Locke would allow students to proceed as far as their interests took them once they had mastered the essentials.

Politics and government, themselves useful studies for a gentleman,

[60] Locke, *Some Thoughts Concerning Education*, pp. 154–155.
[61] *Ibid.*, p. 157.

also provided students with a superior foundation for the study of civil law. So all three had Locke's support. He refused, however, to say anything good about logic or to recommend it as a school subject. His antipathies were not based on any abhorrence to logical processes as such, but on his disapproval of the stilted formalisms and artificial distinctions that dominated logic. If the use and end of right reasoning is the formation of correct judgments and the ability to distinguish between truth and falsehood, then students, he said, should be discouraged from any exercises in disputation. The ordinary outcome of logic's study, Locke claimed, was a wrangler, or a person taught to sacrifice truth—the real end of reasoning—to the empty and useless devices of certain victory in argument.

On the lighter side, Locke added some acquirements (almost in the manner of personal and gentlemanly ornaments) to be obtained in regular social intercourse. For example, he mentions dancing as being particularly worthwhile because its cultivates graceful movement and confidence; fencing and riding, considered essential to good breeding, are recommended too; and, finally, extensive travel is endorsed with enthusiasm. Every gentleman, Locke thought, should have certain social skills enabling him to act effectively—and we know he singled some out for special attention. But the greatest agent for social education was travel, for it broadened and matured persons in a way that nothing else could. Somewhat surprisingly, Locke also speaks favorably of gardening and carpentry, telling his readers that both have considerable value to businessmen who may use either or both as diversions from their ordinary occupation, and to promote good health.

This program of study and training, proposed for making gentlemen, should be completed at about age twenty—after which, Locke assumed, most young men would marry, and thus be engaged in responsibilities leaving no time for formal study.

Locke's criterion of fitness and suitability for any subject in a gentleman's syllabus of study is utility. Anything failing to fulfill this test should be ignored. But this criterion sounds worse than it was, for almost any subject, even Greek, could demonstrate its use for the young man aspiring to a career of scholarship. What Locke meant to say was that assumptions about the worth of subjects should be tested and retested, and nothing should be retained in a curriculum simply because of its traditional status. Locke, it is clear, had almost no interest in making experts, or even scholars, out of his students. Schools, he believed, should endeavor only to kindle a love and esteem for knowledge, and motivate students to improve their minds and bodies. Learning was adequate, Locke said, when it met a student's needs.

When we examine the whole range of subjects whose worth and method are discussed by Locke, we come to the conclusion that history, civil law, English law, foreign language, and a command of the mother tongue, together with what is implied in these or found necessary as preparation to them, constitute Locke's idea of a desirable curriculum for a student. Added to these, perhaps as extras, we find the books of Euclid, plus accounting (for every man of good standing must be able to care for his finances), astronomy, and French. By applying his criterion of utility, Locke narrowed the curriculum to the point where broad cultural accomplishments, once so highly prized among earlier educators as an avenue to moral formation, were no longer in evidence.

LOCKE'S METHODOLOGY

While Locke insisted on making the curriculum more meaningful, he was equally demanding in the matter of methodology. He wanted teaching to be more efficient, and at the same time he wanted compulsion removed from all learning and teaching techniques. Learning must never be a task or a burden, nor must a child be kept at it until he is tired. Above all, children should never come to associate the idea of punishment with learning. In learning, as in discipline, he strongly opposed the use of punishment, for a child cannot learn, Locke argued, when he is emotionally disturbed, and a mind filled with terror has little room for other impressions. Learning should be made attractive and pleasant. The introduction of games and play in the school in connection with lessons to be learned would do away with the drudgery and boredom.

Another salient point to be observed in his methodology is a strict order of learning beginning with the simple and moving to the complex. The learner must first grasp an elementary idea before moving forward to another simple idea, which the teacher proposes because it comes next in the total pattern. With such gentle and sensible steps, confusion is avoided and understanding is opened and extended. The tutor should accustom the pupil to order and show him the advantages to be gained by clear thinking. Inductive and deductive reasoning should be exercised, and, with their repeated use, the student will see what methods are proper for gaining different ends.

Locke recognized the need for diversity in methodology. No two children have the same temperament, background, and capacity, and therefore no two children can be taught effectively by using the very same method. Here Locke is setting forth a pedagogical principle which today is universally recognized: education must adapt itself to the learner.

The criticism that Locke leveled at contemporary education was not entirely negative or destructive. When he rejected something, he was always ready with something to put in its place. His most general criticism was that education relied too blindly on the past, but when he rejected the authority of the past, he called upon parents and tutors to use their reason and ingenuity in directing the education of youth.

LOCKE'S PRINCIPAL EDUCATIONAL VIEWS

From the foregoing we can summarize certain of Locke's educational views that have made the greatest impress on modern education.

1. Locke rejected the doctrine of innate ideas. This doctrine, which had been respected for centuries, held to the belief that certain abstract propositions—or even the idea of God—are innate. Locke argued that if there were innate ideas all people should have them in common. This, he claimed, they did not. The only source for ideas was experience. He put it this way: "Whence has it [the mind] all the materials of reason and knowledge? To this I answer in one word, from experience; in that all our knowledge is founded; and from that it ultimately derives itself." [62]

2. From the rejection of innate ideas it was but a short step to a theory that captured the imagination of modern educators, although it may have done very little to change their academic practices. This was the *tabula rasa* theory. According to Locke's theory, man's mind is passive and, like a wax tablet, can receive only the impressions made on it. He wrote: "These simple ideas, when offered to the mind, the understanding can no more refuse to have, nor alter, when they are imprinted, nor blot them out, and make new ones itself, than a mirror can refuse, alter or obliterate the images or ideas which the objects set before it do therein produce." [63]

As a result of the *tabula rasa* theory, two new emphases were welded to modern education: environmental determinism, and equality among men. Both emphases eventually gained doctrinal standing in their own right and elicited support apart from Locke's theory, yet in

---

[62] Locke, *An Essay Concerning Human Understanding*, Book II, chap. 1, p. 2. See also James Gibson, *Locke's Theory of Knowledge and Its Historical Relations,* Cambridge University Press, New York, 1960, pp. 52–55.

[63] Locke, *An Essay Concerning Human Understanding*, Book II, chap. 1, p. 25.

tabula rasa they found their initial theoretical validity. (Neither influenced school learning immediately, for Locke's impact was not so direct, but neither was ignored as education moved forward for the next two centuries.) If men begin with nothing, no innate ideas or original impressions, then whatever they are to become depends on their experience. To put it another way, environment makes the man. It Locke was right in using his famous wax tablet analogy, then all men are created equal: all begin from the same point. Locke did not, it is true, elaborate the full meaning of this equality for teaching and learning, but the theory was clearly stated, and its theoretical implications for education were easy to draw. He knew and appreciated the fact of individual differences, and neither philosophically nor psychologically was prepared to ignore their implications—but on a more practical pedagogical level, where a theory of equality among men could be translated into a doctrine of equality of educational opportunity, Locke's performance was far from being praiseworthy. With all his talk about equality among men, the educational processes he recommended had meaning and application not for all men, but only for the upper classes.

3. Never wavering from his belief that education's first purpose was moral or character formation, Locke felt compelled to justify private teaching at the expense of public education. Such assertions are familiar to us, for we have met them before (as far back as Aristotle and Quintilian), and Locke added nothing new to the old arguments. Perhaps his fear was genuine when he averred that teaching in common should expose students to contagions against which they might be effectively protected in a tutorial situation. In any case, Locke's dogmatism on this point, coupled with traditional aversions to educating common men, retarded the advent of popular education.

4. From what has been said about Locke's curricular attitudes, he quite plainly wanted to restrict the range of studies only to useful subjects, although his definition of utility took use out of any narrow technical context. Clearly, his philosophical and psychological expressions put him on the side of experience as the only source of knowledge, and in this single-minded attachment to experience he made empiricism respectable and left it as a legacy for modern education.

5. Despite what has been written for decades, alleging Locke as the inventor of formal discipline, his position with respect to this theory was never clear or definite. In some of his books, especially in *An Essay Concerning Human Understanding*, he seemed to say that mental habits—for example, an ability to reason correctly, and the capacity to arrive at prudent judgments—were superior to information. And he

regularly insisted on distinguishing a sound and orderly mind from merely an informed one. But this argument may have been made for emphasis rather than to discount knowledge's value. In any case, we can be fairly certain that Locke preferred a mind able to think clearly, reason scientifically, and judge correctly, to one merely filled with information. Yet we are far from certain that this left Locke an advocate of formal discipline, for he never tired of measuring the validity and worth of a curriculum of study, of judging its adequacy as an instrument for learning, by referring to criteria of use and utility. Even when he discussed memory and took a position now acceptable to most educational theorists (disapproving of a common practice, in his day, of taxing students' minds with rote memorization), his affinity for formal discipline was disguised or absent. Furthermore, he did not believe that the memory could be improved by exercise, for he states that a good memory is due to a "happy constitution." Here he brings into the discussion his peculiar conception of the soul, which is but a *tabula rasa*, an empty and inert capacity, and not a collection of living forces that can be strengthened by exercise. He rejects the idea that any faculties are capable of growth and development. Learning pages of Latin grammar or literature by heart does not fit the memory for the retention of anything else.

On the other hand, the major aim of Locke's pedagogy was to qualify the pupil to use his reason and to subject all his actions to its guidance and control. He did not expect that any of the students who were educated according to his plan would become experts. Rather, he wanted them to have an acquaintance with certain areas of knowledge, or an inclination to travel the avenue that led toward them. Locke sought mental power and activity rather than knowledge, and it was as part of his search that he wrote *The Conduct of the Understanding*. In this work he elaborated many principles for the development of the reasoning process, and described many common-sense methods for ridding the mind of defects which stand in the way of better reasoning. But at the same time he could define education as a practical pursuit which should aim to prepare youth for social living.

As an educational theorist Locke has been variously classified. He has been called a humanist, a realist, a utilitarian, an empiricist, and a disciplinarian, and there are grounds for each designation. Our interest in Locke, however, has not been in finding a neat category wherein his thought may be put, but in evaluating his services to modern education by means of a pedagory that he hoped would come to grips with reality and meet the social tests of adequacy.

Summary

The seventeenth century was just about the most active hundred-year period in the history of education. All the educational developments of the century centered around realism. In education, realism meant putting curricula, methods, and students in direct contact with reality for the purpose of preparing young people for the world as it existed in their century, not as it may have existed in the mind of some classical writer.

The greatest educator of the century was John Amos Comenius, a clergyman, a schoolmaster, and an educational theorist. His famous work was *The Great Didactic*. Before him, as ground breakers for philosophical ideals that supported realism, were Francis Bacon and René Descartes. A contemporary whose work constituted an awkward beginning of many of the educational techniques of the nineteenth century was that curious teacher, Wolfgang Ratke. Despite Ratke's real contributions to realistic education, his so-called secret method has probably kept his name in the history of education.

With all the emphasis on realism in education, there is a tendency to forget religion. The two seventeenth-century educational movements that were intimately related to religion were Pietism, with its champion, August Hermann Francke, and the Brothers of the Christian Schools (Christian Brothers), with St. John Baptist de la Salle.

Finally, there is John Locke, a many-sided thinker, who by the end of the century had converted realism into empiricism. He endeavored to center the educational process about the child by noting individual tendencies and capacities, and in this way he foreshadowed the doctrine of individual differences. He is most often remembered for his *tabula rasa* theory, for his views rejecting the doctrine of innate ideas, and for his connection, or supposed connection, with the doctrine of formal discipline.

XIII

Naturalism
in Education
in *The* Eighteenth
Century

Educational Conditions

The seventeenth century was something of an educational crossroad. In it, humanistic-religious education was reevaluated and partially rejected; and in it, too, the theories of realism came to light. Comenius was no doubt the great educational personality of the age, but inevitably his influence was short-circuited because language and religion were ominous obstacles to an understanding of his proposed reforms, and thus to their adoption. Locke spoke clearly and decisively about a new approach to education, and justified the utility of learning while seriously challenging, and sometimes jettisoning, broad segments of the old humanistic curriculum. But Locke spoke only to England (at least at the start), and even then limited his message to persons of the gentlemanly class. Had realism been taken more seriously by school-masters, fundamental changes might have occurred in teaching and learning, but—again—it was easier for scholars, philosophers, and educators to talk about reforms than to adopt them.

In the end, it is probably fair to say, seventeenth-century schools were little affected by the revolution that had taken place on the level of theory. The Christian Brothers began their schools in 1682, and, properly speaking, the educational reforms of La Salle also belong to the latter part of the seventeenth century; yet their fulfillment was incomplete, for the last two decades of the seventeenth century were unreceptive to a real educational awakening. Later centuries may take credit for the practical accomplishments of the Brothers. Pietism, we know, had bold plans to distribute a basic religious-literary education in a generous way to persons who formerly enjoyed almost no chance for schooling. Francke's schools, his teacher-training institutes, and his impression on public attitudes for education were all good omens, but they did not bespeak an authentic educational revolution, nor did they, despite the number of schools credited to Francke's genius for organization, come close to approaching universal opportunity for formal learning.

Even if the seventeenth century was not a perfect educational catalyst, if it could not recover all the ground lost during earlier periods, and if it was, in fact, unable to generate popular schooling, we should nevertheless like to think of it as a transitional century wherein ideals were brought nearer realization and a foundation was laid for subsequent progress. In other words, we should like to believe that eighteenth-century education was a principal beneficiary of seventeenth-century ferment. This, though, was not the case.

Eighteenth-century schools were severely criticized by men fully sensitive to their weaknesses. The charge was made, and with plenty of evidence to support it, that the elementary schools of the period were hopelessly inadequate. In a nominal way their curricula paid heed to reading, writing, and arithmetic, but in day-to-day practice (although this century, like every other, could boast excellent teachers possessing skill and dedication) the great majority of schools were incapable of offering their students a decent education. Most common people were unable to attend any school, and went through life without even a bad education. Teachers, either poorly prepared or totally unfit for the classroom, accepted teaching positions when they could find nothing else to do, or accepted their appointment and tried to teach besides engaging in their regular occupation or trade. Classes were ungraded; boys and girls—if girls went to school at all—were herded into the same schoolroom, and studied whatever the teacher happened to be able to teach. Neither a student's maturity nor his scholastic achievement counted; everyone was treated alike. The fortunate boy who attended school was treated to a brief and perfunctory course which, by the time he reached his twelfth birthday, was over. And what he had learned during his brief scholastic career bore little, if any, relationship to the kind of life he would lead in society, nor did it have much meaning for moral formation.

Elementary schools were bad, and the grammar or secondary schools were not much better. These schools may have been able to claim that their teachers were somewhat better prepared than those of the elementary schools and that their curricula were more orderly and more carefully designed. Yet, in spite of this, the schoolwork did not have much relevance to the life in society that young people were expected to lead. Secondary schools were classical schools, and it was claimed almost universally that they were of very low standard. It was said, too, that regardless of its theoretical quality, a classical school could not offer a meaningful educational experience. The pitiful inadequacy of the elementary and secondary schools was duplicated and, in a way, reinforced by the inadequacy of the higher schools—the colleges and universities. It was not unusual or surprising that men of ability, who under ordinary circumstances would want to be associated with institutions of higher learning, refused to have anything to do with the universities.

The picture of education at the beginning of the eighteenth century was a bleak one. There was, however, a redeeming feature: Certain perceptive persons recognized principal weaknesses in educational opportunity and practice and, following their pedagogic intuitions, tried again to initiate reform. In some respects, as we shall see, they were successful (despite the fact that their motives were fed more by feeling than hard knowledge), for their demands for better schools and more fully prepared teachers often brought results. Moreover, in generating an awareness of education's importance to society, and of the serious defects then plaguing it, they broke ground for far more revolutionary adventures in the nineteenth-century educational establishment.

The Brothers of the Christian Schools, we know, upgraded elementary education in France, and later in other countries, and in refining classroom teaching practices added some thrust to a yearning for popular education. But they were by no means alone. In England a charity school movement was sponsored with the goal of teaching reading, writing, the catechism, and prayers to all children able to use the opportunity its schools offered.[1] Also in England, and especially under the auspices of the Church of England, the Society for Promoting Christian Knowledge was organized in 1698. The most obvious purpose of the schools of the society was to promote Christian knowledge by teaching the catechism, but the schools that came into existence—more than two thousand of them in England and Wales—offered instruction in the elements of education as well.[2] Somewhat later in the eighteenth century, England inaugurated the Sunday school movement. This effort to achieve educational reform and greater educational opportunity was undertaken principally by Robert Raikes in 1785. The idea of the Sunday school was to offer instruction in reading, writing, and religion to children who could not come to school during the week.[3]

The educational institutions that resulted from the inspiring work of August Hermann Francke—elementary schools, boarding schools, teacher-training schools—have received brief notice before. Their direct influence upon German education should not be minimized. But they had also an indirect force that was of considerable consequence for the future of education in Germany. Largely as a result of the favorable impression made on him by the Pietistic schools, Frederick William I, the king of Prussia, came to appreciate the need that the common people had for education. In the example that these schools provided he thought he saw a practical way to offer the common people some educational opportunity. In 1717 he promulgated a decree that made attendance in the elementary schools compulsory in Prussia. And later, in 1763, Frederick the Great issued the General School Regulations, which made attendance in school compulsory for all children between the ages of five and fourteen.[4]

We do not need to go into any detail here concerning these school

[1] See John W. Adamson, *English Education, 1789–1902*, Cambridge University Press, New York, 1964, pp. 132–133; Howard C. Barnard, *A History of English Education from 1760*, London University Press, London, 1961, pp. 79–87; Mary G. Jones, *The Charity School Movement*, Archon Books, Hamden, Conn., 1964, pp. 280–287; and Bernard Mandeville, *The Fable of the Bees*, The Clarendon Press, Oxford, 1957, Part I.

[2] Joseph Kay, *The Education of the Poor in England and Europe*, J. Hatchard and Son, London, 1846, pp. 198–207; and Betsy Rodgers, *Cloak of Charity: Studies in Eighteenth Century Philanthropy*, Methuen, London, 1949, pp. 66–91.

[3] Joseph Stratford, *Robert Raikes and Others: The Founders of Sunday Schools*, Sunday School Union, London, 1880, pp. 15–31.

[4] Henry Barnard, *German Teachers and Educators*, Brown & Gross, Hartford, Conn., 1878, p. 595; and Gerhard Ritter, *Frederick the Great: A Historical Profile*, University of California Press, Berkeley, 1968, pp. 109–119.

regulations, but we should stress the fact that Prussia's example had far-reaching effects in Europe. It provided the historical foundation and some of the political justification for state control of education.

Not only on the level of lower schools was this precedent for state control effective; the higher schools felt its impact too. The tendency to reform higher schools, the colleges and the universities especially, was of course much less in evidence than the efforts to alter the existing patterns of elementary and secondary education. Higher education touched so few people that reform movements within its institutions naturally lagged considerably behind reform directed at other parts of the educational enterprise. Yet what was done on the level of higher education in Prussia shaped the direction and the tone of higher education for centuries to come. In the first place, the curriculum of the universities in Germany became broader. The change was due largely to the realistic movement, and the new curriculum was permeated with the spirit and method of science and modern philosophy. This was an important step forward. Equally significant, however, was the development and finally the acceptance of the doctrine of academic freedom. In the German university, for the first time in the history of higher education, the principle of research and freedom—the freedom of the teacher to study and teach and of the student to study and learn—was accepted as a fundamental foundation for university life. The principle was recognized and affirmed by the government. In the third place, the method of the university was altered radically. The old university, following the medieval model, had honored the practice of lecturing on standard works. The new method was to present the facts and interpretations of scientific findings in lectures, and in seminars to help the students to consolidate what they had learned and to find inspiration for the continuation of their study and research. Finally, the modern university, following the German model, began to serve the rising spirit of nationalism; all the lectures in the modern university were delivered in the vernacular. The whole spirit of modern higher education centered around independence and progress. The university's purpose was to serve mankind, not knowledge.[5]

On the level of secondary education—and still in the German states—we find that the *Realschule* was established. It was a practical school in the sense that it prepared boys for the various vocations in life and did not confine its goals, as the classical schools had done and were doing, to the preparation of boys for the established professions. Johann

[5] Friedrich Paulsen, *German Education, Past and Present,* translated by T. Lorenz, Charles Scribner's Sons, New York, 1912, pp. 122–123.

Julius Hecker (1707–1768) was the man who advanced and implemented the idea for a secondary school with a practical orientation. He established such a school in Berlin in 1747.[6]

Educational Ideals

Except for a relatively few privileged people, the chances for schooling in the eighteenth century were, as we have seen, not appreciably better than they had been in the seventeenth. The common man or even the middle-class man was in no position to lead theoretical or practical movements to bring about much-needed reforms in education. We have seen a few of the practical changes that were inaugurated. But the theorists were not inactive, and actually the changes in educational theory had their effects not only in the eighteenth but in later centuries as well. There are big changes and big names in this century. The eighteenth century, no less than the centuries that preceded and followed it, was a time of educational ferment.

In the eighteenth century, Germany stands out as the country in which practical educational reforms were most widely and actively instituted. Yet Germany is not the country that attracts our attention when we look for the national home of theoretical reforms in education. This honor belongs to France. More than any other place, France was the scene of the Enlightenment.

The educational effects of the Enlightenment are notoriously difficult to assess. It would be hard to find a document of the Enlightenment that was distinctively educational, or to find any leading figure in the movement who could be called an eminent educator. In spite of this, the educational ferment of eighteenth-century France was certainly generated principally by the Enlightenment. We may ask, of course, if there was not something in its doctrine that could explain its influence over education. But the answer would have to be that the doctrine of the Enlightenment is almost undiscoverable and practically inexpressible. In the main, the Enlightenment was a revolt against the established order; it was critical and destructive and individualistic. What did the men of the movement have in common? Such a question either has no answer or else has so many answers that both the question and the answers lose their meaning. Yet we may suggest that the bond which held the men of the Enlightenment together in a kind of loose relationship—not a bond of friendship but an affinity of ideas—was the rejection of authority. It could be called antiauthoritarianism. Nothing that could not be recommended by reason or common sense was accepted; the Enlighten-

[6] Henry Barnard, *op. cit.*, pp. 437–438.

ment was coldly and critically rationalistic. And as a reaction to this movement the reformer of the century appeared. He was Jean Jacques Rousseau.[7]

The Enlightenment, with the Encyclopedists as its guardians in France, had glorified reason and had rejected authority. Rousseau was willing, even anxious, to go one step beyond this: Not content with rejecting authority, he rejected reason itself, or, at least, he attacked it with such force that skepticism was the logical outcome. So Rousseau became a reformer who was to reform the reform. He could not agree with the Encyclopedists, however much he might have wanted to see established the reform that they also wanted. Rousseau's position was made quite clear in his *Discourse on the Sciences and the Arts.* It may be said that Rousseau's educational interests began with the *Discourse,* for in it, as elsewhere in his later work, he emphasized the nobility of man and the freedom that ought to be extended to him. With Rousseau we see the first clear signs of the conflict that marked the educational thought of the eighteenth century. On the one hand are the theorists, of whom we shall see more later, who stressed the social objectives of education and the control that the state ought to exercise over it to ensure the attainment of those social objectives. On the other hand is Rousseau, who expressed a doctrine entirely acceptable to a great many common people, that the only justifiable purpose of education was to produce a man. Not a political man or a social man or any other special kind of man, but just a man. On this fundamental level the conflict rested: Are the goals of education social or individual? One compromise, offered in the eighteenth century and more or less honored since, was that a social-political man can be formed as a by-product when man is educated as man. Another idea, sometimes accepted, is the converse of this: The perfect man may be produced by aiming first at the preparation of a good citizen and a good or worthy member of society. Although these statements were the bases for later disputes in education, they were not the only theoretical positions taken. In addition to the educational work of Rousseau, of which we shall see more later, Condillac and Helvétius contributed to the ferment characteristic of this century.

Neither Etienne Bonnot de Condillac (1715–1780) nor Claude Adrien Helvétius (1715–1771) achieved any special eminence in eight-

---

[7] See William Boyd, *The Educational Theory of Jean Jacques Rousseau,* Longmans, Green and Company, New York, 1911, pp. 66–67; F. C. Green, *Rousseau and the Idea of Progress,* The Clarendon Press, Oxford, 1950, pp. 1–20; and Peter Gay, *The Enlightenment: The Rise of Modern Pragmatism,* Alfred A. Knopf, Inc., New York, 1966.

eenth-century educational thought or practice, and neither is much re-membered in the history of education. This neglect is no great historical crime, yet the full picture of the restlessness of the eighteenth-century educational world would not come into clear focus without a word or two concerning their theories. Both expressed what have been called sensationalist views on education, and both are indebted to the philo-sophical and psychological thought of John Locke.

In his *Treatise on the Sensations,* a psychological-philosophical work written in 1754, Condillac attempted to develop an idea gleaned from Locke's writings: Man's senses are not naturally useful to him; in other words, it is necessary for a child to learn to see, to hear, to smell, to taste, and to touch. Condillac was apparently laying a foundation for a formal training of the senses, but he did not elaborate it. Rather, he proposed the theory that the senses are trained not as detached faculties but as a result of understanding; their development and more complete usefulness follow the evolution of judgment and the improvement of understanding and insight. The first goal of the educator must be, then, not the training of the senses but the awakening of understanding and judgment. At the same time, Condillac's position was that the instruction to which young people were exposed should be graded to fit their intellectual maturity, for their sensitivity to experience de-pended upon this instruction much more than it depended upon the senses. His ideas, which were not without merit, were more fully de-veloped in a work that appeared in 1775, with a dedication to the grand-son of Louis XV, under the title of *Course of Instruction.*[8]

Claude Adrien Helvétius, while he belonged to the same general sensationalist company as Condillac, made an application of his views to education which was quite different from anything proposed by Condillac. In his book *On the Soul,* which appeared in 1757, he set out to prove that all of man's faculties have their foundation in the senses. Observable inequalities among men are not due, he maintained, to the differences that are supposed to exist in innate capacity, for there are no such differences. There are differences in men's experiences, and these experiential differences account for variations among men. The mind, as Helvétius said in his last book, *On Man, His Intellectual Faculties and His Education,* is nothing more than the sum total of all of a man's experiences. When one mind is better than another, this excellence is due to the quality and quantity of the experiences it has had; any other

[8] Zora Schaupp, *The Naturalism of Condillac,* University of Nebraska Studies in Language, Lincoln, 1926, pp. 80–107; and E. B. Condillac, *Treatise on the Sensa-tions,* translated by Geraldine Carr, University of California at Los Angeles Press, Los Angeles, 1930.

interpretation, especially one affirming qualitative differences among men due to varying gifts from nature, he deplored and rejected. In addition, he maintained, if two men were educated in the same way and exposed to the same environment, then their minds would be exactly the same.[9]

Although philosophers are prone to downgrade the work of Condillac and Helvétius as having an extremely limited impact on psychology—excepting possibly on behaviorism—and on philosophy, we should not dismiss them too quickly, for education was affected by their views. Whether coincidentally or otherwise, beginning with Condillac and Helvétius, educational philosophers began to think more and more of the influence that the social environment was having on the formation of mind and character. Another view, also, received wider acceptance—namely, that there is a common mold from which all men are made and that the development of men depends primarily upon opportunity. Whatever we may think of these ideas, we can hardly disassociate them from the democratic movement in education in the nineteenth and twentieth centuries. There is still one other line of thought to be mentioned in this connection: If men are really the products of their environment, then society is in a position to control its future by carefully controlling the education it offers. Here, of course, we see the foundation being laid in the modern world for education as an instrument for social reform. Who can doubt that this was not a sharp departure from the role that pre-eighteenth-century education was expected to play?

The eighteenth century offered a framework in which Condillac, Helvétius, and Rousseau could express their views on education. But these men were not alone. A year after Rousseau's *Emile* appeared, another book on education was published, which was to be especially influential in the last forty years of the eighteenth century. This was *Essay on National Education* by Louis-René de la Chalotais (1701–1785).[10]

La Chalotais' name is prominently associated with the expulsion of the Society of Jesus from France, a political-religious coup engineered in 1764 largely as a result of a literary indictment La Chalotais made against the order. This tract, entitled *The Constitutions of the*

[9] M. Grossman, *The Philosophy of Helvetius*, Teachers College Press, New York, 1926, pp. 152–153; Ian Cumming, *Helvetius: His Life and Place in the History of Educational Thought*, Routledge & Kegan Paul, London, 1955, pp. 240–247; and Irving Horowitz, *Claude Helvetius: Philosopher of Democracy and Enlightenment*, Paine-Whitman, New York, 1954, pp. 81–85.

[10] Francois de La Fontainerie, *French Liberalism and Education in the Eighteenth Century: The Writings of La Chalotais, Turgot, Diderot, and Condorcet on National Education*, McGraw-Hill Book Company, New York, 1932, pp. 14–71.

Jesuits, was prepared over the years 1761 and 1762 and appeared in print in the latter year. Basically, La Chalotais was opposed to political and religious privilege, but it was safer to oppose the Jesuits and religious privileges in the eighteenth century than it was to challenge the monarch and political privileges. Yet La Chalotais did not object to the Jesuits just because they were a religious society, but because they had almost complete control over French education.

His bill of particulars was an imposing one: The Jesuit system of education, he argued, was inefficient, and he refused to consider the testimony—and ample testimony it was—that could contradict this part of his argument. Students in Jesuit schools, he admitted, learned Latin, but he insisted it was bad Latin. Beyond this, he contended, such scholars knew nothing of the principles of religion, little of the elements of practical composition (not enough, he said, to write a good letter), and nothing of the fundamentals of right reasoning or prudent argumentation. These charges were made, and generally countenanced, in spite of a reputation for excellence the Jesuits had in these very areas of instruction. He also called attention to the Jesuits' way of life, especially their isolation from the world, and declared that men in such circumstances were unfit to prepare boys for their role as citizens. It was not that their methods were ineffective, for La Chalotais could not really have feared the Jesuits if this were so, but that they placed the Jesuit system—the individual Jesuit, the Society, and its Constitutions—above citizenship, the rulers of the state, and the state itself. With such dedication and devotion sustained by solemn vow, the Society, he claimed, could not be trusted to educate the youth of the French nation. We need not try to test the authenticity of La Chalotais' charges, for on the level of history they were effective quite apart from whether or not they were true.

The two books of La Chalotais are simply two outlets for his total argument: *The Constitutions of the Jesuits* was instrumental in depriving the Society of its opportunity to do educational work in France; *Essay on National Education* was really a document that seconded all of the charges made in *The Constitutions* and added that with the vacuum created in education with the departure of the Jesuits, a national system of education was needed more than ever. In his plan for a national system of education, La Chalotais did not exclude clerical or religious teachers. It is true that he did not place education in the hands of the religious or of the Church—this was the main point of his opposition to the current state of educational affairs—yet he would not have driven clerical teachers from the schools. He left no room for doubt when he said that clerics who were prepared to teach might teach, or when he called attention to the work of the priests of the Oratory for whom he had a good deal of admiration, or when he demanded that a system of education which was intended for the national good be controlled by the people of the nation, and that laymen, who were the first citizens of the state, should have the first claim on teaching in such national schools. In other words, it is possible to detect both an anticlerical bias and a pro-lay bias in the views of La Chalotais. Considering the near monopoly that the clerics had over education in France, it is not at all surprising that sensitive Frenchmen who were devoted to the spirit of reform should have taken such a stand.

If we were to stop here with a summary of La Chalotais' work and writings, our impression of the man would be quite incomplete and could lead to inaccurate judgments. Perhaps La Chalotais was right when he demanded that education be controlled by the people rather than by members of the clergy or religious orders. He may have been on solid ground when he argued that laymen should play a larger role in shaping the educational future of the French nation. Yet, as we read on in *Essay on National Education,* we find that he is not unequivocally an educational reformer committed to progress: La Chalotais did not want to extend educational opportunity any more generously than the current practices allowed. As a matter of fact, he would have been in favor of curtailing some of the educational opportunities that the children of France then had. He believed that France had too many students and too many schools. He opposed the educational work of the Brothers of the Christian Schools, not because he did not commend their methods or recognize their successes in teaching poor boys, but because he was convinced that educating people beyond their needs was both dangerous and unnecessary: dangerous for the common welfare and unnecessary for the happiness and welfare of the people involved.

After having settled the questions of who should teach and who should be taught, at least to his own satisfaction, La Chalotais turned to the problems of what should be taught to the privileged few who did attend the schools. Only a word need be said about this phase of La Chalotais' work because, in the first place, it has little to do with the national education theme for which he is so well known and, in the second place, what he had to say on the subject is not very significant. Perhaps the most remarkable thing about his excursion into the realm of practical education was that he completely ignored Rousseau's writings on education. Although he relied heavily on other authorities—Locke, Milton, Bacon—for he was no expert in this area himself, he chose to turn his back on the advice that Rousseau had given. And this is all the more surprising because of the sense of urgency which surrounds the advice of Rousseau and the need for urgency of action which permeates the outlook of La Chalotais. It is said that La Chalotais despised Rousseau and was unwilling to give him any further recognition by an endorsement, or even a mere mention, of any of his proposals. In spite of this antipathy, it is clear that in their attitude toward sense education—what we call sensationalist psychology—Rousseau and La Chalotais had much in common. But there were important differences too; the most important, it would seem, lay between La Chalotais' complete approval of an academic and a classical curriculum and Rousseau's advocacy of natural methods of teaching and learning.

National education is a big subject, much larger than La Chalotais, although he gave it much of its direction and impetus. Behind national education itself there were many pressures for the reform of education, but in themselves these proposals for reform were just recommendations and were in no way patterns for educational revolution. Even the views of Rousseau cannot be called revolutionary, although on one point, the point of control, they contained revolutionary features. And, of course, it may be argued, many of the reform recommendations were made within the context of hope for changes in the administration of education. Thus, behind all of the changes that were proposed for education in eighteenth-century Europe, especially in France, was the radical idea that the control of education should be vested in the nation. Although this was a new, and in some respects a revolutionary, concept, it was accepted quickly in many European countries. It found ready acceptance in Germany; its application in France was somewhat slower. Even in England, where very little in the way of a national system of education was established in the eighteenth century, the proposition was viewed with more than mild interest.

The principal shift in emphasis among advocates of national education was away from La Chalotais, who withheld educational opportunity from common men, toward a more liberal doctrine wherein the educational needs of the common people were clearly affirmed. Now, at least in theory, the common man came first. He was given this primacy of consideration, logically enough it would seem, for he was the one person in society who could not provide for his own educational needs, even assuming that he was in a position to judge what they were.

In England the nearest thing to a national system of education evolving in the eighteenth century was a plan for monitorial schools devised and put into effect by Joseph Lancaster (1778–1838) and

Andrew Bell (1753–1832).[11] This system of monitorial or mutual instruction had a liberalizing influence on education, although the quality of monitorial teaching was seldom praiseworthy and the generosity of its opportunity was often overrated. The monitorial schools' main appeal was financial: One teacher should be able to instruct extremely large elementary-school classes (Lancaster himself taught classes of one hundred) most inexpensively. According to the plan, a regular teacher taught the older children, who in turn taught children younger than themselves. These monitors or student teachers worked their way down the instructional ladder, so from the highest grades to the lowest all children in school were exposed to some formal, though nonprofessional, teaching. The cost of elementary education was affected directly by this plan, for only one teacher had to be paid.

While it is easy now to find the weaknesses in monitorial schools, we should be prepared to admit their temporary success during a period when schools were few, and good teachers hard to find. In the long run, and from a purely pedagogical point of view, the experiment conducted by Lancaster and Bell was a failure. Yet it taught a useful lesson to a public becoming more sensitive to the need for more and larger schools: Decent teaching and learning opportunities were impossible in schools conducted largely by persons who were themselves only on the threshold of education. In other words, good teaching was the key to quality learning. Still, monitorial schools were not at first tested on their instructional worth, for the plan of Lancaster and Bell failed, not because the quality of instruction was low, but because such schools became entangled with sectarian religion and taught, among other things, the doctrines of England's Established Church. After several decades, then, monitorial schools fell out of favor and lost their chance to represent England in its tentative quest for a national system of education. Yet, despite all its inadequacies, the monitorial school whetted the English appetite for broader public educational opportunity, and its significance in the history of education must rest mainly on this fact.

Although England was slow to read the signs of educational reform, Germany made considerable progress in establishing national education in the eighteenth century. We have already seen how as early as 1619 the Duchy of Weimar had required the attendance of boys and girls in school, and how Frederick William and Frederick the Great had accepted this practice and applied it to Prussia. In the eighteenth

[11] John Griscom, *Monitorial Instruction*, M. Day, New York, 1825, pp. 91–110; and Joseph Lancaster, *Improvements in Education*, Collins and Perkins, London, 1807, pp. 140–168.

century, however, the possibilities of national education were even more fully realized in Germany, where Johann Bernard Basedow (1724–1790) stood as its most ardent advocate.[12]

The educational ideas of Basedow were apparently distilled from the educational writings of Rousseau and La Chalotais. Basedow was impressed especially by Rousseau's assertion that men learn through natural experiences, and he made every effort to put Rousseau's theory into practice by suggesting methods for teachers. These reformed theories and techniques of learning were to be set in the context of a national system of education, like that which La Chalotais had proposed, although Basedow was not very favorably impressed with La Chalotais' commitment to limiting educational opportunity to the privileged classes.

Despite Basedow's profound and long-standing interest in education, it was not until about 1768 that he was able to translate his interest into action. In that year he wrote a book containing the bases for all his later educational theories and practices. This book had the rather imposing title of *Representations to Philanthropists and Men of Wealth Regarding Schools and Studies and Their Influence on Public Well-being.* Two ideas seem to dominate the work: one, all education should be approached as if it were play; and two, the state should create administrative machinery for the control and support of an educational program adapted to a class society. One system of schools should be organized for the common people and another system for the elite. Dualism in education now had a theory to support it. Also, although religious teaching was never a subject to be dealt with summarily, Basedow recommended rather cautiously that schools in the dual system delete it from their curricula.

Basedow's first book was followed by two shorter ones dealing with the practical business of managing schools: *The Elementary Book* and *The Book of Method.* Neither was intended as a full expression of Basedow's attitudes on educational issues, for both were fragmentary and centered on the classroom. In 1774 he published a full-length book purporting to elaborate, integrate, and refine his earlier pedagogical statements. This was *The Elementary Work,* and it contained Basedow's best thoughts on what should constitute a school's curriculum, and how teaching methods should be deployed.

Perhaps Basedow tried to fill his book with everything he knew, and in his great enthusiasm for educational reorganization may, in fact,

---

[12] Henry Barnard, *op. cit.,* pp. 380–385; and Carl H. Becker, *Secondary Education and Teacher Training in Germany,* Teachers College Press, New York, 1931, pp. 77–92.

have neglected a clear and orderly presentation of his plans. In any case, critics have sometimes said that his chaotic expressions in *The Elementary Work* betray a confusion of ideas. But this evaluation is too harsh. Despite the book's defects, Basedow had exceptional insights into school practice, and his ideas were given a good deal of sympathetic attention, especially when he was able to demonstrate them in his own school. One of these ideas reflected his interest in physical education, nature study, and agricultural training, the studies of which were furthered greatly by his close associate Christian Salzmann. Salzmann wrote *Gymnastics for Youth,* a book which exerted a permanent influence on German physical training, and as Basedow's lieutenant he managed a school in the Thuringian Forest for nature study and agricultural training.

Basedow had always wanted to test educational theory and teaching recommendations in real school situations. He got his wish to do so in 1774 when persons who believed in him and his work became the patrons of the *Philanthropinum,* a school located in Dessau.[13] In this school Basedow began by segregating students according to their stations in society, and then he tailored a curriculum for them. Although the various curricula had some common features (there were, Basedow said, certain things all classes of men should know), the general content in them was meant to keep the social classes apart rather than to integrate them. Children from common homes followed one educational track; boys and girls with middle-class status followed another; and "students"—supposedly children with real intellectual and scholarly promise—followed a third track. Basedow apparently accepted the class-structured society of eighteenth-century Europe and tried to devise an instructional program to reinforce it. But, on a more progressive side, he continued to rely on his "playlike" methods to make learning an enjoyable experience; and while he conducted the school he continued to recommend public support and control for education.

In 1784, for personal and professional reasons, Basedow severed his association with the Dessau *Philanthropinum;* yet his departure in no way affected the institution's popularity. It continued to stand as an example of educational innovation and, at the same time, served as a model for similar schools all over Germany. Even in other countries pedagogical enthusiasts succeeded in founding a few *Philanthropinums,* but in Prussia Basedow's influence was felt most, and there the cause of national education was served best. The person to be mentioned in this connection—the one who took Basedow's ideas seriously

[13] See Hugo Göring, *J. B. Basedow's Ausgewählte Schriften,* H. Beyer und Söhne, Langensalza, 1880, pp. 480–489.

and made them work on a grand scale—is Baron von Zedlitz, Frederick the Great's minister of education from 1771 to 1789.

Von Zedlitz's name is an important one in the history of national education, for as minister of education in Prussia he advanced the doctrine far beyond anything previously seen or heard.[14] He was responsible for the reorganization of the classical schools—the German Gymnasia that had their origin with Sturm—and for the promotion of a scientific study of education. As a result of the minister's encouragement, and for the first time in history, a university chair of pedagogy was established at the University of Halle in 1779.[15] And he added further luster to his name by bringing into existence in 1787 a Supreme Council of Public Instruction—the *Oberschulcollegium*—and making it responsible for directing all education in Prussia. Ten years later an additional, and almost conclusive, step was taken in Germany toward finishing a national system of schools by the enactment of a law making state institutions of all colleges and schools.

What little needed to be done to complete the job involved the sensitive issue of sectarianism. The vast majority of German schools were now confessional schools—schools conducted to accommodate the various religious preferences of the people.[16] They worked this way: a student from a Catholic home would acknowledge (confess) his religious belief and be assigned to a school wherein Catholic doctrine was taught; a student from a Lutheran home would similarly confess his religious allegiance and be enrolled in a school where Lutheran teaching prevailed. While this system undoubtedly had the approval of many Germans, and had in fact been in operation for several years, it appeared inconsistent with the new ideas of state control of education, for it allowed the churches to exercise too great an influence over the schools' curricula. Moreover, since it would unquestionably result in a greater number of schools, because various religious preferences had to be satisfied in any one community, the cost of teaching was increased sharply over what it would be without confessional schools. Thus in 1803 the tradition of confessional schools was suppressed by law, and the German system of national education was finalized.

---

[14] Henry Barnard, *op. cit.*, pp. 479–480.

[15] Friedrich Paulsen, *German Universities and University Study*, Charles Scribner's Sons, New York, 1906, pp. 179–180.

[16] Henry Barnard, *German Educational Reformers*, Brown, Russell and Gross, Hartford, Conn., 1878, pp. 308–313; and see also, C. E. Elwell, *The Influence of the Enlightenment on The Catholic Theory of Religious Education in France, 1750–1850*, Harvard University Press, Cambridge, Mass., 1944, pp. 109–111.

Other countries lagged behind Germany in the creation of national systems of education and had to wait almost another century before these systems became realities. France, although almost violently active on the level of theory, made only slight practical progress toward nationalizing its education in the eighteenth century. We have noticed some of this theory before in the books of La Chalotais, and we see it once more in the work of Rolland, Rousseau, Helvétius, Turgot, and Diderot. All of these eighteenth-century authorities shared one common conviction: The state alone should be responsible for the education of future citizens, and teachers should be laymen. Rolland expressed this view in his *Report;* Rousseau's ideas on the subject were contained in his *Considerations on the Government of Poland;* Helvétius followed suit in his *On Man,* Turgot in his *Memoirs,* and Diderot in his *Plan for a University* (which he prepared for the Empress of Russia). In spite of the ferment in France, very little of practical worth was accomplished; educational theorizing did not lead to effective action. With the outbreak of the French Revolution, inertia was uprooted and the influence of conservatives was destroyed. In 1789 educational reform and reorganization could begin to see some hope, although the educational reforms of the Revolution itself were abortive, whether they were initiated by Mirabeau, Talleyrand, Condorcet, Lakanal, Lepelletier, Robespierre, or any of the other revolutionary figures. The numerous educational schemes contained all kinds of ideas, ranging all the way from the most conservative to the most radical. Yet out of the new framework for society that the Revolution devised, the French system of national education took its form. The chief mover was the Marquis de Condorcet (1743–1794). He prepared a *Report on the General Organization of Public Instruction* for the French Assembly in 1792. It contained recommendations for taking control of education from the Church and putting it under state control; for replacing religious with lay teachers; for compulsory and universal free schooling; for civic rather than religious educational goals; for secular teaching to replace denominational indoctrination; for five levels of instruction beginning in the primary school and ending in a national university; for freedom in teaching and uniformity of pedagogy; and for new curricular emphases on natural science, history, geography, and citizenship. More than any other document, the *Report* was responsible for bringing a national system of education into existence in France.[17]

[17] La Fontainerie, *op. cit.,* pp. 230–235; and Howard C. Barnard, *The French Tradition in Education,* Cambridge University Press, New York, 1922, pp. 17–33.

Jean Jacques Rousseau (1712–1778)

Jean Jacques Rousseau, who became a controversial figure, appeared, as many great thinkers do, at a time in history when what he had to say needed to be said. These men of ideas seem almost to vocalize a ferment and desire for reform which exists unexpressed in the people's subconscious mind. Right or wrong, for good or bad, they have inflamed the people and the times in which they lived. Because a man achieved popularity with humanity for what he said at one time, does not mean than his words had universal value or even that they have any validity for later periods. He may have merely possessed a volatile eloquence, while the ideas he thus made attractive may have rested on a fallacious philosophical assumption.

This inflation is especially prevalent in the field of education, where so much has been said and written by so many for so long a time. It is, therefore, constantly necessary to reevaluate an educational thinker to determine what actually his influence was in his own times, what it has been in subsequent periods, and what it should be for the present and the future. This reviewing is important because if he was a great expounder of verities, he should be constantly studied for what he has to offer to teachers in educating the young. If he was not a thinker of consequence, then it would be better to put him out of the main stream of educational history. It would seem, at least at this point in history, that the work and the words of Rousseau cannot be put aside.[18]

ROUSSEAU THE MAN

Born June 28, 1712, in Geneva, Jean Jacques Rousseau camę from middle-class French Protestant stock. He lost his mother at birth and for some time thereafter was in the guardianship of a paternal aunt whose care was no substitute for that of a real mother. W. H. Hudson states that "under the aunt's care, the precocious boy learned nothing of restraint, obedience, self-denial, but rather conceived against all rule that deep aversion which was to mark him through life."[19] The absence of maternal influence in Rousseau's early childhood affected his life considerably, and the lack of maternal care resulted in an ex-

[18] Gabriel Compayré, *Jean Jacques Rousseau and Education from Nature*, translated by R. P. Jago, Thomas Y. Crowell Company, New York, 1907, pp. 69–75; and E. H. Wright, *The Meaning of Rousseau*, Russell & Russell, New York, 1963, pp. 150–155.

[19] William H. Hudson, *Rousseau and Naturalism in Life and Thought*, T. & T. Clark, Edinburgh, 1903, pp. 4–5.

cessive extolling of motherhood and its responsibilities in Book I of his famous *Emile*.[20]

Indeed, this lack of respect for authority, which is everywhere evident in Rousseau's writing, seems to have been nurtured by his father, who was himself an eccentric. Imitation, always a potent force in learning, was Rousseau's only teacher during his first years of youth when, because of lack of either encouragement or opportunity, he never attended school. Yet, despite what we should call neglect, Rousseau was never critical of his father, for whom he entertained lifelong respect. As a matter of fact, he approved of the way he had been handled in his youth, idealized the freedom he enjoyed, and used his own life as evidence against institutionalized instruction. He was himself, he averred, an example of natural education whose mild processes had allowed him to become a natural mature adult.[21] How much of Rousseau's moral and intellectual formation may be attributed to nature and how much to social and institutional forces which affected him negatively remains an open question, although some authorities are willing to take Rousseau at his word on natural influences and agree that nature was not only his master, but imbued his whole being.[22]

It may be too easy, even a kind of evasion, for Rousseau to concentrate on the virtues of natural, undirected learning, for, despite his lack of formal education, he was by no means illiterate. Together with his father the boy read widely, if unselectively, from among all kinds of cheap, ephemeral literature. French romances, which were often sensational and sensual, caught their fancy and they devoured them in long literary orgies. Caught up in the passion of romance, family life was allowed to go uncultivated. There was, one commentator says, an absence "of any sense of home ties and duties [which] was part of that general spirit of vagabondage which seemed a tradition in the Rousseau family." [23] An older brother, who somehow earned the reputation of a scoundrel, ran away from home and was never heard from again; even Rousseau's father, always quarrelsome and unreliable, fled from home to escape the authorities and left Jean Jacques to fend for himself.

Now the boy had to adjust to new surroundings and different

[20] Jack H. Broome, *Rousseau: A Study of His Thought*, Barnes & Noble, Inc., New York, 1963, pp. 116–121.

[21] Jean Jacques Rousseau, *Emile*, translated by Barbara Foxley, E. P. Dutton & Co., Inc., New York, 1938, pp. 176–177.

[22] Romain Rolland, *French Thought in the Eighteenth Century*, David McKay Company, Inc., New York, 1953, p. 7; and Jacques Maritain, *Three Reformers: Luther, Descartes, and Rousseau*, Charles Scribner's Sons, New York, 1928, p. 236.

[23] Hudson, *op. cit.*, pp. 7–8; and see Thomas Davidson, *Rousseau and Education According to Nature*, Charles Scribner's Sons, New York, 1898.

values in the home of his maternal uncle, Gabriel Bernard. But he left this home shortly and was kept, for two years, by a clergyman who had definite ideas about discipline and moral education. Yet, Rousseau's habits were already fairly well fixed, and the rigid atmosphere of a minister's house was so unbearable that he escaped from it whenever possible, to roam around the countryside and commune with nature.

Between 1725 and 1728, Rousseau was articled to a notary, who discharged him because he was undependable, and apprenticed to an engraver, who, Rousseau felt, mistreated him. In 1728, at age sixteen, Rousseau finally—and, one might add, almost inevitably—ran away. Falling in with an elderly curé during his wanderings, Rousseau was given a letter of introduction by this man to a Mme de Warens, a recent convert to Catholicism. These associations seem to have continued the pattern of unusual life experiences begun as early as his infancy. This Mme de Warens exercised "a despotic force [in] the life of the shy yet sensuous youth, who had accidentally drifted under her spell." [24] Under her influence, Rousseau was sent to a monastery at Turin, where he was baptized a Catholic. This conversion was apparently not an affair of the soul but only an expedient means of getting along at the moment, for when it later suited his purposes he became a Protestant again. The monastery gave him money and secured employment for him as a lackey in the household of the Comtesse de Vercelles.

While in this situation Rousseau was accused of stealing, lied to protect himself, and put the blame on a young servant girl. His resulting unpopularity from this devious action prompted him to leave this household and move to that of the Comte de Gouvon, where he was taught Latin and Italian by a young son of the family. Here, too, he was influenced by a Savoyard ecclesiastic after whom Rousseau modeled the Cicaire Savoyard in Book IV of *Emile,* wherein representations are made for a natural, deistic religion.[25]

Rousseau was dismissed from this position too, so shortly we find him wandering again from place to place until he returned to Mme de Warens. But the renewal of this association was short-lived, and we find him next in Paris, on his first visit to that great French city. His reaction to Paris was unfavorable, and rather than live in the city he took refuge in the countryside, where he encountered the peasants and where, it is said, he gathered some of his ideas for social reform. R. L. Archer maintained that "his youthful wanderings brought him into contact with the French peasant and convinced him that French society

[24] Hudson, *op. cit.,* p. 14.
[25] Rousseau, *op. cit.,* pp. 228–278.

rested on a wrong basis." [26] Whether or not this short visit to Paris and its environs had a decisive effect on Rousseau's social ideals cannot be determined. In any case, he did not remain near Paris long, but returned to Mme de Warens in 1732. He was ill for a time, worked intermittently at odd jobs, and in 1740 tried tutoring, unsuccessfully, for a very short period of time. Though this was his only encounter with an experience in teaching, he seems to have gained enough insight into pedagogical method to comment on it at great length in *Emile.*

Shortly after this, in 1741, he returned to Paris and tried to make a place for himself. After trying to do several different things with indifferent success, he became secretary to the ambassador to Venice. But this position did not suit him either, and in 1743 we find him back in Paris again. At this time in his life Rousseau met and formed a lasting association with Thérèse de Vasseur. Several children were born of this union, and all of them were abandoned, for which cruelty Rousseau blamed society, which did not provide him with the wherewithal to support them. Once again we see his refusal to accept responsibility and his habit of absolving himself from all blame, although as Cassirer correctly suggests, "the fact that Rousseau confesses to abandoning his five natural children at a foundling home does not affect the merits of the educational plan in *Emile.*" [27]

Meanwhile, Rousseau became the intimate companion of people of social and literary prominence. Among them may be noted Richelieu and Diderot, for whose encyclopedia he wrote an article on music. A certain notoriety attached to Rousseau from these activities, as well as from the essays which he wrote for contests sponsored by the Academy of Dijon. One dealt with the effect of the progress of civilization on morals; it was in this article that Rousseau proposed the paradox of the superiority of the savage state. The other included a discussion of "The Origin of Inequality." Archer believes that "the question propounded for a prize essay by the Academy of Dijon, whether the progress of the arts had contributed to human happiness, suggested to him the further stage in his thought that modern civilization was not wrong merely by accident but in virtue of its inherent character as civilization.[28] Such views appealed to Rousseau's confreres and to a sophisticated part of

[26] R. L. Archer (ed.), *Rousseau on Education,* Edward Arnold & Co., London, 1928, p. 8.

[27] Ernst Cassirer, *The Question of Jean-Jacques Rousseau,* translated and edited by Peter Gay, Columbia University Press, New York, 1954, p. 15.

[28] Archer, *op. cit.,* p. 8; and Roger D. Masters, *The Political Philosophy of Rousseau,* Princeton University Press, Princeton, N. J., 1968, pp. 390–393.

society with an unlimited capacity for self-criticism. Perhaps Rousseau's readers did not take him seriously, but they liked to toy with the unconventional and dangerous social gospel he was preaching.

This brush with fame was terminated for Rousseau by another period of illness, which caused him to retire for six years, from 1756 to 1762, to the Hermitage, a place secured for him by a patroness. It was here that he became involved, in 1756, in an argument in writing with Voltaire over the social significance of the catastrophic Lisbon earthquake. Here, also, he published his major writings: *Julie, ou la Nouvelle Héloïse* (1760), *Le Contrat Social* (*The Social Contract*, 1762), and *Emile* (1762). The publication of these works and the subsequent public reaction brought an end to his stay in the country in 1762. *Emile* was banned by the Parliament of Paris; the book was also banned by Catholics and Protestants alike for its rejection of institutions and authority and for its decided deistic bias. Because of imagined or real persecutions, Rousseau fled first to Geneva, then into asylum granted by Frederick the Great, and, finally, to England, under the auspices of the philosopher, David Hume. In 1770, at the age of fifty-eight, Rousseau returned to Paris. In 1773, at the suggestion of a Polish count, he published a tract entitled *Considerations on the Government of Poland and on the Reformation of It Projected in April, 1772* The tract contains a solid analysis of political reality in an era of intense nationalism, and to protect and preserve the national state Rousseau recommended careful attention to education as a civic instrument. If Poland created a national system, Rousseau said, and educated every child in patriotism and good citizenship, the stability of Poland would be assured. Rousseau died at Ermenonville on July 2, 1778.[29]

ROUSSEAU'S *EMILE*

Rousseau's *Emile* is a thought-provoking book. It is all the more so in the light of Rousseau's life and experiences. He possessed the ability to observe glaring faults in the French social and educational structure and to call attention to them in his writings in a dramatic way. He appeared at a time when man's social and educational institutions had become so solidified and stratified that they had lost touch with changing times and circumstances. Rousseau believed that the needs of educational reform included a return to nature, a development of the natural man, a simplification of the whole scholastic regime, a reassertion of the wholesomeness of childhood, and a removal of cramping restraints and

[29] F. C. Green, *Jean-Jacques Rousseau, A Critical Study of His Life and Writings,* Cambridge Unversity Press, New York, 1955, pp. 340–347.

clumsy educational machinery. *Emile* was published in 1762 when Rousseau was fifty years old. The fundamental idea on which all the proposed educational reforms were based was that the essential liberty of natural man should be safeguarded by education and really assured by the lawmakers.

The book is organized into five parts, or books. Book I deals with the years from infancy to age five; Book II, from age five to twelve; Book III, from age twelve to fifteen; Book IV, from age fifteen to twenty or twenty-two; [30] Book V discusses the education of women. The first four books represented what Rousseau believed to be the natural and important periods in the growth of the child. Much more than a discussion of educational theory, *Emile* is an example of education in action told through the story of a child selected for experiment. The child is Emile, who, according to Rousseau, is educated in three ways: by nature, by things, and by men. In his book Rousseau wants to show how these three sides to the educational process may be managed harmoniously for the good of the child, and as we read Rousseau's *Emile* we need never doubt his sincere and genuine devotion to educational reform.

Rousseau approached the issue of educational reform from the point of view of social theory; he began, in *Emile*, to remold society by remolding the individual. His aim of education was to make the person a unit, a whole being, capable of finding himself in society. His theory of education was concerned with facilitating the direct and unconscious unfolding of the individual, with assuring the right of a natural man through thwarting outer hindrances and everything that might cause distortion. He felt that education must perform both negative and positive functions; it must clear away hindrances and must open a way for the natural development of the powers of the individual.

A main thesis of *Emile* is that "everything is good . . . as it leaves the hand of the author of nature; everything deteriorates in the hand of man." Indeed, the first sentence of Book I is, "God makes all things good; man meddles with them and they become evil." [31] Rousseau asserts that man develops in, rather than is molded by, society. The educational process he advocates is based on the assumption that the child's autonomous tendencies are sound, and that he need not, therefore, be subjected to authority. The order in which human abilities mature must be observed; this is the key to the education of natural man.

Emile is rather difficult to read because it is full of repetitions, digressions, and extraneous matter, and everywhere it is clogged with

---

[30] See Rousseau, *op. cit.*, pp. 5, 41, 128, 172, 321.

[31] *Ibid.*, p. 5.

detail. Understanding of Rousseau's thought is further complicated by the fact that his philosophical system is unscientific, superficially rational, based on emotion, and more prophetic than philosophical.[32] This difficulty of reading is further increased by Rousseau's facility for coining happy phrases which catch attention and tend to obscure the more significant parts of his discourse.[33] Rousseau, moreover, never wasted time on empirical data, preferring instead to deal in rational and abstract propositions where both his style and vocabulary—he used words in an uncommon way—put additional burdens on a reader. And finally, when what Rousseau said is compared with how he lived and how he treated his own offspring, the impediment to fair interpretation is magnified. Rousseau himself may have anticipated this charge of inconsistency when he wrote: "My words are often contradictory, but I do not think there is any contradiction in my ideas." [34]

Book I of *Emile*, dealing with the years of infancy to age five, explains how a child's life should be made simple and rugged, and if this alone is done enough has been accomplished. With such a beginning the child is able to preserve life and he has besides, Rousseau assumes, the two arts indispensable to life and happiness: self-knowledge and self-control. Thus Rousseau's basic educational doctrine is expressed quickly and succinctly (education should enable the child to live naturally and well), and he can go on to discuss more general considerations. Although teachers in the ordinary sense should have little visibility here in the first years, or elsewhere, in Rousseau's program, he devotes a good deal of attention to who teachers should be, what they should know, and what their relationship should be with students. We find that Rousseau was a confirmed advocate of the tutorial method: No teacher should have more than one pupil; the teacher should himself be exceptionally well educated, for otherwise he cannot lead his pupil; he must always guide more than instruct; and he must whenever possible withdraw to allow the pupil to learn for himself. Without going the whole way in justifying self-education, Rousseau unquestionably prized learning by discovery; and after reading the whole of *Emile* we should not be criticized for asking why schools or teachers were necessary at all.

But there is more in this prefatory book, and some of it permits us to report on Rousseau's extraordinary empathy with poor people. They, as a class, are more in need of sound education than are the

[32] Rolland, *op. cit.*, p. xx.
[33] Cassirer, *op. cit.*, pp. 13–17.
[34] Rousseau, *op. cit.*, p. 72.

so-called "upper classes," for their status in society is imposed on them, and their only chance for human freedom is through educational means. Throughout Book I Rousseau equates life and learning, asserts that education begins even before a child can speak, that learning precedes instruction, that habits are formed out of the froth and foam of emotional experience, and that sense experience is the raw material of thought.[35] What were then bold assertions are not now especially exciting, for what Rousseau had to say about education generally and about the childhood years in Book I have long since been recognized as worthwhile and are almost taken for granted. But in the eighteenth century this was novel stuff, and only the avant-garde were receptive to the proposed reforms. As a matter of fact, Rousseau's first drafts of Book I paid less heed to the formative years of youth than the final one, and it was only after his friends alerted him to the significance of the innovative features in his view that he agreed to rewrite Book I and elaborate his tentatively-held theory of childhood education.[36]

By the time we reach Book II of *Emile*, where education from ages five to twelve is studied, we know a little about Rousseau's fundamental ideas. Clearly, he is not searching for a compromise wherein some of the good features of an old teaching program can be grafted to a reformed pedagogy. In other words, he began by affirming that everything in conventional educational practice was bad and ought to be rejected. Besides, we detect a determined effort to defend the rights of the child to find his own personality and construct his own value system. Rousseau's *Emile*, intended originally as a letter to a mother interested in the education of her son, has outgrown its first boundaries to become a *magna charta* for a natural, unencumbered, and undirected adventure into learning and life.[37] Yet, this freedom of youth which Rousseau regards as an unavoidable condition to natural learning is everywhere in jeopardy from men and institutions who insist on imposing their values on succeeding generations of children. How can education be natural, how can a child be himself, if the institutions of society are constantly trying to mold him? Of course he cannot, so Rousseau advances what has always been the most noticed feature of his theory, and he applies it especially to the level of life and education represented by ages five to twelve: "Do nothing and allow nothing to be done." This is Rousseau's doctrine of negative education which may, at first, sound worse than it is. He means only that children should be protected from the evils of organized society, and thus that the very

[35] *Ibid.*, p. 31.
[36] Boyd, *op. cit.*, p. 9.
[37] Rousseau, *op. cit.*, p. 1.

best education for this time of life forms a shield to vice and error.[38]

Put another way, Book II counsels an almost unlimited freedom of the child to learn what interests and has meaning for him. The values of adults, values they are always trying to impose on children, must be immunized, and the only way Rousseau can think of for doing this is to isolate children from society—to offer them an environment wherein their intercourse with nature can be both constant and complete. Rousseau's best advice to teachers and parents is to love children, to encourage them to be themselves, to indulge them in their sport, their pleasures, and their delightful instincts. This is his reason for elaborating the doctrine of negativism, and (he goes on) if it is taken seriously, children will follow their own inclinations, which are at once both natural and right. The foundation for the best education, Rousseau tells us, and what he himself should regard as a pedagogical law, is "not to gain time, but to lose it." [39]

Up to this point, Rousseau writes, learning has been a mere preliminary to what must come next during the years twelve to fifteen. And no doubt he has misled us somewhat, for in Books I and II there is no sign whatever that what has been said is relatively less important than what will follow. We are entitled to wonder, moreover, if his own evaluation of the respective books was sound, for there are many perceptive insights in the early pages of *Emile*. In any case, the first years have been treated, and in Book III he can grapple with something that is really important: the business of work, instruction, and inquiry. Now intellectual education occupies the center of the stage, and it is to be motivated only by curiosity, interest, and pleasure, for Rousseau, in having rejected all forms of compulsion before, sees no good reason to recommend them now. Yet the tutor is not entirely helpless, nor is it necessary for him to stand by merely watching his pupil trying to grasp important things all by himself: he can create an environment for learning, and endow it with a spirit wherein his pupil is confronted with things that are both useful to learn and well within his range of comprehension.

In some ways, perhaps, Emile is tricked into believing he is learning everything for himself, but this is only a condition and does not detract from the fact that what is learned is firsthand, is real knowledge, and has been achieved by discovery. Rousseau usually appears reluctant to offer examples of his theory in action, but here he points to

[38] *Ibid.*, p. 35.
[39] *Ibid.*, p. 134.

science with the counsel that students should not be given, or instructed in, the data of science but should discover them.[40]

Rousseau's interpretation of intellectual education is different from anything we have met before in educational philosophy. Locke, in many respects Rousseau's mentor, had willingly jettisoned parts of a curriculum he considered archaic and useless, but nevertheless had nailed reason to his educational mast, and consistently prized it as an outcome of formal learning. Rousseau values reason, too, but it is never the sophisticated rationalism of the learned world; it is reason on the level of refined instinct. Locke's student might possibly become a scholar who could be called learned; Rousseau's student could only be called shrewd.

So in this context of natural education, and with an unconventional attitude toward cultivated intelligence, Rousseau opposed both authoritative teaching and all forms of bookishness during these critical adolescent years. He had seen how children had been subjected to literature, and how reality was restricted to the printed word in most schools, and he was led to believe that books were learning's worst enemies. With most books proscribed from the syllabus Emile should follow, life itself must be a textbook—and we must assume that Rousseau meant what he said, for he writes very plainly when he eliminates all literature, save *Robinson Crusoe,* from the scholastic regimen mapped out for Emile. *Robinson Crusoe* is allowed to remain because it alone, among all books Rousseau has seen, contains a treasury of natural education and illustrates an education in self-preservation along with a clear recognition of the dignity of physical labor.[41]

Three criteria are advanced by Rousseau to govern the period of intellectual education covered in Book III: necessity, usefulness, and moral suitability. But he is actually talking more about character formation than about intellectual development, and this allows considerable range for his ideas. Truth appears to be important, but it is always the truth of pragmatism, and even then is subordinated to what must be done in order to live fairly satisfactorily in human society. Whatever truth may reside outside the contexts of necessity and use can easily be—and, perhaps, should be—ignored, for knowing things that can never make any real difference in life was, Rousseau thought, the great deficiency of the so-called "educated" person. Following a course of artificial and insignificant learning, a student is distracted from acquiring useful knowledge. Thus, Rousseau advises his readers, the great

[40] *Ibid.*, p. 151.
[41] *Ibid.*, pp. 161–163.

danger in life and education is not ignorance, for ignorance never harms anyone, but error, which, if allowed to go uncorrected, can be fatal.

Still, if error is so dangerous, we wonder why Rousseau, barely five pages after he registers this warning against it, acknowledges that the person who never makes a mistake never learns anything well. It is possible, moreover, to assert that if trial-and-error pedagogy were completely withdrawn from Rousseau's plan, the plan for natural education would disintegrate completely. Apparently Rousseau's warning must be understood as a charge to eliminate error by continuous testing, and thus not allow error to go unchallenged wherever it is found.

Of the three criteria superintending intellectual education, the principal one is use, for, Rousseau says, "This is the sacred formula by which he and I [Emile and his teacher] test every action of our lives." [42] From this formula it is possible to distill the following principles: Never tell the child anything he is unable to understand; begin teaching by cultivating a desire for learning; and emphasize learning how to learn more than the acquisition of knowledge. These, Rousseau asserts, are "assuredly fundamental principles of all good education." [43]

Although there are all kinds of learning (some difficult, some easy), educators, Rousseau charged, had tried over the centuries to make all learning difficult—and, for the most part, had succeeded. "We surround ourselves with tools and fail to use those which nature has provided everyone of us." [44] We should, Rousseau argued, ignore the clever techniques invented to aid learning, and depend instead on our real teachers: experience and emotion. Every educational situation should be organized with learning by doing always preferred to learning by listening to a teacher's words; only when doing is impossible should the latter technique be countenanced at all. In this kind of teaching, assuming that Rousseau believed that learning by doing was a kind of teaching, well-trained minds should be an inevitable outcome and form "the pillars on which human knowledge is most deeply engraved." [45]

Book III is finished, and we are supposed to know how to plan for the intellectual education of an adolescent. What we have learned would not take up many pages in a teacher's manual, although Rousseau's somewhat fragmented pronouncements on this level of learning are by no means inconsequential. Mingled among extravagant hopes

[42] *Ibid.*, p. 142.
[43] *Ibid.*, p. 135.
[44] *Ibid.*, p. 139.
[45] *Ibid.*, p. 147.

and promises are ideas and inspirations making a good deal of educational sense. More than anything else, Rousseau reconfirmed a pedagogical principle always understood by good teachers: The content of education must be adapted to the capacities and interests of the student, for unless this is done a tremendous amount of human time and effort shall be wasted.

In Book IV, which treats of the years from fifteen through the early twenties, Rousseau is preoccupied with ethical and moral training. He assumes (although we may not agree) that the education of the earlier years has not been ethically and morally oriented—and this is not an oversight. By now we can see how he reserved certain periods of development for special kinds of training; at this level morality has its turn, and rests on a trained intelligence, or at least on an intelligence trained according to the advice given in Book III. Everything Emile has learned before is important to what must come next, for, Rousseau says, "to announce a truth to those who are not intellectually mature enough to receive it, is equivalent to indoctrinating the mind with error." [46]

Still, we are uncertain of the moral objectives Rousseau has in mind (although we know Emile must be acting naturally), and he does not enlighten us much. To be moral means to act according to the dictates of one's heart, and, however nice this may sound as a generalization, it remains barren advice to the educator faced with the problem of organizing a program for moral training. Perhaps Rousseau would want moral teaching to begin with two great truths—God, and man's soul—and with these as a foundation seek to direct natural self-love, and its equal potentiality for good and evil, toward a concern for the welfare of mankind.

Rousseau unquestionably had humanitarian tendencies and was vitally concerned about moral relationships among men, but he refused to call on institutionalized religion for help, and never regarded it as being especially interested in man's most fundamental human problems. In a very broad, undenominational sense, Rousseau was religious, and he wanted Emile to be religious too, but he also wanted him to stay away from churches. Morality could be formed naturally and should, Rousseau thought, take the following steps: Beginning with self-love, Emile should shortly become selfish because of his natural inclination to compare himself with others, and out of this selfishness he should, again, naturally begin to realize that all men are fundamentally alike. In this realization he will generate a love for the human race, and this love can be translated into sound ethical action. It sounds simple enough, and was a satisfactory explanation of moral

[46] *Ibid.,* p. 200.

foundations for Rousseau, but it remains largely a personal affair in which neither example nor precept should seem to have much place.

Direct moral teaching finds no favor with Rousseau, for he was never confident that it could accomplish much. Yet, some studies might be useful, and history is the best illustration he can think of. The essential function of education at this point is to guide a grown man toward more profound insights into human nature, and to accomplish this the teacher must, Rousseau says, reverse the process employed to train a child. The worth of history is that it reveals men as they are and provides us with some bases for judging them. But not all history should be taught, and what is taught must aim at insight rather than information. In this respect the ancient historians were preferred by Rousseau, because they were nearer nature in their historical approach, and from among the ancient historians Rousseau liked Thucydides the best.

Men, Rousseau tells us, are born twice: to existence, and to life. The first three books of *Emile* are intended to elaborate the principles governing the former; Book IV takes us face-to-face with life when a person must go outside himself to learn what he must know to get along with others. This type of learning—an informal study in human relations—is what Rousseau thinks of as moral education, and, although to follow Rousseau through the pages of Book IV is always wearisome, it is nevertheless evident that he put unusual emphasis on moral formation.

The passions, no doubt, need to be controlled, but Rousseau counsels a natural approach wherein truth replaces deceit, where language is used to clarify rather than conceal, and where natural curiosity is rewarded by simple, straightforward answers: "It is much less dangerous to satisfy a child's curiosity than to stimulate it." [47] Yet, Rousseau was not as unconventional as he may sound, for this honest response to questions pertaining to human passion is recommended only when the subjects of reproduction and male-female relationships cannot be ignored. At best, of course, curiosity should be neither hastened nor retarded, but on an issue now called "sex education" Rousseau does not go beyond advising us to surround the child, and thus protect his innocence, with persons who respect and love him. Here, as elsewhere, Rousseau avoids positive teaching.

Throughout *Emile* Rousseau has said that the education of children should take place away from society, which is always filled with evil influences. His negativism is no less pronounced in Book IV where, in effect, he recommends that social education be commenced, and that Emile learn by living, but that he be kept away from society as

[47] *Ibid.*, p. 177.

much as possible. Since it is inevitable that he shall come in contact with persons and institutions, all social contacts must be carefully supervised: only good companions are allowed; large towns and immodest women are to be avoided. Yet, Emile must taste life as it is; he must know about illness and suffering; so the process of immunization from society and its effects on men must not be total. Emile must be touched but not hardened by the sight of human misery.

During this period of social education Emile will discover what it means to be a man. He will become aware of his own weaknesses not by being told of them, but from experience. He will become moral in a natural way, but this natural moral formation will studiously ignore the agencies and dictates of organized religion. Rousseau wants Emile to be religious, and he wants him to be moral, but both are natural consequences of right living and neither, Rousseau asserts, is cultivated by the yoke of arbitrary religious opinion. Emile should be on good terms with God and should fittingly seek the benefits and pleasures of a promised afterlife, but only after he has managed to use his present life effectively. There is nothing otherworldly in Rousseau's educational dogmas.

Now Rousseau turns to Emile's desire for a wife and explains how other diversions, such as reading, trade, travel, and agriculture, are unacceptable substitutes for what Emile now feels he wants from life. The qualities Emile should look for in a wife are discussed at some length, and we are led to believe that Emile will be capable of choosing a suitable wife whose taste for simplicity and standards of natural goodness match his own.

Emile is ready to approach the altar to take a wife, but his education is not yet complete. More must be done to refine his taste, to add something to his culture. To this end Rousseau leads Emile to the sources of pure literature: he allows him to review everything contained in the literary treasures of mankind. Emile, as we might have imagined, rejects everything but the classics, and from them selects only the few that will best help him to perceive beauty and remain constant to his natural appetites. Thus we see Rousseau sharing a common tradition in finding educational value in the classics, although it must be admitted that his allegiance to the classics was compromised by his naturalism. The worth of the classics is not in their purity of language, or even in their faultless style ("He will be none the worse if he knows nothing of them. . . ."), but in their power to reveal taste to any person who can think. And if Rousseau's educational prescription is valid, Emile is able to think.

At the end of Book IV we are keenly aware of Rousseau's preoccupation with character education, but are unable to find many recommendations that might prove useful to a schoolmaster in helping him direct his students toward this goal. Rousseau refused to budge from his negative principle voiced early in the discourse: Do nothing, and allow nothing to be done.

Book V is concerned with Emile's search for a proper life companion and his eventual marriage. This part contains more narrative than the previous books, and it terminates with the expectation of Emile's first child. The task of education by the teacher is complete; the father now assumes that role for his child. Most of this part of the book is concerned with the education of girls, and much of it is today anachronistic because of the drastic changes in the status of women. The basic theme is the same—natural development in education. Rousseau begins by pointing out that woman differs from man only in degree. He suggests, again ironically, that in man and woman nature has contrived to make two beings alike and yet different. The man should be strong and active; the woman should be weak and passive; the one must have both the power and the will; it is enough that the other should offer little resistance. Rousseau contends that "woman is specially made for man's delight." [48] The passions are restrained in men by reason, in women by modesty. Woman's inequality before the law is acceptable to Rousseau because she is less affected by reason. Yet, curiously, stronger men are produced because of strong women, and weaker (in the sense of softer) men from weak women.

The difference in the sexes necessitates a difference in education. A woman's education must be planned in relation to man, for she is the source of his early education. The ends of women's education are to be pleasing in men's sight, to win men's respect and love, to train men to manhood, to counsel and console them, and to make men's lives pleasant and happy. Of prime importance in achieving these goals is the teaching of self-control. In other words, utility governs man's education while "what will please man" governs woman's education. Since woman is not governed by reason, she needs more authority and guidance in education. She should be taught to love duties by considering the advantages to be derived from them. Since men reason and women observe, the latter's studies should be thoroughly practical and directed toward the study of man and the formation of taste. The ultimate objectives are taste without deep study, talent without art, and judgment without learning.

Epitomizing this approach is Sophy, Emile's perfect mate, whom he finds, naturally, while wandering through the countryside. Her prac-

[48] *Ibid.,* p. 322.

tical accomplishments include needlework, lace-making, and house-keeping. Her religion is reasonable and simple, with few doctrines and fewer observances; her morality has been taught in the guise of pleasure and fun. Sophy comes from the lower level of society, for, Rousseau admits, in a class society, it is better to marry beneath one's station than above.

Another portion of Book V is concerned with the culmination of Emile's natural education, the final phase of becoming a social being. He begins by suggesting that we, as human beings, are bound to be what nature has made us at any given age. In developing his social theory of education, we must remember that all our natural inclinations are right. Rousseau advocates a theory based on this principle, the theory of the social contract: "Every one of us contributes his goods, his person, his life, to the common stock, under the direction of the general will; while as a body we receive each member as an indivisible part of the whole." [49] Rousseau maintains that the social contract is, or should be, the foundation of all civil society, and it is in the nature of this contract that we must seek the nature of the society formed by it. This is natural because there is not and cannot be any other fundamental law, properly so called, except the social contract. The two contracting parties are the individual and the public. This contract, in operation in society, will admit the existence of free individuals, who do what is right voluntarily, because they desire it, and not through a sense of duty. Rousseau adds that "the further we get from equality, the greater the change in our natural feelings." [50] This socializing process is to be achieved in education by the processes already set forth: first, self-love; then, selfishness; and finally, love of humanity.

The book is concluded by Emile's acknowledgment that he owes much to his teacher, that he will always need him and his example, and that it is now his turn to do the same for his anticipated son. In *Emile* Rousseau has proposed, not a plan for education, but a doctrine to inspire it. He was fully aware of what he was doing, and never for a moment did he believe that he was providing anything more than literary inspiration and broad educational goals for those who follow in his footsteps. It is impossible to point to the direct results of Rousseau's views on education, yet it is easy to find educators who were influenced by him; perhaps it is impossible to find one who was not. Of all of the educators of the modern world who looked to Rousseau for inspiration and consciously tried to apply his theory in practice, none stands out more clearly than Johann Heinrich Pestalozzi.

[49] *Ibid.*, p. 424.
[50] *Ibid.*, p. 369.

The Natural Methodology of Pestalozzi (1746–1827)

Johann Heinrich Pestalozzi was born at Zurich on January 12, 1746, of Italian Protestant refugees who had settled in that city toward the middle of the sixteenth century. His father died when he was five, and after this his mother had to practice a most rigid economy. "My mother," Pestalozzi was to write later, "sacrificed herself with the most utter self-devotion to the bringing up of her three children, depriving herself of everything which at her age and in her surroundings could have had attractions for her." [51] Pestalozzi attributes to this exclusively maternal influence his exaggerated sensitivity, and the lack of manly qualities which a paternal example would have helped to develop. Throughout his school life he was awkward and clumsy, and he always lacked the polish and social graces of the typical gentleman. While he was in school he made few friends and was often the brunt of his schoolmates' jokes. Equally disappointing to him was what he considered to be an extremely unrealistic education. "We imagined we could prepare ourselves thoroughly for the petty civic life in one of the Swiss cantons, by a superficial school knowledge of the great Greek and Roman civic life." [52]

Almost by accident Pestalozzi became a professional teacher. His own schooling had prepared him for the ministry and his profound humanitarianism led him to the pulpit. But his brief pastoral experiences were dissatisfying and he began to doubt that his interest in social reform could be served by an ecclesiastical career. He resigned his pastorship and looked elsewhere for means to achieve the betterment of mankind, although in abandoning the ministry he never entertained any thought whatever of rejecting religion, and all his later educational plans made the development of keen religious sensitivity a primary objective.[53] Wherever possible he tried to weld a solid religious dimension to Rousseau's naturalism, and while he essayed to be a true follower of Rousseau's ideals he often departed from Rousseau on some important points.[54] Religion in formal education was one such point.

[51] Quoted in A. Pinloche, *Pestalozzi and the Foundation of the Modern Elementary School*, Charles Scribner's Sons, New York, 1912, pp. 3–4.

[52] *Ibid.*, p. 7.

[53] See H. Holman, *Pestalozzi: An Account of His Life and Work*, Methuen and Company, London, 1908, pp. 44–45; Hermann Krüsi, *Pestalozzi: His Life, Work, and Influence*, American Book Company, New York, 1875, pp. 112–116; and P. H. Pullen, *The Mother's Book*, S. P. G. F. P., London, 1820.

[54] See Edward J. Power, *Evolution of Educational Doctrine*, Appleton-Century-Crofts, Inc., New York, 1969, pp. 275–278; and Henry Barnard, *Pestalozzi and His Educational System*, C. W. Bardeen, Syracuse, N. Y., 1906, pp. 61–68.

At some time during Pestalozzi's early life he read Rousseau's *Emile* and became strongly attached to its doctrine of educational reform. Almost as a matter of faith, he accepted the Rousseauistic doctrine of natural education, and to implement this doctrine in a practical way he bought a farm on which he hoped to conduct a school according to the broad principles Rousseau had laid down. Although Pestalozzi's good intentions should not be questioned in connection with this school, he was not, it must be admitted, prepared to manage the education of children. Later he admitted that his lack of technical pedagogical knowledge was responsible for the school's failure. An overabundance of worthy ideals was an ineffective substitute for basic methods of teaching, and so Pestalozzi's first educational venture was doomed almost at the outset.

Pestalozzi knew in a very general way what he wanted to accomplish; the failure of his school-farm experiment led him to develop a more thorough plan. The first steps in this plan were made when Pestalozzi undertook to educate his own son according to the ideas contained in Rousseau's *Emile*. He even went so far as to name his son, Jacques, after Rousseau. Pestalozzi envisioned an educational environment which would offer opportunities for work experiences and elementary learning. At the same time, he never lost sight of Rousseau's proposals; he was consistent in seeking a method that would follow the order of nature, and he was resolute in organizing a curriculum of significant experiences that would lead to high goals.

Almost from the beginning of his ventures into education, Pestalozzi engaged in writing books and pamphlets on various social topics, including education. The first part of his most important work, *Leonard and Gertrude*, appeared in1781. In it he described a village community, and called the attention of his readers to the conditions under which so many of the lower classes lived. Throughout *Leonard and Gertrude* Pestalozzi stressed two points which are fundamental to his theory of education: the necessity of extending sympathy or, at the very least, justice to the poor, and the importance of a mother's love, personified in Gertrude, the heroine of the story.

In 1785, he published the second and third parts of *Leonard and Gertrude*. In the second part, he drew up a list of the various kinds of injustice and tyranny that were prevalent. In the third part, he pointed to the remedies that should be put into force to alleviate the sad conditions. The first reform, he advised, should begin with the schoolmaster, the second with the school. "After all," he said, "we can do very little with the people, unless the next generation is to have a very different training from that which our schools furnish. The school ought really to stand in the closest connection with the life of the home, instead of, as now, in strong contradiction to it." [55] He went on to condemn the unprogressive, old-fashioned schoolteacher who could neither read nor write, and he criticized, in particular, the sanitary conditions in the village schools.

Leonard and Gertrude is a didactic novel. In Pestalozzi's story the old-fashioned schoolmaster is replaced by a young lieutenant, who is a disabled war veteran. Like the hero in an old-time melodrama, the lieutenant begins his crusade against filth, laziness, and disorder. Gertrude lends moral support by insisting that what she has done with ten children, the new teacher can do with forty. When the new type of education begins in the story, the children do a great deal of manual work and receive instruction in the three R's. Teaching methods are much emphasized: how to maintain good order without harshness, how to encourage good habits, and how to instruct from nature in those things that are most essential. The children are taught to pay particular attention to what they see and hear because accurate observation through the senses is the first step toward real knowledge. The author puts it this way:

> Besides reading, all were to learn writing and arithmetic, which previously had only been taught to the more wealthy, in private lessons. . . . He [the lieutenant] cared for their heads as he did for their hearts, demanding whatever entered them should be plain and clear as the silent moon in the sky. To insure this, he taught them to see and hear with accuracy, and he sought to give them a thorough training in arithmetic; for he was convinced that arithmetic is the natural safeguard against error in the pursuit of truth.[56]

The third volume of this educational novel was intended to demonstrate how the same beauty and strength that characterized nature could likewise be found in men, and in the fourth part, Pestalozzi was concerned with the inadequacies of the legal system and drew up long lists of suggested reforms. The young, up-to-date schoolmaster was shown to be the only person who could bring about any great improvement in the laws that govern society, and his views and suggested reforms inspired the ruler of a neighboring principality to put into effect laws that would protect his subjects against corruption, abuse, and the miscarriage of justice.

[55] Johann H. Pestalozzi, *Leonard and Gertrude*, translated and abridged by Eva Channing, D. C. Heath and Company, Boston, 1906, p. 118.

[56] *Ibid.*, pp. 153, 157.

After completing the four parts of *Leonard and Gertrude,* Pestalozzi believed that he had communicated his message to the world. He was surprised and dismayed to discover that it was not understood. Thereafter, almost everything that he wrote, including *How Gertrude Teaches Her Children,* was written to explain the deeper meaning in *Leonard and Gertrude.* Almost everything that he did was a practical implementation of the ideals that were clothed in the fiction of *Leonard and Gertrude.* Pestalozzi became a schoolmaster in the most practical sense.

At Stanz he assembled and instructed a number of children who had lost their homes because of the ravages of the French Revolution. He tried to do in the orphanage school at Stanz what the lieutenant had done in the novel. But there were factors in the real situation at Stanz that could not be found in the fictional community he had described. He met hostility from the predominantly Roman Catholic population, who considered him to be an intruder and a heretic. He tried hard, nevertheless, to create a family spirit in the community, with mutual feelings of love, gratitude, and unselfish regard for others. In spite of Pestalozzi's high ideals and his hopes for achieving good, the school was closed and the children were moved elsewhere. By this time, Pestalozzi's knowledge of teaching techniques and practical school problems and children's broad interests had been greatly enriched. When he started out to be an educator he was only a theorist; now, in addition to the theory, to which he remained true, he had all the knowledge that the practical schoolmaster must have.

As far as teaching techniques were concerned, Pestalozzi was especially interested in those that would cultivate the powers of attention, observation, and memory. It is interesting to learn how his insights into methodology were formed; he has given us a glimpse of this formation. "As I had to teach the children single-handed, I learned the art of teaching many at once, and as I had no other means than that of repeating aloud to them and making them repeat what I had said after me, the idea occurred that they should draw, write and work while they learned." [57] Pestalozzi felt that this oral repetition by the children while they were actively engaged in another job, not only formed the vocal cords, exercised attention and memory, but at the same time prepared the children for doing work in a lifetime activity in which the attention had to be divided without being distracted. [58]

[57] Quoted in Pinloche, *op. cit.,* pp. 33–34.

[58] Pestalozzi's first assistant at the school in Burgdorf leaves us his impression of this method: "He [Pestalozzi] had almost brazen lungs, and anyone who had not, would have to give up all idea of speaking or rather shouting continuously as he

While he was at the Burgdorf school, Pestalozzi attempted to concentrate on the teaching of reading by one simple method of instruction. Since he believed sound to be the first elementary means of instruction, he collected combinations of syllables and had the children repeat them aloud. It appeared to him that it was only common sense that sounds should be stamped on the mind before the first letters are put before the child's eyes and any exercises in formal reading are begun. This type of approach, somewhat similar to phonetic analysis, made his students appear more advanced than students taught by the conventional methods, though whether their greater achievement was apparent or real remained an open question. Herbart, for one, had some doubts about the method, although he was in general agreement with Pestalozzi on many points about the educative process. In commenting on the method, he said: "The committing to memory of names, sentences, and the apparent lack of concern as to whether it was all understood cause me to doubt and put questions." [59]

In the Institute of Education which he opened and in the book, *How Gertrude Teaches Her Children,* Pestalozzi advanced both actual and written educational principles which he hoped to perpetuate. The book, published in 1801, was made up of a series of fourteen letters. The main idea expressed in *How Gertrude Teaches Her Children* was that first impressions of objects or sense perceptions are the basis for our knowledge, and that it is possible to establish a natural method of classification for them. Education would and should become a science, obeying definite laws. The knowledge gained from sense impressions could be clarified and developed by means of three concepts: number, form, and language. This is the way Pestalozzi put it: "When a confused conglomeration of objects is brought before our eyes, and we wish to dissect it and gradually make it clear to ourselves, we have to consider three things: (1) how many things and how many kinds of things there are before our eyes, i.e., their number; (2) what they are like, i.e., their form; (3) what they are called, i.e., their names." [60]

---

did. Even if I had had such lungs myself, I should often have desired that he and his class, might have used more moderation and lowered their voices. There were other points on which I could not entirely agree with him: He wanted to teach two subjects at the same time: he tried especially to combine exercises in speaking with freehand drawing and writing." (Quoted in Pinloche, *op. cit.,* p. 41.) See also Kate Silber, *Pestalozzi, The Man and His Work,* Routledge and Kegan Paul, London, 1960, pp. 129–134.

[59] Johann F. Herbart, *Outlines of Educational Doctrine,* translated by A. F. Lange, The Macmillan Company, New York, 1901, p. 91.

[60] Johann H. Pestalozzi, *How Gertrude Teaches Her Children,* translated by Lucy E. Holland and F. C. Turner, 5th ed., C. W. Bardeen, Syracuse, N. Y., 1915, p. 47.

According to this view, children should be taught to consider each object that is brought before them both as a separate unit in itself and as a member of a family of related objects; and they should consider in the same way the words which apply to or describe the object studied.

Through the use of objects which gave the child the sense perceptions so essential to learning, the child could see that the data assembled by his own observation were real and meaningful. The teacher, in turn, could present a problem mainly by questions phrased in terms of the child's observations, and the child's interest would stimulate his mind to work on a solution. This was the beginning of the "object lesson" as a formal approach in teaching methods. Counting objects would provide for significant experiences in arithmetic; drawing them would give lessons in form and would be related to writing; instruction in their names could develop a knowledge of language. Good teachers would develop techniques that would engage the student (self-activity), and this activity would produce the best results when it followed the psychological order of learning, passing from the simple to the complex, from the known to the unknown. Pestalozzi was certain that by this time education would have provided the means of giving the right experiences, the right training and environment, to produce the right kind of citizen for the state. Both of Pestalozzi's chief goals—improving the condition of the individual man and improving society by the cumulative bettering of members of society—would be achieved by education.

It was largely through Pestalozzi's insistence upon the three main principles of his method that educators began to place more stress upon teacher preparation. The reduction of all subjects to unanalyzable elements, the teaching of these subjects by carefully graded steps, the use of the object lesson and the oral teaching of all subjects, the subordination of the textbook and the greater emphasis placed on perception, individual judgment, and generalization made the preparation of a better-educated and more skillful teacher an imperative.[61]

[61] The object lesson, especially, became an important tool in methodology. It may have been that it was used excessively, as is suggested by the following: ". . . just as the spirit of classical humanism degenerated into concentration on the form of the classics to the virtual neglect of their contents, so did such Pestalozzian ideas as the use of objects in teaching and the principle of proceeding from the simple to the complex degenerate into emphasis on the mastery of isolated steps in a given procedure, attention to minute detail . . . without much attention being given to the content of the sense experience." (Walter B. Kolesnik, *Mental Discipline in Modern Education*, University of Wisconsin Press, Madison, 1958, p. 17.) See also Michael R. Heafford, *Pestalozzi: His Thought and Its Relevance Today*, Methuen and Company, London, 1967, pp. 52–57.

PESTALOZZI'S INFLUENCE AND THE MAIN POINTS OF HIS PEDAGOGY

A quarter of a century before Pestalozzi's death, he achieved the kind of stature and fame that no one could have predicted for him when he was forty years old. He was made a citizen of the French Republic, was honored by kings and heads of state, and was accepted as a man worth listening to by philosophers, psychologists, and educators. His influence on the educational patterns of European states was impressive. Every country in Europe looked to him for some advice or inspiration. Prussia was especially marked by his influence. American education, too, was to come under his magic spell.[62]

The main achievements of Pestalozzian pedagogy may be summarized as follows:

1. The aim of education was nothing more or less than the betterment of mankind. This ideal provided the kind of inspiration that modern states needed, along with the humanitarianism that it generated, to move in the direction of democratic education. Whatever steps were taken along the road to greater educational opportunity, national education was always set in the context of the practical, and this concern was, in every way, in keeping with the views of Pestalozzi.

2. Education was given its initial impulse toward becoming a scientific study. Up to this time, knowledge of education was largely unsystematic and indefinite and sometimes invalid. When Pestalozzi appeared on the educational scene, no one thought that teaching and learning were in any way scientific, or if they did think of education as a science, they said very little about it. Although Pestalozzi himself was not a scientist, when his work was finished the bases for a science of education had been laid.

3. The order of learning that Pestalozzi emphasized, without always knowing the technical points involved, brought out the importance and relationship of developmental psychology to teaching techniques and curriculum building. The whole movement toward child study may be traced to Pestalozzi.

4. The object-lesson technique brought the senses and sense training—realism of a kind, directed toward idealist ends—into sensitive positions in teaching and learning.

5. Pestalozzi's whole approach to education made a new kind of

[62] See J. Payne, *Pestalozzi: The Influence of His Principles and Practice on Elementary Education*, Methuen and Company, London, 1875, pp. 99–111; and W. S. Monroe, *A History of the Pestalozzian Movement in the United States*, C. W. Bardeen, Syracuse, N. Y., 1907, pp. 206–209.

teacher absolutely necessary. Now the teacher needed to be well edu-cated and skilled in the art of teaching. Since no magic could produce such an expert instructor, formal teacher training was begun.

Summary

In many important ways the circumstances surrounding education in the eighteenth century were no more conducive to quality or to opportunity than in previous centuries. Yet the eighteenth century was more sensitive to the needs for education and more fully aware of its values and of the possibilities for national good and national greatness that might flow from it than any other century had been. In every European country sentiments on the subject generated ferment; in some countries, notably in Prussia, this ferment was translated into practical educational reforms; in other countries, chiefly in France, the tendencies toward reform were channeled into theories. So Prussia was the place for action; France provided many of the ideals. The best illustration of this point is found in the history of national education in the eighteenth century: La Chalotais in his *Essay on National Education* laid the theoretical groundwork that Prussia put into operation. In Prussia we see the first concrete steps taken toward creating a national or state system of education, and there, too, we see the clearest example of com-pulsory attendance in schools.

The great historical figures of the century are Jean Jacques Rousseau and Johann Heinrich Pestalozzi. Though there is no evidence that the two ever met, they did share an intellectual comradeship. Rousseau, much dis-mayed at what he saw in schools and teaching, and prompted by his own undoubted genius, proposed a return to national education. In his great work, *Emile*, he proposed principles for education that were almost com-pletely negative. "Do the opposite of what is now being done," he advised, "and you will almost always be doing right." For all his interest in education, it must be admitted that Rousseau was no schoolmaster and showed no interest in becoming one. He expounded theories; their application was left to others.

Pestalozzi took up the work where Rousseau stopped. He tried to con-struct an educational process based on Rousseauistic ideals. Naturally, be-cause he was operating on the level of a schoolmaster, he could not afford the literary flights of fancy that had engaged Rousseau. Pestalozzi's work was far more practical and could be applied. Two principal books set forth his main doctrines and educational practices: *Leonard and Gertrude* and *How Gertrude Teaches Her Children*. In the areas of methodology, child study, motivation, and teacher training, Pestalozzi made important contribu-tions to the modern educational scene.

XIV

Science,
National
& Education

The nineteenth century reaped the rewards of the educational philosophizing of the eighteenth century. Rousseau had awakened the educators of the world. Not all of them were followers of Rousseau, of course, but none, not even those who opposed him most violently, could afford to ignore what he had said. Even in what appeared to be his most flagrant rejections of common sense, there were some things to be learned. And if the influence of Rousseau began to wane, there was the work of Pestalozzi still going on for twenty-seven years of the nineteenth century to remind the schoolmasters and the educational theorists that Rousseau had spoken and that educational practitioners were still trying to apply his theories. Pestalozzi continued to be a force in education well into the nineteenth century. It is fair to say that his work had more effect on the educational patterns of this century than that of any other educator.

In addition to the theoretical and practical questions that educators met in their own research or in discussions with an aroused public, other movements added to the intellectual ferment of the nineteenth century. This was a century of many reforms and changes, and as it faced new conditions, it tried to keep intact its inheritance from the eighteenth century.

One of the inheritances was the economic realignment that had been undertaken sometime in the eighteenth century. What we have in mind was, of course, the onset of the Industrial Revolution. This change in the economic picture almost immediately brought about changes in the social structure; changes in the social structure, while not necessarily demanding changes in educational opportunity, did, in fact, impel men to argue heatedly for them. Then there was the political inheritance that the century had left, with its burden of political philosophy that both went into and grew out of the French Revolution. Liberty, equality, fraternity: these were words that had profound meaning and unusual appeal. And who could deny that both their meaning and their appeal affected the destinies of education?

But politics took education down many roads. It was not enough to argue for greater opportunity for the individual. There were many complexions of political thought to be considered, and education was asked to adjust to them. The most significant adjustments were expressed in the form of national education. This was the time when the great national school systems began to take their shape. Later in this discussion, we shall look at their evolution and their significance for the nineteenth century.

Finally, there was the question of faith in education. Sometimes faith meant a kind of humanitarian conception that could see nothing but good coming from an unequivocal commitment to national education. But this was only one side of the coin. Faith could mean also the commitment to the kind of education that would offer opportunity for students to develop their religious faith. Thus, in the movement for national systems of education directly under the control of the state, the desire for an education with some religious perspective was retained. Of course, not every national school system made provisions for religious education; some did and some did not. It was at this point that the whole matter became involved in controversy.

We might say, with some justice, that the distinctive characteristics of the nineteenth century were nationalism, democracy, and anticlericalism. With these preoccupaions in mind, men could argue for a national system of education that was open to all and that provided opportunity of various types for the variety of individuals who would come to school, and also for a control vested in the people themselves rather than in religious communities or persons.

We shall see something more of these characteristics as they influenced educational thought and practice in this century. National systems of education involved both the first and the last characteristics. Outstanding educational leaders and thinkers—Herbart and Froebel are probably the best examples—translated into practical school programs the democratic principles that heretofore had been discussed only by philosophers and political theorists. Because the democratic tendencies were felt in the national school systems that came into clearer focus in this century, we shall begin with the men who were largely responsible for furthering democracy in education.

Johann Friedrich Herbart and the Science of Education

Herbart (1776–1841) was both an educational philosopher and a teacher. He had all the abilities of a Rousseau, yet at the same time he had the pedagogical interests of a Pestalozzi. Perhaps the most interesting and significant thing that can be said about Herbart is that he tested his own theories. Had Herbart not been able to carry his theories down to the level of proof, we should probably not be studying about him today. He was a thorough and searching thinker, and an educational scientist.[1]

Herbart was born in Oldenburg, Germany, in the year 1776. His early childhood was spent under the watchful eye of his mother. He received his elementary education from the local pastor, and his secondary education, which was completely classical, in the local Gymnasium. At the age of eighteen the young Herbart was ready for the university. Since his father had decided that he would follow the profession of law, young Herbart entered the University of Jena. The only unusual feature about Herbart's university studies, aside from the fact that he was especially successful, was that his mother accompanied him to college and looked out for him while he was there. Her indulgence extended to the point where she cultivated relationships for him; her solicitude was responsible for the special friendship

[1] See John Adams, *The Herbartian Psychology Applied to Education,* D. C. Heath and Company, Boston, 1897, pp. 135–139; and Edward J. Power, *Evolution of Educational Doctrine,* Appleton-Century-Crofts, Inc., New York, 1969, pp. 311–312.

that sprang up between Herbart and Schiller. Largely as a result of this friendship and also of Herbart's lukewarm feeling for the law, the young man's attention was turned to philosophy and education. About the time that Herbart came in contact with him, Schiller was writing his *Letters on the Aesthetic Education of Man,* and this book may have been the original spark that kindled Herbart's interest in education. From being interested in education in the early nineteenth century to becoming a disciple of Pestalozzi was only a short step, but, contrary to the general view, Herbart did not take this step very quickly. He left the University of Jena in 1797 and undertook a commission offered to him to tutor the three sons of a Swiss government official. It was not until after he had finished this assignment, in 1800, that Herbart met Pestalozzi, and even then Pestalozzi was hardly in a position to exert a great influence on him. Besides, Herbart had already laid some of the foundations for his educational theory by the time he first came in contact with Pestalozzi. That Herbart followed his own road does not detract from the fame of Pestalozzi, but it does give greater credit to Herbart's dedication to the work of education. Although it should be denied that Herbart was a disciple of Pestalozzi, it can be admitted that there was some cross-fertilization of their thoughts.[2]

Herbart's position gave him far more power to exert influence than Pestalozzi had ever been able to achieve; from his exceptional record at the University of Jena it was easy for him to move to the position of tutor for the children of a well-placed family. When this tour of duty came to an end, Herbart was ready to share his thoughts with others. He wanted to write. His writings, plus the general reputation that he had already achieved in the academic world, brought him a university appointment. He became professor of philosophy and pedagogy at the University of Königsberg in 1809. By this time, however, he had already formed quite definite views with regard to education, and had also worked out the philosophical positions which he defended throughout his career.[3]

When we speak of Herbart, we often find it necessary to distinguish between Herbart the philosopher and Herbart the educator. Of course we should not assume from this that philosophy and education

[2] See Johann F. Herbart, *Pestalozzis Idee eines A B C der Anschauung, Göttingen,* 1802; *Über den Standpunkt der Beurtheilung der Pestalozzi'schen Unterrichtsmethode,* Bremen, 1804; and *Ueber Pestalozzis neueste Schrift "Wie Gertrud,"* Göttingen, 1802.

[3] J. W. Adamson, *English Education, 1789–1902,* Cambridge University Press, New York, 1930, pp. 71–73.

are so far apart that a man who is both a philosopher and an educator is a divided man. For Herbart the difference between philosophy and any other field of knowledge was certainly a matter of emphasis. In his philosophical writings (and generally speaking, it is possible to distinguish Herbart's writings into two categories, philosophical and peda- gogical-psychological) he is critical of the separation that was more or less regularly being made between philosophy and other sciences. He was consistent in his belief that academic philosophy was not a kind of supernatural wisdom that could lead and direct other fields of knowl- edge. In an early work on philosophy, entitled *On the Study of Phi- losophy*, Herbart expressed simply and sincerely his view as to the role that philosophy should play:

> Which relationship should Philosophy set up between herself and the other sciences, and between herself and life? Would she like to be considered as ruler, superior through her new and unknown weapons, menacing and formidable? Or would she rather prefer to be considered a native in her environment, as kin and friend, needy of ever-new acknowledgment and approval? . . . If the power of the human mind is strong enough simultaneously to expand itself into the width as well as the depth of life, then all the sciences, each separately and yet all united, ought to produce philosophy as their indispensable comple- ment, and they ought never to cease in this endeavor. It is the limita- tions of the human mind which force us everywhere to divide labor, and which split knowing into portions of knowledge that philosophy has been severed from the totality of thought. . . . Thus philosophical thinking, unfortunately, has led to philosophy as a special and isolated branch of scholarship.[4]

Perhaps a word more should be added on Herbart's philosophy. Though it is not unusual to call Herbart a philosophical realist, this designation is only partly true. Apparently he was a realist only in the sense that he believed there was a world of real things behind the appearances that we know. He believed, also, that the soul's nature, simple though it is, is totally beyond our knowledge and will always remain so. We do, however, have some knowledge of the experiences or the impressions that are made on the soul—what we call mental states—but we are not in a position to know anything of their origin or the nature of the real soul on which the impressions are made. At the same time Herbart accepted the view of the soul or the mind that

[4] Quoted in Robert Ulich, *History of Educational Thought*, American Book Com- pany, New York, 1969, pp. 272–273.

had been offered somewhat earlier by John Locke.[5] For Herbart, as for Locke, the mind was originally a *tabula rasa*. All ideas are, without exception, the products of time and experience. Although this is only a brief and sketchy treatment of Herbart's philosophical views, it does provide us with some foundation for looking more closely at his educational doctrines. These were presented in the following works: *ABC of Sense Perception, The Application of Psychology to the Science of Education, Letters and Lectures on Education, Outlines of Educational Doctrine, The Science of Education: Its General Principles Deduced from Its Aim and the Aesthetic Revelation of the World,* and *A Textbook in Psychology.*

In Herbart's thinking about education he tried to integrate and accommodate theory to practice. He was convinced that the aims of education could not be arrived at or even discussed without reference to the meaning of human existence, and that the starting point for any theory of education, therefore, is the nature of man. Now his question is this: What is the best way for us to get at the fundamental meaning of man's nature? Here is where he turned to psychology, or more specifically, to the empirical approach, in the hope that it would throw additional light on the central issue. In other words, Herbart was by no means turning his back on the traditional answers that had been given concerning the nature of man; he was only seeking additional information that could supplement and perhaps confirm what was already known. But psychology was something more than this. It provided a basis upon which the technique of teaching could be more firmly and scientifically established. In the history of education, it would be hard to find a man who devoted more attention to laying a foundation for methodology than Herbart. And he was especially successful; his efforts produced results. He established an institute for the training of teachers, not the first such school, it is true, but the first so scientifically oriented, where men and women were instructed in techniques of teaching that could be established on an experimentally verifiable foundation and where they were imbued with some of the spirit that had inspired Herbart to begin such work in the first place.[6]

[5] See Johann F. Herbart, *The Science of Education: Its General Principles Deduced from Its Aim, and The Aesthetic Revelation of the World,* translated by H. M. and E. Felkin, D. C. Heath and Company, Boston, 1908, pp. 201–205; and John Locke, *An Essay Concerning Human Understanding,* 28th ed., T. Tegg and Son, London, 1838, pp. 8–21.

[6] H. B. Dunkel, "Herbart's Pedagogical Seminar," *History of Education Quarterly,* VII (Spring, 1967), pp. 93–101.

HERBART'S AIM OF EDUCATION

In the opening sentence of his *The Science of Education,* Herbart comes right to the point on the subject of the end of education. "The one and whole work of education may be summed up in the concept of morality." [7] Herbart meant that the goal of education is the production of good men. This was not the first time in the history of education that the formation of men had been called the goal of education. As a matter of fact, education in its broadest meaning could have no other objective. Yet the educational traditions with which Herbart was most familiar and the point of view that he had met at the university looked upon education as principally an intellectual enterprise. So there was something new in Herbart's outlook, although it was only a newness of emphasis.

But when we say that Herbart regarded the proper and ultimate end of education to be moral, we must add that Herbart was thinking of education on the most basic level; he was not writing about what might be done in school or at home or elsewhere, but rather, about everything that is or can be done to form the individual under all possible auspices and at all possible times. It was Herbart's impression—and it has long been a common religious expression—that the worth of a man is measured by his will and not by his intellect. Herbart would have the educator, who is not necessarily the teacher or the instructor, concern himself with all those things that go to make up the good man. [8]

This generalization would be sufficient for most educational thinkers; it had satisfied many in the past. But the various parts of morality had to be spelled out for Herbart, for generalization was not good enough for him. Morality was made up of what he called the "five moral ideas": freedom, completeness, goodwill, right, and equity. [9] Education was thus aiming at making a man who would know what he ought to do on every occasion and how to do it. It would be concerned with giving him the bases of instruction so that he would be a broad man; and this was the teacher's task. It would be a matter of cultivating in him the right ideas with respect to what we today call brotherhood. Education would, in addition, have the job of establishing in the individual an attitude that regularly respected the rights of others, both their persons and their property. Finally, there was the moral idea of equity. The educational assignment here was to inculcate the idea of

[7] Herbart, *The Science of Education,* p. 57.

[8] *Ibid.,* pp. 192–197.

[9] *Ibid.,* pp. 28–30.

reward for good behavior and punishment for bad or evil behavior. The man who had assimilated these five moral ideas and had made them part of his system of values was, as far as Herbart was concerned, a good man. When education had produced such a good man, it had done its work well.

Producing the good man was, then, the great aim of Herbart's pedagogy. But, as we have suggested above, not all of this was the proper work of the teacher; only one part was especially his responsibility. This is what Herbart referred to as the idea of perfection or completeness, which needed instruction to fulfill its task. And this is where Herbart's celebrated doctrine of interest made its appearance.[10]

Although Herbart's doctrine of interest has had its greatest effect in methodology, it played an important role in the objectives that he assigned to all of education. On this level Herbart thought of interest in terms of breadth. The interest that he advocated was to be many-sided, and he expected that the teacher, more than anyone else, would have the responsibility for developing broad interests in the children who came to him for instruction. To have many interests would give a person a number of obvious advantages, but for Herbart the most important was that an individual with wide interests would be in a better position to form character and persevere in good action. But the teacher could go farther. It was really his task to create in the mind of the learner an interest in the good life, the life of sound character. Of course, this was not a responsibility that rested solely on the teacher's shoulders, for other institutions that were engaged in the general work of education would share it with him to a certain extent. But since it was the school's role to deal with matters of instruction and since interest was related to instruction, the teacher had a responsibility for developing interest.[11] But Herbart's work did not stop with setting goals. He tried to formulate scientific procedures whereby teachers could be more certain of the results of their work and reasonably sure that they were actually contributing to the formation of a child's character. In other words, Herbart was trying to find out, by scientific methods, how knowledge, the outcome of instruction, might be converted to virtue. His research carried him over into the science of education, and in this area he achieved his greatest reputation.

We should not leave this phase of Herbart's educational thought without making it clear that Herbart was always willing to distinguish

[10] Johann F. Herbart, *Outlines of Educational Doctrine*, translated by A. F. Lange, The Macmillan Company, New York, 1901, pp. 76–93.

[11] *Ibid.*, pp. 60–66.

between education and instruction.[12] It has often been said that Herbart deplored attempts to make such a distinction, yet without it a great deal of his thought would not have made much sense. Education was the total cultivation of the individual, a lifelong and lifelike process. Herbart never doubted that it was more important than instruction, but on the other hand, he never denied that instruction was a necessary part of education. Its role was to emphasize the moral ideal and impress upon the student the wonder and value of the good life. Herbart never tired of repeating that the final aim of education was the formation of character. He recognized that the teacher would have to exercise extreme care, even in carrying out his commitment to character building, so as not to cripple the individuality of the child through an overzealous approach to his mission. Still, the foundation for the formation of character was, according to Herbart, to get the learner to accept transcendent values so that the criteria for morality would be his own.

METHODS OF TEACHING

The foundation on which Herbart's methodology rests is psychological. By the time he was ready to present a method for teaching, he had pretty well abandoned speculative psychology and embarked upon experimentation. Herbart's methods of teaching are based on an experimental psychology.[13] From the experimental approach he tried to develop a scientific and systematic theory of learning, and from learning it was only a short step to method. At the same time, he opened the gates of education to influences from other sciences, especially from medicine and psychology.

One of the foundations in psychology that Herbart laid for his method had to do again with the matter of interest. This was his explanation of the dominance of one idea or interest over others that might be contending for places in the mind. According to Herbart, the contest was simply a struggle on the part of these various interests or experiences to command the attention of the learner. The most recent experiences had some advantage in the contest and would tend to rise more quickly into consciousness and persevere more stubbornly than older experiences. While this theory may have been nothing more than an application of the so-called "law of recency" to learning experiences,

[12] Herbart, The Science of Education, pp. 135–142; and A B C of Sense Perception and Minor Pedagogical Works, translated by W. J. Eckoff, Appleton-Century-Crofts, Inc., New York, 1903, pp. 99–106.

[13] See Charles A. McMurry, The Elements of General Method Based on the Principles of Herbart, The Macmillan Company, New York, 1903, pp. 113–121.

it did have an influence on methods. If the teacher wants to utilize certain ideas that the child has or build on certain experiences that are part of his background, he must help these ideas and experiences to emerge on the level of consciousness. He must aid them in their struggle for supremacy over the other ideas of the child.

This is all part of a kind of conditioning process. The interests of the child are put into a certain frame of reference, and certain ideas or habits of action are derived from them. New experiences will be made to fit into the background of these past experiences and become part of a preformed frame of reference. Manipulating interest, then, was for Herbart an important part of the educative process.[14] But this matter of interest could not be touched without certain dangers. Broad interests were eminently desirable, but broad interests that were held with a kind of passivity were really of no great value. It was necessary that a certain intensity should be coupled with the many-sidedness of which we have already spoken, provided it did not become exaggerated and lead the child away from vitally held interests. A mind that concentrates on one single interest to the exclusion of others is a one-sided mind. Method, then, becomes to a large extent a matter of controlling the voltage of interest. Neither too much nor too little, but always broad.

The question may well be asked: How broad should these interests be? Herbart thought the range of interest should be equivalent to the range of life itself. Yet he was quick to realize that such a wide approach to interest would not give much guidance to the teachers who were faced with the problems of dealing with schoolchildren's concerns. For pedagogical purposes he classified interests into those that had to do with nature, on the one hand, and with society, on the other— interests that had to do with the physical world in which the child lived, and interests that arose regularly and appropriately from the social world in which he also lived. Neither source of interest (that is, neither world) could be neglected in the education of the child. This twofold classification of interest received further analysis and classification. Herbart divided the child's interests in the physical world and the social world into knowledge interests and ethical interests. The knowledge interests, which, of course, are subsumed under both the physical and the social world, would have to do with information about these worlds, interpretations of this information on a normative level, and finally, attempts to see the aesthetic values, the beauty, in them. Ethical interests, of no less importance than the knowledge interests, were directed at man, that is, at the individual man with whom students

---

[14] Charles DeGarmo, *Herbart and the Herbartians,* Charles Scribner's Sons, New York, 1904, pp. 88–101.

would come in contact; at men, that is, at societies or civic communities that men organize; and at God. Herbart was neither oblivious to, nor opposed to, the interest that men have in the Divine Being. He saw this as a social relationship.[15]

Herbart's classification of interests had meaning right down to the level of the teacher who is teaching and the student who is learning. The classification of the objects of interest was relevant first to the curriculum and then to the techniques of teaching. According to Herbart (and he is still operating well within the logical limits of his theory of education), the curriculum should consist of two main groups of studies, the historical and the scientific.[16] Of the two, he considers the historical the more important, because the historical studies are obviously more humanistic. It is remarkable that this man, who has been called the father of the science of education, should have felt that human questions were always to be in the foreground of the educational process. It should be understood, however, that this was a matter of emphasis, and that Herbart by no means intended to relegate the scientific parts of the curriculum to second place. He could not have been true to his doctrine of many-sided interest nor would he have been optimistic about the attainment of the goals he set for education, if he had reduced part of the life of man to a definitely subordinate role. He wanted education to produce the moral man, but he did not believe that morality could be achieved by the presentation of moral ideas alone. "Do you believe," he asked, "that by moral ideas alone you can teach man how to act? Man stands in the midst of nature . . . he must know himself and his powers, and the forces around him who can help him." [17] The work of the curriculum is not simply to present material from the various fields of knowledge. This must be done, of course, but there must also be some principle of integration, if the desired outcome of education—the truly moral man—is to emerge from the process. Herbart's argument brings us to the point where we should look more closely at the actual methods of teaching that he endorsed.

The Herbartian teacher would have to be concerned with three things primarily when he begins his presentation to the students. Before we touch on these three things, we should make clear that Herbart assumes that the teacher will be in a position of authority and that his purpose is to teach the child what he does not know. If there is any question about this, that is, about the fact that there is knowledge which can be taught or communicated, then Herbart's system and all of

[15] Herbart, *The Aesthetic Revelation of the World*, p. 72.

[16] Herbart, *Outlines of Educational Doctrine*, pp. 223–228.

[17] Herbart, *The Science of Education*, p. 221.

his thought become a meaningless jumble of words. The principal concerns for the teacher are: to relate the new lesson to what the child already knows; to help him to retain what has been taught; and to seek to maintain a high level of interest in the student, not only for what is currently being learned, but for learning in general. All of this means, of course, that teaching and learning are dynamic processes. Instruction depends on the dynamics of description, analysis, and synthesis.[18] These are, or may be, discrete types of instruction, but Herbart emphasizes the teacher's obligation to employ them all in the effort to achieve good instruction.

Perhaps interest is central to all of this. As we have said before, the teacher's presentation must begin with ideas that are meaningful to the student. The teacher must find the student's level of maturity, it is true, but he must also find his level of experience. If either level is not found, then it is a foregone conclusion that the student's interest cannot be aroused to the point where it can lead to instructional goals. If the various levels are not reached, then the school is really standing in the way of the children's growth and development. Yet we know (and Herbart had no difficulty in seeing this) that individuals must do certain things in society, and that society will not always wait for them to become interested in learning how to do them. In practice, the student may have to accept some teaching for which he is neither psychologically nor experimentally ready.[19] The nature of things demands this, and it can hardly be opposed by the nature of learning. But on a broader and more significant level the question arises of how individual and social motives may be served by instruction in school. The social motives—better expressed as the needs of society—may open to the learner broad avenues of human knowledge and human experience, and may eventually disclose to him social values upon which the very foundation of civilized society rests. All of this means that the teacher should follow students' interests whenever such a procedure is to their advantage, but it means, too, that the teacher should lead students into those experiences that will be good for them and for the society in which they are to live. They will need the experiences if they are to share in protecting the stability and vitality of society. The students who are instructed on this broad level, where their own interests as well as the needs of society form the basis for their instruction, are exposed to what Herbart called a liberal education.

There is nothing in education for which Herbart is more famous

---

[18] *Ibid.*, pp. 154–169.

[19] *Ibid.*, p. 155; see also Alexander Darroch, *Herbart and the Herbartian Theory of Education*, Longmans, Green and Company, New York, 1903, pp. 177–181.

than the "five formal steps of instruction." This fame is somewhat misplaced, for such a recipe for teaching was not of Herbart's making. He
never supposed that teaching and learning could be put on a simple
mechanical level.[20] The steps of instruction, although they may find a
basis in Herbart's pedagogical theory, should not be attributed to him;
they belong rather to those of his disciples who were associated with
the nineteenth-century normal schools and were looking for a clear-cut
and precise method of teaching which could be communicated to the
students. The five steps attributed to Herbart were: preparation, presentation, association, systemization, and application.[21]

As we have said, Herbart never intended that the stages of instruction which he outlined should be followed mechanically, for he was
acutely aware of the complexity of learning processes and of the instructional procedures necessary to meet them. He could not have
advocated the employment of a simple, set, and mechanical method
of teaching. Still, we must not divorce Herbart so completely from these
steps that we fail to see the basis for them in his work. In *The Science
of Education* Herbart used his theory of psychology and his theory of
education and instruction to devise four steps, or levels of approach to
instruction: clearness, association, system, and method.[22] By the use
of these steps Herbart hoped to indicate that a unified and coherent
method of instruction ought to be followed if the child was to be
helped to concentrate on the material that was presented to him, to
learn it, and to retain it.

By "clearness" Herbart meant that the child should not be confused
by an inappropriate presentation of a subject, but that he should be
able to understand what he is being made to learn. He would not
understand it thoroughly, of course, for then there would be no need
to present it to him, but he would understand it at least on the level
of recognition. The presentation, then, would develop this level of
recognition into a level of more complete knowledge, where the child
would grasp the information that had been presented. The next step
was "association." Herbart talked of apperceptive masses, by which
he meant those bodies of experience already stored or held by the
learner. Association was a matter of relating the new experience,
the material which had just been learned, to old experiences, ideas,
or convictions already in the mind of the student. The next step was

[20] See G. Compayré, *Herbart and Education by Instruction*, T. Y. Crowell & Co.,
New York, 1907, pp. 155–167.

[21] Herbart, *Outlines of Educational Doctrine*, pp. 69–75; DeGarmo, *op. cit.*, pp.
60–66; and McMurry, *op. cit.*, pp. 155–161.

[22] Herbart, *The Science of Education*, p. 126.

"system." By this Herbart meant that once the new learning came into the mind and was associated with past learning, it should be organized into a more meaningful and systematic order. New learning would be put into the proper categories of past experience and would thus take on greater significance for the learner. Finally, there was the step of "method." Method meant that the student, as a kind of an end result of this order of learning, would be in such possession of his knowledge that he would be able to apply it. He would be able to make the transfer of the things that he had learned to the practical realities of the life that faced him.

In other places Herbart referred to his steps in different language: He spoke of instruction that was illustrative, consistent, elevating, and applicable. When he used these terms in this context, he meant nothing really different from the terms clearness, association, system, and method. Herbart did not cast method into an unchangeable mold, although the same cannot be said of his followers. No part of Herbart's educational theory was ever admired more or followed more closely than that part which led to the formation of the five formal steps of teaching. As a partial evaluation, we may add that even though Herbart's method was misused by his followers, there were some good results from this misuse. No methodologist in the history of education ever took a more positive stand with respect to a systematic order of teaching than Herbart, and his followers paid regular allegiance to this order.

More generally, and including method but not limited to it, Herbart's educational perceptions influenced great segments of modern education. His pedagogy affected Germany first, where teachers and school directors paid heed to his definition of educational aim—morality; to his distinction between education and instruction; to his psychological conceptions of mental activity; to his sensitivity to feelings, emotions, and will in the educational process; to his elaborations of a doctrine of interest, later recognized as the most fundamental of his pedagogic principles; to his theory of ethics and culture, which argued for a restructuring of curricula; and, finally, to his method which put all these on the important level of day-to-day teaching techniques.

Once imbedded in German educational theory and practice, Herbart's scientific pedagogy was ready for export. In the late decades of the nineteenth century, American scholars—Charles DeGarmo, C. C. Van Liew, Charles and Frank McMurry are good examples—studied in European universities, became aware of Herbartian principles, and returned to the United States determined to reform the processes of formal instruction along lines suggested by Herbart. This led almost at once to a crusade for making education scientific, and the crusade was stimulated by books on Herbart, translations of his educational and philosophical works, pamphlets and articles on scientific teaching, and the creation of the National Herbartian Society (later the National Society for the Scientific Study of Education, and now the National Society for the Study of Education), whose aim was to concentrate on the independent and scientific study of education.

Most leading American educators of the late nineteenth and early twentieth centuries were involved in this many-sided movement which had its origin in Herbart's doctrines. And allegiance was paid to Herbart and to science in education until the great John Dewey raised his voice to caution American educators against following too closely the pedagogical footsteps of an educator and philosopher who saw education's purpose through nineteenth-century European eyes. Dewey's warning, while not meant to discard what was valuable in Herbart's system, was a reminder that Herbart's words on the complex business of teaching and learning were neither final nor definitive. Thus, while some of Herbart's theory would seem to have permanent value to the teacher (some of his methods are still in use), we should also know that much of his science has been refined, corrected, or discarded.

Froebel and a New Dimension to Education

Friedrich Wilhelm August Froebel (1782–1852), a German educational reformer, was born at Oberweissbach, Thuringia, in central Germany. Because his father was fully occupied with his duties as a Lutheran pastor and his mother died before he was a year old, young Froebel was left to the rather negligent care of brothers and servants. His stepmother lost interest in him when her own son was born. An uncle later retrieved some of the neglect and chaos of the boy's life by taking him in and providing him with an opportunity for education. But Froebel's mind was not on his books, and the uncle, thinking that the boy did not have the capacity of mind necessary for learning, apprenticed him to a forester. At seventeen he left the forest. By this time his insights had matured sufficiently for him to see that somehow the schooling that he had received had missed the point. So we may say that Froebel's interest in educational reform dates from an early period in his life.[23]

In 1799 Froebel went to the University of Jena, not apparently as a student but only to visit his brother, and while he was there he became intrigued with the possibilities of obtaining a higher education

---

[23] See H. C. Bowen, *Froebel and Education by Self Activity*, Charles Scribner's Sons, New York, 1901, p. 47.

himself. The story is that, because of his own inadequate educational background, he enrolled in university studies of a somewhat preparatory sort. His stay at Jena was short. From the university he drifted from one position to another, was imprisoned for debt, and finally accepted a position as teacher of drawing in a Frankfort normal school. It was in this position that Froebel found the fulfillment of his overwhelming desire to serve mankind. In his *Autobiography* he reported that he had found something he had never before known but had always longed for in his life as a teacher. After two years with the Pestalozzian Institute of Frankfort, Froebel realized that his preparation for the profession of teaching was not all that it should have been and that he could not continue without a more substantial scholastic background. He decided to pursue his studies and obtain more experience with children. At the same time he seemed to realize that there was a dimension to teaching and learning that had not yet been fully exploited. He began to see that the method of instruction must be directed by the laws of development of the human mind as well as by those of the subjects to be taught. He had, at this early date in his career, the intuition that the essence of method is the art of adapting to the momentary stage of development in the student the corresponding aspect of the subject. This law of development became the central principle in his pedagogy and he was determined to understand it fully.[24]

To arrive at this end he studied more of Pestalozzi, at Yverdun, and experimented with a model group of boys whom he observed particularly at play. From the Pestalozzian surroundings Froebel emerged with mixed emotions. According to his own testimony, he was impressed by what he saw, but he was puzzled and disturbed too. In 1811 he went to the Universities of Göttingen and Berlin in pursuit of knowledge which would be helpful to him in the educational reform that he hoped to bring about. There is every indication that with his newly found zeal for educational reform, Froebel did remarkably well in his university studies despite the impediment of a faulty background. In 1814 he interrupted his university studies and enlisted in the Prussian army. His purpose in entering the military forces was wholly patriotic, for he was intent upon defending his fatherland in this renewal of the Napoleonic wars. But the military experience, besides satisfying his sense of patriotism, enriched his thinking on other subjects. He saw more clearly than ever before the values of discipline and united action,

[24] James L. Hughes, *Froebel's Educational Laws for All Teachers,* Appleton-Century-Crofts, Inc., New York, 1904, pp. 115–118; and P. R. Cole, *Herbart and Froebel: An Attempt at Synthesis,* Teachers College Press, New York, 1907, pp. 27–36.

and he met two men, Langethal and Middendorff, who later became his associates in promoting the new educational ideal.

In 1814 Froebel and his associates settled in Berlin, where Froebel obtained a situation in a museum. This gave him time to study in preparation for the opening of a new type school, and it gave his followers time to catch up with him in their educational thinking. Within a year or so he was ready to apply his theory of education by development. He began on a trial basis for a short time with a few students in Berlin. After this he engaged in a two-year trial period at the village of Griesheim and then opened his first formal school at Keilhau, with twelve students. This was in 1817. Froebel remained with the Keilhau school until 1831, when he turned it over to his associates and went to Switzerland. During all this time the school with which Froebel was connected was an elementary school. It was still too early for Froebel's ideas on the kindergarten. In 1826 Froebel published his *The Education of Man*. This extremely complex book contains the one formal exposition of his educational views; it sets forth his high hopes for the educational enterprise. In 1836 Froebel turned his attention to the education of young children. It was in education on this level that Froebel was to make his indelible mark on the history of education. In 1840 he opened the Universal German Kindergarten, and for the next twelve years devoted all his attention to the progress of these institutions throughout Germany.

FROEBEL'S PHILOSOPHY

Froebel's philosophy, which is basic to all of his theories about education, places him squarely in the tradition of idealism.[25] Some writers have seen enough similarity between him and Rousseau to call Froebel a German copy of the French philosopher. On the level of educational ideas, ideals, and practices there are many similarities between Froebel and Rousseau and Froebel and Pestalozzi. On the more basic level of philosophical principles there is little, if any, similarity.

Unity is Froebel's dominant principle. All things are related, connected, unified, whether or not this unity can be detected. The ultimate source of the unity, the principle of all unification, is God. The whole purpose of education is to enable men to fulfill themselves, to complete themselves, to attain unity with God.[26]

[25] Friedrich Froebel, *The Education of Man*, translated by W. N. Hailmann, Appleton-Century-Crofts, Inc., New York, 1892, pp. 16–18.

[26] *Ibid.*, pp. 69–71; and John A. MacVannel, *The Educational Theories of Herbart and Froebel*, Columbia University Press, New York, 1905, pp. 147–161.

Although Froebel was an idealist and a pantheist, he did not go so far in his idealism as to deny or ignore the facts of the world. It was by means of the facts of the world, by finding in them the clues to unity, that men would become educated and would be completed. Added to Froebel's principle of unity is his general conception of organic evolution. He believed that man grew much as plants and animals grow, with this difference: Plants and animals develop according to a definite inner law of their nature; man, being endowed with a mental nature, is able to shape many of the elements of his own development. Here again education, which may be simply the opportunity for development, becomes extremely important. Step by step, stage by stage, man moves forward, building on what he has constructed before. No stage of development is unimportant; possibly the first years of life, the foundational years, are most important. In the various stages of development men will be confronted by different problems and opportunities. The principle of unity that flows through all these various stages is self-activity. By being self-active, man comes closer to God, who is an ever-active spirit. The challenge that faces education, then, is to bring man closer to God and while doing so to enable man to become more completely himself.

FROEBEL AND EDUCATION

Although Froebel's philosophy was basic to his educational theory, it is a complex, idealistic philosophy which is difficult to understand and more difficult to explain. For this reason we shall not dwell on the philosophical phases of Froebel's thought but shall go directly to his educational plans and practices.[27]

1. Most educational thinkers concerned themselves first with the aims of education. Froebel was no exception. He saw quite clearly the relationship between goals and means. Froebel envisaged a twofold aim for education. One part of the general aim was to produce in the individual a firm, pure, and strong will.[28] The other part, which is somewhat difficult to interpret, is to "lead and guide a man [through education] to clearness concerning himself and in himself, to peace with nature, and to unity with God." [29] In brief, Froebel was saying that education's chief purposes should be moral and, in a broad sense, social.

[27] See Ulich, *op. cit.*, pp. 284–291.
[28] Froebel, *The Education of Man*, p. 96.
[29] *Ibid.*, pp. 4–5.

2. Froebel's theory of development had considerable relevance to the means of education, curriculum and methodology. He believed that there were definite, and for a time, discrete, periods of development through which children passed. These periods were knit together or unified in an educational experience by self-activity. Learning by doing, as a principle in education, knew no more ardent champion than Froebel. What should the child learn? According to Froebel, the fundamental object of instruction was not knowledge, but habits, skills, will, and character. The curriculum, then, would not need to have an orthodox or even a uniform content. It could be made up of those activities and experiences which would seem to lead a child toward the strength of character or will that was prized so highly.[30] This attention to the steps of development in the learning processes made Froebel a forerunner of the whole developmental movement in psychology and in some ways an anticipator of the progressive movement in education.

3. One of the first steps in the maturation of the child is play. Before play begins, the child becomes aware of his surroundings, of the physical world in which he lives. Then he begins to play in and with that world. According to Froebel (and this was a principle that formed an important role in his building of the kindergarten), play is an outward expression of the child's inner action and life. It was, Froebel believed, the most spiritual activity in which a child could engage. Much of education, certainly most of the activities in the kindergarten, should be set in the context of play. This was, of course, just a step in the developmental process, for in Froebel's educational plan children did not always play. Play which combined attention with relaxation, purpose with independence, and discipline with freedom led the child up the ladder of maturity.[31]

4. Besides coming in contact with the world in a playful way, the child should be given every opportunity and every encouragement to get in direct contact with nature. Froebel would not release the boy in the pasture or in the woods in quite the same way that Rousseau would have done. Yet he was every bit as convinced as Rousseau that the study of nature forms one of boyhood's deepest interests, and Froebel's own devotion to nature and nature study carried over into his school plans. In the programs of studies that he constructed for the schools with which he was associated, he always included weekly excursions out into the fields, so that children could come in contact with

[30] *Ibid.*, p. 16.

[31] Friedrich Froebel, *Pedagogics of the Kindergarten*, translated by Josephine Jarvis, Appleton-Century-Crofts, Inc., New York, 1905, pp. 66–69; and William H. Kilpatrick, *Froebel's Kindergarten Principles Critically Examined*, The Macmillan Company, New York, 1916, pp. 47–59.

nature. This same interest led Froebel to endorse mathematical studies, by means of which man could measure or describe nature, and literary studies, especially those that had nature as their subject, and all forms of art and artistic skills that could come in contact with nature.[32]

5. Froebel made two outstanding contributions to modern education. One was the kindergarten; the other was social education. Before the time of Froebel, social education was not unknown nor did it go completely uncultivated; still, educational theorists and practitioners did not devote much space or time to the development of the child's social nature. The school was a place for intellectual or moral formation, and social formation could and would take place outside the school, outside the ambit of formal education's responsibility. Much of this was changed by Froebel. First of all, his philosophical principle of unity envisioned the child as part of a whole, destined to a fuller and more complete life by sharing more fully in the life of the whole. Knowing and participating in the totality of mankind's hopes and aspirations was the supreme purpose of social education. No educator before Froebel and few after him perceived more clearly than he the importance of human relations and the role the schools could play in advancing them.

6. Froebel's most important single contribution to education and the thing for which he is most of all remembered is the kindergarten. This was a school—a preschool perhaps, in the strict sense—which did not have preparation for later schooling as its chief purpose. The kindergarten was a place in which children could grow, develop, and learn in an entirely natural way.[33] Froebel's first kindergarten was established in Blankenburg in 1837. It met with some difficulties that first year and did not operate on a permanent basis until 1840. From Germany the kindergarten spread to many parts of the world. In America, the kindergarten was introduced by Mrs. Carl Schurz, a coworker of Froebel's in Germany, in 1855, at Watertown, Wisconsin. This was a German-speaking kindergarten. The first English-speaking kindergarten was opened in Boston, Massachusetts, in 1860, by Elizabeth Peabody. The kindergarten became a part of the public school system in the United States in 1873, in St. Louis, Missouri, under the direction of the superintendent of schools there, William T. Harris.[34]

[32] Froebel, *Pedagogics of the Kindergarten*, p. 67.

[33] *Ibid.*, p. 75; see also Irene M. Lilley, *Friedrich Froebel: A Selection from His Writings*, Cambridge University Press, New York, 1967, pp. 126–131.

[34] See Kurt F. Leidecker, *Yankee Teacher: The Life of William Torrey Harris*, Philosophical Library, New York, 1946, pp. 560–563; and Ruth M. Baylor, *Elizabeth Palmer Peabody: Kindergarten Pioneer*, University of Pennsylvania Press, Philadelphia, 1965, pp. 125–136.

The Development of National School Systems

While Herbart and Froebel were organizing and rearranging patterns for educational experience in the nineteenth century, the great states of the world were undertaking the work of reorganizing their school systems. Reorganization also went on in a number of smaller states, but it was from the great states that the impetus for educational control usually came. The great states had obviously more to gain or lose through an educational system. Germany, France, and England became deeply involved in nationalistic education, and because of their historic roles in world affairs must be given principal attention (on a topic that is really too large for these pages). Russia, too, because of her dramatic rise as a world power, will be included in this historical survey.

EDUCATIONAL REFORM IN GERMANY

The immediate motive for educational reform in Prussia was lodged in the bitter experience of defeat which that nation suffered from the army of Napoleon. In 1806 the French routed the Prussians in the battles of Jena and Auerstedt, and in 1807 imposed on them a severe peace in the Treaty of Tilsit. A weaker people with less fiber might have taken this humiliation with philosophic resignation and used it as an excuse to withdraw from the main currents of European political life. Not the Prussians. Instead, defeat was interpreted as a challenge to recoup loss of status, and again become a nation of power and prestige.

What were the means? A principal one was stated by Johann Gottlieb Fichte (1762–1814) in his *Addresses to the German Nation*, wherein he chose to concentrate on education as an instrument for social and political reform and revitalization. His choice had two apparent justifications. First, schools and instruction were ignored by the French, who were then supervising the terms of the imposed peace and who gave every indication of an unawareness of the power of education even though for at least a century French thinkers had been talking about the significance of education as a weapon for achieving national purpose. Second, the history of education proved how the schools could be used to gain political, economic, religious, and social objectives. We know something of that history and Fichte knew it, too, so it was natural for him to stress the instrumental character of education to achieve both social solidarity and national autonomy.[35]

[35] G. T. Turnbull, *The Educational Theory of J. G. Fichte*, University of Liverpool Press, Liverpool, 1926, pp. 41–53.

The image we have of Fichte delivering inflammatory speeches in public, unmindful of the presence of the French sentries patrolling Unter den Linden, tends to emphasize patriotic tub-thumping rather than social philosophy, and this is inaccurate. Fichte's public addresses were not the audacious acts of an imprudent man, and while they bespeak a courageous person, it is only fair to add that, as far as the French were concerned, education was a neutral issue, stripped of political significance, about which Fichte could say anything he wanted. The French were wrong of course, and being wrong they allowed Fichte to talk and permitted the Prussians to shape their educational affairs to suit themselves.

German educational organization showed marks of genius and disclosed, moreover, how much schools can really accomplish. On a purely political level, education in the German states can be credited with having provided the essential social foundations for national unification. It was employed to generate patriotism and national identity, and in the end was a chief factor catapulting Germany into a position of European and world prominence. Guided and guarded by the state, German education endeavored to (and to a large degree did) inculcate an almost fanatic devotion to the fatherland. In part this reverence for their nation meant that the German people wanted to blot out of the national memory the humiliation of Jena and Tilsit, but if history could not be rewritten, its mistakes, at least, should not be repeated. Education was commissioned to maintain and enforce this monumental guarantee.

What was the main thrust of educational reform in Germany? On the most fundamental level it was to redirect educational opportunity and prepare persons for life in society. Here moral education (or, more accurately, patriotism) was accorded pride of place, and intellectual training—for which some German schools eventually became famous—was made to play a secondary role. But the distance between primary and secondary purposes, while rigorously maintained, need not be great, and any reading of the record of nineteenth-century German achievement along truly intellectual and scientific lines proves that German educational policy could maintain the hierarchy of moral purpose without allowing intellectual effort to be neglected.

Inevitably, educational reform was accompanied by drastic changes in the German schools. Friedrich Wilhelm von Humboldt (1767–1835), appointed minister of education (director of public instruction) in 1808, was commissioned to implement the broad goals of reconstruction and, although in office for only eighteen months, his work was amazingly successful and permanent. Even today the basic structure of German schools wears Von Humboldt's mark.[36]

Von Humboldt began by establishing a new university, the University of Berlin, at a time when, from financial considerations, its founding was inopportune. Yet such action confirms our belief that a new, or at least different, kind of higher education was considered essential to educational reconstruction. The University of Halle some years before had incorporated the idea of academic freedom as an internal guarantee of the professor's right to search for truth and teach it, but the University of Berlin, a state institution, went even further: At Berlin the university was granted full liberty to manage its own affairs—namely, everything connected with study, teaching, and the administration of university life.[37] Few universities of Europe or anywhere else had ever enjoyed such freedom. In addition to exercising its independence (which, as time proved, it was not prevented from doing), the University of Berlin set new horizons for higher learning. By choosing to emphasize scientific research and by minimizing the university's teaching function, Berlin set standards of excellence in scientific investigation that other German universities were anxious to imitate. When they did, German higher education began to wear a new face. In the end, all German universities became research-oriented, and their reputation for high quality made them the envy of the academic world. It also made them models for universities throughout the world to study and follow. In the United States, for example, the German university was the prototype for several private and public universities. Among the former type were Johns Hopkins University, and among the latter the University of Michigan.[38]

Simultaneously with alterations in the universities, German secondary education was transformed from a narrow classical course to broader instructional programs more nearly meeting society's needs. Traditionally, at least since the time of Sturm, the only secondary schools capable of preparing students for the university were Gymnasien, and such schools, we remember, were committed by their founder to the objective of literary and linguistic exactitude. Yet, among Gymnasien there existed sharp variations in quality of teaching and

[36] Henry Barnard, German Educational Reformers, Brown, Russell and Gross, Hartford, Conn., 1878, pp. 601–617.

[37] Friedrich Paulsen, German Universities and University Study, Charles Scribner's Sons, New York, 1906, pp. 114–121.

[38] Charles F. Thwing, The American and German University, The Macmillan Company, New York, 1928, pp. 201–212.

standards of student performance, and thus university officers and the minister of education were often uncertain about the scholastic competence of the Gymnasium graduates. This uncertainty could not be tolerated by Von Humboldt, so in an effort to control the quality of instruction he instituted teachers' examinations. And while it may be true that such examinations cannot eliminate entirely the intrusion of poor teaching, they can identify teachers whose knowledge of school subjects is inadequate.

The outcome of Von Humboldt's tactic was in effect a purging of many clergymen from teaching positions, and also to serve notice that secondary-school teaching could not any longer be a sinecure for men of the cloth or, for that matter; for any unqualified person. Teaching in secondary schools was henceforth regarded as an important public function open only to qualified men, and such men were endowed with prestige and status previously unavailable to them. The curriculum of secondary education was broadened and its teachers upgraded. The traditional Gymnasium, we know, was a classical school; the new Gymnasium, while still a classical school, discarded Sturm's commitment to pure, idiomatic Latin in order to approach the classics as repositories of the great ideas of mankind. With these ideas in his grasp the serious student could deepen his insights and ponder the fundamental issues of the day.

In addition to the Gymnasium, two types of German secondary education were developed in the nineteenth century: a Realgymnasium and an Oberrealschule. All three types had these common features: They admitted boys only, for coeducation on the secondary level was unknown in nineteenth-century Germany, although some girls attended special female academies; they were nine-year schools with prescribed curricula for each year; graduates from a secondary school were admitted to any German university on the basis of their secondary-school diploma; [39] twenty was the normal age for graduation in all types of secondary schools because the difficulty of the course made it almost impossible for anyone to complete it by age eighteen (a graduation age easy to assume, for the boys usually entered the school at age nine); and all taught religion, German, history, music, and physical education. What was unique to each type of secondary school was its curricular emphasis. Thus the Realgymnasium taught Latin, the classics, science, and modern foreign languages; the Oberrealschule discarded Latin,

[39] James E. Russell, *German Higher Schools: The History, Organization and Methods of Secondary Education in Germany*, Longmans, Green and Company, New York, 1899, pp. 380–386.

Greek, and the classics and taught instead mathematics, science, and modern foreign languages.

All three types of secondary education also offered part-courses, or six-year schools intended to accommodate boys who were unable for academic reasons to complete the full course, were too poor to afford a longer time in school, or who lived in a town unable to support a nine-year school. By adding diversity and curricular variety to secondary education, the new German Gymnasien eroded the exclusiveness of the classical Gymnasium.[40]

The changes in elementary education, although somewhat less dramatic, nevertheless were of equal significance to the total objectives of educational reconstruction. All elementary schools were public and free; attendance in school was compulsory from ages six to fourteen; teachers were selected with greater care and almost all were men; methods of teaching aimed at the development of practical intelligence; and the broad purposes of elementary education centered on the generation of allegiance and devotion to national ideals. With such a system—and such a system did become a reality—illiteracy practically disappeared in Germany.

The educational ideas and plans of Pestalozzi, it should be added, made a deep impact on German elementary schools.[41] Fichte, of course, had made many references to Pestalozzi in his analysis of educational conditions, and was inclined to put Pestalozzi on a pedestal as an educational savior. Besides, the German government sent a number of teachers, educational supervisors, and directors to study firsthand the Pestalozzian schools. Yet, even with all this apparent admiration, there were elements of distrust, for Pestalozzi was clearly a spokesman for popular and democratic education, and German elementary schools, despite their excellent features, were not democratic.

German children, depending on their social status and the promise that might be expected from them, attended different kinds of elementary schools. First, there were the Volksschulen, the schools for the people (the common people) wherein reading, writing, arithmetic, and religion were taught and where every effort was made to inculcate patriotism and to achieve the highly significant goal of social solidarity. Such elementary schools were brief academic excursions of seldom more than four or five years' duration, and students left them to go to

[40] Friedrich Paulsen, *German Education, Past and Present,* translated by T. Lorenz, Charles Scribner's Sons, New York, 1908, pp. 280–286.

[41] See, for example, J. Payne, *Pestalozzi: The Influence of His Principles and Practices on Elementary Education,* Methuen and Company, London, 1875.

vocational or continuation schools where they might master skills necessary for economic life. The possibility of a student's moving from this level of elementary education to any Gymnasien and then on to a university was so remote as to be practically nonexistent.

Another kind of elementary education, intended for the "better" classes in society, essayed to prepare its students for secondary education and, in turn, the university. Because elementary school curricula are not subject to much modification (almost always dealing with the fundamentals of education), we should not expect sharp curricular differences between the two types of German elementary schools. They did much the same educational work, but they did it to or for different classes in the German society. The dual system—one set of schools for common people and another set of schools for aristocrats—was everywhere evident in nineteenth-century Germany, and this second type of elementary school was the first step on an educational ladder intended to perpetuate an aristocracy of position, power, and wealth.

We should mention one last outcome of nineteenth-century German educational reconstruction: a further development of educational theory and practice. Education had at last come of age; it was accorded full recognition as an important national instrument, so it was only natural for capable persons to pay it heed. On the level of school practice, however, the outstanding feature appears to have been the attention devoted to teacher education. In this connection, and to ensure a supply of properly qualified teachers, schools for teachers were organized throughout the country, sometimes in collaboration with universities but often independent of them. Now, and on a broad scale, the educational recommendations of Herbart were listened to, for most of the techniques taught in such schools came directly from Herbart's books.[42]

EDUCATIONAL RECONSTRUCTION IN FRANCE

Nineteenth-century Europe neither escaped nor tried to avoid the tides of nationalism affecting domestic education. In France, however, the changes that occurred were less clearly reforms, at least for three-quarters of the century, than tendencies toward a simple reorganization allowing a national system to take hold without any fundamental overhauling of the curricula or goals of the schools. In a word, French national education was unable to produce the aims it must have sought to achieve. Moreover, it was less permanent than the system which

[42] See Dunkel, *op. cit.*, pp. 100–101.

attained dominance in Germany,[43] for France was subjected to at least
five changes in government in the nineteenth century and this political
instability, while it may not have destroyed educational structures, undoubtedly affected fundamental educational commitments and scholastic objectives. Then, too, France was ambivalent about the role of the
Church in education, sometimes allowing it complete autonomy over
certain levels of education, and at other times proscribing Church
educational action altogether.

By the time Napoleon assumed power in France, the educational
doctrines of La Chalotais were fairly well known and quite generally
accepted among the controlling elements in French society. Therefore,
when Napoleon issued decrees in 1806 and 1808 making French education a tool of the state, there was little reason for alarm, and, generally
speaking, there were only isolated pockets of opposition. This is somewhat surprising because the Napoleonic policy of absolutism in education contradicted any educational policy that might be mined from
Revolution ideology. The Revolution, if nothing else can be said for it,
aimed at freedom, and Napoleon's policy, along with the decrees putting it into effect, denied the doctrine that the principal purpose of
education is to build personal individuality, and from a foundation of
individual strengths to proceed to the formation of a strong and resilient
society. To state it more bluntly, Napoleon's policy was an obstacle to
progress, for it reversed a twenty-five-year trend in French educational
practice that had given many evidences of future promise.[44]

With no more than a cynical nod in the direction of the educational traditions and ideals of the French, Napoleon took control of
all education in France by creating what is called the University of
France. We are aware of the place of France in the history of education,
and we recognize that some of the solidest traditions in higher education had their foundation in France. The University of Paris, the mother
of universities, had its birth on French soil; and in no other country
were the purposes of the university or the freedom that higher teaching
and study entailed more energetically defended than in France. But
the Revolution changed much of this. Suffice it to say that when the
Revolution had accomplished its work, the universities of France had
disappeared. In the aftermath of the Revolution, central schools came
into existence. These schools, in many ways part of education's higher
level, tried to combine interests in literary and industrial studies. Their

[43] Howard C. Barnard, *The French Tradition in Education*, Cambridge University
Press, New York, 1922, pp. 79–93.
[44] See Isaac L. Kandel, *The Reform of Secondary Education in France*, Teachers
College Press, New York, 1924, pp. 66–71.

career was brief, and the record was not too precise, nor was it especially distinguished. It was at this point in history that Napoleon created the University of France.[45]

Educational institutions engaged in studies above the elementary level were made part of the University of France. It should be made clear at the outset that the University of France was an administrative unit, established to control education, and that it had no teaching function as such. Its control over education in France, however, was extensive, except that the University showed no interest whatever in elementary education, which, for the most part, was left to wither and die. The university system inaugurated or reestablished practices in education that were almost always open to suspicion. It was a rigid system: Schools were run along military lines; teaching and learning were present but instruction was narrow and illiberal; thinking was discouraged, for thought could be dangerous. Everyone, every student and every teacher, was under the most severe form of discipline. Nothing could be done without authorizations in the regulations of the University of France.

It may be noted that the French system had many admirers in other countries. There is little reason to doubt that it was an efficient system—a good way to control education, but a poor way to bring about the intellectual and moral autonomy of persons. Some of the states of the United States were anxious to follow the French model, although it may be said that they were usually unwilling to accept the authoritarianism with which French education in this period was branded.

We have already said that the scheme of Napoleon for controlling education left elementary education pretty much out of the picture. True, Napoleon required the schools—especially the *collèges* and *lycées* —to offer some training classes for the teachers who were or would be in the elementary schools. Yet, even so, it could hardly be claimed that the French had anything remotely resembling a system of elementary education. Most of the opportunity for elementary education was provided by the schools of the Christian Brothers. The Brothers were permitted to continue their work because Napoleon happened to approve; still, in a country as vast as France and with her growing population, it was simply impossible for any one teaching congregation to provide all the opportunity that was needed on education's most elementary level. No special indictment of the Brothers is intended when we say that private means for elementary education were inadequate.

[45] Henry H. Walsh, *The Concordat of 1801: A Study in the Problem of Nationalism in the Relations of Church and State*, Columbia University Press, New York, 1933, pp. 187–191.

In an absolute sense, private elementary education was a failure, although in a relative sense, one might well admire its many remarkable accomplishments. Neither the monitorial school idea, imported from England, nor any other plan devised during the first thirty years of the nineteenth century solved France's educational problem. If the Revolution had hurt education more than it helped it, the Restoration brought about no renaissance in education on any level. An inquiry into the state of French education in 1833 revealed conditions that were exceedingly bad.[46]

With education in the hands of the state, the vitality of French educational thinking began to evaporate. The minds that would have turned to educational questions saw the futility of doing so and turned their attention to other fields of intellectual endeavor where obstacles were not so awesome. Yet there were a few sparks of inspiration left. The activity in French educational thought took two main directions. One was toward domestic education, especially the education of girls. This, with the exception of Fénelon's *Treatise on the Education of Girls* [47] written in 1687, had been a neglected subject for centuries. The other was the creation of new societies in which education could play a special role.

In connection with the first direction, the name of Mme Necker de Saussure (1765–1841) stands out especially. Despite a new theoretical emphasis, it should be mentioned that on the practical level the education of French girls had not been completely neglected. Catholic teaching sisterhoods were conducting more than five thousand schools for girls about this time. Besides Mme de Saussure, Mme de Staël, Mme Campan, Mme de Remusat, and Mme de Guizot are some of the other names to be mentioned in this connection; but it was Mme de Saussure, in *Progressive Education*, written about 1838, who made the greatest impression. Without all of Rousseau's negativism, Mme de Saussure was a feminine Rousseau; yet she differed with Rousseau very pointedly on the education of women. The third volume of her *Progressive Education* takes up the issue, and in this volume she rejects almost everything that Rousseau had written in his last book of *Emile*. In her plan, education for girls would be much broader than anything Rousseau proposed. To put it briefly, according to Mme de Saussure, a girl was to be given the opportunity to develop her personality to the fullest. In

[46] This was the inquiry following the 1832 report of Victor Cousin (1792–1867) on the structure and standards of Prussian education.

[47] François Fénelon, *Fénelon on Education*, translated by H. C. Barnard, Cambridge University Press, New York, 1966, pp. 18–28.

doing so she was to become a qualified member both of the household and of society.[48]

If Mme de Saussure's views were somewhat novel, they were not, it would seem, really revolutionary. This approach was left to St. Simon (1760–1825), Fourier (1772–1837), Jacotot (1770–1840), and Edouard Séguin (1812–1880). The latter may not have been a true revolutionary but apparently he did share the ideals of one who was, St. Simon. Only a word can be said here about the role these men played in French educational thought.[49] St. Simon's aim was to break with most social traditions and create new communities that would not be controlled by the interests then controlling society. Since these new communities would be somewhat isolated and mainly self-sufficient, education would have to turn more and more in the direction of vocational preparation and training. St. Simon's social views also endorsed strong moral purposes for the schools. Fourier's plan was more drastic: Children would have been taken from the home when they were infants, and all their upbringing would have been conducted in small communities under the care of special persons. Fourier's views on education, which were for the most part eminently practical, were contained in his *Natural Education*. Jean Jacques Jacotot's *Universal Education*, which appeared in 1822, made at least a temporary impression on teachers, when it set forth ideas advocating the startling and truly revolutionary view that a teacher could teach things of which he himself was ignorant if he had the right method. Jacotot proposed to give teachers the right method. The implications of Jacotot's thought are surely evident when one considers that a great deal of attention was being given at this time, for political reasons, to broadening the base of educational opportunity. A universal method that required of teachers almost nothing in the way of competence caused education-minded politicians to look a second time. When they actually did look a second time, they found very little that was substantial, very little that was educationally attractive.

Finally, there was Edouard Séguin. The significance of his work is by now clear. He was a pioneer in the educational work for retarded children. One author has called him the "apostle of the idiot" because of the principles he laid down with regard to the education and training of such children. In his book on *Idiocy*, Séguin established important positions for the education of defectives. Maria Montessori (1870–

[48] See William Boyd, *From Locke to Montessori*, Henry Holt and Company, New York, 1914, pp. 88–129.

[49] *Ibid.*, and F. E. Farrington, *French Secondary Schools*, Longmans, Green and Company, New York, 1910, pp. 113–128.

1952) demonstrated their validity when she began her work many years later.[50]

Although the principal thrust of French education during the nineteenth century was on a level of theory (and we know enough of the history of educational theory to know how far behind theory practice lags), there were post-Napoleonic educational developments in France well worth noting. Centralized control of French education was a legacy from Napoleon's era—a legacy that remained uninterrupted during the Restoration Monarchy (1815–1830), when almost nothing was done to improve education or even to change it, save to invite the Church to become more active. After 1830, however, leaders in the July Monarchy (1830–1848) became concerned about the lack of educational opportunity for the common people, and commissioned Victor Cousin (1792–1867) to study the whole question, investigate other systems, and prepare a report on what might be done. While Cousin was busy examining Prussian education, an exercise leading to his famous *Report on the State of Public Instruction in Prussia* (1831), Guillaume Guizot (1787–1874), the minister of education, conducted a survey of French elementary education which revealed an almost total absence of public elementary schools.

The work of Cousin and Guizot led directly to the Primary School Law of 1833. This law established primary and higher primary schools —both for the common man, leaving private schools to care for the elite. It called for an annual appropriation of funds to support these schools, required the certification of all teachers, and founded thirty normal schools for the education of teachers. It also directed such schools to conduct a curriculum consisting of French, reading, writing, spelling, grammar, composition, and arithmetic. Religion could be taught only to the children whose parents approved such instruction. Primary schools could charge fees, but children unable to pay were supposed to be taught in any case. Attendance was not compulsory, but, in an obvious attempt to stimulate attendance, the law required towns to conduct schools whenever they reached a certain level of population.

Some of the gains made during the July Monarchy were lost during the periods of the Second Republic and the Second Empire (1848–1870). So French national education either marked time or regressed until the Third Republic, when it reached maturity. Due mainly to the

[50] See Mabel E. Talbot, *Edouard Seguin: A Study of an Educational Approach to the Treatment of Mentally Defective Children*, Teachers College Press, New York, 1964; E. M. Standing, *Maria Montessori: Her Life and Work*, Hollis & Carter, London, 1957; and E. M. Standing, *The Montessori Method: A Revolution in Education*, Academy Library Guild, Fresno, Calif., 1962.

work of Jules Ferry (1832–1893), who served as minister of public instruction from 1879 to 1882, education became a state function to be jealously guarded by the state and to be used to achieve national goals. Ferry's code did not destroy private education in France, but it clearly made private schools delegates of the state, and none was allowed to operate unless it submitted to state regulation and inspection. Elementary education, too, was upgraded; all fees were abolished in primary schools; higher primary schools, abandoned in 1850, were restored; school attendance was compulsory for children between ages six and thirteen; and the curriculum of both levels of primary education was enriched. Secondary education was subjected to the searching scrutiny of the ministers of the Third Republic: the classical course, long the staple of French secondary schools, was dethroned; Latin study, although not jettisoned entirely, was deferred to the later years of schooling; scientific subjects were made welcome in all secondary-school grades; and the admissions' policies of secondary schools were liberalized in order to increase the opportunity for the sons of common people to improve their status in life.

The French brand of national education did not succeed in creating the same deathless devotion to the fatherland as education did in Germany, yet in its own social context French education, in addition to reducing illiteracy to almost nothing, and by stressing especially the national language in all schools, helped to generate a high degree of national consciousness and unity.

ENGLISH EDUCATION

Steps taken for the establishment of a national system of education for England were somewhat retarded. While both Germany and France were making some progress in connection with popular education, England's attitude seemed to be one of indifference. The reluctance on the part of the state to take any action did not mean that no one in England was interested in educational reform or that it was not needed. The industrial revolution had ushered in many changes in English life. Most importantly, the factory system motivated certain changes in, or realignments of, living conditions; the factory system led to conditions in urban living that were so bad that they obviously had to be reformed first. Such things as education would have to await more basic social and economic reforms. The common man, when he or his leaders became articulate, demanded change, and in education he demanded greater opportunity. The middle class, on the other hand, was in a position to resist many of the demands of the common man because it, too, was strong and articulate. Mercantilism seemed to support the conditions that were so prevalent in England.

Yet it is not true that nothing at all was done. As early as 1802, the "Health and Morals of Apprentices Act" was passed. This act limited the working hours of apprentices to twelve a day and directed that every apprentice be given some instruction in reading, writing, and arithmetic during the first four years of his apprenticeship. This instruction was to be given according to the age and ability of the apprentice, and the costs of such instruction were to be borne by the master. The instruction that this act required was to be given in a place especially prepared either in the factory or in the workshop. In spite of the legislation, which was, no doubt, a step forward, little was done. It would appear that the law was not enforced with any vigor. Thus the English child, especially the child of the workingman, had to mark time until 1833, when another act that had relevance to education, The Factory Act, was passed.[51]

The act of 1833 prohibited the employment of children under nine years of age, made two hours of instruction each day compulsory for children between the ages of nine and thirteen, and appropriated £20,000 for the purpose of building schoolhouses in which the children of the poorer classes might receive some instruction. By 1870 England had made enough progress in the direction of a national system of education to include all children in the elementary system. From that date on, English education was engaged in consolidating the gains that had been made in the previous seventy years. This consolidation took the form principally of broadening the requirements for compulsory attendance in elementary schools and, in time, of making more adequate provisions for secondary education so that it became more nearly on a popular level.

Two nineteenth-century figures stand out especially as English educational reformers and theorists: Robert Owen (1771–1858) and Herbert Spencer (1820–1903).

Owen was one of the nineteenth century's most ardent proponents of popular education. According to his views of education, expressed in *A New View of Society*, or *Essays on the Formation of Human Character*, education, more than anything else, was responsible for the making of men, and society was man's teacher as much as the school. Thus, Owen sought to bring about social reforms that would provide a more suitable frame of reference in which education or schooling could do its work. But this was not enough; he sought to reform education, too.

[51] Adamson, *op. cit.*, pp. 136–141; and Mary E. Lawrence, *Friedrich Froebel and English Education*, Philosophical Library, New York, 1953, pp. 191–198.

Toward this end he suggested that a number of changes should be made all the way up the educational ladder. The infant school was unquestionably his best known effort at reform. The infant school was really an elementary school that offered opportunity for elementary studies to poor children between the ages of five and ten. Owen's educational experiment, a school called the New Institution, was conducted in the community of New Lanark, near Glasgow. It would be hard to believe that anything of any great consequence for educational practice could have made its way out of this institution. On the other hand, it is surely true that Owen generated a great deal of sympathy for the cause of education with his work, and he formulated the humanitarian outlook that was absolutely confident of the power of education to regenerate men and reform societies.[52]

If Robert Owen was important to the future of education, Herbert Spencer was even more important. Naturalistic education of the twentieth century is almost entirely indebted to him for its foundations. Besides, Spencer was very much opposed to national education, since he was convinced that only harm could come from creating a system of education under political control. At any rate, Spencer was not powerful enough to stop national education, although he and other Englishmen of like mind did retard its development in England for a number of years. His place in the history of education, however, is reserved not because of any of the stands that he took in opposition to national education, but because of his views as to the purposes of education in general. In an essay written about 1861, "What Knowledge Is of Most Worth?", Spencer discussed the aims of education. It may be fair to claim that this essay, more than any other educational document of the nineteenth century, gave direction to the educational thought and practice of the twentieth century. What was Spencer's answer? What knowledge is of most worth? According to Spencer, it is scientific knowledge and especially that kind of scientific knowledge that leads to individual development. For him the individual's development is always first; social formation is always second. Literary education is nothing more than a "poor relative" in instruction. It is practically meaningless when compared with the kind of knowledge that can help individuals solve life's problems. This distrust of traditional knowledge is found not only in the essay "What Knowledge Is of Most Worth?" but also in Spencer's other essays, "Moral Educa-

---

[52] Frank Smith, *A History of English Education, 1760–1902*, University of London Press, London, 1931, pp. 76–91; G. A. M. Lowndes, *The British Educational System*, Hutchinson & Co., Ltd., London, 1955, pp. 116–131; and Harold Silver, *The Concept of Popular Education*, MacGibbon & Kee, London, 1965, pp. 270–280.

tion," "Intellectual Education," and "Physical Education." [53] In general, it can be said that Spencer completes the educational traditions that had their inception with Rousseau and Pestalozzi. His views, moreover, exemplify the individualism that was so characteristic of nineteenth-century English education.

Despite this ardent quality of individualism in English society, a quality implicitly endorsing the educational principle "each man according to his own means," the history of nineteenth-century English education reflects an awareness of needed reforms and a ferment for incorporating some of the features of French and German education into an English system. Here neither the monitorial-school idea—the work of Robert Owen, Herbert Spencer, Andrew Bell (1753–1832), and Joseph Lancaster (1778–1838)—nor the early nineteenth-century laws or commission reports counted for much. What did count was the Elementary Education Act of 1870 (Foster Act), whereby school districts controlled by elected school boards were created and empowered to establish elementary schools where they were needed. Such schools—now authentically public—were supported by taxes and, following the act of 1891, were made entirely free. Private schools, always recognized as worthwhile in English tradition, were eligible for public support, too. So now the stage was set for compulsory attendance in elementary schools.

Secondary education was almost untouched by nineteenth-century developments in England, but before the century closed this oversight was partly redressed. The Bryce Commission, in 1895, recommended an articulated public system of elementary and secondary schools, a recommendation implemented in the Balfour Act of 1902. Thus, without the same intense motivation as Germany or the rage for centralization as in France, England took halting, though important, steps toward nationalizing education in the nineteenth century.

EDUCATION IN RUSSIA

It is hazardous to compare the nineteenth-century developments of national systems of education in other European countries with those of Russia. Russia's educational consciousness was slow in forming. Peter the Great and Catherine the Great, who belong to the seventeenth and eighteenth centuries, were responsible for the foundations of Russian

[53] Herbert Spencer, *Education: Intellectual, Moral, and Physical,* Appleton-Century-Crofts, Inc., New York, 1927; and Jay Rumney, *Herbert Spencer's Sociology: A Study in the History of Social Theory,* Atherton Press, New York, 1966, pp. 330–336.

education. In the nineteenth century we may mention Czar Alexander I (1801–1825) and Nicholas I (1825–1855) in connection with Russian education, but we cannot easily indicate the contributions that they made. More often than not, educational historians are content to say that they continued the work of their predecessors, although the educational work of their predecessors is not very obvious. Alexander II (1855–1881) was responsible for what one may call the beginnings of a national system of education in Russia, by establishing a state system of elementary schools that were open to all children. There was no such thing as compulsory attendance in these schools, however, and it is not possible to be precise about their effects. Apparently the ideal of popular education was accepted slowly, if not reluctantly, in Russia.[54] About the time of the Bolshevist revolution (1917) no more than one-fourth of the school-age children were attending school, and less than one-quarter of the population of Russia was literate. The great educational advances in Russia belong to the twentieth century.[55]

Yet, while recognizing both what amounted to indifferentism in vast areas of Russian education, and a long-standing Russian tradition to turn its back on Western Europe, there are some interesting historical data which may serve to illuminate the Russian educational scene. In the eighteenth century the czars were apparently willing to accept things as they were—which, in educational terms, meant that only an aristocracy could hope for learning. Too often, however, even this hope was unrealized; so in 1719 Czar Peter decreed that the children of priests and nobles be taught to read and write. And to ensure respect for the decree, he instituted state examinations. The extent to which these decrees were honored can be debated; in any case, the next prominent forward step was taken at the insistence of Catherine the Great in 1764, when she caused the Educational Society of Noble Girls to be founded. Using the Society and a multitude of other means at her disposal, Catherine improved the quality of female education for Russian gentlewomen, although, for the most part, what was accomplished would have to be classified as "polite" or finishing-school education.

In 1786 the Commission for the Establishment of Schools was created by Catherine, proving that her perceptions of educational need

---

[54] Leo Tolstoy, *On Education*, translated by Leo Wiener, University of Chicago Press, Chicago, 1968; and Nicholas Hans, *History of Russian Educational Policy*, P. S. King & Staples, Ltd., London, 1931.

[55] See William H. E. Johnson, *Russia's Educational Heritage*, Rutgers University Press, New Brunswick, N. J., 1950; and F. C. Barghoorn, *The Soviet Cultural Offensive*, Princeton University Press, Princeton, N. J., 1960.

were not limited to schools for girls. And the report of the commission, largely the work of Jankovitch de Mirievo, the minister of education, became the *Statutes for Public Schools in the Russian Empire.* The *Statutes* recommended a complete school system almost universal in scope, free, and under the direct control of the state. Primary schooling was charted as a two-year course consisting of reading, writing, arithmetic, grammar, and religion. Higher schools and private schools had broader curricula and were preferred by students who could afford them. But in the public schools prescribed methods, syllabi, and rules reigned supreme; nothing was left to chance. Yet, considering what the new system was expected to replace, it earned commendations. Two obstacles stood in its way, however, and in the end spelled its doom: inadequate financial support, and an almost total absence of qualified teachers.

In 1802 the Ministry of Public Education replaced the Commission for the Establishment of Schools and almost at once began the hard task of making a public system of education work. As a first order of business the schools were reorganized, costs were estimated and sometimes budgeted, curricula were specified for various school levels, teachers were trained, and a good beginning was made. A centralized system seemed to be a reality and good omens were in evidence. But again cost, geography, and social barrier proved too much, and the system's promise deteriorated. Then, too, partly because of Russia's military encounter with Napoleon, the mood of the country changed, and educational goals were subjected to some rethinking. Rather than putting confidence in education as a way of strengthening society, Russian spokesmen and leaders began to see it as a dangerous threat. All schools were suspect, but the universities, which had been fairly progressive in absorbing European thought and culture, were singled out for special scorn and abuse. In the end, the benefits of literacy were doubted; religious instruction was enough. Here, at least, was the educational philosophy of Nicholas I.

Against this background of suspicion toward schooling, Alexander II came to power in 1855. Being more enlightened than his immediate predecessors, he directed that schools be opened and upgraded. So in 1863 the universities were restored and, in fact, became somewhat easier to attend. In 1864 the Secondary School Code reestablished the classical school, which was for a long time the only Russian representative of secondary education; and at about the same time elementary schools were revived, although they never went beyond a simple curriculum of religion, morals, and the three R's, nor did they lead a student to the threshold of secondary school studies. By the end of the century, after the numerous reforms we have noted, Russian secondary and higher education won good marks for quality, although opportunities for attendance were severely limited to an aristocracy. But elementary education, for which the need was so great, was plagued again by faulty support and ineffective teaching, by the Church's intrusion to deemphasize secular in favor of religious teaching, and by the state's inability or unwillingness to make elementary-school attendance compulsory for all persons. Twentieth-century Russia inherited the educational problems of the nineteenth century, and without much solid guidance from tradition, law, school organization, or commitment to learning was left to work them out as best she could.

Summary

The nineteenth century was anxious to accept its educational inheritance. The ferment that characterized the two preceding centuries was still in evidence, and the outcomes from it were directed along practical lines toward the improvement of education. Two prominent educators attract our attention, Herbart and Froebel. As a result of Herbart's many accomplishments in education and psychology, it is possible to refer to him as the father of the science of education. His work made its greatest impression on the methods of teaching. Froebel was an idealist, who tried to reshape education along idealistic lines. In the main he failed. Yet in one area he was eminently successful. He founded the kindergarten—an institutional outgrowth of his educational philosophy—in 1837, and this institution has been his most important contribution to education.

The large educational movements of the nineteenth century had to do with national education. States began to see the relationship between education and national life and national goals. State systems came into existence. National education had its first and highest development in Prussia, then in Germany, then France, and finally England.

PART IV

The Growth *of* American Democratic Education

The colonists who came to America brought their social institutions with them. Whatever their religious preferences and economic interests, they were not cultural innovators. Colonial schools, for example, bore undeniably European marks. Colleges imitated the curriculum of European higher schools, adding only a dimension to purpose whereby these schools could prepare clergymen for the churches. Secondary schools borrowed freely from the classical models in England and on the Continent, and in the end were little different from the schools we met during our study of Erasmus, Sturm, and Cordier. Elementary schools lacked the support of public policy and those on a secondary and higher level followed the old instructional patterns as well. Even the town school, so famous in American educational history as a prototype for local school organization and control, has no authentic claim to make for originality, for once we sharpen our historical focus we know we have seen signs of it before.

Had the American social order remained static, these transplanted schools would have remained the high points of colonial and national education; but the social order was dynamic, and social change occurred on the levels of both ideals and practice. Thus the old schools were found wanting and being unable or unwilling to keep pace with society itself, were either reformed or transformed. These reformations or transformations, beginning about 1750, breathed new life into American education and put it on the track to social progress and responsiveness. But the new era was ephemeral and, in the last analysis, it must be admitted, was incapable of realizing its ambitions for making educational opportunity conform to the new idealism in American life. Franklin and Jefferson were spokesmen for a social system, including education, which should match the promises of human freedom and aspiration in the new world. Yet for all their wisdom, and not discounting the cogency of their thought, their voices went unheeded, and the new educational era was made to heel to the tested traditions of previous centuries. The trial took a hundred years—and in the end the schools were back where they had started.

But if education could not live in the past, neither could it mark time in the present: After two decades of the nineteenth century, dedicated educational reformers were anxious to try again. In the next half-century, educational history in the United States records the common-school movement led by Horace Mann, the upgrading and broadening of elementary education, the creation and development of the high school (aided greatly by the favorable Kalamazoo decision and later by the *Report* of the Committee of Ten), and an almost total reorientation of higher learning.

With an educational system intact—one capable of instructing in the elementary schools all the children of all the people, and more liberal in admitting them to high schools and welcoming them to the colleges—the time was ripe to reinforce the educational visions of nineteenth-century educators with an authentic theory for democratic education, and a dependable science of education to support this theory. John Dewey must be singled out for special praise in connection with the former, and for a science of education, Edward L. Thorndike's name must be ranked above all others. With theory and science as education's partners, the early decades of the twentieth century produced lasting and significant contributions both to education's popularity and to equality of educational opportunity.

XV

Education in the United States

During the sixteenth and seventeenth centuries Spain, France, and England, all vitally interested in North America, undertook to establish through active colonization their claims in that vast frontier continent. Thus it is possible to speak of a New France and a New Spain as well as a New England in connection with the settlement and civilization of North America. Indeed, wherever France and Spain held dominion in the New World their political, social, and economic systems, as well as their distinctive colonization policies, were evident. However, though both countries acquired a colonial American educational history, both histories were abbreviated, and neither was destined to play a decisive role in the educational future of the United

States. For that reason alone (which should seem to be highly convincing), having taken brief note of the presence of France and Spain in colonial North America, we move on immediately to English America, where the permanent foundations were laid for education in the the United States.

A Period of Transplantation (1635 to 1750)

The colonists in English America were neither directly exposed to, nor even indirectly affected by, seventeenth-century European educational experiments. Indeed, the tentative and experimental pedagogies of realism and naturalism were almost totally ignored by most colonial schoolmasters. While colonists were busy clearing the wildernesses and extending frontiers, it was only natural for them to give little attention to the kind of educational ferment common in the more settled social order of Europe. Yet, because they shared a cultural tradition which had its roots in Europe, they tried their best to be true to their past; and for this reason, with the passage of time the foreign educational example finally made impressions in America. Eighteenth- and nineteenth-century European educational theory and philosophy not only crossed the Atlantic, but found in America a new and rich environment in which to thrive.

A common political and social attitude in colonial New England scorned democracy and most of its claims for equality among persons. So if we look to the colonies for the basic policy of modern American education—democracy—we look in vain, for it was not there. The dominant intellectual interest which made itself felt in society, politics, and education, and one which could absorb almost all a colonist's attention, was religion. In all the colonies of New England, with the exception of Rhode Island, the men responsible for the course of events were primarily concerned with the establishment of Bible commonwealths, and with the maintenance of an ecclesiastical social order sustained by a class-structured society.[1]

The status of education in the New England commonwealths was defined and limited by an unequivocal repugnance for democracy, a circumscription of suffrage and social standing, and a dogmatic assumption that the state should be subordinated to the Church. Wherever

---

[1] For further study of the conflicting views of the early system of education in New England, see Samuel Eliot Morison, *The Puritan Pronaos*, New York University Press, New York, 1936, p. 30; Edgar W. Knight, *Education in the United States*, 3d ed., Ginn & Company, Boston, 1951, p. 85; and Merle Curti, *The Social Ideals of American Educators*, Charles Scribner's Sons, New York, 1935, pp. 4–5.

schools were found in New England, their teaching reflected these fundamental attitudes held by the educated members of the community, who were at once the framers of all public policy.[2]

In New England, where we find the earliest permanent beginnings of education in America, there was a definite commitment to mental and moral training (although possibly not to schooling under formal auspices for all the children of the colony) which had its source in the religious ideals entertained by the governing class. To put it briefly, their religious beliefs led them to a conviction that a learned ministry was absolutely essential to the well-being of their creed. Without educated leaders, they knew, their sect would wither and die, and so they advocated the creation of schools and colleges capable of producing and sustaining a competent ministry. Opinions differ as to why the colonists of New England, especially those in Massachusetts Bay, wanted schools and education. These opinions range all the way from the desire on the part of New England Puritans to cultivate liberal education, to their conviction (shared by leaders in other colonies as well) that education must and would serve the needs of institutionalized religion and the interests of a class-structured society. Just where the truth lies on this question of educational motive is hard to say. But we see little evidence to support the belief that the educational intent of the Puritans was liberal or that the institutions they founded, or the intellectual ideals they cultivated, could lead very naturally to liberality of mind. The typical attitude of the New England colonist was that educational goals had to subserve superior interests, and that the most superior of all interests was religion. Education, then, was set in a practical context, and was always religious in content and purpose.[3]

This attitude did not necessarily retard educational progress, for institutionalized religion is not required to stand in the way of educational opportunity or intellectual enlightenment. It was precisely because their respected ideals demanded education that the colonists of New England showed such energy in making provisions for schooling. Almost from the beginning some colonists took a progressive position on the question of opportunity for education, favoring more and better

[2] Harvey Wish, *Society and Thought in Early America,* Longmans, Green and Company, Inc., New York, 1950, pp. 37–41.

[3] Morison, *op. cit.,* pp. 30–40; Knight, *op. cit.,* pp. 85–89; Curti, *op. cit.,* pp. 15–18; and in connection with curricula and schoolbooks, see John A. Nietz, *Old Textbooks,* University of Pittsburgh Press, Pittsburgh, 1961; Charles C. Butterworth, *The English Primers,* University of Pennsylvania Press, Philadelphia, 1953; Paul L. Ford, *The New-England Primer,* Teachers College Press, New York, 1962; and Cloyer Meriweather, *Our Colonial Curriculum, 1607–1776,* Capital Publishing Company, Washington, D. C., 1907.

schools for most, if not all, children, but their recommendations were paid scant heed. It was easier to stay within the familiar precincts of tradition and to follow the conventional pattern wherein each man was educated according to his means, and wherein society itself should not be expected to assume any responsibility for the education or training of its members. This, indeed, was the accepted and acceptable theory, although it ran counter to an advanced but minority opinion advocating social responsibility for education, and community support of schools. Although this liberal educational doctrine was largely ineffective in producing broad educational opportunities for the children of the colonies, it must be admitted that in the end it was responsible for the organization of town systems of schools. The famous educational acts of the Massachusetts Colony were logical expressions of this principle.

The town, of course, arose out of the peculiar circumstances and needs of the New England community and was not created for educational purposes. It was a compact type of settlement capable of adapting itself to the needs of the people. The inhabitants of the town may have been farmers, fishermen, or businessmen. The town's area was seldom less than twenty square miles or more than forty, but in every case the size of a town depended upon the colony's legislative body. If a congregation or a group of people wanted to organize a town, they did so by petitioning the colonial government; and if the colonial government granted their petition, it marked out the boundaries of the town. The title to the land was assigned to proprietors, the affluent members of the community. The town, therefore, was a kind of corporate entity. With its legal creation, the town assumed an important place in colonial political life. Now it was able to send representatives to the colonial legislature, and it was given a good deal of freedom in the conduct of local affairs. There were broad areas for local action at this time; in some things—possibly education could be included—the local town unit was autonomous. But to return to town organization: When the town received its legal recognition from the colonial legislative unit, its officers began to assign plots of land in the village on which the proprietors and inhabitants could build their homes. Other plots were assigned for other purposes. A farmer would be allotted another plot of land on the outskirts of the village where he could till the soil; an artisan would be allotted a place in the village where he could build his shop. This land was assigned to the inhabitants of the town and was legally held by them. Yet not all the land of the town was assigned to private ownership. Pasture land and wooded areas, for instance, were reserved for common use, and there was no individual ownership of the commons.⁴ After all the inhabitants of the newly formed town had had their property designated, the town may still have had some undistributed land. Such land was simply held by the town for future assignment. A newcomer to the town could apply for a portion of the land that remained unclaimed, and if the town board voted its approval, a plot of land would be assigned to him.

In New England the town meeting came into prominence as a forum in which the affairs of the community were conducted. In such a system, although there were many signs of democracy, there was no such thing as popular government even on the town level. Only qualified members of the town could participate in the discussions of the town meeting and vote the decisions, and usually the qualifications were stated in terms of an individual's status in the town: Was he a householder? What was his estate worth? Did he have a good reputation? All of these questions demanded a proper answer. In addition to these other requirements, an attained age of twenty-four was usually demanded.⁵

Thus, the town was governed by an oligarchy, although this was an impermanent arrangement, for the seeds of the system's destruction were there from the beginning. The original system of political control established in New England was indebted to institutionalized religion for its support. As religion became weaker, authoritarianism in government tended to become weaker too. New England was, after all, a frontier, and democracy has always thrived better on the frontier than anywhere else. Repression and regulation are the weapons of authoritarianism, and these weapons were becoming progressively less effective in the New England of the seventeenth century. Church leaders were aware of the diminution of their authority, and in spite of their desperate efforts to maintain control and power over the people, the ministers of the gospel saw this power gradually slip away from them. At one time their political, economic, social, and even religious authority went unquestioned. This condition of affairs changed. Magistrates and gentlemen as well as ministers were losing their power. The man who was coming into the picture, not yet a man to be given control in any democratic sense but a man to be reckoned with, nevertheless, was the common man. There were a number of reasons for these decided

⁴ For an appraisal of the town in New England life, see John Fairfield Sly, *Town Government in Massachusetts,* Harvard University Press, Cambridge, Mass., 1930, pp. 81–106.

⁵ *Ibid.,* pp. 75–76.

shifts in society which we cannot consider here.[6] We are concerned mainly to know that in this social ferment the initial steps were taken in the interest of education.

The first advance, which was also the most famous and perhaps the most effective, was made by the Massachusetts Act of 1642. In this act we have the first example of compulsory education in the English American colonies. Between 1642, when the Massachusetts statute was passed, and 1671, all New England colonies except Rhode Island enacted similar laws setting minimum educational accomplishments for all children. It must be noted, however, that compulsory education did not necessarily mean schooling. None of these early acts required the communities to establish schools or required anyone to attend a public institution. The legislation making education compulsory put upon the home the burden of offering what were considered to be the minimum essentials for a Bible commonwealth. If the home would not or could not accomplish the goals envisioned in the law, the child could be removed from the home or taken from the master to whom he had been apprenticed and put in a place where he could obtain the required education. This was a departure from the English laws on which these statutes were based—the Statute of Apprentices of 1562 and the English Poor Law of 1601—for the first English laws had not made anything more than the care of children a social obligation. If for any reason a child was removed from the home, from his parents or master, the responsibility of society was to see that he had food and shelter, nothing else. New England, slightly more humanitarian in its outlook, went a little beyond this and required that such a child receive not only some trade training but some academic education as well.

The Massachusetts Act of 1642 was, then, the first law in English America to make education compulsory for children. It was up to the selectmen of the town to determine whether or not the requirements of the law had been fulfilled. If they were not, if the children were not taught a calling or a trade and could not read well enough to understand the principles of religion or the capital laws of the colony, the parents could be fined, or the children could be removed from the home or from the care of the master. The Massachusetts law of 1642 was the model legislation for other colonies enacting similar laws; its main features were preserved in a new law in 1648. In this new law

[6] For this point, see M. W. Jernegan, *The American Colonies, 1492–1750*, Longmans, Green and Company, Inc., New York, 1929, pp. 179–185; and Ralph Barton Perry, *Puritanism and Democracy*, Vanguard Press, Inc., New York, 1944, pp. 71–78.

the selectmen were commissioned as educational inspectors and were empowered to test the children's ability to read perfectly in English and, moreover, to assess their understanding of the colony's laws. Besides this, the law had a religious dimension: Every child's knowledge of the orthodox catechism was tested by the age-old technique of catechizing. The provision for teaching a trade or calling remained much as before; parents or masters were "to bring up their children and apprentices in some honest lawful calling, labor, or imployment." The selectmen, with the help or advice of two magistrates, could remove children from situations wherein the law was not being fulfilled and apprentice them to some master who would abide by the law. Under such conditions boys were apprenticed until they were twenty-one and girls until they were eighteen.[7]

These colonial laws were evidently inspired by economic, religious, and educational motives. By now the two former are fairly clear and reflect deeply ingrained social atttitudes, but the educational motive stands on less certain ground. Had the colonists really nailed a vision of decent learning to their educational mast? Or were they merely being practical in using the means of education to preserve the status quo? Was reading, for example, stressed because it could open up to people the world of literature, or was it recommended because of its value as a political tool? It should indeed be a pleasant exercise to report that the former was true, but this would be a distortion of colonial educational history. In the last analysis, colonial education was an instrument for controlling the people in a political and social system bent on regulating every detail of personal life.[8]

As we have said, all the New England colonies save Rhode Island passed such statutes. And we may now ask: How carefully were these laws enforced? Although a serious effort was no doubt made at enforcement, many children in the colonies never enjoyed any of the vocational or educational opportunities prescribed by law. The cause of popular education, we must believe, was served well by the example and effects of the Massachusetts law of 1642 and the laws modeled after it; but the laws themselves were not permanent, and the legal foundation for compulsory education met with at least temporary frustration. Late in the seventeenth century (from 1686 to 1689, to be exact), all New England colonies were united in a dominion under the governorship of Sir Edmund Andros. Colonial charters were revoked

---

[7] See M. W. Jernegan, *Laboring and Dependent Classes in Colonial America, 1607–1783*, University of Chicago Press, Chicago, 1931, pp. 91–95.

[8] Perry Miller, *American Puritanism,* Doubleday & Company, Garden City, New York, 1956, pp. 171–176.

during this regime, and the laws pertaining to compulsory education were repealed or rendered ineffective. Thus, as the seventeenth century came to a close, the seeds sown for popular education had been uprooted, and the traditions shaped by the Massachusetts Act of 1642 were sidetracked and stalled.

But before these unfortunate obstacles arose to interrupt educational progress, some of the colonies had taken another step forward. They passed laws to establish town schools, and thus redressed the legal inconsistency of compelling children to show evidences of formal learning without the benefit of schools they might attend. Again leadership was assumed by Massachusetts when it passed the famous "'Old Deluder Satan Act" in 1647. Yet, even before Massachusetts took what is often counted the most important legal step in furthering the cause of free public schools, a few colonial towns anticipated this action to make provisions for publicly supported schools.[9] Compulsory-education statutes, it is easy to see, often put unequal and, in some cases, impossible burdens on parents and masters, and some parents and masters simply refused to use their own resources to educate their children or apprentices. But the law was clear and, in general, town officers tried to obey it, sometimes by demanding strict enforcement and sometimes by using the resources of the town to found schools.

The school-establishment movement was by no means a popular one, however, and perhaps not more than a half-dozen towns established such schools before 1647. When they did, the schools were supported in various ways: Some towns taxed their citizens and used revenues for school support; others used income from town lands to help defray educational costs; still others appealed to the charity of wealthy inhabitants and asked them to donate the funds necessary for school support. In every instance, however, regardless of whatever other sources of income were available for school support, students were charged tuition, rates, or educational fees. Despite evidences that public support for schools was being tested, the free school idea had not yet matured. Nowhere in New England—not even in the famous Boston Latin School—was free schooling a fact.[10]

Apart from any consensus on ways to support schools, or any general acknowledgment that schools should be free, an observable heightening of interest in town schools provided a popular basis for the Mas-

---

[9] See Robert F. Seybolt, *Apprenticeship and Apprenticeship Education in Colonial New England and New York,* Teachers College Press, New York, 1917, pp. 111–121.

[10] Jernegan, *Laboring and Dependent Classes in Colonial America, 1607–1783,* pp. 72–82.

sachusetts Act of 1647. This is but another example of law following rather than leading public opinion, for, although encountering strong pockets of resistance, the act of 1647 probably expressed the people's will. And, it should be observed, the act's provisions were consistent with European trends toward national education as well as with the earlier Massachusetts law of 1642. The legislation of 1642 required Massachusetts towns with fifty or more householders to appoint a teacher to instruct children in the skills of reading and writing. Support for teachers was provided for in this way: "[Their] wages shall be paid either by the parents or masters of such children, or by the inhabitants in general, by way of supply, as the major part of those that order the prudentials of the town shall appoint." [11] A warning was inserted to discourage teachers from charging more than the customary fees for teaching, but this was probably an unnecessary precaution, for schoolmasters in the colonies were never in an enviable bargaining position. The law was clearly interested in providing for elementary education, but it did not stop until it had also required towns with populations greater than one hundred householders to open a "grammar school, the master thereof being able to instruct youth so far as they may be fitted for the university." [12] In assigning to towns a legal responsibility for elementary and secondary education the law also set a scale of fines to be levied against any town refusing to comply with its provisions.

This act, a model for later colonial laws, was followed in every New England colony save, again, Rhode Island. So there are good reasons for accepting the "Old Deluder Satan Act" as a fundamental plank in the platform of American public education. Yet the motives behind its passage should perhaps be summarily rejected today, for they were really blind to the most fundamental possibilities of public education. The people of the colonies, we must admit, wanted the advantages of learning, knew that reading of the scriptures and good literature were worthwhile, and were for, rather than against, literacy. But this was only part of the picture, and a rather inchoate part at that. The real motives behind the Massachusetts Act of 1647 and other laws like it had to do with religious and political authority and control. The fundamentals of learning enabled the masses to understand and obey the regulations of the Church and the laws of the state. The act was religious, civic, and social in its outlook, but literary values, or the human dimensions to a decent education, were not uppermost in the minds of the

[11] *Report of the Commissioner of Education, 1892–1893*, p. 1232; or *The Colonial Laws of Massachusetts*, Boston, 1889, pp. 190–191.
[12] *Ibid.*

legislators who voted for it. Perhaps the primary outcome of the law
of 1647 was its recognition of the state as a legitimate agency of education, and thus it established a permanent precedent in American educational law.[13]

Although we are on entirely safe ground in recognizing the act
of 1647 as an important beam in the structure of American education,
we are nevertheless uncertain about its acceptance during the half-
century following its enactment. A good deal of dispute among historians centers on this point: some say the law was ignored, others are
impressed by evidences of observance.[14] In any case, in this same half-
century education and schooling became more popular, and the means
of education were more generously distributed. Whether or not these
were direct effects of the law of 1647 and the precedents it generated
may be debated.

Colonial Schools

In the New England colonies provisions were made for formal education in four different types of schools: the dame school, the town
school, the Latin grammar school, and the college. Each of these schools
had a counterpart in Europe, and each was content to transplant instructional practices having their origin in Europe.

THE DAME SCHOOL

The dame school, imported from England, made its appearance in
America at a time when such a school—standing between town effort
in education and home instruction—should not have had much to
recommend it. This was a simple school where the elements of reading,
spelling, and religion were taught to any child who could afford to
attend, but it was always outside the boundaries of genuine public
education. Rather than fitting into the tentative mold of public schooling and instruction outside the home, dame schools were extensions of
the home's teaching function. As such, the dame school's days were
numbered, and it disappeared when elementary schools commissioned
by the towns became more common. The dame school, however, did not
pass quickly from the colonial scene, and the principal reason for its
tenacity was that early town schools—the types of schools generated in

[13] John Hardin Best and Robert T. Sidwell, *The American Legacy of Learning*,
J. B. Lippincott Company, Philadelphia, 1967, pp. 10–11.
[14] Bernard Bailyn, *Education in the Forming of American Society*, University of
North Carolina Press, Chapel Hill, 1960, pp. 15–49.

the legislation of 1647—usually demanded a reading ability of their entering students. Although in retrospect we find it hard to justify such an entrance requirement to an elementary school, its imposition kept colonial dame schools relatively intact. The teacher in the dame school was usually a woman of the community who had the time, the necessary literary skill, and the room in her home to conduct a school. She kept the school in her kitchen (thus the name "kitchen school"), and charged fees for her teaching. Because these schools were outside the ambit of public responsibility, the record of their work is little known and, moreover, because they were always private ventures, there was no need for them to follow conventional patterns of instruction. A general historical portrait of dame schools is difficult to draw.[15]

If the dame school appears to us as an oddity, we must remember that it was a more logical expression of seventeenth-century colonial educational theory than was the town school. Despite the good record of progress toward more public responsibility for education, as evidenced in the Massachusetts laws, the most fundamental of seventeenth-century educational beliefs was that the individual, not society, was responsible for his own education. We have already remarked that two sides to this question were then being debated, but, it should be clear, the dame school found the bulk of its support in the view that the child's education is first, and probably exclusively, a home responsibility. If the home decided to delegate some of its functions or to seek help in teaching, the dame school was usually available.

THE TOWN SCHOOL

When the town school first appeared as an import from England, its curriculum consisted of writing and arithmetic. This was a continuation of the scribal tradition in education; the school's main purpose was to educate clerks. But in New England, it was almost impossible to keep reading out of the elementary school's curriculum, for the most necessary of the elementary skills was reading, not arithmetic or writing. Thus, the town school in New England, following the prescript of the Act of 1647, became at first a reading school. Before long, however, the school was devoting its attention to the three R's—not the three R's of the twentieth century, but of the seventeenth: reading, writing, and religion. Arithmetic was thought to be a mercantile skill and was not commonly taught except in the towns that enjoyed a commercial status. In spite of this tendency to isolate skills as they had been isolated be-

[15] Walter H. Small, *Early New England Schools*, Ginn & Company, Boston, 1914, pp. 162–170.

fore, the colonists soon came to include in their schools the content that is now universally accepted as proper to the elementary school.

The town school was not always an elementary school. When a town had more than one hundred householders, its obligation was to have a school which would "fit youth for the university." Clearly, the law of 1647 intended that the town school should go beyond elementary subjects in its offerings. In spite of this legal obligation, the towns apparently employed one master and charged him with the responsibility of teaching youth the first elements of education and of instructing more advanced students in the mysteries of the Latin language and the classics.[16]

The town school, then, was, as the law required, a reading-and-writing school. There seems to be no need to distinguish between the reading school and the writing school after compulsory-school laws were adopted in the New England colonies. For a few years before these laws were passed in Massachusetts in 1647, it may have been true that a reading school was maintained separately from a writing school, but we have little historical assurance for this statement. It should not be forgotten that the town system provided also for the more advanced education of youth. In many respects the town school was a secondary school and a Latin school, although it is surely true that most of the boys who came to the colonial colleges had attended, not a town school, but a private Latin grammar school.[17]

THE LATIN GRAMMAR SCHOOL

The first permanent school established in English America was the Boston Latin Grammar School. This was a school that could trace its educational inheritance all the way back to the schools of the Hellenistic period. In a number of important respects it had changed but little from the schools common in that age. Its more recent progenitor was, however, the classical school, the Gymnasium, of Sturm. The Latin grammar school came to New England recommended highly by the traditions of the Protestant Revolt and the Renaissance. It would be a mistake to think that the colonists of New England could create a Latin school modeled exactly after the Latin grammar schools of England, and it would be overgenerous to think that they could or would

[16] Frank T. Carlton, *Economic Influences upon Educational Progress in the United States, 1820–1850,* Teachers College Press, New York, 1965, pp. 10–11.

[17] George Paul Schmidt, *The Liberal Arts College: A Chapter in American Cultural History,* Rutgers University Press, New Brunswick, N. J., 1957, p. 61.

create an institution with the liberality of purpose that the English Latin grammar school came in time to have. The Latin grammar school of New England was first and foremost a religious institution. Its curriculum contained the usual classical subjects, although no attention was given to mathematics, science, modern language, or history. The fathers of the colony and the founders of the school had little real interest in the classics, but they were interested in the making of minds, and they followed the theory of the day which maintained that the best way to form the mind was to study the classics. They followed the theory of mental discipline and insisted that it be applied without exception to all secondary school subjects.[18] What a boy learned was much less important than how his mind was formed. This must have been an unavoidable conclusion, for it would surely be hard to prove that the Latin tongue and the literature of the classics could have had a practical value for the people of New England. Even the boys who were thinking of the ministry as their life's work could not be sure that the knowledge of the classics that they obtained from their studies would have any real utility for them. Yet the Latin grammar school had only one commission: to prepare boys for college. Since the colleges were classical schools, the New England college was in a position to dictate objectives to the Latin grammar schools for many years to come.

The Latin grammar school was never a highly popular institution in New England or elsewhere in America. It was a school that catered to the so-called "better" classes; it pretended to be a school for the elite, and it maintained an exclusive policy of admissions. In addition to this, it was a school exclusively for boys.

The Latin grammar school was the best evidence that the New England attitude toward education was undemocratic. A boy's education was primarily a matter for individual initiative and means. Although the Latin school did at times receive some public support in the form of money or land grants, this support was never regular, and it was never given in such a way that the private control of the institution was jeopardized. To a greater extent than the colonial colleges, the Latin grammar school repelled the threat of state or colonial intervention and control. Even the law of 1647 and its educational aftermath did little to disrupt the placid existence of the Latin school. The grammar master that the towns employed was really no threat to the established Latin school. The prestige of the Latin school was such that boys who wanted to go to college and maintain their position in the class-

[18] Robert Middlekauff, *Ancients and Axioms: Secondary Education in Eighteenth-Century New England,* Yale University Press, New Haven, Conn., 1963, chapter 8.

structured society could ill afford to ignore the opportunity that the school offered.

Although we may charge the Latin school with lack of democracy and with an inability to update its curriculum to accommodate to evolving social, political, and economic systems, we cannot prove that the Latin school was incapable of achieving the objectives that were prescribed by its masters. It never pretended to be anything other than a classical school. The records of these schools, their permanency and their long history of success, as well as the generally good standing of their graduates as men of affairs, all surely command our respect, even though we may want to qualify our endorsement of the educational theory that dominated them.[19]

THE COLLEGE

A year after the Boston Latin Grammar School was established, the General Court of Massachusetts Bay Colony, granting an appropriation of four hundred pounds (sterling), founded the first college in English America. This school became Harvard College.[20]

Why were colonywide resources used for education? More exactly, why were they used to establish a college? What compelling circumstance motivated the Massachusetts magistrates to support the founding of Harvard College? Harvard's historians, as well as other historians of colonial education, offer several motives, including a profound interest in liberal learning, but the basic motive was a determination to perpetuate a learned ministry. Seventeenth-century Congregationalism demanded more from its ministers than an ability to follow ritual or preside over religious ceremony, for the creed was neither ritualistic nor evangelistic. It was fundamental Puritanism, and as such was both an intellectual outlook and an assent to a religiously oriented life as well as a denominational confession. A college was founded in order to maintain intellectual standards and to sustain the denominational doctrines embraced by colonial leaders. In this primary religious purpose standards of scholarship and literary quality were heeded, and the college which was established outside of Boston was an entirely

---

[19] The theory was mental discipline. For its principal educational constituents, see The Yale Report in Richard Hofstadter and Wilson Smith, *American Higher Education: A Documentary History*, University of Chicago Press, Chicago, 1961, vol. I, pp. 275–291.

[20] See Samuel Eliot Morison, *The Founding of Harvard College*, Harvard University Press, Cambridge, Mass., 1935, p. 168.

respectable academic institution. Yet, it was by no means a school committed solely to liberal objectives. Although not all of Harvard's seventeenth-century graduates became ministers, the first reason for the establishment of the college was to prepare men for that calling. In this objective the college founded in Massachusetts stood on common ground with the vast majority of colleges to be founded later in colonial America.[21]

Harvard's chief purpose was to produce future ministers. But how was this purpose accomplished? What constituted academic, social, and religious life in the college? How was college life organized and governed? What precedents were set in this college to influence the future of American higher education? To these questions we can give only a partial answer here.

The preparation of ministers for the Congregational Church departed somewhat from what might be called orthodox seminary training. This departure was possible because, as we have said, the creed demanded little in the way of ritualistic compliance and, as a matter of fact, when the prospective preacher left the college he was not yet ordained. Ordination into and by a congregation was left to the church that called him. More importantly, however, from an educational point of view, the minister was expected to be a leader in society, a learned man, and a teacher. This lattermost role had been welded to the ministry in the early days of Christianity and had become so permanent that it was impossible to separate the offices of teacher and preacher. A Congregational minister, although there were certain points of doctrine on which he had to be orthodox, was expected to examine and analyze the truths of Christianity, and to interpret them to his congregation. He was not expected to be a purveyor of church doctrine. He had to be an educated person to fulfill the role created for him, and the education best suited to prepare him for it was the traditional classical education reshaped by humanistic scholars of the Renaissance. The divinity student, and every other student too, who passed through Harvard's halls followed an instructional program strongly resembling the ancient liberal arts. Grammar, logic, rhetoric, geometry, and astronomy were taught, as were ethics, metaphysics, natural science, and sometimes some Hebrew, Greek, and ancient history. Latin occupied its familiar position as a prominent study and the language of instruction. One curriculum was enough at Harvard; regardless of a young

[12] Richard Hofstadter and C. DeWitt Hardy, *The Development and Scope of Higher Education in the United States*, Columbia University Press, New York, 1952, pp. 5–6.

man's vocational aspirations, this was the course of studies and he had no choice but to follow it.[22]

A small college with but a few students needed only one professor (who was also the president) and a couple of assistants, or tutors. The latter were charged with the instruction of lower classes and with the superintendence of the more routine affairs of college life. Almost always these tutors were young men, recently graduated from the school, waiting to be "called" by a congregation. While associated with the college they undoubtedly took their work seriously, yet almost to a man they regarded college teaching as nothing more than a convenient steppingstone to the active ministry. The president was himself a minister who often divided his time between college and congregation.[23] While at the college he was its principal teacher and chief disciplinarian; in addition, he held the keys to the college's future, for if it was to progress, its educational compass should have to be set by the president. Beginning with colonial schools, college presidents occupied a sensitive and central position in the evolution of American higher education.

Despite their multiple responsibilities, however, neither Harvard's president nor the presidents of other colonial colleges enjoyed complete authority to govern their schools. College government was exercised from the outside. That is to say, the men who ruled the college, the trustees of the institution, were not part of the teaching staff or the administration. They were ministers, magistrates, and businessmen, who saw nothing unusual or incongruous about their taking the reins of control and making the basic decisions for an institution with which they had had only a very limited experience. Perhaps this was the major precedent forged in Harvard's early years, for with few exceptions the control of American colleges and universities continues to be from the outside.[24]

In addition to Harvard, the colonial college that preceded all the rest in America, the following permanent colonial colleges were founded before 1769: William and Mary, 1693; Yale, 1701; Princeton, 1746; Columbia, 1754; the University of Pennsylvania, 1755; Brown, 1765; Rutgers, 1766; and Dartmouth, 1769. These colleges set a tone for American higher education, and to some degree they are still exercising a function of leadership. And with the exception of the University

---

[22] Schmidt, *op. cit.*, pp. 88–90.

[23] Hofstadter and Hardy, *op. cit.*, pp. 28–29; and George Paul Schmidt, *The Old-Time College President*, Columbia University Press, New York, 1930, pp. 31–37.

[24] See J. E. Kirkpatrick, *Academic Organization and Control*, Antioch College Press, Antioch, Ohio, 1931, pp. 112–121.

of Pennsylvania, founded as the College, Academy, and Charitable School of Philadelphia, all were created with a definite denominational affiliation. At least in the beginning, they shared the common objective of providing ministers for the churches.[25]

Colonial Education Outside New England

Early education in New England served such clear purposes, and was organized according to such definite patterns, that it often obscures education elsewhere in the colonies. Of course a preoccupation with education in New England is justified in the light of history, but we should not on this account ignore the really fruitful developments and precedents for education generated elsewhere in colonial America. No one will find the beginnings of the American public school system in Pennsylvania, New York, or the Southern colonies, but in spite of the lack of striking innovations in educational policy, these regions were responsible for attaching some almost indelible traditions to American education.[26]

When we examine the educational position of the Middle colonies and the South, we realize that the people's customs, their motives for colonization, and their social and political environment were all sharply different from those in the North. We can hardly expect to find in these places an educational consciousness comparable to that of the evolving policies of Puritan New England.

In New York and Pennsylvania the accepted educational policy dictated an almost studied indifference to public responsibility for education. Of course in these two colonies Church domination of public policy was out of the question. In the first place, the state was too strong to let the Church exercise control; and in the second place, far too many denominations were represented for any one to gain a dominant position and retain it. The policy, one of educational laissez faire as far as the state was concerned, made schooling either a personal matter or a matter for the separate congregations or sects to deal with. Here in the Middle colonies we find a social climate capable of generating parochial systems of schools.[27]

[25] Frederick Rudolph, *The American College and University: A History,* Alfred A. Knopf, Inc., New York, 1962, pp. 48–49.

[26] Allen O. Hansen, *Liberalism and American Education in the Eighteenth Century,* The Macmillan Company, New York, 1926, pp. 141–153; and Charles H. Maxson, *The Great Awakening in the Middle Colonies,* University of Chicago Press, Chicago, 1920, pp. 61–90.

[27] See Francis J. Grund, *Aristocracy in America,* Harper and Row, Publishers, New York, 1959, chap. 10; and Carlton, *op. cit.,* pp. 26–27.

The South, following an educational policy honored for so many decades in England, was indifferent to public action in education, too. The economic and social conventions of the South tended to sustain this policy so effectively that anything resembling public responsibility for schooling, except in the case of orphans and paupers, was difficult to find. Since the colony itself was reluctant to provide any other kind of educational opportunity, endowed, charity, and denominational schools of various types came into existence. Denominationalism in education in the South was so pronounced that the University of Georgia, often credited with being the first state college, was actually (although not nominally) a denominational school in its first years.[28]

On the whole, the institutional provisions for education in the Middle and Southern colonies reflected the inherited traditions and customs of the colonists as well as the dominant economic, social, and political conditions of the colonies. The most characteristic feature of education on all levels in this block of colonies was its diversity, whereas in New England the outstanding quality was uniformity.

The Transition (1750 to 1820)

The second period in the development of American education opened with the founding of the academy and closed with the creation of the high school. These are events, however, that should be taken as landmarks; in actual fact they are more the effects than the causes of educational ferment.

RESHAPING THE AMERICAN MIND

When education was first brought to America, it reflected in institutions and ideals its indebtedness to the country from which it had been transported. The colonial period proper, that is, the years from 1635 to 1750, was in educational matters an old and conservative period, however venturesome it may have been in settlement and colonization. The ideals by which men lived were the tested and true ideals of the past, and no one questioned their validity. It never entered the minds of the thinking men that the world was passing them by, but this, in fact, was what was happening. The question was not whether the ideals were valid for all time (for who could test them in any ultimate fashion?) but whether they were relevant to the present time. As far as education was concerned, it became clearer and clearer that the theories

[28] See E. Merton Coulter, *College Life in the Old South*, University of Georgia Press, Athens, Ga., 1951, pp. 151–152.

dominating it were not entirely relevant, but even this realization did not bring about any educational revolution. The period which we have under consideration now was a period of marked evolution, which affected the schools and all education in a very significant way. On the other hand, this evolution was never forceful enough to upset all the old schools. There were many pockets of resistance to change and many outposts of inertia, and some of the outworn ideals of the early period were never discarded.

By way of summary, the fundamental characteristics of the old society were: (1) The colonies had a close political tie with the mother country; (2) the culture was inherited from the mother country, and the conservative wisdom of the age prescribed its preservation; (3) society was organized into a fairly rigid class structure; and (4) the religious tradition, especially that of Puritan New England, dominated almost all of life. These characteristics may be listed by way of summary, as we have said, but they may be placed also in juxtaposition with the characteristics of the new period. The new period concerns us most now, and in its changed character we find the American mind taking on a new, broader, and more democratic dimension.[29]

The fundamental question was: Who is man and what sort of society is best for him? This is an unavoidable and constant social and human inquiry. What the world is like in any period influences the answers men give. We must indicate at the outset that the answers to fundamental questions were not what they had been before. This change in philosophy led to a distinctive intellectual climate, one in which new and sometimes radical ideas concerning man, society, and education might be generated.

As much as anything else, the Enlightenment was a factor in causing men to reevaluate their thinking. The Enlightenment was not a very positive force in the history of thought, but if it did nothing else it motivated men to examine the assumptions upon which they had operated. The general code of the Enlightenment was to denounce authority, whatever its source, and to depend only on those assumptions that could be tested in the clear light of pure reason. Whatever the evils of such a system may have been, a new life invigorating science came, in part, from the Enlightenment. We need mention only the names of men of the stature of Rutherford (1749–1819), Cavendish (1731–1810), Bergman (1735–1784), Lavoisier (1743–1794), and Volta (1745–1827) to make the point a little clearer. Yet, in spite of the unmistakable influence generated by the Enlightenment, we must

[29] Rush Welter, *Popular Education and Democratic Thought in America*, Columbia University Press, New York, 1962, pp. 112–131.

not think that scientific thought rushed through an unguarded door and was welcomed with open arms by those who waited inside. Actually, the higher schools and the American colleges wanted to reject Enlightenment thought.[30] The higher schools especially were distressed by the representations of science, and the lower schools were never in any position either to embrace or discard such advanced ideas. The latter, almost inevitably, must transmit the values society has tested and accepted—and this limited, although necessary, commission constitutes a marked difference between higher and lower education. Higher schools, both colleges and universities, should form a cultural vanguard and be deeply involved in intellectual ferment; secondary and elementary schools, however, should be codifiers of a cultural and intellectual heritage. Neither the Enlightenment nor science actually invaded and dominated these American schools, yet both came in time to influence them. Slowly but surely the movement contributed to changes in the purposes and curricula of the colleges and in the hopes and aspirations of lower schools, and paved the way for a democratic system of education in the United States.

Faith in the power of knowledge, coupled with the unwillingness to accept the conservative wisdom of the previous age, a wisdom that made human progress unlikely if not impossible, brought about still further changes. The root of this new way of thinking may be called humanitarianism. Its most important constituent was the idea of human progress.[31] Man was able, according to this view, to control the world and other men in such a way that progress would be inevitable and possibly even infinite. The key to the whole program of human progress was knowledge. And who could speak of knowledge without thinking at once of schools and the means for education? With such a deep and sincere faith, a faith not to be despised or scorned, education came to be a kind of religion. Men could become excited about it, and they could defend its virtues with infectious arguments and seductive devices. Of course it would be unreasonable to suppose that this new humanitarianism was not challenged by the old order, for it contained in it the seeds that could destroy the old order. If society's stamina is to be found in knowledge, and if knowledge is available and waiting to be found and is not an exclusive prerogative of an aristocracy, the aristocracy loses its position of influence. No one gives up easily those

[30] George Paul Schmidt, "Colleges in Ferment," *American Historical Review*, LIX (October, 1953), pp. 19–42; and "Intellectual Crosscurrents in American Colleges," *American Historical Review*, XLII (October, 1936), pp. 46–67.

[31] Norman Woefel, *Molders of the American Mind*, Columbia University Press, New York, 1933, pp. 51–66.

things that he values highly. Who could expect the so-called "better classes" to capitulate without a struggle?

Ideas are contagious. When the Enlightenment called upon reason to testify, it did not merely suggest that revelation and authority based thereon were undependable; it stated so explicitly. As the effects of the Enlightenment moved across the land and as men became more and more enamored of humanitarianism, there was greater and greater secularization of thought and feeling in America. The first step in this direction was recorded when religion began to lose its hold on the intellectual life of the eighteenth century—and a clear illustration of ground lost by denominationalism was the demise of official established Churches. Before the Revolution, nine colonies recognized such Churches, but after the Revolution the established Church was almost everywhere rejected as an anachronism.[32]

The philosophical idea was expressed, and more often than not in clear and precise language: Men are equal before the law and they should have almost limitless opportunities for political and social equality. The testing ground for this theory of social equality and social mobility, as well as for freedom and self-reliance, was the vast frontier waiting exploration and settlement, and on this frontier democratic ideals were further incubated.[33]

Democracy as an ideal is one thing; democracy as a reality, both political and social, is another. The idea came first; the reality was a long time in being achieved. Yet the first steps in translating ideas into reality were taken in this context when a new political order was established in which social democracy and democratic institutions could be born and where they could grow. This was the framework that education needed for its rebirth. It was possible within such a framework to construct new ideals and generate new patterns of instruction. Finally, we come to the question of means—not means on the level of the internal functioning of a school, but means of a broad social type. Where was the support for education to come from? Although questions of school support had been raised before 1820, their vital significance to democratic school processes was seldom fully understood. Fundamentally, this was an economic rather than an educational issue, and it involved a variety of considerations that had to do with production, distribution, and consumption. Although we look in vain for what can be called a definite economic theory, that is, a theory in a formal and

[32] Neil G. McCluskey, *Catholic Education in America*, Teachers College Press, New York, 1964, pp. 4–7.

[33] Alice Felt Tyler, *Freedom's Ferment: Phases of American Social History to 1860*, University of Minnesota Press, Minneapolis, 1944, pp. 200–220.

completely authentic sense, we can see that a number of economic inter-ests did come into conflict.[34] The most noticeable were those of the capitalists, on the one hand, and the agrarians on the other. There were the interests of the businessmen, the bankers, and the professional men, and there were the interests of the farmers, the artisans, and the com-mon men. More often than not these interests were at odds. Each side formulated a set of doctrines and expressed them as coherently as pos-sible in the hope of defending vested interests. The period that contained all this ferment, from say 1750 to 1820, was the period of transition. During these years intellectual battles were being waged whose outcomes made a foundation upon which democratic education could rest. The greatest strides in the direction of democratic education were taken by the two most important men of the period, Benjamin Franklin and Thomas Jefferson. Each contributed a great deal to Amer-ican educational theory and practice.

BENJAMIN FRANKLIN (1706–1790)

Benjamin Franklin had an engaging personality, an inventive mind, and a character capable of appreciating practical achievements. These traits were of considerable importance to him and to the country he served. Franklin, more than anyone else in this country or in Europe, understood the desire of the common man for independence, success, and intellectual illumination. This insight into men's desires and mo-tives may have come to Franklin because he himself was once one of these common men, who, by reason of his own great ability and the learning he had obtained through his own efforts, had become an un-common man. Besides this understanding of man's drive to lift himself out of his mediocrity, Franklin had a vision of America: He sensed its untapped potential and he refused to admit that Old World standards and aspirations were suitable for Americans. Yet in the reforms he advocated for education, Franklin avoided the extremes of reaction, on the one hand, and revolution, on the other. He wanted to remake education, but he chose conventional means to do so.[35]

When we read his *Proposals Relating to the Education of Youth in Pensilvania* (1749),[36] we see the commitment Franklin was willing to make to change, for what he thought was a decent education was in

[34] Carlton, *op. cit.*, pp. 83–102.

[35] Francis N. Thorpe, *Franklin's Influence in American Education*, U. S. Bureau of Publications, Washington, D. C., 1903, pp. 18–21.

[36] Theodore R. Sizer, *The Age of the Academies*, Teachers College Press, New York, 1964, pp. 68–76.

many respects greatly different from the practices followed in the best schools of the day. In addition to Franklin's willingness to embrace change, we must note his indifference to any theory incapable of practical application. After setting forth his proposals for education containing a recommendation for a new school, the academy, he concentrated his best efforts on founding that new school.

The academy, a secondary school, embodied in its program of studies and its creed for education everything Franklin had said in his famous *Proposals*. Its dominating theme, or basic philosophy, was this: "As to their studies, it would be well if they could be taught every thing that is useful, and every thing that is ornamental: But art is long, and their time is short. It is therefore proposed that they learn those things that are likely to be most useful and most ornamental. Regard being had to the several professions for which they are intended." [37]

Franklin could introduce "modern" ideas to learning without being entirely original in restating the theories of many earlier educators. Yet he contributed two rather original emphases, largely the products of his own thought and experience, that had far-reaching and lasting effects on American education. One had to do with the nonsectarian context in which American public education came to be set, and the other involved the emphasis upon utility in education. The first is easy to detect; American public education has a long history of nonsectarianism. The second may be found in the attention that has, in the past century, been given to the study of English. This concentration of attention has led to a shift of emphasis from the study of other languages which amounts to a virtual exclusion of them from the curricula of American schools. Perhaps Franklin may not be held responsible for the monolingual type of education that has become so common in America, but it is clear that he supported the inclusion of utility-centered subjects such as mathematics, the mechanic arts, and the methods of scientific experimentation in the secondary school program.

Following the model that Franklin provided in the Academy of Philadelphia, the secondary school in this country tended to become an English school rather than a classical school. We do not mean to imply that all the classical schools were closed with the advent of Franklin's school, nor should we think that this tendency toward English education in the secondary school was never challenged. Yet, if Franklin had had his way, they would have been closed and English education would not have been challenged. Franklin had little time for the dead languages. As it was, the academies became exceedingly popular. They

[37] Thomas Woody (ed.), *The Educational Views of Benjamin Franklin*, McGraw-Hill Book Company, New York, 1931, p. 178.

were generously supported by states, towns, and counties, and their founding was encouraged in every section of the country. The academy movement probably reached its height about 1850, when there were more than 6,000 academies, with more than 12,000 teachers, and about 260,000 pupils. It should be remembered, however, that despite the generous public support they received, academies were tuition schools and therefore closed to many children. They were never genuine public institutions.[38]

The conviction that Franklin expressed everywhere in his writings is that man's general welfare ought to be and must be improved. Man's welfare is dependent on internal as well as external factors. Perhaps it depends most of all upon the intellectual illumination of each man. And this illumination, Franklin would say, was not gained merely by coming in contact with disparate kinds of knowledge, but by pursuing all knowledge that would lead to the improvement of the general state of man. Franklin was utility-minded, there is no doubt of that, but he was not a narrow utilitarian. He understood the meaning of utility in the very same way that his age understood it, namely, anything that would lead to the betterment of mankind. Of course intellectual cultivation could not always be developed independently. A social agency was implied, and this social agency, the school, was charged with the mission of "making men" who in turn could make better worlds in which men could live. There was nothing ignoble or small about Franklin's educational vision. He stimulated America to move toward a commitment to universal public education. The realization of this ideal did not come in Franklin's day, but without Franklin it might not have come at all.

THOMAS JEFFERSON (1743-1826)

Thomas Jefferson's major interest was the preservation of the democratic experiment. He was proud of the system of political organization that he had helped to bring into existence, and he wanted it perpetuated for the generations of Americans who would follow. This could best be done, Jefferson was convinced, by a system of public education. Education was the chief guardian and the principal lifeline of democracy; without education, democracy would perish. We cannot doubt the validity of Jefferson's view.

In order that education in the new world might provide the kind of foundation that Jefferson thought necessary for democracy, it would first of all have to be secular. It was not enough to distinguish educa-

[38] Sizer, *op. cit.*, pp. 22–23.

tion from religion; it was essential, Jefferson thought, to free the people from the coercion of religion. This meant creating a social environment wherein men would be entirely free to do as they pleased on matters involving religion.[39] There were good reasons for the views that Jefferson held. History holds all kinds of examples of religious tyranny, and he wanted none of it in this country. Jefferson was not merely a theorist on this question of religious freedom. He was a member of the committee for the revision of the Virginia constitution (1776–1779), and as a result of his work on this committee an Act for Establishing Religious Freedom was passed by the Virginia Assembly in 1779. Another result of the committee's efforts, equally important to the future of America, was the Bill for the More General Diffusion of Knowledge. This bill contained the essentials of Jefferson's educational policy. Although it never became law in the commonwealth of Virginia, this bill did create an ideal of universal education without which American democracy surely could not have prospered. This bill is worth looking at a little more closely.

According to the proposal, Virginia would be divided into sections, called "hundreds," and each of these sections would have a school wherein reading, writing, and arithmetic were to be taught at public expense to all free children in the section. This opportunity would be given to each student for a period of three years, after which, although the public would no longer bear the expense of instruction, the child could remain in school if he wanted to. For every ten sections an educational supervisor would be appointed; he would presumably be a man fully qualified in learning and in the business of keeping schools.

In addition to the elementary system, Jefferson's plan provided for the establishment of secondary schools on a statewide basis. Twenty secondary school districts were to be organized in the colony. Each was to have a grammar school, which would be built and maintained by the public. It was to be located on a hundred-acre plot of land, and it was to have all the equipment necessary for keeping the boys in residence while they attended the school. Many of the boys would pay tuition, but provisions were to be made for giving scholarships to boys who could not pay tuition fees. The scholarship system was worked out with considerable mathematical intricacy. It is doubtful that it would have worked had it been put to a test, yet it did embody the practical realization that all the boys chosen for the scholarship program would not succeed in school. The scholarships would be diminished each year until by the end of six years of instruction there would be only one-half

[39] Gordon C. Lee (ed.), *Crusade Against Ignorance: Thomas Jefferson on Education*, Teachers College Press, New York, 1961, pp. 7–11.

as many scholarship students as in the beginning. The school was to have been a combination of the Latin grammar school and the academy. Although not a high school in the twentieth-century sense, it was a prophetic anticipation of the high school.[40]

This secondary school system was intended to prepare qualified students for the College of William and Mary. Although this purpose was noted because William and Mary was already operating, the private college was not to be a permanent part of the system. Jefferson asked that a state university, the University of Virginia, be established. This would give the state a publicly supported college in which religion would not intrude. A system of state scholarships was planned for the state university: twenty students from the grammar schools would receive such scholarships. In addition to the scholarship students, anyone who was qualified and could afford the costs could attend the state university.

The plan that Jefferson proposed was not accepted in 1779, and when he offered it again in 1817, it was again rejected by the legislature. This is evidence, surely, that most people were not ready for universal elementary education. It is evidence, too, that Jefferson was far in advance of the people and that he was giving them a goal toward which the educational enterprise might strive. Although the bills which he proposed did not become law in Virginia, his efforts were not totally without success. In one area especially, state activity in education, the effect of his influence was felt: Many state leaders, now sensitive to Jeffersonian political theories and more alert to the close relationship between educated citizens and political objectives, began to attach to their state constitutions and statutes provisions indicating the state's willingness to assume some responsibility for education. Jefferson undoubtedly moved the states closer to a political doctrine wherein education became a matter of public policy.[41]

It would be difficult indeed to overestimate Jefferson's influence on American elementary education, especially the popularization of the ideal of universal education. But Jefferson's idealism went beyond the lower schools to affect higher education, too. Common men should be prepared for self-government, so much may be admitted, but in order to ensure an open society where reason rather than religion or tradition prevails, the colleges and universities must be cured of their anti-intellectualism and purged of their denominationalism. When Jefferson

[40] Roy J. Honeywell, *The Educational Work of Thomas Jefferson,* Harvard University Press, Cambridge, Mass., 1931, pp. 112–121.

[41] Herbert B. Adams, *Thomas Jefferson and the University of Virginia,* Contributions to American Educational History, no. 2, Washington, D. C., 1888, pp. 77–91.

spoke for reform in higher learning, he was demanding a jettisoning of old preoccupations and in their place an erection of authentic intellectual commitments to science and social responsibility. In his view colleges should be concerned with real life; they should, moreover, prepare leaders for contemporary society. But above all, the colleges should be responsive to public need and control. With such progressive attitudes toward higher learning, we should not be surprised at Jefferson's keen disappointment with the verdict in the Dartmouth College case of 1819, for in this verdict he detected a reversal of the trend to make higher education socially and politically responsible.[42] These broad statements were important to the future of American higher education, but along with them, we should remember, Jefferson could go inside the college and recommend some changes. Chief among them was electivism. Jefferson tried to replace the rigid curriculum of the earlier centuries, one in which students had no choice as to what they would study, with a curriculum broad enough to allow for a selection of courses according to their interests and abilities.[43]

The American Educational Awakening (1820 to 1900)

The third general period of American educational history spanned most of the nineteenth century. At the beginning of the period it would have been impossible to speak in any strict sense of an American educational system. When the period came to an end, the system was complete, and the structure was present for democratic opportunity in education. We cannot easily determine which of the three periods—transplantation, transition, or awakening—was the most important, but neither can we overestimate the importance of the years of educational awakening.[44]

EDUCATION FOR CITIZENSHIP

About 1820, although there were tendencies in the direction of nonsectarianism in education, the American school was set in a religious atmosphere; the purpose of education was religious, and the content of education, although it was not mere catechism, was also mainly re-

---

[42] Charles F. Arrowood, *Thomas Jefferson and Education in a Republic*, McGraw-Hill Book Company, New York, 1930, pp. 171–178; and see Edgar W. Knight and Clifton Hall, *Readings in American Educational History*, Appleton-Century-Crofts, Inc., New York, 1951, pp. 213–214.

[43] Adams, *op. cit.*, pp. 60–65.

[44] Sidney L. Jackson, *America's Struggle for Free Schools*, American Council on Public Affairs, Washington, D. C., 1942, pp. 116–131.

ligious. It would be fair to say, then, that although early American education was not medieval education all over again, its ultimate objective was otherworldly. The directors of education were churchmen; for the most part they decided not only what would be taught but who the teachers would be. The teachers, although not much can be said for their qualifications, generally measured up to the expectations that were held out for education. The period after 1820, sometimes called the period of educational awakening, was heir to much of the secular thought of earlier years. Both Franklin and Jefferson were listened to. Although religious perspectives were not immediately altered in the schoolroom or religious content expurgated from the school syllabus, the educational interests of the people were no longer set in a narrow religious framework. Education was beginning to have a new mission. Education for citizenship was the new goal, and soon it was accepted in all publicly supported schools.

The extent of public education in the early years of the period is a matter sometimes disputed. By 1820 or 1830 many of the states had enacted statutes that promised the establishment of public school systems. Yet the meaning of *public* was not always precise, and the provisions for education made by the various states did not go much beyond an endorsement of the general expectation that all the children of the state should learn to read and write. Not even in New England did all the children of school age always attend public schools at public expense. And, of course, 1820 or 1830 is still too early for compulsory-attendance legislation, although such legislation did become a reality during the early part of the period of awakening. The most progressive legislation up to 1820 was the Northwest Ordinance of 1785. According to this legislation (an excellent example, incidentally, of national interest in education), section 16 of every township in the Northwest Territory was to be reserved for school purposes, and the income from such land was to be used for the schools. But this land produced little revenue, and no state could have afforded to conduct a system of universal elementary schooling on the income from the national land grant. Not all the states, moreover, participated in this grant from the national government.[45]

Though the ideal of public education may have been acceptable, the idea of free education was somewhat repugnant to the American temperament. A long history of charity schools and pauper schools had made the American public understandably suspicious of the practice of free education. A great deal of evidence indicates how reluctant

[45] See Howard C. Taylor, *The Educational Significance of the Early Federal Land Ordinances,* Teachers College Press, New York, 1922.

parents were to send their children to free schools. James Carter, in his *Essays on Popular Education,* referred to the unwillingness of the people of as progressive a state as Massachusetts to send their children to schools supported out of public funds, because such schools were considered inferior. And not only the public free schools were affected by such an attitude. In the second decade of the nineteenth century, the Jesuit college in St. Louis found that if it adhered to the rule of the Society and offered instruction to its students gratuitously, the students of the quality that the Jesuits wanted would not come to the school. In the interest of preserving the ideals of education which their school was founded to serve, and in order to make the school appear academically respectable to the people of St. Louis, the Jesuits had to charge tuition. The tuition levied, while very moderate, was nevertheless enough to induce students to come, for now the school could not be regarded as a pauper school.[46] How curious it was that the free school idea had to fight two very different kinds of opposition. On the one hand, some people opposed the free schools because they did not want to pay for them or did not believe them to be consistent with democratic principles. On the other hand, other people were unwilling to send their children to schools that did not charge fees for instruction.

Opportunities for free public education were extremely limited at the outset of this period. One of the major accomplishments of the years after 1820 was the establishment of the principle that elementary schools, open to all, should be provided for the children of the country and that they should be able to attend such schools without either paying rates or being exposed to the ridicule of attending a pauper school. Some historians think that the foundations of free public education are to be found in the Eastern United States, and their view is supported by a great deal of evidence. Others think that in the Eastern United States the traditions of private education and of pauper and charity education were so strong that the free school idea could not readily take root, and that the West may have been the section of the country in which the free public school was accepted and developed. The free schools about which we are talking, it should be understood, were, with few exceptions, simple elementary schools which offered the rudiments. Despite opposition, the free school became an accepted and tested institution. By 1840 the free school, open to all the children of all the people, was the foundational institution in the American educational system. It may be called the common school.

[46] See Edward J. Power, *A History of Catholic Higher Education in the United States,* The Bruce Publishing Company, Milwaukee, Wis., 1958, pp. 161–165.

THE COMMON SCHOOL

The common school grew out of the idea that the needs of a democratic government and of a democratic society require the majority of the people to be literate. The first objective of the common school was literacy. In time, of course, the common school was confronted with the problem of broadening and deepening its educational program, but in the beginning these schools were reading-and-writing schools and nothing more. Educational ideals are one thing; educational practice is another. It was a long step from the ideals expressed in the writings of Jefferson to the erection of publicly supported schools in which universal elementary education was possible. This long step was retarded at many points. The first and probably the most effective opposition came from people who refused to pay for public schools. The argument made then, and one occasionally revived for use later in order to retard the progress of free schools and broader educational opportunity for all classes of citizens, was grounded on economics: The resources of the country, it was fervently maintained, were insufficient to support a system of schools to educate all the children of the land.

The second point of opposition was to be found on the level of educational control. In order to have an effective system of public elementary education, it was felt necessary to curtail the power of the districts.[47] These pockets of educational control had operated with near autonomy since the early years of the nineteenth century, and they were reluctant to give up any of the precious control that tradition and the disuse of state educational authority had won for them.[48] In the light of history it would seem obvious that the demand for more effective state supervision was unavoidable if the system of schools promising universal elementary education was to become an effective reality. Yet the light of history casts a clearer backward shadow, and the general opinion of the day seemed to be that although the state could and probably should aid in financing education on the local level, it should not set any of the standards according to which the schools were to operate. Eventually state supervision became a fact, but its realization was slow, and it was achieved only by overcoming concentrated and diligent opposition.

Finally, organized religion's hold on education was not relinquished without a fight. The churches, so long effective instruments in providing opportunity for education and exercising control over it, were no more willing to give up their schools than they would have

[47] See Small, op. cit., pp. 33–41.

[48] See Lawrence A. Cremin, The American Common School, Teachers College Press, New York, 1951, pp. 36–49.

been to give up their church buildings; the ministers were as reluctant to give up their dominant positions on school committees as they would have been to cede their pulpits to the deists. In time they had to relinquish the control they had exercised over education, and in time it was necessary to take denominational religion out of the common school. Had it not been for the decision to make public education nonsectarian, the experiment with universal elementary education might not have succeeded. The continued existence of the common school hung in the balance. Here were the alternatives: either to keep sectarianism in the common schools and sacrifice them, or to remove sectarianism and save the schools. In 1827 Massachusetts took the lead in requiring that all its common schools exclude denominational teaching from the school syllabus. Neither God nor religion, in the general sense, was expelled from the school, but the distinctive teachings of the sects were no longer welcome, and according to law, they were not permitted. Thus, we see, before the common school could prosper, before it could be the instrument for extending democratic opportunity, three important battles had to be waged and won: the battles of support, supervision, and sectarianism.[49]

Public men of vision, educational organizations (the Western Literary Institute, the American Lyceum, and various conventions called to support educational causes), educational journalism, foreign example, and a generation of educational statesmen led the fight for the free common school. Space does not permit anything more than a word about these sources of support, except for the last, the educational statesman. It is impossible to overlook the work of Horace Mann in the history of education in the United States, and to Mann's name may be added those of James Carter and Henry Barnard. There were many others, it is true, but these men were the great figures. The greatest and most influential of all was Horace Mann.

HORACE MANN (1796–1859)

Horace Mann, following the rational rather than the religious philosophies of his genre, put a good deal more faith in the capacity of human beings than conventional traditions allowed, and for this he may be classed among the humanitarians. After having had intimate connections with Puritan thought in his youth, Mann rejected the Calvinistic doctrine of human depravity and substituted one wherein education became an important instrument for human perfection. Putting reason before religion was a revolutionary doctrine, and it ran counter

[49] Jackson, *op. cit.*, pp. 81–99.

to the accepted and central tradition that education was to be offered to those who could profit from it. Although a person's capacity for education depended upon many things, unacceptable social status and background were usually sufficient reasons to exclude otherwise capable children from the opportunities good schools afforded. From Mann's point of view, or from any point of view, the doctrine of perfectibility, coupled with education as its chief instrument, had broad social implications. This doctrine, reinforced by practical proposals for education, urged upon the American public the idea that if education were more generously distributed, not only would individuals be better and more humane, but society, too, would be free from vice, crime, poverty, and other social ills. In a way this doctrine might appear to have a socialistic flavor. Yet, if it had implications for the status of the individual in society, it had, also, the advantage of promoting the industrial welfare; and thus, though perhaps indirectly, it was a doctrine that came in time to claim capitalism as an ally.

Mann appeared on the educational scene when a reformer of his type was most needed. Irrespective of the quality of his ideas, he was a resolute, even a stubborn reformer. After having once made up his mind, he never turned aside, never doubted for a moment that the decision he had made was the right one.[50]

About the time Mann began to take an active role in the affairs of the state of Massachusetts, industrialization, urbanization, and many other social problems were facing the country. All of these issues were related to the question of elementary education. And of course it should not be assumed that Mann was cultivating virgin ground; the way had been prepared for him by others, most notably by James Carter (1795–1849), who had for years been working, writing, and speaking for the cause of popular education.[51] These were days of ferment, and education did not escape the attention of those who were most directly involved in the social upheaval.

Mann's first official connection with education came when he was appointed secretary to the State Board of Education in Massachusetts. This appointment was made in 1837. From this time until he died, Horace Mann was the firmest friend public education in America ever had.

Within a few months after assuming the office of secretary, Mann

---

[50] Burke A. Hinsdale, *Horace Mann and the Common School Revival in the United States,* Charles Scribner's Sons, New York, 1898, pp. 188–204.

[51] See James G. Carter, *Essays on Popular Education,* Bowles & Dearborn, Boston, 1826.

reported on the conditions of education in the state. The report was based on the findings of his own investigation where he found, first of all, that the school committees—the boards responsible for the district schools—were rarely doing their duty. They were practically ignoring the schools and permitting teachers of uncertain quality to teach in them. In addition, he found that the children who needed the common school most of all did not attend it regularly; more than one-third did not go to school in the winter, and an even greater proportion remained away from school in the spring. These shortcomings were magnified by the brevity of the school term, buildings and teaching appurtenances ill-befitting an environment for learning, the total absence of school libraries, the lack of common textbooks for a class, and a general neglect of grading either of instruction or of students. But these features, bad as they were, were compounded by the public's apathy toward the common schools, and its almost certain expectation that their quality would be low.

Hardly any note of optimism prevailed regarding possibilities for improvement, for, generally speaking, private and sectarian academic institutions were assumed to be the custodians of all decent education. Neither these conditions in the common schools nor the public's attitude toward them could, in Mann's opinion, be tolerated for long if democratic institutions were to survive. Most of all, he refused to adopt the conventional opinion that a public school was incapable of offering students good educational opportunities. His principal goal as secretary —and this point is too often glossed over—was fairly simple and straightforward: to improve common schools and make them places in which the people could take pride. At the same time, he was entirely unwilling to countenance the regularly repeated assertion that a sectarian school could prepare youth for their duties as citizens more effectively than any public school. He was determined to demonstrate the fallacy of this assertion, and to a great extent he succeded.

Yet, however Mann's purpose as a reformer may be stated, his task, it must be admitted, was not an easy one. First, it was necessary to change public opinion, not only about the existing common schools but about all public education as well. So he inaugurated a public relations campaign with the express purpose of calling attention to the worth of schooling to men and society. Once this was done he could work for a more general acceptance of a healthy public policy toward public education.

Throughout his long and illustrious career as an educational statesman, Mann played an important role in laying a stronger foundation for American public education. This foundation included public support, public control, nonsectarianism, and the broadening of the curriculum and the recruitment of qualified teachers in order to give the child in a public school a sound educational experience. Perhaps we should add, in the interest of presenting a balanced view of the man, that he was often arbitrary in his actions and very determined and uncompromising in his beliefs. Mann made enemies more easily than most people, and he seemed to thrive on controversy; besides, he found controversy an extremely useful device for promoting his views on educational reform. What better way was there to attract attention to education than by engaging in a fully reported controversy? So Horace Mann quarreled with churchmen who disliked his nonsectarianism, with newspapermen who represented traditional attitudes, with publishers who saw some threat in his proposed reforms, and with schoolmasters who believed he was endangering their positions.[52]

One last point should be mentioned before we leave this great educational reformer. Among persons sincerely convinced of the essential relationship between education and sectarian teaching, Horace Mann's name is usually anathema. Their wrath, however, is misplaced, because neither Mann's record as a school leader nor the writings for which he is best known, the twelve *Annual Reports*, contain documentation to support an indictment citing his antagonism toward religion. Quite the opposite, in fact, is true, for Mann was always friendly toward religion (although he wanted sectarianism purged from common-school classrooms), and he held the Bible in awe, recommending its regular use in moral education (but objecting to sectarian commentaries on it in common schools). In *The Common School Journal,* a periodical founded, edited, and largely written by Mann, and in other public utterances where he displayed his uncompromising allegiance to common schools, Mann spoke out clearly in favor of a system of public education which would be free from the crippling influences of sectarianism, and wherein the various sects would not be fighting one another and using the schools as a main battleground. History told him of the unsettling effects of contention and religious dispute, and how such animosities would eventually destroy public schools, so he supported nonsectarianism in common schools as a principal safeguard. This stand could of course be easily misinterpreted, yet it was not tantamount to antireligious convictions, and it would be impossible

[52] See Raymond B. Culver, *Horace Mann and Religion in the Massachusetts Public Schools,* Yale University Press, New Haven, Conn., 1929, pp. 65–81.

to prove that Horace Mann was responsible for (so to speak) driving God out of the American schoolrooom.[53]

Much of what Mann accomplished in Massachusetts was repeated in Rhode Island and Connecticut under the leadership of Henry Barnard. In addition to his work as an educational leader and reformer in Rhode Island, Barnard became the first United States Commissioner of Education in 1867. Barnard's image is one of a scholar and writer who, on occasion, could involve himself directly and successfully in day-to-day issues of school organization and administration. Besides, he produced a huge body of educational literature, was an inveterate traveler and investigator, both in the United States and abroad, and may properly be called the first education scholar of the United States.[54]

THE CONTENT OF THE COMMON SCHOOL

Before we leave the common school of the nineteenth century we should discuss briefly its content, its organization, and the experiences a student in such a school might have. Irrespective of. changes constantly taking place in a society the school was expected to serve, the school itself, its character and its curriculum, changed but little. It took a minor educational revolution to make the common school a graded school; it took a good deal more to broaden its program in such a way that young men and women could get from it an adequate social, civic, and economic education.

Gradually overcoming a definite resistance, changes came slowly but surely to the common school. At the beginning of the period of awakening it was a considerably different institution from what it was at the end of the nineteenth century. The early common school had been a reading-and-writing school. Spelling was added and became part of the reading-and-writing syllabus, and geography had a fairly early introduction to American elementary education. What was taught in any of the subjects offered was, for the most part, what the textbook had between its covers, for the teachers in those schools were seldom able to go beyond the printed text. So the expansion of the common school curriculum, because it depended so much on the texts, had to await the appearance of new textbooks.

[53] Horace Mann, *Report, Together with the Report of the Secretary of the Board, 1st–12th,* Dutton and Wentworth, Boston, 1838–1849; reprinted, Washington, D. C., 1947 and 1952.

[54] Richard E. Thursfield, *Henry Barnard's American Journal of Education,* Johns Hopkins Press, Baltimore, 1945, pp. 118–131.

Reading and writing, studying the Bible, and spelling made up the usual common school program. The materials used for reading and writing were often religiously oriented; this may have been one of the reasons for the proscription of such materials from the schools of Massachusetts in the law of 1827. Spelling was taught first from the text prepared by Noah Webster, *The First Part of the Grammatical Institute of the English Language.* Although the whole work extended to three volumes, the latter two were devoted to grammar and reading. From 1783 to 1836, when Parsons' *Analytical Spelling Book* appeared, Webster's book had the market pretty much to itself and to a great extent controlled the curriculum of the common school. Parsons' book was probably a little better fitted to the needs of the time and of the school that was opening its doors to more and more people. There was a challenging and intriguing statement in the preface to Parsons' speller: "Parents who have little skill in teaching can learn their children to read, where there are no schools, and adults with little assistance can learn by themselves." [55] The study of arithmetic, heretofore reserved for schools in commercial districts, was stimulated by the introduction of Colburn's *First Lessons in Arithmetic on the Plan of Pestalozzi.* This book appeared in 1821. The book itself marked the beginning of a pedagogical revolution, for the lessons that Pestalozzi had taught brought the teaching of arithmetic down to the level of the object lesson. It is reasonable to expect that the students who had to use Colburn's text were, to say the least, more satisfied with their mathematical experience than the students who had studied the subject in the earlier schools.

There were signs that the curriculum would be broadened when geography was added to the elementary school syllabus. Up to about 1821, when Woodbridge prepared his *Rudiments of Geography,* the subject had been reserved pretty much for the classical schools and colleges. After 1821, geography was a fairly common subject in the lower schools. Of course, to take a subject from the secondary school and put it in the elementary school's program was not an extraordinary procedure; this shift is a regular occurrence in the history of curricula. But in the years when the elementary school was experiencing its greatest growth in the United States, such happenings were even more understandable, for the common school student had no real hope of going further up the educational ladder. The common school was to be his only formal educational experience. He was to be exposed to the things that were best for him individually and that would best prepare him to be a good citizen. Goodrich's *Method of Telling about*

[55] Quoted in Clifton Johnson, *Old-time Schools and Schoolbooks,* The Macmillan Company, New York, 1904, p. 226; and Nietz, *op. cit.*

Geography was published in 1830, and for some time these two texts held a position of considerable authority in elementary education. History, too, was added, for it, more than any other subject, could contribute to the formation of good citizens. With the strong emphasis on citizenship, it is not surprising that the teaching of history was set in a definite nationalistic context. But of all these new materials of instruction, none could command the attention of the student and the educational historian as do the *McGuffey Readers,* published first in 1836.

As the school program became broader and the number of years to be devoted to elementary education increased, the educators of the day found it imperative that the instruction be graded more formally than first, second, and third readers, etc. Grading, though unavoidable, was a long time in coming, and it stands as one of the principal achievements of the common school of the nineteenth century. But before grading was instituted, children just went to school and sometimes repeated what they had previously mastered. Although it may be argued that grading of instruction and the establishment of an age-grade complex has weakened twentieth-century education, it can hardly be maintained that grading of instruction was not a step forward in the nineteenth century.

Finally we should say a word about the teachers in the common schools. (This was a subject that as early as 1790 had excited Benjamin Rush of Philadelphia, who had sought to infuse the teaching profession with a status and dignity befitting its role as society's most influential profession. Being ahead of his time by half a century, Rush's advice went unheeded, however.) There was always the exceptional teacher, of course, but for the most part the teachers in these schools were really not qualified to be there. The nineteenth century saw a great improvement in the quality of teaching. When the century began almost anyone could teach in a common school; when the century came to an end teacher education and teachers' requirements were observed with considerable care in every state system of education. The normal schools and the teachers colleges offered programs for teacher training and education,[56] but, more than that, these institutions were subject to state supervision, and after 1852 prospective teachers were usually required to attend them. For all its shortcomings, no century may claim

[56] For the history of teacher education in the United States, see Vernon L. Mangum, *The American Normal School: Its Rise and Development in Massachusetts,* Warwick and York, Incorporated, Baltimore, 1928; and Jessie M. Pangburn, *The Evolution of the American Teachers College,* Teachers College Press, New York, 1932.

greater developments in the teaching art, or greater improvements in the opportunities offered youth for education.

SECONDARY EDUCATION

Up to nearly the end of the first quarter of the nineteenth century, the only secondary schools in evidence in the United States were Latin grammar schools and academies. Neither fully met the country's needs for secondary education. By the time the high school was founded in 1821, the academy had lost most of its distinctive features and to all intents and purposes was little different from the Latin grammar school which had preceded it in America. Since we have already described these two older types of secondary education in the United States, we need not repeat their features here. In any case, neither was prepared to update and broaden its curriculum or to change its age-old objectives to fulfill the requirements of a larger and different clientele. While popular secondary education was only a distant dream, it was nevertheless indisputable that an obvious need existed for a kind of secondary education not offered in the established schools. To accommodate this need the American high school was created.[57]

The first high schools were founded with practical curricula foremost among their educational goals. They sought to prepare boys for the usual day-to-day activities of nineteenth-century economic life and thus, in some respects, to give the appearance of trade or vocational schools. But they were also committed to a good education in English. The school taking the lead along these lines was the Boston English Classical School, renamed Boston English High School in 1824. Still, a break with the past and what were assumed to be tested traditions in secondary education was incomplete. Amid the usual appurtenances of practical education the classics were retained, although whereas in the old schools they were read and studied in Latin, and sometimes in Greek, now they were read and studied in English translation. The classics contained treasures to be mined, so many were still admitted, but their secrets could now be possessed by boys who knew only English. This shift away from the classical languages as the essential feature of secondary education was an innovation of the first rank, and it did an immense amount of good for American secondary education despite

---

[57] For the early history of the high school and the high school movement, see Elmer E. Brown, *The Making of Our Middle Schools*, Longmans, Green and Company, New York, 1902; Emit D. Grizzel, *Origin and Development of the High School in New England before 1865*, The Macmillan Company, New York, 1923; and *Report of the Committee of Ten on Secondary School Studies*, U. S. Bureau of Education, Washington, D. C., 1893.

the fact that it was only a temporary departure from past practice. The academy had been unable to sustain its original purpose of being genuinely practical; the high school suffered from the same fate. But there was an important difference: Whereas the academy capitulated to the old classical curriculum and became a Latin grammar school all over again, the high school readmitted the classics and the Latin language to the school syllabus only after it had demonstrated the worth of practical studies and had laid a solid foundation for them. Though this readmission had the effect of distorting the high school's original purpose somewhat, the classics henceforth were incapable of dominating the high school's curriculum.

Apart from important curricular innovations, which went a long way toward defining the high school as a new academic institution, another of its important features was its embrace of both boys and girls as secondary-school students. Both sexes were entitled, according to its basic assumptions, to a postelementary education capable of preparing them for life in society. Part of this preparation for life still meant basic entrance studies for college, for all secondary schools were thought to have this as an imperishable function, but high schools were not limited to a college preparatory role. In fact, while college preparation was, as we have said, a legitimate function for the high school, its more general function could be found in the assumption that for the vast majority of students the high school would be a terminal instructional agency. Thus, it must be admitted, the so-called "redefinition" of the high school's purpose by the Committee of Ten in the 1890s was actually a call for a return to the institution's first objective, and an effective plea for it to be true to its original purpose.[58]

Another important feature associated with the high school must not be neglected: The high school was publicly supported and controlled and was open and free to any qualified student.

The high school in Boston was a successful experiment. Yet though it germinated the high school idea, the multiplication of high schools was due not so much to the model that existed in Boston as to the Massachusetts law of 1827—the High School Act, sometimes called the James Carter High School Act—which required the establishment of high schools or the employment of teachers who could teach high school subjects in every Massachusetts town with a population of five hundred or more. Thus began a movement that within two decades had spread throughout New England and to most of the Western states. Still, the high school was not a popular institution. It was recognized as a desirable addition to the educational system, but it was not entirely ac-

[58] *Ibid.*

ceptable as a part of publicly supported and publicly controlled education. Many people were convinced that the high school could never become part of the public school system because it would be impossible for the public to support such an addition. Others, not so much impressed with the financial argument, insisted that the high school was really part of higher education, that it had nothing to do with the preparation of citizens, and therefore that it could not be a legal part of the public school system.

Even though the lattter argument would have little standing in the mid-twentieth century, it did influence many minds in the nineteenth century. State constitutions had generally accepted the commission to provide public education to the people of the state by the constitutional invocation that "the state legislature shall establish and maintain a system of public education." The question was: What is public education? Where does it start and where does it end? Those who claimed that the high school was part of higher education were saying, in effect, that the high school could not be supported by public money, that it would not be constitutional to do so, for the state's constitution had not provided for the support of higher education. This impasse blocked the high schools in many of the states, and retarded high school expansion and development.

In 1859 the Michigan legislature passed a law permitting certain types of school districts to establish high schools and support them out of public money. This law may be regarded as the beginning of the high school movement in Michigan, but compared to the precedents arising out of the interpretation of the law, the law itself is of little historical importance. In keeping with the Michigan High School Act, a number of school districts founded high schools. One such school district was School District Number One of the village of Kalamazoo. But the high school in Kalamazoo met with opposition which arose not because Charles Stuart and others who joined with him were opposed to high school education, but because they doubted the constitutionality of the High School Act of 1859. They took their case to the courts and this litigation led to the famous Kalamazoo decision of 1874, wherein the legal status of the high school in Michigan was assured. In its decision the court upheld the constitutionality of the act of 1859 and in effect defined the high school as part of public education. The decision of the Michigan court served as a precedent for similar decisions in other states. For the first time, then, the supporters of the high school movement knew where they stood; they knew now that no legal obstacles would stand in the way of the high school's natural evolution. The Kalamazoo decision was a great victory for the high school and brought it to the brink of popularity.[59] Achievement of true popularity was due to another important event in the history of the American high school, the *Report* of the Committee of Ten.

In 1890 a committee of the National Education Association was appointed to study the relationship between high schools and secondary schools and colleges on the question of college entrance requirements. For the past several decades the colleges had controlled the secondary schools with their college entrance requirements. In 1890 relatively few students attended high schools who did not anticipate college entrance, and high schools and secondary schools in general could not afford to ignore the curricular demands that the colleges imposed. In a very real sense the high school's curriculum was in the colleges' grip, and this domination curtailed the growth of the high school. The committee was appointed to find some way to resolve the tensions between secondary schools and colleges.

The Committee of Ten, while not conforming exactly to its original commission, decided to take a long and careful look at the high school. As a result of this study, the committee redefined the high school; it made its essential purpose one of preparing students for life. While the college-preparatory function of secondary education was duly recognized by the Committee of Ten, the important purpose of the high school was set in a terminal context. In other words, the high school was to find its objectives in what young people would do when they left school. This terminal context was accepted because it was believed that only a relatively small percentage of the high school population would ever go to college. The high school experience would conclude the formal schooling for most of the students.[60]

The *Report* of the Committee of Ten, along with the Kalamazoo decision, made the high schools popular institutions in the United States. Within a few years after the committee's *Report* appeared in 1893 (the Kalamazoo decision had been rendered in 1874), the high school was attracting about as many students in one year as it had in its entire history up to that time. While the high school did not eliminate other kinds of secondary education, no other kind of secondary education after 1895 could rival the high school in popularity. With the creation and popularization of the high school, the American educational ladder was complete; a student could climb all the way from elementary school through the public university. And now we turn from this brief survey of the high school to the last rung of the American educational ladder, higher education.

[59] *Michigan Reports* (1874–1875), pp. 69–84.

[60] *Report of the Committee of Ten on Secondary School Studies*, pp. 121–128.

AMERICAN HIGHER EDUCATION

Naturally we cannot determine a precise point in history when the colleges of America were freed from the religious control to which they had been subjected since the founding of Harvard in 1636. At best this freedom was only a relative thing, for in a number of colleges, especially those under Catholic auspices, the religious direction of instruction became even more important. The Catholic colleges of the United States began to make their appearance just as the general college movement in America took a turn in the other direction. By the time we get to the last half of the nineteenth century, the day of the denominational college is really in the past, while the day of the state university and the state college is just dawning. We do not mean to say that none of the denominational colleges made significant contributions to the life of America. Even though the period of its greatest influence was over, the denominational college of the late nineteenth century and of the twentieth century, for that matter, was still capable of offering education of high quality to thousands of students.[61]

Two main indictments were drawn up against the denominational college: One, it was undemocratic both in institutional control and in choice of students; two, it either refused to respond to society's needs or was extremely reluctant to do so. Because the old college, with its traditions lodged in a European and colonial background, continued to live in the past and praised the classical course (as was done in the famous *Report* of the Yale Faculty in 1828), unmindful of the pressing need for a different kind of higher learning and unable to discard its old doctrine that everything worth knowing was in the classics, the public lost confidence in the denominational college as an effective institution and, moreover, began to doubt the wisdom of listening to the educational advice of its minister-president.[62]

The public felt betrayed by the old college and looked for a substitute wherein a more practical and useful kind of higher learning would be offered. Francis Wayland, president of Brown University in the 1840s and 1850s, was a principal spokesman for curricular change and an updating of college purposes. Yet, changes in a collegiate system dating all the way back to 1636 could not be effected easily or quickly. One proposed solution—and some precedent existed for this approach—

[61] The aftereffects of the Dartmouth College decision are dealt with in Donald G. Tewksbury, *The Founding of American Colleges and Universities before the Civil War,* Teachers College Press, New York, 1932, pp. 142–154.

[62] Schmidt, *The Liberal Arts College,* pp. 155–161; and Hofstadter and Hardy, *op. cit.,* pp. 88–92.

was to expand public colleges. From as early as 1785 the public college model was current in America and, we remember, Jefferson had championed the idea of public higher education in 1779. Yet, public colleges had always suffered from lack of both support and confidence because throughout most of our early history the dogmatic assumption reigned that higher learning must necessarily be wedded to religion and subordinated to ecclesiastical control. By 1862, however (because, as we have said, confidence was waning with respect to private denominational colleges, and because of a heretofore unfelt urgency for technical higher learning), Congress passed the Morrill Act (the land-grant college act) and assigned land from the national domain to states prepared to found public colleges for agricultural, military, and mechanical learning. Although the Morrill Act was not, in a strict sense, an act responsible for originating the state-university movement, it did, nevertheless, add tremendous impetus to a new public consciousness for public higher education.[63] The states used the federal grant in a variety of ways—some opening new colleges, others expanding and strengthening existing state schools, some assigning the grant to private colleges (although retaining public control over the collegiate unit supported by the land grant), and others, especially in the South, founding separate land-grant colleges for both black and white persons. In all, the Morrill Act was instrumental in creating sixty-nine colleges, presently designated as land-grant schools, and in furthering the future development of state colleges of all kinds.

Even before the drive was made through the Morrill Act and other public evidences to broaden the scope of public higher education, another way had been tested to convert the private and denominational college to more liberal educational and social purposes. This was done in some states when the state legislatures rewrote college charters and thus brought the old private college under public control. The rewards for such state action were obvious and attractive, but they were also extremely temporary; in the end some private colleges mustered the determination to resist this erosion of their independence. In one dramatic legal instance involving Dartmouth College, the state failed in its effort to rescind Dartmouth's colonial charter and replace it with one issued by the state of New Hampshire. In the latter charter Dartmouth College would have lost much of its original autonomy, but this legal move on the state's part was blocked by the famous Dartmouth College decision in 1819. According to the United States Supreme Court decision, the college, with its colonial charter, could not be interfered

[63] See Earle D. Ross, *Democracy's College*, Iowa State College Press, Ames, 1942, pp. 68–121.

with by the state and the state could not bend the college to its will. Thus, not only Dartmouth College but other private colleges as well had their independence assured by this decision. A college with a charter was protected, of course, and this protection extended equally to colleges with old charters and to colleges with recent charters.[64]

This decision dictated two courses of action for the states if they wanted to involve themselves in higher learning: First, to control higher education directly they should have to found state colleges; second, they should grant charters to private colleges with considerably greater care and reservation than before. In connection with the latter course of action, the states promptly enacted laws making it illegal for any unchartered school to confer academic degrees on its students.[65]

Although we could hardly argue that the Dartmouth College decision deprived the state of authority in higher education, the decision clearly marked out a sector for private schools and allowed them to proceed largely free from state interference. Possibly the decision prompted the states to establish higher educational systems of their own wherein a new and more up-to-date kind of higher learning could be promoted. In any case, the state college movement, influenced by the Dartmouth College decision, on the one side, and the Morrill Act, on the other, became highly visible and fairly efficient in the last half of the nineteenth century.[66]

The state universities especially became conscious of a new dimension added to university purposes: research. Although many of the newly founded or newly expanded state schools were unable at once to undertake research programs or highly advanced graduate programs, no state university was oblivious of the attractiveness of such activities. In time these state institutions answered the call for technological development and social science research, and also for medical schools, legal departments, and schools of engineering, all of which departments had a vital social significance. Research was soon being organized, and graduate schools were introduced especially after 1876, when the Johns Hopkins University in Baltimore provided a model which other American universities could copy.[67] And there was another

[64] Tewksbury, *op. cit.*, pp. 144–148.

[65] *Ibid.*

[66] Rudolph, *op. cit.*, pp. 139–155.

[67] See John C. French, *History of the University Founded by Johns Hopkins*, Johns Hopkins Press, Baltimore, 1946, pp. 41–50; and Abraham Flexner, "The Graduate School in the United States," *Proceedings of the Association of American Universities*, 1931, pp. 114–115.

expansion: Higher education accepted new students in its hallowed halls. These new students were women. The first beginnings of the coeducation movement in higher education were made at Oberlin College in 1833 and were followed by Antioch College in 1853, Syracuse University in 1850, and the University of Iowa in 1856. At about the same time, or possibly a few years earlier, the separate woman's college grew out of the academies or seminaries that for some years had been conducted for girls. We find such well-known colleges as Mount Holyoke, Rockford, and Vassar, to name only three. In all, more than sixty colleges for women were founded before 1860, although we may justifiably inquire whether all these schools really merited collegiate rank.

One of the chief reasons for the development of coeducational programs in colleges for men, and for the founding of colleges for women was that women now, in the greater and broader development of popular education, had ways of applying the knowledge gained in college studies. In other words, the lower schools now needed women teachers, and girls could go to college in order to develop salable skills. With this incentive the college programs for women increased spectacularly.[68] But the colleges were not the first institutions to respond to the need for properly educated teachers. The general willingness of the colleges to enter the field of teacher education was not much in evidence before the normal schools and teachers colleges cultivated this area of professional training.

As a public institution the normal school dates from 1839, and as a private school from about 1822. Its purpose was, without pretense or fanfare, to teach people who wanted to be elementary school (common school) teachers something about the art of teaching. The normal school was usually not interested in content and therefore did not offer a college course. Its commitment was to communicate techniques of teaching. The normal school lasted for about fifty years in the United States, and during these years some very famous normal schools came into existence. The most famous of all was the Oswego Normal School at Oswego, New York.[69] Between 1830 and 1880 public and private normal schools could be found in every state in the Union. When the ele-

[68] Louise Boas, *Women's Education Begins*, Wheaton College Press, Newton, Mass., 1935; and Willystine Goodsell, *Pioneers of Women's Education*, McGraw-Hill Book Company, New York, 1931.

[69] Ned H. Dearborn, *The Oswego Movement in American Education*, Teachers College Press, New York, 1925, pp. 17–34; and J. P. Gordy, *Rise and Growth of the Normal School Idea in the United States*, U. S. Bureau of Education Circular of Information, no. 8, 1891.

mentary school program was broadened and when the high school became a permanent and popular part of the educational system, the normal school no longer seemed adequate to the task of preparing teachers for America's schools. A new kind of teacher was needed, and a new kind of institution for teacher education came into existence. This was the teachers college.

Public and private teachers colleges were founded, and both types undertook to prepare men and women to teach in elementary and secondary schools. As teachers colleges grew, normal schools declined. At present, in the mid-twentieth century, the normal school has completely disappeared, and teachers colleges in the United States educate about one-half of the country's teachers. In addition, many teachers colleges, although they may no longer be called by this name, have complete university programs wherein qualified students may earn the advanced degrees usually granted in the graduate schools of the country.[70]

Summary

The first schools in English America were transplanted schools; they were really European schools brought to the New World in the hope that they would help the colonists achieve their ideals and their dreams. Although colonization differed from one section of the new country to another, education tended to follow the established Old World patterns. The first major break with tradition came in Massachusetts in the famous laws of that colony. These laws were passed in 1642 (the compulsory-education law) and 1647 (the compulsory-school law). The typical schools of the transplantation were colleges, town schools, Latin grammar schools, and dame schools (elementary schools).

Eventually it became clear that the old institutions would not do in the new setting, and efforts were made to found new schools or reform old ones. These enterprises were undertaken, generally speaking, during the period of transition, from 1750 to 1820. During this period the new schools that attract our attention are the academies and the state universities. Benjamin Franklin and Thomas Jefferson were active in inculcating new ideals for the educational enterprise of the new country.

With a theoretical foundation inherited from the transition, the period of educational awakening, from 1820 to 1900, translated these theories into practice. In these years elementary education was made nearly universal and became almost entirely free. Elementary schools (common schools) were supported and controlled by the public. High schools came into existence and in time became the American contribution to secondary educa-

[70] See Charles A. Harper, *A Century of Public Teacher Education,* American Association of Teachers Colleges, New York, 1939.

tion. The Kalamazoo decision and the *Report* of the Committee of Ten must be noted in the development of the high school.

Higher education, too, was subject to tremendous change. The most notable changes were in the development of state universities, which brought an entirely new tone to higher education, and in the establishment of graduate and professional schools and programs related to society's needs.

XVI

American Education in The Twentieth Century

The nineteenth century, a century of educational ferment, laid the foundation for a more truly democratic system of education in the United States. The rewards were mainly the products of the next century, however, so when we look for illustrations of a pedagogical reform and a consolidation of ideals in practice, we must turn to the first sixty or seventy years of the twentieth century.

The Popularization of Education

The important forces of the nineteenth century made themselves felt by the last decade of the century, and education on all levels became more popular. By "popularity of education" we mean the place that schools, both public and private, occupy in the public mind. From 1890 to the outbreak of the Second World War, the record of educational history is mainly one of growth. During this period a steadily increasing percentage of the school-age youth of America was attending school; the increase in high school and college enrollments was at a phenomenal rate. The school term was lengthened, and by 1918 all the states had compulsory-attendance laws which made universal education a virtual reality. The schools, from the lowest to the highest, were given more adequate financial support, and the salaries of teachers more than doubled during these years. In 1890, 44 percent of the population from five to seventeen years of age was in school. By 1930 this proportion had changed to 67 percent; in 1960 it was 79 percent. From 1890 to 1930 the school year was increased from 135 to 172 days; and by 1960 the school year in most of the states was at least 180 days.

Throughout this period of growth there were obvious rays of sunshine. The educational establishment was better off than it had ever been before, and the quality of educational opportunity was higher. But there were clouds too. Some sections of the country lagged behind others. The figures of growth given above are averages; some states and some regions were far behind these averages.

When we enter the twentieth century, we find a complete American school system. The educational ladder extends from the primary school through the university. It is possible now for Americans to speak of a nearly authentic democratic system of education. We see, too, that this ideal of democracy in education involved another consideration, namely, how far it was possible and right to control private education. American society was a pluralistic society; its needs were many and varied, and, in addition, America had a strong tradition of private control and support of education, as she had a strong tradition of religiously oriented education. Both private and religiously integrated education had lost ground in the late years of the nineteenth century. There was so much devotion to democratic education as the twentieth century began that private, church-related education was in real danger of becoming extinct. Many people argued that private and church-related education could not be democratic and that it could not serve the best interests of a growing America. Their arguments were heeded, and the call went out for the suppression of all but the state schools.

Another prerogative of the schools was in danger. In the interest of achieving curricular uniformity, the demand was voiced and again heeded, and in some states converted into law, that only certain subjects be taught and that they be taught in a certain way. Some states, Nebraska for instance, proscribed the teaching of foreign languages to children who had not yet finished the eighth grade. About the time of the First World War, the prevailing tendencies threatened to leave little room in education for agencies other than the state, if the state had its way. This was one of the prices that education had to pay for popularity. But it was too high and also too unrealistic a price. In time, both of the extravagant claims of the state, that it alone could be the educator of youth and that it alone could decide what was best for youth to study, were struck down by the United States Supreme Court. In the famous Oregon decision (1925), the Court issued a decree that protected not only the rights of the private schools involved in the litigation, but also the rights of all non-public education in the United States.[1] In 1923 the United States Supreme Court ruled on the Nebraska law that had prohibited the teaching of languages other than English to elementary school students. The Court held that the Nebraska statute was unconstitutional. The Court's ruling thus protected the right of parents to determine what their children should study.[2]

The relationship of these points to the popularization of education may seem, at first, to be somewhat remote. On closer examination, however, we see that the legal foundation given to private education in the Oregon decision had the effect of making education more popular and more generously distributed. In the language question, the Court gave the parents some control over the schools, and in this way enabled the schools to gain parental confidence. Gaining the confidence of those who are first of all responsible for the education of children is more than half the battle for popularizing education.

Educational Opportunity

The question of educational opportunity, as it was asked in the first sixty years of the twentieth century, had two dimensions: first, the extension of opportunity, both horizontally and vertically; second, the opening of schools to all the children of all the people without regard to race, color, or creed. Both dimensions were immensely important to the future of education in the United States and also to the position of the United States on the scale of world opinion.

Many kinds of inequality may exist in an educational system. There is inequality when a student of superior capacity is placed in a

[1] *Pierce v. Society of Sisters*, 268 U.S. 510.
[2] *Meyer v. Nebraska*, 262 U.S. 390.

classroom with children of far less ability and also when a student of inferior ability is put in a classroom with superior youngsters. Yet when we speak of inequality of educational opportunity in the twentieth-century American school, we really have only one thing in mind: the Negro in American education.

The struggle for equal educational opportunity for the American Negro has a long and sometimes disappointing history. Although important progress has been made in the past few decades, equal educational opportunity is not yet a fact and the great quest for it is bound to continue. The Negro has not been alone in his determination to achieve equality before the law. From the introduction of slavery in the colonies to the present day, white men and women have sensed their moral obligation to arouse the conscience of the nation concerning the issue of educational inequity for the Negro. Thus, black men have had private allies who have tried to help, but another important and more powerful ally has been the federal government. Without the active role of the federal government, particularly the judicial branch, it is unlikely that the Negro would enjoy the educational opportunity he now has.

A history of the drive for equal educational opportunity for black citizens can be divided into four fairly distinct periods. In the first period, from 1808 to 1896, the foundations were laid for an articulation of the "separate but equal" doctrine; and during this period the first case involving this doctrine was argued in a court in Boston, Massachusetts. The Dred Scott case forms part of this period as does the first civil rights bill enacted by Congress in 1875 and ruled unconstitutional in 1883.[3]

The second period, from 1896 to 1935, illustrates a consolidation of the "separate but equal" doctrine expressed in *Plessy v. Ferguson*,[4] although there were relatively few litigations involving the educational rights of black citizens, because Negro education was in its infancy and few black citizens were prepared to initiate tests challenging the constitutionality of the doctrine further.

The third period began in 1935 and ended in 1954. During this interval court decisions tended to erode the doctrine of "separate but equal" by making it more difficult for the states maintaining dual school systems to demonstrate that the facilities of the two systems were in fact equal. This period saw more test cases than ever before, because

[3] *The Civil Rights Cases,* 109 U.S. 3.
[4] *Plessy v. Ferguson,* 163 U.S. 537.

by now Negroes were better prepared academically and began to aspire to professional and graduate schools which were not maintained by the states on an equal basis.

The fourth period began May 17, 1954 with the demise of the "separate but equal" doctrine in *Brown v. Board of Education.*[5] With this decision the Court brought to a close almost a century of litigation over the question of citizens' rights in education. The issue was posed first in *Roberts v. Boston* (1849) [6] and last in *Bolling v. Sharpe* (1954).[7] The real meaning of the 1954 decision was that segregation in public education had lost whatever constitutional standing it appeared to have in old Court decisions. In 1954, "With all deliberate speed" was the phrase used by the United States Supreme Court (*Brown v. Board of Education*) in commanding school integration. In many places, however, the response was deliberate resistance. In 1969 (*Holmes v. Alexander*), the United States Supreme Court unanimously ruled that the deliberate speed formula "is no longer constitutionally permissible." Instead, the Court declared: "The obligation of every school district is to terminate dual systems at once and to operate now and hereafter only unitary schools."

Brown v. Board of Education had not dealt with higher education, although the constitutional principles outlined in the decision were soon made to apply to colleges and universities. In 1956, in a case involving the University of North Carolina and three black students,[8] the Court held that the facilities of the university must be made available to black citizens even though the professional courses they intended to pursue were offered at Negro state colleges.

With the enactment of the Civil Rights Act of 1964, the black citizen is legally free to enjoy the full privileges of citizenship. Law, however, is incapable of enforcing attitudes, changing customs, removing intolerance, or even making the Negro economically and socially competitive in a highly competitive social order. So actual, though illegal, segregation continues to prevail in many state and city school systems, and *de facto* segregation and discrimination continue to exist in housing and employment opportunities.

Education's role not only in providing black children with quality learning, but in eliminating vestiges of prejudice, intolerance, and racism has become clear. The school's function in social education and

[5] *Brown v. Kansas,* 347 U.S. 483.

[6] *Roberts v. Boston,* 58 Mass. 198.

[7] *Bolling v. Sharpe,* 347 U.S. 497.

[8] *Board of Trustees of the University of North Carolina v. Leroy Frasier,* 350 U.S. 979.

the contribution it must make to social solidarity have become obvious in the decade of the 1960s.[9]

The other dimension of opportunity tried to find its solution in the realignment of the school system. During the late nineteenth century, when the high school became a regular and legally recognized public institution, the American school system took a definite shape. By 1890 or so it was possible, as we have said, to speak of the American educational ladder, an integrated system of schools that began with the primary school and ended with the university. It was, for the most part, open to all American children; at any rate, there was no dual system such as could have been found in Europe during the same period. In the establishment of such a system, American educational theory committed itself to popular education on all levels. This inclusiveness gave rise to the charge that American schools had no standards, that they were not real intellectual agencies, and that they were definitely inferior to their European counterparts. It must be understood, of course, that in any discussion of the relative merits of European and American education we must consider what the two systems are driving at. We should do the same thing when we debate about education in the United States and in the Soviet Union. Many of the complaints directed at American education are based on a faulty understanding of its purposes.[10] In the next section we shall review the evolution of American educational theory.

To return to the development of the American ladder, we may say that the twentieth century witnessed the following extensions: Elementary schools were extended downward; secondary education was extended downward, and so was higher education. These downward extensions fashioned four new steps for the American educational ladder: nursery school, the kindergarten, the junior high school, and the junior college. The latter is now more generally referred to as the community college. Each of these new educational units was brought into existence primarily to provide greater opportunity for education.

The American Teaching Tradition

Indebted though it was to the educational theory and practice of Europe, American education came in time to have a teaching tradition of its own. Before 1900 it could have been described as European educa-

---

[9] Nathan Glazer and Daniel Moynihan, *Beyond the Melting Pot,* Harvard University Press, Cambridge, Mass., 1963, pp. 41–45.

[10] Theodore Brameld, *Education for an Emerging Age,* Harper and Row, Publishers, 1965, pp. 31–55.

tion all over again. But education and the schools outgrew their parent institutions of the nineteenth century, whether these institutions were found in America or in Europe. Education in America became a big business, and the doors of the schools were opened to all. Public education had a rapid growth, but it was to gain even greater stature in the twentieth century. It was in this growth and in the delving into the ground of theory from which it sprang that the American teaching tradition came into being.

It would hardly have been possible to speak of a native pedagogy in nineteenth-century America. The names of Pestalozzi, Herbart, and Froebel were far too prominent for American educators to think that they themselves could be independent. But the important point to be observed here is that the Americans who had studied under the influence of the best pedagogical minds of Europe were now in a position to prepare a generation of American educators. One of the leaders in building the American teaching tradition was Francis W. Parker (1837–1902).[11] As superintendent of schools in Quincy, Massachusetts, Parker introduced a method which has since been called the Quincy method. Although there is nothing unusual about it when viewed from the perspective of the third quarter of the twentieth century, it was extremely novel when it was introduced by Parker in the waning years of the nineteenth century. The general idea was that the formalism of the old-time schoolroom should be eliminated in favor of a classroom in which learning and living would be made to complement each other. In other words, Parker introduced the practice that was later to be labeled progressive education. It should be noted that Parker's new method and his liberalism in teaching did not go unchallenged; the people of Quincy were determined to see whether or not the methods that had been used in teaching their children were valid. A long and somewhat wearying investigation was undertaken. The people wanted to know whether their youngsters could spell, read, write, and compute. It was found that the pupils who learned these skills by the new method were able to perform as well if not better than those who had learned them by the old method. Parker left Quincy for Chicago, to become director of the Chicago Normal School of Education.[12] His connection with the school was brief, however, for he died in 1902.

In a way, then, Parker was the founder of the American educa-

[11] Jack K. Campbell, *Colonel Francis W. Parker: The Children's Crusader,* Teachers College Press, New York, 1968.

[12] Robert E. Tostberg, "Colonel Parker's Quest for 'A School in Which All Good Things Come Together'," *History of Education Quarterly,* VI (Summer, 1966), pp. 22–42.

tional tradition; but it was John Dewey (1859–1952) who cultivated what Parker had invented and gave it the stature of a real teaching tradition.

John Dewey was born in Burlington, Vermont, in 1859. He attended the public schools in Burlington and the University of Vermont. Following his graduation from college, Dewey became a schoolteacher and for two years or so was the schoolmaster of a country school. During this brief interlude his interest in the world of ideas was stimulated to such an extent that he returned to the University of Vermont to take an informal postgraduate course in philosophy. After a year or so at the University of Vermont, he enrolled at the Johns Hopkins University of Baltimore (a school that had achieved a reputation for excellence in a few short years and one which attracted most of the outstanding students of the United States of that day), where he pursued graduate study in philosophy. At Johns Hopkins he came in contact with the famous G. Stanley Hall (1844–1924) and the leading idealist philosopher in America of the day, George S. Morris (1840–1889). When Dewey completed his studies at Johns Hopkins, he took his Ph.D. degree and accepted a teaching appointment at the University of Michigan. His teaching field was philosophy, although for those who like to think of Dewey as a psychologist, it might be mentioned that his doctoral dissertation was on the psychology of Immanuel Kant. From the University of Michigan Dewey went to the University of Minnesota, where he stayed for two years, and then he returned to the University of Michigan. From Michigan he went to the University of Chicago, and then to Columbia University.[13]

Although Dewey's academic area was philosophy, he began to show unusual interest in education, and within two years after his appointment to the faculty of the University of Chicago he had organized a school, the Laboratory School of the University of Chicago. Dewey's interest in education was not as unusual as it may appear, for he always regarded the school as the best testing place for philosophical doctrines. The laboratory school was, therefore, an entirely natural outlet for his philosophical interests. This school was an experimental school, and the idea caused almost as much excitement as the new methods of teaching and learning that it practiced. Experimenting with children was then thought to be a radical departure from orthodox procedure.

From the Laboratory School at the University of Chicago John Dewey led an educational revolution.

[13] Milton H. Thomas, *John Dewey, A Centennial Biography*, University of Chicago Press, Chicago, 1962, pp. 68–75.

The essential elements of this revolution have been described, praised, and criticized in various ways. Basically, Dewey wanted to turn the schools back to a closer relationship with life.[14] In the early chapters of this book we examined educational practices that tended to separate learning from living or ignored the essential relationship that ought to exist between teaching and reality, between instruction and the world of people and things. Again, and especially in the hands of Dewey and his followers, the school was turned in the direction of affinity with real life situations, and the shibboleths most characteristic of this new direction described education as a matter of "teaching students, not subjects," or of "educating the whole child." Another pregnant statement was "Education is not a preparation for life; it is life." There was just enough truth in the new catch phrases to make them attractive, and just enough unreal pedantry in the old-school situation to warrant a kind of grand rejection. The motives of men are not easy to assess. Yet whatever the educators' motives were in this case, they led men to accept the new kind of education at least on a trial basis, assuming, no doubt, that it could not be any worse than the kind of instruction, arid and incomplete and unreal, with which the age was most familiar.

Aside from a new methodology that was based primarily on the animal nature of man, a method incidentally that educators have discovered should never be overlooked, this new view in education first set out to free the curriculum from the grip of formalism. As the elementary school of the nineteenth century developed, it became a graded school with a fairly rigid curriculum. The age-grade relationship became an unwieldy thing. Regardless of a child's ability, he was put in the grade to which his age assigned him, and he was kept in that grade until he was one year older. Another kind of formalism resulted from the idea that there was a definite and prescribed subject matter waiting to be mastered, a subject matter that could not be altered by anyone. The idea was deeply ingrained in educational practices. Textbooks were prepared for the various subjects in each of the several grades, and it became the teacher's duty to see that the material in the book was covered. Most of the pupil's time was spent in mastering the textbook, a task which meant memorizing the details that were touched on in the book. Too often these exercises had little or no meaning for the children. If these features led to educational unpleasantness in the early years of the nineteenth century when educational popularity was yet to come, think of the wrath they incurred in the early years of the

[14] See Lawrence A. Cremin, *The Transformation of the School,* Alfred A. Knopf, Inc., New York, 1961, pp. 124–125.

twentieth century, when the school population had already attained some of the proportions that phenomenal growth had promised!

The unreality and irrelevance of the elementary curriculum had not been ignored all these hundred or more years. Reform movements were undertaken before Dewey, but they did not enjoy any special success. There was, for example, the Oswego movement. This was an attempt to apply the principles of Pestalozzian methodology, to substitute concrete experiences with common objects for the memorization of textbook content.[15] The movement advocated a diminishing emphasis on the "book" in the elementary school. The kindergarten movement that was introduced to America in 1855 and in 1873 was grafted to the American public school system in St. Louis, Missouri, under the sponsorship of William T. Harris (1835–1909), lent new inspiration to the beliefs that children should be active if they are to learn, and that self-activity is the basis of all learning. Even the Herbartian movement was ready to lend a hand by assailing the prevalent organization of content and by criticizing the outworn methods of teaching that were in use. Perhaps the criticism was not so much that the methods were outworn as that they were without solid psychological foundations. Then there was the work of Parker. In addition to the many other reforms that he advocated, Parker wanted elementary education to be built around a core of common experiences, and he wanted the elementary schools to follow the general educational plan of Froebel. In the end none of these reforms was accepted. Rather, it was John Dewey and the Progressive Education Association that made the greatest gains in attacking formalism and wresting education from its clutches.

It is true, of course, that many of the ideas of these progressives, Dewey included, were not original with them. They borrowed from Rousseau, Pestalozzi, Herbart, Froebel, as well as from others. That they did so does not lead us to criticize them. Regardless of the indebtedness that these progressives may have had to educational thinkers of the past, the main source of their inspiration and the major architect of what may be called progressive education was John Dewey.[16] He challenged the education of the past as well as the education of the present in a number of important books: *School and Society* (1899), *How We Think* (1909), *Democracy and Education* (1916), *Human Nature and Conduct* (1922), and *Experience and Education* (1938). These, of course, are only a few of the books that Dewey wrote, and

[15] Ned H. Dearborn, *The Oswego Movement in American Education,* Teachers College Press, New York, 1925, pp. 124–131.

[16] Cremin, *op. cit.,* pp. 115–126.

hundreds of articles could be added to them. The central purpose of all his writing and teaching was to create the new educational tradition of which we have spoken. The first step in creating such a tradition and one which would have a definite commitment to democracy would be to formulate a new theory of education. And so we find the reason for Dewey's preoccupation with educational philosophy, a philosophy that challenged both the ends and the means of the traditional levels of education.

The Progressive Education Association, organized in 1918, was an especially active agency in promoting and spreading the ideas of John Dewey, although in later years Dewey was often critical of the PEA.[17] It could boast such names as William Heard Kilpatrick and Harold Rugg, but there were hundreds of other, lesser figures who took their places in this movement. Whatever our final evaluation of progressive education may be, we cannot believe that it will be susceptible to the charge of insincerity that is sometimes leveled at progressive educators. Their devotion to the cause of education is one thing that stands out greatly in their favor. In spite of the dedication which the progressive educators felt to the reform they had undertaken, they met with a good deal of opposition, although the record of history will show that the opposition was not very effective. This opposition came generally from essentialists or traditionalists. The labels are not especially helpful in identifying the people who were opposed to progressive education, but in a general way such opposition arose out of the belief that the educational practices of progressives were really antieducational. The practices most commonly advocated by progressives, often following Dewey but sometimes misinterpreting him, were these: To create a school situation in which learners have a great deal of freedom, to stress child initiative and self-activity, to abandon logically arranged and formally taught subjects in favor of projects, to have children themselves formulate meaningful and proximate educational objectives, and to emphasize personality building and social adjustment. In a word, the schools were to be turned back to the children, and, in the best progressive terminology, they were to be places that stressed living rather than learning.

This is probably the place to indicate that a number of educators and teachers who were close to the controversy that was being waged refused to join either side. They thought neither of winning nor of losing a theoretical point; their one object was to organize and conduct the best schools possible for the youth of America. Many educators were actually eclectic in their educational position, taking what they

[17] *Ibid.*, p. 246.

thought was good from the several theoretical positions and trying to fashion the best educational program possible. This is not to say that arguments did not continue from entrenched positions. The progressives challenged the traditionalists and vice versa; the challenge was accepted; and the educational duel was fought and refought. No one was the winner in any of these battles of educational ideology. The question may be asked: Were there not many losers? When the Progressive Education Association disbanded in 1944, its dissolution was not by any means a surrender, for the association did not really disappear; it only changed. It was known as the American Education Fellowship until 1955, when it finally disbanded.

Dewey's kind of progressive education made itself felt most on the level of elementary education. But the revolution that touched the elementary schools and led to such ferment for forty years or more did not ignore secondary education. Progressivism touched the high school of the twentieth century in the following ways: (1) It reinforced the definition of the high school made by the Committee of Ten; (2) it supported a standardizing of the goals of the high schools' curriculum— the goals set forth in the report of the Committee on Reorganization of Secondary Education, which met in 1918 and produced the famous Seven Cardinal Principles of Secondary Education; [18] and (3) it promoted an increase in the number of subjects in the high school so that the differences in ability of students might be served by a variety of curricular offerings. The changes seem laudable, and we can hardly maintain that the high school could or should have taken some other direction. And with the greater perspective of time, we must admit that none of the three points listed above was characteristic of progressivism in any special way. It was the spirit and practice of electivism that committed the high school to the progressive views of the Progressive Education Association. In other words, when the high schools accepted the doctrine of electivism and the theory of equivalence of studies that supports it, the opponents of progressivism claimed that the high schools had been captured by progressive practices in education. The same thing occurred when the "Carnegie unit," a quantitative measure of a student's progress, was applied to the evaluation of high school work. Eventually, in the Eight-Year Study, we find the Progressive Education Association conducting a study to test the merits of the traditional preparatory secondary school program.[19]

[18] *A Report of the Commission on the Reorganization of Secondary Education,* Appointed by the National Education Association, Washington, D. C., 1918.

[19] The general report of the Eight-Year Study was published under the title *Adventures in American Education,* Harper and Row, Publishers, New York, 1942.

In spite of the progressive tendencies that seemed to become attached to it, the American high school was neither regressive nor antiintellectual. The high schools of the United States tried to adapt their programs to the ever-increasing high school population; but at the same time, with the addition of new subjects, with the organization of the curriculum to meet individual needs, and with the introduction of vocational curricula and guidance programs, they achieved an excellence never before dreamed of.

While public education was growing, private education was not standing still. The most remarkable developments in private education in the United States were to be found in the Catholic school system. This system had come into existence with the Third Plenary Council of 1884.[20]

Building a Science of Education

The schools in colonial America as well as those in the early United States were conducted by teachers who were assumed to be engaged in an art. Most teachers, it was hoped, were effective artists, but whethei they were or not depended largely on their own intuitions of good technique rather than on a body of knowledge—a science—about pedagogy. There was, we know, a fairly prescriptive curriculum which the teacher took for granted and communicated in his own way; there were also, by this time, some valid data concerning techniques of teaching, though for the most part they were either unknown or ignored by America's first teachers. The best books on pedagogy, and probably the foremost teachers, talked about child nature and the possibilities of adapting instruction to the child's level, but even the good books and the good teachers were generally unfamiliar with psychological and pedagogical principles and were unable to apply these principles to the instructional process. The social values of education had been underlined by Rousseau and others and were faintly recognized, but even when these values were recognized it was the extraordinary teacher who could translate them into day-to-day school practice. Methods of teaching, of handling curricular materials artistically, were sometimes discussed along lines made popular by Pestalozzi, although, in general, such advanced pedagogical doctrines were understood by only an initiated few. It would be unfair to single out America's early teachers for special blame because they lacked a science of education, because

[20] See J. A. Burns and Bernard J. Kohlbrenner, *A History of Catholic Education in the United States*, Benziger Bros., New York, 1937, pp. 137–144.

the scientific information available on teaching and learning was highly fragmented, and in addition it was often doubted that any sound knowledge about the educational process could be organized. American and European teachers shared a common tradition of doubt and anxiety about the possibilities of a science of education.

Education waited a long time for the right man to come along who could help it to achieve recognition as a scientific discipline. It waited until the middle of the nineteenth century for Herbart, who by virtue of his work in the psychology and methodology of teaching may be called the founder of scientific pedagogy. Students interested in education—and there were many by this time—went to Europe to study under men pioneering in the science of education, men trying to discover and understand the essential nature of the teaching and learning process. Foremost among these European professors was Herbart, whose impact on American education has already been mentioned.[21] Slightly less important than Herbart was Wilhelm Wundt (1832–1920). Wundt published his *Principles of Psychology* in 1874, and from that time on the relationship of experimental psychology to the teaching-learning processes became more and more important. In America the great William James (1842–1910), following the psychological pattern of the day, published his *Principles of Psychology* in 1890. More than any other book on psychology, James' book sensitized educators to the place that psychology must play in teaching and learning. The movement started by James was accelerated by James McKeen Cattell (1860–1944) and G. Stanley Hall (1844–1924). The great figure, however, after American psychology and American psychologists had been impressed by functionalism and behaviorism and various other psychological "isms," was Edward L. Thorndike (1874–1949). No American psychologist has had greater effect on the American school than this man, who developed the theory of connectionism to its highest point.[22]

Thorndike began his studies of learning at Harvard University under the direction of the celebrated William James, and continued them at Columbia University, where he gained a reputation as the world's foremost educational psychologist. In addition to his connectionistic theory, and its profound influence on teaching methods, Thorndike was a pioneer in the field of educational measurement. Besides these important contributions, he made a deep impact on such educa-

---

[21] See also Edward J. Power, *Evolution of Educational Doctrine*, Appleton-Century-Crofts, Inc., New York, 1969, pp. 308–332.

[22] Geraldine M. Joncich (ed.), *Psychology and the Science of Education*, Teachers College Press, New York, 1962, pp. 107–118.

tional issues as transfer of training, individual differences, isolation of certain mental capacities, skill learning, psychological and physiological growth and development, and adult learning.

Thorndike probably will be remembered especially for his theory of connectionism—the stimulus–response bond—and the new ground it broke for classroom methods. This theory, with its S–R bond and its explanation of learning according to the laws of effect, exercise, and readiness, was widely acclaimed by educational psychologists and enthusiastically embraced by classroom teachers. The latter were pleased with the simplicity and precision of learning's laws and the relative ease of their applicability. Questions of validity left them untroubled, although such questions were worth heeding, as did the highly mechanistic setting from which learning processes were viewed. Yet, along with their inherent theoretical weaknesses, the laws of learning emphasized the long-neglected and ignored physical bases to learning, and this, it must be acknowledged, was a good omen for pedagogic practice. With its fairly obvious strengths and despite its weaknesses, connectionism became so popular that most teachers during the second and third decades of the twentieth century acknowledged their discipleship to Thorndike. Textbooks and teachers' manuals were written following the learning principles espoused in connectionism and codified in Thorndike's three-volume work, *Educational Psychology,* published in 1913.

The scientific direction added to educational practice, now reinforced by Thorndike's monumental work, prefaced the mental-testing movement.[23] One of the chief forces advocating the more general employment of tests in schools was the newly formed American Psychological Association. Yet relatively little progress was made in introducing tests into schools on a broad scale until the success of the mental test was more clearly demonstrated by Alfred Binet (1857–1911). Binet, a Frenchman, began his work in 1895, and ten years later America was ready for the mental test. In spite of the recognition that must be given to Binet and to Theodore Simon (1873–1961), the real credit for the testing movement must go to Lewis B. Terman (1877–1956). In 1916 Terman revised and published the Binet test, and from that time on, Terman's scale and subsequent revisions of it have been deservedly popular in the educational world. With this movement the IQ, the intelligence quotient, was introduced to American education. The testing movement received further acceleration from the United States Army, which devised Alpha and Beta scales for the testing of intelli-

[23] Edward L. Thorndike, *An Introduction to the Theory of Mental and Social Measurements,* Teachers College Press, New York, 1913.

gence. The idea was, of course, that the results of such tests would be used to place the First World War inductees in positions for which their capacity most fitted them. In spite of psychologists' inexperience with such instruments on such a large scale and some extraordinary and unexpected outcomes from such use, the army program served to dramatize the value of tests and the variety of uses to which they could be put. The practical character of testing was demonstrated.[24]

With the acceptance of the mental test as a valid instrument for assessing a variety of human capacities, the way was clear for such tests to be widely used in schools. After all, both their validity and reliability were vouched for in the clinical experience of psychometricians, but, equally important, they were standardized. Test scores from the children in one school could be compared to the norms developed through previous administrations of the test, and, by using these highly formalized comparative techniques, test scores could reveal a number of things about a child's aptitude and achievement that were hidden from most classroom teachers. It was intended, of course, that testing should have an effect on both curricula and methods. Although undoubtedly it did, it must be confessed that the promises of the testing movement were never fully realized in school practice.

Another step in building a science of education was the survey movement. The school survey was far from being a novelty in the nineteenth century. Horace Mann's *Annual Reports* had been surveys or reports of surveys.[25] Wilhelm von Humboldt's work in Germany and Victor Cousin's in France were related to the survey. They had examined schools and teaching and had reported on what they found. This is the essence of the survey. In the late nineteenth century and in the early twentieth, school districts began to employ qualified people to conduct surveys. Some of these survey reports were of considerable importance in the field of educational literature. One of the first formal surveys was the one conducted in Boise, Idaho, under the supervision of Calvin Kendall. This began a movement that was followed in most of the nation's larger cities. The school survey became so important that the 1914 Yearbook of the National Society for the Study of Education was devoted to it.[26]

[24] See Frank N. Freeman, *Mental Tests: Their History, Principles, and Application,* Houghton Mifflin Company, Boston, 1939, pp. 18–28.

[25] Horace Mann, *Report, Together with the Report of the Secretary of the Board, 1st–12th,* Dutton and Wentworth, Boston, 1838–1849.

[26] Charles H. Judd and Henry L. Smith, *Plans for Organizing School Surveys, with a Summary of Typical School Surveys,* Thirteenth Yearbook, National Society for the Study of Education, Part II, University of Chicago Press, Chicago, 1914.

The first surveys were simple affairs. As time went on and as school systems became larger and more complex, the survey had to be more extensive and more carefully conducted. Perhaps the best, or at least best-known, survey in the United States was the 1935 cost-and-character survey conducted by the New York State Regents.

In addition to surveys and testing, the educational scientists turned their attention to the curriculum. Without going into the details of this aspect of the science of education, clearly those who advocated the application of science to curriculum believed an academic program needed the invigorating effects of a scientific approach. One of the favorite means for approaching curriculum in the early years of this movement was to analyze the job of living—"job analysis"—and then put into the school's curriculum those things that such an analysis indicated ought to be there. Job analysis was only one of the many scientific approaches to curriculum construction. The general purpose was, of course, to make the curriculum of the school a more useful instrument for forming the minds and characters of youth. Whatever one may think of the outcomes of some of the scientific studies, their general purposes are not subject to criticism. The greatest problem facing the scientific curriculum builder was that no agreement could be arrived at, with science or without it, as to whether the curriculum should consist of subject matter or whether it should provide a frame of reference in which young people could have worthwhile experiences. These problems are still real; they have not been resolved in educational history.

Curriculum, testing, etc., were points in need of attention, but to them must be added the study of the child himself. This was the study in which the science of education made its greatest progress. Modern education has many instruments for coming to know the child better, and it is using these instruments in clinics and study centers the country over. So far as the history of the child-study movement is concerned, one may mention that it received its original impetus from Rousseau, an added impetus from Pestalozzi and Froebel and, in America, from G. Stanley Hall.

Finally, the science of education turned its attention to the problem of exceptional children. From as early as 1817, when Thomas Gallaudet (1787–1851) established a school for the deaf, concern has been shown for the education of exceptional children. There are many categories of the exceptional, and progress of surprisingly high quality has been made in all of them; the curriculum of the schools for such children, the qualifications and the special education of teachers who are to teach them, and the medical and psychological care that the children need, are all matters for study and continuing interest.[27]

Educational Theory

In the eighteenth and nineteenth centuries American educators paid theory scant heed. Theorizing, they thought, was a luxury they could ill afford. More important work awaited them: Schools needed building, money had to be found for their support, and qualified teachers were desperately needed to instruct an ever-increasing student population. With such great practical issues facing American education, it is easy to understand why educational philosophers had a holiday. Whatever theory seemed imperative to guide educational practice could be imported from abroad, for during these same centuries European educational philosophers had been both highly active and remarkably perceptive. What was borrowed was sometimes useful, for, as we have just said, European educational theory had made impressive gains under the prodding of men like Locke, Rousseau, Pestalozzi, and Herbart.[28] But in the long run the worth of European theories was open to question because they arose out of an educational and social system unable to make the kinds of assumptions and commitments that American education wanted to make. Democratic education, equality of educational opportunity, universal opportunity for schooling lay largely outside the European social experience, so there was hardly any way to simply import European educational theories and put them to work in the United States. American education needed its own guiding principles, principles distilled from life in American society. A distinctive American philosophy of education began to make its appearance in the first years of the twentieth century.

An American teaching tradition, we know, was in a formative state, and that emerging tradition served as an added impetus to the building of an American philosophy of education. Yet, despite the progressive nature of that tradition, as time went on it was more and more apparent that a fundamental theory was lacking. What direction, then, should American education take?

America's foremost educational philosopher, who was also responsible for instituting basic reforms on the level of pedagogy, was John Dewey. The job of codifying an American philosophy of education

[27] For example, see Paul Woodring, *A Fourth of a Nation*, McGraw-Hill Book Company, New York, 1957, chapter 4.

[28] Power, *op. cit.*, pp. 244–332.

was left to him. Dewey, however, did not work alone; theoretical ground was broken for him by Charles Sanders Peirce (1839–1914) and William James (1842–1910).[29]

Peirce's contributions to American pragmatism have generally been subordinated to those of James and Dewey. The latter educators were more favorably situated in academic positions, and their scholarly platforms assured them of an audience Peirce never commanded. Still, it was Peirce's formulation of pragmatism's basic idea—"To determine the meaning of an idea, put it into practice in the objective world of actualities, and whatever its consequences prove to be, these constitute the meaning of the idea"[30]—that caught the attention of James and Dewey, and they expanded it into a philosophical system. Peirce's formula for grasping meaning is popularly rendered as "If a thing works it is true," but this is a distortion, or an oversimplification, of his intent. In the first place, he was not concerned with devising a test for truth; and he showed no preoccupation with truth itself. What counted was meaning, not truth, and by following his formula, he believed, meaning could be discovered. While Peirce refused to be confined by tests of truth, he also avoided any special affinity for systems wherein his pragmatic formulation might be elaborated in a dogmatic credo. Education was not for him, as it was for Dewey, the ultimate testing-ground for philosophical precept; further, since he was not a professional educator, he either neglected or failed to sense the pedagogical implications in his pragmatic criterion. In the end, his ideas were unknown except among an initiated few—although, significantly, that few numbered James and Dewey in its ranks.

The popularization of the pragmatic idea or criterion was left to others, among whom the most effective was William James. Few teachers and writers of greater popularity than James have appeared on the American scene. He took the criterion that Peirce had proposed and gave it general currency in philosophical circles. In the hands of James the criterion was used much as Peirce had wanted it used. Both men believed that once the idea was tested in the world of affairs, its meaning could be depended upon; in other words, that a certain permanency

[29] G. W. Allen, *William James: A Biography*, Viking Press, New York, 1967, pp. 512–519; Ralph Barton Perry, *The Thought and Character of William James*, Harvard University Press, Cambridge, Mass., 1948, pp. 312–328; Edward C. Moore, *American Pragmatism: Peirce, James and Dewey*, Columbia University Press, New York, 1961, pp. 270–278; and Murray G. Murphey, *The Development of Peirce's Philosophy*, Harvard University Press, Cambridge, Mass., 1961, pp. 370–381.

[30] Quoted in J. Donald Butler, *Four Philosophies and Their Practice in Education and Religion*, rev. ed., Harper and Row, Publishers, New York, 1957, p. 434.

attached to the outcomes of the pragmatic test. The pragmatism developed by Peirce and popularized by James was changed by John Dewey.

We have already seen something of the background and academic career of John Dewey. He took the pragmatic inheritance of Peirce and James and converted it into a philosophical system that was to bear his distinctive mark. With Dewey, though not with those who preceded him, pragmatism adopted a naturalistic outlook, or, we might say, to the extent that this brand of pragmatism had a metaphysic, its metaphysic was naturalistic. Where both Peirce and James had been willing to believe that ideas once tested had a degree of permanency, Dewey regarded truth as relativistic. This line of thought was all worked out on a philosophical level, although it was not without meaning for education. Applying it, Dewey defined the school as a social institution with social objectives. The school had always had some social objectives, but with this new educational theory the social purposes came to dominate all others. It was not the school's main function to communicate the inheritance of the past, although this might be done, but rather to put the student in direct relation with the society in which he lived. He was to learn what he needed to know not by reading about it but by living it. The school environment was to be informal, and the educational process was to be set in a context in which the student could be given an opportunity to learn what he needed to know. The objectives of education were not to be determined in advance; they were not outlined in long and impressive lists of goals; they were to be elaborated as the children lived and learned in the schools.[31]

It is hard to know where the theories of Dewey stopped and those of his followers began. A long list of names belongs to the general pragmatic tradition, but all these men may not have been close and careful followers of Dewey. Besides, there were changes in Dewey's pedagogical creed. True to his pragmatism, Dewey did not formulate one position on educational doctrine and refuse to budge from it. Thus, it is difficult for the historian of American education to trace the evolution of Dewey's thought and pragmatic practices in education, and such close studies of Dewey's educational philosophy will have to be left for other books. We must be content here with the broad, although at times somewhat incomplete, outlines of that evolution.

In the development of educational theory in America, Dewey and those who followed him more or less closely form a group which, for

[31] John Dewey, *Democracy and Education*, The Macmillan Company, New York, 1916, pp. 158–165.

want of a better name, we call "progressives." Those who opposed the ideas and practices of Dewey and his followers we may call "essentialists."

ESSENTIALISTS

There were, it should be said at the outset, two kinds of essentialism: One was represented by William C. Bagley (1874–1946), a professor of education at Columbia University's Teachers College. Bagley was the leader of a group of educators who called themselves essentialists and who had organized in an effort to give effective opposition to the progressive education movement.[32] The other kind of essentialism, which was not a product of an organized essentialistic society, advocated a return to the fundamentals in education. Among those who associated themselves with the generalized movement, one could find all kinds of educational opinion and educational philosophy. They did agree on one point, however—that a common core to basic culture consists of the essentials of civilized life, and that this common core ought to be communicated steadfastly in all the schools of the land. Eventually this latter essentialistic group broke up into many splinter groups. It was in these groups that the beginnings of certain present-day educational theories are to be found, namely, realism, idealism, rational humanism, and Christian humanism.

Whatever form these various schools of thought took, they maintained in common some opposition to the means used by the progressives, although they may not have scorned the outcomes progressives obtained with their new methods. At the same time, the progressives were not immune to the criticisms heaped on them. In 1930 they attempted to prove that the new education was superior to anything that the traditional or essentialist educators had to offer. They organized the Eight-Year Study. This was an attempt to find scientific verification for the claims progressives were prone to make about the superiority of the kind of education they advocated. It involved a comparison of the performance of high school students who were subjected to the older methodology and the older objectives, on the one hand, and the students who were exposed to the new pedagogy, on the other. Two groups were formed, and they were to be followed from the first year of high school all the way through college. The study, beginning in 1930 and lasting until 1938, issued a report generally favoring the new pedagogy. Although many essentialists took issue with these conclu-

---

[32] See Isaac L. Kandel, *William Chandler Bagley, Stalwart Educator,* Teachers College Press, New York, 1961, pp. 85–101.

sions as well as with the design of the study, the report of the Eight-Year Study was praised by the Progressive Education Association, the Carnegie Corporation, and the General Education Board. The outcome was that the high school's course, and to some extent its standards of achievement, were open to even further liberalization.[33]

Essentialists, however, were unawed by such things as the Eight-Year Study, and returned again to their central thesis that the purposes of education are to transmit a cultural heritage whose significance cannot be gainsaid, and to help students achieve intellectual discipline. From this point on they often differed among themselves on the kinds of services which schools should offer in addition to staple intellectual training. Thus, some essentialists embraced guidance services, school social functions, athletics, and a long list of extracurricular activities. But they were always careful to maintain a distinction between the curriculum, the real business of the school, and the extracurriculum, the pleasant but peripheral functions that might be associated with school life. Should the extracurriculum begin to intrude on the school's principal function it should at once, as James D. Koerner of the Council for Basic Education said, be put back in its subordinate role.

James B. Conant, Arthur E. Bestor, and John Wild would all agree that students in the high school should follow a common core of standard studies—English, social studies, history, government, mathematics, and natural science—plus electives. Academic courses may be elected by good students, and vocational or semivocational courses may be taken to fill out the programs of the less talented.

Teaching, too, is within the essentialist's purview, and educational spokesmen such as Bernard I. Bell, Theodore Greene, Paul Woodring, James Conant talked about the teacher's dual role of teaching an organized body of knowledge, and transmitting sets of tested values. Essentialism puts a high premium not only on a common core of basic culture and on superior teaching, but on the school's role as an institution capable of maintaining standards of human value and of defending its autonomy in a society that is frequently ambivalent about its great objectives. Arthur Bestor, for example, argued that the school, if it is good enough, can stand above, and even ignore, a changing culture in a changing society; perennial and worthwhile intellectual and moral values are the school's business and it should always seek to protect them.

Throughout essentialism's history its spokesmen have assured an educational public that what is essential can be known and validated; that popular democratic education of high quality is possible within

[33] On this point, see W. M. Aikin, *The Story of the Eight-Year Study,* Harper and Row, Publishers, New York, 1942.

the boundaries of essentialistic doctrine; that certitude is possible with respect to knowledge—that truth, after all, is capable of being possessed; and that solid human values can be conserved and transmitted. The essentialists' war with progressive education, or for that matter with any educational pressure-group trying to erode the traditional image of the school as an intellectual agency, is almost certain to continue, for there are no present signs of essentialism's willingness to retreat from its basic thesis.

Higher Education in the Twentieth Century

With the advent of the twentieth century, most educators were confident in the assumptions they made about higher education. Colleges and universities were places where academically-minded young men (and some young women) could pursue their studies and where they could prepare themselves as leaders in the professions and in society. The colleges, however, were as yet unwilling to assume any general obligation for the education of teachers, and, unalterably committed to their old-fashioned ideas of liberal learning, refused to embrace curricula for the professional teacher-education student. The college stood as the last great haven for the education of an elite. Elementary schools had opened their doors to all the children of all the people, and high schools followed suit, but the colleges tried to be exclusive and used tests of admission to select their students. The college of 1890 or even of 1905 was a citadel of academic conservatism; its fundamental character was defined, and every effort was undertaken to immunize it to change.[34]

Yet, as the century wore on and as the country felt the bitter experience of the Great Depression of the 1930s, uncertainties arose as to the colleges' ability to ignore social change and progress which earlier had reshaped the lower scholastic institutions. Because it was not easy for persons to find productive work during the years of the economic depression, more and more students who otherwise might not have thought of continuing their education beyond the high school came to the colleges. Various government and philanthropic programs were instituted to help defray college expenses, and with the admission of these students to college halls the conservative traditions of higher education were forced to face their first test. The motives for higher

[34] See Richard Hofstadter and C. DeWitt Hardy, *The Development and Scope of Higher Education in the United States,* Columbia University Press, New York, 1952, pp. 78–93.

learning that for the most part had dominated the college student of earlier generations were abandoned by this new breed of college students, and new, more liberal motives were substituted. Prescribed curricula and anachronistic studies were challenged; students sought utility from their intellectual labor and were prepared to jettison the traditional courses of study. At best, their projected reforms were mixed blessings, but in the end the colleges were awakened to a new era in higher learning.

Prior to the twentieth century, and in fact as early as 1872, Charles W. Eliot (1834–1926), the dynamic president of Harvard College from 1869 to 1909, introduced the elective program making it possible for students to select the studies in which they were most interested.[35] In discarding the required curriculum and the assumption that only one road led to a B.A. degree, some colleges embraced the theory of equivalence of studies, a theory later incorporated in the *Report* of the Committee of Ten, and one which defended the notion that all school subjects are of equal value. Each course was assigned a credit-hour value, and any student who accumulated a certain number of credit hours was qualified for graduation.

This rather drastic change in degree requirements led to an expansion of college study programs and to a multiplication of college degrees. For most nineteenth-century colleges the only degree was the bachelor of arts, but after three decades of the twentieth century, dozens of new bachelor's degrees were invented.

These changes—they may be called "liberalizations"—had other effects also. Some college officers, becoming concerned about the new directions taken in the colleges, feared that the intellectual talents of the relatively few academically inclined students might be wasted in such experimental democratizing programs as the colleges were following. They decided to establish separate colleges, or separate branches within a college, which would effectively segregate the serious from the ordinary student. This organizational device, operating during the first two years of the traditional four-year course, was called a junior college. While the student attended a junior college, either attached to or separated from a four-year institution, he was expected to demonstrate his fitness for higher learning.

Later, junior colleges entirely separate from four-year colleges

---

[35] Charles W. Eliot, *Charles W. Eliot and Popular Education*, edited with an introduction and notes by Edward A. Krug, Teachers College Press, New York, 1961, pp. 49–55; and Mark A. D. Howe, *Classic Shades: Five Leaders of Learning and Their Colleges*, Little, Brown and Company, Boston, 1928, pp. 175–180.

were organized.[36] Some of these junior colleges, which were both publicly and privately controlled, regarded themselves as preparatory schools for four-year colleges and universities; others were simply going through a period of maturation, waiting with hope and optimism for the time when they could expand their curricula to a full four years. Quite apart from questions of quality in higher education, junior colleges clearly made higher learning available to many students who otherwise would have found college attendance impossible. After the appearance of the *Report of the President's Commission on Higher Education* in 1947, the junior colleges received even greater attention, for this report advocated the establishment of junior colleges on a much broader scale than anyone had proposed up to that time, often in connection with local school systems.[37] The report called such schools "community colleges," spoke of them as new additions to the local public high school, and suggested that their objectives be set in both a preparatory and a terminal context. In other words, the new community colleges then envisioned in the report were to offer academic programs to students who wanted them and could profit from them, and also were to offer nonacademic programs to students for whom, for whatever reasons, academic courses were unattractive. The community college became active in such areas as adult education, continuing education, vocational education, and the reeducation of skilled workers for certain local industries.

In addition to these broadening movements in higher education, which had the effect of changing the face of higher learning, many colleges and universities took further steps to liberalize and update their curricula. Most noticeably, they added summer school sessions, accelerated programs (these were added mainly during the Second World War), and night school courses. Besides, many new professional schools were organized, and colleges expanded their structure to add professional schools of their own. New units in higher education, usually called "institutes," appeared, to offer specialized training or education in a variety of skills and subjects.

The meaning and scope of higher education, by the time we reach the seventh decade of the twentieth century, is evidently considerably different from what it was at the beginning of the century. Contempo-

---

[36] See Leonard V. Koos, *The Junior-College Movement,* Ginn and Company, Boston, 1925, pp. 380–391; and Leland L. Medsker, *The Junior College: Progress and Prospect,* McGraw Hill Book Company, New York, 1960, pp. 300–312.

[37] *"Higher Education for American Democracy,"* Report of the President's Commission on Higher Education, Washington, D. C., 1947.

rary American higher education is schooling or training beyond the high school, no matter what its content or its purpose may be. It may be scientific, professional, academic, nonacademic, technical, or vocational, and, although it is usually commenced after the high school years, it is unnecessary for all who enroll in higher education programs to have a high school diploma.

While the frontiers of higher education were extended considerably during the first half of the twentieth century, and while more and more students came to attend some kind of institution for higher education, many signs warned that some of the conventional values of higher education were in danger of being lost. The loss was not so much in the direction of lower standards for the ordinary college or university, but rather in the direction of overspecialization. There was a time, early in the century, of course, when it was assumed that the high school was the place for general or liberal education. Liberal education, according to the conventional educational wisdom, was intended to give the student a foundation upon which he could build and from which he could go in almost any direction. As long as the high schools remained true to their older purpose, the college could go rather safely down the road to specialization. But with the change in the high school course, many students came to the colleges without the foundational preparation that the colleges felt they should have. This posed something of a dilemma: Should the colleges go on with specialization and ignore the inadequate backgrounds of the students, or should they accept responsibility for giving students foundational experiences? Two important studies of the 1940s addressed themselves to this issue: the report of a committee of the faculty of Harvard University, *General Education in a Free Society* (1945), and the *Report of the President's Commission on Higher Education* (1947). Both reports deplored the lack of attention given to general or liberal education, and both subscribed to the view that the real danger in American higher education was overspecialization, by which they meant specialization without the proper grounding in basic studies of English, literature, science, mathematics, and social science. Both advocated a reorganization of the college curriculum which would make more room for such liberalizing subjects.

Passing from criticism to action, the University of Chicago, beginning with the administration of Robert M. Hutchins in 1929, instituted a program whereby students were to spend their first two years of college pursuing studies in the broad fields of human knowledge covering the humanities and the sciences. At the end of this two-year curriculum, students could present themselves for examinations and, if successful, would be granted the bachelor's degree. Then they would begin their university studies in those areas in which they wished to specialize. The Chicago Plan was by no means widely acclaimed, for by this time American colleges and universities, as well as the accrediting associations they had organized, were committed to a four-year course leading to the bachelor's degree. Despite the Chicago Plan's brave beginning and its promise for creating a renaissance movement in American higher learning, resistance to it became so great that its anticipated prospects were dimmed. Other American colleges were disinclined to follow the Chicago example, and when President Hutchins left the University, the plan was allowed to fall into disuse.[38]

Any survey of twentieth-century American higher education should notice the effects of the GI Bill of Rights, in its educational provisions, on higher education after the Second World War. According to the federal legislation, men and women who had served in the armed services of the United States were eligible for monetary aid to assist them through college, the amount depending on the number of months of military service they served. About six million men and women used the GI Bill of Rights and attended colleges of their choice. More than any other instrumentality devised in the century, the GI bill served to popularize higher education.

After the Second World War (although to some extent this direction was being taken before the war), colleges and universities became especially aware of their obligations to carry on scientific investigation to extend the frontiers of knowledge. Research programs of various kinds, almost all of them devoted to pure and applied research related to science, were undertaken by higher schools. Government, industry, private foundations, and the schools themselves supported these programs. Many such research programs, of course, were (and still are) related to those kinds of knowledge capable of utilization for national defense. Yet, in spite of the practical and critical nature of the work in which the colleges are involved, the college community tends to benefit, and the college and the university tend to achieve a more significant role in the nation's life. At the same time, however, it has been argued, the college, in becoming a research institution for the federal government, is again putting itself in jeopardy and is endangering the humanistic values that colleges and universities, as teaching agencies

---

[38] See C. S. Boucher, *The Chicago Plan*, revised and enlarged (after ten years' operation of the plan) by A. J. Brumbaugh, University of Chicago Press, Chicago, 1940, pp. 367–381.

principally, must continue to cherish and communicate.[39] Regardless of the motives for research, it is certainly apparent that American universities of the 1960s and 1970s are more research- and science-conscious than at any other time in their history.

A word should be added here concerning the students themselves: their interests, their values, and the goals that they seek through the college course. In the nineteenth century, students attended college for the same reasons that students are attending college in this century, for self-improvement and professional advancement. The nostalgic appeal is sometimes made for a return to the college-student type of the good old days. The facts are, however, that the college student of the good old days was much the same as his present-day counterpart. Both attended the college to develop skills and achieve knowledge and understandings enabling them to advance in the world of affairs. This is not to say, of course, that students never studied for the simple joy of learning, but the purely liberal approach to learning in higher education has never had a very warm welcome in reality, whatever theoretical appeal it may have had.

The college student of the twentieth century, especially in the years from 1930 to 1970, came to the college with much better preparation than his predecessors, and he was motivated to seek socially approved goals. Since we have already said something about the college course, what we have to say now will be directed at the fringes of college life, at the college student's amusements, his entertainment, and his recreation. At one time these things were reserved for the free time of the student. In the modern college, cocurricular or extracurricular activities are pointed in the direction of caring for the student's leisure time. Thus it is possible for us to see the activities in which students engage becoming a regular, almost an official, part of college life, whereas before they were thought to be outside the ambit of college influence. The most noticeable among many emphases in this part of college life is upon athletics. The major public appeal of colleges from 1920 to 1950 was in athletics, especially in football, and during certain seasons of the year the public eye was focused on the colleges, not looking for scholars or scientists but for athletes with prowess on the gridiron. Yet in spite of the considerable attention such fringe activities receive, even

---

[39] See C. D. Hutchins, *Trends in Financing Higher Education, 1929–30 to 1959–60,* U. S. Department of Health, Education, and Welfare, U. S. Office of Education, 1961, pp. 100–121; and Selma J. Mushkin, *Economics of Higher Education,* U. S. Department of Health, Education, and Welfare, U. S. Office of Education, 1962, pp. 202–218.

in the colleges' more mature years of the 1960s and 1970s, we can still allege that contemporary colleges offer the highest-quality and most well-rounded opportunities for learning and intellectual development ever presented in higher learning.

Among the many critical issues facing American colleges in the last half of the twentieth century, one stands out especially; it involves the recruitment of an entirely competent faculty. With the ever-increasing enrollments in the colleges, college faculties must continue to grow. But the problem has been and continues to be to find these fully qualified men and women. Faculties of the colleges may easily be downgraded by bringing in teachers from the lower schools, many of whom are fitted neither by temperament, training, nor scholarly instincts to be fully adequate college teachers. But this is a problem for the future to solve; it is hardly one for the historian to settle or even to illuminate.

There are, of course, many features of the academic community that attract people to it, as there are features that drive them away or dissuade them from joining. The most important of the deterrent forces in the years from 1920 to 1955 involved academic freedom. After the First World War and again after the Second World War, many members of the college teaching community were suspected of being, if not actually disloyal to their country, at least of doubtful dependability. Government committees, citizens groups, and the public press began to question the qualifications of many of the members of the academic community. Teachers were dismissed from their teaching positions under supposedly suspicious circumstances and with less than conclusive evidence, when the searching eye of public inquiry was directed at them. History will record that few colleges were willing to stand behind the faculties they had organized when questions were raised concerning an individual teacher's loyalties. It has been said of the colleges that they preferred popular approval to honor.

Unlike day laborers and certain other professional people, college teachers have been reluctant to organize for their own protection. Although college teachers have a professional organization, the American Association of University Professors, fewer than 20 percent of the college teachers in America have joined this professional organization. Yet this Association, with what strength it has, has been in the vanguard whenever the rights and responsibilities of college faculties have been threatened. Without any question at all, one of the major issues touching the teachers of twentieth-century American colleges has been the question of academic freedom.

Educational Issues: 1960 to 1970 and Beyond

Few decades in the history of the United States, or of any other country for that matter, have been so marked by change as was the decade of the 1960s, and much of this change centered on education. Although to impose a hierarchy on shifts in social and educational emphasis would now be a difficult undertaking, some of the changes will undoubtedly prove to be more lasting and more significant than others. So, for a historical overview or summary of the flux in educational events it is probably best to proceed without trying to settle the question of relative importance.

The United States has sharpened its interest in intercultural and international education over the past decade and has tried to capitalize on its brief historical involvement in international education. This involvement goes back to 1926, when the Commission on Intellectual Cooperation was organized with an intention of using education as a means for achieving international cooperation and understanding. At about the same time, the International Bureau of Education was established with the active backing and financial support of several nations. Its basic plan was to collect and disseminate information about various countries and thus, as a clearinghouse for knowledge, promote international goodwill. In addition to its purely informational functions, the International Bureau of Education conducted international conferences which were attended by persons from the various countries, and who, it was hoped, would be able to return to their homelands with clearer perceptions of their international neighbors. Although it is easy to applaud the theory behind an effort of this kind, on the level of practice, it must be reported, the International Bureau of Education was never able to fulfill the promise held out for it. And whether or not this had anything to do with the limited success of the Bureau, it should be said that the United States chose not to become a member of the Bureau until 1958.

In the Americas of the 1930s and thereafter, regional cooperation was emphasized as a means of creating better understanding among the several states of North and South America. When programs were inaugurated, usually with government support and direction, they aimed at facilitating various types of informational and cultural exchanges, and so teachers, students, books, art, and other cultural appurtenances were circulated from country to country. Even outside the Americas such cultural intercourse appeared to be worthwhile, and a good deal of action was taken—as, for example, in the Institute of International

Education, in State Department programs for the exchange of students, teachers, and sometimes just ordinary men, in the Fulbright grants enabling students and teachers to study abroad, and, on the university level, through a new emphasis in serious study of such subjects as comparative government and comparative education.

Finally, of course, in connection with international cooperation and education, the work of the United Nations must be noted, and especially that of the appendage of the United Nations known as UNESCO (United Nations Educational, Scientific, and Cultural Organization). UNESCO was founded in London in 1945 on the premise that since wars begin in men's minds, it is in men's minds that the defenses of peace, and assurances for a peaceful world, must also begin. With "Education for Peace" as a motto, the purposes of UNESCO are to spread information, to promote communication, and to try to create an intellectual climate wherein peace will flourish. As practical programs flowing from its high ideals, UNESCO has sponsored international student exchanges, has promoted teaching programs for reducing illiteracy in all countries of the world (especially in the underdeveloped countries), and has given considerable assistance to all countries seeking it in raising their educational and cultural standards.

Nationalism, isolationism, and exclusivism have plagued the work of the United Nations and its educational branch, UNESCO. Some countries, believing their cultural and educational standards to be peculiarly their own, want no outside interference from an international agency; other countries, for their own reasons, good or bad, prefer to isolate their own cultural reservoirs and choose not to draw on those of their neighbors; and, finally, due to certain interpretations of political morality, some countries, both the large and powerful and the small and weak, are excluded from the United Nations and are therefore unable to draw on its cultural and educational resources.

While it is still too soon to assess the value of UNESCO, it is fair to report that many of its programs have been remarkably successful, while on the other hand—for example, in parts of Africa and Asia, where the need for educational and cultural enlightenment would appear to be greatest—it has made almost no impact whatever.

Only part of the contemporary educator's time is spent looking outside the United States, and this is easy to understand, for there are many issues to command his attention within the American educational structure itself. Beginning almost with the initial explorations of outer space, determined efforts were made by elementary, secondary, and college educators to upgrade the curricula of American schools and to introduce a technology of education to the classroom. Upgrading meant mainly the introduction of new content to science and mathematics courses, so in the 1960s we began to find syllabi referring to the new mathematics and the new science. But, in addition to new emphases in science and mathematics teaching, there was also a determination to keep pace with what was called the "knowledge explosion" by eliminating from the curriculum much that was considered useless or out-of-date and replacing it with the latest findings from the research laboratory. Subjects formerly taught in higher schools were now found on the elementary level, and parents whose opinion of their own mathematical abilities was good found that they were unable to help their children with homework. Subjects formerly common in the first or second year of college were taken for granted when they appeared in the junior or senior high school years. And the colleges, too, were almost forced to restructure their curricula, to pare away what could no longer be justified and replace it with something that was up-to-date.

Despite a fairly obvious preoccupation with rebuilding the curriculum, American educators and teachers retained their traditional attachment for instructional techniques and tried to modernize them along some important lines. This modernization of technique was really an introduction of technology to the school where, in the 1960s and 1970s, we find such things as programmed instruction, and the application of computer techniques to the management and administration of teaching.

Along with the improvements in school life and learning, improvements that may have raised American education to the highest point in its history, there were demoralizing features, however. Thousands of children were either missed by educational opportunity or, if they went to school, attended schools in economically disadvantaged or ghetto and slum areas. There the quality of instruction was deplorably low, and even if teachers were good the discipline was so bad and the goodwill toward learning so low that nothing along the lines of real teaching or learning could ever take place.

Both federal and state governments became involved in what was called a "war on poverty" in a determined effort to eradicate the obstacles to a full and satisfying life in American society. This war on poverty had many battles, one of which involved the schools directly, for the most obvious and recurrent cause for poverty, according to the best sociological evidence available, was inadequate education. We cannot hope here to review all the various federal and state programs dealing with the improvement of educational opportunity in urban and rural deprived areas, but we can say that this war on poverty and the attention paid to education led to massive appropriations of federal funds. Few educators would have predicted, in the 1950s, that the federal government would have entered the field of educational support on such a broad scale, for in its determination to give aid where it was needed it largely ignored many of the old arguments relative to states' rights, separation of church and state, and other such obstacles.

In an age when everything began to cost more, the schools, too, became extremely expensive. Local school districts, no longer able to finance their school programs without making serious inroads on quality, turned to the state for aid, and when the resources of the state became severely taxed, the states turned to the federal government for help. When private and public colleges were beset by inflationary costs, they turned to the states for help, sometimes surrendering their private status rather than accepting bankruptcy, or they appealed to the federal government for assistance in funding programs that had become too expensive for the college itself. The subject of state and federal aid to education is too large for any extensive treatment here, but it is by now clear that many of the historic assumptions relative to the use of public money for public and private educational purposes and schools are badly worn.

Adult education, in connection with both local schools and community colleges, is coming of age. Its programs run all the way from courses intended to improve a person's cultural insights, to training programs wherein a person may prepare for a new trade and thus for a new economic career. But the promise of adult educational programs has only been partly exploited.

Finally, one of the most disturbing current issues on the American educational scene is the one of student unrest in the colleges. The traditions of American higher education have been upset, for those traditions always assumed that the college student would be docile, that he would be receptive to college discipline and college control, and that he would willingly learn to love what he was supposed to love, and hate what he was supposed to hate. The genesis of student unrest—even "revolt" would not be too strong a word—is unclear as yet, and the social scientist shall have to complete his research before he explains it. But unquestionably it is, in part at least, rooted in the United States' involvement in what, in the student community and the university community generally, has proved a highly unpopular war. More than this, it is also an insightful, questioning, even impudent, challenge to the older generation to clarify its values, to be honest, and to be consistent. Part of the trouble may be found in the college community itself, where tradition allowed the college administrator to make academic law and enforce it, and where there was little willingness, on the one hand, and no machinery, on the other, for students to communicate either with their teachers or with college administrators. Excessive enrollment in some colleges made it imperative that the entire process of higher learning be depersonalized to the point where many students were convinced they were nothing but a mark on a computer data card. The announced values and objectives of the college course were, in this context, in serious jeopardy.

While it is not in the province of history to make predictions for the future of education, it appears almost inevitable that higher learning in the decades ahead shall surely wear a different face. But this prediction need not be restricted only to higher education and the current issues surrounding it, for the seriousness of social problems defined by these issues makes it almost imperative that all American education in the future wear a different face.

Summary

Many of the hopes for education in the United States were realized in the twentieth century. Free public schools were made universally available, and opportunity for all children was expanded greatly. The teaching tradition of the past was reformed and reinvigorated in order that teaching and learning might accommodate the expanding needs of a democratic society. Knowledge about the art of teaching and the science of education was organized, and consistent efforts were made to increase the body of knowledge about teaching and learning. The educational consciousness of the twentieth century was capped in a new theory of education called pragmatism. The leading educational philosopher of the century was John Dewey. The last rung of the educational ladder, higher education, was subject to important changes. In a word, higher education was brought more closely in line with democratic educational ideals.

While all these important educational developments have been taking place in the United States, education throughout the world has been reawakening to the needs and hopes of mankind. The greatest need is for understanding among men and nations; the greatest hope is still for peace and human equality.

Index